1 MONTH OF
FREE
READING

at

www.ForgottenBooks.com

By purchasing this book you are eligible for one month membership to ForgottenBooks.com, giving you unlimited access to our entire collection of over 1,000,000 titles via our web site and mobile apps.

To claim your free month visit:
www.forgottenbooks.com/free919020

ISBN 978-0-266-98318-7
PIBN 10919020

CIRCULARS OF INFORMATION

OF THE

BUREAU OF EDUCATION

FOR

THE YEAR 1875.

———————

WASHINGTON:
GOVERNMENT PRINTING OFFICE.
1877.

GENERAL CONTENTS.

The pagination here used is that at the foot of the page.

	Page.
General title	1, 2
General contents	3, 4
Circular of Information No. 1, 1875:	
Proceedings of the Department of Superintendence of the National Educational Association..	9–122
Circular of Information No. 2, 1875:	
Education in Japan	123–186
Circular of Information No. 3, 1875:	
An account of the systems of public instruction in Belgium, Russia, Turkey, Servia, and Egypt...	187–294
Circular of Information No. 4, 1875:	
Waste of labor in the work of education.................................	295–310
Circular of Information No. 5, 1875:	
Suggestions respecting the educational exhibit at the International Centennial Exhibition	311–336
Circular of Information No. 6, 1875:	
Statements relating to reformatory, charitable, and industrial schools for the young	337–542
Circular of Information No. 7, 1875:	
Constitutional provisions in regard to education in the several States of the American Union..	543–672
Circular of Information No. 8, 1875:	
Schedule for the preparation of students' work for the Centennial Exhibition	673–687

ERRATUM.

Page 611. Instead of the first two lines of the third note, read as follows: " ‡ The United States deposit fund is a part of the sum of $28,101,644.91 distributed among the States under the act of June 23, 1836, of which New York received $4,014,520.71."

5, 6

CIRCULARS OF INFORMATION.

7,8

CIRCULARS OF INFORMATION

OF THE

BUREAU OF EDUCATION.

No. 1–1875.

PROCEEDINGS OF THE DEPARTMENT OF SUPERINTENDENCE
OF THE NATIONAL EDUCATIONAL ASSOCIATION, AT
WASHINGTON, D. C., JANUARY 27 AND 28, 1875.

WASHINGTON:
GOVERNMENT PRINTING OFFICE.
1875

9–10

CONTENTS.

	Page.
Letter of the Commissioner of Education to the Secretary of the Interior.......	5
Address of the president of the convention...................................	9
Organization of the convention..	10
Paper on " The legal prevention of illiteracy," by Hon. B. G. Northrop, secretary State-board of education of Connecticut......................................	12
Discussion of Mr. Northrop's paper	17
Reception of the department by President Grant...............................	30
Visit to Corcoran Art-Gallery	31
Paper on " Brain-culture in relation to the school-room," by A. N. Bell, M. D., of New York..	31
Discussion of Mr. Bell's paper..	36
Remarks of the Commissioner of Education.....................................	37
Reception of the department by the Secretary of the Interior...................	51
Paper on " The origin of the alphabet," by Professor J. Enthoffer, of the United States Coast-Survey Office...	52
Paper on "American education at the Centennial Exposition," by Hon. J. P. Wickersham, State-superintendent of common schools of Pennsylvania.......	55
Discussion of Mr. Wickersham's paper...	59
Remarks of Baron von Schwarz-Senborn, minister from Austria-Hungary......	61
Letters presented by the Commissioner of Education from superintendents of States and of city-schools regretting absence	78
Resolutions reported by the committee on the relations of the General Government to public education	79
Remarks of the Commissioner of Education concerning the International Exhibition to be held in Chili in 1875..	80
Resolutions reported by the committee on school-hygiene and the subjects of Dr. Bell's paper...	81
Paper read by Hon. John D. Philbrick, of Boston, Mass., " Can the elements of industrial education be introduced into our common schools?".................	81
Discussion of Mr. Philbrick's paper..	89
Paper on "Industrial drawing in public schools," by Professor Walter Smith, State-director of art-education, Boston, Mass.................................	92
Remarks of Professor Joseph Henry, secretary of the Smithsonian Institution...	104
Report of committee on resolutions...	105
Remarks on the death of Hon. Milton B. Hopkins, late State-superintendent of Indiana..	106
Letter from Señor Manuel de Zamacona, commissioner of Mexico..............	106
Adjournment..	107
Reception of members by Governor Shepherd...................................	107
Visit of members to the Smithsonian Institution	108
Appendix A...	108
Letter of Hon. A. T. Goshorn, Director-General of the United States Centennial Commission...	108
Report of committee of conference with Director Goshorn.................	108
Circular-letter of director-general to State-governors	109

Page.

Appendix B.. 110

Memorial of the department of superintendence of the National Educational Association to the Congress of the United States................ 110

Memorial of the Massachusetts State Teachers' Association to the Congress
of the United States.. 111

Resolutions adopted by the Indiana State Teachers' Association, January
31, 1874.. 112

Resolutions adopted by the Missouri State Teachers' Association.......... 112

Resolutions adopted by the New York State Association of School Commissioners and Superintendents, at Syracuse, December 30, 1874 113

12

LETTER.

DEPARTMENT OF THE INTERIOR,
BUREAU OF EDUCATION.
Washington, D. C., April 10, 1875.

SIR: The proceedings of the recent meeting of the department of superintendence of the National Educational Association have been submitted to me for publication.

They contain, in addition to several important papers upon topics of great interest to educators, which were read before the Department, discussions of subjects of present and permanent interest.

As being of very general interest to educators and as furnishing the readiest and cheapest means for answering numerous inquiries received at this office, I have the honor to recommend their publication as a circular of information.

Very respectfully, your obedient servant,

JOHN EATON, *Commissioner.*

Hon. C. DELANO,
Secretary of the Interior.

Approved, and publication ordered.

C. DELANO, *Secretary.*

13–14

PROCEEDINGS OF THE FIRST DAY.

DEPARTMENT OF SUPERINTENDENCE OF THE NATIONAL EDUCATIONAL ASSOCIATION, WASHINGTON, D. C., JANUARY 27, 1875.

FIRST DAY.

The department of superintendence of the National Educational Association, agreeably to the call of the president of the department and the Commissioner of Education, as previously arranged, assembled at the office of the Commissioner of Education, at 9½ o'clock on the morning of the 27th of January, and proceeded thence to Willard Hall, where the meeting was called to order at 11 o'clock by Mr. J. Ormond Wilson, president, the following members being present, viz:

Alonzo Abernethy, State-superintendent, Iowa; George P. Brown, superintendent, Indianapolis, Ind.; O. A. Burgess, president Christian University, Indianapolis, Ind.; William R. Creery, superintendent, Baltimore, Md.; Richard L. Carne, superintendent, Alexandria, Va.; George F. T. Cook, superintendent colored-schools, Washington and Georgetown, D. C.; R. L. Cooper, superintendent, Stafford County, Va.; William L. Dickinson, superintendent, Jersey City, N. J.; General John Eaton, Commissioner of Education, Washington, D. C.; Alex. C. Hopkins, State-superintendent, Indiana; M. N. Horton, superintendent, Williamsport, Pa.; J. K. Jillson, State-superintendent, South Carolina; George J. Luckey, superintendent, Pittsburg, Pa.: R. McMillan, superintendent, Youngstown, Ohio; A. P. Marble, superintendent, Worcester, Mass.; M. A. Newell, State-superintendent, Maryland; B. G. Northrop, secretary State-board of education, New Haven, Conn.; B. F. Patterson, superintendent, Pottsville, Pa.; John D. Philbrick, ex-superintendent, Boston, Mass.; H. S. Tarbell, superintendent, East Saginaw, Mich.; John P. Wickersham, State-superintendent, Harrisburg, Pa.; and J. Ormond Wilson, superintendent, Washington, D. C.

Prayer was offered by Rev. Dr. Rankin, of Washington City.

President Wilson then delivered the following

ADDRESS OF WELCOME.

GENTLEMEN OF THE DEPARTMENT OF SUPERINTENDENCE: We have assembled pursuant to adjournment of this department made at the meeting held in August last at Detroit, and it is my privilege, in behalf of this city, to bid you a hearty welcome. The United States Commissioner of Education and the officers of this department, who were authorized to make the arrangements for this meeting, found it impracticable to prepare in advance a full and exact programme for your procedure, and in the circular-letter recently addressed to you they have only invited your attention to some of the important topics that will be presented for your consideration.

17

At no time since the foundation of the National Government has the subject of education, especially when regarded as a part of our public policy, demanded more earnest thought, careful discussion, and resolute action than it now does.

It is a time of sharp, bold, sometimes reckless inquiry, that has little respect for venerable precedent and the time whereof the memory of man runneth not to the contrary. It is claimed here and there, by those who are casting about to find a scapegoat on which to load all the evils of the day, that the public schools are failing to accomplish their professed mission; that they are alienating youth from the honest toil and thrift of the fathers, sending them from the rural districts, where

As she fled mankind,
There justice left her last lone trace behind,

and gathering them into the cities and larger towns, often to become the prey of recklessness, extravagance, and dissipation; that they fail in properly interweaving spiritual with secular instruction, or that the moral instruction that is imparted infringes upon the prerogatives of the family or church; that they are undermining the physical constitutions of the children committed to their care and are sowing the seeds of weakness, disease, and deformity; that they are undertaking too much when they pass beyond the boundaries of the rudiments of knowledge and enter upon the work of the high school, the college, and the university. Occasionally it is even asserted that our National Bureau of Education is not needed by the State and local educational organizations, or, on the other hand, that it is, with its limited functions and scanty appropriations, a dangerous centralizing power, and therefore it should be " cut up by the roots."

This apparently unfriendly agitation and discussion should not in the least dishearten the friends of the common schools, for it is evident to the most superficial observer that the country is in need of more and better education, and these assaults may prove to be like the storms that send the roots of the oak deeper into the earth that supports it. The work in which we are engaged will neither go backward nor halt, and we meet to-day to assist in pointing the way to a future that shall more fully meet the demands of an advancing civilization.

The president then announced that motions were now in order. General Eaton, United States Commissioner of Education, moved, in the absence of the secretary, Mr. Stevenson, of Ohio, the appointment of a secretary *pro tempore*, and nominated Mr. George P. Brown, who was accordingly elected; and Mr. Goodwin Y. AtLee, of Washington, D. C., was appointed assistant secretary.

The PRESIDENT. I would suggest that the members of the department hand their names to the secretary, so that he can make a complete record of the members present.

On motion of General Eaton, it was ordered that the president appoint a committee of three on order of business.

General Eaton, Hon. J. P. Wickersham of Pennsylvania, and Hon. A. Abernethy of Iowa were accordingly appointed.

After a brief consultation the committee reported that the papers by Dr. A. N. Bell and Professor Walter Smith should be reserved for the evening-exercises, and suggested that the paper of Hon. B. G. Northrop should be now read, and stated that the committee would report again on the further order of business.

The president then announced that " the first paper to be presented this morning is by Hon. B. G. Northrop, secretary of the State-board of education of Connecticut. His subject is 'Legal prevention of illiteracy.'"

REMARKS OF MR. NORTHROP.

Mr. Northrop prefaced his paper by the following remarks:

MR. PRESIDENT AND GENTLEMEN: In the brief time which I am allowed it will be impossible to discuss in a broad way the general subject announced, and I am undoubtedly expected to speak of the way the plan of compulsory education works in Connecticut, the State where I am secretary of the educational board.

Mr. J. P. WICKERSHAM, (interrupting.) If Mr. Northrop will be kind enough to suspend his remarks one moment, I will make a motion. I move that at a suitable time the members of this department call in a body on the President of the United States and pay their respects to him.

The motion was adopted.

Mr. ALEXANDER C. HOPKINS, of Indiana. There are some gentlemen here, presidents of universities, presidents of colleges, &c., who, perhaps, feel a little timidity in participating in our proceedings. They may think that this is a meeting expressly for the department of superintendence. I merely wish to suggest the propriety of giving an invitation to all such persons present to participate in our proceedings. I would suggest that they be called upon to give their names to the secretary, and thus become enrolled in our list. Thus we may receive the benefit of their counsels, while they will receive whatever advantage can be gained in a free consultation with the superintendents.

The PRESIDENT. If I am not mistaken it has always been considered that all such persons who are members of the National Educational Association are entitled to participate in our proceedings. It has always been considered, as I understand it, that members of the National Educational Association were members of this department. Members of the National Educational Association are cordially invited to participate in our proceedings.

General EATON. May I suggest, Mr. President, that you probably intend now to say that any of the presidents of colleges or friends of education may consider themselves invited to become members of the National Educational Association and participate with us on this occasion?

The PRESIDENT. Yes, sir.

General EATON. My recollection fully confirms what the president has said, that gentlemen interested in the cause of education have always been invited to participate in our deliberations at their will.

Mr. NORTHROP resumed:

I was about to say that my aim would be especially to speak of the working of these laws in the State of Connecticut. With this explanation I will proceed with the reading of the paper upon

THE LEGAL PREVENTION OF ILLITERACY.

Public sentiment is a growing power the world over. In our country its influence is most marked. Here it creates law and repeals it. A law in violation of public sentiment is a dead letter, and therefore demoralizing, for laws habitually violated tend to lawlessness. Reverence for law is a wholesome sentiment, which should be early implanted in the juvenile mind. Laws in reference alike to the support of schools or attendance upon them must depend largely upon public sentiment. Laws, which may be just and right in themselves, adapted, if sustained, to promote the greatest good of the greatest number, may yet fail utterly from the want of popular sympathy and support. The question of the expediency of compulsory attendance at school in any given State depends on the enlightened public sentiment of that community.

Wherever good schools have been so long maintained that the people generally regard them as essential to their individual thrift and happiness and to public security, morality, and prosperity, there laws for the prevention of illiteracy may be wisely enacted. In those States where free public schools are still a novelty or where illiteracy most abounds, where multitudes appreciate neither the advantages of education nor the evils of ignorance, compulsory attendance would be premature and impracticable.

But in those States where the traditions of the people from their earliest history have fostered the general appreciation of the common-school-education as their most precious heritage, as the source of their success and prosperity, as indispensable to their future growth, as the cheapest police-agency, education comes at length to be recognized as the universal right, duty, and interest of man. If the State has a right to hang a criminal, it has a better right to prevent his crime by proper culture. The right to imprison and to execute implies the right to use the best means to prevent the need of either.

In Connecticut public sentiment is steadily growing in favor of the legal prevention of illiteracy. Stringent as are our laws on this subject, they have awakened no public opposition. A few individual malcontents among recent immigrants, mostly those from Canada, have complained because their children could not be continuously employed in our factories. A few parents—I have not heard of over half a dozen in all—openly defied the law, but, as soon as they found that legal complaints were made out against them, they were glad to stay proceedings by compliance with its provisions. Under this law we have had as yet no prosecutions and no penalties. We hope there will be none.

To intensify popular interest in education I have visited every township in Connecticut, and most of them repeatedly. It has been our aim to make the public school the center of attraction and interest, so that attendance shall be regarded as a privilege rather than a legal necessity.

LAWS ADOPTED IN CONNECTICUT.

You ask me to describe the methods and results of our proceedings in Connecticut under the new laws of obligatory education. These laws relate both to employers and parents. The law in regard to employers was adopted in 1869. That form of compulsory education has been in force for five years. An earlier law, copied *verbatim* from a Massachusetts statute, pronounced its penalty against all manufacturers who should "*knowingly* employ children who had not attended school," &c. That one word "knowingly" utterly vitiated the law. It was inserted as an amendment to the original bill on its second reading in the Massachusetts senate, at the suggestion of a manufacturer who knew well "how not to do it." The Massachusetts law still retains that unfortunate word. Practically, it is found impossible to prove the employer's knowledge of the child's non-attendance. "Not to know" is always easy for any employer.

Our law originally applied to manufacturers *only ;* as revised, it relates equally to all employers. According to its provisions, no child under 14 years of age can be lawfully employed to labor *in any business whatsoever*, unless such child shall have attended some school at least three months in each year of such service. The penalty for the violation of this law is one hundred dollars for each offense.

Realizing that the efficiency of the law would depend largely on the department of education, I determined it should not be a dead letter; but, instead of threatening prosecutions at the outset, I sought to conciliate our manufacturers, conferring with them courteously as friends of education and assuming that they would heartily co-operate in the enforcement of the law. To this end, I drew up the following pledge : " We hereby agree that we will employ no children under 14 years of age, except those who are provided with a certificate from the local school-officers of actual attendance at school the full term required by law." I first presented it to ex-Governor James E. English ; then to Governor Marshall Jewell; next to ex-Governor William A. Buckingham, who—each extensive manufacturers—cheerfully signed it. I then started to get the signatures of manufacturers generally ; but the work proved so great and important that a gentleman was appointed as agent of the board of education to canvass the State. He visited the leading manufacturers throughout the State, and, with one exception, they all cheerfully signed the above pledge. This law has proved beneficent in its results. During the five years of its operation it has met general and cordial approval and brought large numbers into our schools. Instances of remissness sometimes occur. Vigilance is needful.

The agent of the State-board of education is now chiefly occupied in visiting school-officers and manufacturers in all parts of the State for the purpose of securing the attendance of children at school.

In a circular sent to every township, I have requested the local school-officers to communicate to me any facts they may learn as to neglect in the schooling of children.

It is not believed that any one of the signers intends to repudiate the agreement above cited. They have shown a degree of liberality and interest in education worthy of commendation. A courteous reminder from the agent or secretary of the board has been sufficient to remedy an occasional remissness attributed to inadvertency.

Nearly four years ago a law of compulsory attendance at school was passed in Connecticut applying to all *parents* of children who were employed to labor at any business in this State and who were discharged for the purpose of attending school. This class of children was supposed to comprise nearly all " non-attendants." The next year this limitation was removed. Our law now requires that " *every* parent, guardian, or other person having control and charge of any child between the ages of 8 and 14 years, shall cause such child to attend *some public or private day-school* at least three months in each year, six weeks at least of which attendance shall be consecutive, *or to be instructed at home* at least three months in each year in the branches of education required to be taught in the public schools, unless the physical or mental condition of the child is such as to render such attendance inexpedient or impracticable." The penalty for the violation of the above provisions is a *fine of five dollars* " for every week, not exceeding thirteen weeks in any one year, during which any parent or guardian shall have failed to comply therewith." As French Canadians are very numerous in many of our manufacturing-villages, printed posters in both French and English, giving the substance of the law both in its application to parents and employers, were widely circulated and posted.

The following notice, neatly printed, was also sent to the manufacturers of the State, to be posted in some conspicuous place :

" In accordance with the statute of the legislature of 1869, no children under 14 years of age can hereafter be employed in this factory except those who present a certificate from the local school-officers of actual attendance at school the full time required by law, which is ' at least three months of the twelve next preceding any and every year in which such children shall be so employed.'"

Printed blank forms of complaint against negligent parents were prepared. In a few instances a legal process was begun against delinquent parents ; but, when it was seen that the law was imperative and its officers in earnest, the law was complied with. Many evasions of this law no doubt occur, but, as a general rule, the people of Connecticut approve its provisions and mean that they shall be observed.

The more thoroughly this law is executed, the less of course will be the *average* attendance. The greater the number who attend school *only* the time required by law, the less will be the average for the whole year. Three months' schooling a year is not enough, but it is a good beginning. "Half a loaf is better than no bread." It is hoped that such interest in school and fondness for books will be awakened as to induce many to attend longer than the time required by law.

Our aggregate attendance last year was 95.65 per cent. of the whole number enumerated, the highest figures ever reached in this State. The whole number enumerated in 1874 was 133,522; the whole number in schools of all kinds was 127,720: since 1869 the increase in enumeration is 9,878; since 1869 the increase in number registered at school is 19,908. The increase of attendance above the increase in enumeration is 10,030.

This result has cost work. We have not leaned upon the law alone, but it surely has been of great service. It has awakened no opposition. Both political parties equally favor it. No suggestion for its repeal has been made in the legislature, nor, so far as I know, in any Connecticut paper. The people of Connecticut plainly sanction the legal prevention of illiteracy.

EDUCATION OF PUBLIC SENTIMENT.

Instead of falling back upon the law to do the whole work, we have made argument, persuasion, and conciliation our *main* reliance. Any statute which should lessen these primal forces I should deprecate. But, with growing faith in moral suasion, I prize the sterner sanctions of the law as a *dernier ressort only* in cases otherwise incorrigible. When paternal pride, interest, or authority fails, and parental indifference or intemperance bars the way to school, legal coercion may be wisely employed.

Whatever may be true in monarchical governments, in *our* country there is every motive to kindness and conciliation in the execution of such a law. The plan is truly democratic, for its entire management is by the people and for the people, through school-officers chosen by the people and responsible to the people. Such a law, in our country, should command popular sympathy more than in any monarchy, for it is not pressed upon the people by some outside agency or higher power, but is their own work, embodying their judgment and preferences. The form of compulsory education which existed in Connecticut for more than a hundred and fifty years was not forced upon the people as "subjects." It was rather a living organism, of which they as "sovereigns" proudly claimed the paternity, growing up with their growth and recognized as the source of their strength and prosperity. After the utmost use of kindness, tact, and persuasion, and every effort to awaken a dormant parental pride, if not a sense of duty, and showing that education will promote their children's thrift and happiness through life, we find that such persuasions are the more effective when it is understood that the sanctions of the law might be employed. We have used the right to enforce mainly as an argument to persuade an authoritative appeal to good sense and parental pride. As thus used, we know in Connecticut that our law has been a moral force. It is itself an effective advocate of education to the very class who need it most. The people of Connecticut plainly approve this law, stringent as are its provisions. It has already accomplished great good and brought into the schools many children who would otherwise have been absentees. Since its enactment no objection has been made to it in the legislature, and no article, editorial, or contribution in any Connecticut paper has expressed disapproval of it, so far as I know.

Individual instances of neglect or evasion still occur, occasioned by poverty or indifference of parents, or by the oversight or selfishness of employers, who do not, however, deny the justice and necessity of the law.

HISTORICAL STATEMENT.

It is objected that compulsory education is monarchical in its *origin* and character. This is erroneous. Massachusetts and Connecticut may justly claim to be the first States in the world to establish the principle of compulsory education. Before the peace of Westphalia, before Prussia existed as a kingdom, and while Frederick William was only elector of Brandenburg, in 1650—two hundred and twenty-five years ago—Massachusetts and Connecticut adopted most rigid laws for coercive education.

The selectmen in every town were then required to see that so much *"barbarism"* was not permitted in any family as that their children should not be able perfectly to read the English tongue, upon penalty of twenty shillings for each neglect therein. Repetition of the offense was punished with still higher fines or by taking children away from their parents and apprenticing them where they would be sure to be educated.

In the early history of Massachusetts and Connecticut this law was strictly executed. It was so heartily approved by the people and the education of all children was so generally desired and secured, that attendance lost its involuntary character. Created by public opinion, it tended to deepen that sentiment. The demand that the barbarism of ignorance should not be tolerated helped to make it disgraceful to keep even an apprentice from school. To bring up a child or ward in ignorance was shameful and *barbarous* in the eyes of the fathers of New England. This is still the sentiment of their genuine descendants. High appreciation of education is one of the most precious traditions of New England. This old law greatly aided, both in awakening and perpetuating this public interest and in fixing the habits, associations, and traditions of the people. For one hundred and seventy years after the adoption of this law an adult native of Connecticut, of sound mind, unable to read the English language, would have been looked upon as a prodigy. Such a citizen of the old New England stock I have never met in Connecticut, though I have mingled freely with the people and visited every township of the State.

Judge Daggett, long professor of law in Yale College, on finding any witness on the stand or criminal in the dock who could not read and write, used always to ask "where were you born?" and with only three exceptions, during his long judicial service, did he receive the answer "In Connecticut." But recently immigration has caused startling figures of illiteracy, especially in our manufacturing-centers. With this ignorance comes indifference to education, and hence the new need of coercion.

ARGUMENT FOR THE LAW.

The *right* of the State to enforce attendance will hardly be questioned by any in this body. It is a corollary from the compulsory school-tax. The power that claims public money to educate all classes may justly provide that such expenditure should not fail of its end through the vice, intemperance, or perverseness of parents. The State has the same right to compel the ignorant to learn that it has to compel the penurious to pay for that learning. Tax-payers pertinently say, "If you compel us, who have no children, to support schools for the good of the State, you must provide that the children fail not to share the advantages thus furnished." The question really is one not of right, but of expediency. "The people will not bear compulsion" is the main objection. In some States this may yet be true, and there coercion would be unwise. On this subject public sentiment is often misunderstood and the discernment of the masses is underrated. It is a significant fact that the labor-unions, both in this country and in Europe, favor obligatory education. Mixing much with the laboring classes for the purpose of promoting school-attendance, I have the best means of knowing their sentiments, and have been greatly encouraged by their appreciation of education, whether Americans, Germans, Swedes, or Irish.

FOREIGN INDORSEMENT OF THE LAW

The workingmen of Europe, in their various organizations, show their approval of compulsory education. At the International Workingmen's Congress, held at Lausanne, in Switzerland, the sentiment cordially adopted after full discussion was, "that education should be universal, compulsory, and national, but not denominational." In England they are earnestly advocating this measure. The opposition comes from the large farmers and property-holders. Attending the National Trades-Union Congress, held for five days at Nottingham, I found that body strongly favoring such a law. One of the members, a leader in the labor-league-movement, habitually addressing large assemblies of workingmen in all parts of the country, said he everywhere found among them great unanimity on this subject and never heard the objection that obligatory education would be a usurpation of parental or popular rights. No man in England so fully represents the sentiments of that most oppressed and depressed class, the farm-laborers of England, as Joseph Arch. He is a most earnest advocate of universal and compulsory education. Denied all early school-advantages, his own bitter experience has taught him to condemn the virtual exclusion of children from school by their constant employment on farms or in factories. His motto is, "Child-labor means pauperism, crime, ignorance, immorality, and every evil." The latest reports from England show that school-attendance has increased most in those towns which adopted the compulsory system. The absence of opposition from the lower classes and the good effects already witnessed are commending this measure to general favor.

The motto of the National Educational League, supported largely by the common people, is, "Education must be universal, unsectarian, and compulsory." This was the unanimous sentiment expressed at the great annual meeting of this association held in Birmingham two months ago. The compulsory plan is now in operation for about 78 per cent. of the borough-population of England, and, as the last number of the National Educational League says, it is working with great success and growing in public favor.

After many inquiries among the laboring classes in Germany, I could nowhere get from them any objection to compulsory education. They evidently favor it, and so generally regard the school as a privilege that attendance is voluntary, in fact, and few think of coercion. Said a resident of Dresden : "Were the question of compulsory attendance to be decided by a plebiscitum to-morrow, it would be sustained by an almost unanimous verdict."

It is a significant fact that Guizot during the last three years of his life stoutly advocated that compulsory system which he successfully opposed when minister of public instruction in 1833. The logic of events had refuted his old theory, that such "coercion was the creature of centralization and bore the marks of the convent and the barrack." A similar conversion occurred in the case of Canon Kingsley, just deceased. He long took a lively interest in the improvement of the working classes, an interest deepened by his service as government-inspector of schools. On finding that the working-people favored compulsory attendance, all his objections vanished.

Switzerland, the country most jealous of liberty and averse to any form of usurpation, has long maintained compulsory attendance in all of her twenty-two cantons, except in four of the smallest. In the recent revision of her constitution this law was made universal in its application. This country—proud of being so long the home of freedom in Europe, glorying in free schools, free speech, free press, free trade, freedom of traveling, and freedom of religion—has now chosen anew for all its people the system of compulsory attendance. No further facts are needed to show that the prepossessions of intelligent workingmen are not against obligatory education.

At the conclusion of the reading, Mr. Northrop said :

I have some circulars such as we have sent to every town in the State in large numbers and I have copies of a notice such as we have had posted in the factories of Connecticut. These have been put forth in English and in French, as the French Canadians are the persons whom we wish especially to inform on the subject. These papers, or sample copies, are here for distribution, if any of the members care to see them.

Mr. JOHN D. PHILBRICK, of Boston. I have listened with the greatest interest and pleasure to the paper which has been read and the accompanying remarks. It seems to me scarcely possible that any subject of greater importance in connection with the educational interests of the country can be presented for our consideration at this meeting ; and I am especially glad that the matter has been brought before us in this practical way, in illustrating what has been so successfully done in the State of Connecticut. I rise more especially to make one inquiry of the honorable secretary. That inquiry is in regard to direct compulsion. If I have understood the remarks that have been made, they have reference mainly to what our English cousins call "indirect compulsion;" that is, provision for compelling manufacturers to desist from the employment of children who have not had a certain prescribed amount of schooling. I should like to inquire, therefore, whether in Connecticut there is any provision of the school-law requiring children to attend a certain number of months; and, if so, whether there has been provision made for executing that law directly, bringing the children into school, compelling their attendance. I understand that the manufacturers are liable to fines or some other penalty for the employment of children who have not received during the year the prescribed amount of schooling. But is there no provision going directly to the child or to its parents, requiring attendance during the prescribed term in the public schools? Is there no provision for punishing the parent if the child does not attend the given number of months?

Mr. NORTHROP. I am much obliged for the inquiry. In the circular to which I have referred, you will find the law on the subject. I will read it:

All parents, and those who have the care of children, shall bring them up in some honest and lawful calling or employment and shall instruct them or cause them to be instructed in reading, writing, English grammar, geography, and arithmetic. And every parent, guardian, or other person having control and charge of any child between the ages of 8 and 14 years, shall cause such child to attend *some public or private day-school* at least three months in each year, six weeks at least of which attendance shall be consecutive, *or to be instructed at home* at least three months in each year in the branches of education required to be taught in the public schools, unless the physical or mental condition of the child is such as to render such attendance inexpedient or impracticable.

The penalty for the violation of the above provisions is a fine of five dollars "for every week, not exceeding thirteen weeks in any one year, during which any parent or guardian shall have failed to comply therewith."

At the outset we began with what may be properly called indirect legislation on the subject. We commenced with a stringent enforcement of the law in regard to the employment of children who had not attended the public school for the proper period. I have spoken of our action under that law. When we had this law in our hands, and were able to specify a penalty for disobedience to its provisions, we went to the manufacturers, in a conciliatory way, and secured their voluntary pledge of co-operation. And I was almost as much surprised as gratified to find the heartiness with which the manufacturers throughout the State came into the agreement; and I think it is really wonderful, as well as a theme for gratitude, to see how our manufacturers, as a rule, agreed to this pledge. We have an agent constantly employed in visiting the factories of the State. His aim is to get the name of every factory-child in Connecticut——

Mr. PHILBRICK, (interrupting.) The gentleman does not understand my question. The point was, whether there was any provision of law, bearing directly on the children or on the parents, compelling school-attendance; and, if so, what is the method of executing that law? I am not inquiring as to whether there are any officers in the State deputized to prepare a list of the children employed in the factories. My question is, whether the children are themselves actually required to attend school during three months in the year? If that is so, what are the provisions of the law?

Mr. NORTHROP. Large numbers of the manufacturers have given their promise, also, that, one week before the time when children must be sent from the factories to the school, they will send such a list of names to the school-visitors as is requisite, in order to facilitate and insure the execution of the law. This is a valuable co-operation. At the outset, before this compulsory law was passed, some parents and some manufacturers said that if children were not employed in the factories they would be idling in the streets. The law was then passed, or modified so as to provide for compulsory attendance of the children and that they should be sent to the schools as soon as they were discharged from the factories. This was the effect of it. The law was then made universal, making the duty of attendance obligatory upon the children and the parents, whether the child was sent from the factories or not. The law is now of universal application.

Professor M. A. NEWELL, of Maryland. I would like to ask the honorable secretary, in his estimate of the good results arising from these compulsory laws, as he ascribes them, how much he really thinks is due to the voluntary pledges taken by the manufacturers themselves. Judging from his argument, the good results appear to be due more to the pledges voluntarily taken by the manufacturers than to the laws themselves.

Mr. NORTHROP. I think we owe much to the co-operation of the manufacturers, but I think the pledge itself was due to the law. I have no certain idea that we could have obtained that voluntary pledge from the manufacturers if they had not known that the moment they refused we would have put on the screws.

Mr. NEWELL. Now, is not my friend from Connecticut well satisfied that if he, or his agent, had gone around among the manufacturers, as he describes, and asked for signatures to such a pledge, without any law in the background, that a great proportion of those who did sign under the law would have signed without the law ?

Mr. NORTHROP. A great number, no doubt, would have done so. Not all, but many.

Mr. PHILBRICK. I am very much obliged to the honorable secretary for the answers which have been given to my questions, and I am very much interested in all that he has said; but I do not yet understand how these children are reached in the State of Connecticut. He has told us how they are reached and designated when employed in factories. Now, there is a large class of children in that as in every State who are not employed in any manufacturing-establishments. Therefore, any indirect compulsion operating through the manufacturers does not touch them, is not brought to bear upon them.

My question is, what is done under the law in the State of Connecticut in such cases where the children do not attend or labor in any of the manufacturing-establishments, where the parents of the children are able to, and willing to, support them without requiring any work in such establishments from them?

Mr. NORTHROP. The law applies directly to them as much as to any other children. I can explain in a few words how we reach them. I will read from this circular, which explains how the school-officers in each of the towns are required by law to inquire into the attendance of children living within the boundaries of their school-districts:

The board of education have appointed Mr. Giles Potter as agent to secure the observance of this law. For this purpose he is now visiting different parts of the State and occasionally lecturing on educational topics. His experience in the legislature, and especially in the revision of the school-laws, in which he took the most active part, will enable him to give needed information to the school-officers with whom he is constantly conferring. *As school-visitors are required by law to inquire into the causes and extent of non-attendance, they are requested to communicate to the secretary of the board any facts they may learn as to neglect in the schooling of children.* While the board of education must take the steps "proper to secure the due observance" of the law, it is hoped the necessity of rigorous measures may be avoided.

Occasionally such information comes to us; and, if the school-visitors cannot meet the exigency, if they cannot meet the difficulty, or wish any help, we send at once to that particular town our agent, Mr. Giles Potter. Even if it be only one family that is complained of, he will go to that town for the sake of reaching a single family. He will say to that family that unless their child or children attend school we shall at once commence a prosecution. In some four or five cases parents have announced that they would defy the law. Then a complaint was laid before the grand jury. When they found that we were in earnest in regard to the matter, their children began to attend school. They were very willing, apparently, to secure the withdrawal of the complaint, by compliance with the law.

Mr. PHILBRICK. Allow me to ask another question, and that is, if the authorities in the State of Connecticut have had to do with parents who were unable to provide text-books or clothing for their children and how it is that the compulsory law reaches that class of children if such have to be provided for? I am quite well aware that there is a class in Connecticut, perhaps a larger class than in any other State, in which the parents have their children employed in manufactories and obtain wages for them, and they are very reluctant to send them to school. But there must be another class of children whose parents at the best are unable to furnish their children with suitable books or comfortable clothing. There is a class of orphans and half-orphans. There is a class of vagrant children whose parents feel or exhibit no great interest in their welfare and are either unable or unwilling to furnish them with proper school-books and clothing. How are these classes reached under the system adopted in Connecticut?

Mr. NORTHROP. No doubt there are some of that class who escape us. We have sent out printed circulars to every town, having reference to such a class; but such efforts as we have made are not claimed as of universal efficacy. We have recommended contributions and the provision of funds for use in supplying text-books for such children as are unable to purchase them; and we have urged strongly that some general plan be adopted for supplying the children of very indigent parents with suitable school-clothing—some such plan as has been so successfully employed in some Sunday-school-enterprises. We don't claim that we have met this difficulty fully, and, as I have said, there are, no doubt, some cases of destitution or perhaps of willful vagrancy.

Mr. PHILBRICK. Then I do not understand that there is any machinery in the State of Connecticut for executing the compulsory law which exists, except such as consists in the visits of this special agent. I do not understand that there are any truant-officers, who make it their special business in certain districts to go from house to house and see that every child is properly in attendance at school. I understand that there are no such officers in Connecticut.

Mr. NORTHROP. The school-visitors are specially invited to appoint one of their number to attend to this duty. It is not always done.

Mr. PHILBRICK. Are they directly required by law to attend to this duty?

Mr. NORTHROP. The school-visitors are by law required to see to the attendance of children within their districts.

Mr. PHILBRICK. They are not required to appoint special officers for this work?

Mr. NORTHROP. No, sir.

Mr. PHILBRICK. There is no compulsion brought to bear on the school-visitors for the execution of this duty?

Mr. NORTHROP. There is no compulsion brought to bear upon them in that respect. There is no penalty attached to their failure in this particular.

2э

Mr. PHILBRICK. Then it seems there is a deficiency in the law when it comes to practical application. You have a resolution calling upon visitors to do this thing, and there is no compulsion by law in regard to it. It seems to me that, if the school-visitors here or there should differ from the legislature in their view of the law, there would be no means of requiring them to appoint any person to see that the children in their neighborhood attended school for the proper period.

Mr. NORTHROP. There are truant-officers in the city of New Haven. You have possibly noticed the fact that during school-hours you cannot find any boy to black your boots. The boys are in attendance upon the school or are playing shy of the officers. There are truant-officers in Hartford, and in New London, and in other cities; and I believe that they are efficient where they are employed.

Mr. NEWELL. I should like to ask one question. I would like to inquire if the secretary has any means of ascertaining the proportion of children in attendance at school all the year round—who are employed and who are idle.

Mr. NORTHROP. We have returns from the manufacturing-establishments, as I have said.

Mr. NEWELL. Have you definite means for determining the proportion of children employed and of children who are idle when not in school ?

Mr. NORTHROP. As I have stated, the aggregate attendance is 95.65 per cent., almost 96 per cent., and is very encouraging, although it is not up to where it ought to be. We hope to bring it up higher. But, when you consider the very large number of children between 4 and 5 years of age, whose attendance at school we discourage, we submit that the result of the calculation is gratifying.

Mr. NEWELL. How near does the average attendance reach your figures ?

Mr. NORTHROP. I can read the figures to you from the report. Of course the average attendance will diminish just in proportion as the aggregate attendance increases; that is to say, the more strictly you enforce the law prohibiting the employment of children unless they have attended three months in the year, the greater will be the number who will attend only three months in the year, the greater will be the number of poor children who will attend school as the law requires and no longer; and so the average attendance will be less. If it will not weary you I will read the figures.

Mr. A. C. HOPKINS. Does this 95 per cent. come within the limit of children between 4 and 16 years of age ? In other words, is the highest limit of enumeration 16 years ? In the schools out West we have persons 16, 17, 18, and 20 years of age attending school. Now, I would like to ask if in your enumeration all such attendants, over 16, are counted in ?

Mr. NORTHROP. They are all counted in.

Mr. HOPKINS. That will make quite a difference.

Mr. NORTHROP. But that number is more than counterbalanced by the number of children at school within the year at which we limit or advise first attendance.

Mr. PHILBRICK. It is not my purpose to occupy the attention of the convention by making any extended speech, but I wish to say a very few words before the subject is finally disposed of. I wish to say that I feel that the experiment in Connecticut is another valuable argument in favor of this principle of compulsion; and I am one of those, Mr. President, who fully believe, who have the firmest and most unshaken convictions, not only in the expediency of this principle as an indispensable element in our system of public schools in the different States, but I also believe, from the evidence which we have in this country and in other countries, that compulsion, direct compulsion—what we call compulsory education in the common sense of the term—is destined to be absolutely universal in every country that pretends to educate its children. That is, in a word, my creed on this subject; and the more I study history, the more I observe the workings of this system at the present day and the great drift of public sentiment in different countries on this subject, the more strongly am I convinced. The honorable secretary has alluded, I think, to the recent movement in England in regard to this subject, and I think, Mr. Chairman, that we have a lesson given us in the experience of England on this subject, which is of the greatest importance. Within the last fifteen or sixteen years, I have come in contact with a great many leading Englishmen—men high in influence, men deeply interested in the subject of popular education in Great Britain. Every one of these men up to the year 1870, without exception, said: "No matter what else we might be able to do in Great Britain to advance the cause of public education, one thing we can never do, and that is, we can never inaugurate a system of compulsory education." "The people of England," they said, "have too much of the sentiment of individual liberty. They are too self-willed, too spirited in resisting everything that looks like a tyrannical coercion. They will never consent to such a system. You may persuade them; you may bring to bear upon them moral suasion; you may make your schools attractive and beautiful, and so appeal successfully to their intelligence, or good nature, or pride. But as for compulsion, we can never think of that."

Well, what has been the result? The leading men of England, who handled the great bill of 1870, which was passed, looking at the experience of Europe, said that they would venture for Great Britain this measure in the interests of popular education. But even in their spirit of venture they were most considerate and cautious. They said: "We will venture to ingraft in this bill a simple provision for local compulsory action. We will claim it as a provision under the principles of English liberty. We will provide the local right for compelling the attendance of children, so that, in any particular city, district, or neighborhood, the subjects of Great Britain may have compulsory education if they desire it." And they draughted that measure in accordance with these sentiments, expecting that it would result in a practical adoption in hardly any instance. This was a feeler. It was thrown out as a tentative provision, to see what the result would be. Now, what has that result been? Why, sir, the facts which are recorded before us are something scarcely less than astounding. The whole city of London has been canvassed, and the name, and age, and residence of every child taken with reference to the execution of a compulsory law. Every portion of that great city has been districted by boundaries of convenient size. And every one of these districts is furnished with truant-officers, appointed solely with the official view and authority, under the law of the kingdom, to go from house to house and see that the children are at school. And over them are local superintendents, whose work is supervised by a general superintendent. So that we may say that, so far as the system is concerned, they are not behind any of our States in this movement; and especially may we say this from the mere fact of the law being upon the statute-book. There they make laws to be enforced and enforce laws that are made. They do not pass laws there to be disregarded. They are well known as peculiar in that respect. To pass a law in view of its being ignored or disregarded is something that they cannot exactly comprehend. They do not know what that means.

When, under the statute, the boards of education adopted these rules, they adopted them with the purpose of executing them. The law and the rules under the law are being executed there, and compulsory education is as fully and completely enforced throughout the whole city of London as it ever was in any part of Prussia, or Saxony, or Brandenburg. And that is only one example. Such is the condition of affairs there. Attendance has already been reported which reaches 79 per cent. of the enumeration. But the most extraordinary thing in connection with this whole matter I am about to state. Mr. W. E. Forster, a man who came up from the people, the father of the educational law, really the great promoter of this work which is being carried on by the national board of education—Mr. Forster, who is, I may say, the coming statesman of England—on a public occasion in England, in August, in Sheffield, at the dedication of the new school-house—declared that he placed himself squarely on the platform of universal compulsory education. Mr. Forster said that he hoped the Disraeli government would have the honor, which they could not claim, but which they would be glad to claim, of making compulsory education universal. Now, it is within the discretion of the school-boards to adopt the system. Now, I say this is the lesson for America to study, for we are of the same race. We have the same literature and the same general ideas of advance in civilization.

It is said that this may be considered as a question of expediency.

Look at the history of this matter in other countries. There is Belgium; forty-four years ago they adopted a system of education somewhat similar to the one that has been considered. But it was determined that the people were opposed to compulsory education. The law was not executed, even as it stood. Where is that people now? These very people have made a careful survey of the illiteracy of the country and spread it before the world. What story does that tell? We have the astounding fact that half of the population of Belgium is unable to read and write to-day. Compare this side by side with the reports from Switzerland. In every country where education is compulsory the ability to read and write is universal. And look at the reports from Prussia, where the system has been so thoroughly enforced. We find that out of the great population of the city of Berlin, only two out of one thousand were unable to read and write, while, from reports coming from France, we discover that twenty-nine out of every one hundred cannot read and write. This, sir, tells the story. And as a great philosopher said thirty or forty years ago, when he urged the introduction of this system in Prussia, with a prophetic vision of the future, "The compulsory features of the law will only be required for the first generation. When the system is once fairly inaugurated, as it will be in one generation, very little compulsion will be needed or known." That proved to be literally true, and it proved to be exactly the same in Saxony. And I will say here, without desiring to impeach the general historical accuracy of my friend, the secretary, that I think, if he will go back, he will find that this principle was promulgated in Saxony and in Massachusetts at the same time. I see that he places Connecticut in the same category with Massachusetts.

Mr. NORTHROP. I put Massachusetts first.

Mr. PHILBRICK. I see that a famous gentleman—a gentleman who has become pretty well known lately—Mr. Henry Ward Beecher, made a speech the other day, in which he said that Connecticut had the honor of inaugurating compulsory education. A law was passed on this subject in Massachusetts in 1847, but that was not the first. The principle of the law was declared and adopted in France in 1580, but it was not carried out. So it was in Saxony, but it was not carried out until about thirty or forty years ago. There was a great pressure in regard to it at first, but now, in these European countries, although it is on the statute-books, it is not necessary to enforce it.

I may speak a word in regard to the system which we have in Boston. We have there a number of truant-officers. The law was passed providing for this system in 1850. The people were afraid to touch it at first. They went up to it, or were led up to it, as a horse goes up to a lumber-wagon at first and takes a little smell of it, and by and by they began to consider that it was not such a very bad thing after all. But it could not be enforced. We could not get a law that would stand the test of judgment of an old gentleman who sat on the bench. Finally we got a lawyer to draw up a law; but that would not work. We finally got one of our judges to draw a law which he was willing to execute. Then we took hold of it. In 1863 the system of bringing in the absentees had a practical commencement, and since 1863 the work has gone on very well. There are now fourteen truant-officers, with a superintendent at their head, in the several districts. The provision is, of course, for compulsory schooling during three months in the year, and we had some circulars printed for distribution among the parents. But the officers advised against their distribution. And for what reason? I will tell you, sir. They are really practicing there what might be called a species of pious fraud. Many, and perhaps the majority, of the parents think that under the law their children must go to school the year round. The officers say that if they take these circulars or cards around the parents will become better informed on the subject, and, finding that their children need not go but three months in the year, many will not send them beyond that time. [Merriment.] As it is, they think they must go all the year round. And one of the most curious and happy effects which I have observed from this work, among the very class of people to whom I have just referred, is the cultivation of such a sentiment and feeling among the children that they consider themselves disgraced by voluntary absence from school. They have come to that belief to a great extent. They want knowledge. They are becoming proud of their school-privileges.

For one, I must say that I am thoroughly in favor of the compulsory system, and believe it will be more and more approved in proportion as it is thoroughly executed.

General EATON. The committee desire to state that they have information that the President of the United States will be pleased to receive the members of the association between 12 and 1 o'clock. The committee would suggest that the members pay their visit at half-past twelve o'clock. It is understood that the department will proceed, under the lead of President Wilson, to the Executive Mansion. Before that time, however, there will probably be a further report from the committee on the order of business.

Mr. NEWELL, of Maryland. I have sometimes been classified as opposed to compulsory education; but if compulsory education is to be understood as it is explained by my friend from Connecticut, as I have heard him here to-day, I must say that I have very little fault indeed to find with it. We really do not need, however, a compulsory law until the public sentiment has been thoroughly conciliated in every State; for after this thorough conciliation and consolidation of public sentiment the law is to be carried out in a spirit of preservation. Then, sir, with regard to such a system, I should be inclined to place myself among its most sincere and hearty advocates; but what I do object to is the introduction of compulsion before the people are ready for it. What I object to still more is the idea that the mere placing of such a law upon the statute-book will prove a panacea for all the evils of which he complains. There would be very little difficulty in having enacted a compulsory law in any State of this Union. The difficulty lies in the enforcement of it; and unless you are prepared to thoroughly organize a body of officers to carry out the requirements of your law, then your law is just so much waste-paper. With regard to the advantages that are alleged to have followed during the past few years, in Connecticut, from the enforcement of a compulsory system, as I understand it, I may say, or may suggest, that it is very doubtful whether all the increase of attendance has resulted from the enactment of the compulsory statute or not. At all events I will give you a figure on the other side. We have no compulsory law in Maryland. The increase of attendance during the past year has been six thousand and some-odd persons. That may be put in comparison with an increase of four thousand which has been stated as the result of the compulsory system in Connecticut. But really the figures do not mean anything. I do not put these figures in opposition. I do not mean to say that they show that the increase would be greater with or without compulsory law. My object is merely to show that the statement given for Connecticut does not prove anything at all in the matter.

I think, Mr. President, that the arguments and facts advanced by our friend from Massachusetts, drawn from his experience and from the history of the European countries, are not exactly in point. There is an institution with which I have been connected in the State of Maryland, the president of which entertains a very exalted notion with regard to the abilities of the English and Welsh people as farmers, and he made up his mind that he would introduce somewhat of the English system of farming into the institution with which he was connected. He entered into correspondence with a friend in England, and had sent over to him a first-class English farming-man. This man understood everything about agriculture in a scientific way, as far as it was developed in the country where he was born and from which he was imported. Being asked to approve the proposition in regard to the salary of this gentleman, I said that I would make no opposition to it. But I desired the gentleman who was responsible in the premises to consider that there was a vast difference between the climate of England and the climate of that part of the United States in which this farm-manager was expected to operate; also that he would find a great difference in the kind of labor in which he was employed; also that familiarity with the crops raised in England was a very different matter from understanding our American soil and adaptibilities. I expressed my belief that unless the president exercised great superintending care his English farm-manager might get him into trouble. Notwithstanding these doubts the gentleman was employed, and things went on after his arrival swimmingly during the winter. [Merriment.]

The season for corn-planting was approaching. The English farm-manager was told to commence his work. He did not know exactly what to do. He went around to the neighboring farms and talked with the common laborers; and, finding one of the most intelligent of the number, he said to him, "Can you tell me how you plant this corn? Do you plant it with the point downwards or the but-end downwards?" That is what he knew about raising corn. Now, had it been wheat he would have been perfectly at home. He knew everything about the raising of that crop, for which Englishmen are celebrated, but in regard to corn he knew nothing at all; nothing in regard to our most important crop; and when our friend was making an application of the history and progress of this movement in England I was thinking that perhaps the condition of our social institutions, and social interests, and social habits was such as to render the argument he would deduce illogical and inapplicable.

I think the whole question of compulsory education has been in one sense given up by the elastic and conciliatory management of it which has been proposed by my friend from Boston. Not only is it not sufficient that we have a compulsory law; not only is it not sufficient in Boston that this compulsory law be executed by a number of truant-officers; but in order to have it thoroughly executed it must be carried out by a "pious fraud." Now I would not call attention to this but for this single purpose and to emphasize the fact that the amount of education we are able to obtain by statute amounts, in the long run, to nothing at all. We need a pious fraud to make it worth anything. Mr. President, what is three months in the year? What is three months in the year, then, to the child who is honestly anxious to be educated and for the parents honestly anxious to send it to school? This absolutely amounts to nothing in the nine months that intervene. Supposing these three months to be consecutive, your child will lose during the nine months he is absent from the school all that he has acquired during the early portion of the year. It is a very different matter where you take a person of 15, or 16, or 17, or 18 years of age; then three months at a night-school or at a day-school may effect a great deal; but your child of 6, or 7, or 8 years of age will most certainly forget in the nine months nearly all that he has learned in the three months. But in regard to the other classes whom you wish to benefit by this law it may be said that you cannot get these three months of schooling consecutively. Their names are upon the books, but their bodies are not in the school-room, and in many instances they will be unable to attend school three consecutive months. There are accidents and sickness or injury to be considered, reducing the amount of actual attendance. I have heard it said that, if a compulsory law does no good, it will do no harm. I say it will do no harm if it is executed as our friend has just described, but it will do a great deal of harm if the people think that that is all that is necessary. I might throw a light chair to a drowning man and say, if it does him no good it will do him no harm; but it may do him a great deal of harm if he trust to it, while it is not sufficient to support him. If this compulsory system is trusted to and relied upon absolutely it will deceive you. We may make use of it, but we want more than that; we want something better than that.

Mr. G. J. LUCKEY, of Pittsburg. I am fully impressed with the importance of the subject which is up before us for discussion. It has been said by our friend from Maryland that he is opposed to the enactment of compulsory laws until the mass of the people are ready for them. If we wait until the people are ready for them, then I may say we will have no use for compulsory laws.

Mr. NEWELL. I object to relying entirely upon compulsory laws; but I stated that, if they were executed as has been reported from Connecticut, I had no fault to find with them.

Mr. LUCKEY. We need compulsory educational laws; and we need them as one of the great safeguards of our republican institutions. I do not suppose that there is a thoughtful person in our country who does not see every day the tendency of the people in large centers of population to override and trample under foot the free institutions of the land and the system of law and order which we claim to have established; and this is to be observed just in proportion as the people are deficient in education and culture. In our country, where our people are intelligent, there is no fear for our republican institutions; but in the States where the great mass of our people are uneducated there is danger that our institutions will be overthrown or impaired. There is such danger always where the masses of the people are ignorant. I would like, therefore, to have this convention give its influence directly in favor of compulsory education. Before we leave this subject, I would like to ask a question of the honorable secretary in regard to the first part of this law of the State of Connecticut, which reads:

All parents, and those who have the care of children, shall bring them up in some honest and lawful calling or employment and shall instruct them or cause them to be instructed in reading, writing, English grammar, geography, and arithmetic. And every parent, guardian, or other person having control and charge of any child between the ages of 8 and 14 years, shall cause such child to attend some public or private day-school at least three months in each year, six weeks at least of which attendance shall be consecutive, or to be instructed at home at least three months in each year in the branches of education required to be taught in the public schools, unless the physical or mental condition of the child is such as to render such attendance inexpedient or impracticable.

That is one of the best provisions I ever saw in any law. But how is it to be executed? I would like some light on this subject. Perhaps we need a provision of that kind as much as we need a compulsory clause in our school-law.

There is another point to which I would like to call the attention of this convention before this subject is dropped, and that is this: In Prussia they have no free-school-system; every parent is compelled to pay for the education of his child, and yet all are required to be educated.

What provision is made in Prussia for the poor children or in aid of the poor parents? I know that in this country, unless we have some provision enacted with this compulsory law which will enable the very poor parents to furnish their sons and daughters with books and clothing, this compulsory provision will be a nullity. I visited in my own State, the other day, twenty families who were living in one house, and not a shoe nor a stocking upon a child in the house with perhaps five or six exceptions. There were twenty rooms in the house and twenty families. These children had to be provided by the charitably-inclined "school-marms" of the State with shoes and stockings before we could ask them to go to school. I would like to know how it is in those countries—particularly in Prussia—where compulsory education is enforced; what provision is made for the children of the poor? As I said before, they are not only required in Prussia to send their children to school, but they are required to pay tuition. This is more than our people are required to do here. I am glad that this subject is being discussed as it is; I hope it will be deferred until our next session for further discussion; but I think that in the mean time our friend from Maryland will change his views upon the subject; because he is a good man to have on the right side of a question, and I do not like to see him on the wrong side. I might remark, with regard to his little anecdote about the English farmer attempting to raise corn in Maryland, that it would kill any man to try and raise corn down there. [Great laughter.]

The PRESIDENT. The Chair will be obliged to suspend the discussion at this point, as the time is approaching for our visit to the President of the United States. A communication has been received, directed to the department, from ex-Governor Shepherd, inviting the members to visit him socially at his house, corner of Connecticut avenue and K street, to-morrow evening.

General EATON. I move that the invitation of Governor Shepherd be accepted and that we return him our sincere thanks for his proffered hospitality.

The motion was adopted.

General EATON. From the President's House we will go to the Corcoran Art-Gallery; and from that place we will proceed to listen to a lecture by Professor Walter Smith, on drawing, before the teachers of this District, which lecture will be delivered at the Jefferson School-Building at 2 o'clock. We will meet here again this evening for business at 15 minutes before 7. At 7 o'clock we will listen to an address by Dr. A. N. Bell, of New York, editor of The Sanitarian, on "Brain-culture in relation to the school-room." Doctor Bell is in the city at present engaged in discussing the subject with other physicians. The committee are unable to proceed in determining any future portion of the programme, as all the gentlemen are not here whose names have been put down in the list of speakers. As far as we can determine, however, we believe that we shall have to-morrow morning, at 11 o'clock, Mr. Wickersham's paper on the Centennial. And it is proposed at some time to have a brief illustrated address from Professor Enthoffer, on the origin of the alphabet. To-morrow evening, at 7 o'clock, we shall expect a lecture from Professor Walter Smith, on drawing, with illustrations. It is proposed that we call upon the Secretary of the Interior to-morrow morning at half-past nine o'clock.

A DELEGATE. Make it 10 o'clock instead of half-past nine.

General EATON. I wish to say to the members present that, as far as the efficiency of the Bureau of Education is concerned, it depends very much on the favor and support given to it by the Secretary of the Interior, and it is due to the Secretary to say that this Bureau has always had his cordial co-operation.

It was agreed that the visit of respect to the Secretary of the Interior should be made as suggested by the Chair.

The PRESIDENT. I wish to state that I have received letters from Mr. Binford, of Richmond, and Mr. Apgar, of New Jersey, expressing their regret on account of their inability to attend the department-meeting; and I would state that the Jefferson building, where Mr. Smith will lecture this afternoon, is situated at the corner of Sixth and D streets southwest, toward the river; either line of cars will bring you within a block of the building.

The department then took a recess and proceeded to the Executive Mansion, where they were received by President Grant in his private office.

REMARKS OF SUPERINTENDENT WILSON.

Mr. J. O. Wilson introduced the delegates to the President, after which he made the following address:

Mr. PRESIDENT: The members of the department of superintendence of the National Educational Association, now in session in this city, have called to pay their respects to you and to say that they highly appreciate the deep interest you feel in education, to which you have given such emphatic expression in your messages to Congress.

RESPONSE OF THE PRESIDENT.

The President responded as follows:

I feel that the advancement of the cause of education would be one of the best reconstructive movements we could have in the country, and therefore I have felt, in addition to other reasons, a deep interest in it. I do not see how a pure republic is to be maintained, unless it is based on the intelligence of the people. That requires educational privileges for all the people. Without a combined interest and effort in every section of the country for the support of educational facilities, it will be impossible to obtain the results which we most desire in this respect. In order that there may be a combination and harmony of interest in this matter, I have always been ready and anxious to give my support to any proper means for this end and purpose.

SIGHT-SEEING.

The visitors then took leave of the President, and were shown through the White House, after which they went to the Corcoran Art-Gallery, where they were most courteously received by Mr. W. MacLeod, curator, and Dr. F. S. Barbarin, assistant curator, who pointed out the many works of art in the building. After spending some time most pleasantly at the gallery, the line was again formed, and a visit was made to the Jefferson School-Building, where Professor Walter Smith, State-director of art-education in Massachusetts, addressed the teachers of the District of Columbia on the subject of " Drawing in public schools."

The large hall was filled with the teachers and their friends, who paid the closest attention to the professor's conversational explanations and blackboard-illustrations of the value and practical methods of teaching drawing.

EVENING-SESSION.

The department assembled at 7 o'clock.

The PRESIDENT. It was considered important to have the subject of school-hygiene treated on this occasion by some one who could speak with authority, and accordingly we have invited the gentleman that I now have the honor of introducing to you, Dr. A. N. Bell, of New York, editor of The Sanitarian. [Applause.]

ADDRESS OF DR. A. N. BELL.

Dr. Bell said:

Mr. PRESIDENT, LADIES, AND GENTLEMEN: The paper which I have the honor of reading to you this evening is entitled

BRAIN-CULTURE IN RELATION TO THE SCHOOL-ROOM.

Education is a primary necessity of man. It is by education that the organs of the body acquire accuracy in their movements. The senses of sight, hearing, taste, and smell all learn to act. And the earliest charm of infant-life is to observe the progress of the education of the senses; to watch the study of a toy; to see the hands holding it at various distances, turning its different sides to view, tasting it, shaking it, and finally, when a little older, breaking it to see whence comes the noise. Who that has watched this process has not learned the first accomplishment of a teacher, to promote the education of the senses by the association of physical exercise, amusement, and study?

The passage from infancy to childhood is but an imperceptible step, marked by the continued expression of new experiences. Everything excites new impressions; everything must be examined with due deliberation; no hurry, no pressure, no fatigue. And during the while, ay, even during the whole period of waking hours, there is incessant motion. Nature has implanted in the young of all animals a pleasure in exercise. Muscular action being not only necessary for strengthening the muscles, but also the bones to which they are attached, the actions of crying and laughing, the deep inspirations of sobbing and joy, both alike tend to develop and strengthen the lungs. And the active exercise of the lungs promotes and develops the action of the heart, which, with increasing vigor, sends the blood to every part of the body. In all this the brain participates to an extraordinary degree, requiring that the young mind be exercised with the utmost care. By experience and habit the child acquires judgment, learns to compare one movement with another, to direct its organs to special objects, to produce this or that action, to take this or that attitude for the accomplishment of its purposes. And all the subsequent capacity of the brain will greatly depend upon the care with which it is cultured during the period of growth.

Imagination, perception, and memory—faculties which are always preceded and determined by the sensations—are all the subjects of education, enlarged and extended in proportion as new excitements and impressions call them forth and give them application.

"Glancing broadly at the whole range of psycho-physical phenomena," observes Dr. Tuke, "it is clear that it would be taking a very contracted view of the relation between mind and body, if we did not include in this relationship a reference to the inseparable *nexus* existing between the two, arising out of the fact that the organ of the mind is but the outgrowth and ultimate development of the tissues and organs of which the body itself is composed; that it not only unites them in one bond, but is, in truth, a microcosm of the whole."[*] Of all parts of the human body the brain is the last to gain maturity. According to Owen, "the brain has advanced to near its term of size at about ten years, but it does not usually obtain its full development till between twenty and thirty years of age."[†] While the brain has not usually more than *one-fortieth* of the weight of the body, it receives about *one-fifth* of the whole volume of the blood. It is scarcely necessary to state in this connection that every organ and tissue of the body is nourished by the blood, and that upon the supply of it, and the condition of it, nutrition and development for weal or for woe depend. During the period of growth there is not only the development of new parts, but, in the brain especially, a change of structure going on until that degree of perfection has been attained which is necessary to the exercise of all the functions. Hence this period is characterized by extraordinary functional activity in every part of the body. It is this which makes the demand for food so much greater during the period of growth than in after-years. Not, however, that the larger proportion of food in demand is wholly required as new material applied to actual increase, for that bears a very small proportion to the amount required for constant renewal which the increase involves, but the extraordinary functional activity in disposing of it and the corresponding necessity for replacing the waste in the building-up and perfecting the structure according to the original plan. For it is characteristic of every living thing to follow out a certain inherent type or pattern, subject, of course, in some degree, to modification under the influence of external conditions, or, when these are aggravated, to acute disease and death; but such circumstances do not effect a permanent change in the original design. During the period of growth and change of structure the modifying influence of external conditions is most strongly marked. The constitution of the individual adapts itself to the circumstances and becomes fixed for the life-time. So that, if a child of originally healthy constitution be subject for any considerable length of time to such injurious physical conditions as produce a tendency to disease, unless the conditions are speedily changed, the effect is to establish a constitutional weakness or disease, not only during the life of the individual, but, it may be, a *diathesis*, with hereditary qualities for several generations. For, when the modification of the individual is once fixed in the growing brain, it becomes part of the general fabric; the different organs adapt themselves to the change and the condition is maintained by nutritive substitution. On the other hand, constitutional vices contracted during the period of growth may be gradually overcome in the progress of new generations, and, by a continued subjection to healthy surroundings, the normal type regained. It is apparent, therefore, that these changes of growth and structure are all affected by and through the circulation of the blood; its condition depends upon the air we breathe.

Air, everybody knows, is the absolute necessity of every living thing. It is the very first element of our bodily tissues, and breathing affords three-quarters of the nourishment of our bodies; and the other quarter, which we obtain in the form of solid and fluid aliment, is also in great part composed of oxygen, nitrogen, and carbonic acid—the elements of the atmosphere.

Chemically, the air consists of a mixture of two kinds of gases, oxygen, or *vital air*,

[*] Influence of Mind upon the Body in Health and Disease. By Daniel Hack Tuke, M. D., M. R. C. P., p. 23, Philadelphia edition, 1873.
[†] Anatomy of Vertebrates. By Richard Owen, F. R. S.; vol. iii, p. 144; London, 1868.

and nitrogen, in the proportion, by volume, of one-fifth of the former to four-fifths of the latter, and, besides these, carbonic acid, or *fixed air*, which exists in the free atmosphere in the proportion of about four parts to ten thousand.

In the small proportion in which carbonic acid exists in the free atmosphere it produces no evil effects; but in larger quantities it is not only dangerous, but frequently fatal. Being heavier than the other gases of the atmosphere, it is usually found in excess in low or confined places, such as mines, grottoes, and wells, and in the holds and steerages of ships, and in unventilated apartments generally. Under all such circumstances it is more or less dangerous to life. The bad air at the surface of close rooms is carbonic oxid, the product, usually, of burning gas and bad arrangements for warming. This, being the lightest of the deleterious gases, in close rooms rises to the surface.*

Pure oxygen will sustain life but a short time, owing to its stimulating qualities; it requires dilution, which seems to be the purpose of nitrogen, which cannot sustain life at all, and alone is deadly from its negative qualities. Carbonic acid pure is not respirable. If an attempt be made to inhale it, the glottis closes and prevents it from entering the lungs. When diluted with twice as much or more of air, it ceases to produce that effect upon the glottis, and is permitted to enter the lungs and the blood, and acts as a narcotic poison directly upon the brain. It is not possible to state how large a proportion of this gas may be present in the air without danger; it doubtless differs with different individuals. By experiments on animals it has been shown that an atmosphere containing 5 per cent. of carbonic acid is fatal in about thirty minutes.

Facts abundantly prove that respired air, or the air of occupied apartments containing of carbonic acid more than one volume per 1,000, is dangerous to health. Such air contains, besides the excess of carbonic acid, not infrequently the more deadly carbonic oxid, dead and decomposing animal matter, and other mephitic gases and exhalations arising from defective sewerage or vaults, but it is deficient in its very first life-sustaining property—oxygen—conditions predisposing to and frequently the cause of many fatal diseases.

The average amount of oxygen consumed by a healthy individual is half a cubic inch to every respiration, which in a day amounts to upwards of 25 cubic feet; and, as oxygen constitutes but one-fifth of the volume of the atmosphere, a single individual renders 125 cubic feet of air unfit for respiration every twenty-four hours by the abstraction of oxygen alone. Meanwhile there is exhaled by the lungs about 15 cubic feet of carbonic acid, 30 ounces of watery vapor, and an indefinite amount of organic matter, variously estimated at from 10 to 240 grains.

The whole quantity of air actually respired in twenty-four hours by a healthy person is about 400 cubic feet. This contains, when once passed through the lungs, 5¼ per cent. of carbonic acid, or more than one hundred times as much as it did when it entered them. It is plain, therefore, that in order to reduce respired air to the same standard of purity it had before it was respired, and to keep it so, the supply of fresh air must be at the least equal to one hundred times the volume of that which is thrown out, and upon this condition rests the importance of air-space, the space required depending upon circumstances. For various practical purposes the limits of space may vary from 300 to 4,000 cubic feet, the smallest proportion being the exaction for lodging-houses and the largest for hospitals, making due allowance in all cases for space occupied by furniture. And no deviation whatever should be made on account of children, whether in regard to the different members of a family or a school-room.

The smaller the space, the greater the necessity of, and the larger the opening required for, the admission of fresh air. If two or three hundred cubic feet only be allowed to the individual, the air must be changed every fifteen or twenty minutes, provision for which necessitates a draught and in cold weather great waste of heat.

* Specific gravity: Oxygen, (unit,) 1,000; atmospheric air, in the aggregate, 1105.63; nitrogen, 971.37; carbonic acid, 1524.5; carbonic oxid, 971.2.—*Graham.*

Hence it is evident that the danger of "taking cold" in a small room, if it is kept ventilated. is much greater than it is in a large one. To reduce the gaseous components of respired air to their natural proportions and to neutralize its deleterious qualities. every person requires from 2,000 to 2,500 cubic feet of fresh air every hour.

To admit this amount of fresh air into a room is not as difficult as persons generally suppose. It has been calculated that with ordinary exposure an open space equal to five inches in the square will admit the passage of 2,000 cubic feet of air hourly; this, of course, implies that there should be an equal amount of open space for the escape of the air displaced. If, therefore, an ordinary window of three feet wide be open about an inch and a half at the top, and there be a chimney-flue in the room, the purpose is accomplished. Or the same by two windows on opposite sides of the room ; or, it may be by crevices equal to this space about a door, in co-operation with one window. The multiplication of persons, it is plain, requires a corresponding multiplication of means.

In the aeration of the blood the organs of circulation and respiration are both no less essential to the maintenance of life than they are to each other. Their combined functions constitute the only means of admitting air into the body. And these functions must co-operate and be maintained, without intermission for one single minute, from birth until death. And yet, they have rest; the heart reposes about one-fourth of its time. and the lungs about one-third, but the periods of repose are too short to allow of any escape from a dangerous atmosphere.

The amount of blood in the human body constitutes about one-eighth of its entire weight, but it is variable within certain limits, depending upon the time and amount of food taken. Air is drawn into the lungs through the windpipe or trachea, which divides and subdivides into numerous smaller tubes leading to the air-cells, which, in the aggregate, constitute the lungs, situated one on each side of the chest and the heart between. The number of the air-cells has been estimated at seventeen millions, presenting a surface, if spread out, equal to about 22,000 square inches, or thirty times the surface of the whole body. The lining membrane of the air-cells, attenuated to the thinness of a cobweb, is the medium by which the air communicates with the blood. But the air in the lungs is not wholly changed with every breath. It cannot suddenly penetrate the membrane which separates it from actual contact with the blood and effect the required change in a moment. On the contrary, the air-cells are constantly full, the quantity contained being from 20 to 30 cubic inches, and of this the amount changed with each breath is only about one-tenth. Each fresh supply mixes with that which remains, and the change goes on incessantly, while that which is breathed out, although about the same in quantity, is, as already shown, very different in its properties. If the wall of an air-cell be examined with the microscope, it will be found to be covered with a net-work of exceedingly small blood-vessels, called capillaries, but much finer than hairs and so closely packed together that the interspaces are smaller than the vessels. These little vessels are the communicating extremities of larger ones, beginning and ending in the heart At every beat of the heart, blood is sent into the pulmonary artery, and through it into the capillaries, where it is brought into contact with the lining membrane of the air-cells and through it exposed to the air; thence it returns again to the heart by the continuation of the capillaries into the pulmonary veins.

It is calculated that at each pulsation of the heart not less than one-twenty-seventh of all the blood in the body passes into the lungs : three times every minute the whole mass of blood is passed through the lungs and exposed to the air. Measured at each circuit, the whole quantity of blood so exposed in a day amounts to fifty-seven hogsheads, and, by weight, five hundred and forty pounds every hour, or twelve thousand nine hundred and sixty pounds in a day.

The quantity of fresh air *imbibed* by this exposure of the blood amounts to 616 cubic inches, or about two and a quarter gallons every minute, or upwards of two hogsheads per hour.

Life has often been compared to a burning flame, a sort of combustion, which, like fire, can never be sustained without the consumption of fuel, and, failing this, it flickers out, never again to be rekindled unless new life be given. The simile is in some respects marvelously perfect. Both flame and life depend upon air. Most persons have witnessed the experiment of placing a lighted candle or a taper under a bell-glass, and know the result; that at first it burns brightly, gradually becomes feeble, and finally goes out altogether. If instead of flame a bird or a mouse be placed under the glass, the effect on its life is precisely the same. In both cases the air is devitalized; it is not all used up, but that which is left will neither support a flame nor sustain life. A large proportion of the oxygen has been consumed and the proportion of carbonic acid and moisture increased. In the one case oxygen has been used to support combustion and in the other to sustain life; and air which has been respired, or in which anything has been burned, is always deficient in oxygen and contains an excess of carbonic acid and moisture. So far, then, as these conditions apply, every living animal represents combustion. In the free atmosphere, no creature ever suffered for the want of oxygen or from an excess of carbonic acid; but in crowded and unventilated rooms great harm often results from both.

Brain-culture is environed by the school-room. Upon the condition and management of the school-room depends the quality of the brain, and the brain is the *soil* of subsequent endowments. Education is the fruit; it contemplates a continuance of mental discipline and exertion far beyond the limits of the school-room or college-life. By education is acquired the mental and moral power to restrain the feelings, affections, propensities, and passions, so that none of these may ever gain the mastery over the intellect, a power which can never be acquired without proper brain-culture. A fruitful harvest can never come of an impoverished soil. Most of the anxieties and miseries of life result from the want of a sound and strong brain; and, as we trace back these to their source, they all seem to depend on the want of power to regulate impulse and feeling. A well-cultivated brain is unquestionably the true road to exalted virtues, and the union of a sound intellect and moral power the only stable foundation of true wisdom, by which health becomes, next to eternal salvation, the most important object of life.

A pure atmosphere is the first need of the school-room. Without it none of the vital functions can be sustained in health. We have seen the wonderful activity with which the functions of life are performed; that within twenty seconds a poisonous gas drawn in with the breath permeates every tissue of the body; that every single respiratory act multiplies the carbonic acid a hundredfold. No teacher, surely, will fail to appreciate the importance of these phenomena; nor should he fail to teach them to his pupils. A new series of questions in arithmetic should be devised for their inculcation, such as: If half a cubic inch of oxygen be consumed every respiration, how many respirations will it take to consume 25 cubic feet? If air that has been once passed through the lungs contains 5½ per cent. of carbonic acid, how many volumes of atmosphere will it require to reduce it to four parts per ten thousand? If a single pupil breathes 70 cubic feet of air in four hours, how many cubic feet will be required for 600 pupils seven hours? If a closet of 300 cubic feet capacity requires 2,000 cubic feet of fresh air every hour to purify the air sufficiently for one individual, how many cubic feet of air will be required every hour to purify the atmosphere of a school-room 40 by 35 by 12 containing 75 pupils? Many other questions of similar practical utility will readily suggest themselves to the thoughtful teacher.

I cannot better close these remarks than by calling your attention to the recent action of the Rhode Island State Medical Society, as being eminently worthy of your serious consideration. This action may not meet with your approval in all its particulars, but it is commendable as being a practical and definite application of general principles and a suggestion to all thoughtful persons who are in any way responsible for the modes and methods of education:

"Whereas, although the present school-system has been brought to a high degree of completeness in intellectual culture and to an exalted position of which its friends and the community may well be proud, yet, entertaining for its welfare a profound interest and viewing it as we do from a physical stand-point and believing that in the haste for intellectual culture the physical is too much neglected, the nervous system is developed to the omission of other portions of the body, thus giving rise to a long train of ills and producing an unsymmetrical and distorted organization in the young, entirely unfitted for the stern duties of life : Therefore,

" *Resolved*, First, that physical culture is of primary importance in our public schools and that gymnastic exercise should be made a part of our school-system.

" Secondly, that the ' Kindergarten-system ' should be ingrafted upon our public-school-system.

" Thirdly, that the school-buildings should not exceed two stories in height.

" Fourthly, that 300 cubic feet of space and 25 square feet of floor-space should be the minimum for each child in a school-room in connection with good ventilation.

" Fifthly, that proper warmth and pure air are of the first importance, and should always be considered before ornamentation.

" Sixthly, that scholars should not maintain the same position more than half an hour at a time.

" Seventhly, that two short sessions, daily, are better than one long one.

" Eighthly, that no child should be admitted into our public schools, as now conducted, under 7 years of age.

" Ninthly, that under 12 years of age, three hours a day, and for 12 years and over, four hours a day, is sufficiently long confinement to mental culture.

" Tenthly, that study out of school should not usually be permitted.

" Eleventhly, that all incentives to emulation should be used cautiously, especially with girls.

" Twelfthly, that the ' half-time system ' should be introduced into our public schools."

The PRESIDENT. The subject is now before the department for discussion, and I would especially invite gentlemen of the medical profession who have favored us with their presence this evening to participate.

Dr. C. C. Cox, of the board of health of Washington, said :

I had hoped, Mr. President, that some other member of the profession better qualified than myself would have availed himself of the opportunity thus presented to respond. I appreciate, however, the privilege that is extended to me of expressing my personal gratification with the proceedings on this occasion.

I have been attracted to this room, sir, not so much by the importance of the subject announced for discussion, nor yet by the wide-spread and well-known reputation of the distinguished gentleman who has treated this subject so ably and exhaustively this evening, as by the evidence, the pregnant evidence, accorded, that this body of intelligent educators has been penetrated by a large share of that wide-spread and growing interest, which is felt at this day as it has never been felt before, in the practical relation of public teaching to the most important development of our race in every regard, and for the dearest interests which lie at the foundation and constitute the basis of our prosperity as individuals, as communities, and as nations.

I say, sir, that the interest of this subject and the reputation of the lecturer would, under ordinary circumstances, be sufficient inducements for me to be present here or anywhere ; but I am more impressed with the fact that these intelligent gentlemen present, representing one of the great interests in this country and forming but a part of the wide-spread feeling which exists everywhere, are, as I have said, penetrated by a deep interest in what they know to be one of the most essential elements in the successful prosecution of public education and instruction of youth.

We know that a healthy mind cannot exist in an unhealthy body, and the history of literature and the science of the whole world demonstrate it. Where do you find thoughts so fresh and glowing and philosophic as come to us from the clime of Scotland, where every man is endowed with strength and where exercise is regarded as one of the necessary adjuncts, as essential as eating and sleeping or any other operation of life.

I was very forcibly impressed, sir, by the resolutions with which the distinguished lecturer closed his remarks. Those resolutions are in accord with the views which I have always entertained. I think no more disagreeable precedent exists in connection with the history of education in this country than the so-called infant-schools which existed some years ago. The intelligence of the age has arrived at the importance of cultivating at that period the physical foundation or basis upon which all mental enlargement and all mental advancement exist. We all know, as physicians and medical men, that a child is born into the world with a large preponderance of the nervous element. He has a large head, a big brain, while the other parts of the system, the muscular and other portions of the constitution, are not developed in a corresponding ratio ; and hence the extreme sensitiveness that attaches to the young child in connection with the peculiar nervous development. The object of that period is not to stimulate the nervous system by too much culture other than that which nature shall suggest in the simple operation of play and exercise, which the child most wants. The effect of such a course of stimulation is still further to oppress the powers and the peculiar condition of the system upon which mental success depends. And just as certainly as the child is forced into that culture, at that age, just as certainly as that system is adopted, just so certainly do you find the child the subject of premature mental decay. The vital powers are taken away, and he drops : a monument to the folly that has forced his mind into exercise before his body is prepared for development.

Now, sir, to the consideration of the principle inculcated by those resolutions as to the time at which the child should be introduced into the school. The number of hours required for the first few years I consider of great importance, and this cannot but be indorsed by this body, every letter and every word of it. Then, sir, the practical relations hinge upon the school-house itself; the architectural construction of it, the amount of space, of cubic feet of atmosphere required for the respiration of each individual, the heating of the house, the time of exercise, the peculiar arrangement of study—these are all practical subjects, which cannot be too fully and too strongly enforced in this day of ours.

These subjects have been elaborately discussed, particularly that in regard to the importance of pure air and plenty of it.

It is not my purpose to take up the time of this body by adding one word to what has been so ably and properly said. I merely arose to make my acknowledgment for the courtesy extended by the president to gentlemen not members of the convention to join in the purposes for which this meeting is assembled on this occasion, and as a member of the board of health of this city, and as one of its humblest representatives.

General EATON. It is my purpose to offer a few observations upon this subject, but not to discuss it.

Few careful observers in this country have failed to note the difference between a country school-house and a city school-house. Those who have attended schools in both have felt the difference and those who have passed beyond this personal experience into a study of the relations of health and education have been startled at every step by the results of the comparison. No one can enumerate the times that Mr. Mann and Dr. Barnard were compelled to call attention to lack of air and defects in furniture and construction. They and their coadjutors smote down certain evils within their reach, but beyond these evils still exist. In our cities, while we have erected many fine school-houses, well adapted to their purposes, and while we have greatly improved the architecture of our college-buildings and other institutions for the instruction of youth, yet any one who has traveled and observed extensively in almost any State will have found that the importance of these primary laws bearing upon the conditions of health, to which the doctor has alluded this evening, are ignored. They are not understood, and therefore are not applied. And while, in certain instances, they have been apprehended and applied, in others new college-buildings are being erected in utter disregard of them; immense sums are being put into brick and mortar which will entail upon coming generations the same evils suffered by those in the past. The effect is not confined to the primary school, where so many are placed together. It can be seen in all manner of institutions; traced from juvenile-reform and orphan-asylums, up through every grade of school to colleges and universities, to law and theological, and even to medical schools. How rarely do we find the lecture-rooms in our professional schools properly lighted or furnished with pure air at a proper temperature.

Now, it does seem that the situation here represented is a scandal to all the professions concerned, a reproach to the architects who erected these buildings, to the officers of the colleges and the boards of trust in our cities and districts who are responsible for their erection, and to the medical profession, for, while it is their function to cure, they alone can best prevent; and we look to them for the means of doing this, and thus contributing to the general health of the community. If I understand the various efforts in the direction of sanitary science now making, some general good results may reasonably be anticipated. While myself interested as a school-officer in collecting facts involving education generally, I have felt that here was a mass of facts bearing on public health and underlying all education, that should be collected. Sound conclusions upon this subject are so absolutely dependent upon a correct knowledge of all the existing facts that a few thousand dollars could be wisely expended every year in making a series of accurate observations throughout the entire country in reference to all peculiarities of climate, of local surroundings, and of all the varieties of construction used in buildings devoted to the use of schools and other public buildings used for audiences, with the different methods in use for lighting, heating, and ventilating. Who can doubt that such a series of observations, properly conducted, would result in such knowledge upon these important points as would correct the present absurdities and evils?

One of the first publications of the Bureau of Education after I took charge contained an article on diseases peculiar to the school-room, and I believe we have every year since said something about health and education, which has brought out many needed facts.

But there is still another class of facts which it has been my desire to bring out and lay before the educators, the parents, and all the people of the country. I mean those relating to the breaking-down of the mind. Our medical friends, who have charge of the insane, and who have earned our gratitude by so far consummating their plans for the cure of mental disease, should also begin to devise means of prevention. Many of them will tell you that "two-thirds of these cases of insanity under our charge could have been successfully treated in childhood, youth, or middle age, by training or by other means within human control." And further they will tell you that a very large number of the insane never come within the walls of asylums. Certainly if the professional skill of the educator is ever to be perfected, a great mass of these facts must be gathered and used. They must be carefully observed, accurately recorded and collected, and the result will be an easy impression on the judgment of educators. Then, in our buildings for educational purposes, whether for primary, elementary, or secondary schools, for colleges, professional, or special schools, we shall begin to understand how to adapt air to life, light to the eye, and surroundings to health. We shall reach a method of health, not only to the body but to the mind. Whereas now, if the facts are correctly stated, with all the good we are doing and trying to do, we must confess with shame that we are doing much to cause the very results we are seeking to avoid.

I remember the impression made upon me in college by having a man at my side break down with insanity. It has been one of those starting-points, beginnings of thought, which will crowd one to the end of life. I have since known similar cases. I have met them in different parts of the country, and followed some into the asylums. In this matter I am confident that, if educators will use the resources at their command, they can so modify the courses of study, and the methods, and time, and surroundings of instruction, as to secure greater health of mind.

Early in my study of education, looking at the child with an anxiety to understand what his normal training should be, I found myself seeking out the most degraded youth in the community, to learn the abnormal side of human nature, that I might better know what it should be in its normal condition; and I was amazed at the philanthropy educators have been compelled to exercise to make their efforts successful. I found it of the greatest possible advantage to visit the prison and the pauper-institution, to study all these conditions of the human being, as full of instruction, showing what was to be avoided and what was to be modified in the methods of instruction that we were pursuing.

Now, on this subject of health, it has seemed to me that professional educators need to go to the physician, as this association has gone to-night; to bring in his experience and expedients; to go over on the diseased side of the human system; to bring to their aid the observations that have been recorded, until the sentiment is roused that should permeate the whole country and the modifications which we all regard as necessary are adopted.

It has been exceedingly gratifying to find a hearty response from the whole country to everything the Bureau of Education has published as the result of·observation on this subject. Boards of health and individual physicians write us what they are trying to do and beg us to go further; many inquiries and suggestions bear on this educational point. I have great hope that those gentlemen in charge of asylums for the insane will begin a series of observations on a concerted plan, from which professional educators shall be able to gather a vast amount of wisdom now hidden from them; that we shall learn from the medical profession what diseases in their practice come from the school-room; what diseases among the young are due to misdirected education in the home or the school; and that this knowledge shall be conveyed in such plain terms that none can fail to understand and heed it.

I hope that this subject will not receive merely sentimental attention, but that there will be organized action. It has been so deeply considered by the National Association for the Promotion of Social Science and by the National Health Association, that they are both making the same inquiries in the same general direction. I hope educators will take hold with them and aid them in collecting facts that will end in a satisfactory result; and that such action will be taken before we adjourn as will have an immediate influence upon the gentlemen here as they return to their respective posts of duty. [Applause.]

Dr. L. H. STEINER, of Maryland, said:

Mr. PRESIDENT: I have nothing to add to the views which Doctor Bell has so clearly presented in reference to the necessity of proper ventilation in our schools. Hardly any superintendent is present who has not had abundant illustration of the fact that 25 square feet of space are not allotted to the pupil of the common school. During my own career as a county-school-superintendent, I had quite a number of schools where I should have been very well satisfied if I could have had 8 square feet to each pupil occupying the room. At the present time—and I do not wish to exaggerate—I can recollect where in one instance 6 square feet was about the maximum to each pupil. The ventilation, however, it is proper to state, in this case, was secured in another way, not by architectural intent, but by the moldering effect of time, which had greatly relieved the chinking and daubing placed properly between the logs, in the first instance, in its erection, and allowed a very free circulation of air. [Merriment.] The difficulty was on the score of heat, and not of ventilation. Possibly the health of our country children is saved from the evil effects of badly-constructed rooms just in this way. I have often wondered, looking at a school where the children were seated upon slab-benches, with not enough sitting-space for each pupil to sit fairly and squarely fronting the desk, how they had the bloom of health on their cheeks. This was due possibly, in the first place, to a naturally good constitution, inherited, and, secondly, as I have already said, to the moldering effect of time, which the architect never contemplated.

One mode of reaching, however, a healthy action in this case, I think, would be by some little instruction in our schools. I do not wish to add another branch to those studies that children are obliged now to take up, but I think some little attention should be paid to this very subject of respiration; what is meant by it; what is necessary in it; how dependent health is upon it. The child will take this novelty home, and the younger the child, I think, the more certainly will he take home everything he hears from his teacher, rather than what he gets from his books. The child will take this home, and thus we will begin just at the right point, with the parents, and not with the legislatures of the State, not with the school-boards. You cannot get school-houses constructed properly unless the people understand what a properly-constructed school-house is.

Now, start in the way I have suggested. Let the parents understand the necessity, and they will demand that the school-house shall be constructed in such a way as to allow not only proper light and proper heat, but also that there shall be the proper ventilation.

I merely throw this out for what it may be worth for the gentlemen who are practically connected with the schools of the United States.

This matter of early instruction in practical science—the every-day sciences—is too much neglected in our schools, probably from the fact that many teachers are unfit to do anything of the kind. Others think they cannot teach unless they have text-books. In other words, they cannot teach unless they are asking questions and receiving answers. If that idea could be thrown aside and if the teachers could at once undertake, little by little and day by day, to give some information to their pupils on these all-important subjects, I am satisfied that it would bear its rich fruits, through the parents demanding of the school-authorities the fullest and most satisfactory evidences of their children's education. [Applause.]

Dr. A. N. BELL said:

Mr. PRESIDENT: May I be permitted to say a word in addition to what Doctor Steiner has said? I hope I do it with no want of deference to the information of teachers generally when I state my belief very emphatically that the teachers do not know enough to teach what Doctor Steiner has stated. That is just where the teaching is needed. The school-teachers throughout the country need that kind of instruction. It is not a very long while ago since I met with the principal of a very large school who did not know the difference between radiation and evaporation as applied to heat in his school-room; and, I think, that is just the kind of work, if I understand General Eaton, that should be organized, of instructing teachers; and that the gentlemen, the superintendents who are here to-night, are here to get that sort of information.

A very valuable suggestion thrown out by General Eaton in regard to the causes of insanity I intended to cover to some extent in my brief paper. I believe no one who has ever studied the subject doubts the effects of narcotics, opiates, and stimulants. It is a common acceptation that they are the chief causes of insanity. It does not seem to be understood that carbonic acid is a more quickly fatal narcotic than opium. It takes a very large dose of opium to kill a person in half an hour, but carbonic acid will do it. During the school-age—during the time of growth—the brain is in a state of organization; the structure of the brain is not yet formed. The brain of the child, before ten years, we will say, as compared with that of the adult, is much softer; it contains more water; contains less solid salt; is different in composition. Hence, the effect of narcotics upon the child can easily be perceived. No doctor, who knows how to practice medicine, will give the same proportionate dose of narcotic as of other medicines. The same rule applies as to stimulants of an alcoholic nature. If I want to give the child medicine, I may give it the third or the fourth of a full dose; but if I wish to give the child a sedative, to quiet its nervous system, I cannot give it over one-fourth or one-sixth, it may be, of the same preparation. Why? Because its nerves are so susceptible to the influence of the narcotic. Is it any wonder, knowing the effect of narcotics in destroying the mind and producing idiocy, that children who are educated under the influence constantly of small doses and oftentimes of large ones, (and one of the strongest narcotics to which the human being can be subjected is that of carbonic acid,) is it any wonder that insanity should be on the increase or that epilepsy should be tumbling them over in their seats?

Now, I am not aware of any statistics going into the etiology of insanity so far as to attribute it to the effects of carbonic acid on the brain; but I am aware that they do often attribute it to the habit of intemperance. We know that we can inherit a weak mind. But why not classify still more, as among the causes which produce this effect, that of carbonic-acid gas, which is produced in great quantities in many of our school-houses by defective ventilation. It is, of course, true that the paper I read here to-night did not cover a large field on this subject, and I would not add the words I now do but for the fact that I feel that the teachers throughout the whole country need to be taught these very lessons. And scandalous as it may seem to the medical profession, if we count our medical colleges throughout the country to-day, we shall find we have less than half a dozen that embody hygiene in their curriculum; and so with our literary institutions throughout the country. An instance has come to my knowledge in the Columbia Law-School of New York. A gentleman of culture and intelligence had a son there, who, coming home, remarked that it was delightful to get back home again after spending weary days in a college that had no means of getting the bad air out or the fresh air in, except through the doors and windows. This gentleman wrote to the president of that law-college and asked him if he did not think it necessary, in view of the great army he had charge of, to devise some means by which to give the students fresh air. This is the case with public institutions of the highest class all over this country. Let me ask which of our various colleges pretends to pay any attention to these things. They know as well as we do—better, some of them—the influence of these poisons. Does it occur to them really in its great magnitude? Does it occur to us present here to-night that by every breath we draw we multiply the carbonic-acid gas a hundredfold as it comes out of our lungs and that we are respiring it over and over again? Let us, for instance, watch some one enjoying his cigar along the street, and we can see by the smoke from it how far around floats the carbonic-acid gas that has been exhaled from those lungs; and I do not think we would care to respire that over.

We should take lessons from these things in order to have some appreciation of how these invisible influences are brought around us.

Mr. WICKERSHAM, of Pennsylvania. I do not rise for the purpose of making a speech at all; but, as a large body of the teachers of the country are not here, I thought it might be well for some one to say a word in their behalf. Something has been said here in reference to their ignorance in regard to the ventilation of school-houses and of physiology, chemistry, and all that. Now, I know they do not know more than they ought to about such things, but the ignorance is not wholly on their side.

Now, I have gone about Pennsylvania with a lantern and tried to find a doctor, or any one, to tell me how to ventilate a school-house.

Now, if you will go into any one of our medical societies or consult the wisest member of the medical profession in any of our cities, you will find that each one has his own particular ideas about ventilating or heating school-houses.

Now, I have looked at this whole matter of ventilation. I think I have read the whole thing from A to Z on the subject, and I cannot find that any body of scientific physicians or scientific gentlemen have come to any positive conclusion in reference to this matter; and are the poor school-masters to be accused of ignorance on this subject when these learned gentlemen, graduates of these learned colleges complimented here, are not fully posted on this matter?

Now, our wise men are assembled at Harrisburg, just now, making laws for the State, as our wise men are assembled here. It has not been a long while since they became dissatisfied with the air they were breathing in the senate-chamber and house of representatives, and they looked about all over the State to find some one who could tell them how to ventilate them. The committee who had this thing in charge received from the various medical associations all sorts of devices. Some told them they ought to ventilate by having the ventilation from the floor down. Some said that would not do; there must be upward ventilation; and some said this way and some that, and the confusion was worse confounded. Finally, they got a gentleman from Boston, I think, [laughter,] who put in a ventilating-apparatus for them. I am not sure that he was from Boston, but he came from the East, anyhow, where we get light, and ventilated all the house and senate. And the other day, just before I left Harrisburg, they swept the whole thing out, and said they had better go back to the air they had before than have such ventilation as that. The members who sat under the ventilators said the cold air all came down, and they did not see that any heat went up. And so the ventilators are closed up.

Now, sir, ignorance of this subject does not lie wholly at the door of the poor school-master; it lies at the door of the scientific man as well.

I cannot find anybody in the State of Pennsylvania to tell me why the school-houses should be ventilated this way or that. One says one thing and another says another. What we want is some scientific principle, some positive principle, that can be relied upon and that can be applied in all cases. And the same demand exists with regard to heating.

And then, besides that, Mr. President, are we not attributing more diseases to school-room-influences than really belong to them? May not the home be to blame? Are not parents, fathers and mothers, to blame somewhat for these diseases, as well as the poor teachers? Are children taken care of as they ought to be at home? Are they properly nursed? Do they eat proper food? Are they provided with proper clothes? Do they never keep late hours? Do they never eat at improper times? Is not their training, up to 5, 6, and 7 years of age, very different from what it should be? If they will send from their homes children who are healthy in every respect—strong and healthy at 6 years of age—I am not so sure, sir, taking our school-rooms as they are, that we are going to cause the death of very many of them. I think the trouble lies back of the school-house; it belongs to the parent, to the home, rather than to the school. And while I say this I do not mean to apologize for the ignorance of teachers or for the bad influences, the seeds of disease, that are sown in the school-room; but at the same time I believe, so far as my observation carries me out in this belief, that more is to be attributed to the bad influences of the home, to the instruction they receive before they go to school; and I would like our medical friends to look into that matter. I do not believe that hard study hurts anybody. I do not believe that three hours a day or six hours a day will hurt a healthy child under proper treatment. But these broken-down children who come into the school-room ; these poor dyspeptic little creatures who are badly nursed and housed, and who come into the school-room with disease all through their system, one hour of hard study will injure them.

I should like our medical brethren to look into this matter as well as into the bad influences which are in the school-room. [Applause.]

Mr. BURGESS, of Indiana. Mr. President, it seems the discussion has mainly centered on the question of ventilation. The general character of the lecture which we are proposing at least to discuss is, I think, one the correctness of which cannot be successfully called in question. But I did not understand the lecturer to limit this question of health to the one thing of ventilation. Exercise was also suggested. Even the amount of time of study and of sitting still at one time—these were mentioned, and these will be found of equal importance, perhaps, with even the question of ventilation. I know of nothing, sir, that has come within my observation—and in the course of twenty-five years of experience I have had some opportunities for observation—I know of no one thing more injurious to a child than to put him into his iron jacket; to place him on a bench, perchance so high that his little feet cannot touch the floor. and punish him if he moves, or turns, or twists—that is the proper word I want to use. This is as bad as ventilation can be, and the lecturer introduced that subject. Give the child plenty of opportunity to move about, to turn and twist, and to get up and go out, and to run and play as well as to learn his A B C's.

The time of study was also mentioned, and this is an important element. Whether a child can be injured by one or by three hours of study in a day will depend largely upon these other questions that are correlative to this.

And then, again, the question of exercise is perhaps as important as any one or all combined. This is true in all stages of study. I doubt if there is a gentleman present to-night, no matter what his training may have been, who can sit down to his books three, five, or eight hours in the twenty-four, every day, without finding himself at length compelled to leave them. What do our summer-vacations mean for public men ? What do our days of rest mean ? What does the clergyman mean when . he tells you that he must have Monday or Saturday for rest—that he must have one day in the week for rest ? It means *rest*, sir, exercise as well.

Recreation has been mentioned—a kind of exercise that is in itself sport; that is, play, (to use the school-boy's word;) that is, fun. This is as important to the child or grown-up student as good air to breathe and good bread to eat, almost.

In the university in which I have the honor to preside, no matter how irregular the classes may be—that is, coming and going to and from their boarding-rooms and recitation-rooms—I have kept up the good old custom of having at least half an hour's recess every forenoon; and I do not simply give it as a privilege to the students to go out on the campus for half an hour, but I require it. Another element mentioned by the speaker which he prefaced by the word "particularly," namely, the girls; and superintendents will do well to note that part, "particularly the girls." We are talking about ignorance, gentlemen, in these departments. We are all ignorant as to that matter, and the profoundest of our ignorance relates "*particularly*" to the girls. There are a very few men in this great country of ours who have yet learned how to educate a girl without ruining her health before she has passed her teens. And I mean to say there are very few mothers who know how to rear their daughters and carry them through their teens safely, and this is certainly as important as good bread.

I do not give it as a privilege to go onto the campus for sports during this half hour, but I require it. I go into the ladies' department, and I see some of the young women sitting with their heads resting on their hands, their faces pale and their eyes sunken. I say, "Get out of here, girls! Get out of this! Get onto the campus." "O, Mr. President, excuse me; I don't feel like playing." They have scarcely breath enough to speak it. "Get out onto the campus. Get onto the campus," I say. (A part of it is fenced off for the ladies, and they can exercise there secure from observation.) And there they have their game of base-ball, their game of foot-ball, or whatever other game they may please to introduce. And this half hour of exercise every day in the open air— will these learned medical gentlemen pardon me the remark—is worth more to those young ladies than all the doctors in the city.

While, now, the learned gentleman has noticed all these items, I have been pleased and benefited by the discussion. But I have thought the discussion turned rather more upon the one question of the ventilation of the school-house than the lecturer intended; and I have, therefore, introduced thus briefly, this other feature, exercise; exercise in the open air; exercise, not such, however, as our fathers used to give us down in good old Yankee homes, in the days of what they call "stint." There may be gentlemen here to-night who remember that word, "stint;" how our good old Yankee fathers used to say, "Boys, I am going away, to be gone so many days, and I will give you your 'stint;' when you get that done you may play till I get back." Well, the "stint" would be large enough to last you quite as long as he would be gone, to say the least. [Merriment.] That was the kind of exercise that we got. Now, that tires a man. I am tired even now, almost, thinking about it. That kind of exercise does not amuse; that kind of exercise does not please. And, gentlemen, I believe that man is the only animal that can stand on two feet and shake his sides with laughter; and I do not think the great Creator made us with that faculty and power simply to mock us. Therefore let us shake our sides and grow fat with laughter if we can. And this is my idea of exercise—something that will make girls and boys laugh, and laugh very heartily.

Only one word more. In the management of this question, whether in the common school, the graded school, high school, college, or university, as the case may be, the teacher must be a man of large observation, of quick perception, of a ready application, a power to readily and quickly observe what is wanted and to apply it to the case in hand. If you see the child is drooping for want of fresh air, send him out doors; if you see he is drooping for want of exercise, give him play; that will please him; and thus through the whole course. But as young ladies or, rather, girls—that is not what I want to say, either—as girls think they become young ladies, there is a wonderful change in affairs. If I could imagine that a boy and a girl were a twin brother and sister, so as to have them equal, presumptively so at least, in their start in the race of life, I think I should observe very little difference between that boy and girl until about the time the girl's mother thinks that running foot-races, and jumping over fences, and climbing apple-trees, and throwing stones at the chickens are not very polite employments for the girl. Up to that time the girl can run as fast as her brother, jump over a fence as quickly, and climb a tree as near to the top branches, and, perhaps, in a good old-fashioned rough-and-tumble wrestle, can throw the boy as often as the boy can throw her. But observe what a drawing-in there is, a drawing-in of the size of the feet, a drawing-in of the size of the body, a drawing-in especially of the size of the lungs. All this drawing-in continues until the girl is scarcely recognizable as that beautiful, brave little girl who, a few years ago, could run a race with her brother.

Medical gentlemen, however, are better able to discuss this matter than I am. It is only sufficient to say that no teacher is qualified to teach a girl or young lady who does not well understand the main question affecting her health and of regulating the course of study, exercise, and air in accordance therewith.

I will not detain you longer. I repeat, again, I have listened with intense interest and profit both to the lecture and the discussion. I think the intent of the lecture has given us a broad field here, a few points of which I have endeavored to mention.

Mr. LUCKEY, of Pittsburg. I move that further consideration be postponed until morning, and in the mean time a committee of three be appointed to express the views of the association upon this subject.

The motion was agreed to; and the president appointed as the committee Mr. Luckey of Pittsburg, Mr. Hopkins of Indiana, and Mr. Marble of Worcester.

Mr. WICKERSHAM. Mr. President, the lecturer of the evening does not belong to this association, and has gone to the trouble of coming all the way from New York here to present to us this very able and interesting lecture ; and I move that the thanks of this association be tendered to Dr. Bell for the lecture.

The motion was unanimously agreed to.

Mr. WICKERSHAM. Mr. President, there is a notice on the programme of a very important subject—an exceedingly important subject—that I suppose we are to have a paper upon from Dr. Ruffner, State-superintendent of public schools of Virginia. I am told that he will probably be here to-morrow. It is a paper that is needed all over the country. I move, therefore, that a committee of seven be appointed, of which Dr. Ruffner shall be chairman, to present resolutions upon the subject of the proper relations of the Federal Government to education.

The motion was agreed to.

Mr. HOPKINS, of Indiana. I move that we adjourn till 9 o'clock to-morrow morning.

The PRESIDENT. I would ask Mr. Hopkins to suspend his motion for a moment, until the committee can be appointed and until the committee on order of business have announced the programme for to-morrow. The Chair will announce, as a select committee of seven, Dr. Ruffner of Virginia, Mr. Wickersham of Pennsylvania, Mr. Jillson of South Carolina, Mr. Philbrick of Boston, Mr. Abernethy of Iowa, Mr. Hopkins of Indiana, and Mr. Northrop of Connecticut.

General EATON. Mr. President, so far as the committee on order of business have considered the programme and are ready to report, it is that the association meet for miscellaneous business at the hour designated, and at 11 o'clock listen to a paper by Mr. Wickersham, taking up the subject of the Centennial. That the subject under Dr. Ruffner's control be taken up next. No definite hour is mentioned. That at 4 o'clock a paper by Mr. Philbrick be received. That we meet in the evening at 7 o'clock to listen to the paper by Professor Walter Smith, on drawing; and that after that we adjourn to Governor Shepherd's house, at 8 o'clock.

Mr. JILLSON, of South Carolina. Mr. President, I move that a committee of three on general resolutions be appointed by the president.

The motion was agreed to.

The PRESIDENT. The Chair will appoint Mr. Jillson of South Carolina, Mr. Marble of Worcester, and Mr. McMillan of Ohio.

On motion of Mr. Hopkins, of Indiana, the convention then adjourned.

PROCEEDINGS OF THE SECOND DAY.

DEPARTMENT OF SUPERINTENDENCE OF THE NATIONAL EDUCATIONAL ASSOCIATION, JANUARY 28, 1875.

SECOND DAY.

The members met at the office of the Commissioner of Education and proceeded in a body to call on Hon. Columbus Delano, Secretary of the Interior, where Mr. J. Ormond Wilson, superintendent of public schools of the District of Columbia and president of the department of superintendence, spoke as follows:

MR. WILSON'S REMARKS.

Mr. SECRETARY: The department of superintendence of the National Educational Association is now holding a convention in this city to discuss educational subjects of importance. They are pleased this morning to call to pay their respects to you as the head of the Department in which the Bureau of Education is located.

They regard that Bureau and its chief officer as their head, and look to it for advice and go to it for the best experience of the country, in order that they may avoid evils and secure benefits.

We have to thank you for the courtesy which you have invariably extended to the Bureau. The head of the Bureau informs us that on all occasions you have exercised the power and authority vested in you with the greatest liberality.

SECRETARY DELANO'S REMARKS.

The Secretary of the Interior responded as follows:

I am very glad to meet you, gentlemen, and to learn that your interest in the work of general education still continues.

I do not ascribe to myself much credit for what is being accomplished by the Bureau connected with the Department under charge of General Eaton. What I have done has generally been suggested by that efficient officer, who is personally, as well as officially and profoundly, interested in the success of its operations.

I think I may avail myself of this occasion to say that every year adds to the evidences of the value of the operations of the Bureau.

I will also remark that the condition of affairs in many of the States under the observation of this Bureau furnishes abundant evidence of the propriety of its organization and the necessity for its continuance. As I have said to you on former occasions, the success of republican institutions, where suffrage is universal, must depend upon intelligence—not the intelligence of the few, but the intelligence of the many. And you will comprehend me when I say that there are sections of the country where it is extremely difficult to diffuse this knowledge and intelligence. And certainly not without your co-operation and assistance can we effect the dissemination of such intelligence in the localities to which I allude as is necessary for the welfare of our institutions.

I am very glad to meet you all again on this returning anniversary of your labors, and I hope that I myself, or some one better able to assist in the work you have in hand, will always be found here to co-operate with you.

From the Department of the Interior the members proceeded to Willard Hall, when the department was called to order by the president, and the session opened with prayer by Rev. Dr. Butler, of Washington.

The president then introduced Professor J. Enthoffer, of the United States Coast-Survey Office, who arranged upon the stage some large diagrams illustrating his conception of the origin and discovery of written language and an analysis of our modern alphabet, made in accordance with his theory.

PROFESSOR ENTHOFFER'S ADDRESS.

Professor Enthoffer said:

Mr. PRESIDENT, LADIES, AND GENTLEMEN: I must first ask you to excuse my English. The subject to which I wish to call your attention, and which the diagrams on the stage illustrate, is the origin of the alphabet. I claim that

THE ORIGINAL LETTERS OF THE ALPHABET WERE NOT REPRESENTATIONS OF OBJECTS, BUT DIAGRAMS OF THE ORGANS OF SPEECH IN THE ACT OF FORMING SOUNDS.

The publication of my topographical atlas made it incumbent on me to furnish the engineer with copies for the descriptive portion of maps, not however in the old, careless manner, placing before the scholar copies good or bad which he had to copy. I was convinced that nobody can learn anything thoroughly by mere copying, those only being successful who possessed natural talents. My aim was to draw up rules of construction which would enable any one to attain to some degree of proficiency. For this purpose it was necessary to inquire whether the letters used in the descriptive portion of maps could be based on a uniform law of construction; and this seemed quite plausible, as the Roman letters presented such a marked geometrical character. This investigation showed the figures on page 55 as the basis of the whole alphabet.

These geometrical and symmetrical figures were very surprising, for who would not, looking at them, be struck by the idea that the original alphabet might possibly have been invented by a mathematician? I did not hesitate a moment to get at the truth of this matter; but great was my astonishment when, in books on paleography, I found the most widely varying views regarding the origin of our alphabet: some derived it from the hieroglyphics; others from the Chaldeans; others from the Phenicians, and some even from the constellations of the zodiac; but nothing had led these inquirers further away from the truth than the names of the letters, seeing in them the picture of the object which had been adopted as the representative of some sound. This would then be the same system of idiographic writing as that of the Egyptians.

It is highly probable that the inventor of our original alphabet knew the hieroglyphics, at least from sight, but it is certainly not to be presumed that he thought of adopting either the construction of the Egyptian system of letters or the manner of shaping them. This is proved by the principle of the phonetic system, reduced to sixteen or twenty-two signs, in contradistinction to the Egyptian system, using eighty letters for writing proper names correctly.

The descendant of Shem viewed the matter in a totally different light; he did not intend to invent a secret writing, as that of the Egyptians had been, giving a mysterious power to the priestly caste, but wished to make letters the common property of all men, and in this he could only succeed if he could confine letters to the principal sounds of the human organ of speech. In this sublime simplicity the great thought, the thought of a genius shows itself, and to this simplicity alone it is to be ascribed that at present five hundred millions of men use the same alphabet, with but few alterations, and merely adding the signs for vowels. This invention of the alphabet was the most important result of the ancient world, and it is the foundation on which civilization began to build, through which alone perfect humanity can be reached if the human race is destined ever to reach that height of perfection.

All those noble agents which unite in furthering the education and instruction of the human race work in the spirit of the originator of the alphabet. And therefore it will be of interest to you gentlemen, who have assembled here in such a sacred cause, to learn in what manner this great philosopher proceeded in firmly fixing the winged word, that no longer it should vanish in the air, but live and continue in assisting in the great work of elevating the human race.

I must inform this honored assembly that at present I can only explain the origin of our alphabet in brief outlines and with few words, and even these few remarks would not be justified before this convention if the discovery of the origin of our alphabet had not likewise had a practical result in furnishing a means of facilitating the instruction in reading and writing of the alphabet.

The chief object of the great philosopher was, above everything else, to *dissect the words and find their component sounds.* To substitute signs for these sounds was a question of only secondary interest. Any conventional signs would have answered this purpose, *e. g.*, the circle with two diameters crossing each other for the figures from 0 to 9. It is very easy, however, for us to say *any signs!* as we are surrounded by all sorts of writings and drawings ; but how different at a time when nothing of the kind existed ! Then it was a matter of great difficulty, moreover, to represent sounds, something only audible to the ear, by visible signs—impossible. Here the connection must first be found, *i. e.*, to shape the sign in such a manner as to lead the person who sees it to the idea represented ; and in this lies the second great thought of the inventor, that in simple outlines he portrays the organ of speech and its construction in the shape it assumes at the decisive moment when forming sounds.

If we now examine the mechanical construction of our organ of speech in its different parts, we first see the mouth with its continuation, the throat, containing the ligaments between which sounds are formed, the lips, the palate, the teeth, and finally, the most important of all, the tongue, or the pedal of the human voice, as it has been called. We do not know what action of the muscles contributes to the formation of sounds, but we can easily observe the process going on in the mouth in modulating sounds. Here there is not only a visible movement, but through the resonance of sounds and noises the sensation becomes quite perceptible, of course, only as we concentrate our whole attention on it. In proof of these facts it may be mentioned that trained deaf mutes understand words perfectly if the speaker utters them slowly.

The first sound of the alphabet certainly owes its rank to mature consideration ; it is the principal one of all the fundamental sounds of the human organ, the first sound a child utters when it attempts to speak, the involuntary sound uttered in pleasant surprise, the standard sound which alone must be sung distinctly and audibly in all the accords and scales. The mere opening of the mouth and letting the voice go forth, produces the sound *a ;* the formation of this sound is therefore a visible one. If you now examine this illustration (see Aleph in the table, at the end of this circular,) and compare it with the oldest signs placed by the side of it, you cannot fail to perceive its origin. The open angle corresponds to the open mouth, and all that requires an explanation is the line which crosses the angle. This line was no doubt originally intended to represent the teeth by small projections, so as to lead the observer to the idea that this sign was to represent a view of the open mouth in profile.

This sign, however, has been transmitted to us with a name, viz, *Aleph.* The object of this is easily seen, and has, as a mnemotechnic means, been very important for the beginning, because the commencing sound explained the value of the sign. This has been the original beginning of every sort of writing, but in order to attract the attention of the observer it was in the beginning necessary to draw the objects which were to be represented as similar as possible to their originals, and only in the course of many centuries did the Egyptians get the idea to obtain their object by abbreviation.

These facts have led paleographers to the assumption that the Semitic **A** likewise represented the picture of its name, viz, a bull, and of this only the head. But if it was the intention to draw a bull, why, do we ask, was the sign not placed in an upright position, ᴠ, which would make it by far more recognizable; and why was it placed in a position only possible in a dead bull? That the writing of this sign was very inconvenient is shown by the fact that as soon as writing came into more practical use it was placed in an upright position, just as we write it at the present time.

The character of the second letter ᗺ likewise furnishes proof of the highly philosophical arrangement of the alphabet, viz, to make the sounds more prominent by their contrast. The sound of opening the mouth is followed by the sound of closing the mouth. The sudden opening of the mouth, brought about by the explosive emphasis of emitting the breath, produces the sound B; and its connection with some vowel makes it audible. Its characteristic features are therefore determined by the lips; and how accurately these have been understood will immediately become clear if we compare the conventional sign with the profile view of the mouth. The name *Beth* means "house," and he who has eyes to see will in vain look for some characteristic sign of a house, but will easily recognize the idea in the representation of the lips.

The labial sound is followed by the palatal sound G, produced by the root of the tongue and the palate. In observing the action of the organ of speech, with a view of giving a graphic representation of this sound, we must confess that this could not be made sufficiently plain in the external movement of the organ. The great philosopher, however, found a way out of this dilemma, and in such a simple manner that we are surprised at the clearness of his perceptive faculties. He gives us an inside view of the organ, and, to avoid all doubts as to which portion is meant, nothing but the palate Γ, as the most characteristic portion in forming this sound; it was of course necessary, in order to make the flat arch of the palate recognizable, to show at the top the beginning of the teeth and at the bottom the beginning of the throat. A glance at Helmholtz's diagram, and its comparison with the conventional sign, will be sufficient to convince us of the correctness of this explanation.

The name *Gimel* means "camel." For further illustrations of these principles I must refer to my pamphlet on the subject.

The palatal sound is followed by the dental sound D, which is produced by leaning the tip of the tongue against the upper teeth, thereby shutting the hollow of the mouth completely. This will become clear if we now compare the section with the conventional sign of the D sound, which goes through many ancient alphabets. The name *Daleth* means door.

The time allowed me will not permit me to present here the development of the whole alphabet, and I must refer those of you who are interested in this subject to the forthcoming publication of my treatise upon it, which will not only be of interest to every educated person, but of special use to teachers.

The investigation and discovery of, I may well say, the key to our alphabet, had the important result to show that the chief signs are at the same time phonetic signs of the formation of sounds. In the English language this is unfortunately only the case with those of Anglo-Saxon derivation; nevertheless, the explanation of most of the forms of the letters with regard to the position of the mouth in pronouncing them will be useful in the first instruction in reading. And if it could be used for no other purpose but to awaken the child's interest, the impression made on the memory will be much more effective if the teacher can tell him, "Here, in the letter A, the open mouth is represented if you imagine the sign laid on its side, thus, ◁ ; in the letter B you see the closed lips," &c. It is well known that nothing rivets the attention of the child's mind to such a degree as a historical communication. Objects with which a short story can be connected are the most welcome of all to the child. The mere assertion is to the child a dead matter: "This is B; now remember it." After a long time we may succeed in this way, but how much pleasanter and how much more lasting will be the impression, if the child is enabled to see why this sign represents the labial sound B.

I have illustrated this by my analytic alphabet, consisting of two tablets, containing the component parts of the letters, and five monograms, each comprising from four to six letters. In fact, the juvenile student has only to study these five figures. These figures or monograms are well known to every child.

The first is called the window-monogram, forming the basis for the rectangular letters, such as I, L, F, E, H, and T. The second is called the envelope-monogram, forming the letters X, K, N, Z, and Y. The third is called the lattice-monogram, forming the zig-zag letters A, V, M, and W. The fourth is called the ring-monogram, forming the ring-letters O, Q, C, G, and D; and the fifth, the serpent-monogram, forming the serpentine letters, such as S, R, B, P, J, and U. The arrangement is the following: The pupil is directed to take, at the teacher's advice, certain component parts from the tablets and insert them in the monogram through loops prepared to hold this component part. Previous to this exercise the phonetic explanation has been given by the teacher. For mnemotechnic exercise the configuration of the letters is also imitated by the children with their fingers after the tableau of the hand-alphabet prefixed to the first monogram-tablets. After this the component parts are taken out from the monogram and placed on a slate, and the contours drawn around it, which exercise gives amusement to the child and is, at the same time, an additional aid to its memory.

Then it is recommended to take up the methodical-writing copy-book in which the same monograms are constructed in a blue or red tint for the purpose of being filled out by pencil-marks according to the head-letter.

This writing-exercise is continued from the transformation of the capital letters to the Roman small letters, thus showing the transformation from the Roman small to italics, and lastly from these to the current letters. This exercise is rather to be called *drawing* letters, which is by far the easiest and most natural way of proceeding. After the conclusion of this exercise the Spencerian system for current writing is recommended. But this methodical copy-book is so arranged that it serves at the same time for the advanced scholars in practicing the so-called draughtsmen-letters, which is nowadays a requirement for a good many technical occupations.

This new system of commencing to learn reading and writing is of still greater practical value for institutions for the deaf and dumb, for the blind, and for those most unfortunate creatures, the idiots.

The student is, so to speak, on a well-constructed track, where he cannot go amiss. The frightful score of twice 26 letters is reduced to only five well-known figures, and it operates on the child as if it were already familiar with the subject it is to learn, for the reason that the basis is really an old acquaintance.

The professor concluded his address by exhibiting some copy-books such as he had suggested—one of them written by a girl of 8 years of age, one by a boy of 10 years of age, and one by a boy of 16 years of age—and calling attention to their excellence.

MR. WICKERSHAM'S ADDRESS.

At the conclusion of Professor Enthoffer's address, the president introduced Hon. J. P. Wickersham, State-superintendent of common schools of Pennsylvania, who read the following paper upon

AMERICAN EDUCATION AT THE CENTENNIAL EXPOSITION.

So much has been published concerning the Centennial Exposition to be held at the city of Philadelphia in 1876 that no statement of its design or account of what is purposed to be done seems now necessary. A brief outline of the progress made in the work of preparation, however, and of the prospects entertained of its successful completion, may be of interest, and will serve as an introduction to the special purpose of this paper, which is, to make some practical suggestions in reference to the representation of the schools and school-systems of the country at the Exposition.

The Exposition will be held. Whether it shall be creditable to the nation or otherwise, we must go on with the work. To stop, to even halt now, would be to disgrace ourselves in the eyes of the whole world. American energy and pluck have accomplished marvelous things in the past; they will not fail us now in pushing to completion this great enterprise. Much has occurred within the last few months to encourage the friends of the Centennial. Obstacles have given way; interests threatening antagonism have been harmonized; help has come from unexpected quarters, and the indications are that the whole nation will make one united effort to secure success.

More money will be needed, but the management of the Centennial have now in hand available funds amounting to nearly $5,000,000. Of this sum, the State of Pennsylvania has appropriated $1,000,000 and the city of Philadelphia $1,500,000. The balance is made up from subscriptions to the stock-fund. Five millions of dollars will go far towards the erection of the necessary buildings for the Centennial; but large subscriptions to the stock are still hoped for, and, without doubt, in the end, Congress will make a generous appropriation.

Fairmount Park, in the city of Philadelphia, contains three thousand acres. Several millions of dollars have been expended in improving and beautifying it. Nothing of the kind in this country is now equal to it, and the day is not far distant when it will compare favorably with the finest parks of the Old World. The Lansdowne Plateau, upon which the Exposition-buildings are now being erected, is an elevated part of Fairmount Park. No better site for them could be chosen. Its advantages are said by competent judges to excel those of the sites of either of the great expositions of Europe.

The buildings are, first, an art-gallery, covering a space of about one acre and three-quarters, the material being of brick, granite, iron, and glass, the law requiring that it shall be perfectly fire-proof. The art-gallery is 365 feet long, 210 feet wide, and 59 feet high to the ceiling and 150 feet to the top of the dome. For the erection of this building the State of Pennsylvania and the city of Philadelphia have appropriated $1,500,000. The inner walls of the building are now erected as high as the square, and the granite is being set with marked rapidity. The contract requires its perfect completion six months in advance of the opening of the Exhibition.

The main exhibition-building, covering a space of twenty acres, and to be constructed mainly of iron and glass, was contracted for some months since; the foundations are now nearly ready and the material is being produced at the mills and factories. This building is in length 1,880 feet, in width 464 feet, and in height 70 feet. Height of central towers 120 feet. It will cost about $2,000,000, and will be paid for out of the funds arising from the sale of stock, and is also to be completed six months before the beginning of the celebration. The remaining buildings are the machinery-hall, of twelve acres; agricultural department, of six acres; and a conservatory, of two and a half acres; all of which within a few weeks either have been placed under contract or are about to be. The funds for the machinery-hall and conservatory are furnished by the city of Philadelphia.

The contemplated buildings are large, but it is said that already applications for space have been received from our own people sufficient, if accepted, to take up nearly the whole of that set apart for the United States. I extract the following summary of what is promised by foreign nations from a recent address on the Centennial to the people of New York.

"The indications as to the display from foreign countries at this date, a year and a half in advance of the beginning, are far more favorable than had been anticipated by the managers. The following-named countries have taken action, to wit: the German Empire has accepted the invitation of the President; France has accepted, and has appointed commissioners-resident in Philadelphia and New York; Sweden and Norway have appointed a commissioner, and have gone so far as to provide for defraying the cost of transportation of goods of their subjects to the Exhibition and return. England's acceptance of the invitation has been communicated by telegraph, but the particulars are not known. In several of the British colonies, especially in Canada, Australia, New Zealand, Tasmania, and others of the Australasian Islands, exhibitions of unusual completeness and interest have been prepared. In Austria a large number of manufacturers and artisans have solicited space in the Exhibition-buildings. The governments of Central America and South America have manifested special interest in the Exhibition, and the President's invitation has been accepted by Peru, United States of Colombia, Nicaragua, the Argentine Confederation, Brazil, Venezuela, Ecuador, Chili, Guatemala, and Salvador, and for these countries commissioners have been appointed and money appropriated for their expenses. Mexico, Honduras, and Hayti have also accepted the invitation. Brazil and other South American nations have made application for space. In addition, the Netherlands, Belgium, Liberia, the Sandwich Islands, China, Japan, and Switzerland have accepted the invitation. Spain has accepted, and appointed Señor Emilio Castelar, the eminent republican statesman, to be her resident commissioner at the American Exposition."

Philadelphia is now well supplied with hotel-accommodations. Projects are now on foot to increase these very largely. Hundreds, perhaps thousands, of boarding-houses will be opened. And if all these be insufficient to accommodate the great throng of strangers, the railroads centering at Philadelphia have agreed to provide excursion-trains, to run at rapid speed and cheap rates, to all the neighboring cities and towns and to New York. These trains will run directly to the Exhibition-buildings, so that visitors coming in this way can enter them without the payment of carriage-hire and under cover.

One of the most encouraging events in the interest of the Centennial was the message of the President of the United States, sent last week to Congress, accompanied by a report from the board, composed of one person named by the head of each Executive Department of the General Government, to secure materials proper for representation at the Centennial. The several Departments of the General Government are prepared, it seems, to enter heartily into the work of putting in shape for exhibition the long lists of interesting articles they have to show. The expense of this part of the Exhibition is estimated at $971,000, not including the cost of erecting a suitable building for the special use of the General Government. The President recommends that an appropriation be made for the purpose of meeting these expenses, and it is thought probable that Congress will make it. But what shall be done to secure the proper representation of the school-interests of the country, and how shall they be represented? A gentleman prominently connected with the management of the Centennial writes me within a few days: "The educational department is, in my humble judgment, one of the most important to be presented by our Government." This is the universal sentiment. We have been boasting of our systems of free schools so long that our own people have come to think them the best in the whole world. They will demand there full representation. Failure here will, I am satisfied, bring severe censure down upon the heads of the Centennial management and prove deeply injurious to the school-interests of the country. More strangers, too, from foreign countries, will visit the Exposition for the purpose of witnessing our school-work, and acquainting themselves with our school-systems, than for any other object, possibly than for all other objects put together. The American school-house at the great French Exposition is said to have attracted more attention than all else from America on exhibition. The test will be a severe one, I admit; but there is now no shrinking from it. Germany, Austria, Switzerland, France, England, Belgium, and Holland will come, doubtless, prepared to submit their systems of public instruction to a comparison with our own, and we must be ready to meet them with the best we have. It was easy to say at Paris, at London, at Vienna, that we left our best at home; but at Philadelphia we will be at home.

I have no doubt that a proper place and ample room will be allowed by the management at Philadelphia for the display of material relating to education. What, then, should be done? What should we do?

A beginning was made here at our meeting a year ago. General Eaton, chairman of a committee on the subject, presented the following outline of plan of procedure, which was adopted with great unanimity:

1. That each State and Territory be invited to prepare a representation of its educational condition for the Centennial.

2. That each State and Territory also be invited to prepare a historical record of its educational progress for the same purpose.

3. That each city be invited to act with the State-authorities in preparing such records, and that it present an exhibit of its own educational growth and condition.

4. That each educational institution be invited to participate in the same way.

5. That a census be taken in 1875.

6. That the Commissioner of Education be requested, on behalf of the educators of this country, to correspond with the prominent educators of the world and invite their co-operation in the matter of the Centennial.

7. That an international congress be held in connection with the Centennial.

This is an admirable plan. I approved it then; I approve it now. But to carry it out there must be a great amount of hard work done, and there will be needed a considerable sum of money. Who is to do the work and where is the money to come from?

In my judgment the head of the United States commission on the subject of education at the Centennial can be no other than the head of the United States Bureau of Education in Washington. He is already a commissioner to the Centennial, appointed by the President. Through him, and in no other way, can character, system, and unity be given to the work, and all these are absolutely essential to success. The educational part of the Exposition must not be a mass of ill-assorted fragments, without order or relation. Foreign commissioners, too, will give attention to an officer representing the United States, rather than to those representing States and cities.

The appointment of General Eaton as chief commissioner will no doubt be cheerfully concurred in by the management of the Exposition, who, in conjunction with him, should select the needed number of competent assistants. The number may be small, but it should embrace several of the ablest and best-known American educators. The commission thus constituted should have full power to act without restraint. Auxiliary to this central commission, but acting for their several localities, there may be individuals or committees representing States, cities, or institutions.

The central commision will need a considerable sum of money, for to do what ought to be done well will require months of hard work ; and, to make the Exhibition a credit to the nation, it is easy to foresee that it will be necessary not only to invite the bringing forward of educational material, but to provide it. The money to be used by the central commission must come out of the United States Treasury or the treasury of the Centennial, or both. Without money, little can be done; with it, I am satisfied the educational part of the Exposition will prove a success. Can an appropriation for this purpose be obtained from Congress? What amount of money can be spared for the educational part of the Exposition from the treasury of the Centennial? These are vital questions, but I am compelled to leave them unanswered. It is hoped that the President's late recommendation will move Congress to take some favorable action.

So far as States, cities, institutions, or individuals make preparation for the Centennial, they will no doubt provide the necessary funds ; but it is time to begin the work everywhere. State-superintendents of schools should ask the legislatures of their respective States for an appropriation for Centennial purposes. The superintendents of schools in cities should insist upon the setting-apart of a fund by their several boards of direction, to be used in the preparation of educational material for the Exposition.

The note of preparation should be at once sounded all along the line and a determination be evinced to achieve success in a matter where so much honor is to be lost or won.

The Exposition must be a full, fair, and systematic representation of American education. No possible credit can come to us by filling our space mechanically with the ten thousand articles that may be offered. Material could be had for the asking, I doubt not, sufficient in bulk to fill the whole Exposition-building. A huge mass of miscellaneous articles, with endless repetitions and duplicates, even though they could be so arranged as to look well to the inartistic or unprofessional eye, is not what is wanted. The whole display must be representative. It must be somewhat of an organism, with its several parts nicely adjusted, if not closely related, to one another. In the selection and arrangement of material, I take it, will be found the most difficult and delicate duty of the central commission ; but, with a fair field in which to work and a reasonable amount of money with which to pay expenses, a presentation of the leading features of American education can be made that will be an honor to the country and a wonder to the older nations that may come across the water to compete with us.

At the close of his paper, Mr. Wickersham said : In connection with this paper, I beg leave to offer the following resolution :

Resolved, That a committee of five be appointed to act for this body, with the authorities of the Centennial, in perfecting a plan for the proper representation of the educational interests of the country at the approaching National Exposition at Philadelphia.

General EATON. May I ask whether the gentleman intends to have this committee take the place of the one appointed last year, or is it an executive committee to act immediately, and in harmony with the committee of last year ?

Mr. WICKERSHAM. The committee of last year was composed of one member from each State, was it not ?

General EATON. Yes.

Mr. WICKERSHAM. I think it is wiser to make this an executive committee. It is necessary that we should have some small body of efficient men to represent this larger body or organization—to represent the educational interests of the country—to act in connection with the Centennial. There is no one authorized to do business with the authorities of the Centennial. Any one that looks at this matter in a business-way (a Fourth-of-July oration on the Centennial is out of place and out of date now) will see that we have come to the time when we must meet this as business-men. In order to do business in a proper way, it is absolutely necessary that this body should appoint an executive committee to do the business for us with the authorities of the Centennial. As it is we cannot do anything. We cannot contract for space. The authorities have, in a general way, set apart already a certain amount of space for educational purposes. They have allowed that it would be necessary that a certain amount of space should be dedicated for educational purposes, but for how large a space, or where that space is to be, remains to be settled. We do not know whether the authorities of the Centennial will allow any one outside of the commission to conduct this business. There will have to be a large amount of correspondence between the representatives of this body and the authorities of the Centennial if we are to make a creditable exhibition. It seems to be the universal agreement that we will have such an educational exhibition at the Centennial, and under the auspices of this department, if possible. It is yet to be seen what the authorities of the Centennial are absolutely willing to do in regard to this matter. I think that, with proper communication with the Centennial authorities through a committee of business-men, representing this body, we can have all our demands satisfactorily answered. Such a committee it is proposed shall be created; a working and an efficient committee, authorized to open communication in a business-like way. Then let the Centennial Commission take charge of the matter under the general rules of that organization. That must be the method if we would be successful in this enterprise. But we never can have any proper communications nor any satisfactory arrangements as matters are now. I am very clear about this one thing. We must have a small, efficient business-committee to take in charge the necessary steps in this matter. They will have to give the preliminary information at once and proceed to act upon it. There is no time to be lost. They are to see that space is allowed and filled, and where the money is to come from to carry on this work. They are to see if Congress is going to do anything for us. They are to see whether the Centennial authorities will appropriate any money for this purpose. Because, as I said before, it is a question of business, and the amount of money at the bottom; and I feel sure of this, that we have the means, both the men and the material, to make a creditable exhibition in this department.

The resolution was seconded.

General EATON. I think Mr. Wickersham has met the full necessity of the case by the introduction of this resolution. I have no doubt that the gentlemen here representing the different States have already had inquiries made of them about how this matter was to be promoted, which inquiries could not be answered. Certainly such inquiries have come to us. I have, in reply to some, stated what was done at the last meeting of the superintendents in regard to the matter. I have said that I would have to wait for additional action before I could say anything further. And it seems to me that this resolution meets the necessity that now exists in the premises. I would like very much, before the resolution is acted upon, to hear from some of these gentlemen on the subject. I have the pleasure of knowing that Baron von Schwarz-Senborn, his excellency the minister from Austria-Hungary, is present. He had charge of the Exposition at Vienna. I hope he will say a word or so on this occasion.

The request made of Baron von Schwarz-Senborn was greeted with applause.

68

REMARKS OF BARON VON SCHWARZ-SENBORN.

Baron von Schwarz-Senborn said:

Mr. CHAIRMAN AND GENTLEMEN: I feel myself highly honored to-day at being present and assisting in this meeting of such enlightened men, and I remark this because nobody appreciates more than myself the importance of public instruction. I regard every teacher as a missionary, for whom I have the highest respect.

You remember, gentlemen, there was an old European general by the name of Montecuculi, who said that, if you are preparing for war and wish to become victors, you must have three necessary things: first, money; secondly, more money; thirdly, much more money. [Applause.] Now I think every teacher is a general; that is, he is a combatant of ignorance and of superficiality. I think, too, that the want of knowledge is the root of all evils that exist in the world, and that they can only be successfully combated by three things. Those three things are : first, education; secondly, more education; and thirdly, much more education. [Applause.]

I also think that the education of a people must begin in the family, and that then every man, every woman, every village, municipality, and corporation, and every State-government, and the General Government itself, must aid and contribute to the accomplishment of this vitally important object.

I have been traveling for thirty years, and I have found that the impression gained in traveling is one of the means of obtaining an education. I think a universal exposition is also like a journey; but with this advantage, that you see in a few hours, and at a trifling expense, that which would ordinarily take years of traveling and a great outlay of money to learn.

You will allow me, gentlemen, to say that, for I am an old exposition-man. I was appointed by my government as commissioner to the exposition in Leipsic in 1850. I was commissioner to London in 1851; then, again, in London at the exposition of 1862. I was at Paris as commissioner, and class-president of the jury at the exposition of 1855, and assisted also at the Paris Exposition in 1867, but on that occasion I did not accept any appointment, as I wished to have the whole time for study and observation, which are incompatible with the duties of an official position. Lately, while I was deputy consul-general of Austria-Hungary in Paris, where I resided as such during seventeen years, I was, after the siege and the commune, called to Vienna by His Majesty, my Emperor, to plan and superintend the Universal Exposition of 1873 in that city. As director-general of that last Exposition, I was more strongly convinced than ever that universal expositions are the very best of schools.

I must say that these expositions are not established to satisfy the idle curiosity or to furnish food for the thoughtless amusement of the people. I also consider these expositions as institutions for the improvement of the public tastes and the enlightenment of the minds of the people, and especially so, as they thereby learn what most nearly concerns the great interests of a country. I think there should be written over the door of each exhibition-building the two golden words of the old Greek, Γνῶθι σεαυτόν, which, you are aware, when translated, mean " know thyself." It is a fact that many persons are ignorant of what exists in their own country, and an exposition is the means of their obtaining that knowledge.

Since I have had the honor and pleasure of being in the United States—only six months—I must say that I have seen in that short time a great many things that are not known, either by the people abroad or by all the people of this country, which ought to be known, and with which they can be made acquainted in the shortest time by an exposition. I know that at these expositions one can learn more of a country in a few days than he could by wandering through it for a long time. I must confess to you, gentlemen, that the United States of America are not well known in Europe, for America has been very badly, or, I may say, not at all, represented in the five universal expositions held in Europe since 1851.

Had it been well represented on those occasions, the people of Europe would have obtained a far better knowledge of your country than they now possess and the intellectual and material intercourse between the people of foreign countries and yourselves would have been greatly increased.

On the other hand, it is true that the number of Americans visiting Europe has been increasing every year during the last decade, but that number is extremely small when compared with your entire population of forty millions.

However, a great improvement in the respect I have mentioned has resulted from those expositions referred to ; and I think we can look forward to still greater benefit from the International Exposition in this country which is now preparing in Philadelphia for 1876. It will be a great benefit in every respect. A large number of people will come here from Europe and other parts of the world. They will profit by the occasion to also see the whole country, as I have no doubt that the various railroad-companies of the United States will arrange for excursions to every part of your broad domain.

All these strangers will be enlightened; they will be cured of prejudice and they will become your very good friends and admirers hereafter. Not only this, but very many people will come from all the different States of your own country to Philadelphia to visit the Centennial Exposition. And I am sure that they, too, will then for the first time fully realize what are the productions of the United States, and also what the educational system of their country amounts to.

Since I arrived in the United States I have taken occasion to visit some small but very notable expositions. I saw the exposition of the American Institute at New York, the industrial exposition at Newark, the exposition of the Franklin Institute at Philadelphia, and the industrial exhibition at Cincinnati, besides many agricultural fairs. It was my intention also to visit the local exhibitions at Chicago and Cleveland, but the shortness of my time prevented. I must confess that at all of these exhibitions I obtained a great deal of fresh information. I saw many things and learned many new facts that I rejoice to know.

I have thus given you, gentlemen, my idea of the value of expositions in general.

Now, as far as my experience in Vienna as director-general is concerned, I comprehended that it would be useful and a great benefit for my country to learn of the different educational systems existing in the different parts of the world; and some of the gentlemen now present, who were at Vienna in 1873, will agree with me that the educational departments of all the nations represented at the Exposition at Vienna were the most interesting and most important part of the Exposition. It was appreciated by all enlightened classes of men, by all those who are the well-wishers of the civilization and welfare of the people. I think such a section of the Exposition at Philadelphia will also be the most valuable and in its consequences the most beneficial feature. I think that every American citizen who may contribute in any way to the Exposition in Philadelphia will thereby bestow a great benefit upon his fellowmen.

And I may add here that I have lately been in Philadelphia, and during the two weeks that I remained there I made what observations I could, assisted by the courtesy and hospitality of all the intelligent men I had the pleasure of meeting there, and I must confirm the remark of the honorable gentleman, Mr. Wickersham, who read the paper, that the locality for the Exposition in Fairmount Park is charming, and really better than that of either of the universal expositions in London, Paris, or Vienna. I had opportunities, through the kindness of the different members of the Centennial Commission, when in Philadelphia, to see all the plans, drawings, and specifications, and I know what they are doing now towards the erection of buildings, and I am not at all flattering, but am simply speaking the truth, when I say that all that has been done and all that is now being done show great skill and ability. The most honorable and intelligent men who are the conductors of the great work are using all the experiences gained in the former universal exhibitions, especially that of Vienna, in 1873.

I am sure that the Exposition in Philadelphia will be a great success in every respect, as I wish from my heart and as I have seen from the beginning that it will be so. [Applause.] I am also sure that all intelligent citizens of America will appreciate

e and more the importance of this Exposition. They will see more clearly every
that it deserves all the support that is required. I am certain that every citizen who
aks of and looks into it and every Senator as well as every member of the House
Representatives will do what he can to make this Exposition a success, as it should
l will be, because—if you will excuse me in saying it—I consider that the Exposi-
a in Philadelphia is not a private enterprise; it is not at all an enterprise to make
ney; it is not an enterprise for serving local interests and for the benefit of the city
Philadelphia alone. I put a much higher estimate upon it, and regard it as an en-
prise to be carried out on the most liberal scale.
I repeat, therefore, that whatever the honorable gentlemen here and elsewhere, as
ll as the Government, will do for the Exposition, it will redound to the benefit of the
iole people of the United States of America. [Applause.]

Mr. HOPKINS, State-superintendent of Indiana. I simply rise, sir, to
iy that I am heartily in favor of the resolution, and I can assign one
' two reasons why I think such action is necessary in order to make
fectual our exhibition.

The State of Indiana has already commenced to make preparations
i have our educational interests represented in the Exposition. That
natter has been canvassed more or less for two years, and, in a recent
eport from the department of public instruction to the legislature,
among the recommendations was one that an appropriation be made for
he purpose of enabling the proper authorities in that State to have a
epresentation in the Centennial Exposition of our educational interests.
I have taken great interest in looking after this matter in our State. I
have already done what I could, and hope to succeed still further in
securing a sufficient appropriation from the legislature to enable the
State-board of education to see that the educational interests of Indiana
are thoroughly represented. Of course this is an independent movement to some extent. And if we can have five men, representative men
of the country, to whom we can communicate our desires, it will certainly facilitate very materially the representation of these educational
interests.

As far as Indiana is concerned, Indiana will be represented in that
Centennial Exposition. And we shall be only too glad if this arrangement could be adopted, so that we can be represented as a whole, and
not so much as independent States.

Mr. NORTHROP, of Connecticut. When I seconded the motion, I did
not intend to offer any remarks. But there is one suggestion which fell
from the lips of our friend Baron Senborn which is worthy of notice.
He tells us, and tells us truly, that the Exposition at Vienna was a
school for Austria and that this proposed Exposition will be a school
for America. It was a school for Austria, especially in the direction in
which Austria needed a school. Unification in Germany and in Italy
was greatly facilitated by unity of race and language; but Austria, in
attempting unification, on account of the many different nationalities,
has had the toughest problem of any government in Europe. How to
unify these heterogeneous and sometimes antagonistic elements has
indeed been a problem. And I believe that that Exposition, showing

as it did the intense earnestness of that government for the education and elevation of the whole people, has been an important school. Our friend has said that it was never designed for money-making, and only some frivolous and superficial newspaper-writers represented the Vienna Exposition as a financial failure. As if the great Austrian government entered upon that magnificent enterprise for money-making! So our International Exposition will be a financial failure if we enter upon it for money-making. And yet I am confident that it was of immense benefit in Austria. That Exposition in its influence effected precisely what Austria needed: a school in the promotion of unification. And, in my judgment, that is the great demand of the United States to-day, if the problem of reconstruction is to have a final and happy solution. Certainly this will tend in that direction. And if we can, in the educational departments, create co-operation and sympathy, and the educators of all the States of America will come forward with their full zeal in this work, it will greatly promote what we most need in America—unification and reconstruction. [Applause.]

Mr. PHILBRICK, of Boston. My judgment entirely approves the suggestions contained in the excellent paper read by the gentleman from Pennsylvania, and my heart is thoroughly enlisted in the project of making a complete exhibition of the education of the country at the approaching Centennial in Philadelphia. I earnestly hope the friends of education in every part of the country will make the efforts necessary to give success to this important department. I do not propose to discuss the resolution now before the meeting, providing for the raising of a committee to confer with the managers of the Exposition in regard to the best plan for accomplishing the object in view. The proposition seems to me practical and reasonable, and I shall cheerfully vote for it. But I want to indorse emphatically the ground taken in the paper in favor of placing the general direction of this department in the hands of the National Commissioner of Education. What is wanted is a complete and systematic presentation of the objects and materials which will best illustrate the condition and progress of education in all its kinds and grades throughout the country, and not a miscellaneous mass of matter, piled up without order or system. To secure the requisite unity in design and discrimination in selection, an authoritative head is indispensable, and it seems to me eminently fit that the Chief of the Bureau of Education should act in that capacity if he is willing to accept it. Austria has furnished the best model for a national exhibition of education, at the Exposition in Vienna, and the remarkable success of that educational exhibition was doubtless largely due to the fact that it had an intelligent supervisor, not only to lay out the plan, but to attend to carrying it out in all its details. Co-operation, advice, and assistance will be needed, of course, but the responsibility should be left in the hands of the Commissioner.

Mr. President, for one, I feel extremely obliged to his excellency the Austrian minister, for his very interesting and instructive remarks on the uses of universal expositions in general and for his wise and encouraging words respecting that to be held in Philadelphia. It is quite certain that nobody is a better authority on this subject. He rightly regards a universal exposition as a universal school. It is for the diffusion of knowledge, and not for mere amusement. It is a new instrumentality for disseminating practical information by means of object-teaching on the largest possible scale. It is an epitome of the civilization of the world, and enables one to see much of the world at little cost of time and money. When his excellency spoke of the use of expositions in helping us to self-knowledge and a true knowledge of our country, which is the most valuable kind of knowledge, I was reminded of some of my own experience at the Vienna Exposition in this branch of learning. I found there was some difference between comparing our productions with those of our next neighbor and comparing them with those of the whole world. I was particularly interested in making comparisons in educational matters, and it was gratifying to find that, in some of these matters, America could stand the test of comparison very well—in school-furniture, for example. In this particular thing what I had supposed to be true was simply confirmed. I was not surprised. But not so in respect to school-architecture. Mr. Mann had told us that there were no school-houses in Germany to compare with even our second-rate ones. That was some time ago; and, taking it for granted that we Yankees had in the mean time been moving faster than the Germans and Austrians, I rather expected that the photographs of our best school-edifices would produce something of a sensation among Teutonic educators. Well, great pains were taken to display our pictures and plans to the best advantage in their gilt-frames, and when the show was ready I looked for the sensation; I failed to discover it. But when I got time to examine the objects in the German and Austrian courts, I saw why. There I found a plenty of illustrations of school-architecture quite superior to any I had to show. Then there was the lesson of the Swedish school-house. I made some effort to take out with me an edifice to illustrate our idea of a model school-room with its fittings. I felt pretty sure that nothing but money was wanted to make this project a complete success; but when I entered the beautiful Swedish school-house and took my seat on the master's platform, and surveyed the spectacle presented by the school-room, with its apparatus and fittings, I felt glad that my attempt to bring over a school-room had failed, for I could not have matched what I saw before me. I reckon that the State of Massachusetts will get paid for the cost of sending me to Vienna a hundred times over by the benefit derived from the knowledge of the German idea of a school-room which I brought home with me.

I will mention only one more particular among the many in which I got a dose of self-knowledge at Vienna, and that is drawing. I knew

73

we were only beginners in this important branch of education, but I was not prepared to find so great a disparity between our productions in this line and those of France, Germany, and Austria. In our exhibitions there were collections of drawings sent from the public schools of the principal cities and from one of the oldest schools devoted especially to drawing. But the drawings from one elementary school in Vienna surpassed all these, both in quantity and quality. On visiting that school I found that other branches of technical education were well taught, and yet there was time for what are called the ordinary branches. Here was a lesson of great import. I mention this personal experience to illustrate the way in which an exhibition teaches. Everybody that goes into an exhibition is compelled to measure himself in some way, and so he gets a better knowledge of his strong points and his weak points. If every adult American citizen could be shown the Swedish school-house to which I have referred, I believe the benefit of its stimulating and enlightening effect in promoting popular education would be sufficient to off-set a large part, if not the whole, of the expense of the approaching Centennial Exposition. And the Austrians built a school-house which was not finished until quite late, but when ready for inspection it turned out to be even superior to the Swedish one in many respects. It seems to me that if the Exposition in Philadelphia in 1876 does not result in giving a new and powerful impulse to the cause of education, the fault will be with the educators of the country in not doing their duty in regard to it. I hope and trust the opportunity will be improved to the fullest extent.

REMARKS OF REV. DR. HAROLD.

Rev. Dr. Harold, of Washington, D. C., said:

I understood from the courteous remarks of the Chief of the Bureau of Education yesterday, when stating the cordiality with which all friends of education were welcomed to these meetings, that any gentleman who felt an interest on the subject of education, might be allowed to submit his views on any topic that came up for discussion.

After remarking at some length upon the appointment of the proposed committee and suggesting the expediency of separate action, Dr. Harold concluded as follows:

And now, I wish to say, in conclusion, that I am very glad we have had the distinguished honor of listening to the representative of the Exposition at Vienna, to hear his wise words adapted from his experience to our needs.

I hope his remarks will go over this whole country and will be duly heeded. And, if they have the weight which they ought to have, and which I believe they will have, in their dissemination through the country, I am positive that all who can contribute to such an end will do their utmost to make this Exposition the crowning success of the age in its feelings and characteristics.

REMARKS OF BARON VON SCHWARZ-SENBORN.

I feel compelled to say a few words about the suggestion which was made by the honorable gentleman who has just spoken in regard to the Vienna Exposition being a financial failure.

am not of the same opinion. It is true that both our houses of parliament granted y \$3,000,000 appropriation for the Exposition. And it is also true that the cost ched more than double that amount. From the sum expended must, however, be lucted the total amount of the receipts. The accounts of the revenues and expendi- es have not yet been closed. Besides, all the exhibition-buildings, built of stone, ck, and iron, and representing many millions, are still standing. I think that not a it has been lost or was uselessly spent in the Exposition; and when you come to ike a balance and consider the value of the buildings, I reckon the balance which nains against us will be very small. I will now prove that even that cost will be rered. The account is very simple. Supposing that we had even expended more in the twelve million florins, or \$6,000,000, which is not the case, we must remember it the total number of our visitors at Vienna reached nearly six millions. Well, if ery person who visited the Exposition gained an intellectual benefit of only two llars in value, there was made an actual gain over the money that really was spent the government, besides the cost of the permanent improvements. I must confess, my part, that I gained more—much more. I would not even give the experiences, owledge, and instruction which I got at that Exposition for many thousands of dollars. m advanced in years; I cannot make materially profitable the knowledge which I ined in the Exposition; but I am sure that a great majority of the younger portion the people who visited there will use that knowledge to their future advantage. you will allow me, Mr. Chairman and gentlemen, I wish to say one thing more, and at is, that in Austria we attach the highest importance to a certain system of lncation which we call object-teaching. May I at first make some remarks upon iblic instruction as it now exists in Austria? The condition of the school-masters ere has been greatly improved. Their position once was a very bad one. We ave now made great advances in our system of instruction and in our regard for he teachers. They did not formerly get as much money for their time as was ecessary for a common livelihood; but in the last ten years we have realized ome of the great improvements of teaching for our children and appreciate the eachers more than ever before; and we are improving every day as much as we can. ur children have better instruction than ever and our teachers are better off. I think he time is not far distant when every child in Austria will not only be compelled to arn reading and writing in the primary schools, but also, at the same time, draw- ng. Thus have we provided for the youth; but what must be done for those grown hildren, the adults, in Austria, who have learned little or nothing? They did not ave such large opportunities of schooling as their children now enjoy. A man thirty r forty years of age cannot go to school; but he can be instructed by eyesight- r object-teaching, such as is afforded by the exhibitors and other similar means. ne of those means I first referred to is traveling. What is travel? Travel is edu- ation. You learn many things in traveling, by observation. You are taught in hat way. Therefore, this is object-teaching. A great German savant, Professor Vir- bow, made a very interesting and a very accurate remark which applies here. Ie said that "nothing which comes through your eyes into your head ever goes ut." And so say I. The impressions which we obtain by the sense of sight affect he brain and change our views in the most favorable manner. That was the mean- ng; and the man who has seen many things, who has traveled a great deal, will have iis intellectual faculties greatly improved. We observed in Austria, as well as in other arts of Europe, another striking effect of these exhibitions. They improve in a emarkable way the public taste. The taste in former times in Austria was a bad one. The people had not seen examples of tasteful and beautiful productions. They had, there- ore, no artistic judgment. They had no museums and schools for applying fine arts to ndustry, for improving and correcting their taste, and for thus giving them the right deas of the beautiful. The consequence was that, in their buildings, furniture, and ther things of common life, no taste was shown. But now, within a few years, and pecially since the Universal Exposition and the establishment of museums and schools, here has been a remarkable improvement in this respect. The same may be said of

England. Every one who visited England on the occasion of the London Exhibition, in 1851, will remember that, although the English manufactured articles were very cheap, useful, and of the best quality, yet the taste displayed therein was awful. And now the English have, as a consequence of that exhibition, immensely improved in their tastes; and in the Vienna Exhibition of 1873 we saw new evidence of this fact. Allow me to say, gentlemen, that a sincere friend should speak the truth; and that, as a sincere friend of America, who has the greatest sympathy for its people, in whose country I have learned since my short stay of six months a great deal, and where I hope to learn much more, it is my duty to say to them, in all truth and candor, that their public taste is in the same awful condition as was the public taste in England before their great exhibition of 1851. [Applause.]

I am sure that the public taste in America can be improved to as great a degree within as short a time after the Exposition of 1876 as that of England was improved after the London Exhibition of 1851. I attach, therefore, immense importance to the cultivation of the fine arts as the means of refining the feelings of every man, and thereby improving the public taste. And I think this most desirable result will be attained among other valuable ones by the approaching International Exposition in Philadelphia in 1876. These, Mr. President, are the few remarks which I wished to make.

Baron von Schwarz Senborn took his seat amid great applause.

Mr. NORTHROP. For myself—and I think I speak for all present—I am truly thankful for the remarks which his excellency the minister from Austria has given us. I fear that, perhaps, my remark in regard to the financial failure, so called, of the Austrian Exposition may have been misunderstood by his excellency. I meant to say that the common rumor to that effect, spread abroad by newspaper-reporters, was a superficial and erroneous statement. I intended to say that the Austrian government appropriated six million florins at the outset, and, as I understood, was ready to foot the bills which might be brought in on account of the Exposition in the end; but there was no idea of going into the enterprise as a money-making speculation. I wanted to set aside that sordid idea for ourselves. Austria, realizing the grand benefits of such an Exhibition, stood ready to pay its cost. The Austrian government heartily approved the project and expected the benefits which would indirectly flow from the Exposition would more than compensate the government for any outlay that might occur. And I will say here that there has been a marked progress in that country of late. During the past eight years no country in Europe has made a greater progress in education and general enlightenment than the empire of Austria-Hungary.

Mr. Z. RICHARDS, of Washington, D. C., remarked that he was not a member of the association, but would like to say a word as to the suggestion made by Dr. Harold. He wished to speak as a friend of the organization—one who had been present at its first meeting. He thought it important that the sympathy of the whole people was necessary to secure success, and suggested that the proposed committee should co-operate with other educational organizations, as well as with the Centennial authorities at Philadelphia; that there might be prejudice against this committee if the impression prevailed that it was undertaking to monopolize the care of educational interests at the Centennial, and that this

mmittee should not act wholly independently of the national associa-
on, but that they should all work together in bringing an influence on
ongress and in arousing the interest of the people.

General EATON. Perhaps a word of explanation may be desirable. At
ie meeting of this department last year, a committee was appointed to
ike preliminary action in regard to the representation of education at
he Centennial in Philadelphia in 1876. This committee consisted of one
iember from each State and city represented.

Now, Mr. Wickersham, as I understand it, does not propose any inter-
rence with the action taken a year ago. That committee remains, and
.s members act in their several localities in awakening an interest in the
oming Centennial and preparing for the exhibition there of their local
ducational interests. This committee, however, is too large and its
nembers too widely scattered to be easily convened or to be able to act
fficiently as a body ; there must be a small working executive commit-
ee formed out of this larger body, if any practical results are to be ob-
ained. The judgment of the national association upon the action taken
)y this department seemed to be that this was a matter that came within
the province of this department and that the association indorsed and
approved the action that had been taken. The proposition now is to
designate a certain number of the gentlemen of this committee to act
as an executive committee. This action commits no one and derogates
in no respect from the dignity and power of the general committee; it
is simply a method of securing practical action, without which the larger
committee will find itself powerless and useless. There must be some
way of finding out definitely what is to be done and how to do it. The
authorities of the Centennial must be communicated with, and this proposed small committee is, as I understand it, designed simply to effect a
business-like connection between the educators who desire to exhibit
and the authorities who control the action and facilities of the Exposition. I would be glad, before I sit down, to say a word upon another
topic. When I introduced Baron von Schwarz-Senborn, I purposely re-
frained from the expression of such complimentary remarks as I should
have felt justified in making. I wished the convention to form their
own conclusions, and I am sure that all who heard his views, the result
of such wide experience, feel that it is a great privilege to have him here
with us to-day. I wish further to pay my tribute to the grandeur of the
conception of that wonderful Exposition as it impressed itself upon me
when, officially, the invitation for America to attend and the programmes
of the Exposition were placed in my hands.

The programme of the department of education produced upon my
mind a most forcible impression. The breadth of view, the all-compre-
hending grasp of the subject, worked out with such perfection of detail,
gave evidence that a mind of no ordinary caliber had originated this
noble conception. It seemed to me as if the man that had worked out
the programme of that vast Exposition had risen above the sphere in

which we move, according to the ideal of a grand principle of vision, and had looked down upon Austria, full of love for every being in the entire population, man, woman, or child, and had recognized the necessities of that people and the process by which their interests would be elevated and harmonized, and by which the whole nation was to be lifted in rank among the kingdoms of the earth. It seemed to me that the author had brought to this conception, not only this great love for the people and original ability for arrangement, but the experience of the world. That is to say, he had successfully endeavored to bring the experience of the world, which belonged to such an enterprise, down to the Exposition at Vienna, and had incorporated and expressed that experience there. It seemed the scheme of a great philanthropic statesman, planning first for the advancement of his own people, but broad enough to include all the people of the world, who were freely invited to come to Vienna and see the great results of civilization. I can never forget the impression made upon me by that magnificent programme, which not even the grand results of the completed design, which it was my good fortune to behold, could obliterate from my memory.

Doctor HAROLD rose to explain his position. He feared that the resolution, as offered, would be prejudicial to the object of the association, which, as he understood it, was to procure the funds necessary for a great national educational exhibition in 1876. He heartily approved of this idea and believed that the association could obtain the funds from Congress more easily by itself than by co-operating with the managers of the Centennial.

He alluded to the prejudices which had been excited against the Centennial, and which he believed still existed, and thought it wise for the association not to commit itself to the virtual approval of all that the Centennial authorities had done by connecting its appeal with that organization. I believe that never before was there so much interest felt in educational affairs in this country. I believe, by itself, no interest can so strongly appeal to the Congress of the United States. Every other interest seems to have been subordinate to this one, and indeed that may be said with reference to the progress of civilization all over the world. From all parts we hear the expression of that interest and an anxious desire to promote the welfare of the people by increasing the facilities for their education. Then let your committee go, I repeat, untrammeled and independent, and ask for your quota of support from the Congress of the United States, and I am sure your petition will be recognized and welcomed, and heard and heeded.

A DELEGATE. I call for the reading of the resolution.

Mr. WICKERSHAM. I think I see the weight which properly belongs to the remarks of the gentleman in regard to this resolution. I confess that there is strength in his suggestions. I believe that some of them have already been duly weighed by those who favor the motion in its present form. Now, sir, it seems to me that it must be conceded that the authorities of the Centennial are the parties with whom we have to do business. They are the real authorities that have collected and are disbursing the means so far provided; they are engaged in putting up this building; they are the officers of the Exposition; they have the control and management of the enterprise; and if we want to be represented there, if we want to occupy a part of their space, it seems to me that we must do business with them, whether they are agreeable to us or otherwise; and I will say, furthermore, right here, I don't attach overmuch importance to the foolish prejudice that has been sought to be raised against the men who are managing this Centennial. The only wonder is that there is not a greater prejudice existing against them; but, having some knowledge of these men personally, knowing quite intimately a number of those who are most active in this matter, I say here to-day for them that they are men above reproach. [Applause.] I stamp down into the earth the charges and prejudices that are brought against the distinguished men engaged in this noble work. Such charges and prejudices were brought to bear against the men who managed the Exposition at Vienna; the same charges and prejudices were brought against the men who had charge of the Expositions at Paris and London; and every man who stands up, who dares to stand up and do a great work for humanity and for his age, will meet with these foolish prejudices. Now, I don't think there is overmuch in them; and as we have to do business with these men, therefore it seems to me the proper thing for us to appoint a committee, which shall be a medium between this body and the authorities that have charge of the Centennial.

Shall we attempt to ignore this authority? The men who are putting up these buildings and assigning the space in them—can we afford to ignore them? Shall we undertake, as an independent body, to go to Congress and ask money for a great educational exposition? I think that, if we travel that road very long, when we come to deal with the Centennial authorities and talk with them about space, they will say to us, that as we have been going along upon an independent basis, that as we have been to Congress and elsewhere as an independent organization, we may make our exhibition outside of the Centennial grounds. I take it that that would be about the result. We have to deal with this matter on business-principles; let us, then, discard this foolish prejudice and look into this matter as it is. Let us appoint a small, active committee, that will transact this business for us; let us give to them authority in the premises and rely upon them to represent our interests in all preliminary matters. I am sure that will be in accordance with the general intelligent sentiment of teachers throughout this country. There is a general call for a central head to this matter. There is a general demand for a committee to take charge of the educational department of this Exposition in co-operation with the Centennial authorities. It is the desire to place at the head of that commission the head of the Educational Bureau at Washington. The propriety and fit-

ness of this action cannot be doubted. Then the correspondence in
gard to the subject throughout the United States can be properly
rected and answered ; and we wish the head of the Educational Bure
to act as the head of this organization ; and then, with three or four
five competent assistants, we shall have an efficient and satisfact<
working central committee. Let that committee be appointed un<
the terms of this resolution, and all doubt as to the success of the p
posed exhibition will be at an end. That executive committee can
right to work preparing for the Exposition. They can communic:
with the proper authorities at Philadelphia. They can make the pro]
application to Congress. The legislatures of the different States m
then be called upon in authoritative form and with an assurance of s
cess in behalf of this Exposition. The whole people of the country c
be aroused in this way. We can go out into our several superinte1
encies and act understandingly, and with proper instructions, from ti
to time. Things will begin to assume shape and harmony. It see
to me that the expediency and propriety of this resolution are establish
acceptably, and that it is a waste of words to advocate its passa;
Some such action must be taken, or we will have no adequate rep
sentation at the Centennial. The whole thing appeals to us as busine
men and as the intelligent friends of the educational interests of t
country. In regard to the suggestion that was made by my friend
the right, if he understood me correctly, I wish to say a word or tv
There will, no doubt, be as full a correspondence as possible, as is ju
cious, with all the superintendents in the different States, from the v<
beginning of practical work for the Exhibition, and there is neither ti1
nor opportunity for calling all the superintendents together to co-oper<
in the details of this business ; and we cannot wait for another meeti
of the national association. At the meeting last year the national assoc
tion appointed no committee. As suggested, they seemed to agree tl
what had been done here by this Department was proper and sufficie1
and we cannot wait until August; we cannot wait until another meeting
the national association, before proceeding with this work. We want co
munication and co-operation with the Centennial commissioners at on<
We want to know what space we are going to have. We want to kn<
how much authority is to be accorded to us in the arrangement of our p<
of the exhibition in general and in particular. We want to know th<
views on this subject. It seems to me that we can do nothing less,
we are to go on with this work at all, than adopt some such resoluti
as this. It seems to me that this is precisely what we want. [A
plause.]

At the request of a delegate the secretary read the resolution pre
ously offered by Mr. Wickersham :

Resolved, That a committee of five be appointed to act for this body with the auth<
ties of the Centennial in perfecting a plan for the proper representation of the edu
tional interests of the country at the approaching national Exposition at Philadelph

Mr. ABERNETHY, of Iowa. It seems to me, if I apprehend this matter aright, that the chief purpose and duty of this committee will not be the securing or care of money. Not at all. The object will be to systematize and unify the educational representation at the Exposition. But I wish simply to express my approval of the views submitted by General Eaton. I am of the same opinion with him. I have come more than a thousand miles to attend this meeting, and I feel a great interest in the question which has been brought under discussion. I am glad it has been so thoroughly debated here to-day. Now, to show the point from which I view this matter, I will refer to the fact that we have a Centennial board or commission in our State; we are taking this year a census, which will be much more complete than any we have taken before. I think it will be the most complete census of any State in the Union, taking, of course, the last United States census as a basis. But a large number of items are to be added to it. The blanks are now in the hands of the officers, and they are taking a very full account of educational statistics; statistics as to the age of children and their advance in education, and in regard to all the school-agencies and the attendance—such statistics as we cannot get in our regular annual school-returns. The State-board, which had the preparing of these statistics, allowed me to suggest any topic which I thought might be properly named in this connection, so that we shall have brought all that I can think of as desirable in such a collection of statistical facts. Now, I say, we desire to co-operate with a central organization in this matter of the Exposition. Our State-board of managers are anxious in regard to it. They have made me the offer of the secretaryship of the groups comprising the educational districts of the State. It is made up of thirty-two groups; it is desired to represent our educational interests in as thorough a manner as the same interests were represented at Vienna by the Austrian government. Now, then, having been tendered the secretaryship, I came here desiring to know how our statistics could be best represented to illustrate our State-system. I understand that it is not desired that we should bring any of our school-houses to the Exposition. Is it desired that we should bring photographs of our best school-houses? As to books, the publishers of text-books will be represented, and I presume it will not be expected that we should furnish samples. So will it be, I presume, with school-manufactures: the manufacturers of school-furniture and the publishers of text-books will probably desire to represent those things. Now, what can we bring from our State? We can give a little brief history of our educational progress; our State-associations will prepare such a history, but it will only make up a few pages. What we desire to learn is, how we are to represent our educational progress, our educational status, at the Exposition. How shall we show the manner in which the work is going on and the standard which has been reached? How are Pennsylvania and Massachusetts and New York going to present their educational interests? If we had answers to these questious, we would know how to begin and how to move on. That is what we want to learn to-day, and I should be glad if the discussion should turn in that direction. We want information upon this very point: how can we represent our educational matters at Philadelphia? We want to know that immediately. If I am to accept this secretaryship, I want to know to whom I am to address circulars; what information we wish to try to gather for the purposes indicated; how we shall present a fair statement of our educational matters at the Exposition. I do believe that our State desires to be fully represented at this Exposition, and I think that, if there is anything in which I take a just pride, it is in our school-system. But I want information on this subject. How are we to present ourselves at the door of the Exposition?

Mr. WICKERSHAM. That is the very question in point. We wish to have this needed information disseminated. Now, here are gentlemen from all parts of the Union seeking this information. I found the same inquiry at Philadelphia. We must have some head, from which this information can be sent abroad. First, we must know what space we are going to have. Then some person in authority must determine the character of the exhibition. I take it that, when this committee is appointed by this body, its members will confer with the Centennial authorities and ascertain what their views are on the subject. And they will make some arrangements with the Centennial authorities which will be specific and thoroughly intelligible and upon which satisfactory communications can be sent to the superintendents in Iowa and to all the proper educational authorities in the various States in the Union. The first duty laid upon this Centennial commission, when our committee is appointed, will be to supply information in reply to these questions. I have been asked similar questions in Philadelphia, but I had to confess my inability to answer them. It is high time we were up and doing. I made inquiries myself, at Philadelphia, of the Centennial authorities, but of course I could not obtain any thoroughly satisfactory replies. I had not the time to press inquiries that were proper, nor had I the authority to do so. The commission will tell you in a general way that they mean to have at the Exposition a large amount of space devoted to educational purposes. Some will say that they want to devote more attention to that department than to anything else, but they have no clear ideas as to its character; when you come to details, they can give you no reply. The question must be put authoritatively, "How many square or cubic feet of space are you going to allow for the educational department?" and in regard to the characteristics of that department there must be courteous consultation with the Centennial authorities, for they are the authorities in the premises. I repeat: It is necessary to get down to business-principles; and when your committee has the proper authority to communicate with the Centennial managers, the information required will be rapidly obtained and promptly disseminated to all parts of the Union. Then we can go into the work of harmonious arrangement; then the different States can fall into line in co-operation and contributions without hesitancy and without doubt, and all the desirable variety of exhibition can be secured to the satisfaction of each State and for the promotion of the general interests of the Exposition.

Mr. A. P. MARBLE, superintendent of schools at Worcester, Mass. As I understand the proposition, it seems to me that this is the most direct method for obtaining the result which we all desire. I understand that an executive committee is, under this resolution, to be formed out of the general committee, which embraces all the superintendents represented in this department. The object will be to have an efficient body of men, who can consult with the Centennial authorities and also raise the funds necessary for securing proper representation in the forthcoming Exposition. I think there will be entire unanimity in debating this proposition; but I rose more particularly to make a remark which I think will bring my friend Mr. Richards into perfect harmony with the last speaker. The action of this body last year was published to the friends of education, and carried more particularly to the officers of the educational boards in the different States. That action was virtually adopted by the National Educational Association. I was an officer of that association and present at its last meeting. It seemed to be conceded that the action taken here was proper and sufficient; and, although I am not authorized directly to speak for the National Educational Association, yet I am convinced that I am correct in saying that the action of this body was virtually approved by the national society and that reliance is placed upon your action here in carrying out the objects which have been set forth by Mr. Wickersham. The National Educational Association looks to this body, to this department, to adopt all necessary means for the end proposed. That, I understand, covers the objection raised by my friend on the left.

Mr. WICKERSHAM. I am very glad to hear the explanation which has been made by the gentleman who has just taken his seat. I think it must remove any objection that can be properly raised to the adoption of this resolution. As far as I am concerned, I take great pleasure in expressing my approval now of the motion as it stands.

The resolution offered by Mr. Wickersham was then unanimously adopted, and the president was instructed to appoint the committee.

The president announced that the names of the committee whose appointment was authorized under the resolution would be given at the commencement of the evening-session.

The PRESIDENT. I stated that the editor of the New England Journal of Education had sent a large number of copies of his journal to me, with the request that they should be distributed among the members. We should be pleased to have members take copies for themselves and their friends, so far as they will go. I presume it is understood by all the members of the department that the New England journals of education have been consolidated into this new publication, which appears weekly.

Mr. PHILBRICK. I would like to say one word in regard to that matter, Mr. President. I would like to say that the gentlemen representing the various educational journals of New England, the editors and principal supporters of those journals in the educational bureaus of the several States, after experience of some twenty-five or thirty years in the publication of educational papers, have come to the conclusion that it would be best to combine and concentrate their influence and their patronage on one journal. They came to the conclusion that, instead of scattering their forces by the publication of a number of monthly journals in the different States, they would combine for the issuance of one journal which should thoroughly and ably represent the educational institutions and interests of the people of New England. They have found a man of eminent ability to fill the chair of editor, who will devote his whole time to the work. He has had a great deal of experience in educational matters, and was lately the superintendent of schools in the State of Rhode Island. It is hoped that the journal will be made to fully answer all reasonable requirements of a thoroughly able and comprehensive medium for the friends of education throughout that section of the country. And even something more is hoped. It is expected that it will assume something of a national character, not in the interests of a section, but the educational interests of the people in every part of the country will be considered. We hope the teachers throughout the country will come forward and examine the journal, and, if they conclude it worth while, lend their co-operation in its support and improvement. It is a weekly journal. It is intended to have it placed at a high standard as an authoritative exponent of the best ideas in regard to educational facilities and improvement. I would suggest that each member take ten or twelve copies of the paper, if he sees fit.

Rev. Dr. HAROLD. I will ask for the privilege of offering a resolution.

The PRESIDENT. I suppose that the privilege of offering a resolution is confined to members of the department.

Dr. HAROLD. I would like to ask the privilege, but, if it is not the rule that such a privilege shall be granted, I will not press my offer.

The PRESIDENT. I think that has been the rule. While we ask the friends of education present to participate in our discussions, only members are entitled to offer resolutions—either members of the department or of the national association. Every friend of the cause of education can become a member of the national association. The treasurer of the national association is here, and may think proper to offer some additional explanations in regard to the matter.

Mr. MARBLE. I state, for the information of all present, that this department has the privilege of deciding who its members shall be, but, necessarily, its members are members of the national association. No one can be a member of this department unless he is first a member of the national association. Any friend of education can become attached to the national association by signing the constitution and paying $2. There is an annual payment of $1, which entitles the member to a volume of the proceedings for the year. I notice in the list of members that there are several members of this body present who are not members of the national association. I wish to say, as treasurer of the national association, of which this is a part, that, while it may not be true that the first and second and third need is money, it is literally true that the fourth need of the association is money. The national association has been accustomed to publish a volume of proceedings each year. This volume, as I have already stated, is supplied to each member of the association without charge. The committee on publication last year published a volume of three hundred and seventy-five pages. It contains very valuable papers. Among them is a paper by Dr. Peabody upon elective studies of colleges, a paper by Professor Clark upon the question of co-education of the sexes, and a paper by Dr. Venable, of the University of Virginia. We incurred an expense of $1,500 in publishing the volume. There was in the treasury about $500, which left an indebtedness of $1,000 to be made up from the sales of the volume. The affairs of the publishing committee are as follows: Entire expense of this publication, $1,524, of which $854 has been paid. leaving a balance of $670 due to the committee on publication. Each member of the association has been furnished with a volume. Now, of this $670 about $200 is supposed to be provided for by gentlemen who have pledged themselves to take a certain number of volumes and pay for them. But that $200 is not yet in any official pocket, and it would not do to count upon any more than $170 of it. So that there is really a deficit of something like $500 to be made up from the sale of seven hundred and fifty volumes of the proceedings. Now, what I am looking to at this present time is this: to change these seven hundred and fifty volumes into $500, to liquidate the debt of the association, and to put these volumes into the hands of leading educators throughout the country. A vast amount of good will be done by putting these volumes into the hands of teachers who will read and profit by them. The plan proposed is this: for each State or State-superintendent to order from the chairman of the publication-committee twenty or twenty-five copies of these proceedings, at a cost of $1.50 for each of the first ten volumes ordered. Let each State order as many as is thought fit, from the chairman of the publication-committee, and pay for them, and let the debt be paid. Then the distribution can be made by the superintendents. I will not detain the attention of the assembly any longer; I will only remark that this volume of proceedings is very valuable and will be appreciated by all who purchase it.

Mr. ABERNETHY. How can copies be obtained now?

The PRESIDENT. By addressing A. P. Marble, superintendent of public schools of Worcester, Mass. He is the chairman of the publication-committee.

General EATON presented and read letters from Hon. John M. McKleroy, superintendent of public instruction, Alabama, who writes:

I regret that the immense amount of labor now on my hands in the office here and the inadequate clerical force at command preclude my attending the approaching session of the department of superintendence.

From Hon. Thomas B. Stockwell, commissioner of public schools of Rhode Island, who writes:

In regard to the superintendents' meeting, it would give me great pleasure to attend and my office-labors, however pressing, would not keep me away, but the health of my family is such at this juncture that I dare not leave home even for a day or two.

From Hon. A. Parish, superintendent of public schools, New Haven Conn., who writes:

The pleasant remembrance I have of our meeting last year renders my desire to visit your city again on a like occasion quite intense; but yesterday the secretary of our board, my chum in the office, fell and broke his arm and is quite helpless, and my presence here is indispensable.

From Hon. John Fraser, superintendent of public instruction, State of Kansas, who writes:

I regret that I cannot attend the meeting of superintendents on the 27th instant The Kansas legislature being in session, I must remain at my post.

From Hon. Charles S. Smart, State-commissioner of schools of Ohio who writes:

I can readily understand the valuable opportunity the meeting of the superintendence department of the National Teachers' Association would afford me for learning much tha I shall want to know. It will, unfortunately for me, be quite impossible for me to b present at that meeting on the 27th instant.

From Hon. J. H. Smart, superintendent of public schools, Fort Wayne Ind., who writes:

I regret that an unusual pressure of business will render it impossible for me to accep your invitation.

From Hon. Warren Johnson, State-superintendent of common schools of Maine, who writes:

I regret very much that I cannot have the privilege and pleasure of meeting face t face my brother-superintendents, of grasping them heartily by the hand, and especiall, of sitting down sociably by the national educational fireside to glean from the observa tions and experiences of my fellow-laborers items of cheer and information for my ow enlightenment.

From Hon. J. H. Binford, superintendent of city-schools, Richmond Va., who writes:

I had confidently expected to be present and had anticipated great pleasure an profit from the meeting, but the condition of my health is such that I dare not leav home at this time.

And from Hon. S. M. Etter, superintendent of public instruction, State of Illinois, who writes:

This morning I received the circular giving notice of the meeting of superintendents on the 27th. I desire very much to be present, but I fear it will be impossible.

After the reading of the letters the department adjourned until 3 o'clock p. m.

AFTERNOON SESSION, JANUARY 28, 1875.

The department resumed its session at half-past three o'clock.

The president announced, as the executive committee of five on the Centennial Exposition, General Eaton of Washington, Mr. Wickersham of Pennsylvania, Mr. Philbrick of Boston, Mr. Abernethy of Iowa, and Mr. Ruffner of Virginia.

Mr. Wickersham, of Pennsylvania, for the committee on the relations of the Federal Government to public education, then submitted a report, accompanied with the following resolutions:

Resolved, That this body reiterate and reaffirm the positions taken at its meeting in this place one year ago, as follows: 1. That the Federal Government should leave to the people and local governments of each State the management of their own educational affairs without interference. 2. That great service was done to the cause of education by Congress in establishing and maintaining a Bureau or Department of Education, whereby appropriate information from all parts of the world may be gathered, digested, and distributed, and whereby much useful aid is furnished to the practical work of education throughout the country. 3. That the proposition to set apart the public lands of the United States exclusively for the purposes of free education meets with our heartiest approval. 4. That it is the duty of Congress to furnish special aid to the school-authorities of the District of Columbia.

Resolved, That as, in order fully to perform the work pressing upon it and make its usefulness still more widely felt, we are satisfied the National Bureau of Education needs increased clerical force; and as it is equally plain to us that the distribution directly by the Bureau of at least ten thousand copies of its annual reports each year, among school-officers and those specially interested in the work of education in the different States and Territories, would do an incalculable amount of good, we therefore respectfully petition Congress, in the interest of the education of the people, to take the necessary steps to bring about these desirable ends.

Resolved, That a reasonable appropriation by the General Government is necessary to secure a full and creditable representation of the educational interests of the country at the approaching Centennial Exposition to be held at Philadelphia, and we sincerely hope that such an appropriation may be made by the Congress now in session.

> J. P. WICKERSHAM.
> JOHN D. PHILBRICK.
> B. G. NORTHROP.
> ALEX. C. HOPKINS.
> J. K. JILLSON.
> ALONZO ABERNETHY.

The report of the committee was received and the resolutions unanimously adopted.

Mr. MARBLE. I move that the same committee who reported these resolutions be instructed to embody the same in suitable form and present them to Congress as a memorial from this body.

The motion was agreed to.

General EATON. There is one matter of interest to which I desire to call the attention of the department for a moment. The people of Chili propose to hold an international exhibition at Santiago in 1875, opening, I think, in September.

The minister of that country has, on several occasions, expressed to me his desire that the educational interests of the United States should be represented at this coming exhibition.

Recently a communication has been forwarded from the Secretary of State to the Secretary of the Interior, containing inquiries in reference to the feasibility of such a representation from this country. It having been officially referred to me, I have made the following reply, which I bring to your notice as showing our status in regard to participation in the exhibition:

DEPARTMENT OF THE INTERIOR, BUREAU OF EDUCATION,
Washington, D. C., January 7, 1875.

SIR: In reference to the letter of Hon. Hamilton Fish, Secretary of State, bearing date December 24, 1874, to the Secretary of the Interior, concerning the practicability and expediency of making an educational representation at the international exhibition to be held at Santiago, Chili, in 1875, which was submitted to me for consideration, I have the honor to report that, so far as such representation may consist of the reports and occasional publications of this Bureau and of the official reports on education published by the several States, cities, and towns, and by them furnished to this Office, it is perfectly feasible and, in my judgment, expedient.

Any attempt at a fuller representation of the educational facilities and appliances existing in the United States, such as was made at Vienna, could not, however, be undertaken by this Office without congressional or executive authority and financial assistance.

The effect of such a full and complete exhibition of the school-appliances, furniture, and public-school-systems of the United States, could hardly fail to lead to more intimate relations between the countries, and would, therefore, in itself considered, seem desirable.

Very respectfully, your obedient servant,

JOHN EATON, *Commissioner.*

Hon. C. DELANO,
Secretary of the Interior.

I wish, also, to say to the gentlemen representing the different States and cities here, that if they desire to send copies of their official reports to the Chilian exhibition they can do so by forwarding them to the Bureau of Education, so that they may be included in material sent from that Bureau. Even if nothing further can be done, these reports will doubtless be of value and interest. It may be, perhaps, advisable for you to communicate the fact of this exhibition to those persons in your several localities who may be interested in exhibiting school-furniture, apparatus, and books.

Mr. LUCKEY. The committee appointed yesterday to report on the subjects embodied in the paper of Dr. A. N. Bell beg leave to submit the following report:

Whereas the health and the mental advancement of pupils are co-ordinates of the same importance; and whereas the doctor has so excellently portrayed the absolute dependence of the one upon the other: Therefore,

Resolved, That we cordially commend the practical thoughts embodied in that paper, and that we will as a body of superintendents enforce more strictly hereafter the valuable rules of hygiene as set forth therein, and that we commend the same to the thoughtful consideration of our school-men throughout the country.

Resolved, That we recommend that the Bureau of Education secure and place before the country statistics showing the need of action by the school-authorities upon this subject.

GEORGE J. LUCKEY.
ALEX. C. HOPKINS.
A. P. MARBLE.

Mr. McMILLAN, of Youngstown, Ohio. Mr. President, I have nothing to say against the report of the committee, but, as the Chair was about to submit the resolutions for the action of the convention, I was about to protest, not against anything that might be said, so much as against the assumption that the school-houses are killing more children than all other instrumentalities put together. Now, I do not know what they are doing in Washington; I do not know what they are doing in Boston. But, so far as I know, in Ohio and Western Pennsylvania, the healthiest-looking children, the happiest children, are those you see flocking in and out of the school-houses; and the healthiest and best-looking of them are those that have gone through this "poisonous atmosphere" and course of hard study, and are in the highest departments of those schools. And I wish to enter my protest against that sort of assumption which has been advanced by nearly all the speakers.

I was very much delighted with the address of Dr. Bell, but that doctrine I did not want to have go out without protest.

The report of the committee was then received and the resolutions adopted.

ADDRESS OF MR. PHILBRICK.

The president then introduced Hon. John D. Philbrick, ex-superintendent of public schools of Boston, who read the following paper:

CAN THE ELEMENTS OF INDUSTRIAL EDUCATION BE INTRODUCED INTO OUR COMMON SCHOOLS?

The peculiar characteristic of the common school the world over is, that it is the school in which the children of the mass of the people receive all their scholastic education. In our country it is true that this class of schools, comprising the ungraded rural district-schools and the primary and grammar-grades of the villages and cities, are expected also to prepare candidates for the high schools, who are to pursue, to a greater or less extent, a liberal course of study. But this is not their main function, which is to give the best possible education for the practical purposes of life to the mass of children who must terminate their schooling at 14 or, at most, at 15 years of age. And it will not be disputed, I apprehend, that to secure to every child the blessing of such an elementary education is the paramount educational problem of the present times, for it requires no extraordinary penetration to perceive that at the present period "the world is resting its future hopes and quieting its future fears

89

In reliance on the education and enlightenment of the mass of the people." One must be blind, indeed, not to see that the future of nations depends on the kind and degree of their education. As Jules Simon has well said, "The first people is that which has the best schools; if it is not the first to-day, it will become the first to-morrow."

I find it extremely difficult to handle this subject satisfactorily in a brief paper, on account of the necessity it involves of considering the whole field of common-school-education, for the instruction in a school-course ought to constitute a complete and consistent whole, all the branches of study being chosen, arranged, and proportioned in respect to each other, by judicious limitations, in such a manner as to produce the desired result. This is the ideal to be aimed at in a programme of studies, which should set forth, in the first place, the general object to be accomplished by the whole course; next, the subjects of instruction required; then the results to be sought at each stage in the course; and, finally, the particular requirements in respect to each subject of instruction in the several stages.

This is what has been done, in a masterly manner, in the common-school-programme recently issued by the Prussian ministry of education. It is the result of the combined wisdom of the most competent experts, and, therefore, its authority must command the highest respect. While it is specific enough to serve as a reliable and intelligible guide to teachers and school-officials, it allows all the freedom that can be profitable in respect to the methods of teaching and management in each individual school. Each teacher is at liberty to make his own particular programme, provided that he conforms to this prescribed general one.

NEED OF REVISION OF PUBLIC SCHOOL COURSES OF STUDIES.

The interests of common-school-education in this country most imperatively demand at the present time the same sort of service. I am not aware that any State educational authority has undertaken this important task. The school-laws designate the studies that may be taught; but a naked enumeration of the studies required or permitted is a most insufficient guide to teachers and school-officers in the work they have to do. Considerable progress has recently been made by city-superintendents towards working out rational schemes of instruction for their respective systems of elementary schools; but these schemes have only a local authority, and they embody the idiosyncracies of the individual officers by whom they have been framed. Looking at our American common schools as a whole, it is not far from the truth to say that they are working on no better programmes for their guides than the lists of text-books prescribed for their use. It is not impossible to conceive of the construction of a set of text-books which might serve the purpose in view; but I am not aware of the existence of such a set. The text-books for common schools have increased in number and swelled in bulk, out of all proportion to the legitimate objects and wants of our schools. And the practical standard of instruction to be aimed at is the contents comprised within the covers of these numerous and overgrown text-books. The result is that teachers and pupils exhaust their time and strength on the masses of details of little worth contained in the text-books of a part of the studies proper for the common school, while other subjects of great practical utility are comparatively neglected. This, I believe, is a grave defect in our American elementary schools. As one of the means of remedying this evil, it seems to me desirable that the educational authority of each State should prepare and issue, with the indorsement of its sanction, such a programme as I have suggested, containing a scheme of instruction irrespective of text-books. This scheme should consist of two parts, the one adapted to the wants and capabilities of ungraded district-schools and the other to the conditions of graded city- or village-schools. I do not take extreme ground against the use of text-books. In teaching most branches, text-books are a convenience, if not a necessity, especially in the case of teachers of ordinary qualifications. But text-books, as they exist, afford no adequate substitute for a rational scheme of instruction.

If the State-authorities should put forth programmes as here proposed, they would at once be compared and criticised in the light of whatever pedagogical experience and pedagogical science we possess, and thus we should arrive at the soundest judgment on this important matter.

It is the appropriate business of educators to adapt educational institutions and means to the wants of the time and place in which they exist. New demands must be met by new provisions, while requirements that have become useless or obsolete should be abolished or modified. Our fathers had no such educational problem as this to deal with. In the earlier history of the common school it was taken for granted that its function was to teach reading, writing, and the rudiments of arithmetic, and nothing more. In fact, reading and writing were the only branches prescribed for common schools in the original act for their establishment in the Massachusetts colony. Our fathers were fortunate that they did not have to master spelling after the modern fashion, else they could not have found time to subdue the wilderness. And when, something less than a century ago, the course of study in the common schools of Boston was enlarged by the introduction of "spelling, accenting, English grammar, and composition," it was feared by some that these new language-studies would occupy the time which ought to be devoted to more practically useful branches, and so the committee were petitioned to allow the boys to devote the whole of their last year of schooling to writing and arithmetic.

All this has been changed. The provinces of the old learning have been greatly extended and vast annexations have been made by modern discovery, "and it is not extravagant to say that the amount of knowledge appropriate to civilization which now exists in the world is more than double, and in many cases more than tenfold, what it was about half a century ago." This enormous increase of knowledge, in connection with the corresponding increase in the demands of modern civilization, for the practical use of knowledge, in supplying the wants, overcoming the difficulties, and multiplying the elegances of life, has resulted in the overloading of the curriculums of study in all classes of educational institutions. When Edward Everett entered Harvard College, two years were deemed amply sufficient for preparation; now six years are scarcely adequate for the task. Much has been gained and much more remains to be achieved by improved methods and appliances of teaching, but the powers of the human intellect for the acquisition of knowledge are stationary, and the limits of those powers cannot be transcended with impunity.

POPULAR COMPLAINTS AGAINST COMMON SCHOOLS.

Our common schools are complained of, on the one hand, because they send out their pupils with so little practical knowledge, and, on the other, because the brains of the children are overworked and the foundations of their health sapped by the excessive application required by the multiplicity of the studies. No doubt, broadly speaking, there is too much ground for both these apparently contradictory complaints, although they do not both equally apply in the case of the same school or the same local system. Not forgetting that the chief remedy for educational imperfections is to be sought in the improvement of the qualifications of teachers, I cannot help thinking that the evils referred to might be greatly diminished and the education imparted in our common schools greatly advanced, both in respect to quantity and quality, if school-authorities generally could be induced to prepare a plan of instruction adapted to the capacities and wants of the pupils, in which should be included all the branches properly belonging to elementary schools and from which should be rigidly excluded all unessential details, and which should, at the same time, *limit the requirements in each study to a moderate and reasonable standard.* I would emphasize the importance of the limitation of standards rather than the limitation of subjects, for I believe that common schools are not so much overloaded by the number of the branches taught as by the extravagant requirements in respect to the individual branches and wrong methods of teaching.

The subject of this paper requires us to consider, especially, what place in such a plan of instruction ought to be assigned to industrial education. An intelligent treatment of this question demands a definite understanding of what is meant by the term "industrial education," which is used rather loosely in the current educational discussions.

Every man has two spheres of activity: the one, his own particular profession or business, be it what it may, that of merchant, mechanic, farmer, seaman, lawyer, teacher, or the like; the other, his general calling, which he has in common with all his neighbors, namely, the calling of a citizen and a man. Now, the education which fits him for the former of these spheres of activity is called special or professional, or, perhaps more properly, technical, while that education which fits him for the latter is called general.

It is the design of general education to impart the training, the culture, and the knowledge, of whatever kind and degree, which it is desirable that a human being should possess, without regard to any particular vocation or pursuit in life. Its object is to make capable and cultivated human beings. But, in technical education, the end in view is not culture and knowledge for their own sake, but information and dexterity with reference to their application in some special occupation. Here the aim is to impart the ability and skill requisite to success in some particular vocation, to teach the knowledge required to fit men for some special mode of gaining their livelihood. By industrial education we mean specifically that large department of technical education which fits men for all those pursuits not comprised in what are called learned professions. As in the case of general education, it has its different stages or grades. Its elementary stage is that which is requisite to form the workman of every class, especially those persons engaged in skilled manual labor. The secondary grade is that designed for those who immediately superintend and direct workmen, such as foremen, masters, and overseers, who ought to have, besides practical skill, a considerable knowledge of science and its application to their respective branches of business. The third and highest grade is for those whose callings do not demand skill in manual labor, but high scientific attainments and a large amount of special knowledge, such as architects, engineers, and practical chemists. Again, in each stage, this education consists of two parts: the theoretical and the practical. The former imparts the principles of science and the knowledge of their application, with the rules of the arts and the results of experience, so far as they can be given in schools; the latter requires actual work under the eye and training of a master; that is, it requires apprenticeship in the work-shop or the industrial establishment.

Now, everybody knows that a man's success in his particular calling or profession depends not so much upon the accident of his apprenticeship as upon what sort of a mind and body he brings to it, what kind of intelligence, of conscience, and of physical soundness and aptitude the system of general education has developed in him. Therefore, not only because men are men before they are merchants, mechanics, or farmers, but as a means of making good merchants, mechanics, and farmers, the first and fundamental aim of all education and of all plans of instruction should be to form capable and sensible men. This general "education makes a man a more intelligent shoemaker, if that be his occupation, but not by teaching him how to make shoes; it does so by the mental exercise it gives and the habits it impresses." General education, therefore, must not be undervalued; it must be amply provided for and rigidly insisted upon; the more of it people have the better for them. To sacrifice it to technical education is to kill the goose that lays the golden egg. But its fanciful superfluities must be lopped off, its non-essentials discarded, and its rubbish thrown overboard, and then, by the side of it, and based upon it, and supplementary to it, technical education, especially that great new department appropriate to all industries, must be universally created, organized in all its grades and varieties, and amply maintained. In brief, to make education as useful as possible, it must be made, as far as practicable in both of its great divisions, simple, limited, practical, acceptable to the learner, adapted to his character and wants and brought home to his particular case by subdivision and selection. A good deal is said at the present day about raising the standard of education. But is there not rather need of providing the means of education, of selecting, organizing, and administering existing knowledge to the best purpose and advantage?

TECHNICAL TRAINING IN COMMON SCHOOLS IMPRACTICABLE.

In attempting to apply these general views and considerations to the common-school-problem, especially with reference to industrial education, it is, perhaps, necessary to say a few words in the first place concerning the practicability of teaching trades or skilled handicrafts; that is the practical department of industrial education in the elementary school. Ever since Rousseau, in his ideal system, prescribed, for his model pupil, apprenticeship to a trade, in connection with his scholastic tuition, the idea of introducing the workshop into the common school has not been without its advocates. In France this question has at different periods occupied the attention of the government, and the system was put in operation in many localities under the auspices of the administration of public instruction. But the experiment was a failure, although made under favorable conditions, and all traces of the workshop have disappeared from the schools where it was introduced. It is safe to say that this idea is condemned by all the best pedagogical authorities in the world. The all-sufficient objections to it are, first, that the whole of the limited period assigned to the common-school-course is needed for general education and the acquisition of useful knowledge; secondly, that at the common-school-age the physical development is not adequate to the purposes of most manual trades; thirdly, that it is too early for the pupils to choose their callings; and fourthly, the impracticability of allowing a choice of trades on account of the cost involved in providing for instruction in several. It must be concluded, I think, that the effect of putting the workshop into the school can be no other than to make a poor school and a poor workshop, and to defeat the great object of common-school-education, that of securing the development of the mind and the acquisition of useful knowledge necessary for success in all industrial pursuits.

HALF-TIME SCHOOLS CONSIDERED.

There is another contrivance for combining school-instruction with industrial manual labor, known as the *half-time system*, which places the workshop, not in the school, but by its side. The theory of this plan is that the pupil is to be kept at school during the period prescribed by law, but that, after arriving at a certain age, say 10 or 12, his time is to be divided between the school and apprenticeship, or manual labor, in some industrial occupation, in the manufactory or on the farm. The schooling is reduced to half the usual number of hours per week. This plan originated in England, where it has found much favor, and it has been in operation to a limited extent in some of the manufacturing-towns of Massachusetts. On the continent of Europe it has not made much progress. Very respectable English authorities maintain that where this system has been tried the pupils make as much progress in their studies as those who attend during the whole time; that the results of three hours' schooling daily are equal to those of six hours. If it is true generally that half a school day is as good as a whole day, there is certainly an enormous waste of time and money in carrying on schools! I can conceive of schools conducted in such a manner that half the ordinary number of hours of attendance would be worth as much as the whole number. But it cannot be true of really good schools. And it is impossible that the half-time course should be generally accepted as the equivalent of the whole-time course, unless the obligatory years of attendance are proportionally extended.

Half-time-schooling, continued from 12 to 16 years of age, in connection with manual labor in an apprenticeship, might be as good as whole-time-schooling, extending only from 12 to 14 years, and perhaps better; but the half-time system, as at present understood, is no solution of the common-school-problem, but only a makeshift, a concession to the pressure of poverty and the demands for cheap child-labor in manufacturing-establishments.

WHAT, THEN, IS THE PROVINCE OF THE COMMON SCHOOL?

What, then, is the function of the common school in relation to industrial education? I answer, that the common school must not be appropriated to the teaching of any specialty, as such. It must undertake to teach only those branches which are generally useful in all callings and in the common affairs of life, and not those which belong exclusively to particular occupations. And yet the common school of the present day must accomplish far more than was expected of it in former times, in respect to the range of subjects taught. The elements of what is called the *new education*, namely, science and art with reference to their application to industrial pursuits, must be included in the modern common-school-course. The introduction of this new education and the re-adjustment of the old, to adapt it to the new condition of things, seem to me to be one of the problems of common-school-instruction. The specific thing to do is to introduce as many subjects of general practical utility as possible without overloading the programme. There is but one mode of accomplishing this desirable object, and that is by a judicious limitation of requirements and a simplification in the handling of the subjects. The branches of this new common-school-education, which are especially applicable to industrial pursuits and at the same time serviceable in the common affairs of life, are drawing, geometry, (with the application of arithmetic to mensuration,) natural history, physics, and chemistry. These are the branches which lie at the foundation of industrial education. I take the ground that a knowledge of the elements of these branches is universally needed, *and that knowledge it is the function of the common school to impart.* This seems to me what is desirable and practicable in the way of industrial education in the schools designed for the mass of children. And in addition to these, or, possibly, in part as a substitute, all girls should be taught needle-work, and the cutting and fitting of garments, and the elements of household economy.

IMPORTANCE OF DRAWING AS A COMMON-SCHOOL-STUDY.

Of these branches of industrial education, I attach the greatest importance to drawing as being the most universally useful, both as a means of general culture and as an instrument of practical utility; it is a thing of use in every department of business and in every condition in life; it is in itself an expressive language, easily depicting to the eye what no words, however well chosen, can represent; it is the best means of cultivating the power and habit of accurate observation and of developing the perception and the love of the beautiful in nature and in art; it is the fundamental branch of all industrial education; it is indispensable for the architect, the engraver, the engineer, the designer, the draughtsman, the molder, the machine-builder, the head-mechanic, and indeed to all skilled craftsmen; it is calculated to afford invaluable aid to the inventive genius of our people; it is an instrumentality for illustration which should be in every teacher's hands; and, if properly taught, it more than compensates for the time it takes, by facilitating instruction in other branches. Scott Russell, an authority of the first order in respect to industrial education, says : "Every bit of work which a man does has to fit into some other bit of work of some other man's doing. Each man should therefore understand the plans of the complete work on which he and his fellows are engaged, in order to work well to the other's hand, and the only way to get this thorough understanding of plans is to have learned to draw them himself. Complete plan-drawing applied to his own business is therefore essential to a good workman." Drawing has been well called the sixth sense of the skilled workman. All our best authorities in industrial science are agreed that the manufacturing-interests of this country are in pressing need of the development of art-culture, and the only adequate basis of this culture is a thorough system of elementary drawing taught in all common schools.

Undoubtedly the cause of our past neglect of this branch is found in the general ignorance in regard to its nature, objects, and utility. Drawing has been regarded as a merely ornamental study, of little or no use in practical life, to be allowed only to those pupils who have time on their hands, after having acquired a competent knowledge of what are ignorantly deemed more useful subjects. But the light is breaking; the reform is now fairly inaugurated, and I trust the time is not distant when every child will be taught elementary drawing. No time should be lost in making drawing an obligatory branch of instruction in the common schools of every State. It is nearly five years ago since this important step was taken in Massachusetts, and at the same time it was made obligatory on all towns and cities containing ten thousand inhabitants and upwards, to open free industrial drawing-schools for adults. This action of the legislature originated in a petition largely representing the mechanical and manufacturing-interests of the State, setting forth the disadvantages under which they had to compete with foreign manufacturers for want of workmen skilled in "drawing and other arts of design." Subsequently a State normal art-school was established, for the special purpose of training teachers of drawing and the other departments of art-education. Each of the State normal schools has been provided with an art-department and a special teacher of drawing. Over all the interests of this department of instruction supervision is exercised by a State-director of art-education, an art-master possessing a rare combination of qualifications for the important task assigned to him. The remarkable success of this movement makes it plain that it was not begun too soon. The productive industries of the State will, at no distant day, reap a rich harvest from this educational provision.

Practical elementary geometry is another of these industrial branches which has been most unaccountably neglected in our common schools. Nearly fifty years ago Josiah Holbrook advocated the teaching of this subject in primary schools, and prepared some charts and a little manual to facilitate this object, and, when a child, a few weeks in a school where this plan had been adopted, gave me all the knowledge of geometry that I carried with me to college; and it was a knowledge which I have always regarded as of no small practical value. Several years ago ex-President Hill, of Harvard College, prepared a little text-book for teaching children from 5 to 8 years of age the elements of geometry. Such instruction, he contended, should precede the logical drill required by such a book as Colburn's First Lessons in Arithmetic. The key to his idea of the treatment of the subject is contained in a sentence in the preface, in which he says, "I have avoided reasoning, and simply given interesting geometrical facts, fitted, I hope, to arouse a child to the observation of phenomena and to the perception of forms as real entities." Practical geometry would be taught, of course, in connection with mensuration of angles, surfaces, and solids, on the one hand, and in connection with drawing on the other, in the solution of geometrical problems by the use of the compasses and ruler. These implements are peculiarly the scholar's tools, and I mention it as a curious pedagogical fact that in Germany and Austria all the pupils of the common schools are required by law to be provided with them. President Hill looked at this subject in its relations to culture, but Scott Russell, looking at it as a technical study, says: "Every workman should, for the most part, be able to conceive clearly and accurately, in his own mind, the shape of everything he may have to make or work with. This makes it a first condition of skill that he should master shape in his own mind, and that mastery requires him to be a geometer. If that were true there might be written over every skilled workshop the substance of the ancient Greek inscription, 'No man ignorant of geometry enters here.'"

It is not necessary in the elementary stage to demonstrate geometrical propositions, but to learn the construction of geometrical forms and to acquire a knowledge of the most important geometrical facts in their relations to practical life.

No one will question the value of the knowledge of physical science as a means of economizing and utilizing both time and labor. The application of science to the productive industries has multiplied the comforts and conveniences of life to au extent which it is impossible to estimate. But there yet remains a rich harvest to be reaped from the advantages of such a general elementary knowledge of the physical sciences as is capable of being imparted in the common school. "Our whole working power depends on knowing the laws of the world; in other words, the properties of the things which we have to work with, and to work among, and to work upon." The mass of people must, of course, rely for the greater part of this knowledge on the few experts who devote themselves to its several departments. But an elementary knowledge of scientific truths is essential for every human being, and this elementary knowledge the common school should give.

The object-lessons in the primary grades serve as an introduction to this knowledge. In the higher classes the most useful truths and facts in natural history, natural philosophy, and chemistry are to be taught, not by committing to memory the words of text-books, but by actual observation and experiment. Every common school should have its museum of natural history and the necessary apparatus for the simplest experiments in physics and chemistry.

PRESENT WASTE OF TIME IN COMMON SCHOOLS.

It may be said, and doubtless will be said, that all this knowledge is very useful, but it cannot be given in the common schools; that there is no room or time for the studies I have enumerated, if justice is done to what are called the indispensable branches.

This leads to the question of the proper limitations of studies and to the question of methods of teaching, questions which can be only touched upon here. But I want to say that I think there is an immense waste of time on the studies usually taught in the common schools in various ways, and that if the time of teachers and pupils were properly utilized all that I propose could be accomplished. Take spelling. Why should a child who will have little use to make of spelling be kept drilling on this barren branch until he can spell a hundred per cent. of picked words? Why should years be occupied in memorizing, or learning in any way, the contents of a large text-book on geography? Why should a pupil be kept on arithmetic until he can solve the most difficult problems at sight? Why should these things be insisted upon to the entire neglect of the fruitful subjects I have called the new education? By the proper limitation and simplification of the old branches time enough might be gained for the new ones.

And then I must take the liberty to say here that I think the prevailing theory in this country, in respect to the method of elementary teaching, is, to say the least, open to criticism. That theory maps out the child's mind into certain faculties and proceeds to administer what is supposed to be the needed discipline to each with a view to produce a harmonious development. I do not mean to say that valuable results may not be produced in this way; but, so far as common schools are concerned, I believe better practical results would be reached, by beginning with mapping out the knowledge which it is desirable for the pupil to possess, and then teaching these branches in their proper order, in the most straightforward and practical way, giving no exercises with special reference to mental gymnastic training. By this course, I think, there would be a vast gain, not only in the useful knowledge acquired, but in the effective mental discipline imparted.

I do not mean to say that a knowledge of the science of the human mind is useless to the teacher of an elementary school. The more of this knowledge he has the better. If he understands the order of the development of the mental faculties he can more intelligently adapt his teaching to the capacities of his pupils, and thus economize their power of learning and his own power of teaching. In framing a course of elementary ustruction, it is necessary to regard both the principles of psychology and the wants of practical life. But it seems to me that the plan of common-school-instruction, which seems to be much in vogue in this country, and which might be designated as the harmonious and symmetrical-development plan, has not been a success, and that it is not likely to meet the wants of our times. For one, I find myself more and more inclined to favor the plan of selecting the most practically useful subjects of instruction, and of teaching as many of them as possible by the shortest and most comprehensive methods. If this course is pursued, I feel sure that, during the proper period of common-school-instruction, not only a competent knowledge of what have been called the common English branches may be acquired, but also a very useful amount of knowledge of the elements of the industrial branches I have mentioned. And this is no mere theory, unsustained by facts of experience. It is actually done where common-school-education has been most systematically developed. The Prussian programme to which I referred affords an illustration. Let such a scheme be carried out in a rational way, and there would be no just ground of complaint, either that our pupils were overworked or that they were not properly instructed in matters pertaining to the practical affairs of life.

Mr. NEWELL, of Maryland. Mr. President, a few thoughts have been suggested by the able and exhaustive paper that has just been read, which I will take the liberty to place before the department.

In the first place I would say, contrary to what Mr. Philbrick advanced in his paper, that in the State of Maryland we have endeavored to map out a programme for the use of all schools under the grade of high school. The plan is uniform. The State-board have undertaken to eliminate from the ordinary course of instruction the matters which they thought might best be dispensed with. They have endeavored to group together the courses of study in the order in which they thought they ought to be pursued. Their object has been to map out a very general chart and to give very minute instructions for both teachers and pupils to pursue. After the 1st of July next the State of Maryland will require all teachers, of every grade, to be examined in the elements of geometry and in physiology, before they can get certificates as teachers. One year has been given them to make preparation for this examination.

I feel a little disappointed, Mr. President, in the contents of the paper that we have heard read. And, in speaking for a very few minutes on this point, I hope the department will indulge me if I speak rather as a person who is doubting and looking for information, and as submitting suggestions to arouse the thoughts of others, than as one who has already come to a conclusion. And, while I have thought a great deal on the matter, but have not come to any conclusion at all, it is clear that there is a difference between the three departments of education alleged in the paper by Mr. Philbrick: that which is scientific, whether of a low or of a high degree; that which is technical; and that which lies intermediate between the two, and which we designate by the term industrial. Between these two, the scientific and the technical, there lies a large arable ground, which can be cultivated if we only know how to do it. It seems to me, Mr. President, that among the just complaints which are mentioned with regard to our common-school system, taken in a general aspect, is this one, which deserves our attention: that the school-room tends to make pupils too much of school-boys and school-girls, and too little of practical young men and young women. We have many instances of boys and girls who have gone through the ordinary routine of school-instruction, who are fair spellers and readers, who can go through the books and answer more questions in geography and in history than I can do, for one, and yet who have no sense of the application of these branches of which they have acquired a knowledge, and who feel utterly lost when they come into active life and attempt to turn these school-room-accomplishments to practical purpose. To illustrate: It was the general belief—and I don't know whether the theory has dropped out of existence yet or not —that a boy might go through the ordinary school-process of book-keeping and be pronounced by his teacher as a very fair book-keeper, and yet when he came into the actual business of life he had to begin at the A B C's and learn anew again before he was competent for the practical work. And this kind of education, this superficial knowledge, which is of no use beyond the school-room, I think obtains almost everywhere.

Still further. The complaint runs, whether justly or not I will not say—and let it be remembered that I am not speaking dogmatically, but merely throwing out these suggestions as they occur to my mind— that the work of the school-room exclusively pursued for eight or ten, and, in some cases, twelve, years, terminates in making the boy or girl an enemy to hard work. Now, I put the case very broadly. Let the boy come out of the school with the idea that what he has learned in school can be transmuted into a force which will stand in the place of hard work. I remember several lines in the spelling-book which illustrate this absurdity:

> For learning was the only thing
> That made poor Pepin's son a king.

And this false idea as to the value of knowledge has taken a strong hold on the minds of the uneducated. They think it is something which will enable the boy to do without work. I have heard over and over again, in my own experience, the admonition, "If you don't go to school and learn, you will have to go to the fields and work."

Now, Mr. President, I hold that this is a false view; that the proper view to be taken is just the opposite: that if you have this education, and will then work, you will be the better workman. But under no circumstances can intellectual cultivation take the place of honest, hard labor.

Just a little further: Is it fair that the cultivation of the head should be to the exclusion of the hands? In other words, that intellectual labor, pursued for eight or ten or twelve years, to the utter exclusion of bodily labor, tends to unfit a man for bodily labor? Should there not be within the proper limits of our common-school-curriculum such a course of training as will teach the boys and girls that, while intellectual labor is great and is good, manual labor must be performed by somebody or other; that there is no disgrace to the girl in sweeping the floor; that it is just as useful for a graduate of the high school to know how to cook a beefsteak as to know how to read and analyze; that, while they may properly learn to trace the earth along the chart from one end to the other and give glowing descriptions of everything they see on the way, it is of more importance to know those little minutiæ of housekeeping upon which the comfort and happiness of human beings depend? And the poor boy, while he plods and toils in absurd problems, should not forget that the knowledge thus acquired is not of so much importance as the cultivation of the hands.

Mr. Z. RICHARDS. Mr. President, I want here to express the gratification I have experienced in listening to the very clear and able paper that has been read by Mr. Philbrick. It seems to me that he has struck at the very root of the matter. I am pleased also with the remarks made by Mr. Newell. I think the suggestions thrown out by Mr. Philbrick with reference to the changes needed in elementary education are such as should impress the mind of every gentleman here to-day. I know that to carry out the views advanced would work a revolution. We all know that it would revolutionize our whole system of elementary education in almost all parts of our country. I ask, ought not the system to be revolutionized? I verily believe so.

I want to allude to one point in the paper just read in reference to what has heretofore been considered as almost all that was necessary in the primary schools, to wit, reading and writing and arithmetic and geography. Now, I think we have placed too high an estimate upon the importance of these branches. The great difficulty, Mr. Chairman, is that nine-tenths of our children go forth from our common schools not able to read. They can call the words; they can repeat them; but they are not able to read in the true sense of the term. I can take a so-called good English scholar, a graduate from one of our grammar-schools, if you please, and put a Latin reader, or Cicero, or Sallust into his hands, and while he can call the words, while he can give them a sort of pronunciation—of course he can give the English pronunciation—yet he cannot read in the true sense of the term. And why? Because he does not know what the language means. And that is the difficulty, Mr. President, with nine-tenths of the scholars that go forth from our public schools. Terms are introduced, expressions are used, forms of description and styles of language with which he is almost as unfamiliar when he leaves the school-room as when he first commenced. We want that he should have the ability to read understandingly. And the first book put into the hands of the child should be that which teaches those elements, those terms of language, if you please, which he will have to become familiar with when he enters upon the active affairs and business of life. Take any of the boys of our schools, if you please who have graduated, many of them from our high schools, our grammar-schools, and how many are there of them that can tell every particular part of that chair, and give me the terms correctly as the mechanic who made it himself would use them ? Take this as in application to every one of the arts and in almost every variety of business that we have in this country. Ask any one of these graduated pupils to describe the difference between two chairs or between any two objects that have similar names, and you will find that nine-tenths of them are barren in the knowledge of terms necessary to give a satisfactory explanation. The difficulty is that our first lessons in reading are defective in this respect. What are we to do ? I would have our books made up of something besides nonsense, as they are almost universally now in our elementary schools. The reading-books should be such as to bring in use those terms which the child shall use in after-life. It is in language that the child needs to be qualified as well as in things. If he understands the meaning of the terms which he sees in his books, he is becoming qualified, not only in the meaning of words, but in things.

This is the true way, it seems to me, for this system which you call practical education to be introduced into our primary schools. It should begin in our primary schools—the first elements, of course.

Now, I am deeply interested in this subject, and I hope gentlemen here will feel the importance of the principles laid down in that paper sufficiently well to use their efforts in carrying them out and in seeing that they are more generally understood and felt in all parts of our country.

General EATON. If there is no special business now before the department, I move an adjournment until 7 o'clock this evening.

The motion was agreed to.

EVENING-SESSION.

The department came to order at 7 o'clock, and President Wilson introduced Professor H. C· Spencer, who said:

Mr. PRESIDENT: It gives me great pleasure at this time to be able to present to each of the individual members of this department a copy of the Theory of Spencerian Penmanship.

Professor Spencer then distributed the work referred to.

ADDRESS OF PROFESSOR WALTER SMITH.

At the close of the distribution the president introduced Prof. Walter Smith, art-director of the State of Massachusetts, who read a paper upon

INDUSTRIAL DRAWING IN PUBLIC SCHOOLS.

This subject, upon which I am to address you, appears to be one that has a daily-increasing interest for educators. It comes under discussion at the meetings of teachers: is the subject of letters and leading articles in educational and other newspapers and of reviews in magazines and periodicals.

Having studied this matter for the last twenty-five years with the incentive of love and the opportunity given by having nothing else to do, it may be supposed that the subject, in most of its phases, is somewhat familiar to me. I have watched the development *ab ovo* of this branch of education in some countries of the Old World, and it becomes an all-absorbing subject to me to observe its development in the New.

It is with much satisfaction that I see the general interest now felt in industrial drawing and its consideration with an earnestness by educators that shows the importance attached to it. And it is fortunate for this country that the attention of leading educators is being given to the matter after its possibility has been demonstrated, so that the subject for consideration is relieved from the theoretical question of whether it is *possible* to teach industrial drawing, and is confined to the practical question of whether it is desirable, and, if desirable, what is the best way of teaching it.

There can be no doubt that in the field of education a great transformation is occurring, so important that the days we live in will probably be regarded in future centuries as a historical epoch of the first order. It has been brought about by the social revolution in the condition and circumstances of the masses of the people which the last hundred years have been gradually developing; and this change has established as an ideal educational standard the thorough and equal education of *all*.

Compared with such a result the education of the past, previous to the last hundred years, had as an ideal the higher education of a few, the few being the governing and professional classes, and a condition in which ignorance was undisturbed bliss for the rest of mankind.

Called upon to express these two ideals of education by two words, I would say, that of the past was classic, that of the future will be industrial, the first being represented by endowed universities, the second by free public schools.

Before the work of the endowed-schools commission began in old England, the subjects prescribed to be taught in the endowed grammar-schools were Latin and Greek, with religious instruction from the Holy Scriptures, and all other subjects were regarded as modern frivolities, to be paid for as extras, so much a year for arithmetic, so much for writing, and so much for every other or groups of other subjects. And before the beginning of the nineteenth century, broadly speaking, the endowed grammar-schools, one in each large town, were the only public free schools in England, so that the people who were not content with a classical and biblical fare, and could not pay for extras, had to go away starving from this educational Barmacide feast.

What was true in the education of children was equally true in that of men. The universities were a reflex of the grammar-schools; both were apparatus for creating rulers in church and state, and the rest of the people were found to be more easily governed in proportion as they were left out in the cold, educationally.

The engineer, architect, artist, scientist, was produced by no university; he came in spite of universities, who, if they noticed him at all, it was to treat him with passive contempt or active persecution.

Though this may have never been the case to so great an extent in this new country as it was in the old, yet it was to a definite degree true everywhere before the latter half of the last century, and now is true no longer in the sense in which it was true then.

The more modern institutions for education have not been molded on the patterns of the old, any more than the New England grammar-school is like that established by Queen Elizabeth. Next to Harvard College the most important agency for the education of adults now existing in Boston is the Institute of Technology, and here, if the truth must be told, the living sciences and arts have usurped the place of the dead languages and Bible-history.

Recently the study of drawing has been added to the elective studies pursued by the students of Harvard, and those who are curious in such matters have only to consult Circular No. 2, 1874, issued by the Bureau of Education, to see that Yale, and Syracuse, and Cincinnati, and New York, and Philadelphia are up and doing in the specialty of art-education, either adding faculties of fine arts to existing institutions or establishing independent schools of art.

The most costly building for education now being erected in England is a technical school near Birmingham, for the study of every branch of industrial art, and which, when completed and endowed, will have cost the donor, who is a princely manufacturer, about a million of money, sterling.

Owens College, at Manchester, a modern industrial university, is a similar institution, devoted more especially to science, and but recently professorships of fine art have been established in the universities of Oxford, Cambridge, and London, while the complete plan of the government-establishment at South Kensington includes schools of architecture, sculpture and painting, navigation, music, mining and engineering, natural history, the science of food, and other educational agencies which may be described as technical; comprising together a National Industrial University, which may be called both an expression and satisfaction of the wants of modern society, as Oxford and Cambridge were of mediæval society.

This change, which is so plainly developing in the education of adults, cannot exist here or elsewhere without having its reflex in the public schools in the elementary education of children.

People have to be prepared for industrial rather than contemplative lives; and the great division of labor which is now the rule in almost every occupation, makes it necessary for each of us to know some one thing very well indeed.

If we consider how large a proportion of occupations depend upon habits of accuracy and powers of observation, we shall see from this stand-point that all education tending to develop these characteristics will be most valuable in practical life, whether the individual be directly employed in constructive industry or not. In the formation of these habits no other agencies are more influential than the seeing eye and the cunning hand used in concert, the one in perception, the other in expression, both being indicative of the mental ability to perceive the truth. At the same time that the exercise of the senses of sight and touch reflects mental perception, it not unfrequently creates the power to perceive.

Over the door of every school of art or drawing-class-room I would have inscribed, in the words of the psalmist, "Thy right hand shall teach thee terrible things;" for the criticism which our right hand makes upon our knowledge, when attempting to draw for the first time something we thought we knew quite well, is apt to be a very terrible thing indeed.

And to any one who doubts this statement, and is a novice at drawing, let me suggest that he take a pencil and paper and sit down and draw a portrait from nature of the loveliest person he knows and admires. When done, submit it to the examination of his subject, and I prophesy that not only his hand but his eyes and his ears will teach him some very terrible things, generally relating to his own utter want of perception of the first notion of the beautiful—a lamentable condition, of which he had perhaps been unconscious until his right hand had made it known to him.

If drawing were of no use when acquired, it would still be worth all the time spent in acquiring it, because of its influence on the faculty of observation and its cultivation of the habit of accuracy. Allowing that drawing may be as remotely connected with a man's daily occupation as half the subjects he studied at school, that it is only a species of mental or manual gymnastics, yet the training he gets while learning to draw would make him a more reliable witness in the witness-box, more faithful in testimony and clearer in his evidence than if he knew nothing of form or had learned but superficially through his eyes, without his right hand having taught him the terrible things we all ought to know. There is, therefore, an educational as well as a commercial aspect of this question of industrial drawing, and it is difficult to realize which is the more important.

It has been the custom in Europe to speak of scientific and artistic education as secondary education; something to be undertaken when general or primary education ·

is either very far advanced or completed; as though a human being could be broken in by a certain set of exercises, and then hitched like a horse to a wagon, able to pull any load behind it.

I doubt whether this is as wise a method of procedure as mixing a little secondary instruction with primary from the first stages. Object-lessons, which are of so universal interest to children, are really elementary-art and science-instruction, and the best preparation for that advanced work in either which would come under the description of secondary education.

It must be taken for granted, then, that the arrangement of elementary education is undergoing a change, partly arising from the changes already made in the education of adults and partly from the increased value of skilled labor.

The change may be of two kinds: First, new ways of teaching old subjects; secondly, new subjects to be taught. My subject comes under the second heading.

Concerning this it may be said that perhaps no other subject has been so generally adopted in so short a time, by all nations of civilized men, as this subject of industrial drawing.

WHAT INDUSTRIAL DRAWING IS.

A painting has been defined as "something between a thought and a thing," the material expression of a thought.

A working or industrial drawing is something necessarily existing between a thought and a thing, between the idea and the fact, between conception and execution.

Only the rudest objects created by savages have been made without this medium of the drawing; and what the object shall be when completed must be a matter of accident, unless the idea be first permanently expressed by a design or drawing, and the same be regarded as a standard by which the work is to be judged.

The quality of this design or drawing governs the quality of the work, for the manufactured article is but an echo of the original design. And the value of the manufactured article in the market depends very largely on the skill displayed in the design; so that we have, by direct relationship, the value of many manufactures depending in a straight line on industrial drawing.

The two great arguments for studying the subject, therefore, are its necessity and its value, commercially and educationally.

Practical industrial drawing may be said to have two departments: First, mechanical or instrumental drawing; secondly, free-hand drawing and design; and by means of these two the constructive industry of the world is carried on.

By mechanical drawing accuracy of work is secured; by free-hand drawing and design, originality and beauty of workmanship are attained. Each is of more importance than the other in some departments of industry. Thus, in designing houses, buildings, bridges, machinery, mechanism, making surveys, &c., mechanical or instrumental drawing is of more importance than free-hand work; while in drawing designs for fabrics, such as carpets, calicoes, laces, stuffs, or for the ornamentation of paper-hangings, oil-cloths, or designing for pottery, glass, metal-work, and furniture, generally, free-hand design is of more importance than mechanical drawing.

Yet each of these departments necessitates a certain amount of knowledge of the other, if great success is to be achieved, for the mechanical draughtsman and designer will sometimes find himself compelled to rely on his hand and eye when instruments fail, because they cannot think; and the ornamentist without a considerable knowledge of mechanical drawing cannot be a practical designer.

In all industrial design, therefore, the two factors of value are, first, accuracy of workmanship and, secondly, knowledge and skill in design, in varying proportions, according to the use for which the object is designed.

To secure the first, *accuracy of workmanship*, the workman must learn the use of the implements by which alone it is attainable, and study geometrical drawing to enable him to apply his skill. In default of this, uneducated workmen have to rely on rule of thumb and on methods and specifics picked up in workshops or copied from others, the reasons for which are not understood, and which, therefore, in any emergency or new condition of the work, would be inapplicable and useless. To attain proficiency in the second, viz, *knowledge and skill in design*, is a longer process than acquiring mechanical skill. Here the eye must be trained to see the beautiful, the mind instructed by the study of good historic examples of pure ornament, the creative powers developed and those of observation strengthened by constant exercise. A long course of practical drawing, from examples, from objects, and from natural forms, in which the pupil learns, first, to see, and, secondly, to express, and, during which intelligent instruction is given to him, and the exercises are made to illustrate the principles and characteristics of good design; this alone can produce in the pupil both knowledge of drawing and skill in design.

The precise value resulting from skill in drawing is not difficult to define, for it is reflected on all sides, the workman, his employer, and the customer who purchases the work sharing in the possession of an increase of value in the object when completed. This leads to industrial wealth, in which all are benefited—the producer, the merchant, and the consumer.

CAN DRAWING BE TAUGHT IN PUBLIC SCHOOLS?

The question now arises, is it practicable to give instruction in this subject, or in the elements of this subject, in the public schools?

My reply to such a query is, that not only is it possible to give such instruction in them, but if you neglect to begin it there you put it almost beyond your power to give the instruction elsewhere. In other words, the public school is the only place where it is possible to teach industrial drawing satisfactorily, and the time to begin teaching it is that when the most elementary subjects are begun, during the first week which the pupil spends in a primary school.

So much of drawing is imitative and so much a matter of memory, that it is impossible to begin teaching the subject too early, when children are in the first stages of the merely imitative period and when impressions made and repeated on the memory are likely to last.

The subject and its several elements must of course be graded to the capacities of the pupils, and I think that has been done by the very elementary exercises with which children in primary schools begin to learn.

FALSE THEORIES.

Before speaking on the subject of how drawing should be taught in the schools, I will refer to the question of what is *not* industrial drawing.

Although it may have been conceded in past times that ability to draw was of some commercial value in several occupations and apparently necessary in many branches of industry, it used to be believed that to be able to draw well was a rare endowment, something for which its possessor had not worked—a gift, it was usually called—and people who were unable to draw never ceased wondering how those who could had come by this mysterious gift. Artemus Ward would have treated it as a conundrum, and have " given it up."

When people failed to find an explanation why some persons had this gift and others lacked it, they sometimes came to the conclusion that art-power ran in families, as some one else remarked that wooden legs ran in some families. Both observations were equally profound.

This false theory was at the root of all the wrong deductions and all the mystery. The gift being assumed, people were put to begin in the middle or at the end of the subject, and, when failure was the result, then the inference drawn (for people who could draw nothing else could draw inferences) was that the gift was not possessed.

Apply this reasoning to any other subject, say reading and composition. Assume reading to be a gift, not acquired by patient toiling through the alphabet and words of one and two syllables. Let the child arrive at 10, 15, or 20 years of age without instruction, and then give him a play of Shakespeare to read or a leading article for a newspaper to compose. When he is found unequal to such preliminary exercises, conclude that reading and composition are divine gifts, which have been withheld from that pupil.

We should hardly have patience to listen to such unreasonable conclusions, and yet, be it said with all respect to inexperience, this is precisely what has been done and said and thought about the subject of drawing and design, and the confused reasoning of many about the subject even to this day and this hour.

The explanation why this has been and is so is that few teachers of the first order have been able to draw or brought into contact with drawing, so as to analyze it and grade it as other subjects have been studied and arranged for educational purposes. On the other hand, artists and draughtsmen have not been teachers, and they have, therefore, made no contribution to the elucidation of the matter.

So we have had the power to teach without the power to draw possessed by teachers and the power to draw without the power to teach in possession of the artists; that is, the teaching power and drawing power held by two different individuals, like the two detached halves of one bank-note, which it was impossible to unite, and which, therefore, remained waste paper to the end of the chapter. The drawing which used to be taught assumed this gift, and pupils were put to make drawings of subjects they could not understand, and, as a rule, generally failed. The subjects were usually pictures of some sort. It was supposed that when people had imitated the pictures made by others long enough and closely enough then they would be able to make some for themselves, original and satisfactory.

The precise relationship of these pictures to either industrial art or fine art was never exactly understood, but it was thought that in the artistic fabric they occupied a place somewhere in the foundation, and so they were thrown into the educational trenches and piled up as chance decided.

DRAWING WORTHLESS AS AN ACCOMPLISHMENT.

The young lady who took drawing as one of the accomplishments was visited by the special teacher, and, having chosen her subject, was put through it somehow. If her gift was for faces, she might choose a lithograph-copy of one of Raffaelle's Madonnas; if for landscapes, one of Turner's pictures, such as the Dream of Carthage; if Providence had bestowed the love of animals upon her, one of Landseer's monarchs of the glen might be her choice to draw.

The only way of describing the accomplishment of that drawing is that she was put through it. Completed, it would be carried home in triumph when the holidays came, to startle her parents and astonish her friends, and the work would be equal to the task, for, like its reputed author, that drawing had been fearfully and wonderfully made.

That sort of drawing treated as an accomplishment or pursued as an amusement was absolutely worthless. It never taught anybody anything. Ask a young lady, whose choice pictures adorned the ancestral walls, to draw you anything you wanted, and you might be sure she would reply that that was not her style. She had been taught to draw some one thing, as a parrot is taught to say one thing, and her skill had the same relationship to drawing as the parrot's would have to language.

This was not industrial drawing. It was trickery, not education; and in considering this subject we may be sure that such quackery and specifics as that must be discarded, root and branch, before we begin to understand it at all.

We must clear the decks of all the "gift" and "genius" cargo, and throw overboard all beliefs in specifics and all disbelief in the equal ability of all to do the work required from each, and then lay over on a new tack altogether, which is to be a rational course leading us somewhere worth going.

HOW IS INDUSTRIAL DRAWING TO BE TAUGHT IN THE SCHOOLS?

The question of how industrial drawing is to be taught in the schools may be divided into two phases: (1) By whom is it to be taught? (2) What are the subjects to be taught?

From experience here and elsewhere it would appear that the only way in which the whole of the school and classes can be reached is by the regular school-teachers undertaking the work of teaching drawing. The employment of special teachers to give instruction in elementary drawing to the pupils of public schools, because the teacher is incompetent to do it, is both a reflection on the ability of the teacher and a magnifying of the difficulty of learning to draw in the eyes of the pupil.

The most satisfactory method of introducing drawing into the schools is for the school-committee to employ a good teacher of drawing to give normal lessons to the teachers of the public schools, taking them over the course of work adopted for the schools and which they will have to teach. Then the special teacher may act as supervisor of the work carried on by the regular teachers in the schools, and also give instruction in more advanced subjects to pupils in the high schools. By such an arrangement the responsibility of the regular school-teacher is not decreased, nor her influence over her pupils weakened, as would inevitably be so if a special teacher took her class out of her hands because she was unable to teach it.

Suppose that the teachers have had no instruction, then they should be taught a few lessons before beginning to teach the subject, and this will enable them to keep well ahead of their pupils. It is always to be remembered that drawing is so much a matter of the understanding, so much a question of arithmetic and geometry, that teachers are more than half educated to draw before they draw a line; and, therefore, it is not unreasonable to say they are competent to teach it before they have had much personal instruction.

I have observed a general agreement among experienced educators that the only practical means by which this subject can be generally introduced is by the employment of the regular teachers to teach it. I may add, also, from a careful scrutiny of the results following both experiments—first, the teaching by special teachers, and, secondly, the teaching by the regular teachers—that the best results follow the teaching by the regular teachers, and, therefore, on all accounts, it is the best arrangement to make.

THE SUBJECTS TO BE TAUGHT

It will be seen, from the description already given of what industrial drawing is, that the two broad divisions of the subject are (1) mechanical, geometrical, or instrumental, and (2) free-hand drawing and design, &c.

What is required in the workshop we must teach in the schools, or, rather, we must make the foundation for workshop-skill and practice by the education given in the school-room. That is really the great revolution in teaching the subject which is now going on. Instead of teaching the child to produce pretty sketches, of no use or value to anyone, we have to teach him accuracy of work and originality.

The basis of all industrial art is geometrical drawing, and, therefore, it forms the most important element in industrial drawing.

Every child should be taught the use of the ruler, square, and compass, as soon as he begins to draw, to a degree suitable to his comprehension. The use of these implements, by which a high standard of accuracy can be attained even by a child, will fix a standard of accuracy in the child's mind that will influence all his work, whether done by the free hand or mechanically. This mental standard of accuracy constitutes one-half, at least, of the power to draw, for it creates the knowledge of good and evil. Hand-skill comes as a necessity of this knowledge of right and wrong; comes by practice, as inevitably as that a hungry child finds the way to its mouth.

Visible expression is a reflex of the mental image. The first thing for us to do, then, is to insure a correct image or idea in the brain. If you want a child to have a correct idea of the difference between a square and an oblong, let him construct both figures with the ruler and compass, mechanically accurate, the work of his own hand, and forever afterward, when he has to draw these forms by the free hand, he will have the true form in his mind and eye, haunting him like his conscience, and a critical power behind his hand which will be content with nothing less than truth.

Forms are either regular or irregular, the first being comparatively simple of comprehension, the second more difficult to understand and interpret. It is by a knowledge of the regular we can estimate the character of the irregular, its irregularity. The obvious progress, therefore, is to become acquainted, first, with the simpler geometrical forms, and then to go on to the more complex shapes, either of curvature or of perspective effects.

How the subjects should be arranged in the natural order of progression, I will now endeavor to describe, taking the schools in the order of—

(1) **Primary**;
(2) **Grammar**; and
(3) **High schools**.

PRIMARY SCHOOLS.

In primary schools, for scholars between the ages of 5 and 8 or 5 and 9, the following subjects of elementary drawing may be taught: (1) Geometrical definitions, forms, ruled or struck; (2) free-hand outline-drawing, from copies on blackboard or from cards on slates; (3) original design, elementary; (4) drawing from dictation; and (5) drawing from memory.

This may seem a formidable list of studies for babies between the ages of 5 and 9 years. It is, however, formidable only at first sight. For, if we look closely into it no one of the subjects alone is difficult if the exercises are kept simple, as they should be. And, if no one is difficult, it becomes the question whether any one should be alone taught, or all five.

You will observe that they are all only variations of the same exercise, and not altogether different subjects. Thus, if under the head of No. 1, geometrical definitions, a square of two inches side be drawn, and under the head of No. 2, drawing from the blackboard, the same square be drawn free-hand, and under No. 3, original design, the square be filled with lines or little circles or crosses, and under No. 4, drawing from dictation, the square be drawn, step by step, from the teacher's description, without a copy, and under No. 5, drawing from memory, the square and the design already made be drawn from memory, without either description or copy, then, you would have five different modes of teaching the same subject, which, by their variety, I claim, will teach it to the child more interestingly and more efficiently than if only one were adopted. In the regularly alternated lessons, more variety of subjects should be actually resorted to by the teacher, for, the less monotonous the lessons, the better the children will draw.

It has been questioned whether children so young as those between 6 and 12 years of age should be allowed to handle ruler and compasses; whether it is possible for them to learn the use of these implements so young.

As to the possibility, I may say that in the English national schools the children are annually examined by the government-inspectors in three subjects of drawing, viz, geometrical drawing, object-drawing, and free-hand outline-drawing. The limit of age of the pupils in this grade of examinations is from 6 to 12 years. Having prepared many thousands of such children for these examinations and seen many thousands pass them, for a period of nearly twenty years, I, for one, am prepared to believe in its possibility.

And if any objector raises the argument that American children are less intelligent than Europeans, I am prepared, from my own observation, to deny so ridiculous a statement.

PERSONAL EXPERIENCE.

It is of some advantage to a teacher to be the parent of a crowd of small children upon whom he has the right to experiment. That is how I am situated, and their occasional presence in my studio, as subjects of experiment, is some compensation for other trials which cannot be imagined by the childless and need not be described by parents. Between the ages of 3 months and 12 years I have had nine children to experiment on, and so I can catch one at almost any age, limited to 12, and test any theory upon him without undue cruelty to the offspring of my neighbors or employers. Of the age of 4 I have a little girl who enjoys the rudest health and a power of destructibility which in itself is a sufficient evidence of original sin. She has been recently introduced by me to two sets of instruments: the first, a knife and fork; the second, a pair of compasses. The use of the compasses she acquired in about five minutes, and her circles have the merit of being round. She soon discovered which point of the compasses would stick into anything and which point made a black mark, and can be trusted to amuse herself with the instrument without imminent danger to anything in particular. But about the use of the knife and fork, the tale is not so satisfactory. Suicide was imminent when she brandished her new weapons and bodily danger to all within a certain radius of her experiments. She eats now with a spoon.

You know the story of the three men who went to sea in a bowl. It concludes:

> Had the bowl been stronger
> My song had been longer.

Had little Winifred's life been less precious she might yet be struggling with a knife and fork.

With this experience I am prepared to maintain that a child can be taught the use of a pair of compasses before it can handle a knife and fork, though from my observation I believe the time will come when she will be able to handle a knife and fork also. Concerning drawing from the blackboard perhaps I need say nothing, because it is generally conceded that children may be taught to draw by use of blackboard-illustration better than by other methods alone. Drawing from dictation, in which the teacher describes the size, position, and shape of simple forms, without illustrating on the board or allowing the children to have any copy before them, and the children have to draw from the mental image created by the teacher's verbal description, is a most invaluable exercise, both in drawing and in its influence on other studies. It creates close attention on the pupil's part and enables the teacher to find out whether the terms used in teaching are understood by the pupil; if not, the drawing clearly shows the extent and nature of the misunderstanding. The exercise keeps the teacher alive to the value of clearly-given instruction, concisely expressed, and the practice of lessons so given is as interesting to the children as solving a puzzle, for they are unconscious of how the drawing will turn out, and their curiosity is aroused as each line is added and the form of the pattern or object begins to develop.

Drawing from memory is as important and as necessary as drawing itself. We draw that we may learn, not learn to draw for the sake of drawing. It is as easy to remember anything we have drawn as to remember how to spell the common words, and will eventually be as easy to reproduce any design we have ever made as an act of the memory, as it is to remember the names of the States or of foreign countries. That is a valuable power, to be as certainly obtained as the ability to draw in the first place.

Perhaps the one subject in the list of studies for primary schools about which people express the most surprise is that of

ORIGINAL DESIGN.

To understand it we must remember that design consists in re-arranging old materials, as well as in inventing new forms. A cipher or unit of design, which may have been in use for ages and in all countries, may be so disposed as to its arrangement as to make an invention or design, and in teaching the subject this is the form which the exercise takes. A leaf drawn from the blackboard, taken as the subject, and some condition as to its use being given, such as that it shall be repeated round a center, to to fill a square or circle, or repeated in a horizontal direction, to make a border, any child who can draw at all will be able to exercise his ingenuity and skill in arranging such material. Or, even if a natural form be considered too difficult, a series of arbitrary signs or forms may be used, such as three sizes of circles, or thick and thin lines, or curved lines only, or a contrast of curved and straight lines, to be so used by the child as to produce a pleasing arrangement.

This is not done so much for the achievement which comes of it as that the child shall feel the necessity of arranging something, feel master of his lesson, and do it well or badly as he can, but do it somehow.

I have seen a room full of children in a primary school absorbed in designing, so completely absorbed as hardly to notice the presence of visitors, and out of a class of forty children I have picked the designs of nearly twenty as being not only original but tasteful.

If I am asked whether it is well to thus tax little children, I should say that drawing is much less of a tax than even the elements of arithmetic, for in the one there is present enjoyment and in the other the labor of remembering tables. Moreover, it has been wisely said by a lady who made mankind her study, " Man is a designing animal;" and, if so, the faculty of design may as well be gently exercised from the first, and in a useful direction, as to let it run to seed or impel its owner into mischief and trouble as a vent for this creative faculty.

But the work of children in primary schools must necessarily be very imperfect. It would be a dreadful catastrophe to find a child in a primary school who could either draw well or do anything else well, except look happy and have a good time. The reeds, however, should be planted early, if they are to grow strong, and every idea which a child fairly lays hold of before the age of 10 is going to influence all the after-life.

GRAMMAR-SCHOOLS.

In the grammar-school-period, extending from 8 or 9 to 15, we have an average of six years, the time when the great mass of the people receive their education.

From the grammar-school the boy goes into the workshop, or office, or store, and his opportunities of improvement afterward are only such as he can find in his leisure time, if he has any. It is here, therefore, where the actual education of the mechanic is given, for, though the professional man passes through the high school, and university, and the technical school before he is supposed to be fit for professional work, the mechanic leaves the grammar-school for the practical duties of life. With the experience already gained in the primary school, the drawing in the grammar-schools may be made thoroughly serviceable to the future mechanic; and before he leaves school, at 15 years of age, he may become a practical draughtsman, wanting only the knowledge of specialties to be able to apply his skill to any industrial process requiring delicacy of hand and nicety of workmanship.

In the grammar-school the pupil should be taught the three subjects of (1) plane geometrical drawing, (2) model- and object-drawing, and (3) original design, occasional lessons only being given in dictation- and memory-drawing.

Concerning the time which should be given to drawing, remembering its importance as a subject of practical education, two hours per week could profitably be devoted to the subject; that is, if strong results are to be expected; and if this be distributed over three subjects, giving 40 minutes to a lesson, a material progress may be made each year.

We have been at work for too short a time on this methodical instruction in drawing to see the results which other countries have already secured. But we have seen enough to prove that it depends on whether we teach drawing sensibly or not at all, which will settle the question as to whether America shall become an artistic country, with her art-wealth created by her own citizens, and not imported in foreign ships. The question of whether drawing can be well taught by the regular teachers and whether designing can be taught in the grammar-schools has been fairly tried and finally settled by our experience in Boston, and settled triumphantly in the affirmative.

Many years ago that most sagacious of educators, the superintendent, Mr. Philbrick, not only decided the matter in the affirmative, but created the examples by which it could be commenced. Our more recent experience has only carried his plans a step further, not altered or changed them; but a more generous confidence in the value of this branch of education has enabled us to develop his ideas into practical, educational results.

The annual exhibitions of the public schools of Boston, when every class displays exercises in every subject taught in it, so far as drawing is concerned, have placed beyond all question or cavil the fact that children can be taught to draw and taught to design. And in the city of Brooklyn, N. Y., where the subject has been introduced into the schools less than two years, I have seen designs for cotton-prints, for wall-papers, for encaustic tiles, and also elementary exercises from each class of the grammar-schools, which were quite remarkable for originality and purity of taste.

All that remains for us to consider is whether the results attained have that practical value in education which has been claimed; the possibility of attaining them is placed beyond discussion.

In the grammar-schools, the elements of building, construction, and planning have been sometimes taught, with much interest to the pupils, and a boy who is set the task of planning a house will soon learn more about houses than he ever cared to know before.

HIGH SCHOOLS.

I look forward to the time when our high schools shall not only educate refined men and women, as they do now, but by the thoroughness of their education in art produce men and women as well fitted to become artists and designers as school-teachers.

There is a place in high-school-education for the study of art.

Some time should be allowed for studying the beauties of nature and art. The Greek poets produced no better work than Greek sculptors, and the study of form, color, and industrial design is at least as important to the human being living in the nineteenth century as ancient history or the geography of Japan.

In our Boston high schools, applied design takes the place of elementary design as practiced in the grammar-schools and I have during the past month examined (1) designs for lace-collars and lace-curtains, (2) designs for porcelain tea-cups and saucers, (3) designs for oil-cloths, (4) designs for cotton-prints for dresses, (5) designs for encaustic tiles, and (6) designs for paper-hangings, carpets, hearth-rugs. Moreover, if these designs do not show the skill of the greatest masters, I am prepared to say that they do show an absence of wrong principles and bad design. The pupils have been taught enough to know what is suitable to the fabrics or objects they are designing; and, though their work is not so refined, chaste, and beautiful as we could wish, it is infinitely better than the noisy vulgarity in design made by people whose sole object is to create a sensation, and to be purchased by those who must be loud, if alive.

We are prospecting, seeing the lay of the land, and can only at present make a provisional report; but, so far as we have seen the promised land of the future, there will come a time when industrial education must, from its very interest and its adaptability to the wants of the young, form a very important part in the education given in the public schools.

The average amount of time spent in schools by children is nearly 10 years. Those years are responsible for something. Life and its duties are serious matters, and school prepares us for all, either well or ill.

There is much talk and discussion in these latter days about the high pressure we are putting on children. Sage committeemen examine the handwriting of a class, and, finding only one flourish in the tail of a g or h, come to the conclusion that we are piling up the educational agony, and must drop all the fancy subjects and stick to reading, writing, and arithmetic.

"We must give up singing and drawing," said a school-committeeman to me a short time ago, "and give more time to geography and spelling; it's not done as well now as when I was at school, when we had none of these new-fangled notions to bother us. The children are crowded up. Why, only a few days ago my neighbor's daughter came into my parlor to examine the design for our new carpet, and spent her evening in sketching it, and instead of that she ought to have been having a good time or been at a lecture. What's the good of singing? What's the good of drawing patterns for carpets? And then it makes the rising generation upstarts. Only last Sunday I overheard a boy at the Sunday-school say my flowered satin waistcoat was an instance of bad design, for it would take three Mr. Browns to show the whole pattern, and happily there was only one. We must stop this high pressure; it's agoing to kill off our boys and girls."

I confess that I sympathized with this gentleman, and asked him how many of his children it had killed off on an average. He replied it didn't matter to him so much, because he hadn't any children of his own, but his neighbor Dobbs had, and it was very hard upon Dobbs. To him I observed that I had the advantage or disadvantage, as it might be variously considered, over him, for I had a whole lot of children of my own, and could study from nature the effect of the high pressure of singing and drawing on average children, and I observed that, when my children were particularly happy, they sang the pretty songs they were taught in school, of their own free will and because they loved to sing; and when they were confined at home by a wet or frosty day they came crowding me out of my study to show them how to make their design for next day or the day after, and took as much comfort out of it as they would in emptying the sawdust out of a doll which had been in a railway-accident.

I said, addressing this same committeeman, " and, therefore, allow me to say to you, whose children are those of the spirit, that when you undertake in your wisdom to legislate for my children of the flesh and indulge in your fantastical and ridiculous ignorance of childhood-nature, and suppose spelling and geography are better for them than singing and drawing, I am going, as a father and a teacher, to stand right in front of your theories and impeach you as being guilty of cruelty to animals, and as one who, knowing nothing of children, are experimenting on an offspring of the brain, a bodiless child, a myth of your sterile conception, and we, who have to wrestle with childhood's sorrows, difficulties, and troubles, have to pay the penalties of your crotchets, mistakes, and unwisdom. Get out."

And so we agreed to disagree. And I claim that, if music lightens the load which human beings have to carry and if drawing helps them to an occupation in the industrial epoch we are now entering, we ought to give the one and teach the other, as valuable helps in different ways to the average child.

There is another phase of the question, not altogether unimportant. It is, that, of all the subjects of education taught in the public schools, the power to draw well by an ordinary child is worth more in the open labor-market of to-day than any other subject taught in the public schools.

Good writing, good arithmetic, good general knowledge, are all worth something. Let the boys or girls who stand at the head of their classes in these subjects apply for employment where their attainments can be utilized, and let a boy or girl standing equally high in the subject of drawing apply for employment in a lithographer's shop or draughtsman's office, and I say, with some knowledge of the subject, that the boy who can draw is worth twice as much as the boy who can write, and can earn twice the wages for his skill. In conclusion, the results arrived at by our experience up to the present time may be thus stated:

(1) This country in its educational provisions has not comprehended the subject of industrial drawing. As a consequence, the skilled labor which results from its study is not generally obtainable from native mechanics. The industrial products of a people lacking taste are less valuable than those in which taste is displayed.

(2) Industrial drawing can only be efficiently taught in the public schools by the regular teachers, and therefore its introduction into any system of education need not be costly, and the extra expense at first incurred is limited to the temporary employment of a special teacher.

(3) It has been demonstrated by actual experience that every sane and physically sound child can be taught to draw well; that, in the large majority of the occupations which children of the public schools will eventually be called to fill, skill in drawing

would increase the value of their labor and endow them with one additional qualification for obtaining employment; that, without this skill of hand and education of the eye, the American mechanic cannot compete with foreign workmen successfully and without it the American citizen is deficient in an important factor in education which is a source to others of both profit and enjoyment.

(4) In a progressive age no civilized nation can afford to stand still without risking what it has and losing prospective developments.

It is time, therefore, that America should consider this subject in earnest, being the only civilized country existing to-day whose educational legislation ignores industrial drawing.

I am often asked for an opinion as to the prospects of success in art-education in this country, when it is fairly introduced and adopted in the schools. Perhaps the best answer to this would be the following statement:

I left my country, in which this subject had already passed the stage of experiment, where, from my apprenticeship and professional practice, I was familiar with all the phases of this branch of education; resigned a more lucrative appointment than I now hold, home, friends, and relatives, to come here and throw in my lot with American schools. I did so because I saw, from the love for education so generally felt by the people, from the liberal views in regard to the whole subject of education so generally prevailing, that, when this matter of industrial drawing was seriously taken up, there would be greater facilities and better organization for a triumphant success than I knew to exist in any other country. From indications, which I see and know the meaning of, the time for this success is not far distant.

And I have only to add, in the language of the old ballad, when that good time comes,

May we all be there to see

[Applause.]

REMARKS OF PROFESSOR HENRY.

The president here introduced Professor Joseph Henry, Secretary of the Smithsonian Institution, who said:

Gentlemen of the Convention: I deeply regret that I have not previously been able to attend the meetings of this association.

My time has been entirely occupied, during your session, by pressing business connected with the Smithsonian Institution and the Light-House Board.

I have come this evening entirely unprepared to make any communication; but I cannot refrain from expressing my high appreciation of the admirable address which has just been delivered by Professor Smith on " Industrial drawing in public schools." The truths which it contains I think should be widely disseminated, and were it not, as I understand, that the address has been adopted for publication in the proceedings of this department, I would certainly ask its reference to the Smithsonian for publication at the expense of the Smithsonian fund.

With Professor Smith, I fully agree as to the importance of drawing as a branch of elementary education, and I think, with him, that it can be taught without interfering with the acquisition of other primary branches of instruction.

The several faculties of the human mind are not simultaneously developed, and in a proper system of education these various faculties ought to be exercised in the order of their presentation.

Among these one of the most early exhibited is that of imitation, and its exercise is a source of great pleasure to the young mind, and it may, therefore, be taught without interfering with and almost as a relief from the drudgery of the acquisition of the other branches.

Further, as to the importance of drawing, I think that, as an aid in various pursuits in the every-day-business of life, in addition to its use in improving the powers of observation and of accurate discrimination, little need be said. I would, however, add one remark bearing on the subject, namely: that education tends to render men impatient under the infliction of brute labor. As an illustration of this, I have been told that, in New England, it is quite difficult to obtain a native of that section, who has had the advantages of a high-school-education, willing to submit to the labor of the plow or the ax. Such persons seek more intellectual employment, and, although they desert the toil of the husbandman, the loss they thus occasion is supplied more than tenfold by the invention of labor-saving machines.

Now, nothing, therefore, is of greater service in the line of invention than a knowledge of mechanical drawing, and therefore, to the persons whom I have mentioned, it becomes an invaluable aid; but, as the hour of adjournment has arrived, I must refrain from detaining the audience with further comments on the address of Professor Smith, to which I have listened with much interest and instruction. I will, however, before concluding, beg leave to assure you that this association has my warmest sympathy in the great work in which you are engaged of advancing primary education; and I would be gratified to have the association visit the Smithsonian, which, although not primarily an educational establishment, yet indirectly does service in that line.

Mr. MARBLE moved that the thanks of the department be tendered to Professor Henry for his expressions of sympathy and his invitation to visit the Smithsonian Institution.

The motion was unanimously adopted.

Mr. MARBLE. I move that Baron von Schwarz-Senborn, who has taken such an active and valuable part with us, be made an honorary member of the department of superintendence.

The motion was adopted unanimously.

Mr. JILLSON, of South Carolina, presented the following report:

The committee on resolutions respectfully beg leave to report the following resolutions:

Resolved, That in the death of Hon. Milton B. Hopkins, late State-superintendent of public instruction of the State of Indiana, this department has lost an active and efficient member and the cause of common education a zealous advocate and an earnest and faithful friend.

Resolved, That the thanks of this department are due, and are hereby tendered, to Hon. B. G. Northrop, Dr. A. N. Bell, Hon. J. P. Wickersham, and Hon. John D. Philbrick, for the able and instructive papers read at this meeting.

Resolved, That the thanks of this department are especially due to Prof. Walter Smith for his very valuable paper on industrial drawing in the public schools.

Resolved, That the thanks of the department of superintendence are due to its president, J. Ormond Wilson, and his associate officers, for the comprehensive and well-arranged programme provided for this meeting and for the other general provisions made to secure its success.

Resolved, That the thanks of this department are especially due to the board of education of the city of Washington, for the excellent and generous arrangements made by them for this meeting.

Resolved, That the hearty thanks of the department are tendered to the representatives of the Washington press, for their full and accurate reports of the proceedings of this meeting.

Resolved, That the thanks of this department are tendered to Gov. A. R. Shepherd, for his courteous invitation to meet him, socially, this evening, at his residence.

Rev. O. A. BURGESS, president of Christian University, Indianapolis, Ind., spoke at some length in support of the resolution upon the death of Hon. Milton B. Hopkins,* superintendent of public instruction for the State of Indiana. He gave a statement of his services during the two terms of his superintendency and paid a feeling tribute to the high character of the deceased. It is regretted that by accident no report was made of these remarks.

REMARKS OF GENERAL EATON ON THE DEATH OF HON. MILTON B. HOPKINS.

General EATON, in support of the same resolution, said:

The death of Mr. Hopkins is a sad reminder for us all. The resolution of respect for his memory and in sympathy with his friends has my most cordial support. Our first intercourse was through official correspondence. I never met him personally save when he was here in attendance upon the meeting of this department last winter. I shall never forget the deep and favorable impression the growth of this acquaintance made upon my mind. His manner in our intercourse was business-like, but it made one feel that he was engaged in a great business of vast consequences. Few understand what it is to take up the responsibilities devolving upon the executive officer of a State-school-system. The manner in which Mr. Hopkins took them up for Indiana, and met them as they rose, one by one, revealed to me a character that won my utmost respect. He was not hasty. He sought to repel no opportunity for good, but to receive and invite the co-operation of all means that could bring him aid. He apprehended and understood our relations as if by intuition; no explanation seemed to be necessary. Of strong purpose, full of forecast, reflective in his methods of thought, pushing steadily forward in his course, he had perhaps acquired, by some special experience, great facilities of adaptation. Deeply conscious of his responsibilities to God and man, his life was characterized by that zeal and fidelity which come only from a conscientious conviction of duty. His presence with us a year ago I think was enjoyed by all. We felt the weight of his suggestions and valued the conclusions of his judgment. Of sturdy frame, a strong mind, apparent good health, we little thought he would be the first of our number to be called away.

We do well to recall our memories of him, to emulate his virtues, to be warned by his death, and to extend our sympathies as an association to his family and others more directly and personally bereaved.

The president, Superintendent J. O. Wilson, submitted the following communication from the commissioner of Mexico:

No. 1536 I STREET, WASHINGTON, D. C.,
January 28, 1875.

SIR: It is known to you that I have been requested by the government of the re-

---

* Hon. Milton B. Hopkins, superintendent of public instruction of the State of Indiana, died suddenly at his residence in Kokomo, on the 16th of August, 1874, a few months before the expiration of his second term of office. Mr. Hopkins was born in Nicholas County, Kentucky, April 4, 1821. His father, Joseph Hopkins, a talented lawyer, practicing in Indiana and Kentucky, died when his son was 7 years of age. His mother married a farmer living in Indiana. He remained with his mother till 15 years of age. His stepfather refusing to send him to school, he left home, and after that time provided for himself. He secured a good common-school-education, and then supported himself by teaching, taking at the same time lessons in Greek and Latin from a clergyman. At 21 years of age he became a preacher, was afterward called to the bar, practicing as a lawyer for several years, but ultimately was persuaded to return to the pulpit. Although preaching acceptably for many years, he was also, during most of his life, a teacher, and taught in all grades of schools, district-school, high school, academy, and, finally, college. While president of Howard College, he was elected, in 1870, for a term of two years, State-superintendent of public instruction, and was re-elected in 1872.

public of Mexico, which I represent here in the Commission of Mexican and American Claims, to make some inquiries with regard to the school-system adopted in this country and to the progress it has attained in public instruction.

I am happy to acknowledge that, to a very great extent, it is owing to your kind assistance that I may consider myself as already somewhat advanced in my inquiries concerning this subject.

But with as favorable an opportunity as that afforded by the national convention of school-superintendents, and other persons interested in the cause of education, which is at present holding its sessions in Washington, I should not feel as having done full justice to a subject so pre-eminently important, if I should not make an effort to further extend my investigations and to direct them more particularly to certain points, concerning which they are not yet fully completed.

Will you, therefore, permit me to ask, as a particular favor, that you will make yourself the organ through whom I may take the liberty of addressing myself to the gentlemen representing the different States and Territories of this Union, begging of them that, provided it should not cause too great an inconvenience, they would be pleased to indicate to me, and thereby to enable me to procure those publications by the aid of which it will be possible for me to ascertain—

1. What is the course of studies and methods adopted in the primary schools of the various States and Territories represented in the convention ?

2. To what extent has "object-teaching" been developed in those schools ?

3. What are the normal institutions out of which they receive their teachers and professors, or by what means is this corps of public teachers recruited ?

I beg that you will, in my name, assure the gentlemen members of the convention that whatever information their kindness and their interest in favor of human progress will induce them to communicate will be received as a special favor.

With renewed expressions of my sincerest regard, I have the honor to remain, very respectfully, your obedient servant,

MANUEL DE ZAMACONA.

Hon. J. ORMOND WILSON,
President of the National Convention of School-Superintendents.

The department then adjourned to meet subject to the call of the officers, after which the members, with their ladies, proceeded to the residence of ex-Governor Shepherd, corner Connecticut avenue and K street.

On reaching the residence of Governor Shepherd they were ushered into the parlor, where the governor and his lady, Secretary Delano, Commissioners Dennison, Ketcham, and Phelps received the visitors. After this ceremony the visitors were entertained for an hour or more in social converse, after which they were invited into the dining-room, where a sumptuous banquet was spread.

Mrs. Shepherd was untiring in her efforts to make her guests enjoy themselves, as was also the governor, who made the occasion one of the most pleasant character. After an hour or more had been consumed around the board, the visitors returned to the parlor, where they bade the governor and his lady adieu and departed.

Among those present, in addition to the members of the convention, were ex-Governor H. D. Cooke, Rev. J. Vaughn Lewis, Professor Hilgard, A. R. Spofford, Dr. Gallaudet, Professor Chickering, W. W. Curtis, H. A. Willard, and Hon. C. A. Harmer.

On the morning of the 29th such of the members of the association as remained in the city met at Willard's Hotel and at the Bureau of Education, and proceeded to visit the Smithsonian Institution, where they were most cordially received by Professor Henry, who accompanied them through the museums and explained most fully the operations of the Institution in its publications and system of world-wide exchanges, the objects of the various collections, and the plans of the Institution for increased usefulness. In response to inquiries the professor gave a brief history of the Institution, which was of great interest. A couple of hours were passed most pleasantly in listening to explanations of the Institution and its collections, and then, with many thanks for his courtesy, the visitors paid their adieus to their distinguished host.

APPENDIX A.

Information of the action of the department in appointing a committee of conference was immediately forwarded to Hon. Mr. Goshorn, director-general of the International Centennial Exhibition at Philadelphia, who replied as follows:

"INTERNATIONAL EXHIBITION.

" 1876.

" UNITED STATES CENTENNIAL COMMISSION,
" OFFICE OF THE DIRECTOR-GENERAL,
" *Philadelphia, January 29, 1875.*

" MY DEAR SIR: Your note of 28th instant is received. I shall be pleased to confer with the committee of the National Educational Association any day next week you may name. Please advise me of the day and hour that will suit the convenience of the gentlemen.

" Yours truly,

" A. T. GOSHORN, *Director-General.*

" Hon. JOHN EATON,
" *Commissioner of Education, Washington, D. C."*

It was convenient for four members of the committee, namely, Messrs. Wickersham, Philbrick, Abernethy, and Eaton, to meet in Philadelphia, Wednesday, February 3. After a discussion of the subject committed to them among themselves, they met Hon. Mr. Goshorn at the rooms of the Centennial Commission, and had a full, free, and very satisfactory conference upon the whole subject of the representation of education in the Exposition.

The committee called attention to the action of the department of superintendence of the National Educational Association at the meeting a year ago, which recommended:

(1) That each State and Territory be invited to prepare a representation of its educational condition for the Centennial.

(2) That each State and Territory also be invited to prepare a historical record of its educational progress for the same purpose.

(3) That each city be invited to act with the State-authorities in preparing such records and that it present an exhibit of its own educational growth and condition.

(4) That each educational institution be invited to participate in the same way.

(5) That a census be taken in 1875. That the Commissioner of Education be requested, on behalf of the educators of this country, to correspond with the prominent educators of the world, and invite their co-operation in the matter of the Centennial.

(6) That an international educational congress be held in connection with the Centennial.

The committee expressed the satisfaction that had been shown by the different State and city educational authorities that an attempt was to be made to show the progress of education, and stated, so far as they were acquainted with them, what had already been done to carry out the recommendations past last year.

Referring to the resolution under which they were appointed, they stated to the Director-General the embarrassment now felt by the officers of the different State- and city-systems of education and the several institutions of learning, arising from the want of some definite plan and the need of some immediate and authoritative action.

State- and city-superintendents and officers of various institutions are inquiring, "What shall be the educational representation? What shall my State, my city, my institution do?"

No one now feels prepared to answer. It is a public, and not a private, interest. Its exhibition must be made largely from motives of public good, and only partially from any considerations of private profit, such as would arise from the manufacture of furniture and the publication of text-books.

The plans adopted must accord with the methods of public educational action. The vast diversity of systems, institutions, and facts will require time to consider and arrange what shall be done by each and to harmonize the whole.

The committee consider themselves sent by the department of superintendence of this National Association, only as a medium of communicating these facts and impressions from the different educational workers in the country to the Director-General, and of securing from him any communications he may wish to return to them.

The Director-General, in behalf of the commission, expressed an earnest desire that the influence of the Exposition should be thoroughly educational, and especially that the growth of educational facilities in the United States and their results, as shown in our country's progress, should be most successfully represented, and his gratification that this action had been taken by the department of superintendence of the National Educational Association. He had just written to the governors of the several States, calling attention to a class of subjects, of which education is one,* and hoped that this

---

* INTERNATIONAL EXHIBITION.

1876.

UNITED STATES CENTENNIAL COMMISSION,
Philadelphia, January 30, 1875.

Sir: In behalf of the United States Centennial Commission, I have the honor to direct your attention to several subjects connected with the International Exhibition of 1876, of great importance to your Commonwealth, and for which provision should be made this year.

It has already become manifest that a large proportion of the articles to be exhibited will be provided for in a creditable manner by the manufacturers and producers of the several States; but there remain large classes of objects whose collection is essential to a complete representation of the material and social condition of the community, yet which it is not to the interest or within the power of an individual to collect. Of this description are the unwrought natural resources of the land, such as minerals, soils, woods, vegetation, &c. It is so largely upon their wealth in this direction that the growth of the States depends, that this department of the Exhibition will be critically studied by those interested in the problems of immigration and of investment of capital. On merely economical grounds, every State would do well to provide liberally for the thorough and exhaustive representation of the actual and possible products of its soil.

Another department that should be inaugurated and prepared under the auspices of the State-government is that which may be termed historical and statistical. Unless done by official authority, there will not be a complete presentment of such matters as the history of the early settlement of the State, its physical features, climate, geographical position, government, laws, and punishment of crime, system of State and municipal taxation, revenue and expenditures, benevolent institutions and charities, education, scientific, industrial, commercial, learned and religious societies, agricultural and manufacturing interests, the extent and effects of railroads and other means of transportation, the history and growth in population and wealth of the State. All these subjects, among others, ought to be so represented as to afford a summary view of the history, progress, and present condition of every State. Unless this is accomplished, the Exhibition will seriously fail in that part of its purpose which contemplates a representation of the nation's growth during the first century of its existence.

Official resources, only, are adequate to the satisfactory execution of the task thus proposed.

committee would act provisionally, calling attention to the subject, gathering information, and forming plans for his consideration until the meeting of the executive committee of the Centennial and formal action has been taken by them. The committee retired, and agreed to act as suggested by the Director-General, Hon. A. T. Goshorn.

The following statement was made to the United States Commissioner of Education:

"CONTINENTAL HOTEL,
"*Philadelphia, February* 3, 1875.

"SIR: In connection with our duty as members of this committee, we have observed the action taken by you, as it appears in the message of the President, in reference to an appropriation by Congress of $50,000, for general educational representation at the approaching Centennial Exhibition, which shall be in aid of, and supplementary to, any efforts made by States, cities, institutions, or private individuals.

"We wish to inform you that we highly approve of this action, and have so expressed ourselves in appropriate ways to members of Congress. We believe that this recommendation on your part should be made known to educators throughout the country, and that it would receive the universal approval of the friends of education, and that they would take early steps to communicate their views to their several Senators and Representatives.

"Very respectfully yours,

"J. P. WICKERSHAM.
"JOHN D. PHILBRICK.
"ALONZO ABERNETHY.

"General JOHN EATON,
"*United States Commissioner of Education,*
"*Bureau of Education, Washington, D. C.*"

APPENDIX B.

MEMORIAL OF THE DEPARTMENT OF SUPERINTENDENCE OF THE NATIONAL EDUCATIONAL ASSOCIATION.

To the Senate and House of Representatives in Congress assembled:

At a meeting of the department of superintendence of the National Educational Association, recently held in Washington, D. C., the following resolutions, upon "The relation of the General Government to public education," were passed unanimously, and the undersigned, the committee who prepared and presented the resolutions, were instructed to embody them in the form of a memorial to Congress. In the performance of this duty we herewith present the proceedings above referred to, and most respectfully ask for them such consideration on the part of your honorable body as may be proper.

It is hoped, therefore, that each of the States, either by legislative action or otherwise, will adopt such measures as may be deemed necessary to empower existing organizations or agencies to be created, to prepare an exhibition of its native resources and moral and political advancement, as herein indicated. A collective representation of this character will not only be interesting as illustrating the prosperity of the country, but will also be of inestimable value for preservation in the archives of the nation, as a correct history of the birth and progress of the several communities that have contributed during the century to the growth and strength of the union of States.

How far your State will participate in these suggestions is a question that I have the honor to most respectfully submit and recommend to your early consideration.

Your obedient servant,

A. T. GOSHORN,
Director-General.

His Excellency ——— ———,
Governor of ———.

RESOLUTIONS.

Resolved, That this body reiterate and reaffirm the positions taken at its meeting in this place one year ago, as follows:

First. That the Federal Government should leave to the people and local governments of each State the management of their own educational affairs without interference;

Secondly. That great service was done to the cause of education by Congress in establishing and maintaining a Bureau or Department of Education, whereby appropriate information from all parts of the world may be gathered, digested, and distributed, and whereby much useful aid is furnished to the practical work of education throughout the country;

Thirdly. That the proposition to set apart the public lands of the United States exclusively for the purposes of free education meets with our heartiest approval; and

Fourthly. That it is the duty of Congress to furnish special aid to the school-authorities of the District of Columbia.

Resolved, That as, in order fully to perform the work pressing upon it and make its usefulness still more widely felt, we are satisfied the National Bureau of Education needs increased clerical force, and as it is equally plain to us that the distribution directly by the Bureau of at least ten thousand copies of its annual reports each year, among school-officers and those especially interested in the work of education in the different States and Territories, would do an incalculable amount of good, we therefore respectfully petition Congress, in the interest of the education of the people, to take the necessary steps to bring about these desirable ends.

Resolved, That a reasonable appropriation by the General Government is necessary to secure a full and creditable representation of the educational interests of the country at the approaching Centennial Exposition to be held at Philadelphia, and we sincerely hope that such an appropriation may be made by the Congress now in session.

J. P. WICKERSHAM,
Superintendent of Public Instruction, Pennsylvania.
J. K. JILLSON,
Superintendent of Public Instruction, South Carolina.
JOHN D. PHILBRICK,
Late Superintendent of Public Schools, Boston.
ALONZO ABERNETHY,
Superintendent of Public Instruction, Iowa.
ALEXANDER C. HOPKINS,
Superintendent of Public Instruction, Indiana.
B. G. NORTHROP,
Secretary of Board of Education, Connecticut.

WASHINGTON, D. C., *January 29*, 1875.

———

MEMORIAL OF THE MASSACHUSETTS STATE TEACHERS' ASSOCIATION.

To the honorable Senate and House of Representatives of the United States in Congress assembled:

We, the undersigned, respectfully state that, at the annual meeting of the Massachusetts State Teachers' Association, held in Worcester, Mass., December 29, 1874, we were instructed, by the unanimous vote of said association, to memorialize your honorable body in behalf of the continuance and the liberal support of the National Bureau of Education.

We therefore respectfully represent:

1. That the intellectual, moral, and material welfare of the people of the United States depends chiefly upon their general education.

2. That without such education the security of the Government and of liberty itself must always be in peril.

3. That it therefore becomes the duty of those who have the control of national affairs to do, within the limits of the Federal Constitution, whatever can be wisely done, towards promoting the education of the people.

4. That one of the readiest and most effective means of accomplishing this end is the general diffusion of information on educational subjects. *

5. That the information which has already been furnished by the National Bureau of Education has been of inestimable value to educators and to those who legislate on educational affairs, embracing, as it does, knowledge in regard to school-systems established in the several States and in foreign countries; the various modes of organizing colleges, seminaries, normal schools, and educational institutions of every sort; and a vast variety of important facts relating to every department of education, among which are those which show the influence of education upon labor, crime, and pauperism.

6. That, as no State can justly be expected to collate such information and freely disseminate it for the benefit of other States, it is evident that by the national authority alone can so useful and important an object be accomplished.

7. That while we do not ask for, but, on the contrary, should, if need be, protest against, any interference on the part of Congress with the school-systems of the several States, we, in behalf of the teachers of Massachusetts, do earnestly pray that the National Bureau of Education may be continued, and may be so liberally supported as to enable it to perform its functions in the most comprehensive and efficient manner.

All of which is respectfully presented by—

DANIEL B. HAGAR,
JOHN D. PHILBRICK,
A. P. MARBLE,
CHARLES HAMMOND,
A. P. STONE,
Committee of the Massachusetts State Teachers' Association.

RESOLUTION OF THE INDIANA STATE TEACHERS' ASSOCIATION, DECEMBER 31, 1874.

Resolved, That, to enable General John Eaton, Commissioner of Education for the United States, to secure the necessary appropriations from Congress, for which he is now asking, to enable him to carry on more successfully the Bureau of Education, we respectfully ask the Representatives and Senators of Indiana to vote for and render him such aid as the exigencies of the case demand.

RESOLUTIONS OF THE MISSOURI STATE TEACHERS' ASSOCIATION.

Resolved, That it is the sense of this body that, in order to secure an effectul supervision of schools, a law should be enacted providing for the appointment of a competent school-commissioner for each State senatorial district, who shall employ his entire time under the direction of the State-superintendent in promoting the interest of public education, said commissioner to be paid by the counties composing his district, in proportion to their population.

Resolved, That we recognize the value of the work of the United States Commissioner of Education, and fully indorse that work; and we respectfully ask our Senators and Representatives in Congress to render the Bureau of Education every possible facility for collecting and distributing the important facts and statistics embraced in the circulars and annual Report of the Commissioner.

Resolved, That in our opinion no better disposition of the public lands can be made than to set aside the net proceeds for educational purposes as a permanent fund, distributing the interest accruing among the several States on the basis of illiteracy.

Resolved, That, as citizenship under our form of government throws upon each citizen the liability of making laws, as well as the duty of obeying them, this association recommends a more careful study in all our schools of the history and Constitution of the United States and of the State of Missouri, as well as the general principles of the science of government.

Resolved, That we recognize an appropriate and dignified place in our educational work for the academies and colleges not connected with the public system of the State, and that we most earnestly desire the fullest harmony of action among all educators.

Resolved, That, for the purpose of unifying our entire educational work, we recommend to teachers of both public and private schools, in fixing their courses of study and requirements for admission, to consider carefully those things in which they have a common interest, in order that there may be nothing to prevent the proper work of each class of schools or interfere with the complete harmony which is so highly desirable.

Resolved, That a committee of three be appointed to confer with the faculties of all higher institutions regarding the feasibility of a common course or courses of study in these institutions, such committee to report at the next meeting of this association.

Resolved, That the president of this association be, and he is hereby, instructed to appoint a committee of three members to confer with the State-superintendent-elect, in relation to the school-law of this State, and, on behalf of this association, to co-operate with him for the purpose of securing such legislation as the best interests of the schools demand.

RESOLUTIONS OF THE NEW YORK STATE ASSOCIATION OF SCHOOL-COMMISSIONERS AND SUPERINTENDENTS AT SYRACUSE, DECEMBER 30, 1874.

Whereas the people of the United States have admitted, or are rapidly admitting, to full political privileges millions of freedmen and refugees, utterly uninstructed and destitute of that preliminary knowledge necessary to the safe use of the elective franchise; and

Whereas the danger thence arising threatens every State in the Union and the country at large; and

Whereas there are various measures now pending in the Congress of the United States calculated to meet this emergency:

Resolved, That, in the opinion of this body of school-officers of the State of New York, representing eighteen thousand teachers of the State, the policy of the General Government should be no longer to make large grants from its public domain to moneyed corporations, but to consecrate the proceeds of all sales of the public lands, sacredly and irrevocably, to the purpose of aiding and encouraging the States in the thorough education of the people.

Resolved, That, in this view, we respectfully recommend to the careful consideration of Congress the bills introduced by Hon. J. S. Morrill, in the Senate, and Hon. G. F. Hoar, in the House of Representatives, for the consecration of proceeds of public-land-sales, in part for the improvement of instruction in the various sciences applicable to the industries of the country and in part for the establishment and maintenance of public schools, making the distribution as regards the latter object upon the basis of illiteracy, for a term of years, thus bringing education to bear upon that uninstructed mass, set free by the events of the last fifteen years.

Resolved, That we have noticed with deep regret the apparent want of appreciation,

121

on the part of a large number of Representatives, of the Bureau of Education ington, the great value of which we have learned by our individual experien building up a central power in education at the national Capital, which it app inadequate ever to do, but as enabling those engaged in education in th States to have access to the information necessary to make their work thor efficient.

Resolved, That we tender our thanks to those Representatives who have en to carry out a statesman-like policy on this question, and that a copy of the tions be sent to each of the Senators and Representatives from this State at papers for publication.

○

Pl. I.

e change of form

| | Gr. | Etr. | La. | Mod. |

CIRCULARS OF INFORMATION

OF THE

REAU OF EDUCATION.

No. 2–1875.

EDUCATION IN JAPAN.

WASHINGTON:
GOVERNMENT PRINTING OFFICE.
1875.

CONTENTS.

		Page.
Letter of the Commissioner of Education to the Secretary of the Interior		5
Education in Japan, by William E. Griffis, esq		9
Statistics of schools under the immediate control of educational department		13
The number of schools in Fus and Kens		15
Letter of Stuart Eldridge, M. D., to the Commissioner of Education		16
Copy of the official report of Hon. David Murray, superintendent of schools and colleges in Japan, to the vice-minister of education		19
Appendix A		31
Extract from the Report of the Commissioner of Education for 1872		31
Extract from the Report of Mr. Watson, Her Majesty's secretary of legation at Yedo		34

LETTER.

DEPARTMENT OF THE INTERIOR,
BUREAU OF EDUCATION,
Washington, D. C., April 20, 1875.

SIR: I have the honor to submit the following reports of the move-
its now making throughout the Empire of Japan to introduce into
t ancient country a system of public instruction corresponding to the
ems in use in the western nations, and especially those of the United
tes.

he appointment of Dr. Murray to the position of superintendent
chools and colleges in Japan lends an interest among American
cators to his first official report; and the papers prepared by Mr.
liam E. Griffis, with the accompanying statistics from the Japan
l, and by Dr. Stuart Eldridge, are interesting, as being the personal
·rvations of American educators in Japan. I am indebted to the
:ational department of the Japanese government for the courtesy of
arly copy of Dr. Murray's report and for permission to make use of
ind to the two gentlemen named for their kindness in placing the
lts of their experience at my disposal. The summary of the school-
, taken from the Annual Report of this Bureau for 1872, and the
iunt of the condition of Japan immediately subsequent to the first
iblishment of schools under the law, taken from the excellent official
irt of Mr. Watson, Her Britannic Majesty's secretary of legation in
ian, give, in connection with the previous papers, a comprehensive
w of the condition of this remarkable educational movement. (See
pendix A.) I recommend the publication of these papers as a circu-
of information.

Very respectfully, your obedient servant,

JOHN EATON, *Commissioner.*

Hon. C. DELANO,
  Secretary of the Interior.

Approved, and publication ordered.

C. DELANO, *Secretary.*

EDUCATION IN JAPAN.

129 130

EDUCATION IN JAPAN.

By WILLIAM E. GRIFFIS,

Late of the Imperial Japanese College, Tōkiō, (Yedo,) Japan.

r the second time in her history, Japan is attempting the colossal
prise of introducing a civilization. The movement towards the
tion of the external forces, if not the ideals, of European nations,
h began within the last decade and is now attracting the attention
ie civilized world, is no new thing in the history of Dai Nippon.
restless desire of her people for improvement, and the outworkings
iat noble trait in the Japanese character which prompts to the
rtion of an old and the adoption of a new idea, when proved to be
er, are the principal motors of the national desire to enter within
iomity of modern nations and, by mastering their ideas and follow-
heir examples, to become their equals. As in the first instance, in
arly centuries, so now, they have declared their belief that "Educa-
is the basis of all progress."

iat the true position of this recent development of national life in
iistory of the empire may be fully understood, a very brief sketch
ipanese history may fitly open this paper.

ie aborigines of Japan are the Ainos, a race of men now inhabiting
island of Yezo. From the very ancient prehistoric time, the islands
ai Nippon were inhabited by these wandering tribes of hunters and
rmen. About the year 660 B. C., a band of conquerors who had
e from the main land of Asia began the conquest of Southern Japan.
few years they had possessed themselves of Kiushiu, Shikoku, and
central and southern portions of the main island.* Who these con-

---

* great many errors in Japanese history and geography have become stereotyped
ur text- and reference-books, which are reproduced in the notes and letters of tour-
and by book-makers, who, having never visited Japan, have copied from the old
taken authorities. An almost perfectly uniform system of transliterating Japanese
ars into English has been adopted by Anglo-Japanese scholars, which it is hoped
educated people of this country will assist in popularizing. By this method Ja-
iese names are given the simplest orthography, and their proximate pronunciation
i be easily attained.

a is pronounced	as	a in	....	arm.
e "	"	" e "	....	prey.
i "	"	" i "	....	machine.
o "	"	" o "	....	bone.
u "	"	" u "	....	rule.
ai "	"	" i "	....	bite.
ei "	"	" a "	....	bay.

Final n is usually short.

e and i before a consonant are usually short.

Long vowels are marked by a bar over them, thus: Tōkiō.

The five large islands of Japan are Kiushiu, (nine provinces,) Shikoku, (four prov-

querors were, whether Tartars, Coreans, Chinese, or Malays, is not known, though the probability is that they were Tartars. They brought agriculture and the rudiments of civilization with them, though they possessed neither writing, books, nor literature, except oral productions. From the blending of these two races sprang the ancient Japanese, who developed a type of physical structure and national life which later importations of blood, ideas, and customs have not radically altered.

In the later centuries, from the fourth to the eighth of the Christian era, after the conquest of Corea by the Japanese empress Jigō Kōgō, came letters, writing, books, literature, religion, ethics, politics, medicine, arts, science, agriculture, manufactures, and the varied appliances of civilization; and with these entered thousands of immigrants from Corea and China. Under the intellectual influence of Buddhism—the powerful and aggressive faith that had already led captive the half of Asia—of the Confucian ethics and philosophy, and Chinese literature, the horizon of the Japanese mind was immensely broadened. By the more material appliances borrowed from Corea—the pupil of China— the Japanese became a civilized people. In the time of the European "dark ages" the Japanese were enjoying what, in comparison, was a high state of civilization. Nevertheless, so definitely fixed and persistent was the original type of the Japanese national character, as the resultant of original ancestral impress, soil, climate, food, and natural influences, that the Japanese of to-day are a people differing widely from the Chinese in physique, temperament, character, habits, customs, and ideas.

Up to the twelfth century the Mikado was the sole ruler of his people; instead of the usual development of a priestly and a warrior-caste, there arose in Japan the civil and military orders. Towards the end

ınces,) Hondo, (main land,) Yezo and Saghalın, (Russian name,) or Kabafūto, (Japanese name.) Foreign book-makers have, to a man, fallen into the error of calling the main island Niphon, or Nippon. There is no island having such a name. Dai Nippon, or Dai Nihon, (Great Japan,) is the name of the entire empire, or the Japanese archipelago. To restrict the term Nippon to one island is unwarrantable and wholly misleading. Hondo (main land) is the official name given to the largest island, and it is best to use this term. The Liu Kiu islands belong to Japan, and are governed by Japanese officers appointed by the Mikado. They are wrongly marked Loo Choo on our maps. The term Yedo, which can be spelled with but one d, (and is composed of ye, bay, and do, door, hence Bay-door,) has not been used either officially or popularly by the Japanese since 1868. Tōkiō (tō, east; kiō, capital) is the official and popular name of the Japanese capital. Tokei is another spelling and pronunciation used chiefly by those who affect Chinese learning. Ō'zaka is the correct orthography of the name of the second largest Japanese city. Kioto, not miako—a common noun—is the name of the old capital. Hakodaté, not Hakodadi, is the seaport in Yezo, (not Jesso or Yesso.) Nugata is on the west coast. Shimonoseki (not Simonosaki) is the name of the place on which the retainers of the daimio of Hagi, the chief city in Choshui, erected batteries and brought about the foreign naval and financial victory by which the batteries were destroyed, the town fired, and an indemnity of three million Mexican dollars extorted.

f the twelfth century, the military power of the empire fell into the
1ands of the Minamoto family of military chieftains. In old times
every general was called a shō-gun, but Yoritomo, in 1186, was made sei-
-tai shō-gun, barbarian-repressing commander-in-chief or great general.
This was the beginning of that great usurpation that lasted, with some
intermission, until 1868. The Mikado in Kiōto was overawed by the
military usurper at Kamakura or Yedo, though the prestige of the
Mikado never diminished. The reverence of the people never abated,
notwithstanding the people feared their iron-handed ruler, the Shō-gun.
"The Shō-gun all men fear, the Mikado all men love," is a Japanese say-
ng. Foreigners acquired the idea, which still lingers in our unrevised
text-books, that there were " two emperors " in Japan, one "spiritual," the
other "temporal." The truth is that there was but one emperor, the
Mikado, and the Shō-gun was a military usurper. The term " Tycoon,'
properly Tai-kun,) meaning "great prince" or "illustrious sovereign," was
never used in Japanese official documents previous to the Perry treaty.
It was an absurd fiction of authority, a piece of pompous bombast, designed to deceive the foreign envoys and treaty-makers as to the real
relation of the Shō-gun to his master the Mikado. The Shō-gun was a
vassal of the fourth grade, without the slightest shadow of right to make
a treaty. His final assumption of authority in signing the treaties with
foreigners without the consent of the Mikado was the occasion of his
overthrow in 1868. Even without the presence of foreigners on the soil
of Japan the duarchy would have fallen and a reversion to the ancient
monarchy would have taken place. The presence of foreigners merely
hastened what was already inevitable. It added momentum to the machinery of revolution already at work. The Shō-gunate fell in 1868; the
feudal system was abolished in 1871.

It is not within the province of this paper to explain, as far as the
writer may imagine he understands them, the causes and motives that
led the new government to adopt, or profess to adopt, the modern ideal
of civilization and to enter vigorously upon the path of reform. He
can simply give the merest outline of the present state of education in
Japan and contrast it with the old ideals and methods.

Under the old *régime* of the Shō-guns, all foreign ideas and influences
were systematically excluded, and the isolation of Japan from the rest
of the world was made the supreme policy of the government. Profound
peace lasted from the beginning of the seventeenth century to 1868. During this time, schools and colleges, literature and learning, flourished.
It was the period of scholastic, not of creative, intellectual activity.
The basis of education was Chinese. What we consider the means of
education, reading and writing, were to them the ends. Of classified
science there was little or none. Mathematics was considered as fit
only for merchants and shop-keepers. No foreign languages were
studied, and their acquisition was forbidden. Whatever of European
learning, through the medium of the Dutch tongue, was obtained, was

gotten secretly. Etiquette, physical and martial exercises, occupied largely the time and attention of the students. There was no department of education, though universities were established at Kiōto and Yedo, large schools in the daimio's capitals, and innumerable private schools all over the country. Nine-tenths of the people could read and write. Books were very numerous and cheap. Circulating libraries existed in every city and town. Literary clubs and associations for mutual improvement were common even in country villages. Nevertheless, in comparison with the ideal systems and practice of the progressive men of New Japan, the old style was as different from the present as the training of an English youth in mediæval times is from that of a London or Oxford student of the present day. Although an attempt to meet some of the educational necessities arising from the altered conditions of the national life were made under the Shō-gun's *régime*, yet the first attempt at systematic work in the large cities was made under the Mikado's government, and the idea of a new national plan of education is theirs only. In 1871 the Mom Bu Shō, or department of education, was formed, of which the high counselor Oki, a man of indomitable vigor and perseverance, was made head. From the very first, however, the new government had given great attention to the work of education, and had re-organized on a larger scale the old Kai Sei Jō (place of reform) in Tōkiō, as the language-school was called. The Rev. Guido F. Verbeck, a missionary of the Reformed Church of America, who had been in Nagasaki since 1860, had mastered the language, instructed numbers of native young men, and won the confidence of the government, was appointed head of this school, which, under his administration, rapidly improved in organization, disciplne, and standard of instruction. During the whole of Mr. Verbeck's connection with the education-department, his energy, industry, and ability were beyond praise. He acted as adviser, organizer, and general factotum of the education-department. Education in foreign languages and science, foreign school-methods, discipline, standards, ideas, books, appliances, furniture, were all new things in Japan. Jealousy, suspicion, ignorance, had to be met and overcome, confidence inspired, and raw and refractory material for teachers and scholars had to be dealt with. Success finally crowned the efforts, and the Imperial College in Tōkiō is now not only the largest school in Japan, but is the first in disciplne, standard, and organization, having a brilliant corps of professional instructors and hundreds of trained and earnest students.

According to the scheme of national education promulgated in 1872, the empire is divided into eight Dai Gaku Ku, (Daigakku,) or great educational divisions. In each of these there is to be a university, normal school, schools of foreign languages, high schools, and primary schools. The total number of schools will number, it is expected, over 55,000. Only in the higher schools is a foreign language to be taught. In the lower schools the Japanese learning and elementary science translated or adopted from European or American text-books are to be taught. The general system of instruction, methods, discipline, school-aids, furniture, architecture, are to be largely adopted from foreign models, and are now to a great extent in vogue throughout the country. The writer has had nearly four years' experience in actual educational work in Japan, and in traveling through the country has noticed almost invariably the use of new text-books, written in Japanese, but adapted from foreign models, blackboards and chalk, slate and pencils, steel pens, iron ink, chairs, tables, charts, and a host of new improvements, some diverging considerably from our models, according to native taste, fancy, knowledge, or means, but all tending to improvement, and of unquestionable advantage over those of old systems.

The statistics given below were published by the education-department one year ago. The writer regrets that he cannot furnish them for 1874 and 1875 in time for publication in this volume.

In spite of the Formosan affair, the past year has been one of quiet, steady progress in education, though the education-department is compelled to limit its labors and enterprises, from lack of sufficient appropriations. The statistics here appended relate simply to the schools in which foreign languages or sciences are taught. It is quite safe to say that, to be correct up to the present date, their figures should be increased at least 20 per cent. Of the seven or eight thousand public and the large number of private schools, in which the Japanese language is the sole vehicle of instruction, nothing is said in these statistics. Several other schools of high grade under other government-departments are not noted in this list. In order to understand fully the details of the table, a few explanations are here given:

Gaku kō, or *Gakkō*, school—literally, "learning-place;" *Fu*, imperial city, of which there are three, Tōkiō, Ō'zaka, and Kiōto; *Ken*, prefectural division of the empire. Japan has about 72 *kens*.

[For the summary of Japanese educational statistics Professor Griffis refers to the statement in the Japan Weekly Mail of February 21, 1874, from which the following statistics of schools under the immediate control of the educational department are taken:]

[From the Japanese Weekly Mail, February 21, 1874]

STATISTICS OF SCHOOLS UNDER THE IMMEDIATE CONTROL OF THE EDUCATIONAL DEPARTMENT.

I. *Kaiseigakko at Tōkiō, (first Daigakku.)*

(1) 15 teachers—2 Japanese, 13 foreigners.

A. Jurisprudence and philosophy: 1 English and 4 American teachers.

B. Technology: 4 French teachers.

C. Mining: 4 German teachers.

(2) 236 students.

A. Jurisprudence, (preparatory:) First class, 10 students; second class, 15 students.

B. Philosophy (preparatory:) First class, 20 students; second class, 18 students; third class, 20 students.

C. Technology, (preparatory:) Lower class of three years, 10 students; upper class of 1 year, 16 students; lower class of 1 year, 24 students.

D. Mining: Third class, 11 students.

E. Mining, (preparatory:) First class, 11 students; second class, 7 students; third class, 17 students.

F. Manufacturing, (preparatory:) Sixth class, upper portion, 28 students; sixth class, lower portion, 24 students.

(Besides, there are several students not included in the classes.)

II. *Igakko (school of medicine) at Tōkiō.*

(1) 19 teachers—11 Japanese, 8 German.

A. Medicine and surgery: 2 teachers.

B. Anatomy: 1 teacher.

C. Natural history and mathematics: 1 teacher.

D. Physics and chemistry: 1 teacher.

E. Latin and German: 1 teacher.

F. German and arithmetic: 1 teacher.

G. Pharmacy: 1 teacher.

(2) 242 students.

A. Main studies: Sixth class, 34 students; seventh class, 1 student; tenth class, 33 students.

B. Preparatory studies: First class, 7 students; second class, 47 students; third class, 57 students; fourth class, 46 students.

C. Hospital, 17 students.

III. *Igakko (school of medicine) at Nagasaki, (fifth Daigakku.)*

(1) 10 teachers—7 Japanese, 3 foreigners.

A. Medicine: 2 Dutch teachers.

B. German and Latin: 1 German teacher.

(2) 74 students.

A. Main studies: Seventh class, five students; eighth class, 11 students; ninth class, 13 students; tenth class, 12 students.

B. Preparatory studies: Fourth class, 33 students.

IV.—*School of foreign languages at Tōkiō, (first Daigakku.)*

(1) 32 teachers—17 Japanese, 15 foreigners.

A. English language: 5 English and 2 American teachers.

B. French language: 3 French teachers.

C. German language: 3 German teachers.

D. Russian language: 1 Russian teacher.

E. Chinese language: 1 Chinese teacher.

(2) 542 students.

A. English language, upper degree: First class, 28 students; second class, 24 students.

B. English language, lower degree: First class, 29 students; second class, 29 students; third class, 28 students; fourth class, No. 1, 37 students; fourth class, No. 2, 33 students; fourth class, No. 3, 28 students; classes not passed examination, 58 students.

C. French language, upper degree: Fourth class, 32 students.

D. French language, lower degree: First class, 20 students; second class, 14 students; third class, 9 students; classes not passed examination, 21 students.

E. German language, upper degree: Fourth class, 10 students.

F. German language, lower degree: First class, 20 students; second class, 27 students; third class, 21 students; fourth class, 18 students; classes not passed examination, 11 students.

G. Chinese language, lower degree: First class, 9 students; second class, 9 students; third class, 5 students; fourth class, 9 students.

H. Russian language, lower degree: First class, 5 students; fourth class, 9 students.

V.—*Kaimeigakko at Ōzaka*, (*third Daigakku.*)
  (1) 9 teachers—5 Japanese, 4 English.
  (2) 117 students.
    A. English language, upper degree: First class, 1 student; second class, 9 students; third class, 8 students; fourth class, 16 students.
    B. English language, lower degree: First class, 9 students; second class, 27 students; third class, 20 students; fourth class, 27 students.

VI.—*Kowungakko at Nagasaki*, (*fifth Daigakku.*)
  (1) 5 teachers—3 Japanese, 2 Americans.
  (2) 90 students.
    English language, lower degree: First class, 21 students; second class, 29 students; third class, 26 students; fourth class, 14 students.

VII. *Female-school at Tökiö*, (*first Daigakku.*)
  (1) 7 female teachers—6 Japanese, 1 American.
  (2) 36 female students.
(There is no classification established.)

VIII. *Normal school at Tökiö*, (*first Daigakku.*)
  (1) 4 teachers—3 Japanese, 1 American.
  (2) 85 students.
A. Upper degree, 31 students; B. Lower degree, 54 students.
  (3) 85 students for the lower schools—56 males, 29 females. Sixth class, 12 males, 3 females; seventh class, 33 males, 16 females; eighth class, 11 males, 10 females.

IX. *Normal school at Ōzaka*, (*third Daigakku.*)
  (1) 2 teachers.
  (2) 34 students.
(There is no classification established.)

X. *Normal school at Miyagi*, (*seventh Daigakku.*)
  (1) 2 teachers.
  (2) 46 students.
(There is no classification established.)

TOTAL.

  (1) 7 government-schools, 97 teachers—51 Japanese, (45 males, 6 females,) 46 foreigners, (45 males, 1 female;) 1337 students—1301 males, 36 females.
  (2) 3 normal schools established by government, 8 teachers—7 Japanese, 1 foreigner; 165 students, 85 students for the lower schools, (56 males, 29 females.)

Statistics of lower schools, both public and private, established in various Fus and Kens.

A. Number of lower schools... 6,261
B. Number of teachers.. 5,856
C. Number of students 472,047

[From the Japan Weekly Mail, March 4, 1874]

THE NUMBER OF SCHOOLS IN FUS AND KENS.

FIRST DAIGAKKU-KU.

Tōkio-Fu: Schools of foreign languages, 5, (4 of English and 1 of French.)
Irregular schools: 27 of English, 2 of French, and 1 of German language. Besides

these there are 28 where the English, French, and German languages are taught, and books are translated into Japanese or Chinese, and writing is also taught.

Kanagawa-Ken : School of foreign languages, 1.
Tiba-Ken : Irregular school, 1.
Ashigara-Ken : Irregular school, 1.
Tochigi-Ken : Irregular school, 1.

SECOND DAIGAKKU-KU.

Shidzuoka-Ken : School of foreign languages, 1 ; irregular school, 1.
Chikuma-Ken : Irregular school, 1.
Inhikawa-Ken : Irregular night-schools, 6 ; irregular school, 1.
Tsugura-Ken : Private school of middle class, 1.

THIRD DAIGAKKU-KU.

Ōzaka-Fu : School of English language, 1 ; irregular school, 1.
Kioto-Fu : School of English, French, and German languages, 1.
Sakai-Ken : Private school of middle class, 1 ; school of English language, 1.
Okayama-Ken : Private schools of middle class, 2.
Kochi-Ken : School of English language, 1.

FOURTH DAIGAKKU-KU.

Yamaguchi-Ken : Schools of foreign languages, 2, (one of English and 1 of German language.)

FIFTH DAIGAKKU-KU.

Mitsuma-Ken : School of English language, 1.
Shirakawa-Ken : School of English language, 1.
Kagoshima-Ken : School of English and French languages, 1.
Kokura-Ken : Irregular schools, 2.

SIXTH DAIGAKKU-KU.

Niigata-Ken : Schools of foreign languages, 5.
Wakamatsu-Ken : School of English language, 1.
Okitama-Ken : School of English and French languages, 1.

SEVENTH DAIGAKKU-KU.

Miyagi-Ken : School of English and French languages, 1.
Iwasaki-Ken : Irregular school, 1.
Aomori-Ken : School of English language, 1.

The *total number* of this class of schools is 103 ; 4 of which are private schools of the middle class ; 25 schools of foreign languages ; 68 are irregular schools, and 6 are night-schools.

LETTER OF STUART ELDRIDGE, M. D., TO THE COMMISSIONER OF EDUCATION.

HAKODATÉ, *July 17, 1874.*

DEAR GENERAL : I feel that I owe you a sort of report of progress, and you should have had a report before this but for several reasons, chiefly that the information you desired I found it almost impossible to

tain after leaving Yedo, which place is the headquarters of everything
Japan. * * * * For the last two years I have had a
t of medical directorship of the northern district of Japan, which in-
des Yezo and the Japanese portion of Saghalin. There are quite a
nber of government-hospitals and dispensaries scattered through this
trict, the largest and most important being at Hakodaté. I have a
-man-power medical school, also, averaging about thirty pupils, to
ich I devote my chief attention. I lecture daily. We have quite a
pectable hospital at Hakodaté, part of which I found on my arrival
l to which I have added a new building.

send you by this mail a photograph of my school at the close of
3 and also photographs of the hospital, all taken by a native artist.
annot speak in too high terms of the Japanese youth as medical
lents. I have not found the trouble much complained of by instructors
ther branches of knowledge, i. e., that, when the Japanese have ob-
ied the merest smattering of knowledge, they assume to have com-
ed the course, and act accordingly. Perhaps I have been associated
1 exceptionally good men. I have several native assistants who
e pretty well instructed in foreign medicine by others before I came,
who, for *medical* common sense and general education in *the* science,
not compare unfavorably with the average practitioner at home. In
, all Japanese physicians of any respectability whatever (I mean
iectable standing among their own people) practice western medicine
usively, just so far as they know it, having entirely abandoned the
Chinese system. Many of the better class of native doctors have
iained a reading acquaintance with one or more foreign languages,
there are many who have received a certain amount of oral instruction
rom the few translations as yet made, but are unable, from want of
e or other cause, to undertake the study of a foreign tongue. To
it the wants of this class, as well as to furnish promptly to all the
rent news of our science, I have established a bi-monthly medical
rnal in Japanese, of which I am sole editor and which is translated
my more advanced students. My journal, which is called the Kin-
[-Setzu, (or Modern Medical News,) is published at Yedo by the gov-
iment, and is sold at a price just sufficient to cover the expense of
ae. The first number, which was very small and very badly printed,
s issued in an edition of five hundred. Of the second number an
ition of one thousand was called for. I receive no compensation in
iney for the great amount of extra labor which this undertaking
mands, but, of course, expect indirect benefit. I send you by this
il the first and second numbers. Pray remember that I labor under
: disadvantage of being five hundred miles from the office of publica-
n, and that I am, by necessity, my own artist. You can hardly
igine the labor necessary to secure a correct translation of technical
rature into Japanese. Everything is first translated from my manu.
ipt by one hand, and translated back into English by a second hand
139

unfamiliar with the original. I then compare the original with this re-translated version. That you may be able to form some idea of my journal, I give below tables of contents of Nos. I and II.

CONTENTS OF NO. 1 OF KIN-SE-I SETZU, MARCH, 1874.

1. Introduction, by editor.
2. Introduction, by native assistant.
3. Removal of tumors by ligation with India rubber, (with cuts.)
4. On the relief of pain. No. 1, (with cuts.)
5. Quarantine hygiene, and the cholera.
6. Diagnosis of fatty tumors, by cold.
7. Ergotine in hemorrhage.
8. Extemporized surgical needles.
9. Removal of foreign bodies from ear.
10. Necessity of government-inspection of imported drugs and medi-cines.

CONTENTS OF NO. 2, MAY, 1874.

1. Lectures on urethral stricture, by editor. Lecture 1, (with cuts.)
2. Surgery without hemorrhage, Esmarch's method, (with cuts.)
3. Apparatus for dislocated fingers.
4. Necessity of government-inspection of coal-oil.
5. Necessity of education of midwives in Japan.
6. On the relief of pain. No. 2.
7. Use of copper salts in cholera.
8. Nitrite of amyl, a *new remedy* for asthma.
9. Rules for administration of arsenic.
10. Oxide of zinc in infantile diarrhea.
11. Tinctura ferri chloridi in small-pox.
12. Gelatine suppositories in fecal accumulation.
13. Treatment of syphilitic onychia.
14. Tinctura ferri chloridi in post-partum hemorrhage.
15. Ergotine in hemorrhage. No. 2.
16. Glycerine as an excipient.
17. New sign of death.
18. Worms in the heart and blood-vessels of dog in China and Japan.

* * * * * * *

Pray remember me to our common friends, and believe me, with grateful recollections of many kindnesses, yours,

STUART ELDRIDGE, M. D.*

General JOHN EATON,
United States Commissioner of Education,
Washington, D. C., U. S. A.

---

* Stuart Eldridge, M. D., now in extensive private practice at Yokohama, is an American gentleman, born in Philadelphia, who entered the Volunteer Army from Wisconsin as a private and was mustered out at the end of the war as a first lieutenant and brevet major. He was subsequently librarian of the Department of Agriculture

OF THE OFFICIAL REPORT OF HON. DAVID MURRAY,
ERINTENDENT OF SCHOOLS AND COLLEGES IN JA-
, TO THE VICE-MINISTER OF EDUCATION.

Honorable FUJIMARO TANAKA, *Vice-Minister of Education :*

ie close of the present year (6th Meiji) I desire to submit some
ents and suggestions in regard to the progress and prospects of
on in this country.

aware that my arrival in Japan is still too recent to justify me
ning such a knowledge of its educational affairs as would entitle
clusions to any considerable weight. In the subsequent years
which I may have the honor to serve the Japanese government
to be able to lay before the department of education the results
: mature observations and that these may be more worthy of
ration than the preliminary views which I now submit.

s been to me a great satisfaction, not indeed unexpected, to find
und an interest in the cause of education among all classes of
and so earnest a determination on the part of the government
oy every means for its promotion. The encouraging words which
sed His Imperial Majesty the Tenno to address to me on this
when I was honored with an interview, have been everywhere
ed in all my conferences with members of the goverument since
val. I feel, therefore, that I cannot go beyond my imperial in-
ns, nor beyond the wishes of the goverument, in my endeavors
s the claims of education upon the attention of those to whom
portant work is intrusted. The highest well-being of a nation
y be secured by educating its population. This function may
e considered the very highest belonging to a government. The
l comfort, the intellectual activity, and the moral integrity of the
uals of a nation are dependent on their proper education. In its
ise education has to do with all parts of a man's nature. It must,
is possible, provide him with a sound physical constitution, by
g him how to exercise and care for his body. It must develop and
te his intellectual and moral capacities; powers of mind, to plan;
owers, to discern and maintain the right; bodily powers, to exe-
hese constitute the educated man. And to produce educated
numbers and force sufficient to energize the whole nation is the
great duty of the government of Japan.

of the demonstrators of anatomy in Georgetown Medical College, D. C. He
nied the American agricultural commission employed by the Japa iese govern-
secretary, and was afterward appointed by that government chief surgeon of
ict of Hakodaté, in Northern Japan. In all these positions his energy, indus-
intelligence have gained him the merited confidence of his superior officers
general estimation of those among whom he has lived.

JAPAN NOT AN ILLITERATE NATION.

In the first place, however, let it be premised that Japan is in no sense to be regarded as an illiterate nation. Tried by a standard which we apply to the western nations, Japan will not fall far behind the most favored. The number of persons in the population who cannot read and write the Kana is comparatively small. If the estimates which have received from intelligent sources are even approximately accurate Japan will rank in the general diffusion of education with the most ad vanced nations of Europe or America. It is well known that even the most degraded classes of the population are able to write the ordinary Kana and to read the books printed in that style, and that this is true of the women among them as well as the men. And when again the nation is tried by a higher standard, it must be conceded that the edu cation which has given to the governing classes the wisdom to maintain an organized government for an unbroken period of twenty-five hundred years must have some title to our respect. It may have had its defects; it may have failed in giving to the nation that impulse towards material de velopment and that strong sense of individual dignity and responsibility which western civilization has developed, yet it must be admitted to have shown a marvelous power of imparting stability to national insti tutions.

TEACHING MUST BE IN THE NATIVE LANGUAGE.

In devising, therefore, a future educational system for Japan, we are not called upon to start from the beginning, but we have already a good foundation of national intelligence on which to build. Educational insti tutions are so much a matter of growth, dependent on external circum stances and national temperament, that it would be folly to ignore what has been done in the past when we make plans for the future. There are certain fixed elements in the problem which, whatever else may be changed, must remain essentially unchanged. In the present case, one of these is the language in which the education is to be communicated No system of universal education can be successfully carried out which shall not employ as its vehicle the common language of the people. I must be confessed that the Japanese language presents very serious difficulties in the way of using it as the medium for modern learning And yet, until the means are provided for conveying this learning in the language understood by all, education can only be enjoyed by a favored few. It must, therefore, be fully understood that the efforts to carry forward the national education in the languages of Europe are only tem porary expedients. Just as in the Middle Ages in Europe the Latin was employed as the learned language for imparting the education of that day, so at present, in Japan, the English, French, and German must be regarded as the temporary media for the introduction of the new branches of learning. From the very nature of things, only a very limited number can ever receive their education through these languages.

Hence the few thus educated must in turn be employed to impart their acquisitions in the vernacular to their less favored countrymen. They must be looked upon as the future educators of the nation. It is to them we must look to prepare the books and organize the schools. They must show the better methods for developing the industrial resources of the country. And having themselves enjoyed the advantages of a higher intellectual and moral culture, they must assume the task of adapting what is good in this new civilization to the wants and circumstances of their country.

NEED OF JAPANESE TEXT-BOOKS.

While, therefore, institutions for teaching foreign languages and the sciences which as yet are found only in these languages must for the present be considered an essential part of the educational system of Japan, and must be fostered and increased accordingly, the future aim of the department of education must be to *naturalize* education. There are two chief means at hand for effecting this object: the *one* is to prepare and introduce Japanese text-books on the various branches of western learning. A beginning has already been made in this direction. A number of books have been translated and compiled from foreign sources and have already been quite extensively introduced into the schools. They consist of reading-books, arithmetics, algebras, books on elementary natural sciences and on political and social science. Charts, models, and blackboards have also been prepared, and are now widely used in elementary Japanese instruction in the place of the more cumbrous methods previously in use. This department of work requires to be carried forward with judgment and energy. Many more books in the various branches of learning and science are required. And the department of education ought both to encourage private enterprise and to employ the best available talent in order to provide the books necessary to meet the demands of the increasing intelligence of the country.

NEED OF SCHOOLS FOR TRAINING TEACHERS.

The second means which is at hand to be employed in reforming the system of vernacular instruction is the training of teachers. The work of a school-teacher is one of the most difficult, as well as most dignified, of employments. To teach children the best things in the best ways is an accomplishment worth some effort to attain, and cannot be attained without effort.

Normal schools for the training of teachers have invariably, in Europe and America, been found to furnish the most efficient means for improving the education of a nation. They have been extensively established, especially in France, Germany, and the United States, and have resulted in the most wonderful improvement of the primary and middle schools of these countries. They are even more necessary in Japan than in any of these countries, because the new method of teaching and the new subjects to be taught differ in a greater degree here than elsewhere from those formerly in use. It is therefore with great satisfaction that I refer to the work of the department in this direction. The normal school established at Tokei has shown its usefulness by the excellent results already attained. Under the guidance of its efficient foreign principal, the students there are receiving a training for their future profession of teachers which will give them an immense advantage over others. The methods of teaching children in classes instead of singly; the use of charts and blackboards for illustrating the subjects of instruction; the method of classifying and grading the scholars of a school so as to economize time; the enforcement of rules in regard to order and punctuality; all these are matters which are being impressed upon the mind of the future teachers. And besides these things, which relate to the organization and management of schools, they are carried through a regular course of instruction in western learning, so far as it can be imparted in the Japanese language. The Arabic system of numbers and computation, which possesses such advantage over the Chinese system as to make it certain that it must supersede it, is taught to them.

They receive instruction in the elements of western science and in the history and geography of the great commercial nations with which Japan has such intimate relations. Much remains here still to be done.

Higher text-books than have yet been prepared are needed to enable the students to carry their studies still further. They must have a longer and more varied experience in the methods of modern teaching. That experience should run through not only the grades of a primary school, but should include those of the middle school as well. To this end the training-school attached to the normal school, which has been of such service in the education of the teachers, should be enlarged and carried as rapidly as possible up into the grades of a middle-school-course. The teachers will there have both a better education themselves and have the means of developing their talents for teaching in more varied and difficult branches. From my observations of the operations of this institution and the wide field of usefulness in this direction, I unhesitatingly pronounce it the most promising work in which the department of education is engaged, and I bespeak for it the fostering care and the cordial support which it has received in the past.

And I equally desire to commend the new enterprises of this kind which have already been commenced in other parts of the empire; one in Ō'saka, in the third grand school-district, and another in Miyagi, in the seventh grand school-district. The system on which these institutions are established is the same as that at Tokei, and, if they are conducted with equal intelligence and energy, may fairly be expected to furnish equally valuable results. The teachers for these new institutions are selected from those who have already finished their course of training in the Tokei normal school, and they will bring to their task, it may be hoped, the spirit which they receive from the parent institution.

As the training of native teachers is, in my estimation, the most direct and the most rapid means for reforming the system of education in Japan, I may be pardoned for pressing earnestly the duty of making every effort for this end. It is possible, it seems to me, not only to train up by means of the normal schools a body of new teachers, thoroughly qualified for the new work required of them, but also to do something towards helping the present body of teachers to prepare themselves for doing in much better ways their tasks. To effect this, we may employ a method which has been found efficient in other countries. This consists in calling together the teachers in any conveniently-situated district of country, and for a short time submitting them to a course of instruction in regard to ways of teaching and in new branches of study. The best graduates of the normal school under the supervision of the superintendents and inspectors might be employed to carry out this plan. Each ken in a grand school-district might thus be visited in succession, the teachers in that ken all be summoned together at the kencho, their schools in the mean time being suspended; and for the allotted time, say, one month, they may be formed into classes under the normal teachers, and by them be instructed in the way they in turn are to teach their scholars. The methods of using the reading-charts and blackboards and the new text-books may readily be explained; they may be shown how to classify and arrange their schools so as to save themselves much time and labor; they may learn the importance of making and enforcing proper rules and regulations; and, finally, they may imbibe some of that spirit of progress and improvement which they see in the apostles of this order of things. After a training of this kind, even for a short time, it may readily be seen with what new spirit and energy and intelligence they would go back to their former work.

EDUCATION OF WOMEN.

I come now to a branch of my subject which I am well aware has already received from this department very earnest consideration. Yet its importance and the urgent necessity for early action in reference to it will, I trust, justify me in referring to it here. I mean female-education.

The importance of educating the women of a country cannot be over-rated. To them are necessarily intrusted the care and training of children in their earliest and most impressible years. The influence which they exert is not merely due to the direct instructions which they give them, but the example which they present to them in their manners and conversation. If, then, the future men of the nation are to be inspired with the best motives and be guided by the best principles, the mothers must first be educated up to the standard. The home-life of a country depends upon the women. To make this happy, the women must be so educated that they may understand and sympathize with the plans and pursuits of their husbands and brothers. In Japan, as elsewhere, a distinction has always been made against her in distributing the benefits of education. It is time to place her upon the same level in privileges of education which the men of Japan have begun to claim for themselves. Hence the present efforts to advance female-education deserve the encouragement of all friends of Japan.

In various parts of the empire we find both public and private institutions designed to give a better education to females than their old schools were intended to give. It is a great pleasure to me to refer to the foreign school for girls under the care of this department now in operation in Tokei. It is creditable alike to the department and the directors and teachers. It may well be taken as the nucleus for a much larger institution, which may extend the same advantages to a much larger number.

At present it only accommodates day-students, and can only, therefore, be resorted to by those living in the vicinity. Larger grounds and buildings are needed for it, so that besides day-students the institution may admit girls to reside in it. In the home provided the resident students could learn not merely the usual text-book-studies, but also something of home-life and home-occupations.

As it has always been found in all western nations that females are the best teachers of children, it seems very desirable to make use of their agency in carrying forward the education of the country. They have more tact and patience than men in dealing with children and know better how to render them the assistance they need in their education. But, in order that women may be fitted to undertake the work of teaching, they must first be trained for it. And hence it becomes a duty of the department of education to provide some adequate means of preparing a corps of female teachers. To effect this, it may be possible to employ an expedient which has been successfully used in Europe and America. This consists in connecting a normal department with a well-organized school of the primary or middle grade. For example, let the plan be tried in connection with the girls' school near Hitotsubashi. Here are classes of girls pursuing the studies of the primary grade according to the new methods. In no long time there will be classes of the middle grade as well. It would be an easy and natural step to form here a class of young women who desire to prepare themselves to become teachers. The first step would be to give them some preliminary education in the new subjects of study prescribed for the schools, and then, when prepared for it, they may be admitted to observe the methods employed to teach the classes of the girls' school. And, finally, they may be employed to teach the classes of the school as a preparation for their teaching after graduation. The same system would be adapted to them as has been successfully employed in the normal school. The plan would have all the advantages of an independent normal school, besides being better fitted for a small number of applicants. If the normal branch at any time became too large to be thus provided for, it would be easy to separate it from the girls' school and establish it as an independent institution. For several years this would not be necessary.

The first step, then, in carrying out these plans for female-education, would be to enlarge the buildings and grounds occupied by the girls' school in order to give room for a greatly-increased number of scholars. Provision should be made to admit also a considerable number of pupils as residents in the buildings. This would allow girls from a distance to enjoy the advantages of the school. Proper arrangement for their care and education, not only in branches of study, but also in home-accomplishments, should be made. At the same time a normal class should be established, larger or smaller, as the case may be. They must have the best of instruction, at first in the necessary studies, and then, as soon as prepared, in the methods of teaching.

The code of education adopted by this department and published during the year 1871 has in its principal features commended itself to the nation. In foreign countries the nature and object of this code were to some extent misunderstood. It was in many cases regarded as a system which, having been once adopted, was immediately in all its details to be put in operation. Such a course would have been utterly impracticable, and was indeed never contemplated. The code was an outline of a system to be carried out as the circumstances of the empire would justify. The realization of the scheme in all its parts must necessarily be the work of many years, and experience may suggest many modifications in the practical working and details. Much has already been done. Seven out of the eight grand school-districts contemplated in the code have already been organized, and in each the superintendents and inspectors are engaged in hastening forward the organization of schools and in introducing into them improved methods and apparatus of study. Their work thus far has chiefly had to do with the establishment of primary schools, which must precede and create a demand for institutions of a higher grade. In this work there has been much to impede and discourage. The plans and objects of the educational department have been in many places misunderstood by the people. The old teachers have in many cases been averse to the introduction of the new methods. Communities have in some cases been unwilling to submit to the additional burdens of taxation which the support of schools required and in other cases have shown an utter apathy in regard to the subject. These obstacles have required the utmost persistency of the superintendents to overcome, and they have been compelled to travel from ken to ken and from town to town, to explain and encourage and assist in the organization of the schools. It only requires a consideration of the difficulties of the work to make the progress thus far made seem most encouraging and satisfactory. The future character of the work to be done can readily be foreseen. The work of establishing and remodeling schools throughout the grand school-districts must go on as in the past year. The new methods of instruction and the use of improved text-books and charts must be explained to the teachers, and their introduction pushed forward. And while this goes on the establishment of higher schools must be encouraged. There are many important centers of population where men of enterprise and wealth are to be found. Such communities must be encouraged to organize institutions of a higher grade. Buildings and grounds should be secured, and, if possible, permanent endowments, so that they may be placed on a stable footing. Such institutions would be of so much advantage to the communities in which they are located that the leading citizens may very justly be urged to give them their countenance and support.

Wherever schools of this kind are already in existence, it is the plain duty of the department of education to give them encouragement and help. It has been the policy of the department in many of these institutions to defray the expense of foreign teachers where these seemed desirable.

The presence of these representatives of western education in the interior districts has done much, not only to improve the education, but to stimulate the native teachers. I cannot avoid feeling that it is of the utmost importance that the schools and colleges in other parts of the empire should not be neglected in comparison with those of the capital. General interest in education can only be maintained by distributing institutions of learning in various central localities. To require students to be sent to great distances, and to incur great expense in obtaining their education, will always prevent any considerable number from being educated. The presence of a college in a community stimulates a desire for education. While, therefore, it is without doubt a wise policy to establish a small number of institutions of the very highest rank, it is equally a wise policy to distribute those of a second and lower rank in all available localities. Nor must it be forgotten that institutions of learning are in their nature like plants, which must have a regular growth. They cannot, like a house, be built of their full size at first; nor can it always be predicted where they will grow the best. Circumstances unperceived at the time may influence their prosperity. What seemed a favorable location may turn out unfavorable, and where least expected the college may take root and grow. In establishing the higher institutions contemplated in the code of education, therefore, too much influence must not be allowed to mere geographical positions, but, wherever there is the proper soil and atmosphere, there the college must be planted.

The growth and prosperity of the institutions of learning in Tokei are justly a subject of pride and satisfaction to the department. Nearly one thousand students are now gathered in the imperial college at Hitotsubashi. The organization and equipment are rapidly becoming what its position would demand. There are in it completely-organized schools in all the three great languages—English, French, and German. The teachers are chiefly men devoted to their profession, and the progress of the students may be fairly compared with that in similar colleges elsewhere. The buildings into which it has only recently been removed, and whose inauguration was rendered memorable by the presence of His Imperial Majesty the Tenno, are among the finest in the empire. It is my conviction that, under its present director, whose education and residence in America and Europe give him exceptional fitness for the position, the university will continue to win, in a higher degree, the respect of men of learning and the confidence of the nation. It will still require the continued care of the department in providing it with the best attainable professors, in procuring apparatus and books, and in fitting up its laboratories and museums. Its internal regulations are already undergoing changes which will render its instructions more efficient, the health and comfort of the pupils more secure, and the intercourse of the students, professors, and directors more satisfactory.

The medical college and hospital, also established in Tokei, may be here referred to as among the most important educational institutions under the charge of the department of education. The foreign professors of this college are all Germans, and they have engaged in their work with characteristic energy and thoroughness. The institution has been opened about two years, and much work of a preparatory kind has been done. The students who thus far have been prepared to engage in professional studies have of course been limited in number, but now the students who have been undergoing a preparatory training are beginning to enter upon their professional course. It is believed that the Japanese have a real aptitude for medical studies, and not a few have already, by studies at home under foreign physicians and abroad in medical colleges, attained a very considerable knowledge in medical science and art. The success of this medical institution will, therefore, put this most important branch of science upon a firm basis. There are, by the latest reports of the college, 68 pupils pursuing the principal medical course and 157 the preparatory course, making a total of 225. It must be stated that the buildings now occupied by the college and hospital are most unsuitable. The grounds are low and unhealthy, and hospital-patients are often very injuriously affected by the miasma. It therefore becomes important to make all possible haste to provide the new buildings and increased facilities which the department has already in contemplation.

In concluding this report, in regard to the subjects which under my commission are intrusted to me, I have only to offer two additional suggestions. The first is, that full and reliable statistics in regard to all school-matters are most important aids in prosecuting the work of this department.

I know the extreme difficulty of obtaining this kind of information and the commendable efforts employed by the officers of the department in endeavoring to collect it. The form for the school-statistics provided in the code of education is perhaps too complicated to be easily filled up. It might be possible to obtain more satisfactory responses from the different fus and kens, if the information called for were of a simpler kind. At least the repeated efforts of the officers and the general diffusion of information concerning education will make the task of collecting these statistics more easy in succeeding years.

My only remaining suggestion has reference to the subject of text-books, as used in the foreign-language-schools of the empire. The selection of books has in most cases been made at the suggestion of the foreign teachers employed. Some of these selections have been excellent and some have been unfortunate.

Each new teacher has thought it necessary to insist upon the use of his favorite text-book and to discard the one his predecessor had used. In the same school may sometimes be found the same branch of study taught by different teachers from different text-books. It amounts to a serious inconvenience in these cases, where a pupil is to be transferred from one class to another or where a whole class is to be advanced from one teacher to another. It certainly would be an important step in this matter if the department of education should issue a carefully-selected list of books which should be permitted to be used in the schools under its charge. These lists should be made after consultation with the experienced and trustworthy professors in the several departments of study. From these lists of approved text-books the directors of the schools should be required to make their selections for their classes and should be required to pursue, whenever possible, uniform systems throughout all the classes of their schools. These books should not be unnecessarily changed, nor, on the contrary, ought they to be so fixed as not to permit the introduction of a new book on any subject whenever it is plainly an improvement over the former ones.

In addition to this, the time when each book will be wanted should be known some time in advance, so that means may be taken to procure the necessary supply, and thus the class not be compelled to put up with an unsuitable text-book merely because no other can be had.

These considerations make plain what has become an urgent necessity in such extensive and advanced institutions as the Japanese university at Tokei.

Heretofore it has been thought sufficient to keep the statement of the organization and courses of study of these institutions upon the Japanese records of the department and of the school. But great advantages would arise from the publication of such a statement in the principal foreign language in which the education was conducted.

Such a statement should give the different divisions of the school, the departments of instruction, with their professors and teachers, the courses of study, the conditions of admission and graduation for each, the text-books and books of reference to be used, and the terms of study and vacation, together with the rest-days and holidays. A knowledge of these facts would assist both teacher and pupil. Knowing in advance how much time was to be allotted to each subject and what subject was to be taken up next in order, they could more intelligently employ the given time to the accomplishment of the required result. The directors, too, knowing in advance the books which will be required for the succeeding terms, can make suitable arrangements for procuring the necessary supply. Such a statement, if issued also in Japanese, would make known to the public the educational privileges which the institution affords, and would bring to its doors the youths who are in search of learning.

All of which is respectfully submitted.

DAVID MURRAY,
Superintendent of Schools and Colleges.

DEPARTMENT OF EDUCATION, *December* 31, 1873.

151–152

APPENDIX A.

The foregoing article by Mr. Griffis and the official report made by Dr. Murray to the Japanese educational department give the latest statistics accessible to this Bureau of the present condition of education in Japan.

The following summary of the school-law of Japan is extracted from the Report of the United States Commissioner of Education for 1872. This proposed law was substantially adopted, and, in accordance with its provisions, schools have been established throughout the empire as rapidly as circumstances would permit.

[From the Report of the Commissioner of Education for 1872.]

JAPAN.

[Absolute monarchy, (empire,) area, about 156,604 square miles ; population, about 35,000,000.]

Minister of Public Instruction, OKI.

Through the kindness of Mr. Mori, Japanese minister at Washington, we are enabled to give an outline of the new Japanese school-law, which, though perhaps not yet actually carried out, will, no doubt, soon be in force.

AIM OF THE NEW SCHOOL-LAW.

There have been schools in Japan for many years, but, from their imperfection or misdirection, they benefited the upper classes only. Farmers, mechanics, traders, and women were left in ignorance. Even among the upper classes education was very imperfect, and more devoted to art, literature, and useless discussions than to anything practical. The new school-law aims at leaving none in ignorance in any class, male or female.

HIGHEST EDUCATIONAL AUTHORITY.

The management of educational affairs throughout the whole country shall be in the hands of one central authority, the department of education.

EDUCATIONAL DIVISIONS OF THE COUNTRY.

It is proposed to divide the empire into eight grand divisions, called collegiate divisions. Each division has a central office, located in some large city, with an officer in charge.

The eight grand divisions are made up of 72 provinces and 3 cities. Each grand division or collegiate district is divided into 32 academical districts, each to contain a middle or high school, and each academical district is subdivided into 210 school-districts, each to contain one school. There being 256 academical districts, the whole number of school-districts is 53,760. The exact localities of the school-districts are to be determined according to the population and convenience of access.

SCHOOL-ADMINISTRATION.

There shall be appointed in every academical district by the local authorities from 10 to 13 directors, (superintendents,) each to superintend and control from 20 to 30 schools. The

153

salary of these superintendents shall be paid out of the fund derived from local taxes. If this is impossible, it shall be paid out of the treasury of the central government for the present.

Every child, male and female, of all classes, is to be sent to school from the age of 6 years, and must attend school long enough, at least, to finish the course in the elementary schools.

The rules and by-laws of all schools, public and private, must be submitted to the educational department every year, as also a report of the number of scholars and their progress.

Every collegiate division shall have one bureau, with a director and a sufficient force of clerical assistants, who shall watch the progress of the scholars and observe the practical working of the system. In consultation with the local authorities, the director may so modify or amend the rules as to suit the particular locality, but such amendments must be limited to unimportant matters and be reported to the department of education.

The director of each collegiate division shall transmit all the reports from the school-superintendents to the department of education, where these reports will be printed for the public use.

DIFFERENT KINDS OF SCHOOLS.

There are to be three classes of schools, viz: great learning, (superior:) middle learning, (secondary;) and small learning, (elementary.)

ELEMENTARY SCHOOLS.

The different grades of elementary schools are common schools, schools for girls, village-schools, charity-schools, private schools, infant-schools, evening-schools, and schools for imbeciles, &c.

Infant-schools are for children under 6 years of age, both male and female.

Private schools must have a license.

Charity-schools are for the children of indigent parents.

Village-schools are to be established where the population is sparse, and in these schools the rules may be somewhat modified to suit the condition of the people.

Evening-schools may be provided for those who cannot afford to attend school during the day.

The schools for girls, besides the regular studies, will embrace in their course some of the domestic arts especially appropriate for females.

The common (public) schools shall have two grades, the lower and upper.

In the lower grade the following branches shall be taught: Spelling, writing, conversation, vocabularies, reading, morality, letter-writing, grammar, arithmetic as far as division, instruction by lectures upon health, outline of geography, outline of natural philosophy, gymnastic exercises, singing, (the last-mentioned not for the present.)

In the upper grade the following subjects will be taught: Outline of history, geometry, trigonometry, outline of botany, chemistry, physiology. According to the wants of particular localities the following four subjects may be added: One or two foreign languages, book-keeping, drawing, and constitution of government, (political economy.) The lower grade is for children between 6 and 9 years and the upper for those between 10 and 13.

SECONDARY SCHOOLS, (MIDDLE LEARNING.)

In the secondary schools, (academies,) scholars are admitted who have received the education prescribed for public schools; and these shall be divided into two grades, upper and lower.

Lower-grade academies will teach the following subjects: Japanese language, arithmetic, writing, geography, history, foreign languages, natural philosophy, drawing, ancient Japanese words, geometry, algebra, book-keeping, natural history, chemistry, moral science, physiology, constitution of government, statistics of the country, music, (the last not for the present.)

Upper-grade academies will teach the following subjects: Japanese language, foreign languages, natural philosophy, trigonometry, ancient Japanese words, geometry, algebra, book-keeping, chemistry, moral science, surveying, political economy, zoölogy, botany, geology, mineralogy, mental philosophy, astronomy.

The lower grade is for scholars between the ages of 14 and 16 and the upper for those between 17 and 18.

Private schools which receive a certificate giving permission to teach an academical course may be called private academies.

Agricultural academies are those specially designed for instruction in agriculture.

Academies for foreign languages are for those who are to enter into commercial business. All the schools which teach languages only may be placed in this class.

Commercial or business-academies are purely for commercial purposes, and shall be established in cities.

Industrial academies shall teach all kinds of industrial arts.

SUPERIOR SCHOOLS, (GREAT LEARNING.)

These schools will teach professional branches, viz: Logic, literature, law, and medicine.

NORMAL SCHOOLS.

Normal schools are to be established to provide the teachers required for the public schools.

TEACHERS.

Teachers in the public schools are to be selected from those above 20 years of age, irrespective of sex, who have a certificate that they are graduates of a normal school or have graduated from an academy.

Teachers in academies must be over 25 years of age and must present a college-certificate of graduation.

Teachers in colleges must have obtained the title of "professor."

SCHOLARS AND EXAMINATIONS.

All scholars are required to go through the regular course; and in passing from one grade to another they must be subjected to examinations. Examinations must also be undergone before passing from one class of schools to another.

Poor scholars of decided ability will be pecuniarily assisted by the government, and obliged to refund the sums advanced in course of time.

STUDENTS ABROAD.

All students sent abroad at the public expense shall be under the control of the central department of education. There shall be two classes of students sent abroad; one shall be called freshmen, or the second class, and the other the first class, the former to be selected from among the graduates of academies and the latter from among the graduates of colleges. In order to become a student abroad an examination is to be passed and certificates of good moral character must be produced. The limit of the period for students abroad of the second class shall be five years, and that of the first, three years. The number of second-class students is limited to 150 and that of the first class to 30. While abroad, such students will be under the supervision of the ministers resident in the respective countries.

GENERAL EXPENSES FOR EDUCATION.

The public money for the purposes of education shall be exclusively controlled by the department of education. The government will assist as much as possible all classes impartially in gaining an education.

The public support of education shall be in accordance with the following conditions for the present:

1. For the salaries of foreign teachers and other incidental expenses.

3 B

2. For buildings and repairs of school-houses and colleges, books and apparatus, &c.
3. For academic buildings, repairs, books, apparatus, &c.
4. For the educational fund to be advanced to poor students.
5. For the expenses of the various bureaus of school-superintendents.
In every class of schools a tuition-fee has to be paid.

The following interesting account of the condition of affairs in Japan, shortly after the enactment of the school-law, is taken from the admirable official report of Mr. Watson, Her Britannic Majesty's secretary of legation at Yedo, Japan. This report, which was presented to Parliament in June, 1874, is dated November, 1873, and has but recently been published. The provisions of the law and the detailed courses of studies for the different schools given by Mr. Watson have been omitted, as the summary in the Report for 1872 contains all the details that seem now desirable, since the statistics furnished by Mr. Griffis are of later date than those given in Mr. Watson's report.

JAPAN.

[Report by Mr. Watson, Her Majesty's secretary of legation at Yedo, on the present educational systems of Japan.]

Sir H. Parkes to Earl Granville.

YEDO, *December* 29, 1873.

MY LORD: I have the honor to forward a report which has been drawn up by Mr. Watson with great care on the present educational system of Japan. It details the measures adopted by the government since they entered on a course of educational reform based upon foreign principles and it describes the beneficial results that can already be pointed to and the prospects that may be anticipated in the future.

I think I may add to the completeness of this account by inclosing a series of four papers on the foreign and native teachers, the Japanese students, and the Japanese educational officials. These papers have been written by the same gentleman who supplied the description of the normal school embodied in the report, and it is only due to him to say that his personal experience of the subject enables him to furnish a description of the working of these new educational institutions which is as accurate as it is attractive.

I have, &c.,

HARRY S. PARKES.

———

[Inclosure 1.]

Mr. Watson to Sir H. Parkes.

YEDO, *November* 30, 1873.

SIR: In accordance with the existing regulation which requires that statistical reports shall be drawn up yearly by Her Majesty's secretaries of legation, I have the honor to lay before you the following notes and observations in regard to the present state of education in Japan. I have tried to take advantage of such sources of information as I had access to, with the view of arriving at a just estimate of the actual working of the new Japanese educational system and of its results up to the present time, but I need scarcely say that there are many obstacles which stand in the way of compiling a correct report on the subject in question. In Japan the science of statistics is in its infancy; and the difficulty of obtaining information on any special subject is greatly increased in the case of one who, like myself, is dependent on others in communicating with other persons in the Japanese language.

Although the study of the English language seems in a large degree to have occupied the attention of so many Japanese students, it is nevertheless the fact that there is a great difficulty in the way of finding even an indifferent Japanese interpreter of English; and I have thus been prevented from making inquiry into some details which, under other circumstances, I should have tried to investigate. I have, however, received every assistance from the Japanese secretary of this legation, Mr. Satow, and likewise from the Japanese interpreter, Mr. Aston, whom I have to thank for being enabled to lay this report before you.

I propose to state in it, first, in what the general system of Japanese education now in force consists, specifying, so far as I can, the sources from which the youth of Japan are deriving instruction: and, secondly, to make such observations as may seem to be warranted respecting the progress of western manners and ideas in the dominions of the Mikado.

PART I.

About sixteen months ago, a law was promulgated by the imperial Japanese government, which decreed that there should thenceforth be established 53,760 schools in Japan, there not having been, up to the date of the promulgation of this enactment, any national educational system in the Japanese Empire. Instruction was formerly conveyed in Japan, as it was among the ancient Greeks, by men of learning to their individual followers.

Since the promulgation of the new law above referred to, many schools have been established in all parts of the empire; but this law, as is the case with many other legal enactments of the Japanese government, has, up to the present time, been only partially carried into effect. To what extent schools have been established in Japan, I shall endeavor to show

The following are the more prominent provisions of the law in question, and they explain the manner in which the necessary funds are to be provided, with the objects of organizing and maintaining the proposed school-system.

*   *   *   *   *   *

[Here follow eighty-nine sections of the school-law, which are omitted, as they are given substantially in the preceding summary taken from the Report of the United States Commissioner of Education for 1872.]

LXXXIX.

The education-department will have the sole control of the appropriation for the schools. (Abstract.) It must be, however, understood that as education is for the benefit of the individual, the cost ought not to be paid out of the imperial taxes, but should be paid by the people. At the same time it is at present too early to throw the whole burden on them, and the government will therefore assist.

The government will, in no case, provide food and clothing for students.

The only expenses which will be paid by government in whole or part are—

Salaries and expenses of foreign teachers.

The cost of building high schools and that of providing books and instruments; the same rule will be observed for the middle schools.

Allowances to students in foreign countries.

Expenses in aid of the school-district, to wit, 90 yen (dollars) per 1,000 of the population, or for all Japan the sum of 295,527 yen 61.1 cents.

Then follow a number of forms and forty-three more regulations for the guidance of students in foreign countries.

As the above law was only promulgated in the seventh month of the year 1872, it might be presumed that its extensive provisions would not, as yet, be found to have been carried into actual effect to their full extent; it is rather a matter of surprise to find to how great an extent they have, within so short a time, been complied with. According to the statement of Mr. Tanaka, the enlightened Japanese vice-minister of public instruction, the following is the result of the official inquiries which have recently been instituted by the government on this subject, namely, that throughout Japan there have been established 1,799 private schools and 3,630 public schools; total, 5,429. At these schools there are now under instruction 338,463 males and 109,637 females, making a total of 448,100 ; but to the above numbers, which do not include the higher schools, may be added, Mr. Tanaka considers, some 30,000 other persons who are also now under instruction, making in all nearly 480,000 persons, or, if there be 33,000,000 of inhabitants in Japan,[*] 1 in 68 of the entire population.

Mr. Tanaka was careful to point out to me that the government did not mean to enforce the compliance with the provisions of the law above given to any greater extent than local circumstances might seem to render advisable, but that it should rather be looked upon as a model of a state of things which the government desire shall eventually be attained to.

The educational establishments now actually in operation in Yedo are, so far as I have learned, the following, namely :

The "Dai Gakko,"[†] or University, which includes several separate colleges for the study of medicine, jurisprudence, philosophy, and mining, as also a polytechnic college. The veterinary, commercial, and agricultural colleges, as likewise the college of arts, have not as yet been opened.

The "Go Gakko," a school for instruction in foreign languages ; several private schools, designed likewise for imparting instruction in foreign languages ; the "Shi Han Gakko," or normal school for the instruction of Japanese teachers ; a principal female school ; several preparatory schools ; and certain establishments in connection with some of the public departments, which are designed for imparting knowledge of special subjects.

To describe all of these minutely would occupy a very large space. It will, I think, convey a sufficient general idea of the system of education now being pursued in Japan if I give a detailed description of the course of instruction as observed at certain establishments, to which I shall subjoin the opinions of some gentlemen who are qualified to form a fair estimate of the progress which has been made up to the present time by Japanese pupils in their respective studies.

The following are the statistics of the college of medicine and surgery, which was opened on the 4th of September, 1871, at Yedo :

(1) A preliminary school, in which German and Latin, mathematics, chemistry, natural philosophy, natural sciences, geography, and history are taught. The course—for the present, two years—is to be extended gradually to three and six years.

(2) The college (academy) proper, in which medicine and surgery in all their branches are thoroughly taught, both theoretically and practically ; as also, for the present, German, chemistry, natural philosophy, and natural sciences.

The prospectus (*Studienplan*) is calculated on a course of six years, at the end of which the students will be entitled, after having passed an examination, to a doctor's diploma and government employment.

(3) To the college will be added in the autumn of 1874 an apothecary-school, the students for which will be obtained from the preliminary school ; course, three years. It is the intention to some of the qualified doctors for the purpose of being sent to Europe to complete their education either as specialties or as professors for the college.

The teaching is conducted independently by the German professors, without any interference on the part of the Japanese authorities. The readings take place in the preliminary school in German by means of interpreters, but in the college proper they are conducted among the more advanced students without interpreters. New admissions and distributions take place in the autumn ; age of admission, nominally 16 years.

In addition to the regular students, a number of Japanese doctors have hitherto been admitted for the purpose of qualifying for the requirements of the native hospitals. Their education, of course, is incomplete and one-sided.

This kind of teaching will be discontinued. The number of scholars for the present is as follows :

Qualified subdoctors or assistant doctors.. 30
Academicians, first 35

---

[*] The estimated number of people in Japan as stated in the census recently taken is 33,089,777.

[†] The word here translated as university must not be understood as corresponding in too strict a sense to a European university.

Academicians, second 33
First-class preliminary school 53
Second-class preliminary school 51
Second-class preliminary school 43

Total 245

The students are supplied with board, lodging, clothing, fuel and light, from the institution. The instruction is free, and the students receive, by way of loan, the necessary books and instruments. or, if they wish to buy them, they will be charged cost-prices. For this they pay a monthly contribution of $10. If they cannot pay, they can wait till they have received their diploma and government-employment, when one-fifth of their salary may be deducted until the debt is paid. Should they be unable to pass their examinations as doctor or be dismissed before they have completed their studies, they will be liable to serve the government in some subordinate capacity until the debt is redeemed.

Professors: Dr. Muller, staff-surgeon, major of the Prussian army, for surgery, and as oculist and accoucheur; and Dr. Hoffman, staff-surgeon Prussian navy, for internal medicine.

Directors of the institution: Dr. Doenitz, for anatomy and physiology; Dr. Cochins, for chemistry and natural philosophy; Dr. Heilgendorf, for natural sciences and mathematics; Dr. Funk and Mr. Holz, for languages; and Mr. Nieuwerth, apothecary.

The following account of the working of the normal school for the instruction of Japanese teachers was recently contributed to the Japan Mail by a gentleman who has practical acquaintance with that establishment.

"The Shi Han Gakko, or Tokei Normal School, is one of the schools under the education-department in Tokei and is designed to fit Japanese young men to be teachers in the schools of Japan. These young men will teach in their own language, according to western methods and with discipline. The Shi Han Gakko is, therefore, a training-school for Japanese teachers.

"The buildings now used for the purpose are in the northern part of the city, about a mile from the Imperial College, and are situated within the grounds of the old Chinese College, close by the temple of Confucius.

"The two divisions of the school are the academic and the normal. In the former, Japanese young men receive a good education and are instructed how to teach after the manner of foreign teachers. They thus receive as good a subjective education as a professional teacher ought to have, and are instructed in the best methods of imparting their knowledge to others and how to manage a class of scholars. In the latter, the Japanese young man is actually given a class of boys and girls, and, under the eye of a skilled foreign teacher, learns to instruct his pupils, to put his theory into practice, and to govern according to the discipline of American schools. To the description of these two, academic and normal, we now proceed.

"There is only one foreigner connected with the institution, and it is by his advice, supervision, and work that the organization and results have been so. He is a professional teacher of several years' experience in the United States, and was formerly the superintendent of the San Francisco High School, and was afterward in the Imperial College in Tokei for about one year.

"The normal school was established in order to obtain a supply of properly-trained teachers for the new graded schools, which, according to the scheme of the education-department, are to number over 50,000. It was begun in the following manner:

"A class of twenty-five picked young men was formed and began the study of English. They were fresh and unspoiled and learned with great rapidity. At a certain point, as soon as they could understand the ordinary expressions of their foreign instructor, the study of English was dropped. They had been taught so far simply for the purpose of becoming familiar with the manner in which a foreign teacher instructs a class and maintains discipline. It was something very different from what they had been accustomed to. In Japanese schools the teacher usually takes a class of six or less and instructs each scholar separately. They know nothing of reciting in concert, and the discipline in a large school

159

is, in respect of noise and irregular attendance, about equal to that of the very worst country-schools at home.

"As soon as these young men had learned how a class in a foreign school is taught and managed, little children were brought in, formed into classes, and the young men set to teach them. This they did in the presence, under the eye, and by the aid of their foreign instructor. The latter did not know Japanese, nor did he need it.

"At present there are one hundred and fifty young men in training to be teachers. They are from almost every section of the country. According to the rules, the prospective teacher must not be over 25 years of age, but no applicant is very severely cross-questioned as to his years. They are arranged into classes of about thirty each and are first drilled in the correct pronunciation of their own language. As they come from all sections of the empire, most of them use provincialisms and a style of pronunciation that varies greatly from the standard language of the capital. The importance and significance of securing a uniform pronunciation will be appreciated by all readers of this article at once. Starting thus, the young men begin a regular course of study in and by means of Japanese and Chinese, which is to be equal to that of a good high school in the United States. They study foreign learning and science by means of text-books translated from English into Japanese. At the start they are supposed to have a fair knowledge of Chinese and Japanese, and to be assured of this they are subjected to an examination before they can enter the school. Of all the young men who apply only about one-third of the number are chosen.

"The very best Japanese teachers procurable are set over these young men as instructors. The foreign superintendent visits the class-rooms at intervals, to see that the general foreign methods and discipline are observed. No unnecessary talking, no smoking, no awkward positions, nothing that would be out of place in an American school, is allowed.

"It must be kept in mind that these young men learn no English whatever. They use the following text-books, translated into Japanese, printed and bound in Japanese style. Willson's series of reading-books, four in number; Robinson's series of mathematics, comprising simple and advanced arithmetic, algebra, mensuration, and geometry; Monteith and McNally's System of Geography; Cutter's Anatomy and Hygiene; Willson's Outlines of Universal History.

"Most of the above books have been already translated, others are in progress, and the series will comprise those in an average American high-school use.

"The young men study and recite five hours daily. They number at present one hundred and fifty. They are divided into relays of six each, and take their turns at teaching the boys and girls for a week at a time. At present the turn of each young man comes round about once in three months.

"In getting his education proper the young man is simply a pupil. Besides his actual acquirements of knowledge, he is taught how to impart his knowledge and how to manage a large class. He is taught how to use the slate and pencil, globe, map, phonetic and pictorial charts, blackboard, &c, as a child would use them. He is actually taught how to teach properly before he leaves his Japanese teacher. This is his theoretical training as a teacher. For his practical training, for his induction into the actual work of teaching and managing a class, the normal department exists. For success in class-teaching, such as is pursued in the best foreign schools, three qualifications are essential: 1. Knowledge of what is to be taught; 2. Ability to impart that knowledge; 3. Power and skill to govern a class.

"The young man gains the first requisite in the academic department, to prove whether he has the second and third; and to gain them he enters the normal department.

"To serve the double purpose of a field of practice for the young men who are to be teachers and of a primary school for the instruction of children between the ages of 6 and 9, there were brought in last April one hundred boys and girls who had never before been taught, and hence were unspoiled. They are now arranged into five classes and are under the instruction of the young men who have been already trained in the art of teaching. It is proposed to increase in a few weeks the number of pupils, and to put fifty in a class, as in the primary schools of the United States. A new brick building in foreign style is also to be built. There will then be ten classes of fifty pupils each, making five hundred in all.

"The children are to be taught, through the primary and secondary, up to the average

American grammar-school-course. There are to be eight grades of study and the course will require six years for completion. Boys and girls study together, the former being in the majority. The average age of the pupils is 8 years.

"The apparatus for these pupils consists of Willson's series of readers, translated into Japanese; slates and pencils; blackboards and chalk; improved copy-books for writing; text-books of arithmetic, translated from the English; and a system of charts, both phonetic, ideographic, numerical, and pictorial. The charts number thirty in all and contain about eight hundred objects. No. 1 contains the "kata kana," which is learned by the eye and ear and with the voice, slate and pencil, and pen and paper; No. 2, the "hiragana," learned in like manner; No. 3, the Chinese numerals up to ten; No. 4, the "niigori" marks and letters; No. 5, the Arabic numerals; No 6, the Roman numerals. Other charts contain the Chinese, Arabic, and Roman numerals up to one hundred, and combinations up to one thousand are made. The pupils are practiced in counting from one to one hundred to one thousand, backward, forward, skipping one, two, three, four, five, &c.; then by odd and even numbers, and in every possible way, until they can handle numbers as easily as words. Mental and written addition, subtraction, and the multiplication-table, adding up columns of figures and notation, are next taught. The pictorial charts contain colored drawings of the most familiar objects of every-day-life, with the Chinese ideograph beside them, so that the name of the object and the sound and form of the character are fixed in the memory at once. This differs from the Chinese and Japanese method, which is to learn the sound first without regard to the meaning of the character. By the method of charts the eye and ear assist each other. Next follow the names of vegetables, household-articles, furniture, &c., and from these the pupil is gradually led to more complex objects, such as flowers, trees, rarer animals, clocks, thermometer, &c. From those the ascent is to abstract terms, feelings, the relations of life, uses of various parts of the body, weights and measures, lines, geometrical forms, angles, colors, &c. Practice in reading and writing Chinese and Japanese consumes a large portion of the time. It is intended to study the geography and history of Japan first, and then that of other countries. In due course the other elementary branches of learning will be introduced.

"The scholars under this system not only make very rapid and sound progress, but the young men acquit themselves with great credit as teachers. The progress already made is more than encouraging; it is astonishing.

"The foreign instructor is engaged in overseeing both departments, the academic and the normal. Any dereliction of duty, any breach of discipline, or slovenliness of work, or lack of attention, is at once corrected. Under the easy and pleasant, because natural and graded, methods pursued in this school, learning is made almost as attractive as playing, and the boys and girls seem to like it as much. The teachers are taught that the very first requisite of a good teacher is to interest his class.

"The children are kept in school five hours a day, but ten minutes for play are allowed at the end of each hour. Gymnastics outside and calisthenics in the class-room are practiced by the young men in the academic and by the teachers and children in the normal department and primary school.

"The young men who finish their course of study and succeed well in the actual work of teaching and managing large classes, are to be given a diploma by the Mombusho, certifying their acquirements and ability. Those who cannot succeed as teachers or fail to become good students will receive a certificate specifying what they have done—in other words, a partial diploma.

"The charts and translated books referred to above are now made by hundreds and are sent out to be used in the various schools throughout the country. A good Japanese grammar, by a native scholar, is said to be in preparation, but of this we cannot speak with certainty. It is proposed to establish other normal schools as necessity arises and means allow."

The government of Japan, like that of nearly all civilized nations at the present day, is composed on the departmental system, and there is a minister for each department. These ministers, however, are not necessarily cabinet-ministers, though they happen to be so at the present date. These departments are foreign affairs, treasury, justice, education and religion, public works, army, navy, imperial household, and colonization, (for Yezo and Saghalin.)

All these departments employ a certain number of foreigners for educational purposes, but the principal one is the Kobusho, or department of public works, which comprises the following subdepartments, namely: (1) railways, (2) telegraphs, (3) light-houses, (4) mines, (5) surveys, (6) engineering, and (7) mechanical.

At the survey-department there are twenty-one Japanese students; at the engineering there are thirty students.

In connection with the department of public works is the engineering college; principal, Henry Dyer, C. E., M. A., B. Sc., University of Glasgow.

Professors for the general and scientific course: natural philosophy, W. E. Ayrton, University College, London; mathematics, David H. Marshall, M. A., University of Edinburgh; chemistry, Edward Divers, M. D., F. C. S., Queen's University, Ireland; drawing, Edmund F. Mondy, A. R. S. M., Royal School of Mines, London; English language and literature, William Craigie, M. A., University of Aberdeen.

Secretary, William Craigie, M. A.

Modeler, Archibald King.

General assistants, George Cawley and Robert Clark.

TECHNICAL COURSE.

It is expected that this course will be completely organized in two years from this date, August, 1873.

I. OBJECT OF COLLEGE AND CONDITIONS OF ADMISSION.

This college has been established under the orders of the minister of public works, with a view to the education of engineers for service in the department of public works. The course of training will extend over six years; during the first four years, six months of each year will be spent at college and six months in the practice of that particular branch which the student may select. The last two years of the course will be spent wholly in practical work. By this alternation of theory and practice, the students will be able during each working half year to make practical application of the principles acquired in the previous half year. The system of instruction will be partly what is usually termed professorial and partly tutorial, consisting in the delivery of lectures and in directions and assistance being given to the students in their work.

The session will last from 1st October to 31st March, with the intervention of certain holidays, marked in the calendar. During the months of April, May, and June a short preparatory session will be held for students entering the college, when the elementary parts of the scientific course will be taught, so that the students may be able to enter more thoroughly into the work of the session proper. At the end of the summer-session certain subjects will be prescribed for study during the vacation, and in these an examination will be held in the beginning of October. The college-vacation will take place during the months of July, August, and September. During these months first-year students will be employed in the work-shop. Students of the second, third, and fourth years will serve from 5th April to 26th September of each year as pupils, under a properly-qualified engineer.

Admission to the college will be obtained by competitive examination, for which all Japanese subjects between the ages of 15 and 18 years, inclusive, and of sound constitution, who can produce satisfactory testimonials of good moral character, will be eligible.

The competitive examination will embrace the following subjects: (1) reading in English; (2) writing to dictation; (3) arithmetic; (4) elementary geometry; (5) elementary algebra; (6) geography; and (7) rudimentary physics.

The examination in these subjects will, for a session or two, be of the most elementary kind, but the standard of admission will be raised year by year, till it attains that of European schools.

II. FORM OF APPLICATION AND OBLIGATION OF SURETIES.

Being desirous of studying engineering, I beg that permission be granted me to enter college after due examination.

I am, &c.,

(Signature.)
(Province of applicant)

(Date.)

Declaration of successful candidate.

As a successful candidate for admission to the Imperial College of Engineering, I hereby bind myself to conform, in all respects, to the prescribed regulations, and, after six years of combined theoretical and practical training, to serve seven years under the government.

(Signature.)

(Date.)

Declaration of surety.

A. B. being a successful candidate for admission to the Imperial College of Engineering, I hereby declare myself responsible for his strict observance of the regulations and for his serving seven years under the government, after the completion of the prescribed six years of theoretical and practical training.

In the event of his violating any of the regulations, I likewise bind myself to act according to the rules laid down for such cases.

(Signature.)

(Date.)

OBLIGATIONS OF SURETIES.

In the event of a student leaving college before he has finished the entire term of training or his resigning his appointment under government before the completion of the stipulated term of seven years, his surety will be required to pay all expenses incurred on the student's account up to the date of his leaving.

The same law applies to the surety of any student who may be expelled, either for insufficient proficiency in the examinations or for misconduct.

The surety is also held responsible for the cost of any damage done to government-property within the college by a student.

III. BRANCHES OF TECHNICAL EDUCATION.

It is the aim of the college to train students in the following branches of technical education: (1) civil engineering; (2) mechanical engineering; (3) telegraphy; (4) architecture; (5) practical chemistry; (6) mining; and (7) metallurgy.

The student will be allowed to select a special subject; but, when that selection has been made, he must strictly adhere to the course of study herein laid down.

The student's whole course of training may be thus divided: (1) the general and scientific course; (2) the technical course; (3) the practical course.

IV. GENERAL AND SCIENTIFIC COURSE.

This course forms the foundation of the technical applications and is common to all the special divisions into which the students are separated. It includes (1) English language and composition; (2) geography; (3) elementary mathematics; (4) elementary mechanics, theoretical and applied; (5) elementary physics; (6) chemistry; and (7) drawing, geometrical and mechanical. This course will be taught during the first and second sessions of the student's career at college.

V. TECHNICAL COURSE.

Each student will be required to attend the special technical course for that branch of engineering which he selects. These special courses are as follows:

(a) Civil engineering.

(1) higher mathematics; (2) higher natural philosophy; (3) civil engineering, with special reference to the branch selected by the student; (4) mechanical engineering; (5) geology; (6) surveying; and (7) drawing-office.

(b) Mechanical engineering.

(1) Higher mathematics; (2) higher natural philosophy; (3) mechanical engineering, with special reference to the branch selected by the student; (4) naval architecture; (5) physical laboratory; (6) drawing-office; and (7) workshop.

163

(c) *Telegraphy*

(1) Higher mathematics; (2) higher natural philosophy; (3) surveying; (4) strength of materials; (5) chemical laboratory; (6) physical laboratory, with special reference to electricity; and (7) drawing-office.

(d) *Architecture.*

(1) Surveying; (2) strength of materials; (3) geology; (4) architecture and building-construction; (5) drawing-office; and (6) free-hand-drawing.

(e) *Practical chemistry.*

(1) Surveying; (2) geology; (3) mineralogy; (4) physical laboratory; and (5) chemical laboratory.

(f) *Mining.*

(1) Geology; (2) mineralogy; (3) geological surveying; (4) practical chemistry; (5) machinery; (6) mining; and (7) drawing.

(g) *Metallurgy.*

(1) Surveying; (2) geology; (3) mineralogy; (4) practical chemistry; (5) metallurgical laboratory; (6) machinery; and (7) drawing.

The technical course will be taught during the third and fourth sessions of the student's career at college.

VI. EXAMINATIONS.

The progress of the students will be tested by periodical examinations and by assigning values to drawings, reports, &c., executed by them at college, as well as to work done by them during the summer in the department of public works.

At the end of the second year a general examination will be held in all the subjects of the scientific course, in which a certain minimum of average proficiency will be required. Should any student fail in attaining this qualifying standard, as fixed from year to year, he will not be allowed to proceed to the technical course.

At the end of the fourth year an examination will be held in the technical course. The proficiency of the students will be recorded in the order of merit, as determined by the aggregate number of marks gained in all the subjects.

Each student who attains the prescribed qualifying standard will receive the diploma of "licentiate of engineering," (L. E.,) and will be appointed assistant in that branch of the public-works-department which he has selected.

VII. PRACTICAL COURSE.

During the last two years of the curriculum, the student will be engaged in the practice of the special branch he may have selected. At the end of every half year he will be required to send in to the principal of the college a report on the work in which he has been engaged. At the same time the student will undergo an examination in the principles and practice of uch work.

At the end of the sixth year a final examination will be held, in which the student's knowledge of the works he has been engaged in, and those of a similar nature, will be tested. He will also be required to send in complete drawings, specifications, &c., of a work on a prescribed subject.

Each student, on passing a satisfactory examination, will receive the diploma of "master of engineering," (M. E.,) and will be appointed engineer in the board of public works. The position of the student in the service will be determined by the final examination at the end of each course.

*   *   *   *   *   *   *

[Some twenty pages, consisting of regulations, schedules of studies, and examination-papers, are omitted.]

There are at present in this college, which has been very recently opened, thirty-one cadets and twenty-five day-students.

The following statement shows the complement of the Imperial Naval College, which has been established at Yedo:

rector 1
ce-director 1
ofessors 4
.vigating officers, *i. e.*, lieutenant and sublieutenants 4
.achers, first class 6
.achers, second class 4
.achers, third class 4
.acher, fourth class 1
.achers, fifth class 12
.achers, sixth class 14

    Total 51

.dents 129
.ndents at the elementary preparatory school which is attached to the naval college 69

    Total 198

The 129 students now in the college are divided under the following heads, namely:

.dents of the duties of lieutenants 63
.dents of the duties of navigating lieutenants 17
.dents of the duties of engineers 36
.dents of the duties of naval architects 13

    Total 129

The English officers and seamen serving in the college are the following: 1 commander, 'aptain Douglass, royal navy,) 1 gunnery-lieutenant, 1 navigating lieutenant, 1 chief en-
.eer, 2 engineers, 2 gunners, 2 boatswains, 1 carpenter, and 23 petty officers and seamen; al, 34.

At the elementary preparatory school there are 2 European teachers and 51 cadets.

The course of instruction followed at the naval college, as well as the discipline which is forced, is similar to those observed at the like institutions in England. The cadets wear usual naval uniform.

As the naval college was only reopened under the present direction in the course of the -sent autumn, a sufficiently long period has scarcely yet elapsed to admit of a well-based inion being formed as to its probable results; but so far everything promises favorably respects this establishment—an establishment from which Japan may derive more real vantage, from a material point of view, than from any increase of her importance as a .val power. The class of engineers in particular may prove very useful in the interests the shipping-trade of the country; and Mr. Sutton, who superintends that class, told me at he was greatly pleased with the progress so far of his pupils. He hopes that after eight-n months of study the college may send out engineers capable of working engines, .ugh it may require from six to seven years before their men become capable of repairing .achinery. Captain Douglass seems on the whole to be quite satisfied with the condition f the establishment, and Admiral Sir Charles Shadwell, who lately inspected it, expressed imself in similar terms in regard to it.

There is a naval medical school at Takanawa for the education of young naval surgeons. .s the Japanese navy is organized on the English system, so the surgeons are educated by .ro English teachers. The students average from thirty to forty in number. They go trough a regular course of study, there being a winter- and a summer-session. The great .fficulties hitherto experienced in the way of their progress have been the want of prac-.cal dissections and *post-mortem* examinations; but it is hoped that in the session of .73-'74 dissections and *post-mortem* examinations will be allowed.

INSTRUCTION OF MARINES.

In connection with the naval college at Yedo may be mentioned the system of instruction which is being pursued with the view of organizing a Japanese force of marines and of marine artillery. In January, 1871, an English officer (Lieutenant Hawes, royal navy) was employed by the Mikado's government, and charged with the duty of organizing the system of instruction and discipline to be observed in the Japanese men-of-war. He accordingly, in the first instance, arranged the complement of officers and men to be appointed to the partly armor-clad corvette Riu Jho, and selected a uniform for them. He abolished the then existing practice of having the officers and men in a ship all belonging to one clan and likewise that of wearing two swords. He was allowed to engage the services of an English petty officer who should assist him and he was required to report as to the competency for their duties of the Japanese officers whom he instructed, and who were maintained in their posts or otherwise, according to his recommendation. A regular course of instruction in the branches usually taught to this service was given in turn to each ship of the squadron, and during the course of drill on board of the Riu Jho Kan, each commanding officer of the Japanese men-of-war in harbor attended on board daily, and made notes, with a view to carrying out the same system in his ship. The officers, more especially the Satsuma men, I have been informed by Lieutenant Hawes, showed extraordinary zeal and, on an average, excellent ability.

That officer seems to think that the Japanese are likely to produce better seamen than marines or soldiers, the equality existing between men of the same class or the same clan among the latter standing much in the way of discipline. The seamen are selected from an inferior class.

The term of enlistment for marines is for five years, with the option to re-engage for two years, or the term may be for seven years and three years further. The men, in the first instance, often evaded their duties, and especially complained of being compelled to sit at meals instead of squatting; but they eventually appeared to like their new mode of life, and they have shown great capacity to become naval gunners and have well adapted themselves to the discipline imposed upon them.

The instruction of the cadets for the marine artillery has been confided to Lieutenant Brinkley, royal artillery; and the Japanese government are fortunate in having obtained the services, in this capacity, of one who takes rank among the very foremost foreign Japanese scholars.

The class of artillery-cadets numbers twenty-eight lads, averaging about 18 years of age. They are a selection from one hundred and thirty candidates and comprise members of eleven different clans, one-fourth of the whole number being from Chochiu. The selection was the result of an examination conducted by the native professors of the naval college, the election of subjects resting with the candidates themselves. The cadets, without any exception, were acquainted with the European system of notation and some few had a tolerable knowledge of the first four rules of arithmetic. The object of the instruction being a theoretical knowledge of artillery, mathematics were made the basis of the course laid down, and for the first four months, viz, from May 1, 1872, to September 1, the whole body were instructed as one class, the hours of instruction being six per diem, of which four were devoted to mathematics and the remaining two to language. The instruction has been entirely oral, the book adopted as a text-book being only placed in the student's hands when he had been entirely taught its contents. Up to the present time (November, 1873) the cadets have studied the whole of arithmetic, (except stocks, par of exchange, and duodecimals;) the first six books of Euclid, (except the fifth;) algebra, to the end of permutations and combinations; a considerable amount of language. (English;) likewise of fortification and the use of drawing-instruments; the examples worked out in arithmetic and algebra comprising all those in Galbraith and Haughton's Arithmetic, Wood's Algebra, Wrigley's Examples, the Woolwich Course, and Cape's Mathematics. No interpreters have been used and all the instruction has been given in the Japanese language. Examinations by written questions have been held monthly and half-yearly, the object of the former being to supply the place of repetitions, which are found to be distasteful to the Japanese.

The general result of the studies appears to be most satisfactory, and in some particular cases remarkable aptitude has been shown. Of the whole number of twenty-eight lads, there are not more than two, according to Lieutenant Brinkley's statement, whose diligence iight not be called exemplary, and, on the whole, their conduct has been equally good. Admitting that this progress is attributable mainly to the diligence and aptitude of the adets themselves, there yet remains a surplus which may be entirely placed to the credit of ie fact that, in the case of this instruction, it has been possible to convey all the mathematical explanations in the Japanese language, and thus to impart in a few hours a knowllge of matters which, under ordinary circumstances, it would have taken weeks to aproach, and which might perhaps never have been passed. Lieutenant Brinkley believes iat, in the present condition of the Japanese, it is quite impossible to impart to them any ctensive knowledge through the medium of interpreters. He has met and conversed with early all the best English scholars in Japan, and has no hesitation in saying that there are ot more than three or four of them whose linguistic attainments could carry them over the .nguage necessary to explain, say, the theory of variation. Moreover, he thinks it would s difficult to find a body of men so deficient in moral courage as the Japanese interpreters ow in the employment of the Government; in nine cases out of ten they will convey their wn fortuitous ideas to a pupil rather than confess that they have not comprehended the rords of the instructor.

Teaching carried on under such circumstances inevitably lapses into practical demonstraion and gesticulation; and, as the limits of these aids are very soon reached, the maxims of apartible theory lie within a very narrow compass. It has thus come to be a received fact unong Europeans that the Japanese mind is incapable of arriving at mathematical attainments, but Lieutenant Brinkley's experience leads him to give this conclusion a most unqualified denial; for although he found it quite impossible, with all pains and patience, to mpart mathematical knowledge through interpreters, yet he observed that that impossibility lisappeared so soon as he was able to dispense with interpreters. Moreover, the whole tendency of the system of education carried on among the Japanese themselves is to magnify the memory of things imparted through the senses and minify the reasoning power. "What," says Mr. Brinkley, "could be more completely technical than the acquisition of ien thousand hieroglyphics by sound and sight without a knowledge of the meaning of one? And in dealing with minds that have been thus maltreated, it becomes absolutely necessary io avoid every medium that might tempt the student away from quiet reflection and original malysis; and such a medium undoubtedly is a language that he only in a very small degree comprehends."

With reference to the opinion of Lieutenant Brinkley, as above expressed, in respect to the class of Japanese interpreters, it has been pointed out to me by Mr. Edward House, an American gentleman, who for some time held an educational post in the Kaisejo at Yedo, that a marked distinction ought to be made between the class of interpreters who are at present employed and that of Japanese youths who are being brought up as students of the English language.

The latter Mr. House states, from personal experience, to be possessed, in many instances, of an excellent knowledge of English for general purposes, although they may not be capable of accurately conveying abstruse ideas on certain technical subjects. Several letters which he showed to me, and which had been received by him from some of his former pupils, were admirably expressed.

However desirable it may be that the teacher should be capable of conveying instruction in the Japanese language, it would be quite impossible, even in the course of many years, for the Japanese government to find a sufficient number of otherwise competent instructors who should fulfill this condition.

The best practical course, as it seems to me, is that which is now being pursued, with certain exceptions, as in the case of Mr. Brinkley, namely, to urge the student to perfect himself as far as possible in the knowledge of one or other foreign language, and then for the teacher to convey instruction to his pupil in that language. In any case a large proportion of foreign words must be made use of, as the Japanese language does not contain the terms necessary for explaining many ideas the elucidation of which is requisite for the comprehension of modern science.

I may next, in connection with naval subjects, refer to the docks at Yokoska, near Yokohama. These docks are connected with the naval department, and are under the manage-

ment of M. Verny, the French director, who has under his orders a staff of French
structors. Of these, who number twenty-four, five receive salaries ranging from $250 ;
mouth up to $600; the remaining number, salaries ranging from $60 to $165 per month.

I need not describe this most useful establishment in detail, but no report on Japan
education would be complete without some reference to it. I may add that I had the
portunity of going over it with Admiral Sir Charles Shadwell, who expressed himself
being exceedingly gratified by all be saw of the system there pursued. The advant
already derived by the public from this institution will be at once apparent when it is c
sidered that but for its existence all large vessels in Japanese waters which might req
repair would have to be sent for that purpose to China.

At Yokohama there is a foundery, which is also attached to the naval department. 1
staff of Frenchmen there employed is six persons. A foundery is likewise being construc
at Yedo. To complete the statement of the principal establishments connected with
Japanese navy or mercantile marine, it is necessary to refer to the hydrographical dep
ment which has been established in connection with the admiralty. The arrangements
placing this department under foreign direction or supervision have not as yet been c
pleted, and I am thus unable to give any statistics respecting it. As the task of organi
the Japanese marine has been confided, with the above-noted exceptions, to English officers
that of setting on foot and giving instruction to the army has been intrusted entirely
French officers. About eighteen months since, a military mission, at the head of wh
is Colonel Marquerie, arrived at Yedo, and at once commenced the work of organizin
considerable military force on the French system.

The mission is composed of a colonel and seven other officers, with twenty-two suboffic
or civilian instructors in details relating to an army.

There does not as yet exist any military school under foreign direction, but I underst
that some thirty thousand men are being or have so far been taught French drill-exerc
in the different branches of an army, either under direct French instruction or under tha
Japanese instructors. On the same system eight thousand are now being instructed un
the supervision of the French officers at Yedo.

The army is not as yet by any means in a complete state of organization ; but at seve
reviews which were held by the Mikado at Yedo, when some eight thousand troops passed
review, the foreign officers then present were unanimous in expressing their approval of
general appearance of the troops. as well artillery and cavalry as infantry.

I believe that the remarks of Lieutenant Hawes, above quoted, as to the Japanese marin
with reference to the difficulties in the way of establishing discipline, are equally appli
ble to the army; but the military forces certainly present a highly creditable appearaı
when on parade.

New barracks have been constructed on the European model in different parts of Yed
and the foreign mode of life, as well as a foreign uniform, must be adopted without reser
by the troops, who are enlisted by conscription from all classes of the population.

Military bands have been organized, as well for the army as for the marines, under Fren
and English supervision, respectively ; and the Japanese have shown great aptitude for 1
ceiving instruction in this branch and still more diligence in endeavoring to master t
work set before them.

I may next refer to one or two other special educational establishments which have be
created in connection with certain governmental departments.

There is at the Yezo colonization-department a girls' school, which is presided over l
two Dutch ladies. This school is attended at present by fifty-one girls, varying in age fro
seven years to perhaps three and twenty. They are the daughters of Japanese governmet
employés in different parts of the country, some of them coming from the island of Yez
These girls are being educated and maintained at the expense of the state, and it is 1
tended that, at the end of their three years' course of instruction, they be disposed of by the stal
They are taught to write and to read the English language and some of them also study Frenc
They all likewise are taught needle-work and other branches of an elementary foreiţ
education. They study for four hours a day under the two ladies above mentioned, after whic
they go through a further course of daily instruction in Japanese, under the direction

a master and two Japanese ladies. These pupils wear the Japanese female dress, with the addition of foreign shoes and stockings. Although all of these girls are, I believe, being educated at the cost of the state, yet the school is open to the daughters of Japanese government-officials, on the payment of $100 on entrance and on the further payment of $3 a month during the three years' course of instruction. On payment of the above-mentioned sums any of these girls may be redeemed from all obligation to the state. They receive from their instructresses the character of being very intelligent, industrious, and promising.

With reference to this school, I may mention that the Empress, (who has shown a great interest in the progress of female-education in Japan, as has the Mikado in education in general,) on visiting the school a few days ago, caused her photograph to be taken in a group formed of her majesty and the two Dutch ladies who are in charge of the school, and that the latter are to receive copies of the photographs. Those who are conversant with the exclusive ideas which were formerly entertained in Japan will appreciate the change thus indicated.

There is attached to the foreign office at Yedo a school which was founded in the year 1871, with the object in view of providing for the future an adequate number of public servants (interpreters and instructors) in connection with the different branches (legations and consulates) of the Japanese department, which is presided over by the office in question. There was also at the foreign office a school for students of German and Russian, but this school has recently been transferred to the superintendence of the educational department. The former school, which is under the direction of an American gentleman, (Mr. Jourdan,) contained at first ninety pupils. The director, however, finding that number to be impracticably large for his superintendence, reduced it in the first instance by about one-half, and even this number proving to be too great, he still further reduced it until the remaining scholars, who were selected by examination, numbered only twelve. Six of these being students of the English language and six of the French, a preference was given in their selection to such youths as were at the same time best acquainted with Japanese. Their progress, though slow, has on the whole been very satisfactory. The expenses of this educational establishment, which is under the supervision of the foreign office, are defrayed by the state. It was found difficult, on first starting, to establish discipline among the pupils, but this difficulty has now been overcome. No special subject is made an object of study in the school, except in illustration of the language under study, and only one of the two languages above mentioned (English or French) is studied by any one student at the same time. Among the private schools in Yedo should be mentioned that of the Père Nicolai, a Russian ecclesiastic, who possesses an unsurpassed knowledge of Japanese and whose time is exclusively devoted to giving instruction.

Notwithstanding the general tendency of the course of education which is being pursued in Japan, it should not be forgotten that there is a conservative party in the country who follow the system of instruction as pursued among the Japanese previous to the adoption of the resolution to establish European institutions in the dominions of the Mikado.

To what extent Chinese instruction is still conveyed in the provinces I am unable to say, but in Yedo there are only ten private schools, containing perhaps thirty pupils each, at which Chinese letters and literature are alone taught.

The following is a list of the schools in Yokohama, as supplied by the governor of that port :

Schools founded by private persons... 2

Schools for children, founded by government..................................... 14

Foreign teachers are employed in the above-mentioned schools at the rate of from 50 yen (dollars) to 350 yen per month.

Teachers of the schools founded by private individuals............................ 4
(NOTE.— These four are Americans.)

Teachers of the children's schools 49
(NOTE.—These are Japanese.)

Number of pupils... 2,247

The average age of the pupils is about 10 years and 6 months.

The ordinary subjects of instruction are those tending to expand the intelligence of the pupils.

The books used are the books mentioned in the rules for the instruction of children. (given below.)

In the schools founded by private individuals the English language and moral precepts are taught.

The pupils make good progress, but by slow degrees.

Although the distinction between the schools for boys and those for girls does not now exist, still in the schools there is a separation between them. The number of boys who are pupils is 1,430 and the girls who are pupils number 815.

I subjoin the following further information respecting the schools of Yokohama, for which I have to thank Mr. Russell Robertson, Her Majesty's consul :

There are in Yokohama two or three schools for girls, one under the patronage of the vice-governor of Iseyama; one under the direction of the American Women's Union Mission, at the head of which is Mrs. Pruyn; and, lastly, the school of the Sisters of Charity.

Query. The number and nationality of teachers and pupils respectively in the schools, and likewise the general age of the latter ?

Answer. The light-house-works school has 2 English teachers; the number of pupils is somewhat under 50.

Takashimaya's (a Japanese gentleman of Yokohama) school has 2 American teachers and 135 pupils.

The school under Dr. Brown's charge has 3 American instructors and 56 pupils.

The ages of the pupils range from 8 to 24 years, with but few of them at these extremes. Their average age is about 16 years.

Q. What are the subjects of instruction and the books generally used in the school ?

A. The course pursued in the "Shin bun Kwan" under Dr. Brown may be taken as an example: daily lessons in speaking, reading, spelling, penmanship, and composition. The first object sought is to impart a knowledge of English, both written and spoken. A three-years' course of study is also marked out in geography, primary and practical arithmetic, general history, grammar, and natural philosophy. One half-day in each week is also devoted by the whole school to declamation in English, one-half the pupils being listeners and the other half declaiming, on alternate weeks.

American school-books are used in the school on Noge Hill (Dr. Brown's school) and at Takashimaya's school.

Q. What is the average capacity of the pupils ?

A. It is good. Probably the capacity of the Japanese is much the same as that of persons of other nationalities if placed in like circumstances for its manifestations.

Q. Can you give any particulars in regard to girls' school ?

A. The school on Iseyama, already spoken of, is taught in by 2 American ladies and has about 50 pupils.

There are some sixty pupils in Mrs. Pruyn's school, at No. 212. Both of these are interesting schools from the number in attendance and the progress which the pupils make in their studies. The former is the older school, and has been under very able instruction, so that perhaps the pupils are, some of them, more advanced in their studies on that account; but in both the progress made is very encouraging.

Q. Do Eurasians show any exceptional physical or intellectual qualities ?

A. The number of Eurasians is so small and they are so young that nothing special in these respects has as yet developed itself.

There are two or three difficulties which schools have to contend with in Japan. One arises from the circumstance that the Mombusho (educational department) at Yedo, which controls them, is a department which very few Japanese are competent to fill. Hence crude experiments are often tried and changes made by the department that only tend to obstruct the progress of the pupils and otherwise damage the schools.

Another difficulty is that the Japanese, who have not yet been put through a systematic course of study sufficient to show them that intellectual culture and knowledge are not to be attained by long and sudden leaps, but step by step, beginning at the beginning, are

ras to grapple with the higher studies before they have had any thorough fundamental
ing.

attended, on Monday, the 14th instant, (July, 1873,) at the examination of the pupils
inese) at the school on Noge Hill, until lately under the management of the Rev. Dr.
n, (American.) The school is known as the Shin bun Kwan.

There was a fairly large attendance of visitors, principally Americans. The governor
inagawa was present. The pupils' ages appeared to vary from 8 to 23. The school
livided into four classes—about twelve boys in the lowest or further class, some twenty
e third, eleven or twelve in the second, and four in the first.

The fourth class was examined first in reading and spelling, and the performance was
table. The reading consisted in short, easy lessons, much the same as those met with
iglish primers, and easy words were selected in spelling.

The third class was put through the same course, only of a more advanced stage.

The second class was examined in reading and in arithmetic.

The examination of the first class did not come on until a late hour, and I was com-
l to leave before it came off.

The general appearance of the scholars was characterized by intelligence, though a few
ones were scattered here and there. The very young ones seemed in most cases to be
harpest and most advanced.

Geography formed part of the examination of the second class. A blank map of the
l was hung on the wall, and one of the boys, a lad of 15, was asked to point out
ent places on the map. This he did with great accuracy, naming and pointing to the
ent oceans and seas, the principal countries, rivers, and some of the towns.

Such attention had, I think, been paid to the pronunciation of words, always a diffi-
with Japanese when speaking English. With but few exceptions, the words were
ored very distinctly.

cannot but think, however, that, with such good material, the boys might all have been
ght to a higher degree of proficiency with a better system. Thus I found many with a
rledge of English, written and spoken, that would have enabled them to read many
i, as of history, travels, biographies, &c., that would have given them a good general
ledge of subjects that all lads should know, and would, while increasing their knowl-
of language, leave on their minds a deposit which would go on increasing from day to

In the higher classes the books seemed altogether too elementary. The answers to
r questions in examinations seemed to be given with parrot-like fluency, and I was
to observe no attempt at construing sentences. I cannot but think that most of the
ers had been learned by heart and that there existed but a vague idea of the construc-
of what was learned.

It is scarcely fair, however, to attempt to criticise on the strength of the slight experi-
I had during a brief visit of three hours to the school. Whatever I might see faulty
e system, there was enough to show that great labor had been expended to bring the
s to the attainment of such knowledge as they exhibited."

r the following information respecting the Kioto primary schools I am indebted to Mr.
. Wilkinson, who visited that place in April last. He was informed by Mr. Makimura,
nce-governor of Kioto, that Kioto had been divided into sixty-six divisions and that
orimary school had been established in each division; that the householders contributed
e support of these schools; and that no school-fees were paid by the children. He was
that this arrangement had been in operation for about five years.

e visited the primary school in the twenty-ninth division or ward. The building in
h it is held is also the office and assembly-room of the ward. Here the registers are

One register is kept in which is inscribed the name of every householder in the
l. One page of it is given to each family. Births, deaths, and marriages are recorded,
also the fact of any of the members of the ward-families having left the ward to travel
side elsewhere.

is register enables the ward-officers to know all the children in the ward. An attend-
roll is kept, and when children do not come, an explanation is required from their
its.

The school-hours are from 8 a. m. till 12 noon and from 1 p. m. till 4 p. m., or seven in all daily. Of these seven hours about three are occupied in learning to write, one peating from memory, and three in learning reading and arithmetic.

The writing-room occupies nearly all the ground-floor. It is furnished with Jaj mats and low Japanese writing-desks.

Above stairs is a large room in which the pupils are taught the other branches o education. In this room are desks and benches in the European fashion.

A list of books to be used in primary schools has been published by the Kioto Fu. intended, however, to adopt the scheme of the education-department, and to exclu Chinese classics from this scheme.

Of the two books which pupils first use as reading-books, one is written in square acter and in the Chinese order, and one is written in the grass-character, with "hiral mixed.

In arithmetic the pupils learn the Japanese method on the "Soroban," and al European method. They are provided with slates and use the Arabic numerals.

The scheme of education is exactly the same for girls as for boys. The girls of one were reading, while Mr. Wilkinson was present, the book of Instruction to Street-Offic

Two hundred and fifty pupils attend this school. Their ages vary from 4½ to 12 years.

Mr. Wilkinson was informed by Mr. Nakamura that the attendance in the different se varies from 100 to 500.

INTERMEDIARY SCHOOLS.

There had been in Kioto both a superior and an intermediary school, but both had abolished by the education-department.

The material, however, for an intermediary school exists, and a new building has erected and will shortly be opened. The main feature of this school is that foreign guages are to be taught in it. The new building is arranged as follows:

Front.

French department.   German department.

Offices.

English department.   English department.

There are four buildings to be used as school-rooms, and one for the use of the officers school, not the foreign teachers. These, with one exception, are to be provided with ac modation outside. Of the four school-rooms, one is to be devoted to pupils learning Fi to pupils learning German, and two to pupils learning English. The proportion is at 130 for French, 170 for German, and 300 for English.

his school is to be opened to every person. The fee is about 2 bus (2s.) a month, or 4 ($4) a year. At present there is not any accommodation for resident pupils, but intended to provide accommodation for a few.

he pupils who are to be collected in this building are now scattered in separate schools the city.

r. Wilkinson visited one of these schools which had lately been under the superintend- of an English gentleman and his wife. It was divided into two departments. In the ' department there were 160 girls on the roll and 136 in attendance on the day of his . In the boys' department there were 131.

he hours of attendance are from 7 a. m. till 2 p. m., with an interval of one hour between ad 12 o'clock for lunch.

he girls are taught reading in the morning and sewing in the afternoon. There are lve sewing-machines in the school and two looms, but the latter had only lately been oduced.

he school-books are English. One from which the pupils read is the Illustrated Spelling Reading Book published by Messrs. Cassell, Petter & Galpin.

he pupils read in English and then translate into Japanese.

he following are the schools in the Nagasaki Ken, namely: One at which the pupils are ght by European teachers, under the direct control of the Mombusho, (educational artment.) At Yedo 65 pupils are studying the English language, of which there are 2 hers, and 5 pupils the French, of which there is 1 teacher. The pupils' ages vary n 12 to 18 years.

here are three primary schools in which foreign languages are taught by Japanese in- reters. School No. 1 has 219 pupils, of which number 198 are boys and 21 are girls, ying in age from 6 to 15 years. School No. 2 has 101 pupils, 77 boys and 24 girls. ool No. 3 has 52 pupils, 43 boys and 9 girls. These three schools are under the direct trol of the Nagasaki "Kencho."

.t the government-hospital in Nagasaki there are 41 students studying medicine under the ervision of two Dutch doctors. A Prussian has lately been engaged, who will teach e students the Dutch and Latin languages.

mong the other provincial schools which I may mention is one at Shidzuoka, in the vince of Tzuruga, which is under the direction of Mr. Clark, of the United States, and ich has about 500 scholars.

There are also a hospital- and a medical school, under the direction of Dr. Junghams, a rman North-American, at Saga, the capital of Hizen. Medical instruction is also im- rted at Kagoshima, in the province of Satsuma, by Dr. Willis, formerly of Her Majesty's ation, but I have not yet received from him the details for which I have applied respect- t his sphere of operations.

The following are the details which I have procured relative to the Hakodaté government- ool, and to the hospital and the private schools which have been established at that place: Teachers: Of English, 5, (Japanese;) of Russian, (M. Sartoff,) 1, (Russian;) of Rus- in, 3, (Japanese;) Chinese, 3, (Japanese;) arithmetic, 3, (Japanese.)

Pupils: Resident scholars at government-expense, learning English, with Chinese and ithmetic, 15; resident scholars at private expense learning English, with Chinese and ithmetic, 13; resident scholars at private expense learning Russian, 3; day-scholars learn- g English, with Chinese and arithmetic, 38; learning Russian, 38.

The pupils' ages vary from 8 to 21 years. There are three officers in charge. Total num t of persons connected with government-school, 125.

GOVERNMENT-HOSPITAL.

nerican doctor, (Dr. Eldridge)	1
panese doctors	5
othecaries	4
icers	3

Students, resident, at government-expense... 9
Students, resident, at private expense.. 6
Day-students.. 2

    Total connected with hospital.. 30

Private schools in the town of Hakodaté... 14
Teachers in private schools in town of Hakodaté....................................... 14

    Pupils :
Boys... 580
Girls.. 284

    Total.. 864

In the above-mentioned schools the ordinary Japanese writing and reading are taught.
It was proposed last year to extend the government-school-system at Hakodaté, but this has not yet been done further than as above stated.

To the above specific items I may append the following general observations which were made to me by Mr. Tanaka, who, I may remark, seemed to possess much acquaintance with the systems of public instruction which are being pursued in other countries and who was familiar with the name and measures of Mr. Forster.

There are, he said, at the present time 150 young Japanese who are students of medical science, 220 young Japanese who study special subjects and 300 young Japanese who are pursuing their studies abroad. At Yedo, 50 Japanese girls are being put through a course of instruction by an American lady. There are, including all, about 1,100 young men who, having completed their course of instruction, are now employed in the service of the state.

There are in all 72 foreign instructors who are employed by the educational department alone, the professional adviser of that department being professor David Murray, of the United States. There are 3 normal schools at present in operation ; one at Yedo, one at Osaka, and one at Shendai, each containing 200 scholars, who are supported by the government ; 256 schools are at present in receipt of governmental aid.

In reply to my inquiry, Mr. Tanaka said that it is the intention of the Japanese government to make education in Japan, so far as the state is concerned, entirely secular, in as far as is consistent with the fundamental tenets of the Shinto faith.

I have since learned from a reliable source that the government have resolved that, while they will not interfere with private missionary-enterprise in Japan, no Christian divine will be employed, even as a secular teacher, by the government. It would appear that they have become convinced that some reverend teachers have been imperceptibly inculcating the doctrines of Christianity into the minds of their pupils, and consequently the above-stated resolution has been arrived at. In furtherance thereof, the Rev. Dr. Brown, a United States missionary of long standing in this country and to whom the Japanese government are indebted for excellent service, has been removed from his office as teacher, as has also the Rev. Dr. Verbeck, formerly principal of the chief educational establishment at Yedo. I have been informed that all of the clerical teachers who still remain in the Japanese service have likewise received notice of the termination of their respective engagements.

I may add that, in all of the educational establishments where pupils are being educated at the expense of the state, these pupils are required to conform their habits to western usages. Instead of being allowed to squat on mats, they must sit on chairs, and work, and eat at tables. While no material alteration is attempted in the costume of girls, the boys are, in many cases, as for instance in the naval college, required to adopt foreign uniform or clothing, and all are supplied exclusively with food prepared in the European manner and are attended by European medical officers.

PART II.

I have been led to devote a large space to the first portion or this report, which does not, I think, admit of being very much abridged ; but I do not propose to enter into detail with respect to the second portion of its subject, namely, the indirect agencies which are now in operation tending to the spread among the Japanese of the ideas which influence the conduct of western nations; it will, I think, be sufficient if I merely specify those which I conceive to be the more prominent among them.

It will be supposed that the introduction of steam as a motive-power is exercising the same great influence on the habits and ideas of the people of Japan that it has exercised on those of all countries into which the steam-engine has found its way. There is now a line of railway of eighteen miles in length in operation between Yedo and Yokohama, and the average number of persons who travel upon it each day is about 4,000. Another line of about twenty-three miles will be opened in the course of a few weeks, which will connect Hiogo with Osaka, and the preliminary surveys have been undertaken with the view of prolonging the latter line to Kioto. The habit of punctuality and a greater regard for the value of time cannot fail to be the results in the case of a large portion of the population of the introduction of railways into Japan. The line now in operation has so far been worked with complete success, and its advantages are thoroughly appreciated by the Japanese of all classes.

Steam-vessels, too, now ply in the Japanese waters in many directions. Not to mention the various foreign lines whose vessels touch at the Japanese ports, and by which the Japanese have the opportunity of traveling, a considerable native steam-mercantile fleet, speaking, of course, comparatively, has already sprung up. Native companies have recently been formed in various parts of Japan with the object of organizing a steamer-coasting-service, and there is, likewise, a steamer-service on Lake Biwa. As the companies above referred to are chiefly of this year's formation, it is not within my power at the present time to state to what precise extent this marine has been developed; but so far as it has been so, I believe it is chiefly, though not entirely, conducted by the Japanese themselves, even the engineers on board of a number of vessels being Japanese.

Another proof of the progress of new ideas in this country is the astonishing extent to which, in the course of the last three years, the use of wheeled conveyance has become general. Not only in the cities, but also along the whole length of the high roads, where the nature of the country admits of the use of wheels, the "jinrikisha," or wheeled chair drawn by one man, has been introduced, and the saving of power which is implied by the substitution of this vehicle for the old "kago," or litter borne on two men's shoulders, may be thus estimated. It requires, on an average, the labor of two men to convey a traveler in a "kago" over thirty miles in a day, whereas one man is capable of drawing a light weight after him in a "jinrikisha" over thirty-five miles in like circumstances in the same time. One man with a "jinrikisha" can, therefore, do 2¼ times as much as could be done by one man with a "kago."

The cost of a day's traveling for a Japanese in a "kago" is, I am informed, 5¼ bus, (shillings;) that of a day's journey in a "jinrikisha," 3¼ bus. The original cost of a "jinrikisha" is about $15.

Another influence which may be expected to make itself felt in the course of time in Japan is the introduction of telegraphs, but up to the present time the introduction of the telegraph has by no means been attended with success similar to that which has followed the introduction of the railway, owing, I believe, partly to the absence of the sense on the part of the Japanese clerks of the necessity of punctual attendance to their duties, and partly, also, to the confidence in their own powers, which induces them so often to take to pieces instruments which they as often find themselves incapable of reconstructing.

Foreign machinery has, to a certain extent, though not to a large extent, been introduced into Japan, as well by private persons as to be used in mines and other establishments belonging to the government.

The demand for foreign machinery would be greatly increased, and the consequent production of wealth in Japan greatly augmented, but for the reluctance of the Japanese to permit foreigners to carry on industrial operations on their own account in the interior of Japan. The Japanese are anxious to exclude foreigners as far as possible from competing with them, while at the same time they are, as yet, incapable of successfully conducting many branches of industry without foreign aid. I have shown in a previous report how, for instance, in the case of the island of Yezo, immense facilities for the production of wealth are being utterly wasted, owing to the palpable mismanagement of the Japanese officials and the narrow-minded commercial policy of the government.

As this jealous policy is no doubt in part based on the conviction that, were foreigners admitted into the interior of Japan and to take part in industrial operations, the gains of Japanese merchants would be curtailed, I fear a long time will elapse ere the policy in question is likely to be reversed. It is defended by the government on the ground of their dislike to extend the extra-territorial jurisdiction which now prevails over foreigners within the treaty-limits. The judicial system of Japan and the ways of thinking of its people are so entirely different from those of western nations that, even were the code of laws set in force which is now in course of preparation under the superintendence of some French and other lawyers, it must, I think, be expected that many years will elapse before the Japanese as a nation will have acquired the power of understanding law and administering justice which would be accepted as such by the citizens of western nations, and consequently before the latter would be inclined to renounce extra-territorial jurisdiction in Japan.

In the mean time it is gratifying to know that one result of the intercourse of western nations with Japan has been a very marked tendency to mitigate the severity of the penal laws of the latter country. Many modes of punishment which Christian nations look upon as being barbarous have either been entirely abrogated or are now only applicable in a much smaller number of cases than it was formerly the law that they should be. This tendency to milder legislation applies equally to religious toleration. The edict forbidding the profession of Christianity, which formerly was posted throughout this empire, ought now not to be seen. Such would be in accordance with the decree of the imperial government; and if, in point of fact, the edict in question may still be found standing in a great many localities, although the fact subjects the government to the imputation of neglecting to enforce its own orders, yet the liberal intention of the government with respect to religious toleration can scarcely be called in question, since some 1,900 banished Christians (all that remained of those driven from Urakami in 1869) were, in the spring of this year, sent back by the government to their homes, and since numbers of Japanese are now permitted to attend churches regularly and without molestation at Yedo, Yokohama, Hakodaté, and elsewhere.

Another proof of enlightened legislation is to be found in the recently-promulgated enactments prohibiting compulsory servitude of every description and annulling all immoral contracts for service of this nature, such as those by which in many thousands of instances girls were bound down by their parents or guardians to serve for a stated number of years in brothels.

Another educational influence which is now actively at work in Japan, and the power of which may be expected to extend itself from day to day, is the native press that has sprung up throughout the country.

There are in Yedo the following journals, namely, 18 newspapers, some of them published daily, others every fifth day.

The three with the greatest circulation are the Nishinshinjishi, a daily paper of which on an average 1,500 copies are sold: the Tokionichinichi Shimbun, a daily paper, with a sale of about 860 copies; and the Shinbunsashi, a daily paper, with a sale of 860 copies.

Of the other 15 journals some appear daily, and the sale of each is about 200 copies.

There is likewise a provincial press.

A postal system has likewise been organized throughout the country.

I need only refer to one or two more indications of the progress which western civilization has already made in Japan.

A system of light-houses has been established under European direction, which is being extended along the entire circuit of the coasts of these seas.

Quays have here and there been constructed.

Lock-hospitals have been introduced at several of the treaty-ports.

A mint is in operation at Osaka, under the admirable management of Major Kinder, at which the total number of pieces passed for issue last year was 26,151,206, and the real nominal value $29,154,633, showing an increase on the previous year of 10,647,228 in the number of coins, and the increase, in value, $8,076,022. And while, on the one hand, the custom of wearing arms on the part of the two-sworded class has so far been discontinued that, in the course of a long walk in Yedo or in that of a long drive in at least many, if not in all, parts of the country, only about two persons wearing the sword are generally to be met with, on the other hand, the social consideration of the merchant, in comparison with that of the formerly-privileged classes, has been raised to an extent which those who were conversant with the former social hierarchy of Japan would be almost unable to realize.

In bringing to a conclusion a report on education in Japan, I think I ought to point out that, while very many educational influences are at work, such as I have endeavored to specify, yet it cannot reasonably be expected that the progress of newly-introduced western customs and ideas should work a revolution throughout an entire race in the course of even a few years. According to all experience a sufficient length of time must be allowed for at least one freshly-educated generation to arise before any radical, general, and lasting change may be expected to take place in the ideas and habits of the mass of a people.

The introduction of foreign manners, as that of foreign costume, which has come about in Japan, is as yet mainly confined to members of the court or of the official classes; the domestic and industrial habits of the bulk of the people remain as they were in former years.

I have, &c.,

R. G. WATSON.

Sir H. PARKES.

————

[Inclosure 2.—Extracts from the Japan Mail.]

EDUCATION IN JAPAN.

I.—FOREIGN TEACHERS.

In the articles descriptive of the educational institutions of the Japanese capital which have lately appeared in the columns of this journal, we confined ourselves to plain statements of facts, refraining from comment or criticism, so far as it was possible to do so. We shall in this and future numbers point out what we believe to be defects in the system of education in Japan and shall endeavor to show how they may be remedied. The statement will not, we think, be challenged by any one competent to judge it, that, in a system of education, the most important instruments are the teachers.

We need spend no platitudes in this article to prove the vast influence of a teacher upon his pupils. We presume all our readers to be familiar with the significance of the teacher's position in England and America. The very mention of such names as Ascham, Arnold, Temple and Nott, Wayland and Hopkins, will do more to serve our purpose of magnifying the teacher's calling than columns of argument. The simile of the bended twig becoming the inclined tree is photographed on the memory of all whose speech is English. When, however, the teacher and the pupil are of different civilizations, the tremendous significanc of the position of an instructor of the young is manyfold enhanced. If a people living under a state of national life which is fixed and not liable to change need the best of teachers, what shall we say of the Japanese? We see a people busy above all else in destroying their past. We see their old ties broken, their old sanctions weakened, and their old virtues defamed. To their foreign teachers more than to any other men, they look for help and guid ance. Upon them may depend the future of this nation; whether of sound growth and fruitful maturity, or of reaction, stagnation, and decay. We must be pardoned for attempting to sketch an ideal of the true teacher, such a one as should be charged with the well-nigh sacred office of assisting to lead the rising generation of Japan into a new life.

Among the qualifications of a teacher of Japanese youth, that of a sound moral characte r should be the first. Among a people who put etiquette above morality, the foreign teacher, as a representative of a different, and, as he believes, a better, civilization, should put morals before etiquette, and be himself a moral man. In truth, honor, devotion to duty, purity of life and personal chastity, temperance in eating and drinking, loyalty to his country, to her principles and best traditions, the spurning of all shams, the refusal of all bribes, detestation of flattery, and disdain to pander to the vanity of his employers, the foreign teacher should be firmly established. He should have a sensitive pride in his profession; he should magnify his calling; he should have thorough command of his tongue and temper; he should conscientiously perform his work, shirking no disagreeable parts of it and never allowing his enthusiasm to flag under the monotony of daily and often very prosaic toil in the class-room. Though these virtues should be cultivated and exemplified more than etiquette, yet in this the teacher should not be found wanting and should be as polite as his scholars. The interchange of daily courtesies, patience with halting pupils, when the spirit is willing but the brain is weak; the avoidance of all personal epithets and coarse language and attention to the amenities of dress, posture, and conduct, are absolutely necessary and help to make the teacher what he ought to be. Besides having these moral and social virtues the teacher should be a real teacher. He should be trained to his business or at least have a natural fitness for it. He should know and understand his subjects and should use the best methods of imparting knowledge, of disciplining the minds of his pupils, and of arousing in them that thirst after and enthusiasm for learning which is worth vastly more than a loaded memory or any number of acquirements. The teacher should be a student of human nature and should suit his ministrations to the varied characters, dispositions, infirmities, or excellences of his pupils. A teacher of such an eager and inquisitive people as the Japanese should have no narrow mind, but should be well read and should keep abreast of the general knowledge of the day.

All this a teacher can be and a large part of it he ought to be. If the Japanese can understand what manner of man our ideal teacher is, (which we doubt very much,) they can get men like him; but not with money alone. * * * [A statement is made that in the eagerness of the Japanese to secure teachers of foreign languages they took persons who could speak a language as teachers without regard to their previous training or personal character.]

We wish to show that the teacher's profession is a high and honorable one, and the Japanese are in duty bound to respect it. If they wish to prove that their educational "system" is not a sham and that all their grandiloquent assertions abroad that they believe "education is the basis of all progress," let them do as civilized nations do and put the proper man in every place in their schools now occupied by an improper person. Let them cease to dishonor the teacher's calling by hiring men who in mind and morals are unworthy of their post; let them learn to value a good instructor more than they value jewels; let them cease from the wretched economy that prompts them to pay niggardly salaries which must of necessity deter the right men from their class-rooms: let them offer such contracts as do not make a true teacher blush to sign; let them cease to make regulations which no man with any self-respect can or will obey; let them put competent officers in charge of their schools. If such are not to be found let them confess their ignorance and ask help from men whom they can trust. Until they do these things their system of education, now so admired by those who remain in benevolent ignorance abroad, will not cease to merit the contempt of those who know the facts.

II.—NATIVE OFFICIALS.

The idea of a system of education presupposes a teacher, corps of instructors or faculty, and a governing body of trustees, directors, or council of regents. The names of the two bodies may vary in different countries, but, for the successful administration of a large school or university, a body of directors is needed. The functions of instruction and government must be distinguished, even though in small private schools; for instance, they may be united in the same persons.

That the office of governor or director is a very important one; that a competent person in that office is a co-worker with both teacher and pupil, and an indispensable instrument in a system of education, we need not here argue to prove. We suppose our readers to be familiar with the educational systems of their various countries.

It would be an anomaly as strange as it is happily rare were a school of any reputation in Europe or the United States to have a board totally unfit for and inexperienced in their duties.

To state the case a little more strongly, suppose these directors were profoundly ignorant of what ought to be studied and of what the studies proposed really were; suppose them ignorant of the language in which they were taught, and that for any glimmerings of light they could catch they were dependent upon very poor interpreters; and, finally, that, not withstanding these apparent drawbacks, these directors aspire to make all the rules for teachers and scholars, to choose all the studies, to direct all the operations of the school, and to have all the teachers obedient to their will and pleasure; if our readers can grasp such a monstrous conception as this, then they can understand the educational system in Japan. We have not drawn upon our imaginations. We are stating simple facts. We refer not to one institution alone. From Nagasaki to Hakodaté, and from Kanagawa to Tokei, our conception and the reality are the same.

There is a great gulf of difference between the sentimental ideas with which people at home regard their fellow-countrymen who have been called to Japan to be teachers and professors and the actual facts. The gentlemen in the educational service of Japan, when at home, were informed by their polite Japanese friends that if they would come to Japan they would be treated with the highest honor. "No position is more honorable than the teacher's," and "if our teacher dies we mourn for him as for our father," &c., were the honeyed words which the Japanese, eager to attract an instructor from his honored post to their own "college" or "university," used. The teachers came from many countries, and great was the honor which Japan received. The American and the English newspapers were full of her glory. Every one, including the happy dupes themselves, believed all the fair promises of the flatterers. "The teacher's position is an honorable one in such highly-civilized nations as England and the United States. How much more so in Japan?"

But Japan is the land of surprises. Strange to say, the Japanese official does not like the professional teachers, the college-bred men, the professors. He thinks they are obstinate, rebellious, excessively troublesome. Foolish men that they are, they expect to have a voice in the government of the school and even want to regulate the studies. Worse than that, they sometimes ignore the "rules" and trample under foot the first instincts of a "yakunin." It is a fact, but not a wonder, that the native official has a chronic antipathy to a genuine teacher, and prefers the man whom he can pick up and whom he can rule, for does he not hold in his hands the power even to grant contracts?

We need not criticise. The statement of fact is sufficient for our purpose, which is to prevail on the education-department to reform a state of affairs which has become a by-word and a reproach to those who wish them well and the target for the jests and scorn of the unconcerned. Of all the strange chapters in the history of education, the attempts of native Japanese officials to conceive and carry out a scheme of foreign education form one of the most curious and comic chapters. Indeed, our greatest fear is that our statements will not be believed. However, if the Scotch proverb says truly, "seein's believin', but feelin's the naked truth," we are but setting it forth.

We shall speak of the schools of the capital, not merely because they have been the most conspicuous victims of the empiricism of native officials, but because that unique phase of human nature called "yakuninerie" has there received its highest development and brought forth its choicest fruits. We shall take comfort in the thought that, in spite of its baneful effects, nay, under its very shade, the thirst for education among the youth of this land is still unquenched.

Since the first beginning of foreign education in Tokei, the native officials placed over the foreign teachers by the education-department have been utterly unfit for their post as directors of schools of foreign education. Refusing to put any powers in the hands of their foreign servants, they spent their time chiefly in hampering their efforts, impeding progress, and apparently endeavoring to stamp all hope and energy out of the pupils. The typical "yakunin" sat in the chair of ruler of the highest educational institutions in the land, and sits there still.

As the Japanese have the curious custom of changing their own names several times
ing their life-time, true to their customs they changed the name of their chief school
times in little more than as many years. Something deeper than instinct actuated the
this phase of their educational policy. Each change involved appointments, promotions
a vast amount of clerical, carpenters' and contractors' work. In a native official's ey
man can be a "yakunin" unless he makes many rules. Of these rules, there has not
nor is there the faintest likelihood of there being, any end. To pass away time, the so
officials—we need specify no one place of their achievements—showered rule after rule,
lation after regulation, so fast that one poetically inclined was reminded of autumn-le
Many of them were so unnecessary, so unreasonable, and often so trivial, that the fo
teachers could not obey them. The native officials, however, varied their leisure by chai
the course of studies and adopting new ones. It was simply a matter of mensuration
Chinese characters. So many hours per week, so many square inches of paper, fill u
squares with Chinese characters, (which often mistranslate what the native official k
almost nothing about,) and the new curriculum is laid down, not to be taken up aga
several weeks. Having found out, however, that he had not attained to perfection in
cula-making; the official, believing that he had struck the right course this time, trie
other. Having thus in a few months acquired skill in making short roads to lear
gained some routine-knowledge and a faint conception of foreign education, he was
moted to a higher office in the same or another department, and a new, inexperienced
incompetent man stepped into his place.

The students had just grown used to the vagaries of one director and the foreign te
had smothered his contempt for and perhaps gained the confidence of his superior, when
one arises who knows not his own business or the characters of his inferiors.

There are two bright lines in the spectrum of this subject under examination. The t
ers and professors who know their business do it, paying little attention to such annoya
and the scholars, most of them ever eager and insatiable after knowledge, remit no dilig
and yield to no despair.

But enough of this; we have pointed out the grievous errors and abuses in one part o
Japanese system of education. It has given us no pleasure to expose them. We d
make merry over their short-comings, nor would we raise a laugh at the expense of a p
so nobly struggling from ignorance into knowledge; but we wish to show the evil
point the cure. It would be cruel and unfair to sneer at their lack of western science. We a
doing that. We simply deny their ability and fitness to be directors and head-masters
foreign instructors. We have not only felt the galling yoke of the despotism of ignor
but have seen its blight upon noble young minds and know of the fearful waste of tin
money, and of earnest effort which it has entailed upon the Japanese people and their

The remedy is simple. The chief college and the school of languages at Tokei shou
put under the care of a competent and faithful foreign master. In every one of the Japa
schools for foreign education, the teacher, if a professional instructor, as he ought to
should be given power to choose the studies and to govern his classes.

There is plenty of work for the native official to do. He should be warden over the pu
He might have charge of the pecuniary affairs and he should have the control of all th
outside of educational matters, strictly so called. In short, he should attend to wha
knows about better than the foreign master, professor, or teacher, and with what he kr
next to nothing about let him not meddle.

It cannot be objected to this that the proper men who can be trusted are not to be for
The Japanese know and have in their employ men of blameless life and faithful labor. 1
can easily get from abroad, or can find on their soil, men whose record is known. 1
need not complain that no foreigner understands their needs. They can easily limit the
thority of their teachers and principals. If necessary, these men would give bonds for
faithful performance of work and the abstinence from what their employers think will
flict with the peace of the empire. The foreign educator does not wish to usurp the t
urer's office, to make proselytes, to change the social life, dress, food, or etiquette of
Japanese young men. In these things he is but an adviser, to give his counsel when a

or needed. He should have no power in these things, except so far as is necessary for discipline or the inculcation of western language and science. But whether native or foreigner, let each man be master of what he professes to teach or pretends to perform.

III.—JAPANESE STUDENTS.

While almost nothing is known abroad as to the truth concerning "native officials," and but little about "foreign teachers" in Japan, something is known and much has been said about Japanese students. Most persons have formed extremely favorable opinions about them. In order to treat our subject fully, we must examine these opinions.

Japan had been so long sealed from the world that foreign nations regarded it as a land whose people might possess the average nature and capabilities of Asiatic nations. Indeed, it might be said that, of the mental and social status of the Japanese nation, the ordinary westerner knew nothing. When, then, a few years ago, there came upon America and Europe a sudden influx of polished and eager travelers and of bright, earnest, and very polite students, the tremendous reaction of opinion oscillated into extravagant laudation and unbounded generosity. The *entrée* into homes and families closed to ordinary comers was theirs. Every social encouragement and educational aid was given them. The rules of most of the schools abroad were broken or made exceptions to in their favor. Nothing seemed to be left undone to make these oriental strangers feel at home and to give them as complete an education as good schools, trained ability, and faithful labor could secure. When civil war broke out in Japan there were several Japanese students in America and Europe. While those in Europe returned home, those in the United States were supported by the private contributions of American gentlemen and retained in school and home until affairs in Japan were settled and remittances arrived.

The Japanese students abroad were so earnest, diligent, polite, quick and eager to learn that they won plaudits even from those unused to praise. The president of a Massachusetts college said he wished to have a Japanese in every college in America to teach the undergraduates good manners. The principal of a Connecticut high school said publicly that a body of young men of such powers of observation as the Japanese students exhibited could not be found in America. The journals of England and Germany, as well as of America, stinted no praise of the graceful Orientals in their schools. Several of the Japanese students won distinctions at English, German, and French universities and at American colleges, and others would have assuredly done so had not the grave come between them and the goal. All these things tended to produce the opinion held by some that the average Japanese is even superior to the average American or European student.

In order to judge the matter fairly, let us take a full view of the facts.

In the first place it must be borne in mind that the Japanese students abroad are the very best representatives of Japan's intellect, of high social position and hereditary culture. They are not the average of her sons. They are her best by nature, inheritance, character, and selection. They do not go abroad indiscriminately from the mass of the people, as, for instance, American students flock to Germany. About 90 per cent. of the Japanese students abroad are of the *samurai* class, and were carefully chosen on account of their character and ability. By no canon of justice would it be fair to compare them with the average western student. Further, in very many cases, extraordinary facilities were given them to procure tutorial aids which the student abroad could not obtain. Again, those students who won distinctions or prizes were in every case students of special courses or subjects ; they did not compass the entire curriculum prescribed for the regular university- or college-students. Not one Japanese student has yet been graduated from the full course of a European university or an American college ; though that they are fully able to do so, if they take the time, we entirely believe. We have stated these facts simply to get at the truth and to allow the subject to be seen from all sides. We have not spoken of the great obstacles to be surmounted by the Japanese student abroad ; we suppose them to be known and felt. It is because they are known that extraordinary merit attaches to the success of the Japanese students abroad.

We shall now endeavor to give our impressions of the actual status of the Japanese student, his capabilities, and his mental complexion. These impressions, it is but fair to state, have been formed after five years' constant instruction of Japanese youth, both abroad and in this country.

We can treat our subject best by making a contrast between the Japanese and the western student. The first great point of difference which the foreign instructor notices in Japan is the almost utter absence of any necessity of enforcing obedience. In his own country he knows that among his most important needs are physical vigor and a stern will. To govern a class of boys of the Anglo-Saxon race is like holding the safety-valves of as many steam-engines. To control a class of boys at home requires the expenditure of an amount of nervous force that many teachers do not possess, which injures the health of many and makes a day's toil in the school-room severe even to exhaustion. It has become almost a maxim in the United States that no one should be a teacher more than fifteen years of his life. No wonder that the nervous and dyspeptic pedagogue or the worn professor at home looks upon Japan as the teacher's paradise and hails the Japanese student as the embodiment of his ideals. To leave the boys of his own land, who feed their bodies with beef and their brains with the ideas that have made England and the United States what they are, whose constant struggle is to repress their rebellious physical energies, and to come among the quiet, sedentary, and docile race of these islands, is a grateful relief to the nerves of the worn teacher. When, however, the instructor has youth and exuberant health and spirits, he would gladly exchange a little of the easy submissiveness and docility for a little fire and energy, which he misses so much.

The professional teacher comes to Japan with great expectations. In all the typical virtues of the scholar he expects the young native to be superior. In his work the teacher hopes to find the happiness that is to compensate him for his exile from home and congenial associations.

Nor are his expectations too great or doomed to disappointment. He meets as noble young men as ever thirsted for knowledge. He finds that he has but to point the way and his pupils follow. Their perfect trust and confidence in him are as beautiful as their diligence is commendable. It was once said that Japanese youths were fickle, that they changed teachers as often as the moon her form. If this were true in the past it is not so now, at least in the government-schools. The Mombusho have acted energetically in this matter throughout the country and deserve all praise for having enforced their rules requiring a student who enters a school to remain for a term of years. More than this, the very native officials, whose ability to plan and execute a scheme of foreign language we deny and whose utter unfitness to make rules for foreign teachers and to have charge of educational matters, properly so called, we think we have demonstrated by facts, have shown themselves fully able to be the strict wardens and the kind and careful governors of their students in all that is outside of educational matters. In the government of the students, after they leave their foreign instructors, we see little to condemn and much to commend. The native official has demonstrated his fitness to administer discipline and to provide for the daily need of the boarding-pupils and to administer the economics of education. He has done his work, the cost being considered. far better than a foreigner could do it. From the chaos of three years ago, to the order, regularity, and discipline of to-day, is a change that must be as gratifying to the Mombusho as it is to their foreign servants.

The Japanese student of the present no longer scrapes along, untidy in summer and shivering in winter, but comes to school clad as comfortably and appears with as much dignity, all the facts considered, as a critic could desire. The schools of Tokei are rapidly approaching that point when the precision, punctuality, and discipline observed will challenge comparison with the best of Europe or America.

The average Japanese student is bright, quick, eager, earnest, and faithful. He delights his teacher's heart by his docility, his industry, his obedience, his reverence, his politeness. In the course of five years the writer can remember no instance of rudeness, no case of slander, no uncanny trick, no impudent reply, from any of his many pupils. Some teachers complain of deception and lying practiced by their pupils; with them we cannot from experience join. Indeed, in almost all the gentler virtues, in abstinence from what is rude, coarse, and obscene, the average Japanese school-boy is rather the superior of his *confrère* in the west. In the hereditary virtues of respect to superiors, obedience, politeness, and self-control, he is unquestionably the superior. On the teacher's first entrance among Japanese students who are unused to foreigners, he may notice some peculiarities, allowable in the Japanese code of etiquette, but repulsive to him; but these soon disappear or cease to annoy. In fire, energy, manly independence, and all those positive virtues which are exhibited in action and not in abstinence, the Japanese student is quite inferior to the western student.

In intellectual power and general ability, we are very much inclined to believe that the average Japanese student is the equal of the average western student. Even in the perception and conception of abstract ideas, we are inclined to think him not inferior, provided his knowledge of the vehicle employed—*i. e.*, the language—be equal to that of his rival. We have had two years of experience and observation of Japanese, American, and English students in the same class, and have not been able to detect any difference in their capabilities. Whether the Japanese student can hold his equal way through the highest studies of a foreign university, whether he can go beyond a certain point and win independent conquests by his own intellect with ability equal to that of the foreigner, is a question not yet ripe for solution. To express any positive opinion on this point would be presumptuous, and would be almost tantamount to a decision of the question whether the Japanese intellect is peer to that of the Anglo-Saxon. Some Buckle or Lecky may decide the question a century or two hence, but its discussion can have no practical value at present. The necessary data upon which to found a conclusion must be furnished by the future; they certainly cannot be found in the past.

It has been hard to hold the critic's pen while writing this article. We have striven to express unbiased truth, though many happy, many sad, memories have sorely tempted us to write only as admirer and friend. There seems no grander, no more sublime sight than we have seen in the youth of Japan leaving home and country to go to other lands, and there deny themselves comfort and ease to master the languages that would open to them a new world. We have seen them nobly toil, feeding the flame of their intense devotion with their own life's oil. One, two, three, a half-score, have we seen consume with the passion for knowledge, and, dying, regret not their loss, but that of their people, to whom they had hoped to bring back the sacred fire of knowledge and to kindle and pass on the torch in their own dearly-loved, but darkened, land. Some of their sepulchers are with their people and some are on alien but kindly soil. As critic, as friend, we praise the living; but of the dead, what shall we say? There can be spoken no word so eloquent as their tombs. There can come to their native land no honor greater than their ashes and their fragrant memories. Abroad, there can nothing speak more eloquently the praises of their country, there can be no art or monument embodying the new life of Japan more grandly, more solemnly, than that burial-lot in the quiet college-city of New Brunswick, with its six marble shafts, on which are chiseled names strange to the sculptor, but familiar to the fellow-countrymen of those who sleep beneath.

To the dead, all honor; to the living, all deserved praise. The foreign teacher in Japan, however discouraged and weary, finds his joy, his daily cheer, and his exceeding great reward in his students. To have led the humblest sons of Japan over the arduous road to knowledge, and thus to have helped on the civilization of this very interesting people, is an honor, even though his masters begrudge him appreciation or thanks. Whether in social exile in the interior, away from the stimulating energies and social pleasures of civilized life, or whether annoyed by men whose necessity alone tolerates him, the honor of being a teacher of such eager and grateful pupils must be and is sufficient.

IV.—NATIVE TEACHERS.

The study of foreign languages and science, though extremely important, constitutes but a part of education in Japan. A scheme of national instruction for this country must necessarily include more that refers to the education of the people in their own than in a foreign tongue. Only a small portion of the rising generation will obtain a knowledge of foreign languages and science, and a still smaller number will be brought under the direct instruction of foreign teachers. The rest, who constitute a vast majority, will, it is hoped, receive the best sort of education which an improved system of schools and instructors can furnish them.

To the creation of an improved system of public instruction in the vernacular and the training of a corps of qualified teachers, the best energies of the education-department are pledged and will doubtless be given.

At present the demand for intelligent young men, able to speak a foreign language, trained to western methods, and instructed in western learning, is far greater than the supply. In a few years this will cease to be the case: whereas, of natives well educated in their own language, there is not the slightest danger of there ever being too many. Hence the great importance of that department of the work of the Mombusho which relates to the supply of native teachers.

The new education in Japan will be radically different from the old ; hence the necessity for a new type of native teachers. The Japanese schools of the future will be organized on western principles and after western models, and foreign science and methods of instruction are to be introduced. In these schools the old typical Japanese teacher will be an anachronism.

The need of properly-qualified native instructors is one of the greatest, if not the greatest, of the many needs of Japan. The sudden, almost violent, revolution in educational as well as political ideas, through which this country has passed, has discovered that sore need. It is quite safe to say that hitherto the western idea of a trained teacher and of a science of teaching has been unknown to the natives of this country.

That this is true seems to be abundantly proved by their persistence in employing men in their schools who were unfit to be teachers and also by their treatment of the professional teachers whom they brought from other countries. Further, their ideas of what an education ought to be were as different from the ideas now expressed in the school-systems of foreign nations as those of the mediæval school-men differed from those of Herbert Spencer.

So long as the old education of Japan consisted merely in obtaining what we consider the mere work-tools and so long as they made an end of what we count the means, it could not be expected that instructors, such as are now needed, should appear. Every foreigner who has attempted the study of the Japanese language knows by experience that teachers, such as are numbered by thousands at home, cannot, or rather could not, be found in Japan. However learned the native might be, however diligent and earnest his pupil, it was not possible to make a teacher and to master a language at the same time. The native, knowing nothing of his own language by critical or analytical study, and the idea that a language could be mastered in any other way than by slavish repetition being entirely new to him, was unable to impart to a foreigner what was perfectly familiar to himself. The helpless learner, by dint of much direct- and cross-questioning and at much expense of perspiration and patience, might succeed in making himself a pump-handle and in persuading his teacher to be a pump. Usually, however, the patience of the pupil became exhausted, and the native remained as before, a deep well of Japanese undefiled.

The old typical Japanese teacher is rapidly passing away. Like the ripe scholar of other lands he has fallen out of his place, because his work was done. Learning was the chief qualification of the old native teacher ; skill, ability to impart his acquisitions, were his last requirements. His chief duty was to stuff and cram the minds of his pupils. To expand or develop the mental powers of a boy, to enlarge his mental vision, to teach him to think for himself, would have been doing precisely what it was the teacher's business to prevent. So long as education consisted in a tread-mill-round of committing to memory the Chinese classics, learning to read Japanese history and government-edicts, to write, and to reckon on the abacus, such a thing as mental development was unknown. There was but one standard, the Chinese classics. Every departure from these was a false step, everything new must be wrong. Under the Sho-gun's government, for centuries, the suppression of mental development was reduced to a system, if not to a science. That same usurpation which robbed the true ruler of this empire of his authority sought to crush all mental enterprise

ıackle the intellect of Japan beyond all hope of growth. Science was never taught,
ıtics was confined to the four fundamental rules of arithmetic. Independent thought
ıtigation were branded as criminal. The might of priestcraft hedged in the mind
ection of metaphysical speculation. The Chinese classics dominated, with a despot-
can at the best be but faintly conceived by a foreigner, over the field of politics
als; while the all-overshadowing power of the great usurper in Yedo prevented all
ıl research, study, or composition, except what related to the distant past. Shut off
contact with other intellects, the "ripe scholar" and the "great teacher" of old
·ere but school-men. The intellect of this nation, like the arboreal wonders of the
e florist, with its tap-root cut, deprived of fertilizing moisture, and stinted as to soil,
like the admired dwarf-pines four inches high, and as gnarled and as curious as

ıanner of life of the old Japanese instructor was to squat on the floor with his five or
ls about him on the same seat, who supported their elbows on a sort of table one
ı. Beginning with the first, he taught each pupil the pronunciation of the Chinese
rs; after the entire book had been committed to memory by sound, without any ref-
o sense, the pupil began again, and learned from his teacher the meaning of the char-
On the third reading the book was expounded to the pupil. Rarely did a class num-
e than six pupils. The work of the teacher was simply oral communication and
he pupil imitation; memorizing and copying constituted a Japanese youth's educa-
e old teachers of Japan and the Chinese scholars, though a very respectable body of
l undoubtedly help to repress the intellect of their countrymen, and must be looked
co-workers with the bonze and the official spy.
ld teacher poured in; the new teacher must draw out; the old teacher was a drill-
the new one must be that and more; the old one stifled questioning, the new one
courage it. We believe it to be the right of every student to drain his instructor
ıcholar, unless manifestly endeavoring to waste the time of the teacher and class,
ıe heard and answered. The teacher should be very careful how he calls any ques-
ish.
ative teacher of the future must depend less on traditional authority and more on
urces of a richly-furnished mind. He must be a student himself; he must be able
ıt of the ruts: he must be capable of developing the minds of youth, not merely of
them; he must welcome the appearance of an unusually bright and eager mind as
ı be polished with extra care, and not as a stone to be crushed into regulation-shape
for the common turnpike-road. The new teacher must banish his pipe and pouch,
ıachi" and tea-cups from the school-room; he must taboo his lounges and abandon
t of being regularly sick; he must stand up to his work. The great difference be-
foreigner and a Japanese is that one stands up to his work and the other sits down
le who can stand can do more and better work than he who sits. We have set
r ideal of a teacher in a former paper. Is it too high for a Japanese to aspire to?
k not.
ıeasures taken and the institution established to supply the need of good native
we have described at length elsewhere. Our former article on the Tokei normal
details the method pursued and the system set on foot by the education-department,
h they deserve all praise. If the native officials are not in too great a hurry to dis-
ı foreigner who now serves them, their enterprise will undoubtedly turn out, as it
s fair to do, a splendid success. That the young men now training there have it
to make good teachers, we fully believe. The social customs of this country and
ıs of the Japanese mind are invaluable aids to the native teacher, as we have in
article intimated they are to the foreign teacher. The temptations of the new
e teacher are that he will yield to ease and indolence, undervalue strict discipline,
oo easily satisfied to keep in the ruts of mere authority, and thus lead his pupils
n. We hold to the belief that scholars are largely what their teachers make them,
l they are not changed frequently.
r possible encouragement should be given both by the government and the people to

elevate the social as well as the intellectual standing of the teacher. In a country like this where the government is creator and leader of public sentiment, most of this work must be done by the personal encouragement of high officials. It is very gratifying to know that His Majesty the Emperor and the Empress have so conspicuously shown their great interest in education by visits of inspection to the chief schools of Tokei. " It is the prerogative of royalty to do good by presence alone." Besides this, one who reads of the frequent and often generous private contributions to the cause of education in Japan cannot but believe that the coming native teacher will be appreciated. Certainly the mission of the teacher in Japan is a noble one, and to be envied. His country is passing through social revolution in which he may be not only a helper, but in a large sense a leader. To be one of the " beginners of a better time," to be in the advance of a new and nobler civilization, to rescue his fellow-countrymen from superstition and to shield them from priestcraft, both native and foreign, is a high and glorious aspiration. To all, then, whether enjoying the advantage of the excellent course of the Tokei normal schools or whether attempting self-development under foreign helpers abroad or ´at home, we send fraternal greetings and congratulations. We hope that soon it may be said of Japan as emphatically as Brougham said it of England, " the school-master is abroad in the land." The teacher's office is even more honorable than the soldier's, in that he defends his country from ignorance, a foe worse than foreign enemies. The teacher may be greater than the civil ruler; for while one governs all kinds of citizens, the teacher makes good ones. That it is in the power of Japan, under that divine Providence that is no respecter of nations, to produce as noble specimens of the teacher's calling as are Wolsey, Hopkins, or Hadley in America, and as Temple, Arnold, or Jowett are in England, we do not doubt. Such men, however, are but growths of the social soil and mental atmosphere of their respective countries. To help in preparing the soil and atmosphere necessary to grow the men, character, and intellects who will adorn Japan as the western lands are adorned, is the work of honor and difficulty which now devolves on the department of education.

○

186

CIRCULARS OF INFORMATION

OF THE

REAU OF EDUCATION.

No. 3–1875.

AN ACCOUNT OF THE SYSTEMS OF PUBLIC INSTRUCTION IN
BELGIUM, RUSSIA, TURKEY, SERVIA, AND EGYPT.

WASHINGTON:
GOVERNMENT PRINTING OFFICE.
1875.

CONTENTS.

	Page.
...e Commissioner of Education to the Secretary of the Interior.......	5

TION IN BELGIUM :

...n of the ministry of the interior	9
...struction	9
...f primary instruction	11
...hools under the ministry of justice....................................	11
...hools under the ministry of war.......................................	11
...f illiteracy...	12
...te instruction...	12
...ools for intermediate instruction.....................................	13
...f intermediate instruction...	14
...struction	14
...nstruction in the University of Liége.................................	16
...f Belgian universities..	19
...truction	19
...instruction	19
...schools and work-shops..	20
...l instruction...	21
...tion	22
...struction	23
...struction	23
...struction	24
...s for deaf mutes and the blind	24
...l reform-schools	24
...Belgium...	24

TION IN RUSSIA :

...n	29
...l efforts from 1700 to 1861..	30
...pared with other countries	31
...which Russia ought to pursue..	33
...finances	34
...f the Russian educational report of 1871..............................	34
...f obtaining accurate statistics..	35
...upply teachers..	36
....	37
...nistration	37
...educating the half-civilized races of Russia..........................	38
...lations with Asia...	38
...education...	39
...ussianize Poland and the Baltic provinces	40
...of women	41
...n universities..	42
...e of private individuals	43

Cumpulsory military service and compulsory education ....
Conclusion ....
Statistics ....
Project for educating Russian wandering tribes ....

        EDUCATION IN TURKEY:

Introduction ....
The condition of Turkish women ....
The various kinds of schools... ....
Special schools....... ....
The school-law of 1869 ....
The ministry of public instruction ....
Difficulty of the Turkish language ....
Differences of race and creed...... ....
The lyceum at Galata-Séraï ....

        EDUCATION IN SERVIA:

Introduction ....
Historical development of education...
Primary schools..
Secondary schools ....
The high school ....
The school of agriculture..
The higher school for young ladies ....
The military academy..
School-finances........................ ....
Conclusion...

        PUBLIC INSTRUCTION IN EGYPT:

Character and history of the Egyptian people...................................
Primary Arabic instruction ....
Statistics of primary Arabic schools, (kouttab) ....
Superior Arabic instruction ....
Denominational schools.. ....
Government-schools on the European plan.......................................
Schools of the European and American colony...................................
Statistics of governmental, denominational, and European schools ....
Organic law of 1868 regulating public instruction...............................
Observations by Rev. Horace Eaton, D. D., of Palmyra, N. Y., on education in
    Egypt, Syria, and Turkey, made from notes taken while traveling through
    those countries..
        190

LETTER.

DEPARTMENT OF THE INTERIOR,
BUREAU OF EDUCATION,
Washington, D. C., June 15, 1875.

SIR: I beg leave herewith to transmit for your consideration the following interesting summarized statements of the condition of education in Belgium, Russia, Turkey, Servia, and Egypt, and to recommend that the same be published. Some of this information has been furnished in manuscript to parties wishing it. That in reference to Belgium is gathered from official documents procured in connection with my visit there. The labor of translation has been performed by Mr. Herman Jacobson.

Remote as these nations are from us, diverse as they are from ours in the form of their government and the pursuits of heir people, their experiences unite with ours in bearing testimony to the truth that next to nature itself, education shapes national character and determines national prosperity.

If sanitary science, as it matures, turns to the educator as largely responsible for whatever is accomplished in brain-building, statesmanship, from whatever quarter it gathers facts, finds them illustrating the great responsibility of the educator in building nations.

Agriculture, manufactures, commerce, wealth in any or all of its forms, may be selected as the chief means of national greatness, but the political fabric will be found to rest on a foundation of hay, wood, and stubble if the schoolmaster has not been abroad and laid the corner-stone in the intelligence and virtue of the people. The extent and character of their education will at once shape and measure all else that concerns them.

Education is, therefore, the foremost means to any great national end.

The education of the people clearly is more and more recognized as a factor in determining the power of one nation to cope with another.

England has found German clerks specially trained for commercial pursuits winning success in conducting trade in India over her own sons, who have not had the advantages of similar commercial education at home.

Moreover, if the proposition herein stated, to use education in its broadest sense for transforming the peoples of Central Asia to loyal subjects of the Czar, is carried out, English East Indian policy will doubt less wake up to the fact that it has not taken Russia two centuries to discover the secret of final success in the struggle for supremacy in the East.

The summary in regard to Russia is drawn from articles by Professor de Laveleye,* of the University of Liége, a well-known writer upon education.

The article on Turkey, by M. de Salve, is from a French stand-point and does not treat education exactly as it would be viewed by an American or English observer. But I have thought it all the more important to present it here, as it seems to supplement and confirm the statements already given to American educators in the several reports from this Office. It also contains many facts which have not been brought to the attention of the American public.

Passing to Servia, the reader will be struck with the rapid development of national energy and its intimate connection with the several steps of progress in the educational system.

Turning to Turkey, the facts showing educational effort will indicate whatever there is of national progress, while those pointing to the lack of intelligence will stand as indexes of national decay.

The summary of educational facts in regard to Egypt, presented by an article from the pen of Dr. V. E. Dor, is also a French view, but is believed to have fewer omissions of what other observers would see than the previous paper, and is a monograph of rare merit. Indeed, it is undoubtedly the best statement that has been made in regard to the present condition of education in Egypt. Both of these papers are supplemented by information gathered by an American traveler, both from our consuls and from his own observations in Egypt and Turkey.

Very respectfully, your obedient servant,

JOHN EATON,
Commissioner.

Hon. C. DELANO,
 Secretary of the Interior.

Approved and publication ordered.

C. DELANO,
Secretary of the Interior.

---

* Émile de Laveleye is a member of the Royal Academy of Belgium, author of the work L'instruction du peuple, (Paris, 1872,) in which he reviews the systems of education in all countries of the world, devoting a large space to the United States, and giving a remarkably fair description of our systems and methods, and of their results. He is also the author of many well-known works on political and rural economy, history, and literature.

EDUCATION IN BELGIUM.

193–194

BELGIUM.

Constitutional monarchy, (kingdom :) Area, 11,313 square miles; population, 1,336. Capital, Brussels; population, 314,077. Minister of public instruction, the ister of the interior, Ch. Delcour.]

COMPOSITION OF THE MINISTRY OF THE INTERIOR.

he ministry of the interior is composed of several bureaus, viz: The ean of accounts and pensions; of communal and provincial affairs; nilitia and general statistics; of public instruction; of sciences, litera- , and fine arts; and of agriculture and industry.

he bureau of public instruction has 1 director, 1 honorary director, iefs of division, 2 chiefs of bureau, and 4 clerks. Among the chiefs mreau there is M. Léon Lebon, author of a number of well-known ks on educational subjects. There are 4 inspectors of instruction, : 3 of intermediate instruction and 1 of primary normal schools. A. von Hasselt, a poet and author, who died December 1, 1874, filled latter position.

PRIMARY INSTRUCTION.

he basis of the present system of primary instruction is the law of tember 23, 1842.

he inspection of primary schools, as regards instruction and admin- ation, is in the hands of the communal authorities and of inspectors , as regards religion and morals, in the hands of men appointed by heads of the different denominations.

here is in every province a provincial inspector of primary instruc- appointed by the King. He inspects at least once a year all the ools of the province. He communicates with the cantonal inspectors,) are subordinate to him.

he provinces are divided into districts, each composed of one or ·e cantons, each having its inspector, who is appointed for three rs by the government on the recommendation of the provincial gov- ment. The cantonal inspector communicates with the communal ninistration, visits the schools of his districts at least twice a year, l keeps a diary of his inspections, which must at any time be open to provincial inspector. The cantonal inspector holds at least once a irter a conference of all the teachers of his district, where educa- nal methods, text-books, &c., are discussed. Once a year these confer- es are presided over by the provincial inspector.

The provincial inspectors assemble once a year under the presidency the minister of the interior. This assembly is called the central committee of instruction. Each inspector presents the report of his province, and the assembly discusses new text-books, methods, &c.

Every year a competition is opened in each province between the pupils of the highest class of the primary schools. The number of competitors is at the rate of 1 to 5 pupils, half of them being designated by the teacher and half by casting lot. The examining jury is presided over by the provincial inspector. Stipends of 200 francs each are granted to those pupils who pass the examination satisfactorily, to enable them to pursue their studies in a normal school.

The law provides that every commune must support at least one primary school, where gratuitous instruction to all those children belonging to the.commune whose parents cannot afford to pay anything, is given in religion, reading, writing, elements of French, Flemish, or German language, (according to the different localities,) arithmetic, and legal system of weights and measures. The communal council appoints the teacher and has the right to suspend him for three months, during which time the government decides whether the suspension is to be definite or not. The school-age is between 7 and 14.

Schools for adults.—By the law of September 1, 1866, modified by later laws, the communal councils are obliged to establish special schools for adults. These schools are to be kept in the primary-school-house and by the primary-school-teacher, and are subject to the same inspection as the primary schools. All schools for adults must have two divisions, viz, an elementary and a superior one. Instruction is to be given free of charge in the elementary division in reading; writing; arithmetic; legal system of weights and measures; elements of French, Flemish, or German, (according to the localities;) and in the superior division in French, Flemish, or German; arithmetic; drawing; elements of geography and history, especially of Belgium; the constitution of Belgium; and hygiene. For females, the knowledge of needle-work is substituted in place of the constitution.

Normal schools.—By royal decrees of April 10 and November 20, 1843, two State normal schools have been established, one at Lierre for the Flemish portion of the population, and one at Nivelles for the Walloon portion. By later laws normal sections have been established in connection with a number of primary schools, and by a law of October 25, 1855, the establishment of normal schools for female teachers by private or religious corporations has been sanctioned. Besides these, there are also private normal schools for male teachers.

The course of instruction in the State normal schools occupies three years and embraces the following subjects: Religion and morals; sacred history and church-history; reading; writing; book-keeping; French, Flemish, or German grammar; geography, especially of Belgium; history, especially of Belgium; arithmetic, with special regard to commercial transactions; legal system of weights and measures; elements of algebra and geometry; elements of natural sciences as applied to every-day life; horticulture; theory of education; methods of instruction; school-hygiene; the constitution of Belgium; drawing; vocal music; and gymnastics. Each school has a director and a number of professors, who are appointed by the King. The students live and board in the school, for which they pay a certain amount fixed by special regulations. Examinations are held at the end of every half-yearly term, and a final examination at the end of the whole course, when students who pass it satisfactorily receive a certificate. The normal sections at present differ but little from the normal schools except in name. The course of instruction in the normal schools for females also takes up three years and embraces all the subjects taught in the normal schools for males, adding to it instruction in needlework, &c.

STATISTICS OF PRIMARY INSTRUCTION.

The number of primary schools in 1869 (the most recent statistics) is 5,641, (being an average of 1.12 schools to every 1,000 inhabitants,) with 10,576 teachers and 593,379 pupils, (being an average of 11.7 pupils to every 100 inhabitants.)

The number of schools for adults is 2,620, (an average of 4.3 schools to every 10,000 inhabitants,) with 217,168 pupils, (an average of 43.2 to every 1,000 inhabitants.)

The number of infant-schools (maintained by the communes and by private aid) is 609, with 60,570 pupils.

The number of normal schools for primary instruction is 37, viz: 14 for male teachers and 23 for female teachers, (2 State normal schools, 5 normal sections, 7 private normal schools for males and 23 private normal schools for females,) with a total of 1,896 students, viz, 1,192 males and 704 females.

The total expenditure for primary instruction during 1869 was 8,002,043.07 francs, ($1,600,408,) distributed in the following manner: central government, 3,327,912.97 francs; provincial governments, 318,268.90 francs; communes, 2,934,185.20 francs; school-fees by scholars able to pay them, 935,750.54 francs; private munificence, 358,387.73 francs; balance from last year, 217,537.73 francs.

PRIMARY SCHOOLS UNDER THE MINISTRY OF JUSTICE.

Besides the primary schools enumerated above there are a number of such schools under the ministry of justice, viz: prison-schools, hospital-schools, and almshouse-schools. The number of these schools in 1869 was 6,564, viz, 3,713 for boys and 2,851 for girls.

PRIMARY SCHOOLS UNDER THE MINISTRY OF WAR.

Every regiment of the Belgian army has its school, where illiterates can learn at least reading, writing, and arithmetic. During the year 1870, 2,541 soldiers attended these schools, of whom 306 were entirely illiterate, while 2,235 had a knowledge of reading, writing, and arith.metic. Besides these schools for adults, there are in the larger garrisons primary schools for the children of soldiers. The school-age in these establishments is between 12 and 14 and the condition of admission is a knowledge of reading and writing. In 1870, these schools were attended by 241 scholars.

STATISTICS OF ILLITERACY.

The number of young men of the age of 21 presenting themselves for military service in 1871 was 44,696. Of this number, 10,027 could neither read nor write, 2,319 could only read, 15,823 read and write, 15,716 had a better education, and of 811 the degree of education was not ascertained; 70.56 per cent. therefore could at least read and write and 5.19 per cent. could only read.

INTERMEDIATE INSTRUCTION.

The basis of intermediate instruction is the organic law of June 1, 1850, modified by succeeding laws.

The intermediate schools are either government-schools, those of a higher grade being called royal atheneums and those of a lower grade, intermediate schools, (*écoles moyennes*.) The provincial or communal intermediate schools of the higher grade are called colleges (*colléges*) and those of the lower grade intermediate schools. They are either provincial or communal establishments aided by the state, or establishments supported entirely by the provinces or communes, or private institutions aided by the communes.

The administration of the royal atheneums and of the royal intermediate schools is entirely in the hands of the government. The provincial or communal establishments, aided by the state, must conform to the following conditions: The school must adopt the course of studies prescribed by the government; the text-books used, the internal regulations, the distribution of the course of studies, and the financial status must be approved of by the government; otherwise the administration is left to the provincial, communal, or private authorities.

The highest authority for all intermediate schools is the council of improvement of intermediate instruction, (*conseil de perfectionnement de l'instruction moyenne.*) This council is composed of ten members, prominent educators and men of science, appointed by the minister of the interior and presided over by him. The council has to give advice as regards the course of studies, has to examine the text-books, gives instructions to the inspectors, and discusses all matters of interest pertaining to the intermediate schools.

The directors of all intermediate schools, private or government, must have a certificate of professor of intermediate instruction and the teachers must have a certificate of having attended a university. Every three years a report on intermediate schools is presented to the Belgian parliament.

There are three inspectors of intermediate instruction, viz: One inspector-general, one for mathematical and natural sciences, and one for the "humanities," languages, literature, history, &c. The atheneums are inspected at least once a year by each of the three inspectors and all the other intermediate schools at least once a year by one of them.

Courses of instruction.—The course of instruction in the atheneums is divided in two sections, viz, the section of the humanities and the section of professional studies. The former comprises: Religion; laws of rhetorics and poetry; Greek, Latin, French, Flemish, or German ; elementary mathematics; arithmetic; algebra, as far as equations of the second degree; geometry ; trigonometry; natural philosophy; universal history ; Belgian history; ancient and modern geography ; geography of Belgium; constitution and administration of Belgium; special study of modern languages, such as German and English; drawing and calligraphy; vocal music; and gymnastics. This section has seven classes, each of one year's duration, and the number of hours per week varies between twenty and thirty.

The section of professional studies comprises: Religion; rhetoric; French, Flemish, German, and English ; elementary mathematics, analytical geometry, descriptive geometry, spherical trigonometry, all with their application to the arts, industry, and commerce ; elements of natural philosophy, mechanics, chemistry, natural history, and astronomy ; book-keeping; elements of commercial law and political economy; history and geography, especially of Belgium; drawing; calligraphy; vocal music; and gymnastics. This section has one preparatory class and two subdivisions, viz, the lower one, comprising three classes of one year each, and the higher, comprising four classes of one year each. The number of hours per week varies between twenty-eight and thirty-four.

The course of studies in the intermediate schools usually opens in the beginning of October and closes during the second week in August.

NORMAL SCHOOLS FOR INTERMEDIATE INSTRUCTION.

There are four normal schools for intermediate instruction, viz, two normal courses—one normal school of humanities and one normal school of sciences. The course of instruction in the normal courses lasts two years and embraces the following subjects : First year. French ; Flemish ; geography and history, especially those of Belgium ; arithmetic, and its application to business ; algebra, as far as equations of the second degree; plane geometry ; book-keeping; commercial law; elements of natural philosophy; drawing, especially linear drawing; calligraphy. Second year. Pedagogics and methodics ; French ; Flemish ; algebra continued; trigonometry; surveying; elements of mechanics and chemistry ; natural history.

The course of instruction in the normal school of humanities at Liége lasts four years and embraces the following subjects: Latin language and literature; Greek language and literature; history of ancient literatures; history of French literature; history of Flemish, German, and English literature; psychology; ancient history, (eastern countries and Greece;) Roman history; Roman antiquities; history of the Middle Ages; history of Belgium; ancient and modern geography; physical geography; general grammar and principal theories of Greek syntax of Latin syntax, and of French syntax; pedagogics; and methodology.

The course of instruction in the normal school of sciences at Ghent lasts three years and embraces the following subjects: First year. Algebraic analysis, analytical geometry, elements of descriptive geometry, experimental physics, botany, psychology and logics, exercises in elementary mathematics, linear drawing, and drawing of plans. Second year. First part of differential and integral calculus, statics, descriptive geometry, mathematical methodology, inorganic and organic chemistry, elements of mineralogy, exercises in elementary mathematics and infinitesimal analysis, linear drawing, and drawing from nature. Third year. Second part of differential and integral calculus, rational mechanics, elements of astronomy, elements of geology, zoölogy, chemical experiments, physical experiments.

Special examining juries are appointed by the King or the minister of the interior every year to hold the final examinations in the intermediate normal schools, and candidates who pass satisfactorily receive a certificate.

STATISTICS OF INTERMEDIATE INSTRUCTION.

Total number of intermediate schools December 31, 1870, 161, viz: 10 royal atheneums and 50 intermediate government-schools; 30 communal establishments aided by the government, (17 colléges and 13 intermediate schools;) 3 schools supported entirely by the communes; 64 supported by the bishops, the Jesuits, or religious corporations; and 4 supported entirely by private individuals.

Total number of students in 93 intermediate schools, (all exclusive of the religious and entirely private schools,) 15,822, viz: 3,651 in the royal atheneums, 8,471, in the government intermediate schools, 3,071 in the communal schools aided by the government, and 629 in the schools supported entirely by the communes.

Total number of normal schools for intermediate instruction, 4, with 38 students.

SUPERIOR INSTRUCTION.

There are in Belgium four universities, two supported by the government and two free universities, the two former at Ghent and Liége and the latter at Brussels and Louvain.

Each university has four faculties, viz, of philosophy and literature, of mathematical and natural sciences, of law, and of medicine. The professors are appointed by the King, and no one can be professor who has not the degree of doctor or licentiate in the branch which he intends to teach. Exceptions from this rule are made with men who by their writings or the practice of their science have become famous.

The academic authorities are the rector of the university, the secretary, the deans of faculties, the academic council, and the college of assessors. The academic council is composed of all the professors of the university, presided over by the rector; the college of assessors is composed of the rector, the secretary, and the dean of the faculties.

The rector is appointed by the King for three years, and the administration of the university chiefly rests in his hands. The academic council every year nominates two candidates for the place of secretary, one of whom is appointed by the King. The deans of the faculties are elected annually by the professors of each faculty. The academic council and the college of assessors are convoked by the rector.

Every student must annually pay a registration-fee of 15 francs, besides a fee for the courses of lectures he wishes to attend, varying between 200 and 250 francs per annum.

The academic year is divided into two terms; there are two vacations annually, one from the first Saturday in August till the first Tuesday in October. The programme of lectures is published at the beginning of each term.

The academical punishments are admonitions, suspension of the right to attend the lectures, and expulsion from the university.

The government has charge of the general superintendence of the state-universities. To assist the minister in his duties, the so-called "council of improvement of superior instruction" is called together by him at least once a year. This council consists of eight professors, called by the minister from each faculty, and such other persons as he thinks might be of use in its deliberations on any improvements in superior instruction. With every state-university there is a government-commissioner, entitled "administrative inspector of the university." He has to see to it that the laws regarding superior instruction are properly carried out and that the programme laid out at the beginning of the course is carefully observed, and he has likewise the superintendence of all the buildings belonging to the university.

The state-universities confer a special scientific diploma on persons who, after having obtained the doctor-degree, have applied themselves to certain specialties of science. This diploma is simply an attestation of capacity. For obtaining the doctor-degree and the diploma above mentioned, examinations are held annually.

To illustrate the working of a Belgian state-university, the course of instruction at the University of Liége during the year 1872 is given below:

COURSE OF INSTRUCTION IN THE UNIVERSITY OF LIÉGE.

FACULTY OF PHILOSOPHY AND LITERATURE.

Studies.	Hours per week.	
	First term.	Second term.
Studies required for the examination of candidate preparatory to the doctor's examination :		
History of French literature..............................	2	.
Latin philological and literary exercises	2	.
Political history of antiquity	3	....
Psychology...	4	....
Logics	....	.
Morals	....	.
Roman antiquities with a view to their political institutions	3	....
Greek philological and literary exercises	1	.
Political history of the middle ages	2	.
Political history of Belgium.................................	2	.
Studies required for the doctor s examination :		
Latin literature	3	.
Greek literature...	2	.
History of ancient literature	2	.
Greek antiquities	3	.
General and special metaphysics	3	....
History of ancient and modern philosophy	2	.
Studies not comprised in the above examinations :		
Flemish literature	1	....
Archæology	....	(*)
Modern political history.................................	(†)	....
Political economy	(†)	......
Æsthetics...	2	....
Roman religious, military, &c., antiquities	(*)	....
Oriental literature	6	6

  * Not yet determined   † See law-faculty

FACULTY OF LAW.

Studies.	Hours per week.	
	First term.	Second term.
Studies required for the candidate's examination :		
Modern political history .... }	4½	1½
Historical introduction to the course of civil law .... }		
General principles of civil law	3	3
General review of law, Roman law and its history	4½	4½
Natural law or philosophy of law	....	3
Studies required for the first doctor s examination :		
Modern civil law	4½	4½
Public law of Belgium	4½	....
Political economy	4½	.....
The pandects...	4½	4

FACULTY OF LAW—Continued.

Studies.	Hours per week.	
	First term.	Second term.
required for the second doctor's examination :		
w	4½	4½
dure..	3	3
l law..	3	3
il law..	4½	4½
required for the degree of doctor of political and administrative sciences:		
of Belgium	3	3
tive law	....	....
onomy	....	....
al law	....	(*)
required for the title of notary :		
....	....	....
d financial laws used by notaries	3	3

* Not yet determined.

FACULTY OF SCIENCES.

Studies.	Hours per week.	
	First term.	Second term.
required for a candidate of natural sciences :		
y..	....	....
chemistry	5½	....
emistry	....	4
tal physics	4½	4½
....	4½	4½
....	4	4½
y	4½	....
required for a candidate of physical and mathematical sciences :		
y	....	....
gebra...	4½	....
l geometry	....	....
tal physics	....	....
....	(*)	....
e geometry...	4½	....
al and integral calculus....................................	....	4½
chemistry..	....	....
y...	....	....
required for a doctor of natural sciences :		
orough course of organic chemistry.........................	....	1
orough course of inorganic chemistry.......................	1	....
ive anatomy...	....	4½
ive physiology...	4½	....
anatomy and physiology...................................	....	....
y	....	....
....	4½	....
stronomy	4½	....

203

* See course of special schools.

intend to obtain the diploma of industrial engineer or who merely desire to acquire a more scientific knowledge of industry.

At the head of the school there is a director and a council of improvement of studies, consisting of five members, appointed by the ministry of the interior. The course of instruction in the preparatory school lasts two years and comprises the following subjects: experimental physics and elements of mathematical physics; descriptive geometry and its application to shading, perspective, stone-cutting, and timber-work; organic and inorganic chemistry; applied chemistry; elements of civil architecture, higher algebra, analytical geometry; elements of astronomy and geodesy; differential and integral calculus; analysis; elements of machinery; elementary and analytical mechanics; calculation of probabilities; and social arithmetic. The course of instruction in the special school of civil engineering lasts two years. This school has two sections, the first intended for pupil-engineers, (*élèves-ingénieurs*,) and the second for the education of civil engineers or architectural engineers. The school has an inspector of stud ies and the course of instruction embraces the following subjects: civil architecture, history of architecture, mineralogy, geology, industrial chemistry, industrial physics, social economy, administrative law, hydraulics, construction of machinery, stability of constructions, machinery, steam-engines, the construction and working of railroads, constructing roads, bridges, canals, and harbors.

The school of arts and manufactures has a three-years course, and embraces the application of science s to general and special branches of industry. It is placed under the immediate superintendence of the in. spector of studies of the school of civil engineering.

The school of arts, manufactures, and mining connected with the university of Liége was established in 1838. It has a director, council on improvement of studies, and three inspectors of studies. It has three divisions, viz: a preparatory school, a special school of arts and manufactures, and a special school of mining. The course of instruction is the same in the two first-mentioned schools as in those connected with the University of Ghent. The special school of mining has a three-years course, which embraces the following subjects: the searching and working of mines, mineralogy, industrial economy, industrial organic chemistry, industrial inorganic chemistry, assaying, metallurgy, indus. trial physics, industrial architecture, construction of machinery, applied mechanics, and working of railroads.

INDUSTRIAL SCHOOLS AND WORKSHOPS.

The number of industrial schools is 26; they are almost exclusively communal institutions, receiving aid from the government, which has the general superintendence and the right of inspection. The course of instruction lasts two to four years and is given entirely free of charge. It generally embraces the following subjects: mathematics, mechanics, physics, chemistry, book-keeping, drawing, and modeling, and in some schools, also, mining, metallurgy, and architecture.

An institution peculiar to Belgium are the workshops for learning trades, (*ateliers d'apprentissage.*) The origin of these workshops was the hopeless condition of the weavers in Flanders about 1830, who were suffering much in consequence of the introduction of machinery. A private association was then formed which aimed at spreading the knowledge of improved methods of weaving; the government soon took the matter in hand, and numerous workshops were established throughout the country, where skillful weavers instructed young men in the improved methods of weaving. Many of these workshops are institutions entirely supported by government, and others are supported by the provincial or communal authorities or by private individuals, but all of them are under government-supervision. In many of these workshops instruction is also given in reading, writing, arithmetic, and other elementary subjects during the evening-hours.

In this connection the Industrial Museum at Brussels must be mentioned. It was founded in 1826 and re-organized in 1841, and contains physical and chemical instruments, machinery of every kind, and a technological library. Since 1846 a drawing-school is connected with it and since 1852 free lectures are delivered in the evenings on physics, chemistry, mechanics, political economy, and hygiene, which are very well attended.

AGRICULTURAL INSTRUCTION.

There is one state agricultural school at Gembloux, founded in 1860. This school is located in large and well-arranged buildings and has a model farm and garden, and in the neighborhood are large distilleries breweries, and sugar-manufactories, thus affording the students an opportunity of becoming acquainted with these branches of industry. The conditions of admission are the age of 16 and a good knowledge of the elementary branches, geometry, and geography. The time of entering is the 1st October. The institution is in the charge of the ministry of the interior. Students who board in the institution pay 700 francs annually. At the end of the course, examinations are held and diplomas of "agricultural engineer" given to the successful candidates. The course of instruction lasts three years and embraces the following subjects: elementary algebra, plane geometry, stereometry, surveying, elements of mechanics, linear drawing, construction of agricultural implements, rural architecture, drainage, irrigation, physics, meteorology, inorganic and organic chemistry applied to agriculture, agricultural technology, mineralogy, geology, zoölogy, botany, all with their relation to agriculture; anatomy, physiology, hygiene, breeding, raising, and improving of domestic animals; general and special agriculture, forest-culture, horticulture, and arboriculture; agricultural and forest-economy, various systems of culture, rotation of crops; agricultural laws; agricultural book-keeping. The instruction given is both theoretical and practical.

There are two schools of horticulture, one at Vilvorde and one at Ghent, established by a decree of the minister of the interior in 1855. The conditions of admission are the age of 17, good bodily health, a perfect knowledge of French and of all the elementary branches. The annual charge is about 100 francs, which is, of course, only a nominal charge, as the students are lodged and boarded free of expense. The course of instruction occupies three years, is both theoretical and practical, and embraces the following subjects: French, Flemish, arithmetic, book-keeping, botany, architecture of hot-houses and gardens, flower-culture, culture of vegetables, hot-house-gardening, fruit-culture. Connected with each school are large gardens, nurseries, arboretums, hot-houses, museums, and libraries.

ART-INSTRUCTION.

There are two academies of the fine arts, one at Brussels and the other at Antwerp, both under the direction of the government. The object of these academies is to give gratuitous instruction in painting, sculpture architecture, and engraving, and the sciences relating to these arts, to spread the taste for art, and to encourage and protect those who engage in its pursuit. Councils of administration, most of whose members are appointed by the King, are charged with the superintendence of these academies. The course of instruction is given by professors appointed by the King, is of indefinite length, and embraces the following subjects: historical painting, drawing, sculpture, genre-painting, landscape-painting, portrait-painting, picturesque anatomy, architectural painting, architecture, naval architecture, engraving on wood, steel- and copper-engraving, proportions of the human body, principles of ornaments, modeling, picturesque perspective, history, antiquities and costumes, æsthetics and general literature, comparative architecture, and geometry.

The taste for art is also fostered by the royal museums of paintings and sculpture at Brussels, by the Royal Museum of Antiquities in the same city, and by a number of provincial, municipal, and private museums in every part of the country.

Lower art-instruction is given in drawing-schools chiefly maintained by the communal or provincial authorities, at present numbering upwards of fifty, where gratuitous instruction in drawing and kindred branches is given.

There are two royal conservatories of music, at Brussels and at Liége managed by committees appointed by the King, under the supervision of the ministry of the interior. Each has a director and a number of professors. The object of these institutions is to give gratuitous instruction in music and encourage and elevate the musical taste. The length of the course is indefinite. It embraces the following subjects: thorough bass, harmony, singing, Italian language, elocution, violin, violoncello, double-bass, piano, organ, French horn, trombone, clarionet, saxophone, hautboy, flute, bassoon, trumpet, &c.

BUSINESS-INSTRUCTION.

Book-keeping and kindred branches are taught in many schools. There is a superior commercial institute at Antwerp, established in 1852, for the acquirement of the higher branches of commercial knowledge, at the joint expense and under the immediate patronage of the Belgian government and of the municipality of the city of Antwerp.

The practical and theoretical course of instruction extends over two years and embraces the following subjects: book-keeping; commercial correspondence, in French and English; commercial transactions of every kind; description of merchantable articles and produce; political economy and statistics; commercial and industrial geography; general principles of law; Spanish, Italian, German, and English commercial and maritime legislations compared; principles of international law; legislations of customs; ship-building and fitting-out. The entering-fee is 25 francs per annum, and the general subscription for the first year is 200 francs and for the second year 250. Candidates can enter at any period of the year, but no reduction is made in the terms. Examinations for admission take place only once a year, at the beginning of October, before a commission appointed by the government and presided over by the director of the institution. The subjects of this examination are: a composition in French and a translation from French into German and English; physical geography; commercial arithmetic; elements of algebra, geometry, book-keeping; rudiments of natural philosophy and of chemistry; rudiments of universal history. These conditions are modified in favor of foreigners, especially as regards languages. The students do not live in the institution, but board in the city. A final examination is held at the end of the second year, at which examiners specially nominated by the government deliver certificates to such students as pass the requisite examination; and any student who has displayed special proficiency may obtain a stipend enabling him to travel abroad during several years at the expense of the government and with the title of consular pupil.

MILITARY INSTRUCTION.

There are three institutions for military instruction, all under the supervision of the ministry of war, viz, the school of war, (*école de guerre*,) the military school, and the school for non-commissioned officers of the infantry and cavalry, the first intended for the education of staff-officers, the second for the education of commissioned officers of the infantry, cavalry, artillery, and engineers, and the last for the education of non-commissioned officers. The course of instruction in the two first-mentioned schools embraces: fortification, topography, geodesy, calculation of probabilities, political and military geography, staff-service, higher administration, military history, tactics and strategy, artillery, mathematics, physics, chemistry, general history, French literature, hygiene, knowledge of horses, English, German, and drawing; and the course of instruction in the last-mentioned schools embraces mathematics, linear drawing, geography, history, French, and Flemish.

NAUTICAL INSTRUCTION.

There are two schools of navigation, viz, at Antwerp and Ostende. Scholars are admitted annually during the second weeks of March and October. Instruction is given free of charge in the following subjects: arithmetic, geometry, trigonometry, nautical astronomy, navigation, rigging, stowage, naval steam-engines, commerce, meteorology, English, keeping of the log-book, practical exercises, cruises on the ocean, &c. At the end of the course an examination is held and successful candidates receive certificates as first or second lieutenants or captains.

Statistics of special schools.

	Students.
Special school of civil engineering, University of Ghent	173
School of arts and manufactures, University of Ghent	63
School of arts and manufactures, University of Liége	211
Special school of mines, University of Liége	35
State agricultural school at Gembloux	79
Two schools of horticulture, Vilvorde and Ghent	39
School of veterinary surgery at Cureghem	78
Royal Academy of the Fine Arts at Antwerp	1,588
Sixty-nine drawing-academies and schools	9,389
Conservatory of music at Brussels	538
Conservatory of music at Liége	811
Military school at Brussels	97
Two schools of navigation at Antwerp and Ostende	70
Total	13,171

INSTITUTIONS FOR DEAF MUTES AND THE BLIND.

There are in Belgium no public institutions for deaf mutes and the blind, but the nine institutions which exist have all been founded and are supported by private individuals, aided by the state, provincial, and municipal authorities.

AGRICULTURAL REFORM-SCHOOLS.

There are two agricultural reform-schools supported by the government, one at Ruysselede for 500 boys, and one at Beernem for 400 girls and children between the ages of 2 and 7. The pupils are instructed in agriculture, needlework, housekeeping, and various useful trades.

CRÈCHES IN BELGIUM.

During the last thirty years quite a number of *crèches* (mangers, in remembrance of the manger of Bethlehem) have been founded in most countries of Europe, but especially in France and Belgium. They are all managed and supported either by private individuals or corporations. A complete series of reports of the famous *crèche* Marie-Henriette, (named after the Queen of Belgium,) at Antwerp, from 1867-'72, has come to hand, from which we extract the following:

During the year 1866 the cholera had made great ravages in Belgium, but especially in the city of Antwerp. The misery produced by this epidemic was very great among the poorer classes of the population. Many infants were deprived either of a father or a mother, and, while the parent was obliged to be absent the whole day to earn a scanty livelihood, these poor little infants were left in the charge of careless neighbors, who wanted high pay for their services, but who, in most cases, let the infants suffer from cold and hunger. The same was the case in the family of many a poor working-man whose house had escaped the dreadful scourge, but whose great poverty made it necessary for his wife to go out likewise during the day, in order to contribute towards the maintenance of the family. When these facts became known, a number of benevolent ladies and gentlemen met to propose a remedy, and this remedy was the *crèche*. This first meeting took place on the 4th November, 1866, and on January 23, 1867, the *crèche* was solemnly opened. Since that year it has continued to flourish, and has accommodated, in all, up to the year 1872, 942 infants of the tenderest age, viz, 477 girls and 465 boys. During the year 1872, the number of inmates was 149, viz, 90 girls and 59 boys. The receipts during the same year were 44,306.81 francs and the expenses 26,773.20 francs. To show more exactly the working of a *crèche*, the regulations are subjoined in full:

(1) Every child aged at least fifteen days, or, at most, three years, whose parents are residents of the city, can be admitted to the *crèche*, if it is not afflicted with any contagious disease and if it has been vaccinated.

(2) Persons who desire to place an infant in the *crèche* must furnish a paper showing the residence of the parents and their occupation and a certificate of vaccination.

(3) After these papers have been shown, the name of the child is registered and the time indicated when it can be received.

(4) The children are admitted to the *crèche*, whenever a vacancy occurs, in the order in which they are registered.

(5) Application for admission can be made every day from 9 to 12 a. m., but the admission itself only takes place on Monday.

(6) All children admitted to the *crèche* are treated on a footing of perfect equality.

(7) The charge for each child is five centimes per day, or twenty-five centimes per week, in case of prepayment.

(8) When the time for admitting a child has come, the persons who bring it must answer the following questions: Are the father and mother alive? What is the amount of their daily or weekly earnings? How many days a month do they work? Have they any protectors who help them? Do they receive any aid from the poor-fund?

(9) The *crèche* does not receive sick children, and no child is admitted before having been thoroughly examined by the physician of the institution.

(10) The food of the children at the *crèche* consists—

(a) For babies that have not yet been weaned: Of bread-soup (*panades de biscuit*) made with white bread and arrowroot boiled in milk and water, every day at 10 a. m. and between the hours of 2 and 5 p. m.; and, for a drink, barley-water or gruel, with a little moist sugar. These drinks must be prepared fresh every day.

(b) For children of seven months and more who have not yet been weaned: The bread-soup will be given only in the morning, and at 2 p. m., by a pap of gruel; and three times a week by beef- or veal-soup, (*bouillon*,) from which the fat has been skimmed. This soup is to be prepared with semolino.

(c) For children who have been weaned: At 10 a. m., bread-soup, only a little thicker; at 12.30 p. m., beef- or veal-soup, with rice and semolino, followed by vegetables, of which potatoes are not to form more than one-sixth part; at 5 p. m., slices of bread spread with butter; for drink, ptisan made of licorice.

(11) The following regulations will be observed carefully:

There is to be a continuous ventilation in the *crèche ;* the air will be purified by streams of fresh air as soon as impregnated with any odors, but the children must never be exposed to any draught ; there are never to be any flowers in the *crèche ;* as soon as the number of children in the *crèche* increases, all the windows will be opened and the cradles, &c., be aired ; the children will be taken into the open air whenever the weather permits.

TEMPERATURE.

The temperature of the *crèche* will always be about 15° Réaumur (about 60° Fahrenheit;) towards evening the temperature will be lowered a little. The parents are urged to cover up the children well when they are brought to the *crèche* in the morning and when taken away in the evening.

CLEANLINESS.

The greatest possible cleanliness is to be maintained in the *crèche ;* every child will be washed and combed in the morning and before the first meal ; after every meal its hands and face will be washed. While washing the children they will be kept far from the windows ; they will be completely undressed, and after having been washed they will be rubbed with clean towels till they are completely dry. Every child will be provided with a sponge, a basin, a handkerchief, a cup, and a spoon. From the beginning of May till the end of September, the children will take a tepid bath twice a week, remaining in the bath about 10 minutes ; they will never be bathed till two hours after a meal.

VARIOUS REGULATIONS.

The children will be taken out as often as possible and be made to walk when they are able to do so ; scolding is to be used but rarely, corporal punishment never, and altogether the greatest tenderness in the treatment is recommended ; the children are to be laid sometimes on one side and sometimes on the other, always with the head a little raised ; they are to be covered sufficiently but not too much ; no child is to be left in its chair for any great length of time ; the movements of the children in their swaddling-bands are not to be hindered ; the child is not to be lifted up with one arm only ; the feet of the children are to be kept warm, the stomach easy, and the head cool ; no painted confectionery, or anything which might hurt the children, is allowed in the *crèche ;* the children may be caressed but not embraced ; their sleep is never to be interrupted ; they are not to be excited in any manner ; they are to enjoy their games, and are, if possible, placed near those for whom they show any predilection ; whenever a child has convulsions it is to be at once removed from the sight of the others, and the physician is to be informed immediately.

(12) When a child is admitted to the *crèche,* the parents are informed with regard to the following regulations, with which they must comply :

(13) Mothers must nurse their children whenever their work permits.

(14) Children must be brought to the *crèche* before 8 a. m. in summer and before 9 a. m. in winter, and must be taken back in the evening after the day's work has been finished.

(15) Parents owe due respect to the directress and all the employés of the establishment.

(16) Parents who neglect their infants, and who, after having been duly warned, do not comply with the regulations, lose all their privileges, and their infants are sent home.

EDUCATION IN RUSSIA.

THE PROGRESS OF EDUCATION IN RUSSIA.*

By ÉMILE DE LAVELEYE, *of the University of Liége, Belgium.*

[From the Revue des deux mondes, April 15, 1874.]

INTRODUCTION.

Russia during the last twenty years has shown how a great state may rise from a defeat. Like Prussia, after the battle of Jena, it has profited from a bitter lesson. While the country was recovering from the shock of defeat the time was not spent in sluggishness and fruitless experiments; it has, on the contrary, been a period of radical reform and complete reorganization. In 1854 Russia had really not been conquered, as, after two years consumed in gigantic exertions, the allies had only succeeded in taking one single city, situated on the confines of the empire. The frontiers had scarcely been touched, for the enemy never thought of leading his armies into the heart of the country. The country nevertheless was exhausted, and made peace because it had not the strength to continue the war any longer. The Russian government was fully aware of the causes of its weakness. These causes were three in number: first, the lack of rapid means of communication; secondly, the insufficient development of the productive powers of the country; and, thirdly, the want of enlightenment among the masses of the people. If in 1853 Russia had had railways, the allies would never have ventured into the Crimea, whence they would soon have been driven back into the sea; and if, on the other hand, the natural wealth of Russia had been developed by a free and enlightened people, she could for a long time have defied all the assaults of France and England. To remove these various causes of weakness has been the object which Russia has pursued with indefatigable perseverance and in an intelligent manner.

The beginning was made by tracing a net-work of railroads, which extends every year in all directions. Next, the serfs were emancipated, a reform of far-reaching consequences, which must change the whole economical situation of the empire, since it has awakened in the population that desire for progress which always accompanies freedom. Recently military service has been made compulsory for all, not even ex-

---

*(1) General Plan for the Organization of Popular Education, published by order of the Emperor, by M. P. de Taneef, 1862; (2) General Regulations for Public Schools, prepared by Prince Paul Gagarin, minister of public instruction; (3) Report of the Minister of Public Instruction, Count Dmitri Tolstoï, to the Emperor, for the years 1872 and 1873.

cepting the families of nobles. For some years the government has been earnestly engaged in the enormous work of extending education to all classes of society, both in the rural districts and in the towns and cities. This, in my opinion, is the most important matter, for it is the application of scientific knowledge which makes labor productive. If for the same amount of exertion men reap five or ten times more to-day than in former times, it is because, thanks to science, the domesticated natural powers work themselves and produce everything needed for satisfying our wants. The United States is certainly the country where relatively the greatest amount of wealth is produced, and there more than anywhere else are all new discoveries applied to labor. Open as many schools in Russia as in America, and the power of that immense empire will surpass that of any other country in the world. It must be acknowledged that in this respect everything had to be done, even to laying the very foundation on which to erect the building. In order to understand this we must cast a glance at the past.

EDUCATIONAL EFFORTS FROM 1700 TO 1861.

From the reign of Peter the Great till the abolition of serfdom.

The first attempts to educate the people date from the reign of Peter the Great. In Holland, where even at that time there were many and good schools, the imperial reformer saw the marvelous results produced by them.

In 1714 he established "compulsory schools of arithmetic" for the higher classes.

In 1715 and 1719 stricter regulations were published, and attendance at school was made compulsory for all except the nobility. These excellent measures, far from meeting with favor, were violently opposed. The city-councils of several cities sent petitions demanding the suppression of these schools as being dangerous institutions.

In 1744, it was ascertained that not a single pupil from the middle class attended these schools, and, after special schools had been founded for the clergy and the nobility, they were completely deserted.

In 1775, Catherine II, influenced by the philosophical ideas of the eighteenth century, ordered the establishment of schools in towns and villages. She wished that the school-fee should be as small as possible, in order not to deter the poorer classes from sending their children to school; but this order unfortunately remained a dead letter, for everything was wanting, teachers, school-houses, books, money. Since that time several other efforts were made, but invariably without any result. Considerable sums would have been required to make a beginning, and the government contented itself with passing laws.

In 1782, a committee, with M. Zavadovsky as chairman, proposed to establish two kinds of schools, one with a four-years course for the higher classes, and another with a two-years course for the common people.

In 1786 certificates of ability were required of all persons—at least in the cities—who opened a school.

In 1803 the higher schools were changed to gymnasia, organized on the same plan as the institutions of that name in Germany.

In the common schools established by Catherine II, the "book of the duties of every man and citizen" had been adopted as the basis of instruction; this was replaced by a reader containing pieces on agriculture, hygiene, and natural philosophy. The utilitarian age succeeded the philosophic age.

In 1804 a new effort was made to establish schools on the estates of the Emperor and the nobility; but, owing to want of money, nothing serious was done.

Finally the clergy felt touched in their honor, and decided to show what the zeal and devotion of the servants of religion may accomplish. In 1806 it was stated that in the district of Novgorod there were one hundred and six schools kept by officiating ministers. The report of Prince Gagarin, who mentions this fact, adds that, "unfortunately, two years later they had all disappeared."

It will readily be understood that in a country where slavery exists, where, consequently, individual efforts are necessarily feeble and confined to private interests, the direct and effective intervention of the government is indispensable. Some steps in this direction were taken in 1828, and in 1835 a law placed all the existing schools under the supervision of the superintendents of the school-districts, which were generally of an enormous extent. Several district-schools were founded by the government to serve as models, but the parochial schools increased very slowly.

From the abolition of serfdom in 1861 to 1864.

After serfdom had been abolished, the Emperor Alexander II saw that the indispensable consequence of this great reform must be a thorough reorganization of public instruction. In 1861 a committee was appointed to draw up the plan of a law.

In 1862 M. Taneef submitted to the Emperor a "General plan for the organization of popular education," which contained some very excellent points. The result was the General Regulations of 1864, which are still in force.

RUSSIA COMPARED WITH OTHER COUNTRIES.

Neither France nor England has so fully understood the problem before her. The difficulties which a complete reorganization of popular education meets in Russia are enormous. They are principally caused by the manner in which the inhabitants live, scattered over a large extent of country, and by their extreme poverty.

The following are the expenses of a school according to the report:

	City.	Country.
	Roubles.	*Roubles.*
Teacher's salary...	250 = $200	150 = $120
Remuneration of religious instructor.....................	80 = 64	50 = 40
Books and apparatus..	70 = 56	50 = 40
Total	400 = 320	250 = 200

To support a school in the country-districts costs, therefore, $200, and to this sum must be added fuel and lodging, which makes the total expense even somewhat higher. In order to cover this annual expense, it is estimated that eight hundred persons, or two hundred families, must, on an average, contribute $1 per family, or 25 cents per head. Even in comparison with richer countries than Russia, this seems much. It is true that, in the United States, in the Protestant cantons of Switzerland, and in Denmark, the average expense per head is higher, but in France it is only 39 cents per head, in Norway $27\frac{1}{2}$ cents, in Sweden $30\frac{3}{4}$ cents, in Spain and Greece 25 cents, in Italy $13\frac{3}{4}$ cents, and in Portugal 8 cents.

In Russia 800 persons live on an average scattered over eight hamlets, covering about 20 square "versts." The density of population is so small that there are only 13.6 inhabitants to one square kilometer, ($2\frac{3}{4}$ square kilometers to 1 square mile,) instead of 69, as in France. Under these circumstances only the children from the center hamlet and those living nearest to it could attend school regularly, especially during the winter-months. The remainder of the inhabitants would pay their dues without having any benefit, which would necessarily foster discontent. As Prince Gagarin says, "It has, therefore, not been possible to make education in Russia compulsory, as in Germany, nor even to enforce the establishment of a school in each community."

It is doubtless impossible at present to introduce into Russia the educational systems of the western countries. It is not there that the models for imitation are to be looked for. The geographical and social conditions differ too much, but there is a country in Europe where the same difficulties are met with as in Russia, and where, nevertheless, education is as generally diffused as in Switzerland, Germany, and Denmark, and that country is Norway. In Norway the population is still more scattered than in Russia, for there are only 4.7 inhabitants to the square kilometer. The ground moreover is very much broken by deep valleys and high plateaus ; the climate is exceedingly severe, and deep snow is very frequent; the hamlets are small, sometimes only composed of two or three farms lost in the wilderness. Nevertheless all Norwegians, and even many of the Lapps, know at least how to read and write, and most of the farmers have an excellent education. How have these extraordinary results been obtained ? By means of the itinerant school, the *flyttante skola*. A school-master travels through each of these districts, staying some time in each hamlet. He is received in one of the arms, where he is boarded and lodged, and gathers around him the children of the immediate neighborhood. As they are never very numerous, he can give his whole attention to each individual, and thus they make rapid progress in a short time. When the teacher is gone, the mother, who of course can read, repeats the lessons with her children, and thus prepares them to receive a new installment of instruction on the teacher's return. Popular education in Norway and the north of Sweden is spread almost exclusively by itinerant teachers. In 1840 there were in Norway 7,133 itinerant schools and only 222 permanent schools. Since the country has grown richer and the farmers have made greater sacrifices for the the cause of education, this proportion has been somewhat modified. According to the educational census, there were in 1863 3,560 itinerant schools and 2,757 permanent schools, and in 1866 3,999 permanent schools and only 2,345 itinerant schools.

THE COURSE WHICH RUSSIA OUGHT TO PURSUE.

Russia ought to follow the example of Norway, and make a commencement with the itinerant school. The peddler plays already an important part in the rural life of Russia. He brings the products of distant industry and news from the outside world, thus representing commerce and the press. The itinerant teacher would be the peddler of civilization. Education would thus be brought to every house, and the teacher's influence on the parents and the hamlets where they dwell could not fail to be a happy one. There should be no hesitation to ask the clergy to assist in this work, for, being thoroughly national, it would not become as in Roman-Catholic countries, the tool of ultramontane politicians. It would be well to adopt the ingenious idea recently put in practice in England, of making the subsidies granted proportionate to the result obtained. It is the principle of responsibility and of piecework introduced into the educational field. According to Article 19 of the new code of 1871, the director of a school which is open at least 400 times during the year—either forenoon or afternoon—can claim six shillings for every child which attends school regularly all the year round, and, besides this, for every child examined at the annual examination by the school-inspectors, 4 shillings if satisfactory in reading, 4 shillings if in writing, and 4 shillings if in arithmetic; making a total of 12 shillings.

Let this principle be introduced in Russia; let 1 or 2 roubles be given to the teacher or the priest for every child that can read and write, and the results will be surprising. But if progress is to be made, the government must above every thing grant a liberal appropriation. The Emperor Alexander was fully convinced of the urgent necessity of energetic action; but to do anything at all much money was required. In a recent decree (December 25, 1873) addressed to Count Dmitri Tolstoï, the minister of public instruction, the Emperor, after giving a rapid sketch of the development of education during the last few years, insists in the strongest terms on the urgency of upholding, by constant vigilance, the principles of faith, morality, and public duty in the numerous schools organized with a view to meet the demands of the age. The Emperor says: "That which, according to my view, ought to contribute towards the sound education of the younger generations, should never become an instrument of demoralization, a danger of which some symptoms are already showing themselves. To keep up popular education in the spirit of religion and morality is a task which belongs not only to the clergy, but to all enlightened men, especially the Russian nobility, which has been called to be the guardian of the public schools, by guarding them against dangerous and corrupting influences. To this effect, special rights have been conferred on the leaders of the nobility in their capacity of curators of the primary schools in their districts, and the minister of public instruction, in concert with the minister of the interior, is invited to come to an understanding with them, so as to enjoy their active co-operation in this great and useful work."

THE SCHOOL-FINANCES.

It is an indisputable fact that all the efforts of the nobility and the clergy will remain futile without considerable appropriations by the government. In 1870 Count Tolstoï demanded an increase of 200,000 roubles ($160,000) for the primary schools, and only got 100,000, ($80,000.) It must be acknowledged, however, that quite recently the appropriation has been considerably increased. The sum expended for primary schools in 1871 amounted to 2,742,008 roubles, ($2,193,606,) of which sum 1,271,825 roubles ($1,017,460) were raised by the city- and rural communities, 766,642 roubles ($613,313) by the provincial assemblies, and 703,541 roubles ($562,833) by the government. The government appropriation, which at first was only 100,000 roubles, ($80,000,) has, therefore, in a few years increased more than sixfold. The government, moreover, contributes 216,329 roubles ($173,036) towards the total annual cost of 334,351 roubles ($267,480) of the normal schools. The remainder of this sum has been raised by the provincial assemblies, by the interest from legacies, and by fees paid by the students. We must confess that these sums appear insignificant when compared with those expended for the same purposes in other countries, e. g., the United States or Germany. The city of Berlin recently voted an annual sum of $187,400 for five years for the erection of secondary schools. The wants of the primary schools in Russia are perfectly enormous. Nearly everywhere suitable school-houses are wanting. While official reports usually print everything in the brightest colors, the reports of Prince Gagarin and Count Tolstoï possess the great merit of concealing nothing, however disagreeable the truth may be.

STATISTICS OF THE RUSSIAN EDUCATIONAL REPORT OF 1871.

The Russian report, published in 1871 by the minister of public instruction, states that the regulations of 1864 have never been fully carried out

Of the 34 provinces where the *zemstvos* (provincial councils) have been organized, only 14 have sent in very incomplete reports. In these 14 provinces, the most densely populated and the most civilized of the empire —St. Petersburg, Moscow, Poltava, Tver, Kostroma, Cherson, Jaroslaf, Ekaterinoslaf, Charkof, Tambof, Orel, Kasan, Symbirsk, Penza—with 20,425,294 inhabitants, there were in January, 1870, 4,247 schools, with 4,982 teachers, (of whom 3,516 were priests,) and 143,385 scholars, *i. e.*, 1 scholar to every 142 inhabitants. In Denmark, Sweden, Norway, Saxony, and the Protestant cantons of Switzerland, there is 1 scholar to every 6 inhabitants. In the rural districts, the official report says, teachers are scarce and badly paid. The schools, small in number, are kept in the most unsuitable places, in the entries of large buildings or even by the side of the common prisons. In the district of Toula, according to the report published in French in 1872, only 12 of the 599 schools have a special school-building, 70 are in government-offices, 59 in the guard-houses attached to the churches, and the others in still worse places. The report says: "The bad location of most of the schools explains their very unsatisfactory condition, and is in every way injurious to the cause of public instruction. Badly-located schools, without competent teachers, without books and the most indispensable apparatus, are only calculated to create a general distrust of all education, and such distrust not unfrequently leads to the closing of the schools." Thus, in 1871, there was not a single school in the district of Tsaritsin, in the province of Saratof, because the schools had all been closed by the communal authorities and the buildings sold. "It must be confessed," says the minister of public instruction, "that these are deplorable facts, but they are easily explained by the lack of sufficient funds. According to information furnished by the superintendents of the school-districts, each school did, on an average, not have more than 142 roubles ($113) per annum, a sum which is entirely inadequate, because the minimum for which a school can be supported is 250 roubles, ($200.) The distribution of the funds is, moreover, very unequal. The two-class model schools of the ministry of public instruction receive each from 885 to 1,226 roubles, ($708 to $981,) and among the schools of the provincial assemblies there are some which have from 600 to 1,020 roubles, ($480 to $816.) On the other hand, there are some schools, *e. g.*, in the district of Gdovsk, in the province of St. Petersburg, which receive only 50, 25, and even 10 roubles, ($40, $20, and $8.) In order to put an end to such a deplorable state of affairs, it would be necessary to impose a school-tax on the communities and provinces proportionate to their resources and their wants, and, above everything else, to grant considerable subsidies from the treasury of the empire.

DIFFICULTY OF OBTAINING ACCURATE STATISTICS.

It is rather difficult to find out the exact number of primary schools; it seems that there are no complete official statistics, for the Russian report of Prince Gagarin for 1863 enumerated in 36 provinces (Russia in Europe has 49 provinces) 30,179 schools with 632,471 scholars, while the French report of Count Tolstoï for 1872 gives only 24,000 schools with 875,000 scholars for the whole of Russia in Europe. These numbers are, as the minister remarks, very insignificant compared to the population of Russia in Europe, which is about 65,000,000. Thus there would only be 1 scholar to every 75 inhabitants, while in the New England States and in Upper Canada there is 1 to every 4 inhabitants and 1 to every 6 in Denmark and Saxony. Even the states ranking lowest on the educational scale show a more favorable proportion than Russia : thus, Italy, 1 to 19; Greece, 1 to 20; Portugal, 1 to 40; and Servia, 1 to 48.

EFFORTS TO SUPPLY TEACHERS.

The government is fully aware of the absolute necessity of supplying a sufficient number of good teachers, if education is to prosper at all, and, consequently, makes great efforts to increase the number of normal schools or "seminaries." In the beginning of 1871 there were only 15 normal schools. During 1871 10 new ones were established, and it has been decided to have 8 more, thus more than doubling the number of these schools in one year. In January, 1873, their number was 41. Besides this the provincial assemblies have at their expense organized educational courses in connection with the district-schools in 18 different places. All this is doubtless insufficient; yet it is nevertheless pleasing to see the provincial administrations and the central government rivaling each other in their zeal in such a worthy cause. The central government, for example, appropriates 14,810 roubles ($11,848) per annum for the normal school at Kief, and paid 63,000 roubles ($50,400) besides for the erection of the building. The normal school of Kasan had, in 1871, cost 64,433 roubles, ($51,546,) and 25,000 roubles ($20,000) in 1872. At this price very convenient buildings can be had, and this liberality bears its own reward. In the one year 1872, the government-appropriation for normal schools has been increased by 229,000 roubles, ($183,200.) An important item, which the report neglects to mention, is the number of teachers annually supplied by these institutions and the number of teachers required every year. The extent of the want must be known before it can be fully supplied.

Teachers' conferences, which have proved so eminently useful in the United States, have been introduced in Russia. These conferences are held under the direction of experienced educators appointed by the educational authorities and under the superintendence of the inspectors of primary instruction. The expenses are paid by the provincial assemblies. These conferences have, during 1872, been held in 47 different places, and, according to the minister's report, have exercised a most beneficial influence, spreading the knowledge of better text-books, better methods of instruction, &c. They create centers of educational information, and thus supplement the preparation received at the normal school. It would be well if these conferences could be introduced in every province of the empire, obliging the teachers to attend them, and, of course, paying all their expenses. Teachers' meetings have become so popular in America that families vie with each other in extending their hospitality to the visiting teachers.

ILLITERACY.

Illiteracy is still very prevalent in the rural districts of Russia. According to Mr. Mitchell, British consul at St. Petersburg,* who has thoroughly studied the condition of the Russian rural population, only 8 to 9 per cent. of the population can read and write, and still the Russian peasant is naturally intelligent and learns very quickly everything he is taught. This seems to be one of the national characteristics, for it is well known that no nation learns foreign languages so easily and speaks them so fluently as the Russian. The peasant, who is a good hand at many trades, thereby sharpens his mental faculties. He not only raises all he wants in his household, but builds his own house and barns, manufactures his furniture, his clothes, tools, wagons, harness, and in fact everything which can be made with the few simple tools he possesses. The necessity and habit of thinking of everything, of being prepared for all emergencies, develop in him a taste for work, the faculty of imitation, and thus produce an astonishingly bright and intelligent workman. If education were brought to his door he would make excellent use of it. Educated and better fed, the Russian would make one of the best artisans in Europe. His principal weakness is intemperance. He drinks large quantities of strong liquor—the *vodka*—especially since it has come down in price, and has become *deshofka, i. e.*, cheap drink. The best means to combat this vice, which is actually the plague-spot of the rural districts, is to raise the intellectual standard of the rural population, so as to give them more elevated tastes and a desire for refined amusements.

LOCAL ADMINISTRATION.

The emancipation-law of 1861 accorded to each community an autonomy almost as complete as that of the American township. The inhabitants elect their communal council and their mayor—*staroste*. These authorities do not only exercise the local administration, but also the judiciary-power in the first degree. It is sometimes claimed that the Russian peasants are not sufficiently advanced to make the proper use of such decentralizing and radically democratic institutions, and various abuses springing therefrom are mentioned.† This system, however, is the same as that in force in Switzerland, even among the very

---

*See his admirable report in a Blue-book of 1870, entitled Reports from Her Majesty's Representatives respecting the Tenure of Land in the several Countries of Europe.

† Mr. Mitchell relates the following: Some time ago an inhabitant of Elisabetgrad accused Euphrosine M. of having proved faithless to her marriage-vows. Although no proof is furnished, the husband believes the story; he causes all the inhabitants to as

primitive peasants and shepherds of the forest-cantons, and works exceedingly well. It insures complete and at the same time orderly liberty, it accustoms the people to self-government, and inspires an ardent love of their country and respect for traditional usages. In order to make this system, which was introduced in Russia in 1861, work well, nothing would be required but to give to the Russian peasants that very rudimentary degree of education which the mountaineers of Uri and Unterwald possess. These, it is true, have enjoyed free institutions from times immemorial, but before Boris Godunof (Emperor of Russia 1598 to 1605) had introduced serfdom, the organization of the communities was like that of the Swiss cantons. The same system is in use among the southern Slavonians, in Servia. It would therefore be only a return to national traditions; only, as modern civilization is a much more elaborate system, more enlightenment would be required to administer well even a simple rural community.

EFFORTS FOR EDUCATING THE HALF-CIVILIZED RACES OF RUSSIA.

Russia is making great efforts to spread education among the half-civilized races which inhabit the vast steppes east of the river Don. Schools have been established for the Tartars, the Bashkires, and the Kirghise. The normal schools of Kasan and Irkoutsk are intended to prepare teachers for these Touranian races. This is a far-seeing policy, for it is not only a service rendered to general civilization, but, by thus spreading the Russian language, the assimilation of these foreign races with the remainder of the Slavonian population is gradually brought about. The same result is expected from the Tartar schools of Oufa and Simpheropol, whose chief and essential object is to train teachers who are thoroughly conversant with the Russian language. The Russian government, for very good reasons, attaches such importance to the success of these Tartar and Kirghise schools, that a special inspector, Mr. Radlof, has been appointed, who works among these tribes by persuasion and encouragement, who establishes schools wherever possible and puts them in working-order. He has also undertaken the publication of the most-needed text-books, viz, a manual for the study of the Russian language and an arithmetic for the use of the Tartars, also a Tartar reader. Another very interesting work has been published by order of the ministry of public instruction, viz, maps giving the exact location of all the foreign tribes in the provinces of Kasan, Astrakhan, and Samara, as well as all the German and other colonies.

RUSSIA'S RELATIONS WITH ASIA.

Russia does not neglect anything which tends to make her relations semble at the mayor's office, and has his wife convicted and condemned, without being allowed to plead her cause, to be led, stark naked, through the town and to receive 15 blows with a cane. This sentence was carried out literally, on a very cold October morning. This is certainly primitive and quick justice.

with the nations of Asia more intimate and is calculated to increase her influence in that part of the world. An academy of oriental languages has recently been established, now bearing the name of its first president, lately deceased, Privy Counselor Lazaref. In 1871, 20,000 roubles ($16,000) were appropriated for it. There are eight professorships, viz, of Armenian literature, of Arabic, Persian, Georgian, Turkish, Tartar, history of the eastern nations, and oriental calligraphy. The professors and students enjoy the same privileges as the professors and students of the universities. The recent expedition to Khiva has again shown how useful it is in war to know the language of the enemy. Two Russian officers, thoroughly conversant with the language of Khiva, repeated the bold enterprise of the Hungarian scientist and author, Vambéry, and visited Khiva in disguise, on their return furnishing the Russian commander with exact plans of all the canals and fortifications.

SECONDARY EDUCATION.

Secondary education in Russia is organized almost like that of Germany, especially since the promulgation of the law of 1871, which regulates the studies in the gymnasia, and that of 1872 regarding the real-schools. The gymnasium's course now embraces Greek, Latin, German, and French, besides the scientific branches. The Russian real-schools are very excellent institutions and every way suited to the wants of Russia. Without neglecting general studies like history, they devote nearly all their efforts to mathematics, drawing, chemistry, modern languages, and all those studies which tend to aid industrial activity. They enable young men to acquire a very complete and very superior education without troubling them with the study of the ancient classics, (humanitarian studies,) which frequently drive them into a career leading to nothing. Thus they diminish the number of those mistaken lives, or, to use a common expression, those "dry fruits," which are the plague of families and of society. Holland has likewise recently organized similar schools (*Hoogburgerscholen*) in all the more important towns.

The proof that these schools in Russia really meet an urgent want is seen in the fact that as soon as the ministry had promulgated the law more than forty provincial assemblies and municipalities applied to the ministry to have such real-schools established. Twenty-four at once furnished a building, an endowment, and guaranteed an annual appropriation. The endowments offered during the single year 1872 amounted to 280,000 roubles, ($224,000,) not counting twelve buildings, some of which were of considerable value.

The city of Borissoglebsk, in the province of Tambof, offers a building valued at $30,000; Kief one at $43,000. The city of Rostof, on the river Don, gives annually more than $20,000, a sum sufficient to cover all the expenses of a six-class real-school. Sarapoul annually appropriates $10,000; Krementchoug, $12,000; Rossieni, $8,000; Krasnooufimsk, in the province of Perm, a building valued at $12,000 for a real-school, four classes of which are intended specially to meet the wants of that locality in mining and metallurgy, with agricultural instruction in the fifth and sixth classes and applied mechanics in the select class. These numerous demands, accompanied by such generous offers even from the most distant provinces of the empire, are admirable manifestations of the spirit of progress which is awakening everywhere; they prove that the local authorities are fully alive to the fact that only by the diffusion of scientific knowledge can the natural resources of a country be developed. The funds placed at the disposal of the ministry by the government are, we are sorry to say, as yet entirely insufficient, and most of the above-mentioned requests, so worthy of the strongest encouragement, have consequently been laid over for the present. At the end of the year 1872 there were not more than 27 real-schools, not, however, including those of the scholastic districts of Dorpat and the Caucasus.

On the 1st of January, 1872, there were in Russia 126 gymnasia and 32 progymnasia, with 42,751 scholars, 3,720 more than in 1871. The number of those presenting themselves for the August admission-examinations was 11,068; 2,239 (*i. e.*, 20 per cent.) were unable to pass these examinations, which are extremely rigorous, and in spite of this 44 of the 127 gymnasia had to refuse the admission of 1,048 youths who had passed the examination, merely because there was no room. This is another proof of the eagerness of the people to make the best use of the means of education offered them. What a strange contrast; in other countries the government makes efforts to stir up the local authorities and the private citizens in the cause of education, while in Russia private individuals, city- and provincial authorities outstrip the government in their efforts. It is the most sacred duty of the government to encourage this work of regeneration. During the year 1871 the gymnasia and progymnasia cost 4,467,644 roubles. ($3,574,115,) of which sum the government paid 3,215,889 roubles, ($2,572,711,) or about 72 per cent.; the remainder has been provided by the municipal authorities, the provincial assemblies, private individuals, and by the interest derived from school-funds. It is a curious and significant fact that Russia every year appoints a number of Austrian Slavonians as teachers in her secondary schools, 60 in 1870 and 60 in 1871. If this continues it cannot fail to exercise an important political influence in the future.

EFFORTS TO RUSSIANIZE POLAND AND THE BALTIC PROVINCES.

The official report also speaks of the persevering efforts to russianize Poland and the Baltic provinces. In 1871 there was in Poland only one gymnasium where instruction was not imparted in Russian, and this one happened to be originally a German school. The report says that, in the latter half of 1871, this gymnasium has been placed under the municipal authorities as a German one. The Polish language is thus entirely banished from the secondary schools, and the examinations in the Russian language for admission to the gymnasia are particularly severe. The report says, "that in consequence of these measures parents have their children better instructed in Russian, and the Russian language is studied much more generally than formerly." In the Baltic (German-speaking) provinces—all comprised in the scholastic district of Dorpat—the authorities have gone to work with more precaution. Of the eleven gymnasia in this district there were ten where not only was Russian not the language of instruction, but where the study of Russian left much to be desired. Most families prefer German, which is their mother-tongue and which forms the connecting-link with western civilization. The teachers of Russian are either Germans, who are but very imperfectly acquainted with the language they are to teach, or Russians who have not studied philology. To remedy this defect, which the Russian government considers very deplorable, six free places have been established in the historico-philological institute to educate teachers of Russian for the gymnasia in the district of Dorpat. In Riga a new gymnasium, the Alexander Gymnasium, has been opened, where all branches of study are taught in Russian; and a second gymnasium on the same plan, also to be called Alexander Gymnasium, is shortly to be established in Reval. Both these gymnasia have been richly endowed by the government. It is but natural that the Russian government should endeavor to spread the national language in the provinces inhabited by a foreign population. France has done the same in Alsace and French Flanders and Prussia in the duchy of Posen, but everything which looks like a persecution of the very natural love of a people for their mother-tongue should be avoided. Compulsory measures are apt to awaken a spirit of resistance and make the process of assimilation exceedingly difficult.

EDUCATION OF WOMEN.

There is one branch of education in which Russia does more than many a western country, viz, the education of the daughters of the wealthy classes. With us (in Belgium) lyceums and colleges are opened for young men, but the girls receive their instruction in the convents. The result of this is frequently a very serious difference between husband and wife, the former being thoroughly imbued with modern, liberal ideas, the latter blindly subject to ultramontane influences. In Russia the government, the provincial and municipal authorities, have established gymnasia and progymnasia for young ladies, where a very high standard of education is aimed at, and in most cases successfully, to judge from the knowledge and general superiority of Russian ladies of the higher class who have been educated in these schools. At Moscow there is one school, the Fisher Gymnasium, where the course of studies is exactly the same as in a gymnasium for boys. A professor of the Moscow University has established higher courses of study for ladies, thus enabling them to acquire a university-education; this is carrying out M. Duruy's idea, who would have succeeded in France had it not been for the desperate opposition of the bishops. In Russia, as in the United States, ladies have facilities for acquiring a high degree of his torical, scientific, or philologic knowledge, without running the risk of being excommunicated. The government has increased the annual appropriation for the higher schools for young ladies, in 1873, from 50,000 roubles ($40,000) to 100,000 roubles, ($80,000,) and in 1874 to 150,000 roubles, ($120,000.) At the end of 1871 there were 186 secondary schools for females, with 23,404 scholars, supported at an annual expense of $500,000. The total number of schools of all grades, in January, 1872, was 1,081, with 38,430 scholars, viz, 16,641 boys and 21,789 girls; thus, strange to say, more girls than boys. Nearly all the private schools are at St. Petersburg and at Moscow; 835 of them were primary schools.

THE RUSSIAN UNIVERSITIES.

Russia has eight universities, organized on the German plan. These are: St. Petersburg, Moscow, Charkof, Kasan, Kief, Odessa, Dorpat, and Warsaw. The total number of professors was 512 and that of the students 6,779, of whom 3,247, or almost one-half, or 47 per cent., studied law; medicine was studied by 1,922, or 27 per cent. The number of students studying at the public expense is very considerable; 1,430 are educated entirely free, 2,208 have only to pay half, and 1,732 receive occasional subsidies; thus 80 per cent. are not able to bear their own expenses. This is a curious fact, throwing a peculiar light on Russian society, showing that the wealthier classes do not send their sons to the universities and that the middle classes only do this to a very limited degree. What a contrast to the English universities, attended almost exclusively by the sons of lords and millionaires! The power of the English aristocracy is based on this circumstance, that young noblemen generally study hard and are early inured to political work and made acquainted with political traditions. Russia has been much in want of good professors for the universities, and many professorships have in consequence had to remain vacant for a great length of time. To rem edy this, the government has resolved to establish, under its own au spices, a nursery for young professors. An appropriation of $50,000 has been made for educating young men of talent, at home and abroad, with this special object. Another excellent measure in which Russia is ahead of several western nations is this, that at her universities special scien tific courses have been established on the German plan and have been liberally provided with buildings, apparatus, and scientific instruments Astronomical observatories have been established at Odessa and at Kief. In 1871 a building was finished specially devoted to chemis try, where students have the very best facilities for making chemical experiments, the necessity for which is more and more acknowledged. During the single year 1871 the government has increased the appropri ation for the universities by $105,000.

MUNIFICENCE OF PRIVATE INDIVIDUALS.

The Russian and the American governments have on all occasions given proof of the cordial relations existing between them. Private individuals in Russia seem also desirous of rivaling American citizens in their munificence in the cause of education. We give the following instances: M. Naryshkin has founded a normal school at Tambof, provided it with a large and handsome building, and endowed it with a sum of $370,000. The munificent gift of M. Matveïef has greatly increased the histological cabinet of the Moscow University; thanks to the liberality of the Countess Maussin-Pushkin, instruction has reached a much higher standard in the Lyceum of Negine; a legacy of M. Botkin, a citizen of Moscow, has enabled the university in that city to found an art-museum and to give a prize for works on national history; at Holdingen the nobility has founded a gymnasium; the normal school at Tver has been founded and is supported at the expense of M. Maximof, a citizen of that place. These examples are selected at random from the reports of only two years, 1871 and 1872, and there are very few countries which can equal this. There are patriotic people in all countries, but there are only few whose patriotism is so enlightened as to find out in which way they can benefit their country most.

COMPULSORY MILITARY SERVICE AND COMPULSORY EDUCATION.

The Russian government has recently passed a law making military service compulsory for all citizens of the empire. If it was not for the want of schools, education also would have been made compulsory. The government which imposes barracks on the population ought also to impose schools. It must, no doubt, be regretted that Europe is gradually being transformed into an armed camp, perhaps one day to become an immense battle-field, but this is a necessity to which a nation desirous of maintaining its independence must submit; only, if the state requires every citizen to carry arms for the defense of the country, its first duty is to give in exchange to every one the benefits of education.

Count Tolstoï expresses his opinion on this subject in words which deserve to be quoted here: "It is an absolute necessity that there should be found everywhere primary schools, with competent teachers and a full supply of text-books and apparatus. One of the best means for obtaining this result would be the gradual introduction of a system of compulsory education. As the example of Prussia and the whole of Germany has shown, there is no doubt that this system is the most powerful means of diffusing education among all classes of society. Several of our provincial assemblies are discussing this question." Count Tolstoï then states that in most of the villages and even the cities there is not a sufficient number of schools. A commencement must therefore be made to establish schools; but in the two chief cities, Moscow and St. Petersburg, nothing prevents the introduction of compulsory education. The minister adds: "It seems to me that the time has arrived when this system should be applied to the youth of these two cities, who are placed in an exceptionally favorable condition as regards education. Such a measure would accustom to work and study a large number of young people who now spend their time in idleness, and who thus become useless or even dangerous to society." A census of all the children of school-age has been taken with a view of making education compulsory, so that in this matter Russia will have preceded England and France.

CONCLUSION.

In spite of the relatively great progress made during the last few years, which is shown by the reports of the minister of public instruction for 1871 and 1872, Russia must still make enormous sacrifices in order to bring the country up to the standard of the most advanced nations. As M. Anatole Leroy-Beaulieu has recently demonstrated, (Revue des deux mondes, January 15, 1874,) Russia has been retarded in her progress for several centuries by the invasion of the Tartars, which lasted till the end of the Middle Ages, but to-day all the authorities and all the influential classes of the empire seem fully resolved to make up for lost time, and we can but applaud this zeal. The full and free development of education in this immense eastern empire is of the greatest interest for the whole of the human race. Only through Russia can civilization penetrate the vast regions of Central Asia. We have seen with what success devoted Russian officials organize schools even among the nomadic tribes of Tartars and Kirghise east of the Volga. In the same manner will the pacified principalities of Central Asia be gradually brought within the reach of western civilization. The day will come, for there is nothing to hinder it, when the vast uninhabited portions of Siberia and Independent Tartary will be populated and brought under civilizing western influence. The great Slavonian race has not yet been able to fully develop its genius, because it has been broken up in small groups and has sighed under the yoke of slavery. It has not yet given to the civilization of the world as much as the Latin and Germanic races. It possesses, however, faculties and institutions of its own which ought not to be lost or led into a wrong channel by a servile imitation of western races. The peculiarly Russian element ought, on the contrary, to be respected, giving it scope to develop to its full extent by a general diffusion of knowledge among all classes of the population. We have not hesitated to give accurate figures and details, because the progress of education in the immense eastern empire is of as much interest for the future of Western Europe as for Russia herself. The words inscribed on a pillar standing on the lava at the foot of Mount Vesuvius, *Res nostra agitur*, are applicable here. The destinies of European civilization depend in a great measure on the degree of education which Russia will have attained a hundred years hence. Before one or two centuries have elapsed the Russian Empire will be the most powerful state in Europe, because its enormous extent could easily accommodate three hundred millions of inhabitants, while the growth of the other countries will necessarily be limited by the narrow confines of their territory. If the mass of the Russian people remains ignorant, the form of government will inevitably remain a military despotism; and in that case this gigantic empire will, in the hands of an absolute monarch, be a standing menace to the liberty of Europe; for we cannot with certainty count on a constant succession of wise and peaceful sovereigns like the present emperor. Western Europe would then be at the mercy of the whims of a monarch commanding armies of three to four millions of men. If, on the contrary, the light of knowledge is diffused fast enough to allow Russia to change into a free and constitutional state, by the time she is strong enough to rule Europe the danger to civilization will have disappeared, for a free people has no interest in making conquests or in subjugating other nations. This is so self-evident that it needs no proof. Suppose Russia arrived at the present status of England or the United States; there would be no cause to fear that she would endeavor to extend her boundaries by annexing less civilized countries. The defenders of the old system of European equilibrium will no doubt object to this; but, from a general human point of view, it could not be a matter of regret. Let us wish that the Russian government will not shrink from making the sacrifices which are necessary for the spreading of general education. The future of liberty, of European civilization, demands this as much as the true interests of the great Slavonian empire.

STATISTICS.

Sums expended for educational purposes by the various ministries in 1872-'73.

	Roubles.	
Schools under the "Holy Synod"	1,539,225=	$1,090,284 37
Ministry of public instruction	13,168,125	9,327,421 87
Ministry of war	6,026,356	4,268,668 83
Ministry of the navy	449,922	318,744 33
Ministry of finance	3,513,659	2,488,841 79
Ministry of domains	785,692	556,531 83
Ministry of the interior	338,477	239,744 54
Ministry of public works	159,815	113,202 29
Ministry of justice	402,824	285,335 33
Ministry of Caucasia	508,093	359,899 20
Ministry of foreign affairs	12,800	9,066 66
Schools under the direction of the Empress Maria	1,551,494	1,098,974 91
Total	28,455,482	20,156,775 95

Large sums are annually expended for educational purposes by cities, towns, and private individuals, but nothing definite regarding their amount is known.

Higher schools.—Universities, 8, (not including the one in Finland,) with 543 professors and 6,115 students; lyceums, 5, with about 690 students.

Intermediate schools.—Gymnasia, 122, with 39,270 scholars; progymnasia, 33, with 5,014 scholars; real-schools, 7,[*] with 1,752 scholars.

Lower schools.—District-schools, 423, with 29,709 scholars; popular schools, 21,666, with 875,445 scholars.

Special schools.—Normal schools and teachers' seminaries, 54, with 2,552 students; higher theological schools, 4, with 118 professors and 446 students; intermediate theological schools, 51, with 789 professors and 13,103 students; lower theological schools, 187, with 1,375 professors and 26,671 students; higher military schools, 7, with 1,416 students; intermediate military schools, 25, with 6,330 students; lower military schools, 31, with 6,863 students; naval schools, 7, with 1,109 students; agricultural schools, higher, 3, with 293 students; agricultural schools, lower, 16, with 1,025 students; higher technical schools, 6, with 2,666 students; lower technical schools, 12; schools of art and drawing, 5; schools of music and the drama, 3; business-colleges, 4; law-schools, 1, with 320 students, (each university has a faculty of law;) schools of philology, 3.

Schools exclusively for females.—Institutes, 28, with 5,453 scholars; gymnasia and progymnasia, 195, with 23,854 scholars. No statistics can be obtained regarding the private schools.

The above data are from the Russian Annual of Suworin.

PROJECT FOR EDUCATING RUSSIAN WANDERING TRIBES.

The following project for educating the wandering tribes of the Russian provinces of Central Asia has been prepared by Governor-General Kauffman, and, having been approved by the ministry of public instruction, will no doubt become a law:

(1) The object is to spread a knowledge of the Russian language among all these nationalities; and

(2) To instruct the children in such knowledge as will be useful to them in their daily life.

To accomplish all this, it is proposed to establish schools called district-schools in all the district-towns, each school to have two divisions, a higher and a lower one, and, besides, a class for mechanics. Those in the lowest division learn reading, writing, (Russian,) and arithmetic, and their mother-tongue, written in Russian letters. The study of the mother-tongue, however, is not obligatory.

The older ones continue the branches taught and add to it geography of the country and elements of natural science. Each such school has 50 free places, paid for by the Crown and selected from among the Kirghise. The course lasts four years; the Kirghise free scholars are pre

---

[*] In 1873 twenty-three new real-schools were opened, whose number of scholars is not known.

pared as teachers by the practice of teaching in the lower classes. Those who wish to become teachers remain five years, and are then specially trained in teaching. After having finished their course, they receive a certificate empowering them to open a school, (elementary.) They are not obliged to open a school, but it is hoped that most of them will do so, as the Kirghise are very loth to leave their home.

The idea in opening elementary schools in the steppes is this, that when a teacher gets together a school of 20 scholars he receives a salary from the Crown, as well as the text-books and apparatus. He only loses his salary if in three years his scholars show no progress. To do his duty and encourage him, a sum is paid him for every scholar who passes the examination for entering the higher division. Everywhere the Kirghise is taught in Russian characters. In Tashkend, the capital of Toorkistan, a teachers' seminary is established, with a model school, exactly on the plan of the district-school. No schools will be opened till the first class has graduated from this seminary.

The above information has been kindly furnished by Mr. M. Brodowski, a Russian gentleman who has been associated in service with General Kauffman.

EDUCATION IN TURKEY.

: E

EDUCATION IN TURKEY.

ƴ

By M. DE SALVE.

[From the Revue des deux mondes, October 15, 1874.]

INTRODUCTION.

The commercial and political relations of Turkey with other European nations have not yet produced those changes and that progress which might be expected. The administrative reforms which the Turkish government has thought it its duty to make in yielding to foreign influence are rather imaginary than real, because they frequently shocked national prejudices, were badly interpreted, and did not take into account national customs, which were but little accessible to influences from without. The family-relations, the true basis of all society, have not undergone any modification, the right of property accorded to foreigners is almost illusory, and public offices are held almost exclusively by Mohammedans. At this day, as at the time of the conquest, the Turks show but little taste for agriculture. The richest lands are cultivated by Greeks, and the taxes, in kind, are gathered in a manner calculated to oppress the producer and consumer. Commerce is almost entirely in the hands of Greeks, Armenians, and foreigners. There is no middle class of society to stimulate by its activity the aristocracy, which is dying from indolence.

The sheik-ul-islam, or chief religious dignitary, is one of the most influential men in the empire. His authority has more than once held Sultans in check, and he has to be consulted when any innovation is to be introduced. He is the acknowledged guardian of ancient traditions, and it is reported on good authority that even recently he has demanded that two Turkish *littérateurs* should be condemned to death because in a public lecture they had spoken slightingly of the Mohammedan prophecies. All that was done, however, was to deprive them of their offices. If, as a general rule, the Christian or *Giaour* is no longer exposed to persecutions, he still finds but little sympathy among the Turks. The Koran is the object of general veneration and religious indifference is not considered fashionable. At the time of the *Ramadan*, abstinence is observed with a rigor unknown with us, and I have for several years seen a large number of scholars go to school, during this season of fasting, from morning till evening, without eating or drinking. The English missionaries working in Asia Minor make proselytes among the Armenians, but never among the Turks. This fidelity to the Mohammedan

237

religion is also found in Algiers. Excepting the children of a tender age, which during the famine of 1866 were received in the convents, there are in our African possessions fewer converted Arabs than there are renegades in the one city of Constantinople.

The army, which does not number more than 300,000 men, has been organized on the European model, and the former lack of discipline has entirely disappeared. It is composed of soldiers whose bravery is highly praised and who are remarkably sober; but its numerical weakness and the general incompetency of the officers would not enable it to offer effectual resistance to a well-disciplined invading army. The government has so far refused to admit Christians to the army, and the military service has, therefore, been borne exclusively by the Turks, and proved a heavy burden to them. If Turkey, following the example of other nations, wished to double or treble the number of her troops, the resources of the country would not be sufficient either to supply the required number of men or to support them. The English have not hesitated to enroll the natives of their colonies, and if mixed corps did not prove as valuable as expected, they have found purely national regiments to answer very well.

The sources of public wealth are either not cultivated or are exhausted, and the receipts and expenditures have for some time past been very unevenly balanced. Since the Crimean war the deficiency has increased every year in alarming proportions, and the successive loans have become more and more difficult and onerous. After having used up the certain portion of the revenue, other means have to be employed to meet the urgent expenses, and the interest on former loans is paid by contracting new loans at the rate of 25 to 30 per cent. All the civil and military officers of the government have to wait for the payment of their salaries, usually seven to eight months, sometimes one to two years. Such a situation proves the authority of the government over the nation, but it seems scarcely possible that it can be continued for any length of time.

Education is so little diffused among Mohammedans, even among the higher classes, that the progress which, in other countries, is made in agriculture, industry, and the arts, is unknown or not understood. From pride, or ignorance, which frequently comes to the same, the Turks let the rayahs (i. e., all subjects of the Sultan who are not Mohammedans) enrich themselves at their expense, under their very eyes, and reserve to themselves no other means of acquiring a fortune than public offices or the munificence of the Sultan. The state of education in Turkey would alone be sufficient to explain the weakness and inferiority of the Turkish population, if compared with neighboring nations and foreign nationalities living in Turkey. If a beginning is not made to instruct the masses, no reform can prosper, no effort to fertilize this fallow-ground can be successful, and it is to be feared that the empire will rapidly undergo a process of decomposition.

The French government has made more than one attempt to awaken
the Turkish nation from its torpor; one of the most earnest and perhaps
least known of these attempts aimed at the reorganization of public instruction on a solid basis and to urge the establishment of imperial
lyceums in the principal cities.

THE CONDITION OF TURKISH WOMEN.

There is in Turkey no school for young Mohammedan ladies; it has,
no doubt, been thought that the life in the harem which awaits them
renders all education useless. During the last few years some of the
daughters of pashas have commenced to learn music and a foreign language; that was sufficient for them. Turkish family-life is so walled
up that very little of it is known, and most of the descriptions which
have been given of it are purely imaginary. The Turkish lady, unac-
quainted with serious work, lives in her harem occupied with trifles,
unless she gives her attention to her offspring; she only goes out accompanied by her slaves and eunuchs, and clad in her ancient costume,
which is certainly not deficient in originality, the Paris fashion-plates
being but little consulted. Sultan Mahmoud, who desired to change
the male costume, never attempted anything of the kind with regard to
female dress. A marriageable woman must be veiled; no person, with
the exception of her husband and children, ever sees her face; her name
is never pronounced. This mysterious position pleases her, and she
does not look favorably on the emancipation of woman. Her influence
over her husband and children is great, and I have frequently heard
fathers of families cite the opposition of the mother as a reason why
children did not receive that degree of education which they considered
desirable. As an almost unique exception, I mention a silk-spinning
establishment, founded at Brousa by a Frenchman, who has for a long
time acted in the capacity of consul, where about one hundred Turkish
women and girls are employed. In spite of many attempts made in
this direction, there is only one French manufacturing-establishment
in Algeria where young Arab girls make and sell embroidered work.
Modern nations, by developing the intelligence and the working-power
of woman, occupy a better economical and moral position than those of
former ages.

There is a very general impression that the morals of the harem are
extremely lax. This may be the case, although it is extremely difficult
to get at the exact truth, because but little news reaches the outside
world of matters transpiring within the harem-walls. It is nevertheless
a remarkable fact that during the stay of the European armies in Turkey
on the occasion of the Crimean war, there has not been a single case of
seduction or scandal as far as the Turkish women were concerned.
Polygamy, authorized by the Koran, is surrounded by so many obligations to support each wife in becoming style, that only the rich can
afford it, and even in Constantinople the number of those who are able

to indulge in this frequently ruinous luxury is extremely small. The prodigality of Sultan Abdul-Medjid towards his wïves baffles description. Boys are confined to the harem for six or seven years, and are left to the care of female slaves and eunuchs, of whom the mother generally possesses a considerable number. Such a course is certainly not calculated to develop their morality and to awaken a taste for learning. Later they go out every day to attend the public schools as day-scholars.

THE VARIOUS KINDS OF SCHOOLS.

Three kinds of schools may be distinguished, viz: ward-schools, *ruchdiyés*, and mosque-schools. Each ward or *mahallé* has a small school founded by special bequests, where the *imam* teaches the Turkish alphabet and reads the Koran in Arabic with his pupils. All children attend these schools for five or six years and pay a small fee. On leaving the ward-schools, at the age of 10 or 12, they are admitted as day-scholars to the *ruchdiyés*, schools of a higher grade where instruction is given gratuitously. There they learn to read and write Turkish, the rudiments of arithmetic, history and geography of Turkey. The course at these schools lasts five to six years, and on leaving them the scholars return to their families. Of a higher grade are the mosque-schools, in which the course of instruction embraces Turkish, Arabic, philosophy, theology and history. Instruction is entirely gratuitous and is imparted in Arabic; it does not include any of the natural sciences. The professors of these schools are highly esteemed and their directors are called "rectors." Pupils enter these mosque-schools at the age of 16 to 18, and attend them for about fifteen years; they are lodged free of expense in special houses called *médrézés*, generally occupied by 40 to 100. I have been informed that at Constantinople there are about 500 *médrézés*, while at Adrianople there are only 17. During the month of rest, the *Ramadan*, most of the students scatter through the provinces and earn a little money by giving religious instruction in mosques. Leaving the mosque-schools at the age of 30 to 35, many of these students become cadis, muftis, or rectors. Most of the prominent men of Turkey have been students at the mosque-schools.

During the most flourishing period of the Turkish Empire the mosque-schools enjoyed a very high reputation; at present, the only important studies at these schools are Arabic and religion, so that they may actually be considered theological schools. The principal code of civil and religious law being the Koran, it will easily be understood that religious instruction is of greater importance in Turkey than in other countries. This organization of instruction seems to extend through all Mohammedan countries, as it is found almost in the same shape in Algeria, Arabia, &c.

SPECIAL SCHOOLS.

Besides the above-mentioned schools, which are open to all Mohammedan children, there are a number of special schools, which are in the hands of the government. The more important of these schools are the military academy, the naval academy, the artillery-school, and the medical school. Each of these has a preparatory school, or *idadiyé*. Instruction in all these schools is imparted free of charge. In the *idadiyés* the scholars remain three to five years, according to whether they have attended the *ruchdiyés* or not, and study Turkish, (reading and writing,) arithmetic, elements of Turkish geography and history, and occasionally the rudiments of some foreign language, such as English, German, or French. The course of the military academy and the artillery-school extends over four years and that of the medical school over six. These courses embrace all such knowledge as may be useful in future life to the students of such schools; but the ignorance of the pupils admitted to them from the *idadiyés* unfortunately paralyzes even the most laborious efforts. These young people, who know nothing but reading, writing, and arithmetic, are in six years to become doctors of medicine and in four years officers in the army. If these special schools are to be of any benefit, the reforms must begin in the *idadiyés*. Instruction in the medical school has for forty years been given in French, as the almost total absence of scientific terms and of medical works in the Turkish language justified this measure. From similar causes instruction in jurisprudence, medicine, and philosophy has, with us, for a long time been given in Latin. The *darichoura*, (great military council,) yielding to the reactionary spirit produced by political events, has demanded that all instruction shall be given in Turkish, which is by competent judges considered to be fraught with evil consequences for the study of medicine, and which is at any rate a premature measure.

There are at Constantinople some other special schools of less importance, the best known being a normal school for preparing teachers for the *ruchdiyés*, a school of languages which furnishes all the official translators to the government, a school of forestry with a French director, where all instruction is given in French. This last-mentioned school generally has only 8 to 10 students. Each province has ward-schools, mosque-schools, a *ruchdiyé*, and sometimes an *idadiyé*.

THE SCHOOL-LAW OF 1869.

The school-law of 1869 contains the following provisions:

(1) Each ward or village must have at least one primary school; in towns containing more than 500 houses, primary schools of a higher grade shall be established.

(2) Each town containing more than 1,000 houses must have a preparatory school or college and the capital of each province must have a lyceum.

(3) At Constantinople there is to be an Imperial University and a great council of education.

The excellent provisions of this law have unfortunately never been carried out, and neither new primary schools, nor colleges, nor lyceums, have been established. The funds gave out, and there was a most deplorable want of competent teachers. This want has been so great that four years ago, in a large educational institution, among eleven Turkish teachers, some of whom enjoyed a high reputation, there was not one capable of writing for a young child a complimentary address in Turkish to the grand-vizier, and recourse had to be had to the wisdom of the president of the educational council. It was the intention to establish a university at Constantinople, but the only result has been a few elementary courses, and even this poor attempt has provoked a systematic and blind opposition. As regards the imperial council of education, it has existed for some years, and may exist yet, because it provides for its members a well-paid leisure.

THE MINISTRY OF PUBLIC INSTRUCTION.

The annual appropriation for the ministry of public instruction has for a long time been two millions of francs, (about $400,000 ;) but when, at the end of 1871, Mahmoud Pasha became grand-vizier, he reduced it to 1,300,000 francs, ($260,000,) one-half of which sum went towards paying the salaries of the minister, his secretary and counselors. The whole *personnel* of the ministry is a mere luxury, as it could easily be reduced to one director and a few clerks. The ministry of public instruction has nothing to do with the special schools, the mosque-schools, the *ruchdiyés*, nor with the ward-schools, all these having their own funds and being dependent on other branches of the administrative service. The schools founded by the *rayas* and by foreigners are maintained and managed by them exclusively, so that the functions of the ministry of public instruction extend to only a very small number of schools, *e.g.*, the normal school at Constantinople and some small schools in the provinces.

The law of 1869 has produced no change. Besides the small number of pupils admitted to the special schools and those studying at the mosque-schools, Turkish children, as heretofore, learn nothing but reading, writing, and arithmetic, and are not even well advanced in these elementary studies.

DIFFICULTY OF THE TURKISH LANGUAGE.

The written language of Turkey has no accents and punctuation-marks, but, on the contrary, four different systems of letters, with which only a very small number of persons are familiar. Turkish reading also presents special difficulties, as a written word can be read in different ways, the context of the sentence being in such cases the only guide. The book-language is composed of words in Turkish proper, Arabic, and Persian, and in order to know Turkish well a knowledge of these three languages is required, that Turkish being considered the most elegant which contains the largest number of Arabic and Persian words. It is said that Ali Pasha and Fuad Pasha, who were well versed in their mother-tongue, were not always understood by their colleagues in the ministerial council when they used their choicest language. It is therefore not astonishing that a Turk who can correctly read and write his own language is considered a man of learning, and many high officials might be mentioned who have by no means got so far. Ignorance is far-spread among the Turks, and in order to hide it, and not to be obliged to progress, they prefer to let everything remain *in statu quo*. Fearing that their dominions and riches will pass completely into the hands of foreigners, they refuse all help from outside, and hedge themselves in with an antiquated and exclusive legislation which is their temporary safety. How long will they be able to maintain this state of isolation?

DIFFERENCES OF RACE AND CREED.

The population of Turkey is composed of a number of different races, which are easily distinguished by their habits and customs, and by a sort of autonomy acknowledged by the government. Till quite recently the Turks formed a privileged caste, similar to the old French nobility, and not always free from pride and harshness towards the *rayahs*. This tendency of conquerors to constitute themselves an aristocracy seems to be the natural consequence of every conquest, and is met with in India, England, America, Algeria, and other countries. It is scarcely forty years since every *rayah* had to give way to a Turk on the street and had to salute him. When, some time later, steamers commenced to run on the Bosporus, the deck was divided in two parts, the *rayahs* occupying the fore part and the Turks the stern. These outward signs of inequality have now disappeared, but I would not venture to affirm that there are no traces of it left and that there are no longer any prejudices of superiority on the one hand and a spirit of defiance on the other. During the last months of 1871, while Mahmoud Pasha was vizier, the prefect of Constantinople published an order forbidding Christians to smoke during the *Ramadan* on ships, in the streets, and on porches. It is only owing to the repeated requests of high personages that this order has not been carried into effect.

In no other capital of Europe have the various nationalities and creeds preserved their distinguishing features to such a degree as in Constantinople. Education, which in other countries unites the children of all classes in common centers and by enlarging their views gradually establishes bonds of union and fraternity, has in Turkey tended to widen the distance, because each nationality supports its own educational institutions, where instruction is given in the mother-tongue and where religious traditions are preserved and political prejudices fostered. There is a deep gulf between the Christian and Turkish schools, and only in a few exceptional cases have Christian students been admitted to the medical school and the military academy.

Christians of different denominations, as well as Jews, support a large number of schools. The most important ones at Constantinople are the Greek Phanar school, with 300 to 400 pupils; the Armenian school of Haskeuï; the Jewish school of Ortakeuï; the Italian school at Pera, under the management of the Jesuits; the French schools of the Lazarists and the Brothers of the Christian Doctrine; the German, the English schools, &c. French Jesuits, who were at a later date succeeded by the Lazarists, opened boys' schools at Constantinople more than three hundred years ago. They were followed in their turn by the Sisters of Charity and the Brothers of the Christian Doctrine. The course of instruction in most of these schools is very exhaustive, embracing Greek, Latin, the mother-tongue, history, geography, philosophy, and natural sciences.

It will be seen from this that both Christians and Jews have secondary schools. As regards the Turks, they have primary schools—the ward-schools and the *ruchdiyés*—and superior schools—the mosque-schools and special schools; but there is no system of secondary schools to complete the primary education and prepare for the higher studies, or was not, at least, before the year 1868. This deplorable hiatus has tended to place the conquering race on a lower level of intelligence than the conquered races; it filled the special schools, and, consequently, the public offices, with incapable or insufficiently-prepared men. Endeavors were made to remedy this state of affairs, and forty young men were sent to Paris at great expense, there to study with distinguished teachers, and to fill responsible places in Turkey on their return. This Turkish school at Paris has unfortunately, from various reasons, not yielded the results which were expected, and ought to be closed.

THE LYCEUM AT GALATA-SÉRAÏ.

It seemed natural, under these circumstances, to make an attempt to found, in the country, schools which offered the opportunity to young people of completing their education under the eyes of their families and of acquiring that degree of literary and scientific knowledge which is indispensable to every well-educated person of any nationality. M. Bourée, the French minister, has entertained this idea since his arrival in Constantinople, and urged the Turkish government to establish lyceums for secondary instruction in the principal cities of the empire. He succeeded in awakening the interest of Sultan Abdul-Aziz and his ministers; he inspired them with his enthusiasm and made them adopt measures which assured the success of this patriotic undertaking. The attacks made on him on this occasion showed that his enemies understood the great importance of the undertaking and the services it would render to the Turkish government.

The beautiful building at Galata-Séraï, erected originally for military barracks on the plateau of Pera, fronting the Bosporus, was selected for this first attempt, and it was resolved to start there a model lyceum. The twofold object in view was to introduce a new grade of instruction

iven in a foreign language and to merge the various nationalities of
he empire into one, with the intention of paving the way for the
quality of all citizens in the matter of holding public offices. This was
ertainly a grand plan, but its execution presented so many strange
ifficulties that it seemed almost chimerical. As the whole idea has
een inspired by the representative of France, who introduced into
onstantinople a considerable number of French teachers, and as the
ndertaking tended to increase our influence throughout the East, some
etails on the organization of this institution will not be without inter-
st. I had the honor to preside over the lyceum of Galata-Séraï for more
han three years, and although this position forces me to be somewhat
eserved in my statements, I have had an excellent opportunity of
naking observations, and I shall not fail to point out with impartiality
rhatever good features I have seen.

During the first months of the year 1868, Ali Pasha, the grand-vizier,
nd Fuad Pasha, the minister of foreign affairs, whose combined efforts
ave for a long time been directed to the advancement and grandeur of
he East, came to a definite understanding with M. Bourée, and agreed
s to the basis on which the new school was to be established. The
overnment established 150 free places, divided among the Mohamme-
lans, Gregorian Armenians, Greeks, Bulgarians, Catholic Armenians,
loman Catholics, and Jews. These free places were only open to Turk-
sh subjects, but paying pupils could be admitted without making this
listinction. A sum of 400,000 francs ($80,000) was immediately appro-
riated for buying the building, for school-furniture and scientific appa-
atus, and an annual sum of 500,000 francs ($100,000) was granted for
he current expenses. Objections have been raised to this appropriation,
ut this school in reality cost the state less than any of the other large
chools, and the average expenditure for one pupil has always been less
han in our French lyceums and in the Turkish school at Paris.

The administration and the greater portion of the instruction were
onfided to Frenchmen, selected, at the request of the Turkish govern-
nent, by the French minister of public instruction and made responsi-
le to the Turkish' minister of public instruction. M. Duruy, (at that
ime the French minister of public instruction,) struck, no doubt, with
he success obtained in their schools by the Germans, the Italian Jesuits,
nd the Jews, entertained the idea of establishing French colleges in all
he large centers of population on the coast of the Mediterranean, the
French school at Athens to be charged with the inspection of all these
olleges. The establishment of the Turkish college of Galata-Séraï was
o much in accordance with his ideas as to induce him to favor it with
ill his might.

Instruction was to be given in French, and was to comprise literature,
istory, geography, elementary mathematics, natural sciences, Turkish,
Arabic, and Persian. Latin and Greek courses were to be given in
rder to facilitate the understanding of scientific etymology. Greek was

of almost daily usefulness to the majority of the pupils and Latin was of peculiar interest to all pupils of Slavonian origin. The oriental languages were to be taught by Turkish teachers and the Mohammedan religious exercises were to be conducted by an *imam*.

It will be difficult for any one outside of Turkey to get an accurate idea of the clamorous opposition which was made to an institution organized on such liberal principles. The Greeks, naturally but little inclined to favor anything which might give strength and cohesion to the empire, complained of the little attention given to the study of their language and were exceedingly dissatisfied. The Jews, mostly descended from Spanish Jews who had fled hither from the persecutions of the inquisition, exhibited that religious intolerance from which they themselves had suffered, and would not place their children in a Mohammedan institution under Christian teachers. The least fanatic demanded for their coreligionists a particular food, prepared according to Hebrew rites, which measure would have produced many complications and at the very outset broken up that unity which it was the intention to introduce and foster. Even the Catholics, to a great extent, refused their sympathy to an establishment where all creeds were to be equally protected. Before the lyceum was opened the Pope forbade all Catholic families to place their children in this lyceum under the penalty of being deprived of the sacrament. This prohibition was repeated a few months later and brought to the notice of the public.[*] It seems that fears were entertained for the morals of Catholic children. During the first two years the proportion of exclusions on account of misconduct was five times larger among the Catholic pupils than those of any other creed. The spirit of tolerance had pervaded the whole institution to such a degree that every day children of different creeds could be seen going freely through their religious rites in the midst of their comrades, which was indeed a touching sight. In this fact we see one of the symptoms promising in the future a complete unification of the oriental races.

The foreign powers were not indifferent to this institution, and showed their hostile disposition in every way, fearing that the lyceum, if further extended, might interfere with their own political plans, or alarmed at the part which France might play in Turkish affairs. The Turkish patrons of the lyceum were attacked by a numerous party, who had a solid basis of action. Thus the first Turkish subdirector, appointed by order of the Sultan, was, by intrigue, prevented from entering upon his office. It must be acknowledged that the most sincere sympathizers had reason to be alarmed. The Mohammedans of Constantinople enjoy numerous privileges: they are exempt from military service; they have to pay no

---

[*] " Parentes qui bona fide egerunt, si promittant, quamprimum prudenter poterunt, se filios a lycœo ablaturos, ad sacramenta admittantur. Qui vero vel hoc ipsum promittere renuant vel in posterum obstinato animo filios immittere in lycœum ausi fuerint, a sacramento arceantur."—(Roma dalla Propaganda, April 21, 1869. C. Barnabo, pr.)

taxes, and all their schools are free schools. How could a comparatively high fee be exacted from the pupils of the lyceum? The principle of paying for education is so much at variance with established ideas that even after it had been adopted it was proposed to give to each pupil a piaster (about 4 cents) a day, in order to do away with the inequality which the different positions of the parents might produce among the children. Our love of equality has not yet, however, led us so far.

The common household, the habits of domestic education, the variety of languages, the demands of the various religious beliefs, presented so many obstacles to a system of discipline necessary in a college managed by foreigners, that the hesitation, and even the repugnance, of many families to send their children to it is easily explained. The fear was repeatedly expressed that the teachers would endeavor to make religious proselytes; and in truth this is less surprising than the defiance of the Roman Catholics, refusing at the very outset to have their rites administered in a Mohammedan country.

In spite of all these difficulties and uncertainties the lyceum was opened September 1, 1868, and very soon numbered 341 pupils, of the following nationalities and creeds:

Mohammedans	147
Gregorian Armenians	48
Greeks	36
Jews	34
Bulgarians	34
Roman Catholics	23
Armenian Catholics	1
Total	341

About 240 had no knowledge of French whatever, 60 could read and write French without being able to understand it, and only 40 were well versed in French.

The lyceum had scarcely been opened when the administration encountered new obstacles, which could not possibly have been foreseen, and whose nature will be seen from the following: The Koran prescribes numerous ablutions and baths; it forbids the taking of any food or drink by day-time during the *Ramadan* festival, which lasts a month, and which comes at a different time every year. The calculation of time is not the same in Constantinople as in the western states of Europe. The Turks only use the solar time for dividing the day and the Christians have not yet adopted the Gregorian calendar. Friday is a holiday for the Turks, Saturday for the Jews, and Sunday for the Christians. The civil and religious holidays are not the same in the different creeds, nor even in the different sects of one and the same creed. There are great differences in the matter of food between the Christians, the Mohammedans, and Jews. It became exceedingly difficult to establish uniform and easily-observed rules in this labyrinth of contradictory demands. Even the teachers themselves, some of whom lived in the lyceum, might become the cause of deplorable conflicts, from their different origin, their particular views, and their character, as among them there were Turks, Frenchmen, Armenians, Greeks, Italians, and Englishmen.

In spite of these very unfavorable conditions, the attendance of the lyceum increased rapidly; one month after its opening, the number of pupils was 430 and at the end of the first year it was 530; one year later it was 640, and everything encouraged the hope that this increase might continue, and steps were taken to establish at Constantinople a preparatory school for young Mohammedan children. The progress made in two years was so manifest that the question of establishing similar lyceums in other cities was seriously discussed, and demands for plans and programmes came from several places, among the rest from Beyrout. The Bulgarians made a request for a school of this kind, and based this request on political considerations serious enough to attract the attention of the government; there are few Bulgarian towns where Russia has not her confidential agents who secretly work in creating a sentiment in favor of Russia. Servia, on the other hand, which is almost independent of Turkey, lets no opportunity slip to extend her influence in Bulgaria by opening schools, by paying teachers, and by spreading the Servian language. Turkey could not but see of what vast importance it would be to attach the population to herself by educating the children. A lyceum at Philippopolis would most assuredly have proved successful. The immense conflagration which, on the 5th June, 1870, consumed the greater portion of Pera, and extended to the very gates of the lyceum, marked the end of its prosperity. A few weeks later the war with Prussia broke out, producing new and unforeseen difficulties, changing the destiny of the institution, and preventing the establishment of other lyceums.

Ever since the end of 1870 it was easy to see that a radical change had been wrought in the public sentiment towards France; our prestige being gone, it was found impossible to defend those institutions which we had patronized; it was decided that instruction in the medical school should no longer be given in French, the study of French was discontinued in many Turkish schools, and in the Italian Jesuit college it was proclaimed that henceforth French was only a dead language. This reactionary movement is still going on, and French, which from time immemorial was used before all the civil tribunals of Constantinople, has recently been banished from all courts, only Turkish to be employed in future. The hostile disposition of the Turkish government may also be seen in the regulations regarding the Suez Canal and the Armenian Hassounists.

Sustained by Ali Pasha, the Lyceum of Galata-Séraï resisted, for some time, the fierce attacks made on it, but its prosperity was gone; many families gave it up, and during the scholastic year 1870–'71 the attendance was reduced to 569, and it is actually astonishing that, under existing circumstances, the number of pupils was so large.

In September, 1871, Ali Pasha died very unexpectedly, young in years, but broken down by the fatigues and annoyances of his responsible position. The Sultan immediately took the affairs of state into his own hands. A peaceful revolution took place the importance of which must here be explained. After the destruction of the janizaries in 1826 and the humiliation of the *ulemas*, (teachers of religion and law,) Sultan Mahmoud found himself absolute ruler. His successor, the Grand-Vizier Rechid Pasha, an intelligent and energetic man, conceived the idea of establishing the sublime porte, or council of ministers, as a sort of check to the absolute power of the sovereign, and succeeded in prevailing upon his master, Sultan Abdul-Medjid, that in future nothing should be done without the consent of this council; and it has happened more than once that the council has resisted the will of the Sultan. Ali Pasha and Fuad Pasha continued this policy of Rechid Pasha, and, sustained by the influence of France and England, they succeeded in keeping the privileges of the council intact. When Abdul-Aziz ascended the throne, (in 1861,) he attempted, it is said, to shake off these fetters, and by a personal decree exiled Riza Pasha, the confidential friend of his deceased brother, Abdul-Medjid, but he could not keep up his resistance, and temporarily bowed to a will stronger than his own.

During the latter half of 1871, Fuad Pasha and Ali Pasha died, and left no one to inherit their power and their influence; France was no longer in the condition to make her influence felt and England remained passive. The Sultan lost no time in profiting by this state of affairs and shaking off the yoke which had been imposed on him; he took various measures tending to make all resistance useless, announced his intention to reign supreme, and selected as grand-viziers only such men as would be obedient tools of his sovereign will. The death of Ali Pasha has therefore produced a political revolution in favor of the personal government of the Sultan and hostile to French and English influence. A large party considers this as the liberation of the country and the revival of the ancient power and glory of the Turkish Empire. All recollections of the Crimean war and other services rendered have disappeared like snow in spring. Many acts of the Turkish government during the last four years, and especially the number and impotence of the grand-viziers, can easily be explained thereby.

Ali Pasha, in his weak and sick body, had a great mind, an unusual degree of intelligence, united to a great degree of firmness; all the work of the government seemed to center in him and he possessed an extraordinary influence over the ministers and the Sultan himself. In his almost uninterrupted audiences he was never seen to take any notes, and it is said that in the evening, when at home in his palace, he dictated to his secretary all the acts and occurrences of the day, without ever forgetting anything. His views were broad and free from all prejudices, and still he was considere d a very orthodox Mohammedan, much more than his friend Fuad Pasha, who was freely spoken of as an unbeliever. The diplomatic skill of Ali Pasha is well known at all the courts of Europe. For the sake of Turkey, it is to be regretted that he had no taste for economic matters, and during his long stay in office he did not seek to increase the resources of his country.

It is but natural that the death of Ali Pasha, who had personally created the lyceum of Galata-Séraï, and had for three years extended his special favor to it, still further endangered the already precarious position of the institution. From this very moment the hostile disposition of the ministry became evident, showed itself on every occasion, and finished by the shabbiest tricks, which compromised the very existence of the school. The French director, under these conditions, did not feel justified in staying, and returned to France. When he left, the lyceum had still 471 pupils, but one month later, under the directorship of Vahan Effendi, it had lost 109.

Vahan Effendi, an Armenian, soon resigned, and his place was taken by Photiades Bey, a Greek, who, in his turn, was succeeded by Sawas Pasha. A year ago it had to change buildings with the medical school, and was taken to Gul-Hané, in the neighborhood of Constantinople. This change of location, which placed the school at a greater distance from the Christian quarters of the city and was in every way less convenient, was justly considered as a concession to the enemies of France, and the greater portion of the French teachers therefore considered it their duty to resign. The Lyceum of Galata-Séraï has not ceased to exist, and, such as it is, may still render good service, but it has changed its name, as if thereby to obliterate the last traces of its origin; the course of instruction will no doubt soon be modified, and it is to be feared that French will occupy but a very humble place. Let us examine what have been the results obtained by this school during the first troubled period of its existence.

Before the Lyceum of Galata-Séraï was opened, the question was asked whether it would not be a very chimerical problem to have children belonging to the many different nationalities of Turkey live together, pursue the same studies, partake of the same food, sleep in the same dormitories. Facts have proved that the fears entertained on this score were unfounded. No doubt many susceptibilities and defiances had constantly to be taken into consideration, but the children had the feeling that justice was done by establishing a rigorous impartiality, and thus avoiding all serious conflicts. The unique attempt to break the way through the children for a fusion of the races proved successful, and showed all the results which could reasonably be expected in so short a time; if continued, it would certainly have done away with many prejudices, would have killed the germs of future dissensions, and prepared that assimilation of races which the interests of the country so urgently demanded.

As regards the studies, a single fact will suffice to show their standard exactly. In the third year of the school, in July, 1871, eight pupils received the diploma of bachelor of sciences from a French examining committee, and similar results were obtained during the following years. If one considers the starting-point and the short time, it must be acknowledged that it seemed impossible to hope for such success, and it shows the competence and devotedness of the teachers, as well as the perseverance of the pupils. The progress made in all studies, but more especially in French, and in all the imitative arts, surpassed all expectations, and, through the spirit of emulation awakened among pupils of so many different nationalities, the most surprising results were obtained. It would be very wrong to say that the eastern races had become incapable of receiving any solid intellectual culture and to consign them to final and fatal mental stagnation. It will be interesting to know what nationalities and creeds furnished the most intelligent and best-behaved children. From this twofold point of view the Bulgarians invariably held the first rank ; after them, the Armenians, then the Turks, the Jews, and last of all, I regret to say, the Roman Catholics. The Greeks, with a few honorable exceptions, were badly behaved.

The different origin of our pupils frequently afforded an opportunity for curious studies. Several young Turks pursued their studies in common with their own slaves of the same age, sat on the same benches, wore the same dress, and on more than one occasion interceded for them. Slaves in Turkey do not lead a hard life, and easily obtain a respected place in the family. The Sultan himself occasionally calls himself " the Son of the Slave." Ali Pasha, who, as a politician, appreciated the advantages of a conciliatory education, saw soon that certain prejudices of race against Turkish institutions would not be felt against the Lyceum of Galata-Séraï, and sent us the children of families whom he wished to attach to himself. We thus received a certain number of Circassians, sons of Cretan insurgents, and the last descendant of the hereditary pasha of the Myrdites, a Catholic people of Albania, who is almost constantly carrying on war with Turkey. This child of 12 years, the last of his race, had been taken by surprise among the mountains, with his octogenarian grandmother. The latter is believed to have starved to death voluntarily, in order not to live in the power of the Turks. I seem to see her yet, with her tall figure, her aristocratic bearing, recommend to me with tears her little grandson and express to me her abhorrence of her oppressors. The successor of Ali Pasha wished to place the child in the Turkish Military Academy, but the opposition was so great that he was forced to abandon the idea.

The influence of the lyceum on the pupils, and through them on their families, was very perceptible, and the progress of this influence could be traced from year to year. If, after the Crimean war, when France left a military commission at Constantinople, lyceums like that of Galata-Séraï had been established in some of the provincial cities, such schools would no doubt have been successful during a long period of peace, and would during fifteen years (1855 to 1870) have educated seven or eight generations of young men. Native teachers capable of succeeding the foreign ones would have been educated there and would have given to the whole work a national character which, in the beginning, was of course wanting. The former pupils of these institutions would gradually have raised the intellectual and moral standard of the public officials, of commerce, industry, and the arts, and it is difficult to say what radical changes in the whole country would have been produced. This generous attempt was, unfortunately, not made till on the eve of our national disasters, and their influence therefore made itself soon felt. The future will show whether the Turkish government, in hindering the work which was so well begun, has acted in its true interest, or if, overreaching itself, as is the case in all reactions, it has not subjected itself to influences which, at some given moment, may prove disastrous. However this may be, it will be conceded that it was a great and far-seeing idea to establish in Turkey lyceums for secondary instruction; and impartial judges will count it as an honor to those eminent men who conceived the idea and to the two ministers who carried it out.

EDUCATION IN SERVIA.

EDUCATION IN SERVIA.

[From the Allgemeine Schul-Zeitung, August 15, 1874.]

INTRODUCTION.

The principality of Servia, since 1815 under the rule of native princes, was placed under the protection of the great European powers, as a semi-independent state, by the treaty of Paris of March 30, 1856. The principality preserves its independent and national administration, as well as full liberty of worship, of legislation, of commerce, and of navigation. The election of its rulers is left to the Servian nation, under the nominal sanction of the Sultan.

The area of Servia is estimated at 12,600 square miles and the population (in 1872) was, according to official reports, 1,325,437.

HISTORICAL DEVELOPMENT OF EDUCATION.

While under Turkish rule (1350 to 1815) there was no attempt at education, as the Servians were kept in abject slavery by their Turkish masters.

But immediately after their liberation from the Turkish yoke, the people made exertions to raise the standard of education. These exertions were in the beginning not very successful, but, considering the state of oppression under which they had lived for centuries, they deserve praiseworthy mention.

Twenty years later (1836) the national assembly for the first time gave attention to the subject of education, and the following resolutions were passed: (1) In every district the inhabitants are to support two schools; (2) every community which has a church must also support a school.

At that time there were in Servia only 72 schools, with 2,514 scholars.

September 11, 1844, the first Servian school-law was promulgated, establishing (1) elementary schools, (2) a business-college, (3) gymnasia, and (4) a lyceum. This may be considered the first beginning of a system of education in Servia.

Another law of 1855 provided the necessary means for supporting these schools, every citizen, without exception, being obliged to pay an annual school-tax of about 32 cents.

The revised school-law, which is in force at the present time, dates from 1863. According to this law a school must be established wherever

255

there are 25 scholars. The salaries of the teachers are divided into 10 classes, the highest salary being $285 and the lowest $97.50.

The following exhibit of the educational status of Servia is taken from the official report of the ministry of public instruction, laid before the national assembly during the session 1870–'71:

PRIMARY SCHOOLS.

The primary schools of Servia are grouped in two classes: Village-schools having three classes (course of instruction 3 years) and one teacher; city-schools having four classes (course of instruction 4 years) and 4 teachers. The number of primary schools in 1870–'71 was 484, with 605 teachers and 25,270 scholars. Among this number there were 47 schools for girls, with 64 (female) teachers and 2,882 scholars. There are thus 22 scholars to every 1,000 of the population. Education is not compulsory. There are no separate schools for the poor and the rich, but all citizens send their children to the same school.

Since 1869, libraries have been established in connection with every primary school. At the end of the first two years the number of vol umes in these libraries was 18,000.

A teachers' seminary was opened in 1871 with 25 students. At present there are 62 students in three classes. All these students are supported entirely by the state and are obliged to serve at least 6 years as teachers in the primary schools.

There is also a theological seminary, (established in 1836,) which supplies teachers for the primary schools. The course of instruction lasts 4 years and the number of students is 292, with 8 teachers.

SECONDARY SCHOOLS.

There are three kinds of secondary schools, viz: (1) Small real-gymnasia, with 2 classes; (2) progymnasia, with 4 classes; and (3) gymnasia, with 6 classes.

Besides these there is one large real-school, of 6 classes, at Belgrade.

(1) Small real-gymnasia are to be established in every one of the capitals of the 17 districts into which the country is divided. The course of instruction in these schools is the same as in the two lower classes of the progymnasia and gymnasia, so that scholars leaving the second class of the small real-gymnasia enter the third class of the gymnasia. Each school has at least 4 teachers. The number of schools at the present time is 9, with 430 scholars.

(2) The course of the progymnasia is the same as that of the 4 lower classes of the gymnasia. There are at present 5 such schools, viz: at Belgrade, 2; at Schabaz, Negotin, and at Pozarewaz. There are 5 directors, 582 scholars, and 26 teachers. These progymnasia are of great importance, for from them the scholars enter directly the teachers' seminary, the theological seminary, or the agricultural school.

The progymnasium has 4 classes, the course of instruction embracing the following subjects : Religion, Servian language, Slavic language, German, French, arithmetic, geography, (political, physical, and mathematical,) history of Servia, mathematics, natural philosophy, geometry, natural history, drawing, vocal and instrumental music, and gymnastics; the number of hours per week does not exceed 27 in any class, each teacher teaching, at most, 20 to 22 hours per week.

(3) Gymnasia. Of these Servia has two, at Belgrade and at Kragujewaz. So far they have had 6 classes, but according to a recent order a seventh class is to be added. These two gymnasia have 2 directors, 26 teachers, and 750 scholars. The course of the 4 lower classes is exactly the same as that of the progymnasia. In the two higher classes the following subjects are added: General history, Latin, mathematics, physics, rhetorics, poetry, and history of literature. The teachers' salaries vary from $435 to $330 per annum, with a quinquennial increase of $52.50. After having served 30 years, a gymnasium-teacher receives a pension of $900.

THE HIGH SCHOOL.

This school is located at Belgrade, in a magnificent building, the gift of a patriotic citizen, Anastassiewitsch. It was founded in 1838, but not fully organized till 1842. Till the year 1863 it was called the Lyceum; but at that time it was thoroughly reorganized and divided into three faculties : the philosophical, the so-called technical, (mathematics and natural sciences,) and the law-faculty. There were, 1870–'71, 229 students, 1 rector, and 13 regular and 2 honorary professors. The annual salary of a professor is $637.50, with a quinquennial increase of $97.50. After having served for 30 years, a professor is entitled to a pension of $1,125 per annum.

THE SCHOOL OF AGRICULTURE.

This school was established in 1853, but did not exist very long. Two years ago (1872) it was reopened in the city of Pozarewaz. The students are supported and educated entirely at the expense of the state.

THE HIGHER SCHOOL FOR YOUNG LADIES.

This school opened at Belgrade in 1864. Many female teachers have received their education at this school. It has one director, 7 (female) teachers, 9 honorary professors, and 4 (female) assistant teachers. The course of instruction extends over 4 years. Scholars enter this school from the primary schools.

THE MILITARY ACADEMY.

This academy was in 1837 established at Pozarewaz, and was transferred to Belgrade in 1850. It has a five-years course, 1 director and 10 professors, and 40 students, who, after having passed the required examination, are entirely supported by the state.

SCHOOL-FINANCES.

The annual expenditure for education is $303,000, or the eleven part of the total annual expenditure. The sum expended for the arm is only three and a half times as large, which proportion must be co sidered favorable when we remember that in countries like France t sum expended for the army is 50 to 60 times as large as the one e pended for education. School-fees are not paid in any Servian scho

CONCLUSION.

The above is a brief outline of the state of education in Servia. Co sidering that 60 years ago Servia did not possess a single school, tl results achieved since the establishment of Servian independence a exceedingly gratifying, and the work is still bravely going on. Tl government sends students abroad every year; thus in 1870, 38, of who: 13 studied medicine; 5, technics; 2, pedagogics; 2, law; 4, forestry an agriculture; 3, theology; 1, mining; 1, political economy; 5, painting and 2, the postal service of foreign countries.

Most of the Servian *sarants* are former students of German universi ties and academies.

EDUCATION IN EGYPT.

PUBLIC INSTRUCTION IN EGYPT.*

CHARACTER AND HISTORY OF THE EGYPTIAN PEOPLE.

The most characteristic feature of the Egyptian nation is its stability, its spirit of conservatism, for, in spite of centuries of changes throughout the world, it presents in many essential respects the same picture as three or four thousand years ago.

The ancient Egyptians no doubt came originally from Central Asia, and, as regards their language, belong to the Semitic races. In their religion, likewise, in spite of all its apparent pantheism, very marked traces of the primitive Asiatic monotheism may be found of that one and invisible God who is the original source of all beings.

There is and always has been something sad and melancholy in the Egyptian character, and speaking of their plaintive melodies Mr. Dor has said very truly: "The ancient lamentation of Isis searching her Osiris has never ceased in Egypt, and all along her noble river its sounds may be heard." Ancient Egyptian art likewise has a lugubrious and funereal character, and seems all to center around death and the tomb. Mr. Dor very beautifully remarks: "To the poor laborer who built the colossal temples of Thebes and Abydos, nothing in his work spoke of life and hope; nothing inspired him with that love of country and of art which animated the architect of the Parthenon; nothing spoke to him of liberty or power, as did the Forum at Rome; nothing uplifted his soul from the dust, like the spires of the Gothic domes rising toward Heaven like a crystalized prayer !"

Caste also exercised its baneful influence and contributed its share towards extinguishing in the individual all spontaneousness and spirit of enterprise, and impressing on his character that melancholy resignation which even in our days is found among the Copts as well as among the Mohammedans.

A brief outline of the history of Egypt will not be out of place here. The ten dynasties of the ancient empire, which reigned during about seventeen centuries, were succeeded by those of the middle empire, which changed the capital and the political and social center of Egypt from the north—Memphis and Herakleopolis—to the south, to Thebes. A great change took place towards the end of the twelfth dynasty, when the neighboring Semitic nations of Syria invaded and conquered

---

*Compiled from "L'instruction publique en Égypte," par V. E. Dor, Ph. D.; 399 pp., Paris, 1872.

Egypt. They formed the fifteenth and sixteenth dynasties, and their rulers are known by the name of "hyksos" or "shepherd-kings."

After the expulsion of these kings Egypt rose to new life, but soon, through the tyranny of its rulers, the great mass of the common people degenerated and became little better than abject slaves of the higher classes. From this time up to the reign of Mehemet Ali (1806 to 1849) no great change in the condition of the people took place. Egypt, the richest land in the world, whose soil yields three crops a year, was no longer able to support the population, which in a comparatively short time decreased from about nine millions to three.

Under Alexander and the Ptolemies Egypt externally had a brilliant period of life, Alexandria becoming a great center of civilization, and Egypt for the second time was the leader of intellectual culture; but this civilization was Greek, and foreigners cultivated the arts, philosophy, and literature, while the country itself derived but few advantages from it.

Christianity, which in other countries became a powerful agent of civilization, did not do the same for poor downtrodden Egypt, which remained in her melancholy and desolation.

What Christianity had not been able to accomplish was attempted by Mohammedanism, which brought at least a powerful organization and a profound faith, not only in its aim and its doctrines, but also in the means for carrying out this aim. The passive christianity of the Copts could not for a moment sustain the shock of the youthful and ardent faith of the Arabs, who became masters of the country, to leave it no more. This invasion had a character entirely different from those of the "hyksos," the Persians, the Greeks, and the Romans, and became actually an immigration, a new population settling down beside the old one and in most cases driving it back into obscurity. The two populations lived, if not in perfect harmony, at least in comparative peace. Mohammedanism made numerous converts among the Copt-population, and the number of those who remained faithful to the Christian religion gradually diminished till, in our days, it numbers scarcely half a million.

The new Mohammedan population which has actually become the true and dominant population of Egypt had many characteristics in common with the Copts, and the fatalism of the Koran produced with some slight modifications that same social indifference and that absence of individual ambition which the spirit of caste had produced among the ancient population. After the glories of the great Mohammedan empire had passed away, Egypt entered upon one of those periods of historic obscurity during which it is impossible to follow the development of a nation. One dynasty succeeded the other without taking deep root; kalifs, sultans, beys, and pashas have not even sufficient time to get firmly seated upon their thrones, and it is in vain to expect from them those reforms which alone could have awakened this stationary population from its dreamy prejudices; and the political disorder was therefore constantly on the increase.

This state of affairs lasted till the year 1798, when Bonaparte with his army invaded the country. In whatever light as to its motives we may consider this strange and fantastic expedition, it cannot be denied that in its consequences it became a lasting benefit to Egypt.

Forgotten for centuries, Egypt once more became an active member of the family of nations; statesmen, authors, travelers, turned their eyes toward the ancient land of the Pharaohs and the Ptolemies, which in the hands of a man of genius was now to rise to a new life.

This man was Mehemet Ali, to whom Sultan Selim III intrusted the fortunes of the country after its evacuation by the French. His life and deeds are so well known that they need not be spoken of here, but the character of this extraordinary man and his influence on public instruction in Egypt deserve a more than passing notice.

At an early age he had conceived a strong love for France and every-thing French, and this trait in his character prompted him not only to copy many French institutions, but also to favor the immigration of Frenchmen and to conquer the antipathy to all Europeans which the Egyptians felt. His first care was to organize the army on the French model. In order to bring about a thorough and lasting reform not only of the army but of the whole state, Mehemet Ali recognized the neces-sity of education, and numerous schools of all kinds soon began to spring up throughout the whole of Egypt, and if these schools have not exercised a more decisive influence on the character of the people, this was caused chiefly by the too military or mechanical direction which instruction took. The pasha himself set a praiseworthy example, and it must be confessed that it was a noble sight to see the old chieftain, after having fought victoriously against the Mamelukes, the Turks, and the English, sit down at a ripe old age and learn reading and writing.

From the time of Mehemet Ali, Egypt has been constantly progress-ing on the path of civilization; but, in view of the national character of the people indicated above, the complete ignorance of the lower classes, and the comparative ignorance of the higher classes, it must be said "that, though the Government has done much for education, more re-mains to be done, above everything to acclimatize and nationalize education, which wherever it has taken root has remained too artificial, because it is only an exotic plant, which has not always had the care and the soil necessary for its development."

PRIMARY ARABIC INSTRUCTION.

The primary Egyptian schools, *kouttab*—the remainder of the grand-eur of the Arabic empire—are at this present day in a much higher state of development than is generally believed outside of Egypt; and although they may no longer meet the demands of modern times, hav-ing remained stationary for about eight centuries, these schools nevertheless possessed a great deal of vital force, enabling them to live through centuries of darkness. These primary schools are essentially a creation of Mohammedanism, and the reading and writing of portions of the Koran formed the chief occupation of the scholars.

A peculiar feature of the whole system was the foundation of schools by wealthy persons, the number of such schools gradually growing very large. In many cases the benefactor gave, besides the school-house, an annual sum of money for the teacher; in others, money to be devoted to the clothing of poor children, and in some cases, though more rarely, a library.

These primary schools have not changed much, either externally or internally. The school-room generally measures 15 by 20 feet and is inclosed by a wall only on three sides, and this wall is built up to the ceiling on the two sides only, the greater portion of one side fronting on the street having a sort of lattice-work, to hide the scholars from the gaze of the passers-by and to admit air and a subdued light. The walls are generally covered with verses from the Koran, and on the side turning toward Mecca there is a small niche with a plaster-ornament representing a holy lamp. The floor is sometimes covered with mats or carpets; otherwise there is no furniture whatever; only in rare cases there is a very small desk on which the teacher places his Koran. Occasionally one finds school-houses having a second story, used either as a library or as the teacher's dwelling.

Recently the government has directed its efforts towards establishing schools more in accordance with the wants of modern life, so that the school-houses described above will gradually disappear.

The Egyptian schools are, as regards the way in which they are supported, divided into three kinds: schools with ancient endowments and subject to government-inspection; schools having endowments, but independent of the government, and schools having no endowment and being in nowise subordinate to the ministry of public instruction.

The teachers (*fiki*) are not generally men of any great attainments; all that is required of them is to know the Koran by heart; and this mere mechanical knowledge frequently hides the greatest ignorance. Besides the Koran, the *fiki* does not know much, except a few simple rules of arithmetic and some fantastic notions regarding geography.

The salary which the *fiki* receives is, of course, very small. On the last day of the week (Thursday) the scholars bring each one or two piasters, (the piaster is equal to five cents,) so that the average annual salary comes to about $80 or $100.

The children go to school in the morning not to leave it till about 6 o'clock in the evening, except on Thursdays, when, on account of the coming Sabbath, (Friday,) they leave at noon. They either bring their food along or give half a piaster to the teacher, who supplies them with some dates, beans, and a piece of bread.

The first years of their life the children spend in the harem, which they leave, when about 6 or 7 years of age, to attend school. Mr. Dor gives the following graphic description of a school in full operation: "The teacher and the scholars sit on the floor, the former generally near the door or in that corner of the room which has the best light, the children grouped around him. This assembly of white, tawny, and black figures, with their glittering eyes; their red lips wide open, showing two rows of shining teeth; with their round heads, some freshly shaved, others with short hair; with their long blue garments, from under which the naked feet peep forth—all this, framed by the characteristic Arabic architecture and seen in the dim twilight found in all Egyptian houses, forms a very pretty picture."

The apparatus which the scholar brings to school with him is exceedingly simple, consisting of a wooden slate, sometimes of thin iron; a leather case containing some reeds to write with, and, fastened to it, a little iron box, with a sponge steeped in ink.

The teacher never teaches a whole class at one and the same time, but only one scholar. Every child in his turn comes up to the teacher, sits down by his side, recites what he has learned, shows what he has written, receives a new task, and resumes his place among the other scholars. The scholars commence by learning the letters and the numbers, with their value. They have to repeat them and write them till they are thoroughly acquainted with them. Then follow simple syllables commencing with consonants and then syllables commencing with vowels. From this they progress to the study of words and phrases, mostly taken from the Koran. The teacher writes the words on the child's slate, lets him spell and pronounce them aloud, and then the child practices the writing. When the child can read words or short phrases, the teacher inscribes some characters on his slate in colored ink; and the father, after having convinced himself of the progress made by his child, generally sends the teacher a present of one or two piasters. As soon as the child knows how to read, he commences to learn the Koran by heart, and as there is but rarely more than one copy of the sacred volume in a school, the teacher writes verse after verse on the child's slate, to be learned by heart. All this learning is done aloud, and the noise resulting from it is considerable; still, discipline is rigidly maintained by a prompt and energetic application of the *jus flagelli*. The study of the Koran in the primary schools is entirely mechanical, no explanation or commentary whatever being given. After a child has gone in this manner through the whole of the Koran, his education is considered finished, and, though his knowledge is limited, it must be stated that at any rate he has learned to read and write correctly.

Arithmetic is but rarely taught in those schools which are not under government-superintendence, for the simple reason that the teachers know but very little of it themselves. If a child is obliged to have some knowledge of arithmetic, he studies it with a *rabani* or public weigher or he is apprenticed to a merchant. Other subjects—such as

history and geography—are not taught at all, although it is the intention to make a beginning in this direction in the government-schools.

As will be seen from the above, the study of the Koran is the chief
object of the Arabic schools, and reading and writing are only considered as means for reaching this object. Only very gradually does the
primary school begin to assume a more practical character. This tendency of the school to become more and more a purely lay institution is
shown above everything else in the disappearance of the prayers which,
during the first half of this century, formed an important subject of instruction in all the schools, while at present they are only taught in
some of the country-schools. How beneficial it will prove to the people,
if gradually the light of knowledge begins to shine in Egypt, may be
inferred from the following fact, showing how wide-spread the most
absurd superstitions still are. When, on the 4th of February, 1872, an
aurora borealis was seen at Alexandria, many people believed that it
was produced by the blood of the steer Koutouhia, which had rushed
toward the sky when wounded by Bahamout.

The number of children attending school—quite large in the cities—
is small in the rural districts, where, in spite of numerous schools, the
most profound ignorance reigns. The teachers of many of these schools,
entirely isolated and separated from all intellectual intercourse, are
frequently as ignorant as the poor *fellahs*—peasants—themselves; and
then (in Egypt, as everywhere) it does not suffice to have attended
school in order to acquire a good elementary education; and as the
method pursued does not develop the intellect, the result is in most
cases that nothing of what has been sown in the school germinates and
ripens. As the knowledge of reading and writing is closely united to
a knowledge of the Koran, it gradually vanishes from want of exercise,
and when the child has arrived at the period of manhood but little of
all he learned at school remains. Mr. Jules Simon has proved that in
France one-fourth of the male population is illiterate at the age of
20, while only one-eighth does not attend school; and this decrease
could no doubt be shown to be still larger in Egypt, if there were any
possibility of obtaining reliable statistics on this point.

Once a year, during the month of *Ramadan* (October) or the month
of *Chaaban*, preceding it, examinations are held; clothes and shoes, and
occasionally a small sum of money, are distributed to the children, the
money for such distributions being derived from the endowment-funds
and a procession parades the streets, headed by the best scholars.

Such is the actual state of the purely Arabic schools, which are not
under the superintendence of the government. Some of them are
entirely independent of the ministry of public instruction. These
schools are exactly in the same state to-day as they were centuries ago.
With that tenacity and stability peculiar to Mohammedan institutions,
they have survived all the political revolutions through which Egypt
has passed. They have not followed on the road of reform which Egypt

pursued since the reign of Mehemet Ali; or, rather, the government,
uncing all idea of reforming them, has preferred to raise by the
of them other primary schools resembling those of Europe. The
important innovation has been the introduction of a little element-
arithmetic; and even to this the majority of the old schools have
sed to submit, contenting themselves to teach their scholars the
bers.

iere are no schools for girls, with the exception of the school for
es at Old Cairo and of such as are supported by the Copts or the va-
s European colonies. For years the ministry has talked of opening
mmense institution for the education of young girls; the plans have
i made and the work has even been commenced, but nothing more
eing done.

he education of girls does, unfortunately, in Egypt, not as yet belong
ie domain of public instruction. Whatever progress Egypt may
.e on the field of education, there will always be an immense gap,
the education of women; and consequent upon this the education
he child by the mother. M. Dor remarks, very truly, "However
it may be the number of schools and however ardent the zeal of the
hers, rest assured that a solid, universal, and enlightened system of
iary instruction will only be found where woman is educated. Edu-
woman! ought to be the cry raised before every ministry of public
ruction. Educate woman! for if the mother can read and write,
i not only will the child go to school, but it will reap a double ben-
from its schooling. Educate woman! for the woman of to-day is
mother of the generation of to-morrow. Truly, if the sad alterna-
were placed before me to choose between schools for girls and
ools for boys, I would prefer the former, sure that what would thereby
ieglected would be largely gained in another way by leading mothers
iecome themselves the teachers of their children.

But in Egypt it would be useless to combat against nature and old-
iblished usages. The young girls become marriageable at the age
l2, and it is almost impossible for them to get any sort of solid edu-
ion."

Among the higher classes the girls are occasionally instructed by edu-
ed native women or European governesses, but there is no public sys-
i of instruction for girls.

6 E

Statistics of primary Arabic schools, (kouttab,) 1871.

Moudyriehs or great centers.	Cities and districts.	Details of schools and scholars in cities and districts. Schools.	Scholars.	Totals as far as known by moudyriehs. Schools.	Scholars.	Remarks
	Cairo: Abdyn	16	555			
	Esbékieh	31	1,244			Cairo is divided in
	Bab ech Charieh	24	885			school-districts,
	Gamalieh	64	2,903			ern and the nor
	Darb el Ahmar	34	1,015			of them again
	Darb el Gamamis	23	830			into four distri
	Toumn el Khalifa	18	985	237	8,573	with old Cairo a
	Toumn el Qeysoun	13	405			has a population
	Jewish kouttab	4	155			with a total of
	Copt kouttab	6	192			and 9,883 schol.
	Syrian kouttab	3	84			school to 2,034 i
	Armenian kouttab	1	90			1 scholar to 61 i
	Old Cairo	27	790	27	790	
	Boulak	31	520	31	520	
	Alexandria	42	3,192	46	3,284	1 school to 6,087 i
	Jewish kouttab	4	92			
	Rosette	14	385	14	385	1 school to 2,143 i
						1 scholar to 78 ir
Béhéra	Damanhour	21	582	21	582	Those districts ha inspected.
Ghizéh	Ghizéh	15	244	23	554	1 school to 8,696 i
	Districts	8	310			1 scholar to 361 i
Gharbieh	Tanta	26	500	111	2,661	1 school to 7,207 i
	Districts	85	2,161			1 scholar to 300 i
Dakhalieh	Mansourah	22	663	88	2,656	1 school to 3,750 i
	Districts	66	1,993			1 scholar to 124 i
Gallioubieh	Benha	6	240	44	982	1 school to 3,864 i
	Galioub	6	110			1 scholar to 173 i
	Districts	32	632			
Ménoufieh	Ménouf	13	650	144	6,230	1 school to 1,583 i
	Districts	131	5,580			1 scholar to 37 ir
Charquieh	Zagazig	14	463	33	1,019	1 school to 10,606 i
	Districts	19	556			1 scholar to 343 i
Benisouef and Fayoum.	Bénisouef	10	313	82	2,491	1 school to 4,878 i
	Bouche	4	85			1 scholar to 160 i
	Medinet el Fayoum	24	652			
	Districts	44	1,441			
Miniéh	Miniéh	14	461	41	1,530	1 school to 9,263 i
	Bénimazar	2	75			1 scholar to 248 i
	Fechn	6	252			
	Districts	19	742			
Assyout	Assyout	24	1,330	157	7,812	1 school to 2,624 i
	Districts	133	6,482			1 scholar to 53 ir
Ghirghé	Souhadj	8	300	124	4,130	1 school to 2,984 i
	Akbmin	12	450			1 scholar to 90 it
	Ghirghé	7	280			
	Districts	97	3,100			
	Total			1,293	44,199	

SUPERIOR ARABIC INSTRUCTION.

"To superior Arabic instruction at the time of its greatest splendor may be applied the epithet given to France during the second empire, 'Great centers of light in the midst of dense darkness,' and these cen- ers of light unfortunately had the character of light-houses, seen from ifar, while their immediate neighborhood remained in darkness."

It would lead too far in this place to give a history of Arabic science 'rom its beginning till its period of splendor and its final decline. It rill be sufficient to give a brief sketch of the Mohammedan University if Egypt, El Azhar, its history, and present condition.

This institution of learning is as old as Cairo, having been founded n the year 970, by the Fatimide General Gauhar, and its name, El Azhar, neans "the flourishing." The building was partially destroyed by an earthquake in 1302, but immediately restored, and enlarged and reno- vated in 1596. During the French invasion of 1798 the president— sheik—of El Azhar was called upon to play a part in politics, for to him Bonaparte addressed himself to demand the surrender of the city of Cairo, and on the following day the sheik published a solemn proclama- tion in favor of the French. Under the arches of this venerable building, Bonaparte, clad in Oriental garb, sat down with the learned sheiks, on the 20th of August of the same year, the birthday of the prophet, and recited with them verses of the Koran and an interminable litany on the life of Mohammed.

The extent of the buildings may be judged from the fact that when, on the 21st of October, 1798, an insurrection broke out against the French, fifteen thousand insurgents found a place of refuge within its walls, and did not surrender till Bonaparte brought artillery to bear upon it.

The main building, the mosque, has an irregular pentagonal shape and is surrounded on all sides by different buildings and court-yards, leaving only room for four gates. The southwestern gate is the chief entrance, and leads into a small court, from which an ancient portal opens into the great court, on which the mosque faces. This mosque is a vast hall, whose ceiling, blackened by age and the smoke of twelve hundred lamps, is supported by three hundred and eighty ancient pillars.

El Azhar has always had a great fame, and thousands of students have come here from all parts of the Mohammedan world. Even at this day there are students from India and Soudan, each country or province establishing endowments for the support of their students.

The students are distributed in *riwaks*, or halls, and *harahs*, or quar- ters, the latter corresponding to the country or province of the student. There are thirty-one *riwaks* and twelve *harahs*. Egypt, of course, sends the largest number of students and possesses the greatest endowments, but students come from Tunis, Algiers, Morocco, Sennaar, Darfour, Arabia, Syria, Asia Minor, Koordistan, and India. Though the build- ings are so vast, they are not large enough to accommodate all the

students, and those who possess private means—and they are, perhap
the majority—live in adjoiuing caravansaries.

The Mohammedan religion has seventy-six sects, four of which only a
orthodox, the other seventy-two being considered as heretics. The
four orthodox sects are the Chaféites, the Malékites, the Hanéfite
and the Hambalites; taking their names from their founders. The
are but very slight differences between these sects regarding points
doctrine, and nothing like the sectarian rivalries existing among Chr
tians is found among them. All the students of El Azhar belong
these four sects, each having its own sheik or president.

The chief sheik or chief of the mosque, to whom all the others a
subordinate, is appointed by the government, and his office is consider
as one of the highest in Egypt. He appoints the sheik for each riw
and is attended by a number of choristers, vergers, and ushers. T
chief cook also receives his directions from him. Each riwak has a lar
number of servants, among them twenty barbers.

There are 314 professors, 143 of whom are Chaféites, 97 Malékite
70 Hanéfites, and only 4 Hambalites. Their pay is only raised l
voluntary contributions from the students, their position being consi
ered one of honor rather than of emolument. Many of them hold
the same time other offices, such as that of preacher in other mosque
and professor in the higher government schools.

Till quite recently the manner of appointing professors was very prim
tive, the whole consisting in the advanced students gathering around the
those who had not progressed so rapidly, and thus gradually enlargin
the circle of their hearers. Many abuses, however, had crept in, an
in 1872 the Khédive signed a law which had been prepared by th
chief sheik, intended to regulate the appointment of professors. A
cording to the provisions of this law, candidates for professorships mus
hand to the ministry of public instruction a list of the subjects they de
sire to teach, and will then be examined in these subjects by an examin
ing committee of six ulemas—priests and lawyers. If the result of thi
examination is satisfactory the Khédive will issue the certificate of pro
fessorship.

The students scarcely ever leave the mosque. El Azhar becomes t
them an adopted country, to which they remain faithful all their life
While the European student hastens to leave the alma mater to ente
active life, there is absolutely no limit but death to the studies at E
Azhar, and a student with silvery beard and hair is no unfrequent oc
currence in this republic of letters. The average length of time, howevel
which a student has to stay at El Azhar to finish his studies is two t
three years, although many stay four to six years.

As diseases of the eye are very common in Egypt, there are hundred
of blind students at El Azhar, who have a riwak—hall—to themselve

Every morning all the students attend prayers, and then collect i
small groups around their professors to receive their instruction. Th

course of studies at El Azhar is limited, because its object is solely to educate *fiki*, lawyers, and theologians. There are four divisions, or grades, of study, the first two comprising the preparatory studies, viz, grammar and syntax; the third, called "aëlm and tauhib," is the doctrine of the unity of God and his attributes; the fourth comprises law, and consists of learning by heart innumerable commentaries of the Koran, explaining the principles of jurisprudence. This study is intimately connected with the exegesis of the Koran, which forms the basis of all superior Mohammedan instruction and is divided into two parts, viz, interpretation and tradition, which latter requires long study, as one of the manuals contains no less than 7,275 traditions. There are numerous manuals, both in prose and in verse, to aid in these studies.

Besides the above-mentioned four studies, which are considered the most important, the following subjects are taught to some extent: rhetoric, prosody, logic, arithmetic, and mathematics. Although much is read and learned the results are but meager, as it may be said that all the studies are pursued in by far too mechanical a manner. The students of El Ahzar by constant practice reach a most astonishing facility of committing anything to memory, but all they learn in this manner remains a dead knowledge, their intellect and their reasoning faculties not being developed in the least.

There are similar schools connected with some of the mosques, but they are all more or less perfect imitations of El Azhar, and are not deserving of notice.

The total number of students of El Azhar was in 1871, 9,663.

DENOMINATIONAL SCHOOLS.

Of these, deserve to be mentioned first the primary schools of the Copts, of which there are quite a number. They resemble the *kouttab* in every respect, with the only exception that instead of the Koran the Psalms and the Gospels are read and learned by heart, and that, in addition to reading and writing, singing is taught, confined, however, to the singing of a few religious hymns.

With regard to one point, however, the Copts possess a decided superiority over their Mohammedan conquerors, in feeling the necessity of educating women; thus there are at Cairo two Copt-schools for girls, the one at Esbékieh with 95 pupils, and the other at Hart Saggaïn with 41. The course of instruction in these schools comprises reading, writing, the fundamental rules of arithmetic, vocal music, and needlework. These primary Copt-schools are supported in the same manner as the Mohammedan ones.

The Copts possess two colleges at Cairo, one at Hart Saggaïn and the other near the Metropolitan Church. The former has 3 classes with 125 students and 8 professors. The course of study includes French, English, Italian, Arabic, and arithmetic. The latter and by far superior institution—the great college—numbers 243 students, with 12 professors and 6 assistant professors. It occupies a fine building, with spacious, well-lighted and ventilated school-rooms. The course of instruction comprises the Coptic language, Arabic, French, English, Italian, vocal music, arithmetic, elements of geometry, history, geography, and logic.

Instruction in these two Copt-colleges and in the two schools for girls is entirely gratuitous. The spirit of religious tolerance is so strong in Egypt that the great college is actually attended by about 20 Mohammedans, 4 Armenians, and 10 Syrian Catholics. The Khédive, with his accustomed generosity and entirely overlooking the difference of creed, has donated to the four Copt-schools of Cairo fertile lands to the amount of upwards of 1,500 acres, the income from which amply suffices for their support.

The Jews likewise support a number of schools in Cairo and Alexandria; primary schools, where the children learn Hebrew and Arabic, reading and writing, and occasionally Italian, which language is of great importance to the Jews in their commercial transactions. Some of the Jewish primary schools are also attended by girls, while others are for girls exclusively.

The largest educational establishment which the Jews have founded in Egypt is the college Darb el Iahoud, at Cairo. This institution—founded in 1860—owes its existence to the liberality of Mr. Samuel Rubino. It is in every respect well managed and the pupils receive a good solid education. The course of study embraces Hebrew, French, Italian, vocal music, geography, cosmography, history, and arithmetic. The number of pupils whose age varies between 6 and 15 is 83, who are instructed by two rabbis and three professors, one of whom is at the same time president of the college.

The few schools of the Catholic Copts are nearly all located in Upper Egypt and are attended by about 220 scholars.

The Syrian Maronites have three schools, differing but little from the *kouttab*, with the exception of the Psalms and Gospels being used instead of the Koran and the scholars sitting on benches instead of on the floor.

The Syrian-Greek Catholics have recently opened a flourishing school at Alexandria.

GOVERNMENT-SCHOOLS ON THE EUROPEAN PLAN.

As has been said before, it was Mehemet Ali who began the work of reform in Egypt. He commenced by reforming the army, and went on to establish numerous schools, all organized on the French plan, primary schools, a military academy, an artillery-school, a naval academy, an infantry-school, and even a school of military music, but above all a great college, (to which Mehemet Ali sent his sons,) which at one time numbered more than 1,500 pupils and received the name "School of Princes." A school of languages was opened in the palace of Esbékieh,

60 select pupils of which were formed into a bureau of translation, which still exists, and somewhat later a school of topographical engineering was founded.

All the schools founded by Mehemet Ali were based on the educational wants of a standing army of 150,000 men, and when the army in 1841 was, officially at least, reduced to 12,000 men, the schools of every kind gradually declined, both in numbers and in efficiency, so that when Abbas Pasha, on ascending the throne in 1848, had the original idea of holding an examination of teachers and pupils, he found that they rivaled each other in ignorance. Abbas Pasha, being a man of quick resolution and seeing the necessity of a radical reform, commenced by closing all the schools founded by Mehemet Ali. It had been his intention to start them afresh on a new basis, but other cares engaged his attention, and nothing came of it.

Abbas's successor, Saïd Pasha, who began to reign in 1854, revived some of the schools, especially the school of medicine, and showed himself extremely liberal towards the schools of the European colonies, but the great work of reform was reserved to his successor, the present Khédive, Ismaïl Pasha, who ascended the throne in 1863.

He was the first Egyptian ruler who felt the necessity of not only founding a number of schools, but of an organic law of public instruction. Such a law was sanctioned by the Khédive in 1868.* According to this law all the public schools are of three grades, primary, secondary, and superior; and besides these there are the special schools.

With regard to the primary schools, the *kouttab*, the law provides that arithmetic must be taught in all, and that in the larger cities they shall become, in the full sense of the word, preparatory institutions for the secondary schools, by adding to their programme some modern language and the elements of geography and history. The law also urges the parents to provide more liberally for the teachers of their children.

The most flourishing of all the schools is the school of medicine, founded by Mehemet Ali in 1827, which has had some of the most eminent European physicians as professors, while at present all the professors are natives. Connected with it are a school of pharmacy, a large hospital, a chemical laboratory, (which provides all the necessary drugs and medicines for the government-pharmacies throughout the provinces,) a botanic garden, a library, and a museum of anatomy and natural history. A very important establishment is the school for nurses, which to its students gives not only the special instruction required, but also a more general education than is usually found among women in the East.

At Boulak, the port of Cairo, on the Nile, there are most extensive government-establishments, comprising a foundery for guns and railroad-material, and a printing-office where all the text-books are printed.

* The law is given in full below.

Mehemet Ali had already had the idea of establishing in this great industrial center a school of the mechanic arts, but did not find time to carry out this idea. It was taken up, however; by the present Khédive, and this school is now one of the most admirably arranged in Egypt. The course lasts three years, and the students have the very best opportunities to study the mechanic arts not only theoretically, but also practically, and manufacturers frequently apply to the director for students to become, after having finished their studies, foremen in various factories.

In 1864 the school of Darb en Nasrieh, so called from the street in which it is located, was founded by the Khédive as a sort of preliminary school. The two lower classes study only reading, writing, and the Koran; the study of Arabic grammar commences in the third class and that of arithmetic and French in the fourth. From this class on, the scholars are formed into divisions, according to the language which they choose for their study, viz, French, English, or German. The study of the Koran stops after the fourth class, and its place is taken by the study of the Turkish language, Arabic syntax, and geography. Linear drawing, which was taught formerly, has been replaced by free-hand drawing. Arithmetic is taught very thoroughly in the higher classes. This school has both for boarders and day-scholars.

The polytechnic school—frequently called, after the street where it is located, the school of Darb el Gamamis—is the largest and most important of all the government-schools on the European plan. A spacious building contains the ministry of public instruction, a preparatory school, the polytechnic school proper, a library, the bureau of translation, and a large amphitheater for public examinations. The whole building is built entirely in the modern style and the arrangements for light and ventilation are perfect throughout. Most of the scholars are day-scholars, only the students of the polytechnic school proper being boarders. The students choose between an English and a French division, in which the study of either of these languages is more thorough and serves as a means of conveying other knowledge. Connected with the polytechnic school is a law-school, which no doubt is destined one day to exercise a great influence, when the Mohammedan code of laws shall be reformed. In this school not only Arabic law is taught, but also Roman and French law. One section of the polytechnic school is devoted to book-keeping and surveying and furnishes most of the employés in the government offices. Since 1871 the school possesses a very valuable collection of physical apparatus. The library, already rich, is constantly increasing, and contains a large number of beautiful and highly valuable Arabic manuscripts. The director of the school publishes a scientific and literary review, which is gratuitously distributed to the students and has exercised a very beneficial influence by awakening among them a taste for reading and studying. Many of the students themselves contribute articles to this review.

The school of Egyptology, under the direction of Professor Brugsch,[*] is of no practical importance, but of the highest scientific value.

In Alexandria a school, Ras el Tin, has been founded in 1864, combining two schools, an elementary school and a preparatory school for higher studies.

Similar schools are at Benha, in Lower Egypt, and at Syout, in Upper Egypt.

Two colleges have also been recently started at Cairo, where the scholars pay a small school-fee, and are not—as is the case in the other government-schools—entirely supported by the government.

Two educational institutions, holding the middle place between the college and the *kouttab*, the school of the Wakfs and the school of Ratib Pasha, have been founded at Alexandria, where the Koran, Arabic, Turkish, and arithmetic are taught.

For a number of years the Egyptian government was in the habit of sending annually, at the government-expense, a number of young men to Paris for the purpose of studying there; but as the results of this so-called "Egyptian mission" were not commensurate with the sums expended for this purpose—many of the young men contracting idle and vicious habits—it has been entirely abandoned.

SCHOOLS OF THE EUROPEAN AND AMERICAN COLONY.

In order to remedy the want of European schools, of which the French colony complained, Mehemet Ali, in 1844, called in the Sisters of St. Vincent and the Lazarist Fathers.

The Sisters immediately set to work and opened a school, while the Fathers contented themselves with building a church. Feeling, however, that they had been called to Egypt for educational purposes and not wishing to do anything in the matter themselves, they called from Europe some Brothers of the Christian Doctrine, who founded a free school close to the establishment of the Lazarist Fathers. For six years the two orders lived peacefully together, but it soon became apparent that the Brothers were constantly encroaching upon the rights of the

---

[*]Prof. Heinrich Karl Brugsch, who has recently been appointed by the Khédive minister of public instruction, is one of the most extraordinary scientific men of modern times; as Mr. Dor remarks: "One of those rare men who come into the world with the full panoply of science, like Minerva from Jupiter's head." A brief sketch of his life will not be out of place. H. K. Brugsch was born, February 18, 1827, at Berlin, the son of poor parents, and at a very early age commenced the study of Egyptology, publishing his first important work—a grammar of the Demotic hieroglyphics—while still a scholar in the Berlin gymnasium. In 1854 he paid his first visit to Egypt, and on his return was appointed professor at the Berlin university and curator of the Egyptian museum in that city. In 1864 he was appointed Prussian consul at Cairo, where he has since resided. An indefatigable worker and brilliant writer, he has devoted his whole energy to the study of Egypt, ancient and modern, its traditions, history, language, literature, and social life. His works on the subject—written partly in Latin, German, and French—are as numerous as they are exhaustive. He has also founded a special "periodical of Egyptology," published in the German language.

Fathers, and in 1852 the former were obliged to seek another place fo
their school, while the Fathers also commenced one.

Besides these two schools there are the following Roman-Catholi
schools: Those of the Sisters of St. Vincent de Paul, the Sisters of th
Good Shepherd, and the Franciscan Sisters. All of these have bot
boarders and day-scholars.

The Protestants soon followed. Between 1855 and 1866 the Amer
cans established schools at Cairo, Alexandria, Medinet el Fayoun
Syout, Kous, and Mansurah. The Scotch mission established a schoc
at Alexandria, and Miss Whately opened one at Cairo, under the au
spices of the English mission. The youngest of these establishments i
the one founded by the Chrischona mission near Basel, Switzerland, ii
1865.

These Protestant schools differ from those of the Roman-Catholi
orders by making no distinction between paying and non-paying schol
ars. The school forms one harmonious whole. The principle of gratui
tous instruction is admitted in the American and German schools, an
paying for instruction is made optional in the English and Scotcl
schools. But in all of them there is the most perfect equality between
the scholars The girls' schools have among their pupils quite a number
of young Mohammedan girls.

The mission-schools brought about the foundation of lay schools. The
Greek and Italian colonies especially made great efforts to have schools
where their children would not be under the care of priests or preachers.

In 1860 Raphael and Anania Abed founded a Greek college at Cairo,
which is well arranged and judiciously managed. This college comprises primary, intermediate, and higher classes. Greek forms a favor
ite study, and it is a real pleasure to see with what ease the scholars
read and explain the speeches of Lysias and Demosthenes, the epics of
Homer, and the historic works of Xenophon. The Lancastrian system
is followed in the primary classes. Besides this one there are other
Greek colleges and schools at Cairo and Alexandria.

There are a number of Italian schools, the best of which is the Italian
college at Alexandria, which, in every sense of the word, may be called
a model establishment.

Statistics of governmental, denominational, and European schools, 1871-'72.

Cities.	Schools.	Number of schools.	Number of teachers.	Number of boys.	Number of girls.
Cairo.............	Polytechnic school	1	15	72	....
	Law-school	1	6	44	....
	School of book-keeping and surveying	1	3	44	....
	School of Egyptology	1	3	9	....
	Preparatory school...........................	1	22	309	....
	School of Darb en Nasrich	1	23	570	....
	College of Qérableh	1	10	143	....

tistics of governmental, denominational, and European schools, 1871-'72—Continued.

Cities.	Schools.	Number of schools.	Number of teachers.	Number of boys.	Number of girls.
–Continued....	College of Qalaoun	1	8	122	....
	Italian free school	1	3	45	....
	Jewish college........................	1	5	83	....
	Greek college.........................	1	8	92	....
	Copt Metropolitan College	1	18	243	....
	Copt-college of Hart Snggaïn...........	1	8	125	....
	Italian school of C. Tommasi..........	1	2	30	....
	Free school of the Brothers...........	1 } 26	{	150	....
	Pay-school of the Brothers............	1 }	{	155	....
	Mixed school of the English mission....	1	4	160	60
	School of the American mission.........	1	8	132	....
	Schools of the American mission........	2	5	....	101
	Copt-schools for girls	2	6	....	136
	Day-school of Sisters of the Good Shepherd......	1	3	....	175
	Boarding-school of Sisters of the Good Shepherd ..	1 } 5	{	....	42
	Orphan-asylum of Sisters of the Good Shepherd...	1 }	{	....	48
	Boarding- and day-school of the Franciscan Sisters	1	8	....	67
	Orphan-asylum of the Franciscan Sisters	1	4	....	70
	School for young Greek girls	1	2	....	100
.iro............	School of medicine	1	14	64	....
	School of pharmacy	1	6	21	....
	School for nurses......................	1	6	....	44
:..............	School of the mechanic arts	1	11	40	....
	School of the Franciscan Sisters	1	5	....	45
.dria.........	Schools of Ras el Tin	2	16	246	....
	College of Wakfs	1	4	100	....
	College of Ratib Pasha................	1	5	60	....
	Greek primary school and college......	2	8	187	....
	Greek school for girls................	1	4	....	95
	Mixed school of the Scotch mission ...	1	10	26	54
	Mixed school of the American mission ...	1	5	49	24
	Italian college	1	12	137	....
	Free school, (open to all)............	1	8	105	....
	Jewish free school for boys...........	1	5	104	....
	Jewish school of the late Prospero-Ozima........	1	4	41	12
	Jewish free school for girls.........	1	3	....	85
	Greek school Samaripa................	1	6	28	....
	Greek Catholic Syrian school	1	1	30	....
	Boarding-school of the Lazarist Fathers	1 } 13	{	62	....
	Orphan-asylum of the Lazarist Fathers........	1 }	{	52	....
	Free school of the Christian Brothers........	1 } 38	{	227	....
	Pay-school of the Christian Brothers..............	1 }	{	353	....
	Boarding-school of Sisters of St. Vincent..........	1		{	160
	Orphan-asylum of Sisters of St. Vincent...........	1		{	120
	Asylum of Sisters of St. Vincent..................	1 } 20		100	100
	Free school of Sisters of St. Vincent	1		{	600
	German school for boys............................	1	6	75	....
	German school for girls...........................	1	2	....	28
Said............	Jewish school....................................	1	1	15	....
	School of the Fathers of the Holy Land............	1	3	52	....
	School of the Sisters of the Good Shepherd........	1	3	....	58

Statistics of governmental, denominational, and European schools, 1871–'72—Concluded.

Cities.	Schools.	Number of schools.	Number of teachers.	Number of boys.	Number of girls.
Mansurah	School of the Franciscan Sisters....................	1	4	....	28
	Schools of the American mission..................	2	4	35	30
Benha	Government-school	1	11	30)	....
Medinet el Fayoum..	Mixed school of the American mission............	1	4	35	36
Syout	Government-school	1	10	200	....
	Theological sch^ool of the American mission.......	1	4	24	....
	Schools of the American mission..................	2	3	40	16
	School of the Catholic Copts..........................	1	1	37	....
Takhta..............	School of the Catholic Copts.......................	1'	2	40	30
Akmin	School of the Catholic Copts.......................	1	2	50	15
Ghirgéh......	School of the Catholic Copts.......................	1	2	30	25
Kénéh..............	School of the Catholic Copts.......................	1	1	20	....
Nagadéh	School of the Catholic Copts.......................	1	1	20	....
Kous...............	Mixed school of the American mission	1	2	20	4
	Total	78	475	5, 553	2, 426
	Total pupils...........................	......	......	7, 979	

ORGANIC LAW OF 1868 REGULATING PUBLIC INSTRUCTION.

The old schools founded by the liberality of charitable persons, both in Cairo and in the provinces, will not undergo any change in case their revenue is sufficient.

If this is not the case and if the schools are well located and in a fit condition for the reception of scholars, they will come under the control of His Highness the Khédive and his minister.

If it is necessary to rebuild a primary village-school, the expenses will be borne by the *moudyrieh*, (great center or province.) The plan must be approved by a competent architect.

The expenses for building national colleges in the capitals of the *moudyrieh* will be met by the province concerned. The plan will be drawn by an expert.

Parents will supply their children with text-books, &c.

Care will be taken to avoid as much as possible the former arrange-ment of having the schools inspected by different *mouffatish*, (inspect-ors.)

The *moaddib* (teachers) and the *arif* (monitors) will be supported by the parents, for the sum given them every Thursday is not sufficient.

The preceding applies particularly to village-schools. As regards the schools in the capitals of *moudyrieh*, the government will supply the funds for food and lodging of the teachers, while the parents will bear the expense for school-furniture.

The scholars of village-schools will spend the day in the school-house, only to leave it in the evening.

All the schools will follow strict regulations; the inspectors will make frequent inspections and hold an annual examination for the benefit of the scholars and for that of the government.

According to the report made, it is necessary to found a school at the center of every *moudyrieh* and in all the large cities; the number of scholars should be proportionate to the population.

The teachers, in imparting instruction, will follow a progressive course.

The schools will be located as near as possible to railroad-stations, on government-lands, or, if this be impossible, in a favorable location.

The school-house must be large enough to accommodate all the scholars. Wherever the school has both Mohammedan and Copt scholars, the first class will have two divisions for religious instruction; all the other studies will be in common.

Wherever there are wealthy and indigent scholars, the school-contributions will be divided proportionately among the parents by the government. The children of the wealthy will be clothed by their parents and those of the indigent by the government.

If scholars live far from the school, they will sleep in the school-house; if they live near, it will be optional with them where they wish to sleep.

When the family of a giver of an endowment becomes extinct, the endowment passes entirely into the hands of the school-authorities. A list is kept in the *moudyriehs* and in the provincial archives of all the donations made by parents of scholars. These donations will be transmitted to the ministry of public instruction and will be used in meeting the expenses of public instruction.

All contributions are thankfully received and added to the income from the 22,230 acres of land given to the school by the Khédive, for which the scholars ought to be thankful to His Highness.

Instruction is imparted free of charge.

There will be three kinds of schools, viz: First, primary city-schools; second, primary village-schools; third, primary schools in the capitals of *moudyriehs*.

I.—PRIMARY CITY-SCHOOLS.

According to the report of the committee, there were in Cairo, Old Cairo, and Boulak 222 schools, viz: 8 having more than 100 scholars, others averaging 40 to 50, and some having only 5 or 6.

These schools are divided into three kinds, viz: First, endowed schools under governmental superintendence; second, endowed schools independent of the government; third, schools without endowments, and likewise independent of the government.

All the schools come under one of these three heads. The provincial schools should be placed on the same footing as those of Cairo.

There are schools which are falling in ruins, and yet have scholars, while others entirely new have none; some are constructed in accordance with the rules of health, while others have no regard to these rules whatever; some have rich endowments and others have none. It has therefore been resolved to establish complete equality between all the schools, and with this view the following has been decreed :

ARTICE 1. If a small school has been opened recently without an en dowment and in an unhealthy building, it will be closed. With the consent of the parents, the scholars will be distributed among better situated schools. The building, if it has no proprietor, will be sold, and the money be devoted to the foundation of new schools for the study of the Koran or to some other religious object.

ART. 2. If a school-building is so dilapidated as to be beyond the hope of repair, the scholars will be distributed as above. The building may then be let as a store and the money received for rent be used for educational purposes.

ART. 3. If a school possessing an endowment is in a bad or danger ous state, it will be closed and the scholars distributed as above, till a sum sufficient to make the necessary repairs has been collected. If the amount of the endowment should warrant it, the repairs will be made immediately.

ART. 4. If a competent physician certifies that an endowed school is in a condition dangerous to the health of the scholars, inquiries will first be made whether the endowment will be large enough for the necessary repairs. If this is not the case, the course mentioned in Article 3 will be pursued, unless some charitable person be willing to bear the expense of the repairs; for health of body is the principal thing.

ART. 5. If a school in a town where there are many scholars proves too small, it will be enlarged, either at the expense of the public treas ury or at that of some charitable person, unless the original endowment be sufficient, which, of course, would be better.

ART. 6. If the founder of a school has destined it for the study of some special branch, which is no longer in use, and if the endowment has become extinct, the building can be used for giving instruction in some more modern study, if a person is found willing to pay for it.

ART. 7. If, on the contrary, a school which has been founded for the study of religion is without pupils, but possesses a fund, any person may, by endowing it with another fund, have some new study intro duced.

ART. 8. If any one has made an endowment for his children, but to be used for the benefit of the poor in case his family becomes extinct, the funds are to be applied to schools.

ART. 9. The same rule will be observed if any one has made a similar endowment and appointed an executor.

ART. 10. If there is no objection raised in high places, all the endow ments coming under Articles 8 and 9 will be examined. If the executor is a suitable man, he will be retained; if not, he will be replaced by another. If there is no executor, one will be provided, and the money will be used for school-purposes, according to the directions of the Khédive.

Of the education of children.

ART. 11. If a school has seventy and more scholars, the necessary teachers will be appointed and paid from the endowment-fund. These teachers will teach writing, arithmetic, some commercial knowledge, grammar, ancient history, geography, one modern language, and the rules of politeness.

ART. 12. If a school enjoying an endowment is not subject to the superintendence of the government and the endowment is sufficient, the same action will be taken as mentioned in Article 11. If this is not the case, the required sum will be raised by drawing on other endowments. The endowments designated by Articles 8, 9, and 10 will, if they are insufficient, be distributed to the parents, but their school-fees will be required of them on the first day of every month.

ART. 13. The primary schools, whether under the superintendence of the government or not, ought to limit their instruction to reading, writing, and elements of arithmetic.

ART. 14. Schools which are not under the superintendence of the government ought at least to teach the subjects mentioned in Article 13; but if the founder wishes to have professors of other branches, as in great schools, the "divan" (government-bureau) in charge of the endowments will aid him.

ART. 15. The paying of school-fees will be continued, as well as all the payments made to professors, in all the schools.

Of teachers (maallim) and professors, (moaddib.)

ART. 16. The ministry of public instruction appoints teachers and gives them certificates after they have passed their examination.

ART. 17. Teachers and professors will live up to the precepts of morality, will have good manners, will be thoroughly versed in the Koran, be able to write well, and know the numbers. .

Of teaching and rewards.

ART. 18. Children enter the school at will, and when they have learned everything, pass into higher classes, and are admitted to examination in the government-classes.

ART. 19. During the month of Chaaban (September) the children of each ward will be examined, and those who distinguish themselves will have public rejoicings and a procession.

This applies to the primary schools; in the higher schools the procession will be accompanied by military music.

ART. 20. Every year the government will give rewards to good scholars, consisting, in the primary schools, of ink-stands, small books, &c., with some other objects, in addition, in the higher schools.

ART. 21. Scholars whose conduct has been faultless receive fine clothes for festival-days.

Of school-furniture and apparatus.

ART. 22. The necessary books are the Koran, the alphabet, and man
uals of politeness, geography, ancient history, arithmetic, and drawing
They are printed by the government and distributed by the ministry o
public instruction. The teachers will collect the fees from the scholar
and remit them to the ministry.

ART. 23. The school-furniture will consist of a chair for the teacher
wooden benches for the scholars in the secondary schools, and matting
in the primary schools. In the endowed schools, the furniture will be
paid for from the endowment-fund, while in other schools the founder
will supply the necessary funds.

New schools.

ART. 24. New schools will be built according to a plan submitted to
the ministry of public instruction, which will also appoint the teacher.

Of the sanitary condition of the scholars.

ART. 25. Children afflicted with serious or contagious diseases are not
permitted to attend school, while weak children or those afflicted with
some bodily defect may do so.

ART. 26. The physician of the ward will visit the schools from time
to time and see to it that the sanitary condition of the building and of
the children is properly looked after.

II.—PRIMARY VILLAGE-SCHOOLS.

Of building and repairing primary schools.

ART. 27. Instruction ought to be given in a good building, pleasing
to the children who, by the ministry of public instruction, are called to
pass their childhood there. If the existing school-building answers, it
is well; if not, it must be repaired, and the expenses for such repairing
will be borne by the community.

Expenses for primary schools.

ART. 28. In the capitals of the *moudyrieh*—provinces—the inhabitants will contribute their share towards the expenses for school-buildings, furniture, and the salary of the teacher. If, however, there is an
endowment, all the expenses will be defrayed from it. The text-books
and apparatus will consist of nothing but the Koran and a small slate.
If the children are orphans, the community will take the place of the
parents.

Of instruction.

ART. 29. Instruction ought to be the same everywhere—good and
continued. The text-books used besides the Koran will be approved by

the ministry of public instruction, in order that these books may be suited to the wants of the scholars. In the villages and hamlets it is sufficient to teach the Koran and the numbers. Instruction is not limited to certain fixed hours, but the task set must be learned by the scholars. As regards the time of their leaving school, it rests with the parents in those schools which are independent of the government. Parents may take their children away in the middle of the school-year, even if they are good scholars. This is the only difference existing between such schools and government-schools. The schools are always open and the teachers permanent.

Of the teachers.

ART. 30. As it is sufficient if teachers in small towns, villages, and hamlets know reading, writing, the Koran, and the numbers, the present teachers may remain, but it is absolutely necessary that they know the Koran thoroughly, have a good knowledge of religion, and possess a certificate that they are agreeable to the inhabitants. Their certificate must also state that they are able to teach. This certificate is issued by the " notables" (elders) of the village and by a delegate from the ministry of public instruction. As it frequently happens that teachers who are highly esteemed by the public are blind, it is necessary, if they wish to keep their place, that they have a capable assistant who knows reading and writing, in which case a certificate is given to a monitor who possesses that knowledge. As there are teachers who possess all the requisite knowledge except arithmetic, they may, if they are good teachers, have a leave of absence of one year in order to learn it. This will be of benefit to themselves and their pupils. This regulation only applies to old teachers; new teachers must have all the necessary knowledge.

Books and apparatus.

ART. 31. No books for distribution to the schools will be printed unless approved by a committee appointed for this purpose by the ministry. After a book has been approved a permit for printing it is issued, and a large number of copies are sent to each *moudyrieh*, from which they are distributed as required, the parents of scholars paying for them. The money is sent to the ministry. Ink-stands, pens, and slates (tablets) are furnished by the parents; but if a blackboard and chalk are required, they will be furnished by the ministry, which also supplies drinking-vessels.

Examinations and rewards.

ART. 32. Every year, during the month of *Chaaban*, (September,) the mayor will pay a visit to the school and examine the scholars. Good scholars will be praised, have a procession, and receive other encouragements from the teacher, who keeps a list of the good scholars, especially those who have always been such, so that they may be still further rewarded by letting them enter the higher schools without any previous examination.

III.—SCHOOLS IN THE CAPITALS OF THE MOUDYRIEHS, (SECONDARY SCHOOLS.)

School-houses.

ART. 33. Northern *moudyriehs*: There will be a school at Tantah for the *moudyriehs* of Rhodah and Baharieh, one at Zagazig for Charkieh and the neighboring cities of Galioubieh and Dakalieh, a third at Mansourah; besides these, schools at Cairo and Alexandria. All these schools will receive good scholars, spoken of in Article 32.

Southern *moudyriehs*: For these, four schools will suffice—at Benisouf, Minieh, Syout, and Keneh.

ART. 34. The expenses for school-houses and school-furniture are met by the inhabitants of the *moudyrieh* in proportion to their income. If in the capital a suitable building is found, belonging to the government, it will be forever placed at the disposal of the school-fund. The expenses for necessary repairs will be borne by the inhabitants, unless some charitably-disposed person takes upon himself part or the whole of these expenses. If there is in the *moudyrieh* only a piece of ground belonging to the government, but no building, the government will make a present of the ground, and the expenses for building will be borne by the inhabitants. If there is neither ground nor building belonging to the government, the inhabitants will pay for both; but, in any case, no taxes will have to be paid on such land.

Of the expenditure for the great schools, (secondary schools.)

ART. 35. The expenses for great or secondary schools are of two kinds, viz: (1) expenses for furniture, chairs, benches, blackboards—furniture for the director, which has likewise to be paid for by the inhabitants of the *moudyrieh*; (2) expenses for furnishing the dormitories, for feeding and clothing the scholars, and for the contributions to those schools which are charitably supported by the government, or to the endowments made by the Khédive. If the money accruing from all these sources should not suffice, the remainder of the expenses will fall to the share of the inhabitants.

The expenses will be proportioned to the size of the school, but the professors appointed by the government will have a maximum monthly salary of $37.50 and a minimum of $10. These salaries are paid from the endowment-funds. Each school will have a director, paid by the inhabitants.

There will be two inspectors general, one for the north and another for the south, each having a substitute. These higher officers will distinguish themselves by their knowledge and by their devotion. The professors and all the higher school-officers are appointed by the ministry.

The examiners are appointed every year by the ministry and their expenses are paid by the government.

The local physicians appointed by the Khédive will superintend the sanitary condition of the schools, which will be visited by them once or twice a day. The necessary medicines will be furnished by the Khédive.

Of the number of scholars and of instructions.

Art. 36. The number of scholars in the great (secondary) schools is o be 200 to 300 in each. The scholars born in the limits of the *moudyrieh* are supported by the *moudyrieh*. They live in the school, but are llowed to go out on Fridays, festival-days and fair-days. The number of scholars is to be in proportion to the population of the *moudyrieh*. Scholars from other *moudyriehs* may be received, to a proortion of 20 per cent. If any one wishes to place his child in another *moudyrieh*, he will have to pay for his food and clothing; on these onditions and provided he behaves himself, he will be admitted, but e will have to present himself before the director before the annual xamination in order that the expenses may be accurately calculated. his condition will also be observed if parents wish to have their chilren at home in the evening. If any one wishes to have his child enter a a boarder during the school-year, he will pay up to the end of the urrent year. Scholars for the great (secondary) schools are selected rom among the best scholars of the primary schools. They enter on a ertificate issued by the inspector, the professors, and the elders of the own.

There is to be no denominational difference between scholars. All hildren who are well-behaved may attend school, to whatever religious lenomination they may belong.

Scholars must be healthy and their eyes strong enough not to be iured by reading and writing. Scholars having some bodily defect may e admitted if it does not unfit them for work.

The course lasts four years and scholars are admitted between the ages of 10 and 15.

Scholars are not allowed to leave school before they have finished heir studies. If parents wish their children to leave before that time, hey can only be allowed to do so for very urgent reasons, for scholars attend school to become useful, not only to themselves but to their country.

Orphans and poor children are admitted free of charge.

The course of instruction embraces the following subjects: (1) Araic, comprising grammar, reading, a knowledge of God, the rudiments f religious law and of politeness; (2) some modern European language, Turkish or any other, comprising reading, writing, and translating; 3) the rudiments of geography and of ancient history; (4) the ruliments of arithmetic and some commercial knowledge, linear and geometrical drawing; (5) zoölogy, botany, and the principles of agriulture; and (6) reading and writing of written and printed capital etters and free-hand drawing.

Of text-books, apparatus, food, and clothing.

ART. 37. A committee will be appointed to determine what books shall be adopted in the schools, selecting them from the books already in use or from those which will be written hereafter.

These books have the price printed on them, so that the children may know their value. The children or the parents will pay for the books which they get.

The provisions for the pupils will if possible be bought wholesale for the whole year and kept in the school-store-house.

The meals will always be wholesome and good and similar to those of well-to-do middle-class families.

Bread and other articles of food for the kitchen will always be kept on hand.

The clothes will be of one and the same cut for the whole school. It is desirable that all the scholars should have the same number of articles of clothing, viz, three shirts, three pairs of drawers, three sashes, three uniform tunics, three cotton vests, (these may also be of some other material,) a leather belt, a pair of boots, a pair of shoes, four pairs of stockings, and every second year a winter-cloak.

If a scholar desires to procure other clothes at his own expense, they must be made in such a manner as to be easily worn under the tunic, so that the scholar is always in uniform when at school or when the Khédive visits the city.

Of the means for furthering education.

ART. 38. Every month an examination will be held in the presence of the professors; another examination will be held every half year in the presence of the director, the inspector, and a few invited guests; and, at the end of the school-year, a general examination, after which rewards will be distributed in the presence of the prefect, the examining committee, judges, and other invited guests. The examining committee is appointed by the ministry.

The books in which the names of the good scholars are inscribed are exhibited on this occasion. About a month before the examination the inspectors send the number of good scholars to the ministry, so that the rewards may be in readiness. These rewards, consisting of books, &c., are distributed with great solemnity and to the sound of military music.

At the end of the year all those who have passed a satisfactory examination and wish to enter one of the great government-schools will send a petition to this effect, written in their own handwriting, to the director, who indorses them and forwards them to the ministry, which passes a final decision. The scholars of the primary schools who wish to enter the secondary schools are received in the same manner after an examination, and take the places of those pupils who leave. The ministry has to be informed every year by the authorities of the *moudy-rieh* of the exact number of vacant places in their schools.

If at the annual examination a scholar has not been able to pass satisfactorily, he will have to stay in his class another year.

ART. 39. All funds destined for the schools must be sent to the ministry, which will dispose of them according to the wants of the various schools. Every year the accounts of every school are settled in the presence of the "notables" and the directors. The books are examined by the prefect and are signed by the "notables." At the same time, an estimate of expenses for the following year is made and sent to the ministry.

ART. 40. As the secondary schools are founded and superintended by the government, their directors and professors are appointed by the ministry and receive a pension on retiring.

General observations on the duties of professors.

The professors should be inspired with the same zeal as the Khédive for the education of children, for education should give both knowledge and goodness. The parents will be satisfied with their children, who will be useful to their native cities. The teachers, both in the primary and in the secondary schools, will endeavor to do their duty with elegance and ease, and in a manner appropriate to the age, health, and character of the scholars. They will not get angry; they will avoid all excess, such as insults, blows, &c.; in fact, everything which might lead to a mutiny among the scholars. They will act towards their scholars as if they were their own children, and guide them by their counsel. They will point out to them the consequences of morality and immorality, and the importance of following the path of virtue in early youth. In giving instruction, the teachers will preserve a natural manner and avoid all affectation. The ministry will closely watch over the morality and progress of the schools. In this manner the schools will reach the degree of perfection desired by the Khédive, and the inhabitants in becoming educated will gain the affection of His Highness.

LETTER OF REV. HORACE EATON.[*]

CONSTANTINOPLE, *May* 15, 1874.

SIR: On my arrival at Alexandria I was informed by Rev. Dr. Yule, pastor of the Presbyterian Church in that city, that there was much eagerness on the part of the parents to secure education for their children. Dr. Yule himself has the direction of a school where about one hundred Jewish children are pursuing the primary branches. Mr. Ewing, an American missionary, has also a school of about sixty children from Coptic families. I was assured that the education thus prof-

---

[*] The following letter was prepared from notes made, in accordance with the request of the Commissioner of Education, during a trip through the East in the winter of 1873-'74.

fered by the English and Americans is highly appreciated, and well improved.

My investigations in regard to government-schools in Egypt were more fully rewarded in Cairo. N. D. Comanos, esq., United States consul at Cairo, favored me with an introduction to Ras Pasha, minister of public instruction. His excellency received me with great courtesy and afforded me all needed facilities for visiting the schools. The minister of education in Egypt seems to be sparing no pains to improve and extend education among the people. The higher departments in Cairo are directly under his inspection. His excellency in person favored the consul and myself with a visit to five departments. While they all study Arabic, mathematics, philosophy, one class was reciting in German, another in French, another in English. The sentences presented to us by the students in English were accurate and well written. Another class of young men was studying the laws of the empire. The building devoted to this education was convenient and inviting, surrounded with fountains and gardens. The departments just referred to are supported by the Khédive, with the purpose of fitting students of the greatest promise to serve as engineers, interpreters, and embassadors. In regard to general instruction, I found Hon. R. Beardsley, our consul-general, so well informed concerning the system of public education in Egypt that I asked for and he kindly granted the following clear and instructive statements:

In my dispatch No. 59, of January 25, 1873, to the Department of State, I had the honor to allude to the condition of public instruction in Egypt, which has been so nobly encouraged by His Highness the Khédive, and which is of such vital importance to the welfare of the country. The number of children receiving public instruction had increased from 3,000, in the time of Mehemet Ali, to 60,000 in the first years of the period 1863–'72. The number of scholars in the primary and preparatory schools is now (1873) 89,893, independent of higher and special instruction. This number of 89,893, in a population of 5,250,000, represents 173 scholars for every 10,000 inhabitants. This proportion is less than in most of the European states, except in Russia, where the proportion is 150 to every 10,000.

The obstacles in the way of public education are, however, great and exceptional in Egypt. Among the 89,893 scholars in the primary schools there are only 3,018 girls, all or most of whom are of non-Mussulman families; thus one-half of the population of Egypt is, or has been until now, beyond the influence of education, it being one of the social dogmas of the East that women are not worthy of the blessings of education.

A favorable change, involving an entire revolution of oriental ideas, appears, however, to be guaranteed for the near future. Breaking through the secular prejudices of the country, which have not even the excuse or sanction of religious dogma, the Khédive has resolved that the future women of Egypt shall not be deprived of the blessings of education. By his orders the instruction of girls is receiving the most careful attention of his government. One school, the first in all the Orient for Mussulman girls, has already been inaugurated at Cairo, and extensive educational establishments of a similar nature are in process of organization. It will be no light task to change woman's social status in the Orient and emancipate her from a domestic servitude which has reduced her to a condition of intellectual imbecility; but the Khédive has determined that no efforts of his shall be wanting to accomplish this great work in Egypt. The progress of this social revolution, for it can be called nothing else, will be regarded with unusual interest, for on its success depends the solution of a question which heretofore has been a stumbling-block in the way of all oriental progress towards modern civilization.

A comparison of the number of boys attending the primary schools with the total number of boys old enough to attend them gives the following result, viz: after deducting the male children of foreigners from total number of boys of sufficient age to receive instruction, there remain 350,000 boys old enough to attend the public schools, while the number in actual attendance is about 83,000, being a proportion of 23.6 per 100, a proportion inferior to that of some of the European states, but greater than that of Turkey (10.5 per 100) or Russia (5.7 per 100) and approximating to that of Italy, (31.9 per 100.) In 1862, under the administration of Said Pasha, the appropriation for public instruction amounted to 750 purses, ($18,750;) in 1872, a sum of 16,400 purses ($410,000) was appropriated for the same work, besides several subventions by the Khédive and his sons, to independent schools, native and foreign.

The Egyptians are eager to learn and are susceptible of education to a high degree, and if public instruction receives the official encouragement in the future that it has during the past ten years, Egypt will soon rank with many of the European states in educational attainments.

It will be observed, 1, that the national schools are systematically graded from preparatory and normal up to the higher grades of literature and languages, arts and sciences, medicine and surgery, and polytechnic; 2, that 51 students are being educated in Europe at government-expense; 3, that, at Cairo, Alexandria, and the chief towns and villages, there are 2,067 schools, with 2,381 teachers and 77,292 pupils; 4, that each scholar pays from one to four piasters a month, according to his means, the piaster being equal to 5 cents of our money; and, 5, that these schools are all under the control of the department of public instruction. There are also in the public schools 5,010 scholars who are being educated partly at the expense of the government and partly at the expense of religious estates, making a total of 82,302 students in the national schools. Under the head of European schools are classed all independent schools; these are mostly under missionary-auspices, and the number of scholars here given at Cairo and Alexandria is 5,978, which, added to 82,302, the number of scholars in the national schools, makes a total of 88,280 scholars. Besides those schools, however, there are the many missionary-schools in Upper Egypt and the regimental schools in the army, of which no mention is made in the report in question.

It is safe to say that the number of scholars in all the schools in Egypt will not fall much short of 100,000. A noticeable feature of this report is the mention of the establishment of a school for girls, which is an innovation of oriental thought and custom almost too great to be realized.

It is worthy of notice that for centuries rich Mussulmans have been accustomed to bequeath their estates to the mosques, to support schools and other religious interests. Large sums have thus accrued. These funds are now turned by the Khédive to the instruction of the male children of the Mohammedans. But, though the Khédive co-operates especially with the Mohammedan religion, he is the liberal patron of other schools. He has bestowed valuable sites for educational buildings on foreign residents. Miss Whately, daughter of the late Archbishop Whately, of Dublin, who has devoted her life to the education of Egyptian youth, also Dr. Lansing, and other missionaries from our own land are helped in their educational efforts by the present government of Egypt.

In passing into Syria, now under the direct rule of Constantinople, we met a different intellectual climate. The first school I visited in

Palestine was in Hebron. The room was a basement; no light but through the opening to the street. An old Mohammedan, in full regalia, sitting on the ground, held the rule and imparted instruction. His own example of a see-saw motion was followed by more than 200 boys while they all together read portions of the Koran, written upon pieces of tin. The skill of the teacher may have detected inaccuracies in reading, but it was not evident to the spectator how he could correct mistakes or improve his pupils. The plates of tin were used for teaching both reading and writing. In Hebron, a place of some 10,000 inhabitants, there are five such schools, no post-office, no newspaper published or read. The mechanical arts, the streets, residences of the people, are rude and wretched. Foreign influence seems not to have interfered with the legitimate tendencies of Mohammedan doctrine or rule. The fruit declares the nature of the tree.

At Bethlehem I looked in upon a school taught by the Latin Church. There were gathered 150 boys; instruction in Arabic. Schools for girls, 90 pupils. The order was much like that found at Hebron. At Jerusalem the schools sustained by foreign influence exhibited much careful and well-expended effort. The London Jew Society have a boarding school numbering 47 boys. Arithmetic, geography, English, Hebrew, and German languages are taught. Bishop Gobat has a boarding-school numbering 70 boys. The German orphan-school, 80 pupils. The infant-school under the London Jew Society numbers 70. The German'Deaconesses' boarding-school, 120. Arabic school of the Church Missionary Society, 20. Rev. Mr. Bailey, one of the English teachers, informed me that missionary-schools failed very much to get hold of the Jews, Mohammedans, and Armenians. The communities are jealous of each other, and all unite in opposing the efforts of foreigners who would raise the standard of education among them. If a foreign teacher starts any enterprise for improving the people in the arts, trade, social condition, education, some excuse will be invented for heading off any good to the people for which it was intended.

In Nazareth, the Church Missionary Society have a school of 105 boys. They teach Arabic and English. The same society have a school for girls numbering 50. A Miss McKean has a boarding-school for girls; boarders 18, day-scholars 70. Dr. Vartan, a German physician of the Edinburg Missionary Training Society, has a class preparing for the practice of medicine among their own people. This ministering to the maladies of the body makes the physician all the more acceptable to the people as the director of their intellectual and moral improvement.

Rev. Mr. Zellar, of the Church Missionary Society, has also a small class preparing to be teachers. The school of the Greek Church at Nazareth numbers 84 pupils. The Roman or Latin Church has a school for boys numbering 60; for girls, 35. The only Mohammedan school numbers 18 boys. In passing through Tiberias, Banias, and similar villages, I found no evidences of education, in-doors or out.

Indeed, our consul at Jerusalem assured me there were no native schools worth looking after; that there is not one in a hundred of the Arab population out of the cities that can read or write. Dr. Meshaka, father of our consul at Damascus, a man of learning and acquainted with the Bedouin and Arab population of Syria, also confirmed the same statement. Damascus is said to have a large number of schools. Many of these have extensive buildings, erected by the pride or piety of some rich Mohammedan, but these buildings have frequently been left to fall into decay by their successors. Some of these are still occupied by a few score of boys sitting on the ground and shouting at the top of their voices portions of the Koran, directed by a gray-haired sheik. Small libraries of manuscripts are attached to the more important of these schools. Few of the Moslems have learned to read and write, or advance beyond the mere rudiments of education, though there are some in Damascus well acquainted with literature and not uninformed with regard to the state of science in other parts of the world.

Private libraries of any value or extent are rare, though some ancient families have a few old manuscripts left, heir-looms for successive generations. A military school has been established at Damascus, intended for those preparing to enter the Turkish army. Drawing and engineering are taught by European masters. There are several schools in this city supported by Christian denominations. These are attended by large numbers of boys. That of the Greek Church is the largest and supported by Russian money. The French Sisters of Charity have a school for girls. In these nothing is attempted beyond reading, writing, and the elements of grammar. Arithmetic, geography, history, are not taught. The American Mission have a school numbering 90, and in six neighboring villages they have as many schools, showing an aggregate of 324 scholars. American missionaries have in charge a small school at Baalbek and at Zahleh, an enterprising village half way between Damascus and Beyrout. The people appreciate and improve the means of education afforded them by teachers from America. The intelligent traveler in Syria will be convinced that neither the Turkish government nor native agency is doing much to quicken the mind or to meet and guide those groping for light, but a new element cheers the stranger as he takes the diligence at Damascus for Beyrout. A macadamized road contrasts sharply with the old zigzag along up and down the steeps where a ladder would be an improvement. Telegraph-wires, a modern stage-coach, and merchant-wagons throw into the shade the donkey- and camel-trains. The American will see evidences of new blood as he comes down the west side of Lebanon and enters Beyrout. Convenient houses, fertile gardens, aqueducts, a busy commerce, show new life, thrift, and beauty. From 1861 to 1866, the entire imports into Syria from the United States amounted to $6,000. In 1872 they amounted to $400,000. There was a similar increase in exports from Syria to America.

Now, this increase of enterprise is due in a great degree to the intro-duction of a more perfect system of education. Since 1825, American missionaries in successive generations have here labored and died to stimulate, elevate, and educate the mind. They have adopted education as the handmaid of religion. The armor of the Mohammedans and of other hostile communities was vulnerable only through science. The soul craves truth, expansion. Parents love their children and wish their advancement. Young men see the way to their success in life through education. They pursue education as a means of power and influence. This light and expansion disenthral the mind from ignorance, from old and dark systems; systems that will not bear the light must go to the wall.

It was an enlightened policy of the American missionaries to begin the work of education in Syria at the base of the social pyramid. They have aimed since 1825 to improve and extend common schools till they now number 100 teachers and 2,026 pupils, but in prosecuting primary schools with success there was a necessity of competent teachers. This necessitated higher seminaries. The prejudice against female-education must be encountered. For a woman to read and write was at first an unheard-of thing. Now two female seminaries have ample and attractive buildings and are in successful operation. The female-seminary at Beyrout now reports 105 students; that at Sidon, 60. Similar schools for young men were also established, but the professions demanded still higher and more liberal attainments. The finest minds, quickened in the common school and academy, aspired to the culture furnished by the college.

To send young men abroad for these acquisitions often alienated them from their own people and unfitted them for usefulness. An application for funds to establish a Syrian Protestant college at Beyrout was generously responded to in gifts amounting to $60,000 for buildings and $100,000 as a fund to endow the professorships.

The funds are invested in New York and principally given in New York. The institution was incorporated in accordance with the laws of the State of New York. The frame-work of the building, doors, and windows were framed and fitted in New York. The principal building is 155 by 80 feet, four stories high, and medical hall 80 by 45; also an observatory. All these stand on a plat of ground of about twenty acres, commanding a view of the Lebanon and overlooking the Mediterranean. The college has been in operation six years. One hundred and forty-four students have shared the advantages of the literary department, while the medical school promises to furnish educated and competent physicians to regions as yet destitute.

The natural outgrowth of this educational arrangement is an active and intelligent press. Steam-power is employed in printing Arabic

ibles, books demanded in the schools, monthly and weekly periodicals.
hrough the benevolent enterprise of English-speaking foreigners,
eyrout, so central in its situation, has become a focus from which to
diate light over mountain and vale far away, till 100,000,000 of Arabic-
eaking people shall be reached by the truth of science and Christianity.
Besides the above union of education and the press, some 8 indi-
dual enterprises of foreign benevolence for educating the people are
operation. These foreign influences have provoked the zeal of native
sociations, so that now Mohammedan schools number 1,031; the
thodox Greek schools, male and female, 1,047; the Maronite, 703;
suit schools, 260; Jewish, 105; Lazarist Sisters of Charity, 750.
The Mohammedan communities generally do not sympathize with the
ess. No printed copy of the Koran is acknowledged as authentic,
it other native communities are availing themselves of the printed
ige. In Beyrout alone there are now 15 printing-establishments.
he leaven is working in Syria.
In Smyrna the Roman Catholics have ample provision for orphan-
chools. They gather the poor children, the foundling, into their hospi-
ls. The school of the Propaganda numbers 100; that for girls, under
he Sisters of Mercy, 100; the orphanage, 300. The Greek Church are
till more enterprising in their efforts for education; one school for
irls and boys numbers 800 pupils. The Greek Church lately paid
10,000 for a hospital for the poor and sick. It must be said, however,
f these schools, that they are not thorough, nor their hospital clean and
ell kept. The Prussian Deaconesses have been 25 years in Smyrna.
heir buildings are ample and attractive, adorned with gardens and
owers. They have the most advanced school for girls in the city,
umbering some 220; orphans, 36; ragged-school, 100. The Moham-
edans have been driven to forsake their old position. By the success
f other schools, they too have instituted schools for girls as well as
oys.
May 5, 1874, introduced by Mr. Guaradulo, of the American consulate
t Constantinople, I presented the dispatch of the Bureau to the secre-
iry of public instruction at Constantinople. The secretary expressed
is gratification at the friendly proposition of the Bureau and his high
ppreciation of the system of education carried on in the United States.
le gave his assurance that he would be pleased with any documents
om Washington and promised to send any documents in regard to
ducation published by the Turkish government. He wished communi-
ations to himself to be made in French. The Sultan supports a large
lass of young men in course of training for engineers, translators, and
ther agents of the government. The Khédive of Egypt is also build-
ig an institution on the banks of the Bosporus for female-education.
he mosques at the capital are very richly endowed by bequests before
ferred to, so that a large portion of the land at Constantinople pays a
arly tax, which is designed to furnish means of education to every

child of either sex, so far at least as to fix in their memory a portion of the Koran and certain forms of prayer which the laws require them to repeat five times a day. There are also schools where higher branches of law and Mohammedan philosophy are taught, principally based on the Koran. There are schools in Constantinople where European languages are taught; a medical institution also, whose teachers are French. To these, others than Mohammedans may be admitted. Attempts have been made to establish similar large schools in the empire but the unwillingness of the Moslems to allow their children to be taught what they fear may militate against their own faith has made these schools a failure. Turks seeking a higher education generally repair to Paris.

All the different Christian sects have schools of their own, which each supports without aid from the porte; and the same is true all through the empire. The first impulses were given to education by foreigners Protestant and Romish missionaries taking the lead. This has provoked the natives to improve their own system, but the schools under foreign patronage still serve to raise the standard of education.

Robert College, founded by C. R. Robert, esq., of New York, stand upon a height overlooking the Bosporus, a site not equaled for beauty by any other college in the world. It was founded in 1861 and has 1 teachers and some 200 pupils, commands the confidence of all Christian communities and the respect of the Mohammedans, and promise great intellectual blessings to the Ottoman empire.

The newspaper-press has felt the stimulating power of a higher education. Thirty-five years ago there were only two newspapers in the empire—one published at Constantinople and another at Smyrna, both in French. In 1866, fifty-three newspapers were published in all parts of the empire. There are now published at the capital of Turkey two French dailies; one English, the Levant Herald, the most independent paper in Turkey; four Greek papers; three Bulgarian weeklies; six Armenian, of which two are dailies; three Armeno-Turkish, two of them dailies; one Greco-Turkish; and nine Turkish, three of which are dailies, and one has an illustrated weekly edition. There are nineteen papers published in the provinces, eight of which are in Turkish and two in Arabic, while the remaining nine are in languages of the *rayahs*.

All of which is respectfully submitted.

HORACE EATON.

Hon. JOHN EATON,
United States Commissioner of Education,
Washington, D. C.

○

CIRCULARS OF INFORMATION

OF THE

BUREAU OF EDUCATION.

No. 4–1875.

WASTE OF LABOR IN THE WORK OF EDUCATION.

By P. A. CHADBOURNE, LL. D.,

PRESIDENT OF WILLIAMS COLLEGE, MASS.

WASHINGTON:
GOVERNMENT PRINTING OFFICE.
1875.

CONTENTS.

	Page.
Letter of the Commissioner of Education to the Secretary of the Interior	5
Address by President Chadbourne "On the waste of labor in the work of education"	7
Misdirection of labor shown to be common in other kinds of work	7
Is there similar waste in the work of education?	8
Different causes of waste in education stated	8
Imperfect teaching a source of waste	8
Time wasted on unimportant matters	9
Want of thoroughness a prolific source of waste	9
Waste arising from misapprehension of the real purpose of study	10
Study merely for discipline a waste	11
Mental development gradual and retarded by premature forcing	11
To prevent waste, studies must be adapted to age and development of pupils.	12
Waste arising from want of properly grading schools	12
Rules of discipline should be few and simple	13
Waste arising from toleration of old errors in text-books	13
Absurdity of the old custom of early morning prayers in colleges	14
Waste from want of further classifying students in college	14
Waste from irregularity of attendance of pupils	14
Waste from want of enthusiasm on part of teacher	15
Waste from neglect of moral training	15

LETTER.

DEPARTMENT OF THE INTERIOR,
BUREAU OF EDUCATION,
Washington., D. C., May 10, 1875.

he following paper, by President Chadbourne, of Williams
Villiamstown, Mass., treats of subjects of great importance to
.ors. It has been twice delivered before bodies of instructors,
:d of such interest that I have requested from President Chad-
e privilege of placing it before the teachers of the country;
dially recommend its publication as one of the Circulars of
on issued by this Bureau.

ry respectfully, your obedient servant,

JOHN EATON,
Commissioner.

. DELANO,
retary of the Interior.

ed, and publication ordered.

C. DELANO,
Secretary.

WASTE OF LABOR IN THE WORK OF EDUCATION.

AN ADDRESS DELIVERED BEFORE THE AMERICAN INSTITUTE OF IN-
STRUCTION, AT NORTH ADAMS, MASS., IN AUGUST, 1874; ALSO BEFORE
THE CONNECTICUT STATE TEACHERS' ASSOCIATION, AT NEW HAVEN,
CONN., OCTOBER 22, 1874, BY P. A. CHADBOURNE, LL. D., PRESIDENT OF
WILLIAMS COLLEGE, MASS.

It is supposed that education will prevent a waste of labor; that the educated workman in any productive employment will put his blows in the right place and strike them at the right time, so that his labor shall be more efficient for the good of himself and the world than the ill-directed efforts of the ignorant man. To make labor efficient, schools are established for the education of workmen in every industrial pursuit.

MISDIRECTION OF LABOR SHOWN TO BE COMMON IN OTHER KINDS OF WORK.

It is plain, however, that the world, as a whole, is still far enough from making all labor as productive and effective for good as it ought to be. Through ignorance, carelessness, pride, and dishonesty, a large portion of the labor performed is wasted, in that it fails to produce the desired result or at least adds nothing to the rational enjoyment or progress of the race. We have but to observe for a single day to find too abundant illustrations of this subject. A hundred ignorant laborers, working under their own direction, or rather without direction, in any of the great industrial pursuits of the age, would starve if depending upon the products of their own labor, while that same company, directed by an organizing brain, would support themselves in comfort and leave a handsome surplus for their employer. Through the careless-ness of servants, property is daily destroyed; through the carelessness of owners and guardians of property, ships are sunk, cities burned, and there is a constant, needless waste of property through rust and decay. All such loss is waste of labor. Pride wastes labor for show and dis-honesty wastes labor on poor material or by so cheating in quality of work as to make good material of no account. So we might enumerate a list appalling in magnitude, until we should feel like joining the cru-sade to reduce the hours of labor, that men might learn not to waste it, if for no other purpose. If ten hours of labor are now sufficient to enable the able-bodied men and women to support the world, if we could stop the waste through ignorance, carelessness, pride, and dishonesty, eight hours would be better. After allowing for all needless misdirection and

301

waste, we do not believe that we now get more than six efficient hours out of the ten during which men really do toil. It is safe to say that more than one-third of the time and strength of all who labor is spent in vain.

Does this same waste appear in our own work, the work of education, the object of which is to save all waste? In all honesty, we must say yes. Perhaps I might add, there is waste here from the same causes I have already mentioned: ignorance, carelessness, pride, and dishonesty. I might also add that there is waste oftentimes from the necessity of the case. It often happens, in ordinary work, that we have to labor at a disadvantage. The same is true in education.

DIFFERENT CAUSES OF WASTE STATED.

A portion of this waste from all these causes is due to failure on the part of the teacher, partly it is due to the student, and partly to the parent or guardian. We can only point out the conditions of the waste, and the share belonging to each delinquent will readily appear.

. IMPERFECT TEACHING A SOURCE OF WASTE.

(1) The first source of waste I mention is *imperfect teaching*. I do not so much refer to the defective knowledge imparted in the school-room, although this is often painfully apparent to those who attend examinations, especially in the progressive natural sciences—I do not so much refer to this as to the wretched habits of study formed in some schools. There are schools without system, without any standard of accurate scholarship, and without any enthusiasm; for a genuine enthusiasm for study is impossible under any false system of instruction.

The student labors, but it is as a man might labor piling stones together to form a wall without any reference to the nature of the work in hand, stones of all sorts going alike into foundation and top. Not only is much of the labor in such a school lost, but the habits there formed cling to the student; and it is only in rare cases that they are ever entirely corrected. Those who receive students from such preparatory schools sympathize with the old Greek musician, who charged double price to all students who had ever taken lessons before coming to him—one-half for correcting bad habits.

Much loss comes from the bungling recitations of those who might be trained to accuracy. It is too often the case that the student is allowed to stumble through the recitation, showing only here and there any proper understanding of the subject, so that he gains nothing in clearness of thought, accuracy of information, or precision in language. A little more careful labor on the part of the student, a little more pressure in the right direction, on the part of the instructor, would render the work of both of double worth.

(2) The second point I make is the teaching of *unimportant things*. In connection with some studies are found many things that either have no essential connection with them at all, a mere temporary connection, or one that is worthy the attention of professionals alone. It makes one shudder to think of the trash which scholars have been compelled to learn in connection with the simple studies of grammar, geography, and arithmetic, to say nothing of the waste of labor in connection with classical studies and the higher mathematics. Many grammars insist upon distinctions and definitions which confuse rather than enlighten the beginner. Perhaps no teachers are left who compel their students to commit long lists of prepositions and adverbs, so that they may know them to be such in parsing; but other things as absurd are required, not in common schools alone, but in colleges.

Poor text-books come in here for their share of blame. Small text-books, containing only the essentials of the subjects treated of, only those parts that have life in them, that cannot be eliminated without leaving the subject imperfect, are rare. It takes a brave man, and one merciless towards himself, to make a small, simple, but thorough text-book. Such books we must have, if we use text-books at all. If one doubts the propriety of thus cutting down text-books, let him take his best scholar after completing an ordinary book and ask him to write out all he knows on the subject. The book he makes will be small; and, in general, the larger the text-book he has used, the smaller will be the book which represents his own knowledge of the subject. If this Institute of Instruction would appoint a committee of five to select the best text-books on all the subjects taught in our schools, have this committee solemnly bound not to add a single line, but let each one be encouraged to strike out every rule, list, and problem that he thinks could be spared, my belief is that every author so treated would find his text-book vastly improved. He would probably think at first that the book was ruined, as students are apt to think their essays are ruined when the professor draws his pen through what they consider their finest sentences.

WANT OF THOROUGHNESS A PROLIFIC SOURCE OF WASTE.

(3) In my opposition to the too common method of loading down a subject with what is unimportant, do not understand me to recommend that we should teach but a little of the subject. I wish to throw aside all useless weights, that we may run the better; all non-essentials, that we may make thorough work with the essentials. One of the most prolific sources of waste in the work of education is that we content ourselves with a mere smattering of things that are of no use at all, unless they are learned thoroughly. Those things which we have neither the time nor talents to learn thoroughly should, as a general rule, be left untouched. There are exceptions to this rule, I am aware. How much time is wasted on French by those who never learn to speak or even

read the language; on musical instruments by those who never can, o
certainly never do, get beyond the point where all their performance:
are hard labor to themselves and torture to listeners. In language
and higher mathematics there are many things that some minds simpl
grasp for a moment, if at all, and they are gone, and so completely gon
that they are of no use, directly or indirectly. Some claim here tha·
although the thing is forgotten at once, we have the benefit of the mel
tal exercise in acquiring it, and this is worth all the labor. There i
certainly good in mental exercise. The question is, Can it not be ob
tained on more advantageous terms than by learning a little of difficult
studies to be forgotten?

WASTE FROM MISAPPREHENSION OF THE REAL PURPOSE OF STUDY.

(4) And this brings me to the next statement, that there is waste of labor
in making the studies too hard. There is somehow a notion, ingrained
in many of us, that it is good for us and for the little ones to be afflicted;
and so it is. But it is not good for us to afflict ourselves, or the children
committed to us, except as a rare case of discipline. The whole structure of the world brings all the affliction we need, if we rightly improve
it; and the road of learning, which old authority declared to be no royal
road, is hard enough to tax all the powers of every student to their full
extent, even when his teacher is at hand to direct in every place of
doubt and to lend his aid where the way is hard and the feet are weary
It was an old notion that children must be toughened by exposure to
cold and wet and be made healthy and energetic by calling them out
of bed for hard labor when they ought to have been asleep. Children
lived through such hardships, it is true—some of them did; and for a
time those who had strength to live seemed to improve in health under
the hard usage. But short lives, rheumatism, and broken constitutions
in middle life were the general products of such a hardening process.
A like notion has too often prevailed in regard to intellectual training. The charm of "thoroughness" and "independent work," both excellent—indispensable in their places—induces many ambitious teachers
to make drudges of their students, till all ambition and enthusiasm are
utterly gone from them. By giving such students work only apportioned to their strength, keeping them for a time from all contact with
the knotty points, or lending them a helping hand by showing the
method of untying such knots, they might have gone on with courage
till they could grapple successfully and joyfully with the hardest
problems of any science. Many a teacher has seen such discouraged,
disheartened boys, who utterly loathed all study, simply because it had
always been demanded of them in a kind beyond the mastery of their
unaided strength. And some of us have seen learned and faithful
teachers who tormented themselves and disheartened their students,
because these teachers could not understand the difference between
thoroughness and indiscriminate cramming with non-essentials.

304

STUDY MERELY FOR DISCIPLINE A WASTE.

It seems to be the aim of some text-book-makers, and some teachers too, to make every study as difficult as possible, *for the sake of the discipline.* No doctrine is more fallacious. Get your discipline by doing a greater amount of work and doing it in a better style. What sensible man would turn aside to ride over quagmires and stone heaps for the sake of more exercise for himself or horse? An oak tree might be felled with a stone hatchet, and one would get a deal of exercise in doing the job; but the same time and strength with a good steel ax would give as much exercise and leave something to show for the labor. Leave stone hatchets to savages; let civilized men use the sharpest steel axes they can find. They will thus do the most work and do it in the best manner. This principle of dealing with essentials mainly should prevail in all the work of education. We have too much to do to spend time fooling over complicated arithmetical puzzles which abound in some books—questions which no one should undertake to solve till well versed in algebra and geometry. At the proper stage of education, such puzzles, which are a discouragement to the young scholar because he thinks them essential to the subject, will be solved in the natural progress of his work. They are an annoyance and discouragement simply because they are introduced before their time, before the study of the principles on which their solution depends.

MENTAL DEVELOPMENT GRADUAL AND RETARDED BY PREMATURE FORCING.

In this connection I ought to speak, not only of the attempts to teach the child before he is prepared for the subject by previous study conditional for it, but also of that forcing-system by which things are taught, or the attempt is made to teach them, before the pupil's mind is mature enough to grapple with them. I speak here of the natural maturity of mind through age. In the first place, there is a great difference in children as to the age at which they can profitably engage in the same studies. There is a difference in children belonging to different families, as to the time of the development of their mental powers as a whole and also as to the order of their development. This is plain enough to those who have compared successive classes from year to year and have studied the history of families. Parents ought to understand this, but the majority of them do not. Teachers should study the mental condition of their pupils as carefully, to say the least, as they do the subjects they are to teach. The successful husbandman knows when the ground is ready for the seed, that germination may be sure and the plant become a vigorous grower. The inexperienced farmer or gardener, ambitious for an early crop, puts his seed, at the earliest moment, into the soil, only to find the seed wasted or his plants weakly in growth and failing in quantity and quality of fruit. Some whole schools are samples of this forcing-system. Parents and teachers both join in the work, and rejoice together over the precocious scholars who learn by rote and explain beautifully without ever comprehending what they explain. Such unfortunate prodigies of learning lose by this cramming system all the pleasure and healthful stimulus to vigorous growth that come to the one who, with powers fitted for the work, incorporates the studies of each day into his intellectual life, because he is able to comprehend them fully without weariness to mind or over-draft upon the body. The growth of every day is to the latter healthful; and thus it happens that so many who commence study late in life soon outstrip those who have been delving for years.

TO PREVENT WASTE, STUDIES MUST BE ADAPTED TO AGE AND DEVEL-OPMENT OF PUPILS.

Do not charge me with undervaluing early education. It is a great thing for the child from the first to breathe a literary atmosphere, and in rare instances the crowding I have spoken of makes real prodigies of learning, of which John Stuart Mill was an example—"a fine example," some would say; a sad warning, I should suggest.

In all the early years, say to the age of 14, the studies should be light—just enough to keep the appetite for learning keen—while the physical system has no strain brought upon it by over-confinement or hard mental labor. In these early years, the simple studies of spelling and reading and the simple forms of mathematics, in which the large majority of students who apply for admission to college are wofully deficient, should occupy the chief attention as studies in the class-room. The outlines of geography and history should be so fully given that the reading of the newspaper shall be intelligent work, because the scholar knows where events transpire; and such training in natural history should be secured that the senses may be on the alert for every new form and phenomenon in the natural world. By those who have the opportunity, French or German might be learned orally, without the details of grammar. If this is done, with no more labor than is often wasted in teaching grammar and some parts of mathematics, when the scholar is utterly unprepared for the work; if this is done, and a taste for choice reading secured, at the age of 14 or 15 you are ready to begin the continuous work of education in earnest, so that the student shall not only acquire knowledge rapidly, but shall remember the processes by which he acquires it. And this remembrance of the processes is hardly less valuable than the knowledge itself, especially to one who is to engage in the work of instructing.

WASTE FROM WANT OF PROPERLY GRADING SCHOOLS.

The waste of labor that comes from imperfect classification of schools is so apparent that all understand and deplore it. This evil in country schools cannot be completely remedied, although much can be done by

and tact of the teacher in bringing together all the elements·
ι be combined and in providing in the most efficient manner for
ιptional studies that often range from the primer to rhetoric and

In schools that are classified, there is often no little waste in·
ιss of machinery and multiplicity of rules. We criticise here
ιat caution, for every military man and every presiding officer
ιerative body and every experienced teacher will tell you, and tell·
y, that many rules have borne the test of time as a means of
ιd efficient labor that, to the inexperienced, seem useless or·
ome.

RULES OF DISCIPLINE SHOULD BE FEW AND SIMPLE.

ιfter all, there is too much tendency in large, well-classified
ιnd colleges to make the machinery of government cumbersome,
ιhe rules become such a weight upon the student as to depress
ιd and repress that spontaneity of individual action so essential
ιealthy growth and development of the intellect. Just as soon as
ιt feels that, instead of being dealt with personally, he is only
ι great machine, that is controlled and worked as a whole, much
ιdividual responsibility is lost, except to do his part in the
. Personal responsibility, constant, as though no other student
ιsociated with him, is the true condition of development; and,
ιou secure that condition fully, much of the student's time and
ι is wasted, and your own strength is wasted in managing the
, which, when the school dissolves, is worthless. Machinery is
ιtial in a school as in a cotton-mill, but the simplest machinery
that will accomplish the work is best in both. Simplicity and
ιss are doubly essential in a school, because you are dealing with
ιιngs, and it is the contact of the living teacher with the pupil
ιhole process of education that arouses activity and makes every
knowledge quicken to the fullest development. This is no plea
ιoverument; for the teacher who cannot govern promptly and
· wastes a large portion of his time and strength directly, and
ιchief enough to the character of his pupils to overbalance any
ιhe may impart to them.

STE FROM TOLERATION OF OLD ERRORS IN TEXT-BOOKS.

ιer source of waste is the copying of old mistakes and absurd·
ιext-books and methods of instruction and government simply
ιthey are venerable and have been practiced or recommended by
ιo have been famous in the work of education. We can hardly
ιe this point fully without danger of troubling some one who has
ι book or who still clings to some school-tradition that might
ιunced. We must be content with stating the principle and
ιne or two illustrations.

ιinnæan system of classification of plants was a purely artificial system, understood to be so by its great author, and yet such was the prestige of a name, and so persistent the custom of copying, that this system held its place in our text-books and schools long after it might have been displaced by a natural system that represented botanical truth.

ABSURDITY OF THE OLD CUSTOM OF EARLY MORNING PRAYERS IN COLLEGES.

The early morning prayers, as formerly conducted in many colleges, were an example of the absurdities even wise men will accept from custom. Students were called out of bed before it was light, on cold winter mornings, to hurry to a chapel without fires, and then pass to the recitation-room to recite by the dim light of oil-lamps.

The ill-temper of the students found expression in rebellions and attacks on chapel and recitation-rooms. And yet it was very difficult to change this old custom, handed down from the dark ages, a custom injurious to health and good morals and opposed to common sense.

WASTE FROM WANT OF FURTHER CLASSIFYING STUDENTS IN COLLEGE.

There are two sources of waste in educational labor over which the teacher has but little control. The first is the natural stupidity of scholars, who find their way into every school and college. It is no waste of labor to spend time on dull scholars, if we attempt to teach them only what they are capable of learning and what it is essential they should learn. They are entitled to extra labor, as are the deaf and blind. But the mischief is, stupid students are often forced, by their parents or by their own over-estimate of their powers, into classes where they are a dead-weight upon the movements of all connected with them. The exhaustion that comes to the faithful teacher from daily lifting and pulling and encouraging and driving such students is known only to those who have toiled long and seen their efforts as useless as attempts to warm snow or make the blind see by describing colors. Book-learning is not the *forte* of all men. And while some men attempt only those things for which they are well fitted, others are constantly attempting those things for which they are entirely unfit. Their life is a failure because they never understand their own capabilities. Almost every college has students who would make good business men, good specialists in some science, perhaps, but for whom an attempt to acquire a college education means a great waste of time and effort on their part, a waste of strength and patience on the part of their instructors.

WASTE FROM IRREGULARITY OF ATTENDANCE OF PUPILS.

There is a second hinderance from parents that interferes with every teacher's work; this is their encouragement to irregularity in school-duties. It is marvelous what a number of marriages and special occa-

ne occur in some families, as an excuse for taking sons and daughters
m school. The sons of some families are almost constantly absent
the beginning of the term. The parent sends an excuse which every
cher feels is no excuse. The student is injured by the loss and the
ole class feels the effect. If the lessons are missed or made up there
waste of labor for the teacher, which he can illy afford. His work is
rd enough at best, and thus to load him with extra work or depress
n by rendering his labors, term after term, defective, through the
price of th e student and the ignorance or inconsiderateness of the
rent, is a misfortune to him and a shame to the offenders.

WASTE FROM WANT OF ENTHUSIASM ON PART OF TEACHER.

have but two points more to make, and these relate especially to
teacher. There is failure to secure energetic work and the best re.
ts from lack of enthusiasm. Without this no teacher can have the
t success, however learned and faithful and hard-working he may
Enthusiasm is the heat that softens the iron, that every blow may
. Enthusiasm on the part of the teacher gives life to the student
l an impulse to every mental power. It gives the work of the school-
m a quickening impulse, and by this impulse makes the student a
herer wherever he goes. It gives to the student independent power;
er to go alone. When this is accomplished, there is no more waste
ifting, dragging, or driving. It was the enthusiasm of Linnæus that
d his lecture-room with students from all parts of Europe, and then
t them over the world to gather new treasures for themselves and
ir master. It was the enthusiasm of Agassiz that clothed the com-
est things with new life and beauty; that charmed every listener and
sformed the aged and the young, the ignorant and the learned, into
ful learners. Another man, with the same learning, the same devo-
l, and equal labor, might not accomplish one-tenth as much, because
failed to enkindle that interest that quickens every mental power
lights the fire of latent genius, which, once enkindled, reveals to its
sessor truths far beyond the range of those whose minds have never
n touched by this life-giving power of enthusiasm. It is said one
s this enthusiasm after a while. Then he ought to stop teaching.
e cannot grow enthusiastic presenting the plainest rules of arithmetic
l Latin for the fiftieth time *to a new mind,* then he is unfit for his
k, and should spend his strength on stone or clay, which can only
d to force, but never take form at the mere glow of enthusiasm in
worker.

WASTE ARISING FROM NEGLECT OF MORAL TRAINING.

ut, last of all, there is a waste that brings loss and sorrow to the
ld. This is neglect of moral and religious instruction in connection
l intellectual training. Who are the men who are causing hu-

manity to blush by their dishonesty and corruption, poisoning the wor
at the same time that they are cheating it and astounding it! Wl
men who are educated, but who despise the slow methods of honest ga
and reject the old-fashioned morality of the Bible. There must be
searching for the foundations; and that instruction or that educati
which does not make prominent *justice* as well as benevolence; *law* i
well as liberty; *honesty* as well as thrift, and *purity of life* as well a
enjoyment, should be stamped by every true educator as a waste and
curse; for so it will prove in the end.

We understand the importance of our work, the value of mental and
moral culture. We see the inviting fields that call the student to labor
and the waiting world that needs his time and the strength of his best
cultured powers. Let us see to it that no old notions, no routine of
duty, no shrinking from work or responsibility shall spoil our harvest,
so that at last we shall look back on a waste of energy and time. Let
us work while the day lasts, with our might. Let us see that all our
work is of the best kind. Let us train our students for the *study*, for
the *family*, for the *state*, for the *world*. If we send them forth with the
ability to *labor*, with a love of *truth* and *justice*, and with a spirit of *self-sacrifice*, our work will be a blessing to them and to the world.

◯

CIRCULARS OF INFORMATION.

OF THE

UREAU OF EDUCATION.

No. 5–1875.

SUGGESTIONS RESPECTING THE EDUCATIONAL EXHIBIT AT
THE INTERNATIONAL CENTENNIAL EXHIBITION, 1876.

WASHINGTON:
GOVERNMENT PRINTING OFFICE.
1875.

311–312

CONTENTS.

Page.

Letter of the Commissioner of Education to the Secretary of the Interior 5

Introduction 7

Revised classification by Centennial authorities............................... 13

Practical suggestions respecting the preparation of material for the exhibition of American education at the International Centennial Exposition at Philadelphia in 1876... 15

Elementary and secondary instruction.. 18

Institutions for superior and professional instruction......................... 20

LETTER.

DEPARTMENT OF THE INTERIOR,
BUREAU OF EDUCATION,
Washington, D. C., July 1, 1875.

SIR: The demand is very great and pressing for information with respect to the educational exhibit at the International Centennial Exhibition at Philadelphia in 1876. As the best means of meeting this demand, I recommend the accompanying papers for publication.

Very respectfully, your obedient servant,

JOHN EATON,
Commissioner.

Hon. C. DELANO,
Secretary of the Interior.

Approved and publication ordered.

B. R. COWEN,
Acting Secretary.

INTRODUCTION.

DEPARTMENT OF THE INTERIOR,
BUREAU OF EDUCATION,
Washington, July 1, 1875.

apparent that a representation of education for the century of
tional history, now closing, at the International Centennial Exhi-
at Philadelphia in 1876, can neither be adequate nor successful
t the most extensive consultation in regard to the peculiarities
anifold phases of educational systems and institutions. The in-
in this department of the Exhibition will be very great to all
:ans and all visitors from other countries who attempt to study
ises of our national growth and peculiarities. It should be re-
·red that it is a public interest, and not a source of private profit,
1 reference to its aids and appliances. The producers of these
; would naturally come forward to participate in the representa-
; do all other producers of articles of profit. Yet it is plain that
·ducational exhibit were limited to these appliances, the impres-
ade would be most inadequate; indeed, the value of these aids
cation is best seen in connection with the results obtained in
s and institutions, in respect to which the leading motive must
irily be, not one of pecuniary profit, but of public benefit. For
aiument of this result in the exhibit there must be time for con-
ɔn, harmony of plans, and organization. This Office, as the cen-
ucational agency in the country, has from the first definite antici-
of the Exhibition naturally been addressed for plans and informa-
The recent rapidly-increasing interest has greatly multiplied the
ds for definite plans. Officers of institutions and systems in many
ɔf the country have already fully determined to go forward and
some preparation for the Exhibition, and are now only waiting
·w definitely what to do in each case and how to do it. This
could have promptly projected a theoretical reply to the various
es. There would have been a possibility of its being the plan
to the facts, to be worked out with facility and success. The
of the Office, however, has not been to direct, but to represent,
·rtain what could be done, to gather from every quarter the sug-
is in reference to what should be done and how to do it. In pur-
of this idea, attention was called to the subject in the Reports of
872, 1873, and 1874.
attention must be turned necessarily in two directions: First, to

wards the Centennial Commission, which has entire charge of the classification, and which determines what plans of classification shall be adopted for this, as for all other departments of the Exhibition. Secondly, we must consult with all those who are to participate in the Exhibition with regard to the materials they are to present and their plans of presentation. This Office has been in constant correspondence and communication with the officers of the Centennial Commission, and it is only due to say that they have from the first and always manifested a most earnest desire that everything possible should be done to render this department of the Exhibition thoroughly successful.

With respect to the educators of the country, every means has been taken to gather full public and private expressions of interest, and to act solely and fully in co-operation with them. And while gathering these, whether from personal or organized sources, it has seemed appropriate to consult, as the special representative of them all, the National Educational Association. This association, at a meeting of its department of superintendence, in January, 1874, passed resolutions upon the subject, and, again, in January, 1875, appointed an executive committee to advise with and act through this Office. This committee has since had two meetings, at the request of the Director General of the Exhibition, in Philadelphia, at which the plans of the Centennial Commission were carefully studied, and all indications of what could be done by the different institutions and systems of education, so far as known, were brought into consideration, and an earnest effort was made to answer the two great questions "What to do?" and "How to do it?" One thing has been manifest from the first, that, while certain outlines for a scheme could be laid down, the details must, in the necessity of the case, be announced only as the circumstances upon which they depended were more clearly unfolded in the action of the different sections interested. With a view to giving each institution and system information with regard to the purposes of other institutions and systems proposing to participate, and of putting before the eye a unified scheme to which fuller suggestions could be made, this Office prepared, in January, a " Synopsis of the proposed centennial history of American education." At the first meeting of the committee above mentioned with the Director-General of the Centennial in Philadelphia, it became manifest that a change in the classification there presented was essential for the unity of an educational exhibit. At the second meeting of the committee their views were given in a statement, at the request of the Director-General, and presented to the commission. The committee also agreed upon certain amplifications and specifications, which should be published as a further aid and guide to those wishing to participate in the educational exhibit, when the commission had given a final revision to its classification. The Centennial Commission have now issued their revised classification, and that part of it relating to education is herewith presented. The committee have added their embodiment of suggestions, and hereby

ubmit it as a further step in the development of the work in nand.
While in general the scheme must be executed as it is now established,
t is desired that there may be the utmost freedom of suggestion with
eference to the details. In the prosecution of this work it should be
added that it will be impossible for this Office to perform the part as-
igned to it, save in and by the provision made by Congress at its last
ession for an exhibit by the Executive Departments. The law and execu-
ive orders connected with it are therefore published. The amount of
noney provided for this expenditure is a small share of the $115,000 as-
igned to the Interior Department. It will be obvious, on a moment's
hought, how little of the vast work to be accomplished can be per-
ormed by this Office. It will be seen from what has been previously
published, and, indeed, in all that has been done by this Office, how
nuch more highly we prize the historical than the competitive elements
of the Exhibition. We are thoroughly convinced that no institution,
hat no State or city system, can do better for itself, or can more effi-
iently work for the improvement of its instruction or its discipline,
or the enlargement of its resources or for the increase of its attendance, than by seizing this occasion, when everybody is talking about
he past of our country, to turn the attention of its constituents to the
ncidents of its establishment, growth, present condition, and the con-
iderations which should determine its future plans. Moreover, we can-
ot fail to feel the obligation imposed upon the actors in this memorial
ear to leave all the facts in regard to their institutions and systems in
he best possible shape for the benefit of education in the centuries of
ur Government which are to follow.

Dr. Franklin B. Hough, of Lowville, N. Y., well known for his
istorical and statistical labors, who has already accumulated numerous
nd valuable data with regard to the origin and history of collegiate
ducation, has been invited to co-operate with this Bureau in the prepa-
ation of the exhibit of collegiate and university instruction. The fol-
owing special suggestions are hereby submitted; others will be added
fter consultation and agreement with the officers in charge of these
nstitutions:

The several officers in charge of the institution for deaf-mute instruc-
ion in the county have already appointed a committee to take charge of
he preparation of the representation of this department of education.
The chairman of the committee is Hon. E. M. Gallaudet, president of the
National Deaf-Mute College, at Washington, D. C., who should be addressed on the subject.

The necessity of extended personal intercourse between those familiar
with expositions and the several officers of institutions has rendered it
necessary for the Bureau of Education to invite Hon. John D. Philbrick to
onfer specially with these gentlemen in New England, and Dr. J. W.
Ioyt to perform a similar work, in connection especially with colleges
f agriculture and the mechanic arts, in the Mississippi Valley. Dr. L.

P. Brockett, of New York, whose historical writings on the subject education are well known, has undertaken to aid in the preparation a historical representation of text-books.

Two hundred and forty-eight institutions for the benefit of the youn such as reformatories, asylums, industrial schools, &c., have alread been visited by an agent of this Bureau, and a large collection of fac gathered with reference to their history and administration, which now ready for the printer, and which will be made to constitute a po tion of the Centennial publications upon education by this Office.

The progress of the medical art and medical education prior to th Revolution was the subject of a recent publication by this Bureau, th material having been collected by Dr. J. M. Toner, of this city. N. Davis, M. D., of Chicago, Ill., is now preparing an account of medic education in the United States during the century for this Office.

This Office has also in course of preparation a work on libraries in th United States, past and present, which will shortly appear.

The subject of art-education in the United States during the pa century is also receiving attention, with a view to early publication The attention of all the officers of systems, institutions, and associa tions of an educational character is specially called (1) to the desirabl ness of making the graduating exercises of academies, normal school commencements of colleges, and the several annual gatherings of alumn of teachers, and other promoters of education, in some form commem rative of the centennial anniversary of the foundation of the Republi (2) that the donors of funds for educational purposes be invited to mar this year by the increase of their endowments and benefactions; (that a special effort be made to collect at institutions, offices, and othe appropriate places, busts, portraits, and other fitting memorials of em nent educators and promoters of education, and that these also, as fi as expedient, be made part of the educational exhibit at Philadelphi Other outlines of the great forces of education in the country are und advisement, and all interested are generally invited to offer suggestion

A considerable number of inquiries having come to the Office wit regard to the form of State organizations, the Commissioner of Educ tion takes this opportunity to suggest that, where appropriations hav been made by States, and commissioners appointed to prepare th State representation for the Centennial, a committee be designated b this commission, consisting of the State school officers and others of well-known fitness, to take special charge of the State education. exhibit. This plan has already been adopted in several States with th happiest results.

It is difficult to express in a classification or programme of arrang ments all the details of the methods by which education will be illu trated: (1) as increasing the productiveness of industry; (2) as diminis ing pauperism; (3) as diminishing vice and crime; (4) as increasing th public wealth; and (5) as specially qualifying man for the pursuits

320

life and the duties and privileges of citizenship. It is hoped that no one who has worked out any valuable material which would contribute to this end will hesitate to make it known.

It is suggested that the several annual educational reports in the country may be made to have some special reference to the Centennial Exhibition, and so relieve other documentary statements, and that surplus copies should be furnished at the Centennial with a view to distribution.

The duty of the educator in this matter is twofold: (1) to aid in the exhibit of educational facilities and (2) to use the material thus collected at the Centennial—nay, the Exhibition itself—for the purpose of future instruction.

Among the further details already under special consideration are: (1) the manner of investigating and comparing the work of students so as to bring out the best results; (2) what attempts shall be made to provide special arrangements for formal visitation to the Exhibition by students of institutions of learning, under the guidance of experts, for special investigation and study of the exhibition; (3) the arrangement of an educational congress.

It is hoped that further special consideration will be given to these subjects at the meeting of the National Educational Association in August, at Minneapolis.

JOHN EATON,
Commissioner.

REVISED CLASSIFICATION.

DEPARTMENT III.—EDUCATION AND SCIENCE.

EDUCATIONAL SYSTEMS, METHODS, AND LIBRARIES.

[The following is the educational classification published by the Centennial Commission :]

CLASS 300.—Elementary instruction: Infant-schools and Kindergärten, rangements, furniture, appliances, and modes of training.

Public schools: Graded schools, buildings and grounds, equipments, urses of study, methods of instruction, text-books, apparatus, including maps, charts, globes, &c.; pupils' work, including drawing and penmanship; provisions for physical training.

CLASS 301.—Higher education: Academies and high schools.

Colleges and universities: Buildings and grounds; libraries; museums, zoölogy, botany, mineralogy, art, and archæology; apparatus for illustration and research; mathematical, physical, chemical, and astronomical urses of study; text-books, catalogues, libraries, and gymnasiums.

CLASS 302.—Professional schools: Theology, law, medicine and surgery, dentistry, pharmacy, mining, engineering, agriculture and mechanical arts, art and design, military schools, naval schools, normal hools, commercial schools, music.

Buildings, text-books, libraries, apparatus, methods, and other accessories for professional schools.

CLASS 303.—Institutions for the instruction of the blind, the deaf and dumb, and the feeble-minded.

CLASS 304.—Educational reports and statistics: National Bureau of Education; State, city, and town systems; college, university, and professional systems.

CLASS 305.—Libraries: History, reports, statistics, and catalogues.

CLASS 306.—School and text books: Dictionaries, encyclopedias, gazetteers, directories, index volumes, bibliographies, catalogues, almanacs, special treatises, general and miscellaneous literature, newspapers, technical and special newspapers and journals, illustrated papers, periodical literature.

INSTITUTIONS AND ORGANIZATIONS.

CLASS 310.—Institutions founded for the increase and diffusion of knowledge: Such as the Smithsonian Institution, the Royal Institution, the Institute of France, the British Association for the Advancement of

Science, and the American Association, &c., their organization, history, and results.

CLASS 311.—Learned and scientific associations: Geological and mineralogical societies, &c. Engineering, technical and professional associations. Artistic, biological, zoölogical, medical societies, astronomical observatories.

CLASS 312.—Museums, collections, art-galleries, exhibitions of works of art and industry; agricultural fairs; State and county exhibitions: national exhibitions; international exhibitions; scientific museums and art-museums; ethnological and archæological collections.

CLASS 313.—Music and the drama.

CTICAL SUGGESTIONS RESPECTING THE PREPARATION OF ATERIAL FOR THE EXHIBITION OF AMERICAN EDUCATION T THE INTERNATIONAL CENTENNIAL EXPOSITION AT PHILDELPHIA IN 1876.

he National Bureau of Education at Washington has been desig-
d by the Centennial Commission as the central agency for carrying
the plans for the educational department, and as the organ of com-
iication on the subject with State and municipal authorities, institu-
s, and individuals.

is recommended that the State educational authorities act as agents
heir respective States in the preparation of the representation of
systems, institutions, and instrumentalities within the sphere and
;e of their official connection or authority. Where this recommenda-
is not carried into effect, and in respect to those educational inter-
not within the range of State authorities, all persons, organizations,
nstitutions desiring to participate are invited to communicate di-
ly with the Bureau of Education.

s the time now allowed for preparation is very brief, all will see the
rableness of giving early attention to what they propose to repre-
., and are requested, as above indicated, to communicate their plans,
ing what they propose to exhibit, at their earliest convenience.

i the representation of education, while unity and harmony must
trol the organization of the scheme, it is desired to consult and pre-
;e the individuality of systems and institutions.

'o our education, in its various forms, we are accustomed as a people
.race the desirable elements of our civilization. To our education
attribute the security and perpetuity of our liberties.

t is hoped that educators will embrace this opportunity to illustrate
connection between educational efforts and their results in the pub-
welfare; and that there may be brought to this representation all
iibits showing the effect of education upon individual health; the
itary condition of communities; showing education as a preventive
)auperism, vice, crime, and insanity; and as a means of increasing
products of industry and the sources of personal and social comfort
l confirming individual and civil virtue.

'or the purpose of utilizing and extending the benefits of the Exhibi-
i, one of the most important instrumentalities is that of reports thereon
ompetent experts, and it is therefore suggested as desirable that, in
:ases where it is practicable, educational authorities, organizations,

and institutions should designate suitably-qualified persons to examine and report on classes, groups, or individual objects.

In view of the importance of education in its relation to individual and social progress and well-being; in view of its necessity under our form of government, which gives to all the rights and imposes upon all the duties of citizenship; in view of the probable fact that more foreigners will visit the Centennial Exposition to see our school material and study our school system than for any other purpose, it is urged that all persons connected with the work of education and all educational institutions shall unite in the effort to make the exhibition of our school interests at Philadelphia a credit to the nation.

In order that persons desiring to co-operate may not waste time in trying to learn what the material of the proposed Exhibition should consist of, the following more particularized suggestions have been prepared at the request of the commission:

ELEMENTARY AND SECONDARY INSTRUCTION.

BUILDINGS AND GROUNDS.

There should be full-sized specimen buildings for infant-schools and Kindergarten-schools, the "national school," or the ungraded country school, the graded village school with from three to six rooms, with the whole of their belongings and equipments, from different States of our country and from foreign countries. There should also be exhibited a full-sized American pioneer log school-house, with its appropriate fittings and furniture, as an interesting and significant illustration of an important agency in our civilization, as well as adobe and sod school-houses from the Southwest and Northwest; also a structure comprising a model school-room, with all its belongings, adapted to a large village or city elementary-school-building, with many school- or class-rooms, this structure not pretending to be a model school-house. Views; elevations, perspectives, and plans in drawings; photographs and engravings; historical, representative, and ideal educational buildings; and samples of the best public-school-edifices—rural, village, and city—with working plans, ought also to be presented. There should be graphic representations of heating- and ventilating-apparatus and appliances, photographs and drawings of interiors, photographs of interiors with pupils in various situations, for the stereoscope, (of which interesting specimens were sent from New York to the Vienna Exposition.)

Views and plans should be marked with the dimensions of buildings and date of erection. Representations of buildings unique in character and excellence should be prepared for wall-exhibition. Others should be put up in portfolios, lettered with the designation of the State and city or town, and name of school or institution, and accompanied with printed or manuscript description of the peculiar features, with the cost, material of construction, date of erection, name of architect, &c. Special representations and descriptions of improved arrangements and apartments, such as drawing-rooms, lecture-rooms, chemical laboratories, apparatus-cabinets, assembly-halls, rooms for gymnastic exercises, play-rooms, clothes-rooms, teachers' rooms, teachers' conference-rooms, recitation-school-rooms, vestibules, water-closets, &c., are desirable.

Plans of grounds, with dimensions, points of compass, and location of building indicated; examples of architectural skill in adapting buildings with symmetrical rooms to irregular city lots; maps of grounds, showing the designs for ornamentation; representations of school-gardens, and designs for the same, are also appropriate.

FURNITURE AND FITTINGS.

Teachers' desks, tables, and chairs; scholars' desks, tables, benches, chairs, and settees; approved specimens of such as are in actual use, from State and municipal authorities and institutions; historical specimens illustrating progress; contributions from inventors and manufacturers—only one specimen of a type, and not all the sizes; accompanying statements of peculiar features and supposed excellences and advantages of dimensions, respective heights of seat and desk of each size, and relative position of seat and desk as to distance, (prices in detail;) cabinets for specimens of natural history and apparatus; cases for reference-and library-books, for portfolios of drawings, &c.; contrivances for the preservation and suspension of maps, window-shades, inside blinds, &c., should be exhibited.

All articles of this class should be *samples* in the true sense of the word; that is, such in quality, as respects material and finish, as those in use or made for sale.

APPARATUS AND APPLIANCES.

These should consist of Kindergarten " gifts" and all the materials for illustrative instruction and object-teaching, and for scholars' work in infant-schools and Kindergärten; also model samples of every kind of apparatus requisite for teaching, in the ungraded country school and in the graded village- or city-school, the rudiments of natural history, physics, chemistry, and geometry; specimens of apparatus for the more advanced teaching of the same branches in high schools and academies; globes and maps, the same in relief; maps with special regard to orographical, hydrographical, topographical, climatographical, ethnographical, historical, and statistical particulars; collections and pictures for geographical and historical instruction of different grades; charts and tablets of every kind used in elementary and secondary instruction; atlases, slates, writing-books, drawing-books and cards, copies, examples, and models for drawing, wire and plastic models for teaching projections and perspective, and all other materials and apparatus for teaching industrial drawing; crayons, pencils and pens, blackboards, erasers and pointers; grading, reckoning, and writing machines; ink-

wells and inkstands; clocks, bells, and gongs; merit-cards, merit-roll
registers and record-books, blank forms of statistical reports, diploma
and medals; uniforms and military equipments; book-sacks, book-kna
sacks, book-carriers, and lunch-boxes.

Offers of contributions of all sorts of educational apparatus and a
pliances are solicited from educational authorities, the managers an
proprietors of institutions, inventors, manufacturers and dealers.

TEXT-BOOKS AND BOOKS OF REFERENCE.

There will necessarily be considerable duplication in this division
In the first place, it is desirable to have several complete sets of text
books actually prescribed and used in the unclassified country schoo
and the different grades of classified public schools, from different for
eign nations and from different parts of our own country, as well as i
representative institutions for secondary, collegiate, professional, an
special schools, in their ordinary binding; then from publishers, co
lective sets of their text-book-publications, of whatever description
grade; and, finally, sets from authors of their respective production
samples of the most complete sets of books of reference provided f
elementary schools and in actual use; also the same in respect to se
ondary schools, and accompanying statements of the prices of text-book
catalogues of books of reference in higher and professional school
With collections of books, cases should be sent of suitable size, an
shelving to contain them. The cases should be neat, but without orn
ment, with glazed doors; they should be of uniform height for conver
ience and comeliness of installation, the requisite diversity of capacit
being secured by varying the width according to the bulk of the bool
to be contained or by multiplying the number of cases. The cas
should be exactly four feet high or exactly two feet high, with no bo
.tom or top ornament except simple moldings, and these must not e
tend beyond the above-designated dimensions. The depth of the case
may conform to the sizes of the books to be contained. They shoul
be of dark-colored wood, or stained to resemble such

SCHOLARS' WORK.

This is an extremely important division of the educational exhibition
though, with the exception of drawing, it is not showy in its character.
It is not an easy task to arrange a satisfactory scheme, nor will it be
easy to carry out the best-arranged plan. Much must be left to the
taste, judgment, invention, and fidelity of teachers. Although the results
of instruction belong to the mind, yet they are to a great degree capa
ble of ocular representation, and all written examinations are based
upon this presumption, and upon a little reflection it will be perceived
that the scope of this division is very large. It comprises every exer
cise and performance that is susceptible of a graphic representation
all the work of the pen and pencil, and, in addition, mechanical con

structions and productions, modelings and carvings, whether imitations or original designs.

It is essential that each exhibit should be just what it purports to be, and each collection of papers bound up together, or in any way arranged in a set, and each separate individual paper or production should carry on its face a distinct indication of the facts as to its execution necessary to judge of its merits: such as the grade or kind of institution or school; the class in the institution or school; whether a first draught or a copy; time allowed; age and sex of pupils doing the work; whether selected specimens or work of entire class; whether a general examination, an exercise in review, or a regular lesson, with usual time of preparation; date of the performance; whether a copy or an original design; in draw- ing, whether from flat or round; whether done with reference to the ex- hibition or taken from ordinary routine work; the county and State, with the town or city. It is obvious that productions, without the indication of the essential facts as to their execution, have little or no value for pur- poses of comparison, and therefore for the purposes of an instructive exhibition.

It is hardly necessary to attempt an exhaustive enumeration in detail of all descriptions of scholars' work which might be useful for exhibi- tion. The limits of this programme will permit only the most essential suggestions and directions.

The following should be exhibited:

Kindergarten-work, and the work of pupils in Kindergarten-training- schools.

Primary-school-slates, with printing, writing, Arabic and Roman fig- ures, drawing, and musical notes, done by classes of pupils, put up like drawers in a rack made for the purpose, twelve in a rack.

Writing-books completed, attached together in volumes, of all grades. Specimens of writing should be written on-paper of the size and shape of an ordinary writing-book-leaf, unruled, ruled by hand, or machine- ruled for the purpose, and neatly bound, the work of a school or class in a volume; individual specimens, on larger paper, of ornamental pen- manship, for portfolios or framed for wall-exhibition.

Drawing-books completed, attached in volumes; drawings bound in volumes and in portfolios, also specimens for wall-exhibition; portfolio of two or three specimens of different kinds, free-hand, geometrical, &c., of each grade of a public-school-course, from the lowest primary class to the highest in the secondary or high school.

The drawings from industrial classes, schools of design, technological schools of different kinds, and schools of fine arts will doubtless consti- tute one of the most attractive and useful features of the exhibition. Contributions illustrating the courses in drawing and the results at- tained in each institution of the above classes are desired. They should be loose in portfolios, from which selections may be made for wall-dis- play on an extensive scale.

Models of bridges and other engineering projects and designs; models of building construction; specimens of carving and modeling in clay; samples of the productions of machine-shops connected with technical schools; apparatus of any description made by students.

Map-drawing, from memory and from copy, with and without printed skeleton; paper of the size of the leaf of the ordinary quarto school-atlas; written exercises, comprising English compositions, themes and translations in different languages; exercises in the various elementary branches; exercises in the higher studies, literary, scientific, æsthetic, professional, and technological; specimens of graduating dissertations, orations, and theses.

Written exercises should, as a rule, especially those of an elementary character, be of the regular letter-sheet size, with margin for binding, unruled, ruled by hand, or machine-ruled. They should be neatly and plainly bound in muslin, in volumes of moderate thickness.

As it is desirable to encourage girls' handi-work in school, it is hoped that specimens of both plain and ornamental will be contributed. The smaller articles may be conveniently arranged for exhibition in large portfolios with card-board-leaves. Larger ones may be placed in vertical or horizontal show-cases. If girls have learned, in school, to cut and make their own dresses, samples should be sent.

It is suggested that exercises prepared especially for the exhibition be commenced simultaneously on the 1st of February, 1876.

INSTITUTIONS FOR SUPERIOR AND PROFESSIONAL INSTRUCTION.

So far as applicable, it is desirable that the foregoing suggestions be regarded.

The following additional suggestions are recommended to the authorities of universities and colleges:

DIAGRAMS AND MAPS OF BUILDINGS AND GROUNDS.

The managers of such institutions should present a map of the ground, showing location of buildings, as already located and erected, together with the site, in dotted outline, of those that are to be built according the existing plans. It is estimated that a scale of 1 foot to 1,320 feet, or a quarter of a mile to a foot, would be sufficient for this purpose. The map should include only the college- or university-grounds proper, and not any farming or other lands that may be owned. An exception to this, however, should be made in the case of agricultural colleges, where experimental farms and premises used for practical instructions should be given in detail, while whatever features are incident to this purpose might be fully represented. Where disconnected grounds are occupied by these institutions, separate maps of each might be given, and in some cases a small outline-map of the city or town, showing relative location and distances.

Ground-plans of college-buildings, showing internal arrangements of different parts, would be very desirable. A scale of 1 foot to 270, or about 22 feet to the inch, is thought most convenient for this purpose, and there may be as many of these as are thought necessary for representing the essential features. A marginal table of reference would explain the uses of the various apartments.

PHOTOGRAPHIC VIEWS.

Photographic or other views of buildings, in number sufficient to represent the extent, style of architecture, and appearance, would be very important. They should not be larger than that known to photographers as the 4–4 size, (6½ by 8½ inches,) and might be in sufficient number to fully present the important buildings of the institutions.

SPECIAL HISTORIES.

The present is thought to be a most favorable opportunity for the preparation of special histories of colleges and universities. If prepared, their extent, plan, scope, and mode of illustration would depend upon the judgment of their authors, and would, it is believed, tend greatly to advance the interest felt in these institutions, by making them more fully known.

PORTRAITS OF EDUCATORS.

A series of portraits of presidents of colleges and of faculties and distinguished founders, benefactors, and friends, as well past as present, would be highly desirable.

CATALOGUES.

Series of college catalogues and of other publications would be of great importance, and, if furnished, should be substantially bound and placed under such regulations as might render them convenient for reference. In each of the foregoing objects, its execution must depend upon the interest felt in the subject by the institutions themselves, as no appropriations have been made for these objects, nor can payment be promised. Means will, however, be found, consistent with good taste, under such general regulations as may be adopted by the Centennial Commission, for making known to those desirous of procuring copies the persons from whom or places at which they may be procured.

It is furthermore confidently hoped that the importance of having a permanent collection of these objects at a central repository will be felt by those who may furnish them, and that they will allow one copy of each to remain permanently in the care of the Bureau of Education at Washington, where they will be carefully kept for public reference and use, under such regulations as may tend to prevent injury or loss.

CONCISE HISTORIES OF INSTITUTIONS.

Finally, and as deemed most important of all, because it will be alt(
gether the most lasting and valuable, will be a *concise history of eac
institution embraced in the plan.* This will be included in the official pul
lications of the Government, and will find its way into the princip
public libraries in this and other countries, within reach of any perso
who may now or hereafter have occasion to refer to the informatio
therein contained.

Full credit of authorship will be given to these several summaries
and such generalizations, statistical results, and illustration by map
and diagrams will be made as the subject will admit. It is highl
desirable that engravings of plans and views of buildings and ground
should accompany these condensed histories, but this, if done, must be a
the expense of the institutions. The engravings, or an electrotype copy.
will, however, be returned to those procuring them with a view to thei
use in catalogues and other publications for which there may be occasion in the future. These should be of the octavo size, and advice will
be more fully given concerning them at an early day.

A limit to these summary histories will be stated after some preliminary inquiries shall have been completed ; and every effort will be made
to secure a perfectly fair and impartial opportunity to each institution,
without prejudice or preference.

In the arrangement of these summary histories, and in the deductions
and generalizations that may be drawn from them, the subject will be
distinctly and prominently presented *by States*, preceded by a general
statement of the policy and plan that have been pursued in each for the
encouragement and regulation of its higher seminaries of learning. A
general summary of general results will also be prepared.

As to the subject-matter of these summaries, they should show the
general facts :

(1) Name of the college or university, and its origin and changes,
with the reasons therefor.

(2) Date of organization and incorporation ; denominational or other
control.

(3) Location, and the reasons that determined it.

(4) Brief notices of founders and patrons.

(5) Description of buildings ; extent of college grounds and of other
lands and estates.

(6) General or special objects and original plan of organization, with
its subsequent modifications and present status.

(7) Preliminaries of organization and brief notice of academic or
other institutions from which it may have sprung, with dates of their
establishment, their changes, &c.

(8) Summary of special legislation relating to the institution, and

of the decisions of courts affecting property or rights, with references to documentary and other authorities, in which these can be studied in detail.

(9) Relation to or dependence upon State governments, and patronage or grants from State or General Government, with dates, amounts received, or other information concerning them.

(10) Extent and history of local, denominational, or other endowments; their income, investment, and limitations. These may often be most concisely stated in tabular forms.

(11) Number of trustees, visitors, or other controlling officers; their mode of election and tenure or term.

(12) Organization of the faculty, their mode of election, tenure, powers, &c.

(13) Course and plan of study, with important changes from time to time. Methods of instruction.

(14) Departments of professional or special study, with historical statement of formation and changes.

(15) Libraries, cabinets, laboratories, observatories, apparatus, art-galleries, gymnasiums, and other accessories.

(16) College societies, with facts and statistics, dates of formation, discontinuance, consolidations, and changes. These may often be concisely presented in tabular form.

(17) Financial statements; expenses to students; scholarships; prizes, &c.

(18) Lists of graduates, which will be sufficiently presented in copies of the last general catalogue with supplement added.

(19) Such statements as facts may justify in relation to the work accomplished by the institution, of course avoiding invidious comparisons with other institutions.

INSTRUCTION FOR THE BLIND, DEAF-MUTE, ETC.

Schools for the blind, deaf-mute, &c., are requested to exhibit the peculiar features of their instruction, such as—

For the instruction of the blind: Specimens of printing, with the presses by which they were executed; samples of the literature printed; contrivances for aiding in writing, in teaching numbers and geography.

For the deaf and dumb: Graphic illustrations of the mechanism of speech as applied to articulation and lip-reading, and of the application of visible speech to articulation; practicing-mirrors, and books for teaching reading.

For the feeble-minded: Apparatus for physical development and illustrative teaching in the different stages of progress.

CONCLUSION.

Any communications with reference to the educational exhibit at the International Centennial Exhibition will receive prompt attention on their transmission to the Commissioner of Education at Washington.

Committee on behalf of the National Educational Association :

JOHN EATON,
United States Commissioner of Education.

JOHN D. PHILBRICK,
Ex-Superintendent of Boston Public Schools.

J. P. WICKERSHAM,
State-Superintendent of Public Instruction, Pennsylvania.

W. H. RUFFNER,
State-Superintendent of Public Instruction, Virginia.

ALONZO ABERNETHY,
State-Superintendent of Public Instruction, Iowa.

APPROVAL OF THE FOREGOING PLAN BY THE DIRECTOR-GENERAL.

I take pleasure in approving the plan adopted in this circular, and shall be glad to render any assistance I am able to in its distribution.

A. T. GOSHORN,
Director-General.

APPENDIX A.

INTERNATIONAL EXHIBITION—1876.

BY THE PRESIDENT OF THE UNITED STATES.

Whereas it has been brought to the notice of the President of the United States
it, in the International Exhibition of Arts, Manufactures, and Products of the Soil
d Mine, to be held in the city of Philadelphia in the year eighteen hundred and
enty-six, for the purpose of celebrating the one hundredth anniversary of the inde-
dence of the United States, it is desirable that from the Executive Departments of
Government of the United States, in which there may be articles suitable for the
pose intended, there should appear such articles and materials as will, when pre-
ted in a collective exhibition, illustrate the functions and administrative faculties
he Government in time of peace and its resources as a war-power, and thereby
e to demonstrate the nature of our institutions and their adaptations to the wants
he people:

ow, for the purpose of securing a complete and harmonious arrangement of the
cles and materials designed to be exhibited from the Executive Departments of
Government, it is ordered that a board, to be composed of one person to be named
he head of each of the Executive Departments which may have articles and
erials to be exhibited, and also of one person to be named in behalf of the Smith-
in Institution, and one to be named in behalf of the Department of Agriculture,
arged with the preparation, arrangement, and safe-keeping of such articles and
rials as the heads of the several Departments and the Commissioner of Agriculture
ie Director of the Smithsonian Institution may respectively decide shall be em-
l in the collection; that one of the persons thus named, to be designated by the
ent, shall be chairman of such board, and that the board appoint from their
umber such other officers as they may think necessary; and that the said board,
rganized, be authorized, under the direction of the President, to confer with
ve officers of the Centennial Exhibition in relation to such matters connected
ie subject as may pertain to the respective Departments having articles and
ls on exhibition; and that the names of the persons thus selected by the heads
veral Departments, the Commissioner of Agriculture, and the Director of the
uan Institution, shall be submitted to the President for designation.
r of the President:

HAMILTON FISH,
Secretary of State.

GTON, *January* 23, 1874.

APPENDIX B.

ACT making appropriations for sundry civil expenses of the Government for the fiscal
ing June thirtieth, eighteen hundred and seventy-six, and for other purposes. ·

*by the Senate and House of Representatives of the United States of America
bled,* That the following sums be, and the same are hereby, appropri-

---

itatutes at Large of the United States, volume xviii, part 3, pp. 371, 400.

ated, for the objects hereinafter expressed, for the fiscal year ending June thirti
eighteen hundred and seventy-six, namely:

*   *   *   *   *   *   *

SEC. 5. To enable the Executive Departments of the Government and the Sm
sonian Institution to participate in the International Exhibition of eighteen hund
and seventy-six, the following sums are hereby appropriated, namely: For the Inte:
Department, one hundred and fifteen thousand dollars: for the Treasury Departm
five thousand dollars'; for the |Post-Office, Department, five thousand dollars; for
Agricultural Department, fifty thousand dollars; for the Smithsonian Institution, six
seven thousand dollars; for the United States Commission of Food-Fishes, five th
sand dollars; for the War Department, one hundred and thirty-three thousand dolla
for the Navy Department, one hundred thousand dollars; for show-cases, shelvii
stationery, postage, telegrams, expressage, and other necessary incidental expens
twenty-five thousand dollars; in all, five hundred and five thousand dollars; to be di
bursed under the direction of the board on Executive Departments, appointed in pi
suance of the presidential order of January twenty-third, eighteen hundred and seven
four. And authority is hereby given to the heads of the several Executive Depai
ments to display at the International Exhibition of eighteen hundred and seventy-si
under such conditions as they may prescribe, subject to the provisions of section sev
of the act of June first, eighteen hundred and seventy-two, all such articles in store
under the control of said Departments as may be necessary or desirable to render sm
collection complete and exhaustive: *Provided*, That should it become necessary to ere
any building or part of a building for said exhibition, on the part of the Governmen
the same shall be paid for, *pro rata*, out of the sums appropriated to the several Depar
ments, the United States Commission of Food-Fishes and the Treasury and Post-Offic
Departments excepted, the cost of the building not to exceed one hundred and fifi
thousand dollars; and at the close of the exhibition said building shall be sold an
the proceeds covered into the Treasury as miscellaneous receipts: *And provided furthe*
That the sums hereby appropriated shall cover the entire expense to which the Unite
States Government shall be subjected on account of said exhibition, except the su
appropriated in this act for printing the certificates of stock of said exhibition; an
the board on Executive Departments is forbidden to expend any larger sum than is se
down herein for each Department, or to enter into any contract or engagement tha
shall result in any such increased expenditure; and no money shall be taken by any
Department for the purposes of this exhibition as aforesaid from any other appropriations except the one hereby made: *And further provided*, That of the sum hereby appro
priated the sum of two hundred thousand dollars shall be immediately available.

*   *   *   *   *   *   *

Approved March 3, 1875.

336

CIRCULARS OF INFORMATION

OF THE

BUREAU OF EDUCATION.

No. 6–1875.

STATEMENTS RELATING TO REFORMATORY, CHARITABLE,
AND INDUSTRIAL SCHOOLS FOR THE YOUNG.

WASHINGTON:
GOVERNMENT PRINTING OFFICE.
1875.

CONTENTS.

	Page.
Letter of the Commissioner of Education to the Secretary of the Interior	5
Reformatory schools; (for index, by States, of the names of the institutions embraced in this circular, see p. 205)	7
Homes and schools for children	57
Homes and schools for soldiers' orphans	81
Infant-asylums	93
Miscellaneous charities	99
Industrial schools	135
Appendix A	151
Appendix B	161
Index	205

339–340

LETTER.

DEPARTMENT OF THE INTERIOR,
BUREAU OF EDUCATION,
Washington, D. C., July 3, 1875.

accompanying pages contain the information collected by this
·cting the orphan, reformatory, and charitable schools of the
.tes. While some of these schools are supported by States
most of them are private charities.

. was undertaken at the request of officers of many of these
) found themselves unable to procure the information they
pecting the experience of others, and yet found that such
ι would be of great service to them in the prosecution of

ɔf a permanent or satisfactory character has heretofore been
in an available form, and the statements published were
ιry so much in their scope and character, that, in order to
publication most useful and authentic, from personal obser-
as determined to put the collection of the material into the
qualified person. Mrs. S. A. Martha Canfield* was selected
·pose, and this account is prepared by her. She has visited
d and forty-eight of the schools and charities mentioned in
let, personally inspecting their regulations, arrangements,
ιupervision.

ory schools began in this country in 1825, under the name
ɔf refuge; later, institutions of this description were called
ɔls, and recently they have been established as industrial
ιese changes of names are significant. In the best institutions
, at the present time, the children are subject to family-disci-
·ference to prison-discipline, and are taught useful trades.
pect of the children is thus better preserved and they are
l for actual life.

or orphans were first established in this country at Charles-
Carolina, in 1790.

.t danger to the children in these institutions is that the
l seclusion to which they subject their inmates may prove

---

eld is the widow of the late Colonel Herman Canfield, Seventy-second Ohio
nfantry,) and foundress of the Canfield Home for Colored Orphans at
ιn.   341

unfavorable to their proper social and mental development. The lat war gave rise to an interesting class of these institutions, the soldier and sailors' orphans' homes and schools, for which, however, the nece sity is passing away.

Another sort of charity for children, the infant-asylum, is also notice in these pages. Hospitals for children and various miscellaneous char ties for the benefit of the young are also mentioned.

Many of the schools and charities above referred to are almost entirel industrial in their training, some of them wholly so.

As an illustration of the importance attached to this care of the youn I have appended material kindly furnished by Elisha Harris, M. D corresponding secretary of the Prison Association at New York, showin the loss and injury sustained by the community through the ignoranc and vice of a certain family. (See Appendix A.)

I have also appended the statistical tables respecting orphan ar reformatory schools which appear in the annual report of this office fr 1874. (See Appendix B.)

I recommend the publication of these pages as a circular of informa tion, and am, sir, very respectfully, your obedient servant,

JOHN EATON,
Commissioner.

Hon. C. DELANO,
Secretary of the Interior.

Approved and publication ordered.

C. DELANO,
Secretary.

REFORMATORY SCHOOLS.

CONNECTICUT.

THE CONNECTICUT INDUSTRIAL SCHOOL FOR GIRLS, MIDDLETOWN,

Is designed as a temporary home and school for neglected, vagrant, and viciously inclined young girls, between the ages of 8 and 16 years. It is not a prison or place of punishment, to which its inmates are sent as criminals and by a criminal process, but a house of refuge, to which they are sent as the unfortunate, exposed, and friendless children of the State. They are there to be physically, mentally, and morally trained and fitted for positions of honorable self-support, usefulness, and respectability.

The institution is a private corporation, composed originally of the donors of its funds. By them its affairs were committed to a self-perpetuating board of directors.

It is employed and paid by the State for the custody and education of its dependent and exposed children, thus rescuing them from a life of crime and shame and preparing them for respectability and usefulness.

The form of committal is by a civil rather than a criminal process. Parents, guardians, selectmen, grand jurors, or any two respectable inhabitants of the town where the girl is found, may present a written complaint to a judge of probate or of the criminal or police court of any city or borough sitting in chambers, or to any justice of the peace of the town where the girl is found, who must thereupon take cognizance of and determine the case.

The form of commitment reads, " to the custody and guardianship of the institution till she is 18, unless sooner discharged according to law." Any two of the directors may discharge a girl for sufficient reasons or bind her to service, still retaining the right of control prescribed by law.

The system of discipline and education is specially adapted to the condition and wants of the girls. It aims to be as nearly as possible that of a well-regulated Christian family. Its culture is physical, sanitary, educational, industrial, and truly christian, but not sectarian.

It was incorporated in 1868, received its first inmates January, 1870, was formally opened the 30th of June following, and both homes were occupied in October.

Its present condition is in the highest degree prosperous and encouraging. It has a beautifully-located, well-cultivated and stocked farm, two large family-houses, designed for 72 inmates, but capable of accommodating 80. It has a school-building containing two school-rooms, chapel and box-factory, a superintendent's and farmer's house, two barns, and other valuable buildings. It has a full and well-organized corps of teachers.

More than forty different towns in the State have committed girls its care. The discipline has generally proved salutary and successful. It is believed that not less than 75 per cent. of the inmates will become respectable women.

The box-factory is an important department of the school and a valuable accessory to its discipline and usefulness. It not only aids greatly in the support of the girls, but will afford to them a respectable means of livelihood in addition to the knowledge of domestic duties acquired by them.

The educational department affords excellent instruction in the elementary branches usually taught in the best common schools.

A matron has the charge of each house, its general superintendence and discipline, under the supervision and with the advice and aid of the superintendent. The assistant matron is also the teacher; she has charge of the sewing-room in the morning and the school-room in the afternoon. There is also in each family a housekeeper, who instructs the girls employed with her in the domestic concerns of the home.

Every girl has some specific duty for each day, and all duties are to be performed promptly and thoroughly. Cleanliness of person and neatness of dress are constantly enforced. No girl is kept from school without the permission of the superintendent, and in all cases the teacher is notified at the opening of school. Each one is considered as in charge of some officer, whose duty it is to know where she is at any time.

Punishments are inflicted by giving demerit-marks; by deprivation of amusement, favorite articles of food, privileges, or indulgences; by imposing some irksome duty; by solitary confinement in room or lock-up; and, when absolutely necessary, by corporal punishment inflicted by the superintendent or under his direction.

A record of the time, manner, and circumstances of each case of solitary confinement is kept.

All persons employed in the institution, in whatever capacity, are required to devote their entire attention to the performance of their duties. They reside constantly at the institution, and no officer can leave the premises without permission from the superintendent.

The discipline is that in which obedience and order are maintained with the least reproof and punishment. Self-control and christian love are its foundations.

The recent action of the board of directors is worthy of notice:

" We also petition that the act of incorporation may be so amended as to make the age ot tne girls who may be placed under the care of the school 'between 8 and 17 years.' The reasons for this change are—

"(1) That two-sevenths of the proper subjects of the school are cut off from its benefits by the present limitation, and this too at the most critical period in their lives. On this account the officers of the police-courts have complained of the school, saying that it closed its doors against the majority of those brought before them, and for whose care the school was originally designed.

"(2) The experience of the school thus far shows that its discipline is as valuable and as successful in the case of the girls between 15 and 17 as in the case of the younger. They can more easily be shown the evils and consequences of a vicious life. In not a few cases their sad experience has taught them that the way of transgressors is hard and must ever lead to inevitable destruction. Sometimes they become earnest helpers in the work of saving the younger girls.

"(3) Their labor can be made of much value to the school.

"(4) In case a girl is found incorrigible and her continuance prejudicial to the best interests of the school, the statute provides that she can be remanded to the court which sent her to the school or be placed in any suitable institution.

"We trust, therefore, that your honorable body will think proper to make the changes specified."

The experience of this and of other similar schools teaches that a very large number of the most hopeful subjects are between 15 and 17 years of age.

In many cases the froward and obstinate become quiet and docile; those who have been previously intractable and unmanageable have been subdued, and become grateful, kind, and obedient. The grossly wicked and immoral have been taught to observe the proprieties of life and to feel and acknowledge their accountability to God and to society. In not a few cases have girls who had already entered on a vicious life, and been regarded by themselves as well as others as destined irrevocably to a life-long course of sin and shame, been led to feel that there are even for them possibilities of purity and womanly loveliness and usefulness.

When such hopes have been implanted, a new world has opened to them, and high and noble purposes have been formed and kept. A visible and wonderful change has been witnessed in their feelings and aspirations and conduct. A pure life has begun, and one which will lead to holiness and happiness.

It has long been a general opinion that the proportion of cases of juvenile delinquency in which reformation has been effected is greater among boys than among girls. But the experience and observation of forty years in the New York House of Refuge show the opposite of this to be true.

CONNECTICUT STATE REFORM SCHOOL, WEST MERIDEN, CONN.

This school was opened March, 1854, since which time not less than 2,146 boys have been entered upon its rolls. About three-fourths of these are known to have become orderly and useful members of society.

The building is 300 feet long, and consists of a center four stories high and two wings three stories above the basement. A rear wing, 80 feet long and three stories high, is used for workshops. There is a farm of 195 acres which has cost about $115,000.

Boys between the ages of 10 and 16 may be sent here by the courts of the State for a term of not less than nine months and during minority. Boarders are received by indenture from parent or guardian for a period of six months, not less but longer, and advance-pay for three months is required, at $3 a week.

The inmates are required to labor at some domestic, farming, or mechanical employment six and a half hours a day and attend school four and a half hours. Much attention is paid to the moral training of the boys, which is under the direction of the superintendent, who acts as chaplain, performing devotional exercises with the boys morning and evening, superintending the Sabbath-school, and conducting religious worship in the chapel on the Sabbath with such aid from the clergy in the vicinity as may be necessary.

The superintendent also personally attends to the health of the boys, making sure that they shall receive no detriment from want of sufficient clothing by day or by night, from wet feet, or from any other exposure, and that the rooms and buildings are properly warmed and ventilated.

After the death of Dr. E. W. Hatch, who was superintendent of the school for fifteen years, the position was filled by Mr. S. B. Little, the assistant superintendent, for a period of five months, when Mr. Edward Ingham, formerly superintendent of the reform-school in New Hampshire, was selected for the office. After an experience of seven months in the work at this school, Mr. Ingham writes:

" Our boys are fast coming to feel that this is not a prison, but rather a State-school, in which they can be educated and trained for good citizenship rather than be punished for wrong-doing under influences over which, it may be said, they had little or no control; and the results, present and prospective, are most happy. To be cared for and loved, influences for good the wayward and misled as well as those of fine and tender sensibilities; and often such seed produces a hundred-fold in this life, and gives promise of infinite results in the life to come."

DISTRICT OF COLUMBIA.

THE REFORM-SCHOOL OF THE DISTRICT OF COLUMBIA.

The buildings for which Congress made appropriation are completed. They are heated throughout by steam and supplied with gas, hot and cold water, bath-tubs, water-closets, &c.

ie dormitories contain twenty-four beds each, and it is the practice
lect the best behaved among the older boys and put him as a
ard of honor" in charge of the room. The insufficient accommodations
limited the number of boys, 130 being all that the two new build-
will accommodate.

ie boys are divided into two classes or divisions. One class in the
ing is detailed to the various kinds of labor in the farm, garden,
workshops, while the other division is, during the same time, en-
d in its studies in the school-room.

ie laboring class of the morning attends school in the afternoon,
e the other division takes its place in the field. Thus every boy in
chool performs from four to five hours of faithful physical labor
day, and also spends the same length of time in the school-room
his studies. In addition to the labor performed on the farm and
ie workshops, much has been done by the boys in digging trenches,
ling down Ft. Lincoln and around the new building, which was
ecessary and could have been accomplished only at great expense
e institution if it had been performed by contracting parties.

iair-caning is done for a Baltimore firm, which furnishes all the ma-
ls and pays nine cents for each chair. The boys learn to do it in a
days and work one-half of each day, the remainder being spent in
ol and recreation. An active boy can cane about three chairs a day.
iere is also a tailor-shop, in which a sufficient number of boys are
loyed to manufacture all the clothing of the institution.

ie number of boys at present in the institution is 151. This is more
there are really accommodations for, and notice has been sent to
police-authorities that no more can be received at present.

ie method of discipline and management is parental rather than
il. Those who visit the institution find it surrounded by no high
s. The grounds are inclosed by the same fence which has been in
tence for many years—a common post-and-rail fence, five or six feet
i. In the fields thus inclosed they may see fifty or sixty boys busily
rork, hoeing corn or potatoes or gathering the crops, all cheerful and
py. Only their teachers or the farmer or the gardener is with them,
it would be easy for them to disperse and run. The reason they do
is that they have no desire to. There may be a few among them
would be glad to escape, but they know that if they were to attempt
lo so the others would arrest their flight. The best sentinels are the
s themselves. The boys are more happy, and of course contented, at
school than they have been outside of it, and they are not uncon-
us of the benefit they are deriving from being in the institution.
asionally they escape, but are soon recovered and brought back,
ietimes returning voluntarily.

variety of mechanical employments, it is believed, might be carried
profitably at the institution, especially during the season when out-
r work ceases; but as yet want of means and other reasons have

prevented their establishment. Congress has been asked for an appropriation to enable the managers to erect a building for workshops, and to purchase a steam-engine as a motive power, belting, machinery, &c. The superintendent states that the boys earned in a little more than six months $1,233.93 by caning chairs, done chiefly by the very small boys; but since July, 1874, owing to the general depressed condition of business, no work of this kind has been obtained.

INDIANA.

INDIANA REFORMATORY FOR WOMEN AND GIRLS, INDIANAPOLIS.

This institution was established in 1874, in accordance with a law passed in 1869 by the general assembly of Indiana. The female convicts from the Indiana State-prison were removed here and placed under the charge of Mrs. Sarah Smith, whose previous success in reformatory work in the State had demonstrated her eminent fitness for the position. The result has proved that woman is competent to govern the depraved and desperate of her own sex by womanly measures and appliances, without a resort to the rigorous means which are generally supposed to be necessary in prisons governed by men and intended wholly or chiefly for male convicts.

The condition and surroundings of these women have been greatly improved by the change. Judging from their appearance and deportment, considerable progress has already been made towards the regaining of their own self-respect, which is the first step in the reformation of their lives and characters.

A girls' department is connected with this reformatory, inmates being received between the ages of 6 and 16. To justify the committal of girls to this school, it is not necessary that they should have violated the laws of the State. Vagrancy or incorrigible or vicious conduct on the part of a girl, coupled with the fact that her parent or guardian is incapable of exercising, or unwilling to exercise, the proper care over her, or that she is destitute of a suitable home and adequate means of obtaining an honest living, or that she is in danger of being brought up to lead an idle or vicious life, justify her committal to the guardianship of the institution. There are about a hundred girls in this department of the institution. They are taught half the day in a well-organized school, the remainder of their time being devoted to industrial occupations, principally housework. Washing is taken in from the town to a large extent, the heaviest part of this work being done by the women in the prisoners' department.

The institution occupies a fine new building, erected by the State for the purpose, on ample grounds.

S. A. Fletcher, jr., late president of the board of managers, has recently contributed to the institution a much-needed library.

13

IOWA.

IOWA REFORM-SCHOOL.

itution was organized in 1868, and located in Lee County.
eueral assembly of 1872 appropriated $45,000 for the erection
buildings for the institution and $5,000 to organize a school
he building in which the boys were then kept. A location was
Eldora, Hardin County, the citizens of the town giving to
)0 acres of good prairie-land and 40 acres of timber-land as
ent. The railroad was also pledged to carry all freight and
to and from the school for one-half the ordinary price of
t, &c.
lings were erected at a cost of $3,000 less than the amount
d.
.ely after the boys were removed from the old location, a
;irls was organized in it, having a superintendent under the
he superintendent of the reform-school. While it is consid-
ially necessary that the two departments should be entirely
the institution feels the disadvantage of so great a distance
em, and arrangements will soon be made to erect suitable
ithin a mile of the building now occupied by the boys' de-
This will be a great economy in labor, as much of the work
: boys can better be performed by the girls, and the fruits
bles cultivated by the boys can be furnished to supply the
ie girls' school.

KENTUCKY.

LOUISVILLE HOUSE OF REFUGE.

ghth annual report of this institution is the following state-

the house December 31, 1872 139
mitted during the year 1873 81

le number in the house during the year 220
lished 20
) parents as reformed 15
) parents leaving the city 9
) parents at their solicitation 23
xpiring 3
)mmuted under judge's jurisdiction 2
.... 2
.... 4
ct 1
                                                    79
leaving in the house, December 31, 1873 141

The female department of the house of refuge was opened during the early part of the previous year. The results of this new enterprise have exceeded the most sanguine expectations. Already twenty-eight girls have been admitted; and the management of these refractory girls has been a far more delicate and difficult task than the control of the boys. The success, however, has amply repaid the cost of the very great care, trouble, and anxiety that have been given.

A colored house of refuge, in addition, is now under contemplation.

Every year the work grows in its interest and importance. As experience reveals new and better methods, it also enlarges before the mental vision the boundaries of the work to be done and unfolds new ideals of excellence in it that are more difficult of attainment. It is impossible to overestimate the benefit, not only to individual lives, but to society, which this enterprise promises.

MARYLAND.

MARYLAND INDUSTRIAL SCHOOL FOR GIRLS, NEAR BALTIMORE.

This school is located at Orange Grove, eleven miles from Baltimore. The professed object of the institution is not punishment, but reform; its law being the law of kindness; its aim not simply to restrain from evil, but to educate the mind and heart, and so to train the hands that the inmates may acquire moral and industrious habits. Homes are procured for all who become competent and who may be trusted away from the school; and this is found to be the only proper plan, inasmuch as it thereby removes from the girls' minds the idea of the institution being a *prison-house* for culprits.

There are 31 girls in the institution. They are instructed in the ordinary branches of English education, in sewing, and in housework. Children can be committed at any age under 18 years, to remain until 21. Conditions of commitment are vagrancy, vagabondage of the children or their parents; also those are committed who may be disorderly or incorrigible; those suffering from the poverty, bad habits, or neglect of parents; children of parents out of the State without sufficient sustenance; and illegitimate children.

THE HOUSE OF REFUGE FOR JUVENILE DELINQUENTS OF THE CITY OF BALTIMORE

Was established in the year 1855, and has had under its care 2,421 inmates.

The boys are all employed, chiefly under contracts, at various trades. To each of these six hours are daily devoted, and the same number of hours are given daily to common-school-instruction, which ranges, in six separate schools, from the alphabet to algebra.

In immediate connection with the schools, much attention is given to regular instruction in vocal and instrumental music. Its beneficial influence is greatly confided in, and its value is decidedly demonstrated in the development of much talent that, but for the instruction here received, would probably never have been suspected and most certainly never have been cultivated. The elements of the science are taught regularly to all, to the younger as well as to the older, and hence the striking melody and pleasing effect of their congregational and choral singing have secured marked and general approbation.

By a recent act of the general assembly, girls were excluded from the refuge, and the building which had been occupied by them was set apart as a "house of merit" for the special occupation of the better class of younger lads, as well as to hold it out as an incentive to promotion in grade for moral improvement of other inmates. This is a step towards a better classification. The younger lads and boys of improved character, and boys newly committed, if for no overt criminal offense, and if of fair general character and moral habits, are at once admitted. As far as practicable they are separated from the other inmates; and to be dismissed to the general department of the refuge is considered a degradation, and is resorted to as a punishment only for persistent misbehavior.

The refuge has five schools and one in the "house of merit." The common English branches are taught, and the progress made has been quite satisfactory.

A large majority of the inmates since the beginning of the school are reported to have become respectable and useful citizens. The homes of many of the discharged boys were personally visited by the superintendent or his assistant in 1874, and their reports were generally satisfactory.

The department of labor is one of the most important in the systematic discipline of the house. The boys are the engineers, gas-makers, farmers, tailors, bakers, and shoemakers of the institution. Under proper overseers, they make their own clothing, raise their own vegetables, and do their own cooking and laundry-work.

Besides this, one hundred and fifty-five boys work under contract at various manufactures, and thus are instructed in trades by which they may more readily find useful employment when discharged.

MASSACHUSETTS.

STATE PRIMARY SCHOOL AT MONSON.

This institution was organized in 1866, and has had under its care 2,548 inmates. Eight years since, it established a primary school, and, since its connection with the alms-house was dissevered, has only made the first report of the State Primary School proper. The institution is gradually becoming more distinctively reformatory. Many of the scholars are criminals, though of tender age. The leniency of the law, resting upon the hope of their improvement, operates to save them, if possible, from the fate of the vicious. It allows them to enter the State Primary School instead of forcing them into a position where they must associate with those who are older and more hardened in crime. Yet they are offenders, and their commitment must be regarded in a certain sense as a punishment.

The large boys who work in the shops are allowed a percentage of what they earn. This money is placed to their account, and they can spend it as they choose, or let it remain until they go away. The extra amount of labor accomplished under this stimulus is enough to balance the compensation given to the boys, and no one loses by the transaction. At the same time, their work is performed with a more cheerful spirit than if they were compelled to execute an allotted task.

Boys who are not old enough to work in the shops are employed in light labor upon the farm. The girls, in addition to the ordinary domestic duties of the establishment, which they perform regularly, spend a part of each day in the sewing-room.

Five hours a day are passed by the younger pupils in the school-room. Those who work are required to study but three hours. The classes are arranged with special reference to these half-time scholars. There are seven schools. Nos. 1, 2, and 5 have each two divisions, making distinct classes for morning- and afternoon-recitations, so that they may almost be said each to comprise two schools under one teacher.

Average attendance during the year, 383; average age of pupils, nearly 10 years.

A new feature of the institution is the printing-office, which affords both means of entertainment and of instruction. A Young America press was purchased and set up in June, and the first number of a little paper, called The Dew-Drop, was issued at that time. This paper, which contains the contributions of scholars, as well as communications from their friends, is published bi-monthly. The whole work of setting type and printing is at present divided among seven boys. It is as valuable to them as any school-exercise, inasmuch as it involves a practical application of the rules of orthography at the same time that they are learning the compositor's trade. When there is no printing to be done, the boys set up and distribute type as a rhetorical exercise.

STATE REFORM-SCHOOL AT WESTBORO', MASS.

This institution makes this year its twenty-seventh annual report. For several years a policy has been adopted by which the character of the institution has been gradually changing. It is losing its character as a reform-school for boys and becoming a place of confinement for criminals. The younger and less vicious boys are now sent to Monson, or places are found for them in families, while the older, the more vicious, and the more hardened are sent to this institution, increasing largely the class of incorrigibles.

This change of policy has brought young men, from 16 to 18 years of

any of them familiar with crime and perfectly reckless, into an
tion designed for boys from 7 to 14 years of age, with sometimes
ects on these. This institute has a farm of two hundred and
bree acres, but unfortunately the character of the inmates is
lat they cannot with safety be taken out upon the farm.

ous important changes are being made, and in the present state
gs the government is made more strict. Both the discipline and
uishments have varied somewhat in their nature, as they must
hands of a judicious parent, while the child passes from the
of childhood into youth.

MAINE.

STATE REFORM SCHOOL, CAPE ELIZABETH.

school has been much improved during the past year or two,
n methods and accommodations. Where formerly were dismal
he boys are now placed at night in large, open, well lighted and
ted halls. A classification according to grades in behavior has
dopted, and is found to be the best possible aid in discipline and
ant to study and manliness. The requirements for admission to
st grade are the same deportment that would be expected in any
gulated family and a reasonable assurance that all the members
safely trusted away from the building without an officer. These
ave a more desirable sleeping apartment, better furnished table,
ore luxuries than those in the lower grades. They are permitted
a large part of their recreation in the open fields and pastures,
t their friends when convenient, and are frequently taken out on
ions. The practice has been to discharge and grant leave of ab-
to the members of this grade only. Promotion from one grade
ther and the privileges pertaining to the highest are mainly
upon as incentives to good behavior and reformation.
y one-third of the boys, it has been found, can be trusted entirely
heir honor, and this number is constantly increasing. Some very
ied characters are sent to the school. These are separated, as
s they remain desperate from all who honestly try to be manly
edient. Bolts and locks cannot yet be dispensed with entirely,
ery week a gain is being made in this direction.
reformation of the inmates has been kept steadily in view as the
bject to be attained in the change in the internal arrangements,
stem of grading, and other improvements. The tables are made
form to ordinary family arrangements as much as is possible
the circumstances. The tin plates and basins have been replaced
ne-china cups, saucers, mugs, and plates, and the table covered
narble-cloth, giving the dining-room a home-like appearance.
erience and sound judgment teach us that the tendency of such
es is to elevate the character and lift one to a higher plane of

353

thought and action and inspire him with new incentives to better life. Unfavorable circumstances are a fruitful source of crime, and favorable surroundings may be made available as a means of reformation. Each year has added strength to the conviction that without the influence of Christianity a radical and permanent reformation cannot be effected in these boys. The judicious discipline, however, which has been maintained from the organization of this school has been a necessary accompaniment of those influences.

There is a school in which the rudiments of an English education are taught.

Five hours a day are spent in industrial pursuits, as farming, brick-making, shoe-making, chair-seating, &c. The boys make their own shoes and, with the aid of a sewing-machine, make their clothing.

MICHIGAN.

DETROIT HOUSE OF CORRECTION, DETROIT.

A majority of the inmates here are adults, though a large number of youth of both sexes are admitted. Children are sometimes sent here for petty offenses, in the hope that they may be reformed without being sent to the State Reform-School, to which their commitment would necessarily be during minority. In some cases, too, homeless and friendless children, who have committed no offense, are received upon application from themselves or others taking an interest in them, and are kept until some provision can be made for them.

The school, which is held four evenings in each week, is a part of the prison-life. Teachers are selected from the more advanced students, and it is thought the school has improved under this method. Teachers have a proper ambition to instruct, and students share in the same spirit to learn. The helpfulness of the school is observed not only in its effect on men after they are dismissed, but also while they are in the prison. As to this, an intelligent teacher says: "The time they give to their recitations at school is not all the benefit they derive from the school, but it is the cause of their fixing their minds on their studies while at work and while in their cells. If this were all, I think it would be a great gain, especially where there are two in the same cell."

A library of nearly a thousand volumes belongs to the institution.

THE MICHIGAN STATE REFORM SCHOOL, LANSING.

We have received from this school its seventeenth annual report, and it appears from it that no year has closed with more satisfactory results since the organization of the institution.

The second family-house will afford accommodation, including the one previously erected, for at least seventy-five boys of the smaller and better class, who can be found worthy of trust, without the restraints imposed by bars and bolts and walls. Much confidence is felt in the isdom of this experiment of the family-plan as a means of reformation, e younger and better class being separated by it from those of more ature years and more experience in the ways of vice and crime. For e latter class impassable walls are necessary, or a large number of erseers and watchmen, to prevent frequent escapes, which have a very leterious effect upon the discipline of the school, as one successful cape always has the tendency to induce the attempt on the part of hers.

A suggestion has been made to provide another family-house and labor r the boys who may be, or who may soon become, entitled to their re-ase, where they may be retained for a further probation and where ney shall also be entitled to receive a portion of the proceeds of their bor, thus training them further in their own personal care and man-gement. To this home boys will be permitted to return who fail in the omes provided for them and voluntarily come back to school.

It has been the humane practice of the board of control to release boys who have shown a commendable disposition to restrain themselves and to strive for an honest livelihood, and who have either had parents or friends willing to care for and assist them, or who have had homes found for them before they have reached their majority, (which is the limit of the sentence committing them to the care of the school,) re-turning them, on a violation of the conditions of their parole, to the custody of the school. There is, however, no force to a system of con-ditional release unless this power of compulsory return is authorized by law.

There are frequent appeals from parents and friends to be allowed to send here those who are wayward without the stain of a commitment. Such boys might be sent to such a home, under regulations adopted by the board, and much good effected, and the boys be saved from further progress in the downward path. It is not, in such cases, an effort to release themselves from the duty of providing for their children, but a sincere desire to save the child. Often the parties would be glad to meet the expense incurred in the care of the boy. The industrial occu pation should be imperative upon all enjoying the advantages of the schools, as compulsory as any part of its work, and should form an inte-gral part of this great charity. Industrial training is one of the very essen-tial necessities in their redemption, and without it there is no manhood or moral worth for them in the future.

Their school-department is well sustained and the progress made is highly satisfactory. The establishment of a reading-room during the past year is a very great good to the boys, and they show their appreci-ation of it by the anxiety they manifest for the time to come when they can have access to it, and the care they take of the reading-matter in the room.

Children can now be committed according to law only between the ages of 10 and 16 years. During the early history of the school the limit was 7 years. It has been found that the age of 10 is too late many children requiring reformatory training earlier than this, and the advice of the board of managers to the legislature is that the limit shal be fixed at 8 years. It is regarded, too, as a mistake that the term o commitment should extend during the entire term of a boy's minority first, many magistrates hesitate in committing a boy for trifling cause for so long a term, while yet the child's surroundings may make th school a necessity to his salvation; secondly, the influence which boys larger growth exert upon smaller ones is often of a most deleterio character. And it may be taken for granted that, if boys are found in the school beyond 18 who are still quite indifferent to their characte and are making no effort at self-restraint, for the general interest of the other boys they had better be removed, as their influence will always work against the best efforts of the school.

With such a change the work of the institution will come more within the proper scope of such an establishment, more school-like in its operation. The resources from its labor will be somewhat less, but the spirit and work of the school will be nearer what becomes such a charity.

NEW HAMPSHIRE.

REFORM-SCHOOL OF THE STATE OF NEW HAMPSHIRE, MANCHESTER.

The whole number of pupils at the school during the year which closed on the 30th of April has been 139, 47 of whom have been admitted during the year. In the same time 17 have been discharged at the expiration of sentence; 10 honorably so for good conduct, by the trustees; 5 have had homes found them by the superintendent; 1 has died; 5 have escaped and been recovered, and 101 now remain at the school.

Of those now remaining, there are quite a number of good children, whom the trustees would be glad to discharge, if they had suitable homes to go to, or if such could be found for them; for experience has proved that to return a child to an abandoned home, or to cast him loose upon the world, is to expose him anew to all the dangers and vicious associations which brought him to the institution, and to expose to entire loss all that has thus far been done for him. Many of these children are the victims of cruel neglect and evil example at their own homes.

Of the inmates of the institution 31 are of the age of 10 years and under, 57 of the age of 12 years and under. These children are of six nationalities: Irish, Americans, French, mixed Africans, Germans, and English, and 45 of them are committed during minority.

The average detention of the children discharged during the year was two years and six months.

At the first thought it may seem severe that a small child should be sentenced for a long time at the school, but experience shows it to

be much better for the child. If sentenced for a short time, he feels
hat it will soon be over; and, however well he may behave, he will not
probably be released until the expiration of his sentence, and hence
here is no motive for good behavior; but, if sentenced for a long time,
r during his minority, he sees no chance for liberation before the end
f his sentence unless he behaves well; and he is generally sharp
nough to take that course. Besides, it gives time for bad habits to be
radicated and good ones to be formed, and does not compel the dis-
harge of the child before it is comparatively safe and proper for him to
;o.

The trustees are always happy to send a pupil from the institution as
soon as he is fitted for liberation and there is a good place for him. The
time of detention can thus be fixed as the good of the child may require.

The proceeds of the labor of boys in the chair-shop ($6,222.26) has
been more than doubled in the last year, owing in part to having a
more advantageous job, better shops and appliances for work, and
also to the energy and tact of the overseer.

All the boys that could not be otherwise profitably employed on the
farm, at the barn, or in the house, have been constantly at work, in
working hours, in the chair-seating shops.

Habits of industry may be formed by cane-seating chairs, and such
labor may be made remunerative, but it does not go to the extent of
fully qualifying young lads for the wide world. It does not give scope
enough. Many of the boys realize this, and not unfrequently ask that
they be taught some trade that may be useful to them.

They often go forth to lives of idleness, vagrancy, and crime, satisfactory employment being denied them because they have not the
requisite experience or knowledge of it. If these children could be
sent out from the institution with some knowledge of mechanical business, or at least having some proficiency in the use of tools, they
would be greatly aided in obtaining employment and an honest living.
The introduction of machinery and mechanical business might not increase the net earnings of inmates, but pecuniary profit is not contemplated in the purposes of the institution, but is rather individual
than otherwise. The reformation of "juvenile offenders" and their
preparation for lives of innocence and usefulness are the prime object.

NEW JERSEY.

NEW JERSEY STATE REFORM SCHOOL, JAMESBURG,

Was established in 1867 by the legislature of the State, on a farm of
nearly 500 acres. Since then 534 boys have been under its care, many
of whom are now living lives of usefulness and filling places of trust
and honor. A few are trusted employés in the institution. At present
there are nearly 200 boys under training at the school. Reading,
spelling, arithmetic, geography, and writing are taught. Agricultural

and other varieties of labor are taught and practiced, and there is also time allowed for recreation.

Most of the boys come to the institution bearing sad evidence of both bodily and mental neglect, and the effort is to reform in both these respects. The body is clothed comfortably and otherwise cared for and the mind fed with substantial food. Nearly all those committed here come bringing but little knowledge of books and letters. Many would _ if the matter were left to their own choice, prefer remaining out school to staying in it. Therefore the school-rooms are made as attractive and pleasant as possible, and are well supplied with standard books, maps, &c. The schools will hereafter be made not so secondary in their importance as in the past. Under proper tutelage the boys are employed in the kitchen, laundry, hall, dormitory, in the bake-house, a making bread, the chair-shop at cane-seating, the sewing-shop at making and mending clothes, upon the farm and the grounds immediately about the buildings, and the shoe-shop. All this is not learning a trade, ex- cepting only the shoe-shop. Yet it is being educated to labor, getting steady, industrious habits, and becoming skilled in the use of the hands. It is considered desirable that facilities for learning various trades should be afforded as soon as possible. Cane-seating of chairs is work in which there is a moderate degree of exercise and is quite healthful. We do not encourage our boys to follow this when they leave the school, for it is work not suited to men, nor is it sufficiently remunerative, but in a school like this, having no better employment to offer, it answers well as a stimulant and educator. Labor of any kind is disciplinary and re- forming.

When considered to be fitted for removal, (in not less than a year after admission to the school,) good homes are sought for the boys, either with their friends or by indenture to proper persons, the board of trustees continuing their guardians during their minority.

NEW YORK.

THE TRUANT-HOME, BROOKLYN,

Is under the control of the common council of the city of Brooklyn. The chief aim of this institution is to reform idle and truant boys. Com- mitted because of their indisposition to apply themselves to study, it is difficult to change their natural tendencies, and it is only done by in- creasing watchfulness, industry, and patience. It not unfrequently occurs, however, that after children have been fairly started on the right road, and then discharged at the request of their parents, the subsequent management of them has been such as to again allow them to become idle and truant, and necessitate their recommitment to the institution.

The average age of children committed is about 11 years. The dis- tribution of time for each working-day is from four to six hours for labor, six hours for school, nine hours for sleep, and three hours for inciental duties and recreations. As far as practicable, employment is iven them in the cultivation of the grounds, and financially it has lready saved considerable to the city, as the vegetables raised were early sufficient to supply the inmates of the home through the winter.

The children in their mental and moral improvement make commendble progress.

Some of them evince a disposition to learn, truly surprising, which ne would not expect to find in this class of boys, allowed, as these have een, to attend school when they felt disposed, and wander about the reets, drinking in all manner of evil, forming habits of indolence, culvating a dislike for everything that is good, and taught only those ings that would tend to drag them downward to still worse crimes.

The consequences of this course of life would be fearful to contemplate f not arrested in their career and brought under the humanizing influnce of this or some kindred institutions.

WESTERN HOUSE OF REFUGE, ROCHESTER.

This institution was opened in 1849, since which 3,892 boys have been admitted. The number in the home during 1874 was 606. Of the 210 boys committed during the year, 173 were for petit larceny, 13 were for vagrancy, 9 for burglary, and the remaining 15 for ten different kinds of offenses, the most serious of which, manslaughter, had been committed by one; forgery, one; malicious mischief, one; and obtaining property by false pretenses, one.

The farm belonging to the institution, on a portion of which the buildings are located, contains forty-two acres of excellent land, and lies about one mile and a quarter north from the central part of the city of Rochester, on a slight elevation, between the Erie Canal on the west, and the road leading to the mouth of the Genesee River on the east. Six and a half acres are surrounded by a stone wall twenty-two feet in height, within which stand all the buildings belonging to the institution except the barns. Twenty acres are inclosed by a stockade-fence nine feet in height, formed of cedar posts connected together by iron rods. This inclosure, and some six acres besides, are under constant cultivation. The remaining ten acres are appropriated to pasturage. The grounds within the walls are tastefully laid out into walks, playgrounds, and lawns, and ornamented with trees and shrubbery, which add greatly to the beauty of the place and the comfort of the inmates.

A stone wall eight feet high extends from the center of the buildings to the rear inclosure-wall, dividing the buildings and grounds into two equal corresponding parts, one for the larger boys and the other for the smaller boys, who are thus entirely separated.

Special care has been taken to secure proper heating and ventilation. The rooms are heated by steam and are kept at a perfectly even temperature. while, through the medium of open ventilators and windows slightly lowered, the air is kept pure and fresh without reducing the temperature below the desired degree.

Believing that good citizens generally come from good homes, the effort has been to provide a good home for the boys by having them made clean, comfortably clothed, furnished with a reasonable variety of innocent amusements, with good schools and school-rooms, good beds and pleasant sleeping-apartments, an abundance of wholesome food and cheerful dining-rooms, excellent workshops, and just enough of labor to make them healthy and to teach them habits of industry, treating them with kind, parental care, but insisting at all times on implicit obedience to every rule of the institution.

A large proportion of the boys admitted are found to be sadly deficient in education. Of those admitted during 1874, four were ignorant of the alphabet; eleven could spell easy words; sixteen could read easy lessons; forty-seven could read imperfectly; twenty-four could read readily, and ten could read fluently.

The badge-system, adopted some two years since, is still in force. By this system boys must advance to the highest class of honor by a continued course of meritorious conduct before they can be released; and until the requisite standing is so attained, the efforts of influential friends to secure their release will not avail.

The boys have been furnished with sufficient work, notwithstanding the recent prostration of business.

About 126 boys are employed in the manufacture of women's shoes. They learn the business with facility, and qualify themselves while here to enter any of the large shoe-manufacturing establishments and earn an honest livelihood after leaving the institution.

About 138 are employed in cane- and flag-seating chairs.

The house-tailor-shop employs twenty-eight in making caps and in manufacturing and mending clothing for the inmates. They are thoroughly and carefully instructed in this trade, and on leaving the institution are competent to make a common garment that would be creditable to mechanics of riper years and larger experience.

Thirteen small boys of the first division are employed in the sewing-room, making and mending shirts, sheets, pillow-cases, towels, and knitting and mending stockings.

The remainder are employed in baking, cooking, cleaning, carpentering, farming, painting, steam-fitting, and other labor required in the care of the institution.

NEW YORK HOUSE OF REFUGE, RANDALL'S ISLAND.

This institution was incorporated by the State legislature, under the title of the Society for the Reformation of Juvenile Delinquents in the City of New York, March 29, 1824, and was organized and put into operation on the 1st day of January, 1825, it being the first public reformatory institution for delinquent children, on a large scale, established his country. At its opening, in 1825, it received nine inmates, six s and three boys.

'he institution is under the control of a board of thirty managers sen from the members of the above society, and they are divided) three classes of ten each, to serve one, two, and three years, respect- y. This arrangement allows of an election annually of ten man- rs; the managers serve without remuneration.

he board of managers chooses its own officers and appoints all led employés for the establishment, and fixes their compensation,)f which latter hold office during the pleasure of the board. It also ces all needful rules and regulations for the government of the itution.

he board is authorized, under the act of incorporation, to receive and a into the house of refuge all such criminal, vagrant, or disorderly dren under the age of 16 years as the magistrates having jurisdic- i in the first, second, and third judicial districts of the State, under ir commitment, may deem proper subjects for its discipline and ruction.

'he inspectors of State-prisons are also authorized to transfer any soner at Sing Sing prison, under 17 years of age, whom they may m hopeful of reformation, to this institution; and the United States rts sitting within the State of New York are authorized to commit nders against the laws of the United States under 16 years of age.

ll commitments, except in the United States courts, are during iority, the board of managers becoming the legal guardians of the ldren, to cause them to be instructed in such branches of useful)wledge as shall be suited to their years and capacities. The board lso authorized in its discretion to bind out the children, with their isent, as apprentices or servants, to learn such proper trades or em-)ments as in its judgment will be most advantageous to them.

The managers are required to report annually to the legislature and the corporation of the city of New York the number of children eived by them into the house of refuge, the instruction and employ- nt of the same, and whether they are retained in the institution or ve been indentured as apprentices or given up to friends. They are o required to report the receipts and expenditures of the establish- nt, and generally such facts and particulars as may tend to exhibit ? effect, whether favorable or otherwise, of the management of the ablishment.

All the inmates are instructed daily in the elementary branches of ucation usually taught in the public schools, and they are also taught d employed a portion of the day at some useful occupation or trade. A carefully-arranged time-table is adopted, in which the hours for idy, work, recreation, &c., are specified, and which are scrupulously served.

The introduction of labor is principally for its moral benefits rather than the profit derived from it, and preference is given to those trades which will best enable the inmates to earn a comfortable living on their release from the house.

The discipline is enforced by the grade-system, the inmates being divided into four grades: No. 1 being the best-behaved and freest from faults; No. 2, next best; and so on to No. 4, which is the lowest. These grades are determined each Saturday evening by the number of marks received during the week, five being required to change the grade to a lower degree; four marks make no change, and less than four are few given.

The two rules of the house are: (1) "Tell no lies" and (2) "Always do the best you can."

In entertaining an application for indenture or discharge, three points are considered: first, the conduct; secondly, the progress in school; and, thirdly, the character of the home and the surrounding influences. The first two are determined by the records and the last is ascertained by inquiry or information furnished by the parties making the application. It is insisted on by the managers that the opportunities offered in the application shall be equal or superior to those afforded here.

Careful records of all the inmates are kept, which embrace the ages, parentage, date and cause of commitment, and such knowledge of their antecedents as can be obtained; the conduct and improvement while in the house; the date of discharge; to what business or trade they are put, and such information of their future career as can be gathered by correspondence and otherwise.

These records, covering fifty years, have become valuable in a statistical point of view, and they teach important lessons in the management of juvenile delinquents. These statistics are now being compiled for publication in the next annual report.

The revenue for the support of the institution is obtained from the earnings of the inmates, from a per-capita portion of the school-moneys, from theater-licenses, and from State-appropriations. The earnings by the inmates are about equal to one-half the cost of support.

There have been received into the institution since its organization 15,689 inmates. The ratio of boys to girls is about 5 to 1.

The whole number at the present time is 666 boys and 116 girls— total, 782.

Description of the buildings.—The House of Refuge is located on the eastern bank of the Harlem River, on Randall's Island, and directly opposite that portion of the city of New York which is included between One hundred and fifteenth and One hundred and twentieth streets. The buildings are of brick, erected in the Italian style. The two principal structures front the river, and form a façade nearly a thousand feet in length. The line of their fronts is exactly parallel with the city-avenues. The larger of the two buildings is for the accommodation of the boys' department, the other for the girls. Other buildings are ocated in the rear of these, and are inclosed by a stone wall twenty eet high. A division-wall, of like height, separates the grounds of the oys' department from that of the girls, and in each department walls eparate the inmates into two divisions.

The boys' house is nearly six hundred feet long. The dome-surmounted ortions are devoted to the use of the officers; the central mass also ontains the chapel; while the extreme portions contain the hospitals nd lavatories. There are six hundred and thirty-six dormitories, five et by seven, and seven feet high, in the portion between the center nd the end buildings. In the rear is the school- and dining-hall-build-ng, seventy by one hundred and thirty-eight feet. A central brick wall livides the building in each story into two equal parts, one for each livision. The lower story is appropriated to dining-rooms and the upper story to school-rooms. In the rear of the school-building are the kitchen and bakery, occupying a space twenty-five by ninety feet. The workshops are at the northerly and southerly extremities of the yard, and are each thirty by one hundred feet and three stories high.

The girls' house is two hundred and fifty feet long, the central portion of which contains the apartments of the matron, assistants, and female teachers, while the wings contain two hundred and fifty dormitories for the inmates. In the rear, connected by two corridors or covered halls, is a building for school-rooms and dining-halls; the hospitals, sewing-rooms, and lavatories being at each end, with the laundry in the rear.

The whole establishment is supplied with Croton water, brought across the Harlem River in a three and one-quarter inch lead pipe. Tanks are in the attics of the principal buildings, and a reservoir of one hundred feet diameter, located beyond the inclosure, affords a reserve for extraordinary occasions, as well as a plentiful supply of ice in the winter.

THE NEW YORK CATHOLIC PROTECTORY, WESTCHESTER.

This institution is not experimenting, but claims to be pursuing a course which has for the pledge of its ultimate success the experience of more than two hundred years, which inevitably leads to the realiza-tion of all the best interests of society. It receives children from the ages of 7 to 16, of a class that are deserted and destitute, intrusted to their care by parents or friends, or committed by the city authorities or civil magistrates.

The object is *reform*, and the managers of the institution claim that the best way to accomplish that is to place the child in school. They endeavor to furnish all with a thorough English training, by which they will be able to compete with their fellow-men on a footing of equality. With a corps of thirty-six teachers and assistants, especially trained for this work, they are enabled, by a proper graduation of classes and the most approved methods of teaching, to advance their pupils from the simplest rudiments to the highest form of common-school-education, in the shortest possible time. During the past year or two they have added the elements of algebra and geometry to the mathematical course. In extent, their course of instruction equals that of any public school, while their thoroughness will not suffer in comparison with that of any other educational institute.

Music is thoroughly taught; they have a full brass band, and an orchestra of stringed instruments, composed of the pupils of the institution. Drawing and painting are taught, not only to furnish a pleasant and innocent amusement, but to enable the advanced pupils to find lucrative employment.

With a thorough elementary education they combine the acquisition of useful trades. The industrial department embraces a printing-office, a stereotyping-foundery, a shoe, tailor, blacksmith, machine, wheelwright, paint, and carpenter shop; also chair-caning, baking, farming, and gardening. The boy who leaves the protectory after being there for some time not only possesses the means of earning his living, but also that moral stamina and those habits of industry which will make him a useful member of society.

During the whole period of a boy's stay at the protectory he is never *one moment* without superintendence, and yet, while he learns, from the very beginning, the utter impossibility of violating the rules of the house with impunity, he is never made to feel that this supervision, which rather prevents than punishes his fault, is unnecessary or severe. The constant efforts of the Brothers are to discover and develop the talents and better qualities of their charges, of which even the most degraded are not entirely destitute, and to inspire them with confidence in themselves and in their future.

It is felt that this system leads to ultimate success, but all efforts, it is evident, would fail of success without divine aid. All true reformation must begin at the heart ; in that movement the grace of God alone can help. Without a positive faith, a sure hope, and an enduring charity, the work cannot be genuinely carried out, and only in religion can be found the power to redeem the lost.

The protectory has been in operation twelve years, and in that time has had under its charge 8,771 boys and girls.

The female-department is conducted on the same system as the male-department. It is under the charge of 9 Sisters of Charity, the number of inmates since its foundation being 1,273, and for the year past, 560.

All are taught general housework. Until 14 years of age, or, as their necessities may require, they are kept at school, after which they are taught shirt-making, shoe-fitting, and glove-making.

The proportion of those who have been discharged and become orderly and useful members of society cannot exactly be known, but the institution does know of the well-being and good social position of a very large number of its former inmates.

This institution has been the model for similar institutions in various cities of the United States. Brother Teliow, the rector of the male department, from his large experience and great success in reformatory work, has been consulted, and has given his assistance in several instances to their organization. In 1871 Gabriel Garcia Moreno, the president of the enterprising little republic of Ecuador, in South America, placed at his disposal $24,000 for the purchase of machinery and material for establishing at its capital, Quito, a protectory similar to the New York institution, and also requested his presence and counsel for a short time to inaugurate this important work. On his return, four Brothers and twenty mechanics were sent to continue the work begun under such favorable auspices. The institution is now in a flourishing condition, and forms a monument of the State's charitable and industrial activity, of which the government is justly proud. In grateful recognition of its usefulness, the president has endowed it with a million acres of land.

Several other republics of South America have made application for similar service in their behalf.

The self-denying lives of those devoting themselves to the care and education of the youth committed to them, without any emolument save the plain food they eat and the plainer raiment they wear, doing all for the Master's sake, seems sublime.

On a recent visit to this institution I was most favorably impressed with the uniformly cheerful look, happy manner, and gentlemanly bearing of the boys. They manifested commendable pride in their work, as if they felt that it was honorable to work for a living; and, while they showed marked respect and apparently willing obedience to their superiors, it was evident that in their training they had been taught self-respect.

The libraries number over 2,000 volumes. They publish a monthly paper called The Little Schoolmate.

MONASTERY OF THE GOOD SHEPHERD, NEW YORK.

The House of the Good Shepherd, of New York, is situated at the foot of Eighty-ninth and Ninetieth streets, East River, on a plot of ground containing about thirty-nine city lots.

This institution was commenced at Fourteenth street, on the 2d October, 1857, by five *religieuses* of the order of Our Lady of Charity of the Good Shepherd. By the reception of novices since that period, the community has increased to the number of 110, and 15 out door sisters. Forty of the members are now engaged in conducting similar institutions, which they founded at Boston in 1867 and at Brooklyn in 1868.

The House of the Good Shepherd has for its object the reformation of fallen women and girls, who either submit themselves voluntarily or are placed there by competent authority.

The inmates are divided into four classes, each of which is entirely separated from the others, no communication being allowed between the different classes. The first consists of Magdalens, who are penitents, who have been converted, and are leading the lives of *religieuses*, under the rule of the third Order of St. Teresa. The second class is that of penitent women and girls who have been received in the asylum in order to be converted. The third class is that of the preservation, composed of children who are in danger of falling, and mostly those of bad parents. The fourth class is composed of girls within the age of 14 and 21, committed by magistrates.

The total number of inmates since the foundation of the institution is 4,325; the number of commitments, 2,024. It is supported by charity, industry, and, like other reformatories, receives an appropriation by the city for each commitment.

THE ISAAC T. HOPPER HOME, NEW YORK.

This institution, located at 110 Second avenue, was established in 1845, through the labors and generosity of the person whose name it bears. The following recent statement from the secretary of the home and of the Women's Prison Association, by which the home is managed, gives the objects sought to be accomplished by this charity:

"The Women's Prison Association was incorporated in 1845, and the work has been gradually extended until it ranks among the most important philanthropic institutions in the country. The object of the association is to take care of women discharged from Blackwell's Island and other prisons until they can obtain employment and means of earning a livelihood. The home was established to lend a helping hand to the liberated prisoner, to give her advice and encouragement, to provide her with work—that great safeguard against crime and its consequent despondency—to watch over her during the critical transition from the restraints of prison-life to the dangers of freedom, to save her from her friends—who are often her worst enemies—to shelter her from temptation, until she can go forth into the world strengthened by wise and humane counsels and the wholesome discipline of regular and steady employment, and to provide her with a home suited to her needs, where she will be surrounded by elevating influences. Since the association has been formed they have received into the home over 5,800 women. In the great majority of cases, where the fortunes of the women have been known after quitting the institution, it has been learned that the help and encouragement which they have received in the home have led to a permanent reformation. The principal vice that has to be contended with is the use of intoxicating liquors, but women convicted of many other crimes have been also received and reformed. Their desire to become inmates of the home is the first great step, and the rest follows as the result of the good influences brought to bear upon them.

"The new home in Second avenue is a model of convenience. The rooms are large, pleasant, and thoroughly ventilated, and the inmates take great pride in keeping the apartments neat and orderly. The par lor is handsomely furnished, though the carpets, curtains, and furniture did not cost the association more than cheaper articles, through the generosity of Mr. Ellery. The carpet on the sewing-room was down in the parlor of the old home in Tenth avenue. The dining-room-floor is inlaid with different kinds of wood, and is kept polished with wax by the inmates. The furniture of the sleeping-rooms is very plain, but extreme neatness characterizes the entire establishment, which is very attractive to the visitor. Bathing-rooms are upon each floor, and in the attic is a large one for new-comers. The arrangements of the kitchen and laundry are very complete. Those women who work outside of the home during the week return on Saturday, spend Sunday, and go back to their work on Monday with clean clothing. Their soiled apparel is left at the home to be washed. Whatever wages these women receive is their own, with the exception of fifty cents, which is deducted weekly for their board, washing, and the care of their clothing at the home. The object is to make the women pay the actual cost, and no more.

"The women are not sent out until they have been in the home long enough to enable the managers fully to understand them, and they are always sent to those places where they will be surrounded by good in-fluences. The demand for these women's work is greater than the sup-ply. While in the home the women are employed in the various labors of the household and in sewing. There is a constant and watchful care exercised by the ladies of the association, who pay weekly visits to the home, inspect the house thoroughly, converse with the inmates—taking pains to become acquainted with each case, in order to minister to its especial needs—and provide for the wants of the house generally. On Sundays religious services are held, and the women take great interest in the Bible class in the afternoon. A week-day school has been opened in which many have learned their letters, and others have made con-siderable progress in the rudiments of an education.

"Among the prisoners from Sing Sing in the past year was a Danish woman with an infant. She had been committed for grand larceny, but was believed by the prison authorities to have been innocent. At all events she was friendless and a stranger, her husband having de-serted her. She was received into the home, and arrangements were afterward made to send her to her own country. After she reached Denmark she wrote to the association to express her gratitude and heartfelt thanks for the kind treatment she had received in the home when in direst extremity. Another woman, a seamstress, has 'an ex-cellent set of customers, is doing well, and is truly respectable.'

"The physician of the home reports only one death in the past year, that of a woman who came to the home after a long period of intoxica-tion. Seventeen patients have been sent to the hospital, the most seri-ous disease being that of the kidneys, (albuminuria.) A large propor-tion of those who avail themselves of the benefits of the home are inebriates. To these the home is indeed a friend in need. Here they receive shelter, an abundance of good, nutritious food, comfortable clothing, and all that is necessary for their well-being. Under the influence of favorable hygienic surroundings they are soon restored physically, their resolutions to lead a better life are strengthened, and their moral condition elevated.

"The ladies are doing a good work, and, though they have met frequently with great obstacles and have often been pinched for funds, the influence of the home has been always extending. Their new and commodious building is a great step in advance, and the association can now carry out many plans which were before impossible. The political econ mist has awakened to the fact that it is cheaper to assist criminals to become respectable and support themselves than to maintain prisons where the very discipline hardens and confirms its inmates in following the paths of vice and crime. The most experienced police-officials say that a young person after serving a term of imprisonment is almost certain to return to criminal practices. Imprisonment only makes the convict more cunning and careful not to get caught again. Occasionally there is an exception, but this only proves the rule. The prison-mark is an impassable barrier to obtaining honest employment, and the discharged convict, shunned by the respectable people, is driven to associate with the criminal classes, where a warm welcome is given.

OHIO.

CINCINNATI HOUSE OF REFUGE, CINCINNATI.

The buildings here are of blue limestone, with windows, cornices, casings, and portico of white Dayton stone, and are erected in the Grecian style. The grounds contain about ten acres, five of which are inclosed by a stone wall twenty feet high, within which stand all the buildings except the stable.

The "House" presents an imposing front of 277 feet, and is composed of a main building 85 by 55 feet, four stories in height, with towers at the extremities projecting 2 feet in front, and which are five stories high, besides the basement. In the main building are the offices, superintendent's and officers' apartments, principal store-room, boys' hospital, and dispensary; thirty-six rooms in all.

Extending north and south from the main building are two wings, each 96 by 38 feet, with towers at the extremities projecting 2 feet in front and rear. The wings are four stories in height and the towers five, besides the basement.

The north wing (boys' department) contains one hundred and twelve dormitories, and the basement a bath, 50 by 12, and twenty-six dressing-rooms.

The south wing (girls' department) contains seventy-two dormitories, two sewing-rooms, one school-room, one ironing-room, one drying-room,

d one girls' hospital. In the basement a laundry, wash-rooms, bath-
om, and play-ground.

In the rear of the main building, and connected with it by covered
ssage-ways, is the school and chapel building, containing on the first
or the bakery, kitchen, three dining-rooms, one school-room, and
ree store-rooms, and on the second floor the chapel, 56 by 60, and two
hool-rooms. In the attic over the school-rooms is a large dormitory
cupied by the boys of the first division.

East, and to the rear of the chapel, is the shop-building, 142 by 37,
d three stories in height, containing engine- and fuel rooms, and four
ops; and in the south end of the building, the school-room, forty-two
rmitories, covered play-ground, and wash-room of the boys of the
ird division.

Connected with the shop-building are the boiler-room, 38 by 30; gas-
ouse, 21 by 20; boys' laundry, 69 by 26; two wash-rooms, and two cov-
ed play-grounds, for the boys of the first and second divisions, and
our-room, all one story in height and covered with metallic roofing.
one of the buildings are detached. They will accommodate three
undred and fifty inmates and the requisite officers. The boys are
ivided into three and the girls into two divisions or families. Each of
he five families have separate schools, dining- and wash-rooms, open
nd covered play-grounds, workshops, and dormitories. The buildings
re heated throughout by steam and lighted with gas.

Water for drinking and culinary purposes is furnished from six large
isterns, supplied with filtered rain-water. For fountains and cleansing
urposes, an abundant supply is obtained from the Miami Canal.

The front entrance to the inclosure is through a gothic arched gate-
ay, flanked on each side by gate-keepers' lodges, two stories high, and
ogether containing four large rooms. The whole number of rooms in
he house, including the basements and lodges, is three hundred and
ixty-four.

This institution has been established about a quarter of a century.
t is a refuge or place of safety, where overreached and tempted children
ay be taken out of, and find a refuge from, temptation until right
rinciples are instilled and proper habits fixed.

The boys in the Refuge have been employed at shoe-making, except
hose needed for the work of the various departments.

The girls have done the cooking and dining-room-work for all, the
ashing, ironing, and housework for themselves and the officers, and
ave been taught to sew and to knit and the use of various sewing-
achines, and have attended school in the afternoons.

The schools have been conducted by good teachers, and although the
ajority of the children were very backward in their studies when
ceived, they have learned rapidly. Removed from the diverting influ-
ices of the street, they have been better prepared for active study, and
r that reason have made better scholars.

3 E

The libraries have been well supplied with papers and books, and all who could read have taken great interest in them.

The children generally are orderly and well behaved, and have been easily controlled. They have been shown all the inducements and benefits to arise from doing well while in the institution and after they have passed out to take their places in the busy world again.

In the discipline, kindness has done the most effective work, and it has been used to the utmost, punishment being resorted to only when nothing else would have effect; and if, after trying demerits, which detained them longer in the Refuge, or depriving them of play or food, they still persisted in disobedience, corporal punishment has been inflicted by the superintendent only. These cases have been reported to the board, and examined by them once a month, with good effect.

HOUSE OF REFUGE AND CORRECTION, CLEVELAND.

This is a department of the work-house where the wayward and vicious boys of the city who commit petty offenses, or stroll about the streets as vagrants, or have become incorrigible, with nobody to care for them or control them, are received, trained, and educated so as to fit them to become good and useful citizens. The law consigns them to the guardianship of this department until of age. It is the rule of the directors, however, to discharge them as soon as they appear to have acquired industrious habits, sound principles, and sufficient education to transact business for themselves.

In the process of training which has been adopted, their time, except Sundays, is about equally divided between the school-room and the workshop. In the one they are faithfully drilled by competent teachers in the branches of a common-school-education; in the other they are instructed by skilled foremen in some industrial art or trade. On Sundays they attend Sunday-school and divine services in the chapel. In connection with their exercises in the school-room, they are taught to sing, an exercise in which they not only take great delight, but excel. In their ages they vary from 7 or 8 years to 16 or 17, and in native mental powers are unusually bright, sharp, and shrewd. In controlling them their teachers seldom have occasion to adopt any other than moral forces.

In regard to physical comforts, these boys are not only well fed and clothed, but are provided with large, airy dormitories, and allowed to take regular out-door exercises in an ample play-ground. The kind of care they receive is parental in its character, and hence they seem to feel that they are brothers. They certainly appear to be happy and contented in their family-home.

It is believed, from results already attained, that at least nine-tenths, if not all, the youth who remain for any considerable time in this institution, can be reclaimed and made to become useful and respectable

embers of society. As a philanthropic institution, it is certainly
hieving a great and good work, and is an advanced step in the prog-
ss of modern civilization.

THE OHIO REFORM SCHOOL, LANCASTER.*

This noble and cherished institution, the just pride of the great Com-
onwealth that founded and supports it, began its course of usefulness
a very humble experiment. Its founders groped their way without
ecedent or example to guide them, and, while breaking new ground,
d the foundation of a reformatory, as time has shown, on correct prin-
les, and adopted the true method of securing the objects contemplated
its establishment, so that the Ohio Reform Farm School to-day, in its
anagement, discipline, and success, stands unrivaled in this or any
her land. The credit it deservedly receives at home and abroad is
rgely owing to the sound judgment and wise policy of the State-au-
orities in sustaining a tried and uniform management. Exempted
om change, pursuing a steady course, guided by past experience, the
bors of those intrusted with the oversight of the institution have
en marked with progress and cheering success. The management of
ch an institution is necessarily attended with perplexities and difficul-
s; every day brings its new cares, discouragements, and responsibili-
s. Courage, wisdom, and much patience are indispensable to bear
ch burdens and to perform the duties involved.
The reform-school is located upon a farm of 1,170 acres, near Lan-
ster, Ohio. The farm is situated on what are called the "Hocking
ills," being about six hundred feet above the level of the Hocking
alley. The climate at this elevation is delightful and healthful, and
e scenery and surroundings are beautiful. The soil is thin and unpro-
uctive, and but a small portion sufficiently level to admit of cultivation
ith the plow. The farm, however, is well adapted to the growth of
any kinds of fruit, and the slopes and ravines may be profitably con-
erted into vineyards. Fruit-growing, gardening, and the raising of
rsery-trees, if not always remunerative pecuniarily, have been found
ry profitable employment for the elevation of wayward boys.
The buildings, with yards, lawns, and play-grounds, occupy twenty
res of ground. The lawns are tastefully laid out and ornamented with
ergreens, shrubs, and flowers.
At present the institution consists of eight family-houses, each com-
rtably accommodating from fifty to sixty boys, a large and imposing
ntral building for administrative and domestic purposes, affording
oms for the resident commissioner, guest-chambers, offices, reading-
om, kitchens, dining-halls for 500 boys, and dormitories for employés.
ere are also five shop-buildings, four barns, an engine-house, laundry-
ilding, water-tower, gas-works, bake-house, and a very fine and com-
dious chapel-building that will comfortably seat 800 boys.

* From the last official report.

No high fences, walls, bolts, or bars are used to restrain the boys or prevent them from escaping. By kind treatment and judicious management at least three-fourths of them can at all times be trusted to go to any part of the farm, or even to town on business, without supervision and without any danger of their escaping.

In January, 1858, the doors of the institution were first opened for the reception of juvenile offenders—boys under 16 years of age, convicted of crime and misdemeanor, and sent by courts of record. At their last report 1,822 boys had been received into the school; 1,379 had been discharged and 443 were enjoying its advantages. The boys are classed in families and are cared for by officers called Elder Brothers. Each family contains fifty boys, and is under the supervision of an Elder Brother, an assistant Elder Brother, and a female teacher.

At the time of the opening of this institution on these Hocking Hills, with log-dwellings, almost surrounded by unbroken forests, and with but few comforts and facilities, the first experiment in the United States of providing *a home* and not *a prison*, a school of virtue and not of vice, was made for the wayward, ignorant, vicious, and criminal boys of the State of Ohio. To-day the institution stands as a proud monument of the great success of the humane and philanthropic enterprise. Instead of the wildness of nature, cultivated fields and gardens, extensive orchards, vineyards, and strawberry plantations greet the eye. With one exception, the log-houses have given place to substantial, commodious, and convenient brick buildings, with beautiful surroundings, unmarred by grated doors and windows or massive and frowning walls.

The buildings have a capacity to provide for all the necessary home-comforts of a household of five hundred persons. The school-rooms, shops, and chapel are all that could be desired. The buildings are all neatly and comfortably, but very economically, furnished, and afford all the advantages of a good home to those who occupy them. The original cost of the farm, and of all the improvements made to the present time, has been about $180,000. This makes the cost of each boy for the past year to have been $139.

While it has always been the aim of the management of this institution to be economical in expenditures, and to make the labor of the boys pay the institution towards their support as much as was consistent, still the primary object has always been to make *men* of these wayward boys, rather than to exhaust the energies of the school merely to make money.

A great wrong is committed when the efforts of a reformatory to "make it pay" outrank the higher and more important considerations—the education and reformation of its inmates. Money expended in making reformatory agencies efficacious is always a good investment, not only for the juvenile delinquent, but for the Commonwealth that would save him.

A large number of the boys sent to the institution arrive in rags, filth,

nd squalor, in a sad and most pitiable condition. Accepting the con-
itions and opportunity to reform, with correct ideas of life and duty,
dopting good principles and forming good habits, in due time they
ill be entitled to an honorable discharge. Months and years of care-
il training, followed by a hopeful reformation and fitness for outside
fe, involves much anxiety in regard to the future of the discharged
oys.

At the institution every boy finds a home, employment, and education.
he family building, neat, clean, and comfortable, is his home. Many,
ever having had such a privilege before, feel the happy change, and
ieir improved accommodations are accepted as a potent means to lead
hem to a better life. In the kindness, faithfulness, vigilance, and example
f the Elder Brother and his wife (the officers in charge of the family)
hey find sympathy, restraint, instruction, and encouragement—bless-
igs the poor boys never enjoyed before. Warm attachments spring up
nd are cherished among all the members of the particular family, which
xtend and bind in love and harmony all the families as one great
ousehold. The boys find recreation on the play-grounds and in ram-
ling over the hills and forests, and in gathering and eating the chest-
iuts which are abundant in their season. Hundreds go out into the
roods on these expeditions, but never betray confidence, commit dep-
edations, or give the least trouble.

Employment is a very important and reliable reformatory agency.
Very many of the boys when they enter the institution are confirmed
dlers, hopeless loafers, aimless vagrants, and the companions of evil-doers.
Here, they must settle down and work half of each day. Their physical
condition, age, and tastes are duly considered in their allotment to labor,
and, as far as possible, they are furnished with congenial employment.
Work is made pleasant; and they are trained to be skillful, willing, and
cheerful laborers. Unfortunately, some of the boys are constitutionally
lazy and thriftless, and it is next to impossible to relieve them of this
power of inertia and inspire them with right ideas of life and duty.
After much patient and persevering effort they still remain heedless
drones, and must inevitably gravitate to the dependent or dangerous
classes in society. What to do with such boys, some of them in their
majority, is an important question, difficult of solution. If removed
from the institution to give place for others, and more hopeful subjects,
they are homeless and friendless, and doubtless will never earn an honest
living, but sooner or later become burdens on the industrial energies of
society.

The law strictly provides that the inmates should be the vicious, the
incorrigible, and the criminal; not orphans or dependent and friendless
children. The institution is not an orphanage, or a refuge into which
heartless and unfaithful parents or guardians may send their children
or wards. To send such children, who simply need care, kindness, and
training, is a great wrong—a flagrant abuse of the hospitality and
benevolence of the State. Every such child keeps a boy lodged in jail

or sentenced to the State-prison from enjoying the advantages of the institution. The popularity of the institution has induced the sending of little boys that merely need a home, whereas the worst and most hopeless boys are the proper subjects for reformatory work, and for them the effort should be made to save them from the ways of evil, and restore them to society clothed and in their right mind, with a will and a power to earn honest bread and to be ornaments in society.

The benefits of the institution are not confined to its direct effects, great as they are. Bad boys are received and greatly benefited; idle boys become industrious; vicious and revengeful boys become mild and teachable; profane and obscene-speaking boys soon learn that no evil communications can proceed out of their mouths. Not only this, but it is found that the bad boys of the State, outside of the institution, are very generally aware of its existence and character, and that it is exerting a widespread and beneficent influence even over these. Many boys have been induced to lead well-behaved and useful lives, sooner than be sentenced for a term at the reform-school, although they may know that its discipline would benefit them.

Another beneficial effect of the institution is very apparent. Under the old dispensation, when the jail and penitentiary were the only places for vicious and criminal boys, fond parents preferred to cover up and conceal the faults and crimes of their children sooner than expose them to the disgrace and danger of entering those institutions. Now, however, parents from all classes of society are very ready and willing to place their unfortunate boys here, thus removing the charge, so often made, that the children of the unfortunate poor alone are punished, while the well-to-do in the world are allowed to escape. The children of the rich and the poor, the high and the low, are alike subjected to restraint and discipline, and the encouragement to continue in evil courses, resulting from concealment and immunity, no longer exists.

Physician's report to George E. Howe, acting commissioner of the Ohio State Reform-School:

"Since November 23, 1872, the date of my last report to you as physician of the reform-school, I have not made a single professional visit to an inmate of the institution. This is all I can say concerning the health of those under reformatory discipline at the reform-school.

"D. N. KINSMAN, M. D.,
"*Physician in charge of Ohio Reform-School.*
"LANCASTER, OHIO, *December 2, 1873.*"

PENNSYLVANIA.

HOUSE OF REFUGE, PHILADELPHIA.

On the 1st of January, 1874, there were 566 inmates in the house, viz: 362 white boys and 77 white girls, and 90 colored boys and 37 colored girls.

The inmates are engaged seven hours in the workshops, three in the school-room, and the residue of the day in taking their meals, in innocent recreation, or in their dormitories. They have access to a well-selected library.

The boys are occupied in the workshops in learning brush-making, shoe-making, or blacksmithing; the girls in shoe-fitting, tailoring, dress-making, sewing, or general household duties.

All the inmates have daily morning and evening social worship, and attend divine service twice on Sunday in the chapel. The boys attend Sunday-school in the morning and the girls in the afternoon.

When apprenticed, on leaving the house, they are entitled to two months' day-schooling for every year they have to serve, and those under whose care they are placed are required to satisfy the board yearly that the terms of the indenture are complied with.

A serious obstacle is found in the fact that the destruction of the system of apprenticeship renders it very difficult to obtain suitable places where the inmates can be placed to learn trades.

In the various divisions of the school the pupils are classified with care, and with the single idea of promoting their moral improvement. In regard to their early training, with the exception of a few, some of whom were found to be ignorant even of the alphabet, all had attended school for limited periods. Nearly all were addicted to truancy, and idleness was the prolific source of their vices.

The colored department is entirely distinct from the white. The practical and invariable effect of a different arrangement is the almost entire exclusion of colored children from these schools of reform. In some of them they are not received, and in others their sparsity is most marked, which may be attributed to two causes: first, that the health of the colored child suffers under the regimen of diet and temperature which suit white children; and, secondly, that it suffers also from a recognized inferiority practically displayed towards it, and mostly by those who disclaim the feeling.

The separation provided in the Philadelphia House of Refuge is not made on the ground of any supposed inferiority of either class to the other. It is made, however, for the sole advantage of the colored child, and the increased cost of its maintenance, under such provision, establishes this fact, and also the sound policy of the arrangement; for, whereas, as a general rule, where the two classes are subjected to precisely the same regimen, the mortality of the colored is greatly the larger, in the instance referred to the percentage of deaths in the white department is ten-fold greater. The most pronounced advocates of the equality of the two classes, who have considered the matter, fully approve the plan as both salutary and just.

PENNSYLVANIA REFORM-SCHOOL, PITTSBURG.

This institution was founded twenty years ago, and known as the Western House of Refuge, of Pittsburg, Pa., but by a recent act of the

legislature it was authorized to alter its title. The new name bett
expresses the object and intent of the work which is prosecuted in sc
establishments. The board of managers have purchased a tract of
acres of land, in Washington County, two miles from Cannonsbu
for the purpose of establishing three separate family-homes for the c
dren committed to their care, that a more thorough classification
be perfected and the management and education of the inmates
ducted more in accordance with domestic and home-training.
thought that the principle of discrimination may be more readily app
and more consistently carried out, and that great benefits will
from this policy. Moral influences will have better opportunities o i
pressing themselves upon children whose persons will have at least
semblance of relief from durance, and the country work and the count
air will administer to an improved physical development, which is essential to the healthy growth as well of moral as of intellectual nature.

The institution has had under its charge during the past years 303
boys and 104 girls. The proceeds of the labor done by the large boys
in the workshops amount to $4,604.87. The small boys have been em-
ployed in knitting; and, though no revenue has been derived from their
labor, yet considerable expense has been saved the institution.

The girls have been engaged in the usual domestic duties and in the
sewing-department. All the cooking, washing, ironing, tailoring, and
sewing for the family is done by the female inmates.

The schools of the male and female departments have been in regular
session during the year. They are thoroughly graded, and the course
of study does not differ materially from that usually pursued in our
public schools. The object is to impart such knowledge as will be useful in the position in life which these children are likely to occupy.

The removal of the institution is looked for with great interest. Without doubt it will be an auspicious event in the history of the reform-
school. The change will secure advantages which are sought for in
vain in crowded congregate institutions, however well they may be conducted. The further the education of reasonable human beings is
removed from the artificial and the nearer it approaches nature, the
more it will reach its object and benefit society.

Six fine buildings are now in course of erection on the farm, and it
is anticipated that they will be ready for occupancy during the present
year.

THE SHELTERING ARMS, WILKINSBURG,

Under the management of the Women's Christian Association, devoted
to the work of reforming women, recognizes the necessity of training
the inmates to be skilled workwomen, believing that a trade and education in habits of industry are important aids in the reformation of
character. They propose, therefore, to add to the sewing and laundry-
work already taught instruction in other branches, as they find it
desirable.

RHODE ISLAND.

PROVIDENCE REFORM-SCHOOL.

Since its organization, in 1850, this institution has received a total number of 2,227 pupils—1,770 boys and 457 girls. During the year 1874 there were 220 inmates—179 boys and 41 girls. Youth under 18 years of age are committed by the city. Children are also received at the request of parents or guardians, who pay for their board $2 a week.

The common and some of the higher English branches are taught; also cane-seating of chairs, gardening, domestic work, tailoring, &c.

Since the establishment of the institution, in 1850, 2,244 persons have been committed, about 60 per cent. of whom are known to have become orderly and useful members of society.

WISCONSIN.

THE WISCONSIN INDUSTRIAL SCHOOL FOR BOYS, WAUKESHA.

Organized in 1860 as a house of refuge, this institution afterward changed its name to State Reform-School, and later to its present title.

The whole number of inmates since its opening, in July, 1860, to September 30, 1874, is 1,081; of this number 73 were girls. Since 1870, boys only have been admitted. The average number during the year has been 293, and average age about 12 years.

To make the condition of the inmates as much as possible like that of a good home, they are classified into families, of which there are seven, besides the correction-house and farm. They are presided over by a man and woman, who correspond to parents. Each family has its separate building, play-ground, and appropriate surroundings.

As a last resort, a boy who persists in disobedience is sent to the correction-house, where he is given more work and fewer privileges. This plan has been adopted but recently, but thus far the results are favorable. Boys whose influence is pernicious make much of the disturbance in schools of this character, and if the leaders are removed the disturbance ends.

The school is taught eleven months in the year. Each half day has a session of work and a session of school. The average detention of boys in the school is between two and three years; sometimes they are detained five or six years. Eight hours of each day in winter and nine in summer are devoted to school and work. Saturday afternoon has a short work-session; the balance of the time is devoted to recreation and other miscellaneous duties.

The small boys work one hour less per day than the others.

REVIEW OF REFORMATORIES.

It is now fifty years since the first house of refuge was established the United States, and however sanguine may have been the found as to the result of such establishments, it is believed that their estim of good to be done hardly reached what has been actually acco plished. There is now no doubt of the capability of these instituti to effect the purpose designed, and every succeeding year has stren ened the conviction. The system has undergone various changes modifications and still is by no means regarded as complete in al methods. The public mind, until within a few years, seemed impre with the idea that if a person committed a crime he was truly depra and no hope remained for his reformation. The time of such ignor is passed. An effort towards reformation, and not severe punishm is more in accordance with the principles of Christianity and ph Ia thropy, and after trial it has been found more successful than any other treatment, and far less expensive.

To place the erring youth where he cannot commit depredations; to teach him to restrain his passions; to show him the sure penalty that a course of crime will bring upon him; to speak kindly to him, and tell him how he can be useful and happy; to kindle in his soul the spark of man-hood that has been long latent; to stir up the feeling of self-respect that has too often been crushed by the treatment of others; to find that tender place in his heart, that moral principle which has been so nearly extinct— to do all this is the mission of the reform-school; and statistics show that 75 per cent. of all the youths sent to these institutions have been reclaimed and restored to society, clothed and in their right minds. It is to be remembered that many of these unfortunates are simply delinquents, neglected or wronged children, who of themselves have offended neither the public law nor the public morals.

For these at least it would seem right to provide favorable chances for bettering their condition. They are the unhappy, perhaps erring, members of a large community of children, who, not being cared for by their natural guardians, have become the wards of the public, and who, brought under enlightened tutelage, should repay this public, by future well-doing and prosperity, for her expenditure of beneficence and means in their behalf.

LABOR AS A MEANS OF REFORMATION.

Disciplined physical employment is one of the most effective curatives as a moral agent, without which there can be no such thing as a suc-cessful reformation. Labor is the remedy that God ordained to restore the fallen, and the remedy admits of no substitute.

The formation of the habit of labor, of constant, continued effort in any one direction, is a most difficult part of education; it is rendered loubly difficult by the almost inconquerable aversion to any kind of patient industry, which is manifested by this class of children. This impatience of steady employment is always accompanied by the temptation to obtain property by dishonest means; therefore, if we would make these children honest, we must make them industrious; inculcate in them a habit of labor by affording the means of steady employment, and furnish a purpose by exciting a laudable ambition to excel in all that requires mechanical skill.

A greater variety of trades or mechanical pursuits than are now taught in reformatories would be desirable. Skilled mechanics are needed, and the supply might be increased by introducing the various mechanical pursuits that might profitably be engaged in, and the boys thoroughly instructed in such trades as are best suited to their tastes or inclinations, so that when they were released they might find remunerative employment, become honest as well as industrious citizens, and rise to a respectable position in society.

MENTAL AND MORAL DISCIPLINE ALSO NECESSARY.

The mind, however, must have its proper culture by well-drilled training, more fully to insure that subordination, intellectual improvement, and moral progress, which can give a hope of success to any system. The vagrant mind needs the habit of concentration and exercise of methodic study, as much as the vagrant body requires physical restraint and a rightly-directed exterior.

If it is needful to rightly occupy the body and the mind, it is no less an emphatic and accepted truth that the heart should be moved and the conscience awakened by appropriate religious instruction—Sunday observances statedly performed, the practical truths of the Bible taught, and serious appeals made to the better inner nature.

PHYSICAL TREATMENT CALLED FOR.

Much of the so-called moral turpitude of humanity is the result of physical ailment. This may be inherited or acquired. In either case, it demands treatment skillfully applied and faithfully administered. The feelings and thoughts, and consequently the words and acts, are all modified and characterized by the condition of the physical system.

We may, with as much reason, look for pure water from an impure fountain, as to expect a consistent daily life in one whose system is diseased from the crown of the head to the sole of the foot.

The nervous system cannot fail to transfer its nervous action to the mind and the life. The thoughts generated in the brain through which scrofulous blood flows must be sordid and gross. Cutaneous irritability cannot fail to produce mental irritability and corresponding action.

There must, hence, be a system of medical and hygienic regimen adopted in connection with the other means of good referred to. The services of a skillful and experienced physician must combine with those of a judicious house-mother for the restoration of a healthful circulation and a proper digestion of the food; for only as health comes to a diseased and irritated system can there be tranquil mental action and thorough openness to moral influences for reform.

FURTHER MEANS.

The Industrial School for Boys in Wisconsin has opened a correction-house for the larger and more refractory boys. In this department, work takes the place of play. The boys are given three sessions to work and one in school, studying their lessons during the interval. The correction-house is the last resort for persistent disobedience, and its utility has been fully demonstrated and its results most favorable. Two or three months of this needful discipline has in most cases been all that was necessary to bring the boy into a better state of mind, and it is seldom that a boy is returned for a second trial.

The superintendent of the Wisconsin school proposes a theory, one on which he has expended much thought and made limited experiments. It is as follows:

"A system of compensation or pay to all inmates, after reaching certain limits of age and good conduct, for all the service rendered in the institution, and a charge for all which they receive—a system of debt and credit with each. If this could be so nicely adjusted that a boy, by commendable exertion and diligence, could make a small saving each week over and above his expenditures, it would furnish a motive to action not usually felt by inmates in institutions of this kind. As things are now done, we have little opportunity to cultivate economy. The boy is now fed and clothed whether he works well or not. He learns from the book that ten dimes make one dollar; still he has little idea of its value, and less judgment how to expend it judiciously. In vain he is told the cost and importance of food, clothes, and home. He gets them free, and, like the air and the sun-light, he presumes that they, as a matter of course, are a part of his inheritance. All children are liable to this delusion; the children of the State pre-eminently so. This is seen in the destruction of books and tools. Take the book as an illustration. If the boy is charged seventy-five cents for a reader to-day, and he knows that when he is ready, say in six months, to be promoted or leave the school the value of the book then will pass to his credit, it presents a motive to care for it. The same of tools, clothes, &c. Another most valuable purpose would be saved. When a boy escaped, the cost of his return could be met by the use of his funds and an assessment on the funds of those who were accessory. This would furnish a leverage to find out all who were involved, embracing in certain instances a large portion of the members of a family or shop. A careful examination of the feasibility of this suggestion is solicited."

An odium rests upon the character of *all* children confined in a house of refuge. Many of them unquestionably need the high walls and the invariable key for their restraint and for an evidence of sure means to control and punish. But there are others, and those not a few, who become demoralized by the very precautions which are adopted to reform them, and being prisoners in fact become worthy of the infliction *in their own idea*, and thus a hinderance to self-respect and moral amendment is perniciously interposed.

It is advised that there be established a department in such institutions to which any child may be graduated by a course of good conduct and faithful and ingenuous' observance of such salutary rules as the managers may propose, and that then the child may have the liberty of passing beyond the inclosures, to take service in the shop of the artisan, or the office of the merchant, or any other desirable place for its day's duty, returning to the refuge at its close. The night-school would then be employed for its intellectual instruction, the tone of the institution would be greatly improved, encouragement would take the place of frequent depression, and an aim would be presented to the inmates perfectly legitimate and entirely within their possible reach, which would stimulate their very best qualities to a healthy development. And for such inmates there might be a possible relaxation of the penal discipline and incarceration, which does not now discriminate in such respects in behalf of any.

THE FAMILY-SYSTEM OF REFORM.

In several institutions the "family-system" has been adopted with great success. The children are regarded as subjects of restraint, but not subject to penal infliction or punishment. Walls, bolts, and bars, and all prison-appliances, of whatever description, are dispensed with, and a home and school established for the proper care, training, and education of wayward and neglected children. From these schools the pupils can go forth into the world, prepared for its duties and responsibilities, with no stigma attached to their names, and be received by the community with trust and confidence.

In the "family-system" natural laws are recognized and acted upon by natural principles. The family is a divine institution, and the Creator has so arranged it that every human being is influenced more for good in the family than by any other influence in social life. This influence is indefinable, and runs through the whole social organization; it appeals to our individual self-respect, and addresses our hopes by opening to our vision fair prospects in life. The nearer the approach to the home and the family in the system adopted, the greater will be the power exerted on the hearts and lives of those placed under its influence.

"If our families could be reduced to thirty or thirty-five each, thus giving the family-officers opportunity to establish a more intimate personal acquaintance and a consequent warmer friendship; and if, in addition to this, the superintendent could be so relieved from other

duties that he could consistently spend more time in personal intercour
with the boys, I am sure a marked improvement would speedily be see
To influence another, we must get near him, hand must grasp hai
and heart beat in sympathy with heart. Words spoken softly in tl
ear are more impressive than loud lectures, however eloquent or earnei
from the rostrum. By this means also a healthful public sentime
would be likely to grow up; the better portion of the inmates would
much more inclined to unite their influence on the side of good orde
evil plans and projects would be detected and corrected before the ev
had developed, and, as a consequence, severe discipline would not l
required."

Among the various suggestions for the perfecting of the present sy
tem of juvenile reform, there is one entitled to special attention : a di
criminating and practical scheme of classification. This is a most in
portant and paramount element of success. In looking at the antec
dents of a hundred inmates, almost as many reasons may be found wl
the young delinquent, guilty only of some petty crime, and that perhaj
his first offense, should have no communication with the older adep
with whom crime has become a habit; why the incorrigible, simply
natural disposition or from bad home-government, and why the restiv
truant, should be set apart from the artful and almost instinctivel
vicious; and, finally, why the unfortunate child of destitution or of pern
cious parental example should be cut off from association with tl
turbulent, depraved, and recklessly mischievous.

The superintendent of the Pennsylvania Reform-School, in his repoi
for 1874, says:

"It is evident that the family-system affords very great facilities fc
classification. There are a greater number of subdivisions and more oj
portunity for individualization. Children are not reformed in massei
but reformation is mostly the result of well-directed effort acting upo
the individual heart. In the proposed division of the children int
families, the policy pursued will not depend so much upon age o
character as upon *adaptation*, although the very small children may b
placed in a family by themselves. Special qualifications of the *officer*
in charge of families will be considered, as well as the peculiar disposi
tion of the *child*. The more difficult to manage will be distributed aroun(
in small numbers in charge of those officers who, by tact and executiv
ability, will be enabled to exert the most powerful influence. Care wil
be taken, however, to limit the number of this class of children in an)
one family. By herding together the peculiarly incorrigible and vicious
and rendering them a dishonored class, we give power to evil influence
afford facilities for combination, enable hand to join with hand in wick
edness, and render reformation almost hopeless. *Adaptation*, then
rather than any arbitrary rule of classification, will govern the distribu
tion of the children to the various families. To afford better opportu
nity for studying character, children when first received into the insti

tution will be placed in one of the families occupying the main building, under the more direct observation of the superintendent, and will remain there until a sufficient knowledge is obtained of their character and disposition, when they will be placed in that family where the association and the discipline are calculated to exert the best influence. Thus the individual will never be lost sight of in the crowd; his case will be separately and carefully considered, and the best means adopted to remedy defects in his character or previous training.

"But the question arises, What will you do with the hardened juvenile offender, who has already entered upon a career of crime, and who differs only in age from the convicts in our penitentiary—who is rampant, reckless, and daring, and who defies authority and tramples upon the restraints of society? Is he a fit subject for the mild discipline of a school? Perhaps not. Without doubt there are cases of precocious juvenile depravity, in which offenses against life or property have been of so serious a character, that the courts deal with them and they become subjects of prison-discipline. But we would not reject even these. If there be any influence which will reach them, it will be in the mild paternal discipline of an institution like ours. The very moment you treat these juvenile delinquents as criminals, and consign them to a prison, you place an almost impassable barrier between them and the possibility of reform. In our profession we must have confidence in human nature, however debased and fallen, and confidence in the power and influence of Christianity. When we lose this trust in God and man our occupation is gone, and the sooner we retire from reformatory work the better. I have an abiding faith that there is no human being so low, so degraded, that the light of Christianity cannot reach him and the hand of sympathy cannot lift him up; and I believe this is eminently true of children. I would have the worst of these boys received, then, and with due care and vigilance trained to a better life amid all healthful family-influences. Incessant vigilance is greatly more efficacious with them than any amount of walls and bolts and bars."

NECESSITY FOR SOME EARNEST ACTION.

The prevalence of juvenile delinquency and its fearful evils, and the questions of its prevention or cure, are now pressed upon public attention as never before. All over our country this great evil is truly alarming. Entirely neglected, or very imperfectly taught, great multitudes of youth are growing up ignorant, uncontrolled, idle, and immoral. Children, unblessed with a good home and the all-important advantage of faithful parental training and example, grow up self-willed and debased. Exposed to temptations to evil, and powerless to resist, they gravitate early into a life useless, lawless, and criminal, and find their level in the dangerous classes of society.

Last year over two thousand children between the ages of 6 and 17 were arrested for various offenses and brought before the courts in the city of Boston. In view of this deplorable state of things, and for the purpose of rescuing these wretched children from their evil course, and to save them from being identified with adult and hardened criminals, the board of State-charities for the State of Massachusetts earnestly recommended a special court for their trial.

From the reports of various institutions it is shown that juvenile offenders are on the increase in other States.

The following table, from the report of the Ohio State Reform-School for 1875, shows the cause of commitment of the boys of that institution and the type of character they bear when received:

Nature of crime.	No.
Grand larceny	10
Petit larceny	59
Burglary	8
Assault	4
Forgery	1
Robbery	1
House-breaking and theft	6
Petit larceny and incorrigibility	22
Petit larceny and burning buildings	1
Assault with intent to rape	1
Fratricide	1
Killing animals	1
Vagrancy	6
Incorrigibility	57
Manslaughter	1
Total	179

Another table reveals painful facts illustrating largely the causes of their misfortune and early wandering into paths of sin, presenting the moral and social condition of the inmates before entering the institution:

Moral and social condition of inmates.	No.
Who had lost both father and mother	19
Who had lost father	54
Who had lost mother	32
Whose parents are both living	74
Who had used profane language	63
Who had used tobacco	66
Who had been guilty of larceny	92
Who had used intoxicating liquors	7
Who had been truants from school	110

This is a fair representation of the class of boys in reformatory institutions.

Many of these children never knew the potent power of love, sympathy, and encouragement to be good, nor were they sheltered beneath the roof of a good, safe, and happy home. They were always waifs drifting on the ocean of life and tossed by its tempests. The reform-school was the first safe harbor into which they had entered. Others, with drunken, thriftless, cruel parents, were in a condition worse than orphanage. From the squalor, the wrangling, the poverty, and the wretchedness of such a home, where the father is a confirmed inebriate and the mother powerless to take proper care of her offspring, they are driven into vagrancy and exposed to all the evils of wicked companionship, of idleness, vice, and crime.

There are some boys who, recreant to all the advantages of a good home and culture, rush thoughtlessly into an evil and criminal life, but, subjected to reformatory discipline and treatment, give but little trouble and are considered hopeful cases. Friendless and dependent boys, compelled at a tender age to earn a living, failing to find a home and employment, or a place to learn a trade, become discouraged, and in an evil hour fall from their integrity and are sent to a reformatory, where for the first time in their lives they find a good home with the discipline and training necessary to prepare them to earn honest bread and the confidence of the public.

Boys are sometimes sent to the reformatories ragged, filthy, and in irons. This is a great wrong inflicted on the poor boy, and whoever has the power or interest to send him to the institution should see that he be sent neat and clean in his apparel and person, that on his arrival he may be received and welcomed into the family designated as his future home without showing any outward evidence of his previous life or personal appearance. An unhappy, discontented boy is not in a condition favorable to reformation and improvement. To change a bad boy into a good one, the proper agencies must be adopted and employed. In his new home, he comes under the rulings of the law of kindness and of love. Here the work of reformation is fairly inaugurated, and in a few days the home-feeling is produced and its power realized. His character must be studied, his wants known, and his personal peculiarities ascertained; then reach to him the helping hand of sympathy and encouragement, bring to bear upon his thoughtless mind and stubborn will the power of moral truth and the authority of law, reach his heart through his understanding, let him feel and realize that his recovery from the power of evil is possible, and that by the divine blessing he may become his own deliverer. His dormant energies must be aroused and directed; his purpose to attain a better life must be fixed and avowed; then trust him, and give him the opportunity and the encouragement to do well. This he can enjoy in the school-room and chapel, on the fields and in the shops, in his family and on the play-ground. Some boys are weak and helpless at the beginning of their struggles; but, the intellect aroused, the hand employed, and the heart cheered, a beginning is made, the point of indifference is passed, and, step by step, progress in the right direction is made, the careless become thoughtful, idleness is changed for industry, rebellion for obedience, truth for falsehood, and virtue for vice.

Where the reformatory is a good home, and not a cheerless, gloomy prison; its buildings commodious, light, and airy; its surroundings attractive; its pervading influence elevating, at the very beginning a deep and favorable impression will be produced upon the mind and heart of the new-comer, and he submits cheerfully and hopefully to the authoritative guardianship over and around him. Such a home and such a system of treatment form a wall higher and stronger than granite and iron. It is a better preventive to escapes than cells and manacles. Well fed, comfortably lodged and clothed, taught habits of personal neatness and cleanliness, the boy is ready to take hold of every duty, and his state of mind is favorable to receive moral and religious instruction.

The modes of punishment and the certainty of their infliction should be well known and appreciated by the inmates. The law of punishment is a terror to evil-doers, and, properly used, is an accepted element of power in the discipline of the institution. Slight offenses should receive light punishments, but in cases of grievous transgressions the offenders should know that there exists a power in reserve ready to be used when occasion demands it.

In most cases, kindness is a more effective means of reforming boys than punishment; no boy can be reformed without winning his confidence, and that cannot be won by harsh treatment or force.

THE EARLIER THE ACTION THE MORE OF HOPE.

It is admitted by those of greatest experience that the work of reformation is surrounded with difficulties. To take the neglected, the erring, the depraved, with all that variety of character and life which is ever found in the dark and dangerous undercurrents of society, where the weight of social conditions and vices presses most unfavorably, and endeavor to impress upon it, while immature, something of a redeeming nature, is a difficult but not a hopeless task.

To prevent crime rather than to reform criminals is the truest and most promising work. If the misguided and tempted are shielded, by being withdrawn from the snares that took and held them, until conscience is awakened and made controlling, and the downward progress arrested by placing a barrier between the past and future of the delinquent, giving time and opportunity for whatever of latent goodness and strength there may be within him, beneath the fostering care of a well-conducted reformatory, there is more hope than in what may accurately be called reform. By good counsel and employment these disordered lives are stimulated, encouraged, and regulated; they begin life anew.

When the boy or girl, although not yet mature in years, has cast away restraints of conscience, and, with a precocious development, advanced far towards the meridian of a criminal life, there is less of encouragement, and it is the undoubted opinion of the experienced that for such a more vigorous discipline is needed, and that it is far better they should be placed in prisons, where the most irreclaimable and dangerous ıld have to be overawed by force of the latter than remain to taint less depraved.

'he importance of looking after this class of children early, before ir evil habits become strong and fixed, can be shown by statistics, ich prove that the greatest success is had in the reformation of those ler 14 years of age. As they advance from this point the probability their reformation grows less.

'he histories of thousands of boys and girls show that they became jects for reformatory institutions with few exceptions, more from ;lect, through whatever its cause, than because of any more vicious linations than other children have. It is also rare that a boy or girl is mitted who has had any considerable school-advantages. When :h is the case, it is always found that they have been overtaken by ne sudden temptation, and are not at all hardened cases—a strong ;ument in favor of compulsory law for the education of all classes of ildren.

EDUCATION INDISPENSABLE.

By many it is supposed that it is the churches rather than the schools ıich prevent people from becoming criminals, but the facts indicated the following statistics show the contrary.

The kingdom of Bavaria examined this question in 1870. The result ll-be found in the following table:

	Per 1,000 buildings.		Per 100,000 souls.
	Churches.	School-houses.	Crimes.
)per Bavaria	15	5¼	667
)per Franconia	5	7	444
wer Bavaria	10	4¼	870
e Palatinate	4	11	425
wer Palatinate	11	6	690
wer Franconia	5	10	384

In countries such as Italy and Spain, where the education and moral aining of the people have been exclusively under ecclesiastical con- ol, the following are the results:

(1) A highly educated few; but among the masses general ignorance.

(2) A low grade of morality.

(3) A large pauper and criminal class.

(4) A lack of national progress and development.

If there be any particular system of religious teaching which is supe- ır in its reformatory and saving power, there are ample opportunities test its exclusively potent qualities on the children and youth be- re they are sent to the reformatory. But, if all such systems have iled to save the children from vagrancy and crime until they become ırds of the state, then is it for the state to appoint the system of reformation which it deems best for the moral regeneration of its minor citizens.

One-seventh of the population of the United States over 10 years of age cannot write their names. Fifty per cent. of all the criminals in the country can neither read nor write; one-fifth of all the prisoners in the United States are boys.

A teacher of many years of experience says:

"It was said in the report of a reformatory of last year that there are three methods in vogue of dealing with this class of children, viz, *banishment, punishment,* and *education.*

" *We educate* with earnest and persistent effort. We aim to reach the minds of these youths left in ignorance, to be made the tools of designing men in after years.

"We insist that every child has a right to demand that all his faculties shall be developed to the highest degree to which they are capable, that he may learn to love, respect, venerate, and cherish the institutions under which he lives, and become truly an American citizen in the enjoyment of all the blessings accorded to him as such.

" *We educate* because we *know* that education is reformatory; for while it imparts intelligence sufficient to conduct the ordinary affairs of life, it cultivates, necessarily, habits of punctuality, method, and perseverance; the whole man is toned up, the quality of mind becomes better, and all its strength and activities tend to better acts and nobler impulses.

" *We educate* because Christian character can be cultivated. It is a quality capable of being inbred and inwrought by Christian culture.

"We *know* that our labors in the school-room make a marked change among our boys. It is striking to observe the gross animal instincts departing, the face and form robing themselves in the habiliments of a higher form of manliness, the rigid soul softening and growing warm with life. With new energy infused we find them struggling to work themselves free from the wretched condition in which they have been so long fixed. One of the roughest lads I ever saw said to me, during the past year, 'I *know* I am bad. I have been a burglar for many years. I have been to Blackwell's Island twice. No one ever took an interest in me; no one ever spoke a kind word to me before. I will never trouble you in the school again.' And he did not. Improvement in him was manifest till he left the institution in which he was, saying, 'I can never forget what you have done for me.'

"'With loving kindness have I drawn thee,' are the words in which God declares his desire for bringing back wanderers to his fold. Sensibility to kindness keeps a lingering hold upon our nature. This germ of a dormant manhood seems to outlive all others, as if no degradation could crush it and no depravity extinguish it.

"But underneath all this intellectual awakening there is a grander work to be performed, there is a moral regeneration that can be achieved.

Shall we stand upon the environs of this moral degradation among our boys and shrink from the duty we owe them because they are hardened in sin and apparently given over to evil influences? Would He who came to save the 'lost' have done this? Nothing can supply the place of earnest, faithful, religious teaching drawn from the Word of God. I have the most profound convictions of the inefficacy of all measures of reformation except such as are based on the gospel and pervaded by its spirit. In vain are all devices if the heart and conscience, beyond all power of external restraints, are left untouched.

"There is no grander field than this for the faculties of a man thoroughly in earnest, who will engage in it with intense intelligence of purpose."

REFORMATION OF ADULTS.

The effort to reform adults is necessarily attended with many more dis-couragements than is the case with the same work among children. It is in the impressible period of early youth that the foundations of sound principles and generous impulses are more readily and permanently laid. Nevertheless, the experience of those who have devoted them-selves to the work of adult-reformation gives much occasion for hope-fulness, and most important results have been achieved in those prisons and reformatories in which the idea of punishment has been made sub-servient to that of the help, instruction, and reformation of the inmates. Few are found so hardened in vice, whether it be among men, women, or children, as not to yield sooner or later to the potent influence of love. In direct proportion to the controlling influence of this sentiment in their work and methods, it is believed, is the success achieved by those who have devoted themselves to the reformation of that most un-fortunate and unhappy class of humanity for whom exist magdalen-asylums and midnight-missions. When the erring woman can be con-vinced that the door of hope for this world is not forever shut against her, that there is a career before her of honest industry and its rewards, when the hands of Christian women are ready to steady her tottering steps, and their voices, full of all charity, say to her, "Neither do I con-demn thee," then, in a majority of cases, there is hope. That this large-hearted Christian spirit does not prevail in all the efforts put forth to this end, at least that it is not sufficiently apparent in the methods em-ployed, may account largely for the lack of success complained of by some laborers in this field. When the great effort is to make the mag-dalen feel, not that she is forgiven, but, on the contrary, condemned; that not a whole life-time spent in sackcloth and ashes, nay, that even the blood of our Savior can scarce avail to wash away the foul stain from her life; that association with respectable women is something never to be dreamed of in this world, there is surely little encouragement to pen-itence and reform. Woman craves social recognition. If it be beyond hope to obtain this from the good and reputable, it will generally be sought, and always found, among the bad. The church, in some cases, has recognized this obstacle, and has evaded it by providing a religiou career in the cloister or among sisterhoods, where, by penitence, seve penance, self-sacrifice, and devotion to religion, a certain standing in t church, and even an acknowledged holiness, may be attained.

The Water Street Home for Women, New York, furnishes an examp of the power of Christian love in the work of reform. This " hom offers to the abandoned men and women of that locality a refuge fro temptation, and a helping hand out of the mire of intemperance a prostitution. They are met with kindness and love. They find the selves, not in an institution where rigid discipline is exacted, but in loving family, where they breathe the spirit of a true home. The clerg man in charge, Mr. Boole, states that most of those seeking reformatio are sincere in their desire to be reclaimed; that they are not long accepting Christ, and that a large majority of conversions that take pla among them are permanent. Here the conversion of the person nee ing reformation is made the first consideration, no hopes being ente tained of the permanency of any reform, whether of man or woma without this.

The Midnight Mission, at 260 Greene street, New York, engaged kindred work and upon similar principles, reports a fair degree of su cess.

The Home for Fallen and Friendless Girls, at 86 West Fourth stree during the eight years of its existence, has sheltered and aided 6(women and girls, of whom 219 were provided with situations, 145 we returned to and received by friends, some were respectably and ha pily married from the home, and a very small proportion, it is claime returned to their former course of life.

The House of Mercy, under the management of the Sisters of S Mary and the Lady Visitors of the Protestant-Episcopal Church, is a example of institutions which are doing a similar work, but necessari in a somewhat different manner. The greater number of its inmat are convicted criminals, sentenced by the courts to the House of Merc instead of to a prison. Equally favorable results, therefore, should n be expected from such work as in cases where residence in the instit tion is voluntary. Still, much evident good is accomplished, and muc more is done, the full results of which may never be seen by mortal ey Although necessarily a prison, the house is made to seem as much lik a true home as possible, and the inmates are encouraged and aided b kindness and religious instruction to strive to fit themselves for a bett life in the future. The sum of $110 a year is received from the cit government for the support of each prisoner, the remaining expens being defrayed by their labor. The laundry furnishes their chief occu pation; that and the sewing done by them yield a revenue of abou $1,500 annually. The number of inmates in 1874 was 166; 78 were di missed within the year, of whom 20 were sent to situations, 13 to othe institutions, 37 to friends, 25 left with permission, 6 without, and 2 die

Houses of the Good Shepherd, under Roman-Catholic control, existing in most large cities, combine the voluntary and involuntary system.
Commitments are made by the city-authorities of girls from 14 to 21
years of age. Many, feeling the need for reformation and assistance,
are received on application; others are left at the home by friends, the
age of such not being limited. Those entering voluntarily can leave upon
application to the mother superior; those committed by friends are
retained until withdrawn by them. Much importance is attached to
religious exercises and devotions, the inmates being classified into
various religious orders. Thus, the magdalens belong to the order of
St. Magdalen. St. Mary's class is composed of girls committed by the city-
authorities. The "preservation" class of young girls, who are brought
by friends for the care, discipline, and restraint which they do not find
elsewhere, is called the "detention-class of St. Joseph." In the House
of the Good Shepherd, on East Eighty-ninth street, having 456 inmates,
the class of St. Mary numbers 100 girls, who, under the supervision of 8
Sisters of the White Veil, are employed in laundry-work received from
private families and from the colleges and academies of the city. "The
spirit of self-sacrifice and labor manifested by the children employed
here," say the Sisters, "deserves all praise, sometimes not even interrupting their work at the recreation-hour, and this without any compulsion; yet their spiritual exercises are never omitted. Lectures and
rosaries are interrupted at times by the singing of the Rule, the Litany
of Loretto, or other pious songs." The children in the detention-class
are engaged principally in shirt-making, but also do the washing for
the house.

Another variety of the same work, under Roman-Catholic auspices, is
that done in the House of the Holy Family, an Association for Befriending Children and Young girls, supported by charity and by the labor of
inmates. It is under the control of a lady directress, a board of managers, and an advisory committee.

The Association for Befriending Children and Young Girls, New York,
was commenced in 1860 by a number of benevolent ladies, whose plan
at first was simply to open a school where, once a week, religious and
industrial instruction might be given to neglected and vicious young
girls, and whatever aid and encouragement seemed necessary extended.
The first day of school showed that the work to be done was deeper
and broader than they had supposed. "There were children of 10 years
already confirmed drunkards and girls of 14 fallen to the lowest depth
of vice and depravity." It was immediately decided that the school
must be kept open for two days in the week, and before many months
had passed it became evident that this work would not rest here. Won
by the care and affection shown them, the children would tell their for-
lorn story of want, and misery, and sin; and older girls, long ago lost,
would come to the door of the school, ashamed to be seen among the
children, and implore help for themselves. But they would not go to

institutions which they only knew as places of confinement on conviction for crime. And so a home was opened, a home in fact as well
as in name, where those unfortunates, who desired it, could be reformed,
instructed, and given a fair start on an honest path in life. It had always
been the purpose of the association to give a large share of its attention
and care to that class upon whom society most readily turns its back.
From the beginning it had confined itself to depraved and vagrant
children, but the children were women in the knowledge of evil, and,
when the girl of 14 was as fallen as the girl of 20, it was unreasonable
to draw the line at any age under that. About two-thirds of the inmates are over 16 years of age. They are retained six months, and
longer, if necessary, and on leaving are provided with situations in
Catholic families, or are returned to friends who have been reconciled
to them through the instrumentality of the institution. Younger ones
are adopted by Catholic families, while others regard the house as their
home, and consecrate their lives to God in reparation for the past. In
1874, over 200 were provided with employment and homes in Catholic
families. The work of this institution is confined rigidly to the class
for which it is intended—unfortunate girls, and children of depraved
parents. In every case the applicant comes of her own volition. A
very encouraging degree of success in the work of reformation has been
attained by the good women at the head of this work, and they believe
this is largely owing to the fact that the girls come of their own free
will, in all cases at their own request, and are free to go at any time.
Although numbering among its inmates women and children of the most
abandoned and lawless character, the testimony of this family is that
the instances in which its system has proved unavailing are quite
rare.

Every child under 14 years of age receives secular and religious instruction during the usual school-hours. Those over that age are taught
to perform every kind of household-work, are instructed in a trade, are
prepared for the sacraments, and receive a training in the night-school.

HOMES AND SCHOOLS FOR CHILDREN.

CALIFORNIA.

GOOD TEMPLARS' HOME FOR ORPHANS, VALLEJO.

Children between 2 and 12 years of age are received here, and are retained till after 14. The sources of revenue are: 20 per cent. of the Grand Lodge per-capita tax; State aid, under the law of California relating to orphan-asylums; donations of lodges and individuals, and revenue derived from the support of children whose surviving parent, guardian, or friends may pay a monthly stipend. These sources of revenue are stated to be amply sufficient for the wants of the home, which, in 1874, sheltered 55 children—39 boys and 16 girls.

The report for 1874 states that all the laws of California in relation to granting State-aid to orphan-asylums emanated either from this Grand Lodge or from this board; and the act of the legislature of last session, concerning the guardianship of orphaned and abandoned children, was passed at the suggestion of this board. Under the operation of the statutes now in force, the State contributes a large and satisfactory proportion of the cost of maintaining the orphan-asylums of the State, and in such equitable proportion to each as the number of inmates entitled them to. With the existing laws the board is now content, believing they have been enacted in accordance with the suggestions of experience; and their practical operation has justified their wisdom.

The children here are instructed in the common-school-branches of education and an effort is being made to provide some industrial training also.

CONNECTICUT.

HARTFORD ORPHAN-ASYLUM.

This institution was organized in 1819, and has received on an average 50 children annually. It is well supported, and is doing a steady and creditable work.

NEW HAVEN ORPHAN-ASYLUM.

This institution had its origin some forty years ago in the efforts of about twenty-five benevolent ladies, who, after discussing the needs and sufferings of the destitute children of the city, organized the New Haven Female Society for the Relief of Orphan and Destitute Children, out of which grew the New Haven Orphan-Asylum, incorporated in May, 1833.

Its officers are a board of female managers, consisting of a president, chief manager, treasurer, corresponding secretary, recording secretary, provider, and forty managers. These control the appropriation of the income of the asylum and have the general management of the internal and domestic concerns of the institution. The constitution provides. that the board of managers shall be chosen from the different Protestant evangelical religious denominations of the city.

Besides these, nine gentlemen are elected annually by the society as a board of trustees, whose duty it is to take charge of the property of the corporation, both personal and real. They are *ex-officio* counselors of the board of managers, and act as advisers to them in all cases of necessity.

Many of the children received have friends who pay a merely nominal sum weekly, in order to retain the control of their children, hoping some time to be able to care for them.

·Children are not received before they are 2 years old or after they have completed their tenth year, and they are rarely kept in the asylum after they are 14 years of age. Then they are placed in some family where they can be taught some trade or employment and also attend school during a portion of the year. The by-laws contain the following provisions on the subject :

Persons taking children into their families must be married or keeping house, regular attendants of a Protestant place of worship, and be recommended by their pastor or other respectable persons.

No child shall be indentured to perform labor under 12 years of age; the term of service shall be discretionary with the board of managers.

Employés will be allowed two months' trial, at the expiration of which time, if either party is dissatisfied, the child may be returned to the asylum.

Great care must be taken by the board to secure to the children a comfortable home, kind treatment, and a thorough industrial, moral, and religious education.

The grounds are very beautifully laid out and the building large and convenient. The deep front yard is covered with a soft and rich turf and shaded by a number of large and elegant evergreens, while in the rear of the house are the ample play-grounds and a neatly-kept kitchen-garden. Entering the building, one finds on the ground-floor the parlors and sitting-room of the family, the large dining-room for the children, the capacious kitchen, wash-room, pantries, &c., and the sewing-room, where several sewing-machines are kept in constant operation, making and mending the children's clothing. On the next story are the apartments of the matron and teachers, the boys' and girls' rooms, nursery, bath-rooms, &c. Above these are the sleeping-rooms and hospital. Each sleeping-room contains fifteen or twenty little iron bedsteads, and the care of the beds is delegated to one or two of the larger boys or girls, and throughout the whole house those who are able to work are initiated into all the mysteries of housekeeping.

In the basement, besides the hot-air- and steam-furnaces which heat the building, are two large, separate play-rooms for the boys and girls. Here each child has a little closet or box in which he keeps his own playthings, and they are made the means of teaching the children neatness and the difference between "mine" and "thine."

The present number of children in the asylum is not far from 110, and the total number who have found a home in it since its organization is considerably over 1,000. Of these, 335 were boarders, i. e., whose friends paid something for their board; 52 were orphans; the fathers of 206 were dead and 97 had lost their mothers by death; 116 were the children of soldiers, and 42 were taken from the almshouse; 79 were deserted by their fathers, 18 by their mothers, and 3 by both parents; 49 had intemperate fathers and of 25 the mothers were intemperate, while 17 were the children of two intemperate parents. Divorces of parents sent 14 to the asylum, the fathers of 4 were in prison and the mothers of 6. The mothers of 8 children were in the hospital and the parents of 19 were both sick, while 12 were the children of insane parents; 118 were of foreign parentage, 63 of American parentage, and 8 were colored.

The above statistics are by no means full and complete, as in many cases the records are deficient, but are correct as far as they go. The accounts of the asylum have been very carefully kept, and there is ground for felicitating the ladies on the fact that an institution managed entirely by them has not lost a single cent by carelessness in keeping the accounts in the forty years of its history. The records show that when the asylum was first founded the average cost of maintaining each child was $1 per week; in 1847, it was 75 cents; in 1848, 77 cents; and in 1870, 64 cents.

The discipline of the asylum is of the most careful sort, and every endeavor is made to mitigate in the cases of these desolate children the absence of a mother's care and father's watchfulness. The school connected with it is in excellent condition and reflects great credit on its teachers. It has also a valuable children's library of several hundred volumes, which has been replenished for some time past by an annual donation of fifty dollars.

DISTRICT OF COLUMBIA.

NATIONAL SOLDIERS' AND SAILORS' ORPHANS' HOME, WASHINGTON, D. C.

This institution, sustained in a considerable measure by appropriations from the General Government, is at 1732 G street, Washington, D. C., near the War and Navy Departments. It had in 1874, under its charge, 4 male and 19 female orphans, making 43 in all, well housed and well cared for as respects every material comfort. The elder children are sent for instruction to the public schools; the younger, under the care of a matron and a committee of ladies, are engaged at home in such light household-sports and occupations as may keep their exuberant spirits within bounds. No trades are taught, however, nor does the idea of a special training for any subsequent pursuit appear to form a portion of the plan of government.

ILLINOIS.

PROTESTANT ORPHAN-ASYLUM, CHICAGO.

During its early years the reports were not published very regularly, and more recently some have been destroyed by fire.

The orphan-asylum was rendered necessary by the fearful ravages of the Asiatic cholera, which visited this city in 1849, it proving fatal to many immigrants, thereby leaving their children orphans and destitute.

On the 3d of August, 1849, (a day appointed by the President as a day of fasting and prayer, in view of the spreading epidemic,) a meeting was held for the purpose of affording them a home. A contribution of over $400 was raised and an adjourned meeting appointed for the following Tuesday, when a constitution was adopted and a board of trustees chosen; the 13th of the same month, the board of directresses held their first meeting at the asylum, 13 children having been admitted. Up to the present time, 1,894 children have been cared for at the asylum.

In 1851 the board of trustees (seeing the necessity of a permanent location) purchased two acres of land from the trustees of the Illinois and Michigan Canal, at the first canal-land-sale, for $800, to be paid in annual payments of $200 each. The amount necessary was raised by the ladies from the proceeds of fairs, and the building now occupied was erected in 1853.

In 1870 the location had become so desirable for residences that the trustees built four brick houses, facing on Michigan avenue, two each side of the asylum, which were immediately rented for five years, at $1,000 each. In 1873 four more were built on Wabash avenue, which rent for $1,500 each—$30,000 being still owed for the last set. The rents from the first-named houses are applied towards paying the debt, together with half the rent from the Wabash-avenue houses, the remaining $3,000 being paid for interest on the money borrowed to build the houses. It is hoped that when the debt is all paid the asylum will be nearly self-sustaining. At present it is supported by donations.

The treasury is nearly empty, the panic of last fall causing a marked decrease in the subscriptions, as well as a corresponding increase in the number of children received.

Many of the inmates have one parent, who for various reasons cannot care for children in a home of their own, yet can contribute to their support in the asylum by paying a small amount for board. Frequently

hese are as evidently cases for the exercise of the charities of the insti-
:ution as the orphans themselves.

Many vagrant and homeless children have been surrendered to the
asylum by the mayor who otherwise would have been sent to penal
nstitutions.

All the children of a suitable age attend school, and one afternoon
n each week the girls are instructed in sewing. Much of the light work
of the house is done by the larger girls.

CHICAGO NURSERY AND HALF-ORPHAN ASYLUM.

The object of this charity is the care and maintenance of the children
of poor women, for the purpose of enabling them to find employment;
also, the care and maintenance of such children as are deprived by death,
or other cause, of either parent.

It was originally established as a nursery, where young children could
be cared for during the hours of work, the parents bringing them in the
morning and claiming them at night, paying five cents a day for their
care.

The circumstances of many of the women made it a kindness to supply
lodgings for their children, as well as care through the day, and therefore the plan of the institution was somewhat modified and enlarged to
suit the need.

Several changes were made, until, in the spring of 1870, a lot was purchased, and on it was erected a building, commodious, airy, and suitably
equipped for carrying out its charitable object, and it is doing among
the better class of poor an amount of good that cannot be overestimated.

At the time of the great fire the work was within a few weeks of its
completion, and in the distress of that fearful time those interested in
it were only too glad of its shelter for themselves and families; thus,
for a time, many other children, and even adults, had to be received.
And in a building without doors, only partially glazed, and entirely
without heating-apparatus, the discomforts and suffering endured can
scarcely be exaggerated.

Having struggled through difficulties that can scarcely be appreciated,
during a season of exceptionable hardship, the institution is at last in
admirable working order.

Special attention is given to vocal music, which is considered one of
he most desirable aids to the discipline and happiness of the children.

In connection with the institution there is a day-school, with an average attendance of 86, and the children are making good proficiency in
reading, spelling, and arithmetic. A Sunday-school is also well kept
up, owing to the kindness and energy of its superintendent, who labors
faithfully for its success.

MARYLAND.

THE HEBREW ORPHAN-ASYLUM OF BALTIMORE

Was organized in 1872, under the auspices of the Hebrew Benevolent Society, funds for the purpose having been contributed by the Israelites of Baltimore.

The children attend the public school in the near neighborhood, where they receive instruction in the English branches.

They also receive several hours' instruction daily in the German and Hebrew languages at the asylum, besides being required to devote a reasonable time to the daily preparation of their public-school-studies.

They have the Sabbath and Sunday afternoons entirely at their own disposal.

Their studies are as follows:

(1) Reading and translating the Hebrew Prayer-Book, committing to memory the morning and evening-prayers and the benedictions employed on the various occasions of life and the seasons of the year.

(2) Religious instruction has until now been given more as occasion required, than systematically, because of the absence generally of religious ideas. The orgin and significance of the holidays and festivals and the attributes of God have been fully explained and taught, and the Ten Commandments have been expounded and the children required to commit them to memory.

(3) Biblical history.

(4) German reading, writing, orthography, and grammar.

(5) English—all studies usual in the public schools.

(6) Vocal music.

NEW HAMPSHIRE.

THE NEW HAMPSHIRE ORPHANS' HOME AND SCHOOL OF INDUSTRY

Is located upon the celebrated Daniel Webster farm, in Franklin, N. H.

It was duly inaugurated with appropriate ceremonies, October 18, 1871.

One hundred children have been received at the home since its opening. They are under excellent care and training in every particular, and are contented and happy. The real estate and personal property, amounting to more than $12,000, is paid for, and the title is in the home. The income for the past year was $4,000 and the number of inmates thirty-one.

NEW JERSEY.

NEWARK ORPHAN-ASYLUM, NEWARK.

Some twenty-seven years ago, a little friendless orphan-girl fell from a fruit-tree and broke her leg. Already an unwelcome inmate in the

nily with whom she had found a shelter, this additional affliction
ndered her an unbearable burden. She was about to be sent to the
nshouse, when a kind neighbor opened her home and heart and took
> little sufferer in, and with a mother's tenderness nursed her back to
alth.

This circumstance was known and discussed, and the necessity of
ablishing an orphan-asylum for the benefit of friendless orphan-chil-
:n was pressed upon the minds of the people. Preliminary meetings
re called, an association formed, a building hired, and the Newark
phan-Asylum, the first institution of the kind in the State, and it not
State-institution, was formally opened with appropriate religious serv-
s.

A charter was obtained, and a board of trustees, comprising thirty
lies, chosen from the Episcopal, Presbyterian, Baptist, Methodist,
formed, and Congregational churches of this city. Of those ladies,
are still remaining in the board.

The asylum opened with eight children ; but, as its fame became noised
road, its numbers increased, and in a few years they were compelled
look forward to an enlargement of their borders.

Appeals were made, to which the people of Newark responded, and a
. was purchased for $7,000, and a building commenced in September,
56, and in September, 1857, the house was completed without a dollar
indebtedness, the expense of the house and grounds being $32,000.

The original design of the building is incomplete. It was intended to
finished with corresponding wings, but the funds not being sufficient,
d one wing only being needed for the convenience of the family, the
istees concluded to defer the erection of the other wing until the
·asury should be replenished for that purpose. In 1865 a legacy was
't for this express design, with the condition that it should be used
thin ten years, and it is now hoped that the accumulated interest,
th the principal, will enable the trustees to complete the remaining
ng without appealing to the generosity of its friends.

They are endeavoring to establish a permanent fund, to be so invested
at it will help them to meet their annual expenses and to provide for
seen exigences, for which their present subscriptions are inadequate.

They have now $5,000 or more, but, as the institution has from the
ginning until the present had to depend on the contributions and
nations of its friends to meet its daily wants, it is necessary sometimes
draw upon this small fund to meet deficiencies.

The success of this institution stimulated others, and auxiliaries
rang up in Orange, Paterson, Bloomfield, Morristown, Belleville,
ainfield, and New Brunswick. These all worked cordially and heart-
' with the parent-institution for several years, when Paterson and
range, having so large a number of children to provide for, withdrew
d formed associations of their own, and are both prosecuting their
ork with vigor and success.

and verses of Scripture recited from memory. A Psalm is read, and repeated by them, and thoughts expressed by any one. So far as possible, we aim to make this the most interesting hour of the day, a cleaning-up from heart and mind.

"If one child has left the asylum during that day, it is referred to, and the children reminded that all will eventually go out to new homes; that this is but a temporary one; and that real excellence of character will be indispensably needful for recommendation to those who may seek here for a poor boy or girl to share their comforts and blessings.

"Thirty-two have been put out to good homes during the past year."

THOMAS ASYLUM FOR ORPHAN AND DESTITUTE INDIAN CHILDREN, COLLINS, ERIE COUNTY.

This institution is supported by appropriation from the State of New York, the Indian Bureau, and charitable donations. In addition to reading, writing, arithmetic, and drawing, some industries are taught. It has usually from 80 to 100 inmates.

A gift was received last year from certain benevolent members of the Society of Friends residing in Philadelphia, designed to furnish the children with a fund of instructive amusement. It consists of scientific toys, as magnets, microscope, spy-glass, stereoscope, &c., a working-model for a steamboat, instructive pictures, amusing and interesting books, and a check for $25, to provide table and chairs for fitting up a room for evening-exercises, so as to render the donation available.

The reception of this gift marked an era in the progress of the children, and supplied a deficiency long felt, if not distinctly recognized, in the means and appliances for promoting mental, moral, social, and physical improvement.

Practically, the value of all the other resources of the institution has been greatly increased by it.

THE HEBREW BENEVOLENT AND ORPHAN-ASYLUM SOCIETY, NEW YORK.

The asylum sustained by this society contained, in 1874, 194 children—141 boys and 56 girls—the largest number ever sheltered by the institution. Of these, 113 were natives of New York City and State, 32 were from other parts of the United States, and 52 from foreign countries. The children, when between 5 and 13 years of age, attend the public schools, and, in addition, receive home-instruction. Industrial education receives special attention here after the pupil has attained the age of 14 years, when he is taught a trade, and when able to earn his living is sent out, receiving $200, besides his savings, which he has been encouraged to put by during apprenticeship.

A large amount of relief, in the shape of food, clothing, and cash, is dispensed among the Jewish poor. The ladies' sewing-society, attached

to the asylum, has for years steadily increased in numbers and useful
ness, completing, on an average, over a thousand garments each year
This society has been in existence over fifty years.   It is proposed to ex
tend the idea of the industrial schools so as to benefit others than th
graduates of the orphan-asylum, to furnish sewing-machines to dress
makers, tailors, &c., to procure work for the industrious, and practicall
to impress the principle of helping those who would help themselves
Again, a more systematic co-operation with Jewish and other institu
tions is to be maintained, so that the sick, the infirm, and the aged ma,
be permanently relieved by the proper society, and not constitute
burden on the funds designed for other classes.

ORPHAN-ASYLUM SOCIETY IN THE CITY OF NEW YORK.

This society has made its sixty-seventh annual report.   Their mott
is, "Work while it is day, for the night cometh, wherein no man ca
work."

Many questions have arisen, and are still being discussed, wit
respect to the future of this institution.

Living in this progressive age, they cannot adhere too strictly to tim
honored customs, nor consider the laws bequeathed to them as unalte.
able.   Seeking to enlarge their field of usefulness, it was found neces
sary to form plans and frame resolutions which, while retaining all the
rules and by-laws that can be wisely kept, must receive additions and
improvements to provide for the comfort and accommodation of all
those whom God graciously gives to their care.   During the past year,
this society has amended its charter, increased its number of trustees,
and added two members to its advisory committee.

The asylum is henceforth open, not only for orphans, but for the destitute children of a sick or disabled father or for the children of a desolate widow or forsaken wife.

ST. JOSEPH'S ASYLUM, CITY OF NEW YORK.

Object of the institution: To receive and educate, free of charge, poor
Catholic orphans of the city of New York.

Means of supporting the institution: Collections in churches, donations, rent from buildings, &c.

Fund: The fund of the institution amounts to $16,000.

Officers of the society: A president, vice-president, treasurer, and two
secretaries.   The members are either life-members or benevolent contributors.

THE SOCIETY FOR THE RELIEF OF HALF-ORPHAN AND DESTITUTE
CHILDREN OF THE CITY OF NEW YORK

Has made its thirty-seventh annual report.   The great success of this
charity may be attributed in a large measure to the persevering labor
of its founders and their successors.

Those who have been connected either with the board of trustees or the board of managers have rarely separated from it except by death. The president of the board of trustees was one of the incorporators of the asylum. The secretary of that board has been connected with it for twenty-four years; others, for fifteen and sixteen years. Nearly half of the board of managers have been there for fifteen or twenty and twenty-two years; some still longer. Thus the work has been handed down by trustees and managers of former years, and thus would the present managers leave it to those who shall come after them.

Those who have been engaged in it the longest, from time and experience, recognize its great responsibility and the duty to aid and to protect the poor and destitute, and are thoroughly convinced that this and all kindred institutions should be used only as instrumentalities.

For parents whose daily occupations absolutely preclude the possibility of giving to their children the requisite care, but who gladly do all that they can for their support, such institutions are of the greatest importance, furnishing on the one hand a safe and happy shelter and relieving the keenest anxiety on the other. To such their doors should be always open. But much discrimination is necessary and the utmost care should be taken not to relieve either parents or relatives from a charge which indolence or any other temptation would induce them lightly to throw off. In the family and home are found the most wholesome, safe, and beneficent influences for the formation of character; and observation has shown that character thus formed and disciplined is, ordinarily, far superior to that which is molded within the walls and by the necessary routine of the best arranged institution, whether charitable or not.

The managers frequently discover faults and defects of character in later years, in children who have been with them, which cause them much solicitude. They have reproached themselves with the thought that many of these faults might have been avoided or overcome by greater care and diligence in early training. More recently they have been led to believe that they are not the result of neglect in childhood, but probably the effect of any system of education which must adapt itself to numbers, and not to individuals. They consider it, therefore, a duty to advise all parents applying for the admission of children, to consider well before they place them in an institution, and never, but from necessity, to relinquish the humblest dwelling to which the name of home may be applied. Not that any homes are faultless, but because He who "setteth the solitary in families," has there ordained a special blessing upon family influence.

In this institution the management of the school-room, the sewing-room, and the domestic department—the most important and difficult of all, which must include and supervise the whole, guarding all from infringement and giving to each its full importance—has been unvaryingly faithful and efficient.

ORPHANS' HOME AND ASYLUM, NEW YORK.

This is a well-established and prominent charity of the Protestan
Episcopal Church of the city of New York. Twenty-one years of slo
and quiet growth have brought it to its present maturity, and the litt
seed planted long ago by loving hands has now become a great tree, und
whose branches many hundreds have found shelter and rest. It
supported by subscriptions, donations, and memberships. Its affai
are under the direction of a board of trustees and managers compose
of ladies, representatives from almost every church in the city, with a
advisory committee of gentlemen, of which the bishop of the diocese
the chairman.

The special work of this institution is the care and maintenance
orphans and half-orphans. The larger proportion of its inmates are
the latter class. A most interesting portion of the Orphans' Home
the large and pleasant nursery, with its twenty or more little one
whose rosy cheeks and beaming eyes tell of health and happiness.

The age at which children are usually admitted is between 3 an
8 years. At the age of 12 or 14 years they are placed in situations
returned to their friends, if they desire to take them.

It is the custom of the managers to make up the garments worn
the children, even to the quilting of the quilts that cover their be
This year 646 garments have been made, 36 stockings knitted, and
quilts quilted. A room in the institution is fitted up and used express
for the purpose. The ladies have stated days for their meeting.

COLORED ORPHAN-ASYLUM, NEW YORK.

The managers in their thirty-seventh annual report review their work
with eminent satisfaction. Nearly two thousand children have been
admitted since the opening of the institution. The greater number the
past year were under 8 years of age. One faithful nurse, noted for
her judicious discipline and unwearied patience, has presided over the
nursery for twenty years.

It is a rare sight, this infant-room. Pictures brighten the walls, toys,
innocent of form or fashion, strew the floor, while groups of laughing
little ones are scattered in promiscuous confusion everywhere. Here
are faces lustrous in their ebony blackness and skins fair as our own
Saxon race, yet the stain of a once enslaved people is upon them, and
they are rigidly excluded from all white institutions.

The school is in charge of a corps of six teachers, and shows a fair
progress, many of the pupils fully appreciating the labor bestowed
upon them.

This institution is admirably conducted, the building is well and
carefully ventilated and cleanliness and order are strikingly manifest
in every department of the household.

ROCHESTER ORPHAN-ASYLUM.

This institution was organized in 1837, and during that year received fifty-eight children.

For thirty years no children were received under 2 years of age, but the demand seemed imperative, and in 1867 their doors were opened to infants of the tenderest age, and in five years seventy-one babes were admitted. The average number for the last ten years has been seventy-six, and over seventeen hundred children have shared the fostering care of this institution since its foundation.

TROY ORPHAN-ASYLUM.

This institution is located on Eighth street, city of Troy, county of Rensselaer, N. Y.

In the summer of 1833 a few benevolent Christian ladies, who had long felt the necessity of some organization for the relief of destitute children in the city, met from time to time to talk over the subject and devise the best measures to be taken. They were eventually instrumental in awakening a similar spirit in the hearts of forty wealthy and liberal-hearted gentlemen, who readily entered into proposed plans of action, and immediately formed themselves into an association for work, choosing a board of twenty-one of their number to act as trustees. At the same time the ladies formed a similar association, electing from their number twenty-one to act as a board of managers, auxiliary to the board of trustees, and more or less under their direction.

Their first annual report was issued December 17, 1834. In April, 1835, the board of trustees were made an incorporated body by an act of the legislature of the State.

The asylum began its work with a little group of ten or twelve children from the city. From that time to the present more than a thousand children have been sheltered and cared for, for a longer or shorter time, by its protecting and loving beneficence. Children are received between the ages of 3 and 10, and dismissed as early as the age of 12 years to their friends or permanent homes elsewhere, though many leave at an earlier age.

Among the inmates, native parentage prevails—also half-orphanage. The school connected with the asylum is of an excellent character, being under the supervision of, and supported by, the board of education of the city. Children received are of both sexes, and all confined to the white race. The institution is not denominational, yet strictly Protestant. It is supported by appropriations and contributions. The value of the real and personal estate is estimated at about $75,000. No debts on real estate.

In looking over the first annual report we find that all of that noble band of Christian workers have passed away (from the board of gentlemen) to their higher reward. And, with one or two exceptions, the same may be said of the first board of lady managers. Of one of these we feel at liberty to speak here, viz, the first secretary of the board of ladies. She is to-day still a manager, and one of the institution's heartiest workers, as she has ever been.

Many of the sons and daughters of the original boards seem to have received the fallen mantles of their deceased parents, and to-day are wearing them gracefully, as they are trying to follow in their footsteps, doing like noble deeds of Christian charity.

ST. VINCENT'S FEMALE ORPHAN-ASYLUM, TROY.

This institution was organized in 1848, and was without any funds whatever.

It commenced with a free day-school, and the following year orphans were received, and still continue to be received.

It has been supported by the industry of the Sisters of Charity in charge, voluntary contributions of friends, fairs, and city-, county-, and State-appropriations.

Orphans are received from 3 to 12 years of age, and are placed with good families at any age required.

They are taught orthography, reading, writing, arithmetic, grammar, geography, history, music, drawing, dress making, plain-sewing, general house-work, and domestic economy.

OHIO.

GERMAN PROTESTANT ORPHAN-ASYLUM, CINCINNATI.

Object of the institution: To receive and educate, free of charge, poor orphans of Hamilton County, Ohio, and the neighboring cities of Newport and Covington, in Kentucky; to receive and educate children who have lost one of their parents, if the father was a member of the society and if the circumstances of the family imperatively demand it; to receive and educate wealthy orphans, if their property is by their guardians transmitted to the treasurer of the society as a loan, to be used for the expenses of their education.

Means of supporting the institution: Annual contributions of members, donations, endowments, and the annual sums paid by wealthy orphans for board and tuition.

Fund: All donations and bequests are turned over to the general fund; only the interest of this fund is used, and the capital is never to be touched.

Provision for children who have left the institution: On leaving the institution, children may be bound out as apprentices to some trade or business, but the officers of the institution shall always guard the rights of the children and take the place of the parents till the children are of age.

Members: All German Protestants who are 21 years of age can be

embers of the society by paying an annual contribution of at least
wo dollars. A payment of fifty dollars entitles to a life-membership.

Officers of the society: The officers of the society are a president, vice-
resident, treasurer, two secretaries, and fourteen trustees; the five first
entioned for the term of one year, half of the trustees elected for one
ear, and half for two years.

Candidates for any of these offices are submitted by a committee of
le society.

At the end of his term the president has to make a report.

The institution is at least once a week visited by one of the trustees.

Organization of the institution: The society appoints persons to take
are of the institution, (superintendents,) who must live in the institu-
on and stand to the inmates in the relation of parents.

The superintendent keeps a register of all the inmates, giving their
ame, age, place of birth, time of admission, &c. It is the duty of the
uperintendent to keep the house at all times in good order and to
uperintend the whole household.

Instruction: The course of instruction embraces all the subjects
aught in the public schools, special attention being given to instruction
n German. Religious instruction is given in accordance with Protest-
int principles.

CINCINNATI ORPHAN-ASYLUM.

This noble charity, which has for more than forty years been quietly
and unostentatiously doing its work, can show its magnitude by its
results.

Over sixteen thousand orphan and destitute children have found
beneath its hospitable roof a home and been made to feel that, however
unfortunate, they were not sentenced to a state of pauperism; that
they still had their chances for future usefulness and respectability, and
every encouragement to form habits of hopefulness and self-respect.

No other institution is so thoroughly identified, socially, with Cincinnati. A notice of its contributors would give its social history. Its
large endowments, annual subscriptions, and generous contributions
show that the intention of its supporters is to make the children under
their care comfortable. While care is taken to make the administration
economical, every economy is subordinate to the comfort and happiness
of the orphans. It is resolved that these waifs, before they are sent
adrift again on the stream of life, shall have the advantage of a happy
childhood.

CLEVELAND ORPHAN-ASYLUM, CLEVELAND.

This institution began its work six or seven years before its incorporation in 1853.

Its beginnings were small, but its faithful founders persevered in
heir efforts, struggled against difficulties, solicited contributions from
loor to door, doing their work with much anxious care, with resources

so limited as to be inadequate to the wants of the day, until a charter was obtained from the State. A subscription was then started by friends of the enterprise, who by their vigorous efforts secured $10,000 as a permanent fund. An acre of land was then donated by Rev. E. N. Sawtelle, on the corner of Hinsman street and Wilson avenue. A building was commenced, and a portion completed and put into immediate use.

Efforts were again made to raise funds by subscription, contribution, and otherwise, and the whole was completed in 1859.

The progress of the war diverted public attention and public charity towards the more engrossing claims of the Soldiers' Aid Society of Northern Ohio.

In this emergency, with all means of supply cut off, in December, 1863, came the unexpected and noble bequest of Capt. Levi Sawtelle, a gentleman who, in the course of a long residence in Cleveland, had by frugality and industry amassed a competence, and who, remembering his own orphan-boyhood, bequeathed his whole property for the benefit of the orphan.

The bequest thus made, added to several other smaller gifts and bequests, constitutes the permanent fund, and under the judicious care of the trustees is held as a sacred trust, the income only being available for the working expenses of the asylum, which has always been expended by the managers with the most watchful economy.

THE JEWISH ORPHAN-ASYLUM OF CLEVELAND

Is indebted for its foundation and support to the various organizations of the Israelites in the West and South. Although it confines its charities exclusively to Jewish children, it stands high among the benevolent institutions of our country.

Its system of training and education is of a high order, and special attention is given to each child to direct its studies to that vocation which in its future life it is expected to follow.

It receives from its patrons and friends a noble and generous support.

Its appropriations, contributions, and donations are variable, but always exceed the expenditures.

EBENEZER ORPHAN-INSTITUE OF THE EVANGELICAL ASSOCIATION OF NORTH AMERICA, FLAT ROCK, SENECA COUNTY.

This institution is located on a farm of one hundred and seventy acres, at a cost of $13,500. The building is 50½ by 85 feet and two stories high, and was erected at an expense of $12,000.

It is well managed in all its departments and is a success in its work.

It is generously supported by subscription and endowment. The institution is valued at $55,688.46. The number of inmates during the past year was one hundred. They have a library of four hundred volumes.

PROTESTANT ORPHAN-HOME OF THE CITY OF TOLEDO.

This institution has been in successful operation nearly eight years,
d reports 342 as the number of children admitted since its establish-
ent.

Additional buildings have been recently erected at the cost of
,587.74.

It is supported by life-memberships, annual memberships, and dona-
ns. The average number of inmates for the past year has been 45
r day, and the cost per year for each member would be, taking the
penses as a basis, $71.73, or the small sum of 19 cents and a fraction
r day.

PENNSYLVANIA.

IE ORPHANS' HOME AND ASYLUM FOR THE AGED AND INFIRM OF THE EVANGELICAL LUTHERAN CHURCH.

This institution was founded in 1859 and incorporated in 1863. It is
cated in Germantown, Pa., one of the pleasant suburbs of Philadelphia.
he building is of stone, on a lot containing seven acres of land, and
ie estimated value of the whole real estate is $60,000. The house is
armed by furnaces and supplied with water throughout the building.
is substantially built and will accommodate 150 inmates. Children
·e received between the ages of 3 and 10 years, and sometimes younger.
hree hundred and fifty-six have been admitted since its organization.
The asylum is supported principally by private charity. It is a mer-
orious institution and needs the sustaining care of the liberal-minded
hilanthropist and Christian.

On the same lot is an old frame mansion, which is occupied by twelve
·males in advanced life. The inmates are well cared for in this home
nd are supported and under the control of the same board of mangers as the orphans' home.

OME FOR FRIENDLESS CHILDREN OF THE CITY AND COUNTY OF LANCASTER.

This home is a credit to its benevolent founders, the citizens of Lan-
aster. It was organized in 1858 and incorporated by the legislature
f Pennsylvania in 1860.

The object for which it was established is to take care of and train
he destitute and neglected children of the city and county.

The lot on which the buildings are erected contains fifteen acres, the
ggregate value being $41,042.

The home-building is a substantial brick edifice, 55 feet front by 90
eet deep, four stories high including the basement and mansard-attic.

It is heated with hot-air furnaces, water and gas are conducted to
rery part of the building, and the entire arrangements of the building
re very complete.

Since its organization 750 children have been admitted, over one-third of the present number being soldiers' orphans.

The State has appropriated $5,000, the county of Lancaster has contributed from its treasury $10,000. The children from the county alms-house are all cared for in this institution, which is regarded as one of the best in the State.

GIRARD COLLEGE FOR ORPHANS, PHILADELPHIA.

This noble charity is the result of the beneficence and wisdom of one man, the late Stephen Girard, of Philadelphia, who by the terms of his will bequeathed the sum of $2,000,000, together with such other amounts from the interest on the residue of his estate as might be necessary, to maintain and educate as many poor white male orphans as should be in need thereof, and could be accommodated on the block of ground on which the buildings are located. It is intended that the beneficiaries of this charity shall be limited to very poor white male orphans, all children who have lost their fathers being considered orphans. The expressed design of the founder was to take those boys whose education must otherwise be neglected and train them in practical knowledge. They were to be taught facts and things, rather than words or signs. Thorough training in the common and higher English branches, and also in French and Spanish, is prescribed by the will. The addition of Latin and Greek is permitted, but not advised. Mr. Girard forbade sectarian instruction to the boys, but desired "that all the instructors and teachers in the college shall take the pains to instill into the minds of the scholars the purest principles of morality, so that, on their entrance into active life, they may, from inclination and habit, evince benevolence towards their fellow-creatures and a love of truth, sobriety, and industry." He desired also, especially, "that by every proper means a pure attachment to our republican institutions, and to the sacred rights of conscience, as guaranteed by our happy Constitution, shall be formed and fostered in the minds of the scholars." Mr. Girard's plan contemplated the apprenticeship of the boys to some useful trade or calling, after they should have pursued to its close the prescribed curriculum of studies, but various circumstances have necessitated the modification of such plans to some extent. For instance, the change in the apprenticeship system, which has taken place during the last quarter of a century, rendered it difficult to find people willing to receive boys as apprentices who were unacquainted with labor, and thus it was found advisable to introduce industries in the college. Further, it was found that some of the boys, while they seemed to lack the mental capacity and taste for the pursuit of the higher studies, succeeded well in their industrial pursuits, and these were apprenticed as opportunity offered.

Thus it may be stated, that the Girard College for Orphans, is a home where the pupils are taught and trained, as far as their capacities admit, for their duties and destiny in life. They receive such intellectual edu-ion as they are mentally qualified to acquire and such instruction practical handicraft as is best suited to their usefulness and of benefit themselves. It embraces the home, the college, and the workshop, which these essential qualities, as well as cultivated capacities of nd, morals, and muscles, are developed and educated.

The boys, after entering the college, are, for about two years, when t of school, under the care of five governesses, each one being in arge of a section of about 40 boys. An intelligent supervising gov-1ess also assists in eradicating the evil habits of the boys and in giv-; them religious instruction, moral training, and good manners. Five ?fects, aided by an experienced supervising prefect, have charge of ? larger boys when out of school, and do what they can to guide them ght, as well as to restrain them from wrong-doing. Twelve women d four men give the whole of their time to teaching, three women ve part of their time to instruction in reading and elocution and in e French and Spanish languages, and two men teach vocal and in-rumental music. The band attached to the battalion of College idets is so efficient that their services are frequently sought for out-le, but it is deemed unwise often to grant these requests.

The drill of the College Cadets was found to be so beneficial to the alth and manly bearing of the boys and to the discipline of the insti-tion that a preparatory course of calisthenics has been established. As soon as the question of opening streets through the college-grounds settled, additional buildings will be erected and as large a number of phans admitted as the permanent income of the estate will support, robably 500 additional to the 550 at present in the institution. There re now nearly 100 applicants awaiting admission, and some of them rill be excluded by becoming 10 years old before their names are eached, as in every instance admission is strictly in accordance with he order of application.

The founder of the institution, Stephen Girard, was born in Bordeaux, France, in 1750, and died in 1831, in the city of Philadelphia, where he had lived for more than fifty years. His last will and codicils, dated in 1830-'31, besides other charities, left the $2,000,000 above mentioned for the erection of a college and the necessary out-buildings for the res-idence and accommodation of at least 300 white male orphan-scholars, besides providing for its extension, should that ever be necessary. The corner-stone of the college-building was laid on the 4th of July, 1833, and the main edifice and out-buildings were completed on the 13th of November, 1847, and on the 1st of January, 1848, it was opened with a class of 100 orphans.

THE BURD ORPHAN ASYLUM.

This institution was founded by Mrs. Eliza H. Burd, and is located in Philadelphia. Upon her death, in 1860, she bequeathed funds amount-ng to $400,000 or more, $200,000 of which were expended for the purchase of ground and the erection of buildings, leaving the balance to support the institution. The amount of this balance becoming much larger than was anticipated, the building is to be enlarged so as to accommodate one hundred children instead of fifty, which was the original plan.

The building is constructed of stone, warmed by steam, lighted by gas, and built with all the modern improvements for comfort, health, and recreation. It has a fine library and a chapel, in which services are held every Sunday by a clergyman of the Episcopal Church.

The object of the institution is the care and education of white female orphan-children of legitimate birth, who shall have been baptized in the Protestant-Episcopal Church, to be admitted between the ages of 4 and 8 years, and to remain until they are 18. As far as practicable, they are to be educated as teachers.

THE JEWISH FOSTER HOME SOCIETY, PHILADELPHIA.

This charity was organized nineteen years ago by the ladies of the several Jewish congregations of Philadelphia, for the purpose of providing a home for destitute and unprotected children of Jewish parentage, wherein orphans or the children of indigent Israelites may be rescued from the evils of ignorance and vice, provided for, and instructed in moral and religious duties.

Children are admitted from any part of the country, between 5 and 18 years of age. Only those of the Jewish faith are received. All the children are taught the Hebrew language.

WESTERN PROVIDENT SOCIETY AND CHILDREN'S HOME OF PHILADELPHIA.

This charity is located in Philadelphia. It began its benevolent labors merely as a "soup-house," in the year 1850. Two years later a "home of industry" was added and in another two years it established a "home for destitute children."

This institution is incorporated, and has received appropriations from the State legislature and also from the city of Philadelphia. Sixty children were received during the past year.

ST. JOSEPH'S FEMALE ORPHAN ASYLUM.

This institution is for the accommodation of children of Catholic parents. They are received at quite an early age, and when they are 12 or 14 are placed in Catholic families.

They have a fine brick building erected for the purpose, at a cost of $30,000. A pleasant yard is attached, which is used as a play-ground for the children; their number has exceeded seventeen hundred. Every

partment is clean and shows an air of comfort, while the children seem
right and happy.

The support of the institution is derived almost entirely from private
charity. The city has, however, given $1,000, and the State legislature
5,000, towards its maintenance.

THE ORPHANS' HOME OF THE EVANGELICAL LUTHERAN CHURCH.

This home was established in Pittsburg, Pa., and subsequently removed to Rochester, Beaver County, in the same State, where it was
settled on a farm containing forty-eight acres.

The family-system has been introduced, and the orphan-girls are di-
ided into households, under the care of deaconesses, who devote them-
elves to their care and education. The girls attend to all kinds of
household-duties, under the direction and with the assistance of the
isters. No servants are employed in the institution, and when the
girls are of age they acquire a suitable trade.

The labor of the orphans and the products of the fields and gardens
assist greatly in the support of the institution.

The dwellings consist of four family-houses. The whole property
cost $25,000.

Several of the children are the orphans of soldiers, and, as in other
similar institutions, are supported at the expense of the State.

PROTESTANT ORPHAN ASYLUM OF PITTSBURG AND ALLEGHENY.

This institution was incorporated in 1834. The building is four stories
in height, with spacious halls and stairways, and with sufficient room to
accommodate three hundred children. During the last ten years two
hundred and fifty soldiers' orphans have been cared for and received
their support from the State.

This is a good institution and under excellent management.

HOME FOR DESTITUTE COLORED CHILDREN.

This home is located in West Philadelphia. It was organized and
incorporated April 11, 1856. The lot contains about one acre, upon
which stand the buildings, capable of accommodating about fifty inmates.
Besides this property, the society owns other real estate, the whole
being worth $20,000.

The object of this institution is to afford a home for destitute colored
children of Philadelphia and the neighboring counties until of a suitable age to be indentured. It is supported mainly by voluntary contributions. The contributors are mostly Friends.

The home is under the care of a board of lady managers. It has also
board of trustees composed of sixteen gentlemen, among whom are
some of the most benevolent citizens of Philadelphia. Since its foundation it has received 387 inmates.

THE HOME FOR FRIENDLESS CHILDREN FOR THE BOROUGH OF WILKESBARRE AND COUNTY OF LUZERNE.

This institution has been in existence about twelve years. Its founders, actuated by a spirit of beneficence, began their work of charity and love in a very humble way, and relied upon donations from persons friendly to the object and annual contributions from members of the association. With fostering care it has grown into an institution of no inconsiderable importance, and, in addition to the munificent bounty of individuals, the State has, at different times, made appropriations for the support of the soldiers' orphans placed under its care. It has a large brick building, in one of the best portions of the town, surrounded by fine residences.

The home is well managed, every department being judiciously conducted and liberally sustained by the generous citizens among whom it is located. An effort, which promises success, is being made to raise an "endowment fund" by which the institution shall be sustained.

CHILDREN'S HOME FOR THE BOROUGH AND COUNTY OF YORK.

This home was incorporated in 1865 by the legislature of Pennsylvania. It is located in the borough of York.

The object of this institution is to afford a home for destitute and friendless children, and, when at a suitable age, to place them with respectable families to learn some useful trade or occupation.

The funds for its support are procured by annual contributions from the members of the association and from the State-treasury.

The greater number of the children are soldiers' orphans.

THE ORPHANS' FARM-SCHOOL OF THE EVANGELICAL LUTHERAN CHURCH.

This school was established in Pittsburg and removed to Zelienople, in Butler County, where, on a property containing twenty-five acres of land, substantial buildings were erected, which, six years later, were nearly destroyed by fire. Soon after, the family-system was adopted, and a number of small brick buildings for families were erected, with a large central edifice and school-house, at the cost of $25,000. Additional land has been purchased, and the farm consists now of four hundred acres of wood and arable land. An appropriation from the State-treasury of $6,000 has been made for it.

Only boys are received; they are retained until of sufficient age to learn a trade. They do all manner of work on the farm and in the gardens with their teachers, thus aiding to support themselves while they are acquiring habits of industry and attaining practical knowledge for the future duties of life.

RHODE ISLAND.

PROVIDENCE CHILDREN'S FRIEND SOCIETY, PROVIDENCE.

ts object is to rescue from evil and misery such children as are de-
;ed of the care of their natural protectors. During the thirty-eight
rs of its existence the institution has admitted 987, many of whom
'e indentured to the society and continue under its guardianship
il they arrive at the age of 21 years. Unless in special cases, or
're a child is to be brought up as an adopted child, they are not
;ed out under 12 years of age, and in no case without good refer-
es. No child under 2 years of age is received into the institution.

SOUTH CAROLINA.

CHARLESTON ORPHAN-HOME, CHARLESTON.

'stablished in the year 1792, this is one of the oldest institutions of
kind in this country.
'he administration is wise and successful. Much of the labor of the
titution is done by the children without interfering with their school
studies. They are taught useful occupations here, in order that they
y be fitted to take care of themselves when they go out from the
e and protection of the home hereafter.

TENNESSEE.

THE NASHVILLE PROTESTANT ORPHAN-ASYLUM, NASHVILLE,

is been in successful operation for the last fifteen years; and the
lent desire of the board of managers to establish a home for the
lpless child of want has been happily realized. The erection of a
>arate establishment for boys is now under consideration, and a lot
ground in Watkins's Grove has been donated for that purpose by the
erality of Mr. Watkins.

WISCONSIN.

MILWAUKEE ORPHAN-ASSOCIATION, MILWAUKEE,

charity that has cared for nearly seven hundred homeless and forsaken
ildren, reports : "The Lord has been our Shepherd" and the "Keep-
of our flock," and humbly conscious are we that unless He had kept
e home our labor would have been in vain. Is it not a reproof to our
irs and an encouragement to our faith to remember that for *twenty-
e years* a family of young children, varying in number from twenty to
er sixty, with no endowment-fund, no industry of sufficient magni-
le to be profitable, but trusting only to the "charity that never
leth," has been *maintained without ever suffering a single want or
ling one necessity?* Surely may we exclaim, "I will trust in Thee and
r no evil, for Thou, God, art with me."

NEW YORK.

THE UNION HOME AND SCHOOL.

This institution for the education and maintenance of the children of r volunteers, who may be left unprovided for, is located on the boule- rd between One hundred and fiftieth and One hundred and fifty-first reets, in the city of New York. It was organized in May, 1861. Its ard of officers and managers is composed entirely of ladies, of which rs. U. S. Grant is the honorary president. Ladies also fill the work- g committees. The advisory committee comprises twenty-five gen- men, high in position in military and civil life.

The home is supported by appropriations and contributions and has income of $47,976.38.

In its eleventh annual report it records the past year as being one the most successful in its history.

Since its organization, 3,373 children have been admitted. Of those w in the institution the fathers of 184 were soldiers, 17 were sailors, served in both Army and Navy.

The school is divided into four classes, in which the common English ranches are carefully and thoroughly taught. Much attention is ven to instruction in vocal and instrumental music. They have an rganized band of twenty brass instruments. The progress they ave made is remarkable, and very satisfactory to the managers, and eflects great credit on their instructor.

The value of the real estate and personal property of the Union Home nd School is $215,000.

OHIO.

OHIO SOLDIERS' AND SAILORS' ORPHANS' HOME.

The home is located on an elevated tract of one hundred acres of and, in the suburbs of the town of Xenia, Greene County. The land as donated by the citizens of the town and county. The original orest-trees have been suffered to remain, removing the undergrowth, hus converting it into a woods-pasture, a portion of which is under ultivation.

The Shawnee, a permanent creek, runs near the buildings, from which hey are, by means of a force-pump, supplied with water.

The administrative building is a fine structure, very creditable to the rchitect and constructors. There are twenty cottages, designed to accommodate thirty children each, giving a capacity for six hundred children. The piazzas in front of the cottages add greatly to their beauty and to the comfort of the children.

The children are taught to be industrious and that labor is honorable. The boys assist in the farming and gardening, and whatever is needed to be done by them in the house. The girls are taught to perform domestic duties as far as possible. They make many of their garments, do all of their own mending, under the care and direction of their cottage-managers, besides having the principal care of their cottages. These duties occupy all their leisure time except that needed for necessary recreation. They are in school six hours a day.

From the superintendent's report for 1873 we copy the following:

"Our schools are still under the superintendence of Prof. Edward Merrick, who is, in all respects, thoroughly qualified for his work. He is indefatigable in his labors, and has the hearty co-operation of our excellent corps of teachers. Our schools will compare favorably with the union-schools in our villages.

"Our high school is in charge of Miss Libbie Wharton, a graduate of the Delaware Female College, assisted by Miss Florence Nelson, who is a graduate of the Xenia Female College.

"Miss Phœbe Ensign has charge of the grammar-school. She is a successful teacher, and has been with us ever since the home was established.

"Miss Anna Jones, of Delaware; Miss Frank Summers, of Mansfield; Miss Anna Sanderson, of Xenia; Miss Minnie Hewitt, of Elyria; Miss Carrie Wilson, of Urbana; Miss Mary Briney, of Woodstock; Miss Emma Welch and Miss Ella Cretors, of Xenia, have charge of the other departments. They are all thoroughly qualified, and are deeply interested in their work.

"It is our object to give our children a good business-education and to qualify some of them for teachers. Our course of study ranges from the alphabet to algebra and geometry, including history and physiology. We teach no language but English. Much attention is bestowed upon the moral culture of the children, and this can best be accomplished by the inculcation of the general principles of christianity. No sectarian teaching is allowed.

"Number of children in the home November 1, 1872............... 402
"Number admitted during the last year........................ 177

"Total 579

*　　*　　*　　*　　*　　*　　*

"We have religious services at the home every Sunday morning and Sunday school in the afternoon. The Christian people of Xenia, of the various denominations, still conduct our Sunday-school, and it is a season of great interest to the children. The religious impressions made upon many of their hearts will, I trust, remain with them through life.

7e feel under deep obligations to Mr. J. H. Cooper, the superintendent, nd the teachers, for their long-continued labor of love."

Ohio, distinguished for her benevolent institutions and the ample provision she has made for her unfortunate and dependent classes, has dded to her reputation by her tender care of the orphans of her brave oldiers.

PENNSYLVANIA.

LINCOLN INSTITUTION.

This noble charity is located in Philadelphia. It was organized in 1866, and incorporated the same year. The building is constructed of brick, four stories high, heated by hot-air furnaces, lighted with gas, and has all the conveniences for the use of hot and cold water. It has a parlor, a sitting-room, a reading-room and library, two matron's rooms, two dining-rooms, two school-rooms, a nursery, a sewing-room, ten dormitories completely furnished with single beds, twenty-two small lodging-rooms for the largest boys, each one occupying a room by himself; also a bath-room, wash-room, kitchen, laundry, and rooms for domestics.

This institution receives only boys, and of those admitted the greater number have been soldiers' orphans. They are taken care of during the time they are engaged in acquiring a trade or learning some other occupation, and every boy who graduates at the institution leaves it for a position where he can support himself respectably. During the evening they are engaged in school, and while earning a part of their support by daily work they are acquiring at least the benefit of a common-school-education. The reputation of these boys in the community is such that, oftentimes, the demand for boys for respectable positions is greater than the supply.

The Educational Home for Boys is a branch of this institution, where boys between the ages of 3 and 10 years are received, and remain until they are 12 years of age, when they are transferred to the Lincoln Institution for more advanced instruction and training. Their building will accommodate one hundred and fifty inmates and cost $47,000.

In 1869 the legislature appropriated $10,000 to aid in the erection of the building, and it makes annual appropriations for the support of soldiers' orphans.

MANSFIELD SOLDIERS' ORPHANS' HOME.

The school-room-work of this institution is a deviation from the usual prescribed courses of study. Its success thus far is satisfactory both to teacher and pupil.

The school consists of five grades; these constitute separate and distinct departments and are under the immediate supervision and instruction of one teacher in each. About forty pupils are in each grade, in which three distinct departments of study are daily pursued, viz, language, mathematics, and science. It is believed that the elements of these departments of study may be taught successfully to the youngest child in the school, and a selection from each is made of such branches as seem best to meet the wants of the children and best calculated to develop harmoniously the faculties of body, mind, and heart. Physiology, botany, and local geography in science; the elements of geometry and processes in arithmetic and its tables in mathematics; the constant correction of improprieties in speech, and the no less constant work of teaching how to tell what they know in good English, together with the training of each child to write, so that all his school-requests are in writing—this correlation of accordant branches of instruction is found not only highly useful, but practicable. Teaching, in the main, is given without books. The subject of study, when taken up, is first taken into the mind and heart of the teacher, who seldom fails to give to it a life and freshness that appetizes the class, thus creating a desire for more. After each class-recitation pupils are required to reproduce, in writing, the lesson before the class. It is readily seen that this process secures a closer attention during recitation, greater accuracy in language, and clearness in thinking. It makes teachers more studious in preparation, for without this *daily* exercise the teaching must be a failure. They must of necessity be far more accurate in statement and definition. Such is the plan adopted and the idea entertained in regard to the "new departure," which is under the direction of one of the most experienced teachers in the State.

A new system of labor has also been adopted. One hundred and fifty acres of land have been purchased, to be put under cultivation. Several acres have been assigned to boys desiring it, where each displays his tact and ability in gardening "on his own hook." It is proposed to allow a few of the boys to take a portion of the land to work on shares, thus giving them an opportunity of doing business for themselves, while they can in a measure be guided and directed.

The moral instruction receives daily and hourly attention. Stated times are given for daily devotional exercises, with public services for Sunday and Sunday-school instruction, and it is the constant aim so to blend these with the every-day concerns of life that, when the labors for the children are finished, their development may be symmetrical and in the right direction.

Much credit is due the assistants for their efforts to assist the superintendent. It has imposed upon them labors that the most of teachers know nothing of, labors out of school almost equaling those during the school-session, and they have shown much zeal and earnestness in endeavoring to carry out these new and heretofore untried plans and methods.

M'ALESTERVILLE SOLDIERS' ORPHAN-SCHOOL.

This school is conducted on plans similar to those of the other orphan-schools, and is making good progress in all its departments. An oppor-

unity is given to the girls to become familiar with the various house-
old-duties, and they are taught to operate the sewing-machine, which
hey do very skillfully. The boys are taught shoe- and broom-making
1 addition to the work upon the farm. It has now two hundred and
hirty-four names on its roll of sixteeners, and in each case, as far as is
nown, where an honorable discharge has been given, the recipient is
ollowing some useful avocation, with bright prospects before him.

CASSVILLE SOLDIERS' ORPHAN-SCHOOL.

This institution, supported by an appropriation from the State of
150 per annum for each child, is in most things a success.

Its retired mountain-home, its ornamental grounds, arbors, and groves
re universally admired by visitors and travelers, while the reflex in-
uence upon the children is necessarily most happy.

The sanitary condition of the children is most excellent. This is
ttributed in a large measure to the regularity and substantial character
f the meals, the proper admixture of study, exercise, play, and rest in
he daily routine, and to repeated lectures on the laws of life.

The boys are taught farming and gardening, and are encouraged to
exercise their taste for the beautiful as well as useful.

The girls acquire great proficiency in housework and in sewing, both
vith the needle and the machine.

In the school-room some of the graduates among the soldiers' orphans
lave been employed with very satisfactory results.

The eighth grade of this school received from the State-superintend-
nt, who examined the children, the high encomium of being the best
ighth-grade of any orphan school in the State.

Much credit is due the principal for the great interest he has taken to
lave the whole school introduced to a scientific knowledge of music.
This was an extra expense of several hundred dollars and a free-will
offering of the principal.

Anniversary and reunion.—A prominent landmark in the history of
the school for the year was the "reunion" of the "sixteeners" at the
anniversary on the 6th of November, at which time the school had completed its sixth year under the care of the present administration.
Fifty-six of the one hundred and forty-four sixteeners who had then gone
from these walls returned, no longer children, but well-behaved and
intelligent young ladies and gentlemen. It was a grand social jubilee.
Quite a number of visitors also graced the occasion, while the Broad
Top brass band aided in attracting and entertaining a large crowd.

Rev. J. G. Butler, D. D., chaplain of the House of Representatives,
Washington, D. C., the man who offered the first public prayer with,
preached the first sermon to, and was the first chaplain appointed over, a
regiment of Union soldiers during the war, and who was almost the
only loyal clergyman in Washington at the outbreak of the rebellion,
was present and preached an appropriate sermon to the young, lectured

on life at the national capital, and delivered an appropriate anniversary-address. Suitable addresses were also delivered by Deputy Superintendent Houck and by Mrs. E. E. Hutter, female inspector of our schools, and by several others present. The whole exercises could not fail to have a beneficial and lasting effect upon all present, and especially upon those for whom they were more particularly intended. These sixteeners subsequently, through a committee, presented the principal a suitable expression of their "love and gratitude," in the shape of a handsome gold watch and guard, which will ever be regarded and cherished as a most pleasing memento.

This school has very recently been discontinued.

MERCER SOLDIERS' ORPHAN-HOME.

This school is situated about one-half mile from the old town of Mercer, which, with the immediate neighborhood, furnishes all the supplies of food and clothing, thus making the school a physical advantage to the community in which it is situated.

There are about fifty acres of arable land connected with the school, in the cultivation of which the boys are taught gardening and farming.

Every endeavor has been used to make this a *home* as well as a school for the orphan, and so great has been the success that not only *is* the evidence seen in the smiling and happy faces which greet the visitor, but when they reach the age of 16, the limit of the time for their continuance at the school, many of them are anxious to remain and continue their studies, and arrangements are being made to accommodate them. One marked feature of the graduates is a disposition, on leaving the school, to engage in some useful employment or pursuit, to better prepare themselves for life's duties.

BRIDGEWATER SOLDIERS' ORPHANS' SCHOOL.

The fine building of this institution presents an imposing as well as attractive appearance, located as it is on the Delaware River and surrounded with beautiful scenery. It is surrounded with about fourteen acres of ground, two-thirds of which are under cultivation. The beautiful lawn in front is ornamented with shade-trees; and there are abundant choice bearing grape-vines, with a fine arbor, for the use of the children.

Every incentive to intellectual advancement and every facility for physical development are afforded to make the boys and girls mature into noble men and true model women.

The number of children on the roll has been reduced to 101, showing that the school is rapidly decreasing by discharges on age.

The children have access to five daily papers and thirteen other periodicals, besides a well-selected library of three hundred volumes.

ST. PAUL'S ORPHAN-HOME, BUTLER.

This home stands upon an eminence about half a mile from the town
Butler.

The lot contains 30 acres of land and the house is two stories high.

The institution is supported by the German Reformed Church.

A recent report gives the number of children cared for as 49, of
hom 39 were soldiers' orphans supported at the expense of the State.

PHILLIPSBURG SOLDIERS' ORPHAN-SCHOOL.

In many things this institution might be taken as a model. The
chool follows strictly the studies of the grades ordered by the State for
ts common schools, which is believed to be the best system that can
e devised for the development, the storing, and the strengthening of the
iind, and the best that the orphan-schools can adopt to prepare for
heir work any of the orphans that may desire to teach.

By example and precept much has been accomplished for the religious
raining of the children. When punishment is inflicted, they are made
o feel that God and the State require obedience to the right and good. A
teady effort has been made by them to acquire self-discipline, the im-
ortance of a good character and good principles being constantly
efore their minds; and their good deportment both in private and public
s remarked by all who see them.

The health of those in the institution is remarkable. The attention
ven to the physical culture of the children has produced results the most
vorable, a parallel to which could scarcely be found in any community.
om the report of 1874 we copy the following:

'We receive but very few children in perfect health, and yet have
discharged a single child during the year that was not in perfect
'th and the highest physical vigor. The extraordinary physical vigor
ir children is constantly spoken of by visitors and is exciting wonder
i they are out on public occasions.

'he means of imparting this extraordinary physical vigor are very
e, and tried in over five hundred cases always with the same result,
bsolute cleanliness of the body, pure and abundant *air* and light in
'ing-rooms, nine hours regular sleep so as to give thorough rest to
dent-brain, food suited to repair the wear and build up bone, mus-
ue, nerve, and brain, and moderate and regular physical exercise.
boys' exercise is mostly out of doors, and the girls, mostly in
in the noble and womanly duties of housekeeping in all its
s. The results of the system can thus speak for themselves.
e not had a child in the hospital for twenty-seven months."

ir industrial work both boys and girls receive systematic instruc-
he various duties of the house, and, for their years, are well
i all the departments of work required, particular attention
en to cooking, sewing, and gardening.

TITUSVILLE SOLDIERS' ORPHAN-SCHOOL.

The instruction afforded in this school has been of a superior character from its very commencement, as its recorded lists of experienced and well-qualified teachers for the whole time show. Rapid improvement has been made by the pupils, and quite a number have advanced beyond the grade taught in the orphan-schools, requiring extra instruction at an additional expense. Their attainments were quite as high as are usually required of graduates in our best high schools.

The buildings, although unfinished, are extensive in their plans and are believed to be nearly perfect in design.

The citizens of the vicinity have contributed to aid in the erection of the buildings, and donated generously to supply an immediate necessity occasioned by a recent fire, which consumed the bakery, kitchen, pantries, and dining-room, with all their contents, including groceries and provisions.

NORTHERN HOME FOR FRIENDLESS CHILDREN AND SOLDIERS' ORPHAN-INSTITUTE.

This institution was incorporated in 1854, having been organized the year previous, the object being the care and education of all white children under 12 years of age who should be voluntarily surrendered by their fathers or guardians, and to apprentice them to useful trades, the boys until 21 and the girls until 18 years of age, or to return them to their parents at the discretion of the managers. Another object was that commitments might be made to it by any judge of the supreme court of Pennsylvania, or of the district court and court of common pleas, or by the mayor of Philadelphia, of children needing special moral care. By a subsequent act, this power was extended to the presiding judges of the courts of common pleas in the other counties of the Commonwealth; and, further, it was made the duty of the judges of the common-pleas- and district-courts of Philadelphia and of the recorder of the city to visit alternately the institution at least once in two weeks, to examine into all the commitments, and to discharge such children as have not been properly committed.

The estimated value of real estate and personal property of the institution is $126,000, mostly the result of private efforts and enterprise, only $5,000 having been appropriated by the State for the purpose. For several years annual appropriations to aid in carrying on the work were made by the legislature of the State.

Children are received from all parts of the State, and are well instructed in the branches of a good elementary education.

The institution is conducted on the most liberal principles consistent with economy.

Food, clothing, recreations, and amusements are abundantly provided, and perhaps no other institution is so profuse in its provisions of

422

a domestic and social character for its beneficiaries as the Northern Home for Friendless Children.

At the breaking out of the great rebellion, the Northern Home was the first institution in the United States to open its doors for the children of the brave men who had gone out in defense of the Union, even before any of the fathers had fallen in the struggle. Here these children were kept free of expense, with the understanding that if the fathers fell in battle their orphans would be permanently cared for; but, if they were so fortunate as to return, the children should be restored to them.

After the war had assumed colossal proportions and many children had been reduced to orphanage, the Northern Home was the first to provide a home especially for them upon its own ground.

This Home for the Orphans of the Army and Navy, now called The Soldiers' Orphans' Institute, the first in the country, was formally dedicated and opened in the summer of 1862, the dedicatory services being performed by the late lamented Rev. Dr. Hutter and Rev. Dr. Brainard.

The buildings were both afterward much enlarged, and again rededicated to the good cause of caring for the orphans and friendless. A new and elegant chapel is the latest improvement, and of recent erection.

The Northern Home has thus constantly been spreading itself in good works.

The beautiful park, attached to the "Home" and "Institute" on the eastern side, serves as a play-ground for the large and happy family of children gathered here.

The average number in all the buildings is usually nearly 400. An infirmary is owned across Brown street, and entirely separate from all the other buildings, but the children enjoy such excellent health that an infirmary for the sick is scarcely needed.

During the twenty-one years of the existence of this institution, it has received, cared for, and indentured, or otherwise disposed of, nearly three thousand five hundred children. The average number of inmates during the year was 255. On May 1, 1874, the number of soldiers' orphans in the institution was 240 and of friendless children 113.

The Soldiers' and Sailors' Institute was the outgrowth of a spontaneous and unrewarded charity towards these wards of the nation, exercised long and liberally in their behalf, before any systematic provision was intended by the State or any re-imbursement expected for their maintenance and education. Not only orphans, but children impoverished by the absence of their fathers, were also received, fed, clothed, and educated, to be returned to their homes or adopted and permanently cared for as circumstances required. Several hundred of such children were thus maintained, for whose support no public recompense was ever received.

The locality and the resources of the Northern Home being better adapted to general service than any like institution of the State, it has been continuously recognized by the legislature by yearly grants to aid in its benevolent operations. These appropriations are, however, now discontinued.

UNIONTOWN SOLDIERS' ORPHAN-HOME.

On account of the unusually large number of *young* pupils in this school, but little show can be made of advanced scholarship. Four who left this year have entered the State Normal School.

The boys during their detail hours work in the shoe-shop, stocking-factory, broom-factory, caning-department, and at gardening and farming.

The close of the last year marked the commencement of the numerical decline of the school, the number at that date being fifteen less than at the same time the previous year. The coming year will show a much greater decrease, showing that the work so happily conceived, so munificently carried forward, and already bringing forth such blessed results, will soon be finished.

CHESTER SPRINGS SOLDIERS' ORPHAN-SCHOOL AND LITERARY INSTITUTE.

This is an institution founded by the State and supported by appropriations made by the legislature. Only children of soldiers and sailors are received.

The superintendent and assistants have been very very successful in the moral and religious training of those committed to their care.

Much interest is felt in their Sunday-school and Friday-evening prayer-meeting, and all are expected to be present at the regular morning and evening-devotions, and are most respectful and reverent during these exercises.

The children have all taken the pledge of total abstinence from all intoxicating liquors, and many of the older ones belong to a lodge of Good Templers.

Much attention has been given to instruction in instrumental music. A brass band of thirteen pieces, played by boys under 16 years of age, has received the highest praise for excellent music.

The library of 1,200 volumes, with daily and weekly secular, religious, and illustrated papers and magazines to the number of 50 or more, for the use of the children, is to them a great source of enjoyment.

The system of two hours' labor adopted at the opening of the school has been continued, the boys assisting in the farm and garden, while the girls become quite proficient in the various household requirements.

DAYTON SOLDIERS' ORPHANS' SCHOOL.

The buildings occupied by this school are situated on a slight elevation adjoining the thriving village of Dayton, Armstrong County, and

:ommanding a good view of the surrounding country, which is perhaps unsurpassed in the beauty and healthfulness of its location. The farm ontains thirty-three acres, twenty-three being cultivated, while the remainder, including a very beautiful grove of about five acres, is used or a play-ground.

Over four hundred children have been received into this school. Their ducational progress has been good, and the children of the orphanhools are, on an average, further advanced than children of most other hools.

HARFORD SOLDIERS' ORPHANS' SCHOOL, SUSQUEHANNA COUNTY.

In this school promotions from grade to grade are made quarterly by 1e principal, after a thorough examination of all the classes. Great redit is due to the teachers employed for their faithfulness and general fficiency. Much attention is given to the moral and religious education f the pupils. The sanitary condition is all that could be desired. The ndustrial department is said to be admirably conducted, none working n excess of two hours daily, and the duties of each pupil are varied by , weekly change of the details.

SOLDIERS' ORPHAN-SCHOOL AT ANDERSONBURG.

This school was opened October 16, 1866, and from its commencement 1p to the present time, 174 pupils have been admitted, and 112 still renain on the roll. The last report says:

"Our aim has been thoroughness first, then progress. We believe re have accomplished much in both. We strive to procure the best eachers, tried and proved by long experience in the art and science of mparting instruction and governing youth.

"Our teaching has been attended with great success, as is manifest from he improvement of our children in mind, morals, manners, deportment, nd the ease with which they acquit themselves on examination. Our nstructors being in earnest, with their hearts in the work, impart knowldge with freshness and interest, striving to adapt their teachings to he several capacities of their pupils.

"Self-government has been our aim, and we strive to have all govern hemselves. Holding up to our children that honesty, truth, and honor re noble traits of character, we give them every opportunity in our ower to practice them. By vote they elect their officers, and as nearly s possible control themselves at their work, in their amusements, and 1 the school-room, receiving help only when required. Moral suasion 3 our basis, and we depart from it to use force only when absolutely ecessary, and then enough only to effect the proper purpose. Prompt nd willing obedience to all proper authority is seldom refused. Out of chool-hours the details attend to their work, and the remainder pass heir time at croquet, lee-circle, bat and ball, rope and hoop, and many ther amusements, either arranged for them or invented by themselves for the occasion. Frequently the teachers take the boys to Sherman's Creek, one mile distant, to bathe, and the girls to a wood near the school buildings, where they pass an afternoon at romp and frolic.

"Much care is exercised by all interested to lead the children in the right way, and as a result they are courteous, gentle, and civil, there seldom occurring a wide departure from the path of rectitude. The boys and girls have ample opportunity to become acquainted with each other, and thus the reflex influence has a great tendency to cause them to be polite and agreeable among themselves and to all with whom they come in contact."

A large library is connected with the Sunday-school of the institution, and also a large number of Sunday-school papers are received, besides church-papers and other periodicals sent to the school by friends of the soldier's orphan.

WHITE HALL SOLDIERS' ORPHAN-HOME, MONTOUR COUNTY.

This school has an able and efficient corps of teachers, and steadily and perseveringly the great elementary principles of education have been implanted in the minds of the pupils and cultivated with the most satisfactory results.

A marked religious and moral impression animates many of the children, showing that the seed sown has taken deep root and promises to be lasting.

The boys are drilled in Upton's Military Tactics. In this and all the other orphan-schools a uniform dress is worn by both the boys and girls.

The numbers desiring admission into State normal schools at the age of 16 is largely increasing, and it is to be regretted that but few are permitted to enter, on account of the insufficient sum appropriated for that purpose. The majority of those pupils receiving the one year term at State normal schools have fulfilled their promise, and are now teaching successfully.

The library consists of 350 volumes of standard works, selected especially for the young. Over thirty daily, weekly, and monthly periodicals come to the school and are read by the pupils.

INFANT-ASYLUMS.

DISTRICT OF COLUMBIA.

ST. ANN'S INFANT-ASYLUM, WASHINGTON,

an Catholic,) receives children from birth to 5 years of age; sup-
l by charity; 70 inmates, apparently well cared for.

ILLINOIS.

THE CHICAGO FOUNDLINGS' HOME, CHICAGO,

opened in January, 1871. The object of this home is mainly to
at the crime of infanticide and save the lives of the children to
ate and to the world. As regards admission to the home, no
ications are necessary, no questions are asked; babies who are
to the basket are taken care of, whether white or black, sick or
Most of the babies, no doubt, are born out of wedlock, but many
m are not; the desertion of the father, the death of the mother,
avy hand of poverty, make it necessary to seek other protectors
ne of these little ones. But be the case as it may, all who come
elcomed and tenderly cared for.
worthy founder began this as a work of faith, given him to do by
essed Master. No funds are solicited and no assistance asked,
; of Him whose work it is.
one is appealed to for help except by prayer. As to the workings
s plan, Mr. Shipman says:
it be asked how this plan has succeeded, the reply is, in the main,
The home has had to contend with many hinderances, not the least
ich has been my own faltering and imperfect faith, so that it is at
t laboring under some embarrassments, which God, who knows
st time and the best manner, will surely remove when He sees
at the same time, those familiar with charitable institutions unite
ing that the progress of the home has been unprecedented.
to the charges made here and there, that I have departed from the
at first marked out, and have solicited, directly or indirectly, I
ily say that they are entirely untrue. I have never asked any one
anything for the home but pray for it. The efforts which have
made, in the shape of fairs, festivals, or entertainments, have most
n been made without my knowledge; some of them against my

431

earnest protestations—none of them at my suggestion. From this policy I do not propose to depart. How the friends of the home shall engage others to aid in its support, it is not for me to say, but the home will solicit no one."

Between five and six hundred infants have been brought to the home, and in various ways and from very unlooked-for sources have come the means for their support.

The last legislature of the State passed a law which gives the home a legal claim to all the children left at its door. The home succeeds to all the legal rights of the parents. At the same time it often happens, in course of a few days, that the mother finds she must have her baby at any rate, or the father returns, or a new ray of light comes from somewhere. In such cases—unless there is some good reason to the contrary—the baby is restored to its natural guardians.

MICHIGAN.

HOUSE OF PROVIDENCE, DETROIT,

(Roman Catholic,) receives children under 5 years of age; is supported by contributions; had, in 1874, about 45 inmates.

NEW YORK.

THE FOUNDLING-ASYLUM OF THE CITY OF NEW YORK.

This is in charge of the Sisters of Charity. It was incorporated in 1869. Mothers and children are received, and an effort is made to reform the erring and unfortunate, who are allowed to remain as nurses for their own and others' children. Other women, not of this class, are employed as nurses, and, in addition, many children are placed outside in poor families to be nursed, the wet-nurse receiving $10 a month for this service. In such cases the child must be brought once a month to the asylum, and, if it is not in good condition, the nurse is not allowed to take it again.

This institution receives all infants who are brought and placed in its cradle. More than a thousand are received every year.

"Children 2 or 3 years old in the asylum, under our direct supervision, are found to thrive much better than those outside; and this happens even without the advantage, which many of the latter enjoy, of country air, and in spite of our arrangement, which would seem to preclude inattention, by which each child is brought to the asylum every month for inspection. We do not mean to intimate, however, that excellent nurses are not found among the poorer classes of our city; yet the comparison which our experience affords between outside nursing and that within the asylum warrants the belief that, could we retain in the institution a larger number of the children who have attained their *second* year and keep at nurse only the younger ones, our mortuary

rould be very much diminished. Many reasons may be advanced
pport of this belief. Of them the first, and perhaps the strongest,
at in the asylum the physician is always near at hand, and proper
ment can be immediately obtained for cases of infantile diseases so
ilent, especially during the summer months, in this climate."

NEW YORK INFANT-ASYLUM.

is institution takes charge of foundlings and other infant children
r 2 years of age, and also provides lying-in wards and such
ods of care and guidance as are esteemed useful to prevent the
rnal abandonment of infants and to diminish the moral dangers
personal sufferings to which homeless mothers are exposed.
hen children in the charge of this asylum have attained a suitable
they are placed in families for adoption, or settled at suitable em-
nents, or bound out, or indentured as clerks, apprentices, servants,
until the respective ages of 18 for girls and 21 for boys.
e distinctive feature of this institution is that it aims equally to
the mother and her infant, the mother being retained, as far as
ble, to nourish and care for her child. Experience thus far appears
ufirm the correctness of this policy.

NURSERY AND CHILD'S HOSPITAL, NEW YORK CITY.

e society in charge of this institution consists of persons of all de-
nations, and the objects of its benevolence may be of any creed or
. Its purpose is the maintenance and care of the children of wet-
es, the care of lying-in women and their children, and the support
naintenance of destitute children intrusted to their care. During
rear 1874 the institution had 1,080 inmates—479 women and 601
ren. All who enter as charity-patients are obliged to remain three
hs and give their services without wages in whatever work may
signed them by the matron. Children may remain here until they
years of age. The board charged for infants, $10; for children
can walk, $7; and for hospital or sick children, $9 per month.
ules of the institution, originally strict in excluding all illegitimate
ren, have been modified to some extent; but no woman who has
twice is received, so that no encouragement is given to sin.
stop the exposure of foundlings and to prevent additional crime,
ursery opened a refuge for those about to become mothers, and in
way inculcates the duty of the mother to remain with her child.
man can show penitence for her sin by careful attention to her
rnal duties; and many a woman is reclaimed and led to a virtuous
; the tender love she bears her infant.
ring the winter of 1874 several cases presented themselves of
en in need of the care of the institution in consequence of loss of
oyment or desertion by their husbands; also widows with their

children have been cared for—sometimes whole families have been take
in, for in the city-nursery and country-branch there seems always roo
for more; if there be a spare corner, a spare bed, no one is turned awa;
but sheltered, warmed, clothed, and fed.

THE NURSERY FOR THE CHILDREN OF POOR WOMEN

Was founded by Mrs. Cornelius DuBois, in February, 1854, and cha
tered on the 19th of April, 1854, $10,000 being subscribed by her friend
A child's hospital was added, and on the 22d of June, 1857, the corne
stone was laid in Fifty-first street, and the name changed to Nurser
and Child's Hospital. It was inaugurated May 22, 1858; cost, $25,00(
State-aid to the amount of $10,000 was furnished. A foundling-ho
pital, after the English plan, was established separately by Mrs. C. D
Bois in 1858. It was called the Infants' Home, aided by the common cou
cil of New York, which made a donation of lots of ground at the corne
of Lexington avenue and Fifty-first street and gave $35,000. During th
war, this building was used as a soldiers' hospital; at the close of the wa
it was restored to its original purpose, and the managers of the Nurser
and Child's Hospital were authorized to join the two institutions. A
center building joining the two others was then added in 1869, costin;
$31,500. The whole takes the name of Nursery and Child's Hospital
An act passed by the legislature in 1871 gave $25,000 for the purchas
of a country hospital, amended in 1872 by adding $17,500 additional
This branch is now becoming larger than the city-institution. Th
whole number under care is 725. On Staten Island there is a mai
building and 12 cottages. After the children attain the age of 4 year
they are boarded out in private families, a plan found eminently su
cessful in the moral and mental welfare of the children.

The statistics of infant-mortality show a wonderful decrease sin ·
this nursery was established. It compares favorably with that of a **c**
institution in the world.

ST. MARY'S HOSPITAL FOR CHILDREN, 105 DUANE STREET, NEW YORK CITY.

Children between the ages of 2 and 14 years, suffering from acute or
curable chronic diseases, are admitted free. Nearly four-score children
received gratuitous medical attention and care during 1874, and, had the
accommodations been more ample, many more little sufferers would have
been treated.

PENNSYLVANIA.

ST. VINCENT'S HOME, PHILADELPHIA,

(Roman Catholic,) supported by contribution, has 307 inmates. Children well clothed and apparently well cared for.

THE CHILDREN'S HOSPITAL OF PHILADELPHIA

Admits children between 2 and 12 years of age, and also prescribes for other children outside. It is supported by voluntary contributions, donations, &c., and also by payments for board and treatment from those parents or guardians of patients who may be able to afford it.

RHODE ISLAND.

THE PROVIDENCE NURSERY, PROVIDENCE,

Was founded for the purpose of giving a shelter to the infant children of the poor. During the two years of its existence, 128 little ones have been kept from suffering and death, have been clothed and fed and cared for, till adopted by other homes and friends. Where parents or friends can pay for the board of a child, it is required of them to do so. Many a father has found here a comfortable home for his motherless child, and the burdens of a widowed mother have often been relieved by the temporary care of her little one, enabling her the better to provide for herself and older children.

In case of sickness, the children are furnished with physician and medicines without expense to their parents.

7 E

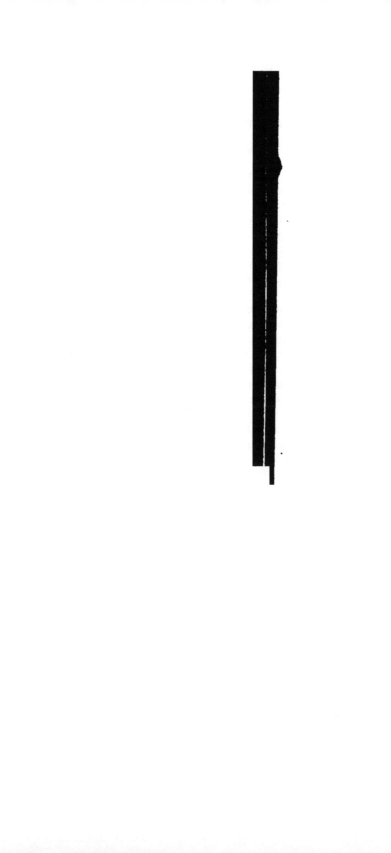

MISCELLANEOUS CHARITIES.

CONNECTICUT.

UNION FOR HOME WORK, HARTFORD.

This benevolent and missionary society, started in 1871 by a few ladies connected with all the Protestant churches, has for its object "the relief of all kinds of suffering, and the physical, intellectual, and spiritual elevation of the women and children of the city." The means used to accomplish these ends are personal visitation; the maintaining of a home or temporary lodging-house; a coffee-house or cheap restaurant; a day-nursery, where working-women leave their young children for the day; a clothing-club, which prepares, for the destitute, garments that are given, or sold at the cost price of the material, according to the circumstances of the persons needing them; a reading-room for girls and one for boys; a sewing-school for girls, and a weekly mothers' meeting for the mothers of the children in the sewing-school, where instruction in sewing and fitting is given them, with a plain, social tea. Tea-parties are also provided for the children, where, with comfortable food attractively set out, china tea-service, and table crowned with flowers, games played and stories told, every effort is made to promote, with the social enjoyment, a love of refinement and goodness.

The day-nursery has been well patronized, and has proved a great blessing, although some women who require its aid live too far away to avail themselves of it. It seems to be the most expensive branch of work, but the matron and her assistants, whose salaries are included in its cost, take care of the home generally, with its lodging-rooms and baths, and do the washing for all. It costs about fifty cents a day to take care of and feed each child, but this amount seems a trifle when we think of the helpless infants saved from neglect, suffering, and danger, while the mother is encouraged in industry, and can go to her work with a light heart, knowing that her little one is enjoying pure air, good food, and patient care.

HOME FOR THE FRIENDLESS, NEW HAVEN.

This institution provides a temporary home for friendless, vagrant girls, and gives them employment and instruction, with the ultimate design of providing for them a more permanent situation or of fitting them to maintain themselves.

The home usually also contains a large number of girls and women who have become friendless and homeless by the force of circumstances beyond their own control, as well as those who have become so on account of their own lack of virtue. To both classes the doors have ever been open, and all have been provided for and helped, according to the exigencies of each individual case.

Many are women with infants, who have left the hospital before they were strong enough to work, and have no other shelter. Some of these have become homeless through the death or desertion of their husbands, and some have none. All are cared for until strong enough to work, and situations are found where an honest living may be earned.

ILLINOIS.

HOME FOR THE FRIENDLESS, CHICAGO.

The Home for the Friendless is an incorporated institution, under the control of a board of lady managers, selected from the various Protestant churches of the city, and is largely supported by voluntary contributions.

The discipline of the institution is strictly parental in its character. Unquestioning obedience is required of the children, and the order and decorum of a well-regulated Christian family are carefully observed.

None are admitted as inmates to the home who will not conform to all the regulations of the house, or who are not hopeful subjects of mental and moral improvement, or who are not desirous of availing themselves of the first good opportunity of securing permanent homes or places of service, except aged or infirm persons, and these at the discretion of the reception-committee.

The object of the institution is the relieving, aiding, and providing homes for friendless and indigent women and children. The kind of persons contemplated are the worthy poor and strangers. Here they find a temporary resting and abiding place until homes are provided for them elsewhere. The large numbers of girls and women who come to the city every year to find employment and search for friends often need counsel and direction to aid them on their way. They come from all parts of the country, and no one is asked, as a condition, *where she* comes from. The home has been a blessing to thousands and has saved many who have been at the very point of desperation. Good food, kind words, and a desirable shelter and bed rarely ever fail to cheer a sorrowing, disappointed heart and change despondent feelings into brighter and more hopeful ones.

The ages of the children who are taken at the home are: girls, from the infant up to the age of 14; boys, from infancy to 12 years of age. It takes the orphan, as well as those who have living parents, and does all it can to assist parents to keep their children. But,

hen necessity compels a mother to give up her children, the home be-
mes the guardian, and indentures these homeless wanderers into good
milies, where they receive an education, are loved by foster-parents,
d become, to a large extent, useful members of society. While in the
me, they have the benefit of a school taught in the building, where
ey receive the elements of an education, and also the principles of
ligion, with thorough Bible-instruction each day.

Two industrial schools belonging to the home are under the direct
ntrol of the lady managers.

The Home for the Friendless co-operates with every charitable institu-
on in Chicago. Many times boys beyond the age of admission find
heir way to the home, or are sent by citizens too late at night to
e sent to the Newsboys' Home, or to places for work. They receive
ood, shelter, and frequently a bath and suit of clothes. Old ladies
ind the home a convenient place to remain while arrangements are
eing made that will enable them to have a permanent place in the Old
'eoples' Home.

Many of the patients from all the charity-hospitals in Chicago are re-
eived at the home to convalesce, after being discharged by their physi-
ians.

Children are frequently kept for a time to enable mothers to get
nough in advance to place them in the Half-Orphan Asylum, an insti-
ution that makes a specialty of boarding at very low rates, to enable
oor people to keep their children. Many other institutions might be
amed, but suffice it to say, that all respectable friendless women and
hildren are received at the home, without regard to creed, color, or
lationality.

The home depends upon voluntary contributions for support. During
he year 1874 it has been enabled to shelter and care for a total of 2,244
ersons, a much larger number than ever before in one year. All need-
ng assistance are welcomed on the broad basis of simply their need,
rithout regard to religion, nationality, or color.

The Home Visitor, a little sheet issued by the Home, presents
he claims of the homeless poor of this great metropolis of the West.
welve times a year it calls upon the friends, bearing its letters for the
lders and stories for the children, giving in a pleasant way all the
ews of the month concerning the inside workings of the home and
oing faithful missionary work wherever it goes.

The price is but fifty cents a year, though few people read it who do
ot give double the amount to the home, either in money or donations
ı kind. And many, who would brook no appeal from an individual,
ill listen, think, and *give* to the little pleader.

The school belonging to the home is a graded one, numbering 266
upils, 40 of whom are also taught in the industrial department. Two
f these have fitted themselves for admission to the normal school and
thers have prepared themselves to enter the high school.

MARYLAND.

THE HENRY WATSON CHILDREN'S AID SOCIETY, NOS. 70 AND 72 CALVERT STREET, BALTIMORE,

Embraces in its home four separate and distinct departments, viz, the girls' home, in which girls of good character are received and boarded at a low rate, taught useful occupations, and assisted in securing good trades and paying occupations; the children's home, in which destitute children of both sexes are received and provided with carefully-selected homes in the country, under the protection of said society, until they attain the age of 18 years, (this "home" is also a temporary asylum for all homeless or destitute children;) the sewing-machine-school, under the management of superior teachers, in which young girls receive free and thorough instruction upon all of the principal sewing-machines now in use; and the school for instruction in cutting and fitting, in which young girls are thoroughly instructed by competent teachers in the most approved systems of dress-making, also in seamstress-work, free of charge.

HOME OF THE FRIENDLESS, BALTIMORE.

For eighteen years this charity has prosecuted its benevolent and successful labors. Its work steadily increases, and a large average of muscle, brain, and soul is trained and molded, and returned to the community in a few years in the form of educated labor. Its annual average of inmates exceeds one hundred, of whom 75 per cent. are under 9 years of age.

The institution is thoroughly catholic in the dispensation of its charities, and is equally so in its administration. Its benefactions are without partiality, without test or qualification, asking of its applicants only the question, "Is it a friendless child?"

The number returned to parents and friends is large; but the temporary assistance rendered to the poor in emergencies of sickness, accident, and loss of employment is one of the noblest missions of the institution.

The annual expenditure is about $7,000. Much is received in the way of donation which cannot be included in this sum, although it does a great deal for the comfort and maintenance of the inmates.

MASSACHUSETTS.

THE HOME FOR FRIENDLESS WOMEN AND CHILDREN, SPRINGFIELD,

Provides "a temporary home for friendless and destitute women and children, and gives them employment and instruction, with the ultimate design of providing for them a more permanent situation or of fitting them to maintain themselves."

Two separate homes are sustained : one for women, the other for children. The charity was founded in 1865, as a home for women; the branch for children grew out of it in 1871.

The class cared for in the women's home embraces many whose need for the aid has been brought on themselves by their own folly and sin, as well as others whose condition is the result simply of misfortune and poverty. But whether the need of the applicant has arisen from her own fault or that of others, the great effort is to do her good ; to create the desire to follow an honest path in life, if it does not already exist; to point out clearly the way, and make it practicable for the woman to follow it by removing otherwise insurmountable obstacles.

The children, comprising about nine-tenths of the inmates of the institution, are taught in a school-room at the home under the management of the public schools. Sewing and simple housework are also taught ; and the children, as opportunity offers, are placed in families where they will be well cared for or perhaps reclaimed by parents whose circumstances have improved.

MICHIGAN.

DETROIT INDUSTRIAL SCHOOL.

This is a day-school for poor children, where, in addition to the regular common-school-studies, sewing and housework are taught the girls. The boys who are large enough split and pile wood, and all are supplied with clothing and a warm dinner. The school is sustained by donations and interest on a permanent fund of $4,075.

THE MICHIGAN STATE PUBLIC SCHOOL AT COLDWATER

Is intended to operate as a preventive of crimes by repressing a criminal growth; that is, the children over 4 and under 16 years of age who are in suitable condition of body and mind to receive instruction, who are neglected and dependent—especially those who would otherwise be maintained in the county-poor-houses, those who have been abandoned by their parents, or are orphans, or whose parents have been convicted of crime— are received into this school, where they are trained for and afterward introduced into good society, or, at least, into society at a better point than would otherwise be possible.

The location at Coldwater brings the school under the scrutiny of a most refined and cultivated public sentiment, a spirit and influence which, preceding the administration in all its departments, is of greatest value to the work in hand. The buildings are unusually attractive, both in the outward appearance and in the internal arrangements and appointments. They are constructed for a mixed system, embracing the main features of the congregate and family-plans, as they are separately applied in other establishments. The central building is for offices and

officers' residence; the wings on either side are respectively for schoo
purposes and for employment, while the rear-wing is for domestic pu
poses. The children dine, work, and school upon the congregate pla
The ten cottages (only seven of which are yet erected) in the rear c
this group of main buildings are of capacity for thirty pupils each an
are under the care of suitable ladies, termed "sister" or "mother."
These cottages are supplied with carpets, with inside blinds, with open
grates for fires, with pictures, birds, flowers, &c., and usually with an
organ or piano; also books, papers, pictorials, games, &c., realizing as
near as may be for the children the true ideal of home.

The congregate school-room is also furnished with a piano, decora-
tions, and other attractions, making it a bright and cheerful place, while
the grounds are ample for out-door sports. The usual impression made
upon visitors is one of pleasant surprise that such provision is made for
such children.

Of the corps of employés it is sufficient to say that it is of the highest
order of qualifications, and that the whole administration is characterized by a regulated sentiment of true christian benevolence.

The system of management adopted differs from others in that it attempts to do more for the children than has been hitherto attempted, as
their superior facilities enable them to do, and in the attempt to adapt
their efforts to the peculiarity of each individual child; that is, the system involves the study of each child, to ascertain inherited defects and
tendencies, as well as the present conditions arising from the circumstances of life thus far. It involves, too, the systematic adjustment of
diet, discipline, employment, and education, to build the best brain possible out of the materials as they come to hand. The difficulty of reaching
this high ideal of treatment seems to be realized, but there is also great
faith that the best results are to come from such a system faithfully followed. Nothing specially novel would be noted in the daily routine as it
could be written out, it being distinguished more for its better spirit and
tone than for its details.

This institution supplies for Michigan an important link in the chain of
preventives between the compulsory-education act as it relates to common schools and the reform-school for juvenile delinquents. Children
falling out of the common-school-system, and for any reason becoming
dependent upon the public charities, are here provided for in a way to
accomplish the most possible for them.

The cost of the establishment as at present perfected is about $75,000,
and will not exceed $100,000 when entirely furnished with the full num
ber of cottages. This is exclusive of the site, which was donated by the
citizens of Coldwater. The institution is administered by three commissioners, who are appointed by the governor, and by a superintendent
and officers appointed by the commissioners.

MISSOURI.

THE HOME OF THE FRIENDLESS, OR OLD LADIES' HOME, ST. LOUIS,

ince 1853, the date of its foundation, has given to about five hundred ged and lone women the comforts of a home, the majority being over 0 years of age, and others past their four-score, and even four-score ind ten.

The original appropriation by the city and county of St. Louis for the purchase of grounds and buildings was $50,000.

The support is partly by endowment and partly by annual contribu- . tions, with an income of about $8,000.

NEW YORK.

BROOKLYN INDUSTRIAL SCHOOL NO. 1, CONCORD STREET, BROOKLYN,

Admits boys of 10 and girls of 14 years. Sewing, reading, writing, and arithmetic are taught. Supported by contributions.

CHURCH CHARITY FOUNDATION, BROOKLYN.

The three institutions known as (1) The Orphans' House, (2) The Home for the Aged, and (3) St. John's Hospital belong to a corporation by the name of The Church Charity Foundation of Long Island, which is under the exclusive control of the Protestant-Episcopal Church of the diocese of Long Island, whose territorial limits are conterminous with that portion of the State of New York known as Long Island, and consisting of the counties of Kings, Queens, and Suffolk.

The charter of this Church Charity Foundation was granted by the legislature of New York A. D. 1848, with amendments thereto A. D. 1852.

The corporators of the Church Charity Foundation are twenty-five clergymen of the Protestant-Episcopal Church of the diocese of Long Island, who are rectors or assistant ministers of parishes in the diocese, and also twenty-five laymen, who are communicants of the Protestant-Episcopal Church, and resident in the diocese. The bishop of the diocese, (now the Rt. Rev. A. N. Littlejohn, D. D.,) is *ex officio* a member of the said corporation and president of the board of managers.

The objects of said corporation are as follows, quoted from Section 5 of the charter: "To establish and maintain one or more houses for such indigent aged persons, and indigent orphan or half-orphan children, and other children left in a destitute and unprotected state and condition, as it may receive and have under its care, and to educate such children; and to establish and maintain one or more hospitals, dispensaries, or other institutions for the shelter, support, and relief of such sick, or infirm, or indigent persons as it may receive under its care or otherwise minister to; and to establish and maintain such other institutions for charitable or reformatory purposes as may be determined upon by the board of managers."

Besides the managers, the Church Charity Foundation has also th customary officers, viz, president, vice-president, secretary, and treasurer, whose varied duties are defined by by-laws. There are also standing committees on homes of the aged and orphans, on the hospital and dispensary, and of ways and means, whose duties are also defined by by-laws. The board of managers elect, annually, fifty or more ladies, communicants, whose duties are to solicit contributions of money and materials for the Church Charity Foundation, and to aid, through their executive committees, in the domestic management of the institutions of the Church Charity Foundation.

There is a resident chaplain, under whose supervision are the services and religious ministrations of the institutions.

The domestic management of the Church Charity Foundation is committed to a deaconess-in-chief, who is assisted by five other deaconesses.

In the orphans' house is a school, supervised by two deaconesses, in which all the branches of an ordinary English education are taught, with special attention to vocal music. Also in the same building are a printing-office and stereotype-foundery, in which are engaged, under the superintendence of a competent gentleman, such of the children, male and female, as show an aptitude for that branch of handicraft. The work consists of job-work, books, and pamphlets, and the issuing of a monthly paper called The Helping Hand.

Beneficiaries are admitted to the Home for the Aged and the Home of the Orphans by the proper executive committee of the board of associates, with the approval of the committee on homes of the board of managers. Certain printed rules and regulations govern their action as to the admission of beneficiaries, &c.

The buildings are three, and mentioned in the order of their erection, all ample and well planned for the purposes to which they are devoted, viz: House of the Orphans, Home for the Aged, and St. John's Hospital, all erected on the same plot of ground. On Sundays and other days, their inmates assemble for divine worship in a beautiful chapel, which is in the House of the Orphans. The plot of ground is situated in the eastern part of the city of Brooklyn, and is bounded by Albany avenue on the west, Herkimer street on the north, Troy avenue on the east, and Atlantic avenue on the south.

Beneficiaries are admitted to the Home for the Aged if *communicants* and *over* 60 *years of age*, and to the House of the Orphans when *over* 4 and *under* 10 *years of age*. The boys may be retained until they are 12, and the girls until they are 14, years of age. The boys are bound out to mechanics, farmers, or merchants, or to those engaged in some

ıer respectable business, according to their own choice, with the
probation of the executive committee of the House of the Orphans.
e girls are bound out to respectable families only, and where there
ᵌ no apprentices, and both sexes are bound out only until they attain
ᵌ age of 18 years.

E HOME OF THE ORPHANS OF THE CHURCH CHARITY FOUNDATION

as organized in 1851 in the city of Brooklyn, and receives its support
ım the Episcopal Church of the diocese.
Large sums of money have been expended in the purchase of grounds,
ᵌction of building, and for furniture; the present value is estimated
$165,500. A memorial chapel is soon to be built; $10,000 have
ready been pledged by one person. The home is supported by volun-
ry contributions. Its receipts for its first year (1852–'53) were $253;
r the past year (1872–'73) they were $37,000. Its work speaks for itself,
ıd with no uncertain accents, to all who come within the sound of its
oice. The most marked event of the year has been the establishment
f deaconesses over the various departments of the charity. The per-
ᵌct success of the same, and the beautiful spirit evinced under all cir-
umstances, have not only elicited the approbation and commendation
f all, but have so completely won all hearts that words are fulsome.
A distinguishing feature of the home is its printing-department. In
his and all similar institutions it is almost impossible to retain boys
ıfter the age of 12 years to their advantage, the comfort of those
·aring for them, and the well being of the children generally, unless
here can be given them some occupation. Great difficulty is found in
ırocuring situations for them, and these facts suggested the idea to the
ıanagers of teaching them printing, convinced that such arrangement
·ould be made pecuniarily profitable to the home and greatly to the
;ood of the boys by giving them a trade which at least would always
·ecure them a living.
In 1869 a monthly paper called The Helping Hand, printed on a com-
ıercial-note-sheet, was sent out by the orphans, the printing being
lone entirely by them. The same gradually increased in size, till it
ᵌas determined at the beginning of the year 1873 to make it a double
·heet, 15½ by 11 inches. It was also decided at that time to increase the
ırinting-department, and give both boys and girls a trade that would
·ecure them a competency in future life. A competent person was made
·uperintendent, and the secretary of the lady associates, as editor of
he paper, consented to co-operate with the superintendent in carrying
ıut the plan. The children, from 11 to 14 years of age, have shown skill
ınd industry, and the success has surprised the best friends of the
ffort. Not only job-printing and the papers have given satisfaction,
ıut two books have been stereotyped; one of 160 pages, the other of 400.
By this arrangement it is hoped that the institution will be able to
old under its salutary influences the orphans until they are from 16

to 18 years of age, and that then, going forth, they will carry with them a somewhat matured Christian character, and such knowledge of a skilled industry as shall insure to them, if rightly exercised, a useful and happy career.

ST. JOHNLAND, ON LONG ISLAND,

An outgrowth of St. Luke's Hospital, New York, is a farm purchased by certain charitable people where several benevolent enterprises are carried on under the auspices of the Episcopal Church. The first of these attempted was the establishment of an office or training-school in type-setting for crippled boys and girls discharged from the St. Luke's Hospital. The next undertaking was the Home for Crippled and Destitute Children, the cost of which was defrayed by three charitable ladies. This house contains all things necessary for the comfort and education of 25 helpless little ones, most of them former patients of the children's ward in St. Luke's. As they become old enough they are transferred to either the boys' house or the grown girls' department, and taught type-setting or some other useful occupation. In 1869 an Old Man's Home was established; the beneficiaries of this are expected to be worthy Christian men, who, through the vicissitudes of life, have become unable to command the comforts of a home. The house will accommodate 40 persons.

The Boys' House, a mother's tribute to a lovely youth, deceased, completed, and appropriately furnished, at a cost of $8,000, is a commodious and cheerful house, of fifty-five feet by thirty, intended for thirty-six boys. It has a school-room, a library or social room, for evening recreation, two good dormitories, a convenient lavatory or dressing-room, and apartments for the care-takers of the household.

An extension of St. John's Inn, northward, contains accommodations for ten grown girls, orphans, under training by Sisters, in the several industrial and household departments of the settlement. It is a provision for the care and instruction of unprotected girls from the age of 14 and upwards.

CHILDREN'S AID SOCIETY, NEW YORK.

This society does a large amount and variety of charitable work among the most wretched and degraded classes of the city, but more especially among the children and youth. Schools, both day and night, where destitute and neglected children, excluded by their circumstances from the public schools, are cared for and instructed; lodging-houses, where children and youth, for a nominal sum, or without charge if they be utterly destitute, can obtain a comfortable night's rest; free reading-rooms, which rival the attractions of the streets; and an emigration agency, which transfers both children and adults to homes in the West at the rate of over 3,000 a year, are among the most important agencies

442

iployed by this society in its efforts to help and save these "dangerous ssses" of New York. There is also a large amount of missionary rk done among the poor by the visitors of the society and by the chers in the industrial schools. In addition to the number regularly ployed, many ladies volunteer as teachers and for missionary work; 1874 there were seventy such, who it is stated were accomplishing a st amount of good. The crowning work of the society, however, is ieved to be its emigration-feature, the placing of orphan and home-s children in good country homes, and, often, the settlement of whole nilies where they can earn a living. For the well-doing and proper atment of the children placed by it, the society considers itself in a asure responsible, and for information keeps up a correspondence th them and their guardians. In 1874 the society provided in this iy for 1,880 boys, 1,558 girls, 242 men, and 305 women, a total of 3,985, 284 more than during the previous year. The number placed in homes icc 1853 is 36,363.

AID SOCIETY SCHOOLS AND THE NEW EDUCATION LAW.

The Children's Aid Society has been for years urging upon the legis-ture of the State of New York the necessity for a law similar to that cently passed securing the attendance of all children upon school a ortion of the year, and the officers of the society have offered their earty co-operation to the public-school-board in carrying it out. In iew, too, of the possible effects of the law, the society has opened a larger umber of night-schools. It is not thought probable that the new law vill lessen essentially the necessity for these industrial schools; first, be-cause most of the children received are too poor to forego the noonday-neal supplied; secondly, they are too ill-clad to obtain admittance into the city-schools, even if they were to seek it; and, thirdly, a majority are compelled to work in the streets a part of the day for their living.

The city pays semi-annually to the society a certain sum for each pupil, as allowed by law.

COUNTRY HOME.

One of the most beautiful of charities was, during the summer of 1874, incorporated with the work of this society. For many years excursions and picnics for the poor children have been provided by this and other societies and by the New York Times fund. These, however, afforded too brief a relaxation to accomplish all the good desired, and a lady, about two summers ago, opened and supported a house on Staten Island as a summer-resort for these children, and especially as a sanitarium for infants. She afterwards proposed to this society the opening of a simi-lar home, on condition that she and the society should raise the sum required, about $4,000. This was soon done; the same house was rented, (a spacious villa with some eight acres of land,) furniture was purchased and borrowed, three cows were bought, and a garden made ready, and early in the summer detachments of 70 from the schools began to go, each remaining a week. It was a gospel of good-will to the poor children. The whole expense was $3,384.84; and this gave a week's sunshine and country air to 1,260 children.

FLOWER-MISSION.

The superintendent of the Rivington-street school and lodging-house has in the rear, and opening out of the school-room, separated only by glass doors, a small green-house. The children are given young plants as prizes; they take them to their homes and after a certain number of months return them to show what care has been exercised, and the result of their efforts. During the past four years Mr. Calder has thus distributed 1,300 plants, besides many bouquets of flowers to the sick. The idea was his own, and it has been carried out at a large pecuniary cost to himself.

A mission, kindred in character, is carried on in Boston by a society organized for the purpose.

CHILDREN'S LODGING-HOUSES.

The Children's Aid Society provides five lodging-houses in New York City, four of them for boys and one for girls, where a night's lodging may be obtained for five cents and a meal for six, all, however, being received, whether able to pay or not. If a child be out of employment or alone in the world, every effort is made to provide for him according to his age, capacities, and necessities. Meantime he or she remains in the home enjoying the benefits of the schools, either day or evening, connected with them, as well as whatever provision is made for industrial training. The demand for a small payment, invariably made of those who are able, is regarded as an important feature in the plan to aid and elevate this class, taking away, as it does, the sting of charity, and making the children feel rather like independent guests in a hotel. Another important feature is the savings-banks which have been opened in the houses, and pay a liberal interest—sixty per cent.—for all moneys deposited by the children, who are thus taught lessons of economy and providence. Girls pay their way by housework, if they have no other means, and are trained in that, in dress-making, and on the sewing-machine.

The newsboys' lodging-house, whose accommodations have long been inadequate, has lately taken possession of a new and commodious building on Duane, William, and New Chambers streets, costing $216,000. It is 109 feet long, with an average width of 60 feet. The building is seven stories high. It contains dining-room for the boys, with accommodation for 400 at table. The school-room has seating capacity for 500 boys. There are comfortable single beds, in well-ventilated apartments, a savings-bank, a school-room, (answering also for chapel,) bath-nd wash-rooms, private lock-closets for each boy, games—as chess and heckers—interesting reading, and every evening a brief devotional cercise.

" The savings-bank," the superintendent states, " has been used by 272 boys, who have saved $3,330.86, being a large increase over last ar—say 38 per cent. During 1874 there were 8,913 different boys who ntributed $6,167.53 towards the expenses, which were $16,470.61, in- nding gas, fuel, food, salaries, rent, bedding, &c., but not improve- ents and fittings up in the new house. The receipts from the boys ere 43 per cent. more than ever before.

" During the year 472 boys were placed in good homes, and 912 lost id truant ones (an average of nearly three a day) restored to relatives id friends. Parents and others often visit the home to learn about st children."

There has been during 1874 an average of 195 lodgers nightly. A tal of 70,681 lodgings were afforded, and 72,567 meals. Since its first stablishment, twenty-one years ago, nearly 10,000 boys have been pro- ided, through its agency, with permanent homes and employment.

The superintendent of the Girls' Lodging House, St. Mark's Place, eports a total for 1874 of 1,507 lodgers, who received 12,750 lodgings; a little more than half of which were paid for. There are, it is stated, seven roomy and well-ventilated dormitories on the third, fourth, and fifth floors, in which are 53 single beds. The girls have the use of the laundry every Thursday, and can take baths at any hour of the day or evening. During the year situations were found for 683 girls; 38 went west. All these express themselves as delighted with the change, say- ing that western people do not treat them as servants.

The lodging-house in the eleventh ward, No. 709 East Eleventh street, lodges an average of 55 nightly. A marked improvement in the boys under its care is reported. The house at 211 West Eighteenth street makes a similar statement. Of the 800 boys connected with this last-mentioned house, 70 were learning trades.

The Rivington-street house reports having provided for more boys, furnished more lodgings, and received more from the boys than during any former year. The great want of the boys, the superintendent has found, is for a sympathizing counselor and friend, in whom they can place implicit confidence and to whom they can always go for assistance and advice; and this want Superintendent Calder is just the man to supply. During 1874, 167 friendless boys were placed by this home in permanent homes, and, from funds contributed by several benevolent gentlemen for the purpose of " setting up boys in business," 254, who came to them utterly destitute, were enabled to commence business and support themselves as newsboys, bootblacks, and peddlers.

The Bethel Home and Newsboys' Association in Cincinnati, and the Newsboys' and Bootblacks' Association in Chicago, are operating in a similar direction to this branch of the Childrens' Aid Society work.

So also is the St. Vincent's Home for Boys, 53 Warren street, New Yor⁻ City, a lodging-house for boys, established in 1870 by the Roman Catﬁ olics, which differs but little in its methods from those already men tioned, the great effort being to surround with wholesome home-inﬂ⁻ ences and supply with the necessaries of life a class of boys who mu . otherwise roam the streets, plying their various vocations, destitute aﬁﬁ neglected. During the past year, so great has been the increase in t ℔ number applying for shelter, it has been found necessary to increase *the* accommodations by adding the adjoining house, thus affording sleeping. room for 200 boys, together with a gymnasium, school-room, 200 small wardrobes with locks and keys, wash-rooms, bath-rooms, &c. During the winter every bed in the house was occupied, and, rather than go elsewhere, many slept on benches and tables; and it is felt that another similar house should be opened for this class of boys immediately.

An evening-school was connected with the home during the winter, in which great progress was made by the pupils, numbers of whom ac-quired a knowledge of the rudiments of education who could previously neither read nor write. Instruction in the higher branches was also imparted to those capable of receiving it. In connection with the school was a singing class, which likewise met with much success. There is also a dramatic club, composed of the members of the home, which is a source of pleasant entertainment and instruction to the boys. An exhi-bition is given once a week by the members, to which all the others are invited. In fact, no means have been left untried to amuse the boys and to induce them to spend their evenings within the home.

Mass is said every morning in the chapel for all who wish to attend. After mass, short instructions on the christian doctrine are given to the boys in the lecture-room before morning-prayers, which take place at 6 o'clock. The hour for breakfast is from 6 to 7 o'clock, after which every boy leaves the home, to pursue his usual daily avocation.

Many bad boys have already been weaned from their vicious habits, steady situations obtained for them, and, instead of being temporary lodgers, have become regular boarders, paying their way weekly, and clothing themselves with the remainder of their wages.

The total receipts for the year were $13,224.55; the expenditures, $15,209.47; leaving a balance of $1,984.92 due to friends, who loaned it without interest.

The Boys' Home Society of Baltimore, and the Lincoln Institution, Philadelphia, while aiming at the same general end, differ considerably from the lodging-houses just mentioned in their methods. Boys are not received for a night or a few hours, but all entering are expected to remain until other provision be made for them, until they shall have served an apprenticeship at some trade, or become established in some business by which a good living can be made. The superintendent finds employment for the boys and acts as their guardian as long as they remain in the institution.

The Boys' Home Society of Baltimore was organized in 1866, and is
der the supervision of a board of directors.

This institution is not properly a reformatory, neither is it an orphan·
·lum. Its object is to provide a home for youths between the ages of
and 20 years, either orphans, half-orphans, or outcasts and homeless.
ey are the material which, when neglected, corrupt the public virtue,
·y our criminal courts, and crowd our houses of refuge, jails, and
·itentiaries. When sheltered and helped they make good men, and
l to the wealth, virtue, and prosperity of the community.

‑ sketch given of this society says :

‘ Before reaching the ages referred to, our orphan-asylums and chil-
·ns' aid societies, homes for the friendless, and other excellent insti-
ions look after and care for them.

‘ In former years, at 10 years of age and upwards, boys were appren-
ed to tradesmen or mechanics, to learn the so-called " art, trade, and
·stery" of some useful handicraft; but the whole system has fallen
o disuse, being practically prohibited by the trades-unions of the
·es and other associations.

" For boys of the ages referred to, therefore, there is very little pro-
·ion. The street is their home; idleness and, consequently, vicious-
·ss their heritage.

" Even if his hand were willing and his heart brave to struggle for a
·elihood, how could the boy hope to be successful? for insuperable ob-
·acles are in his way. On the one hand, the high cost of living, and
· the other the low value of his unskilled labor. It was for the
·rpose of aiding him in this unequal fight that the Boys' Home Society
·s formed. At this critical period in his history it reaches out to him
e helping hand; it invites him into a cheerful home; it finds work
·r him at fixed wages, however small; it extends over him shelter,
·otection, guardianship, in all his feeble struggles; it speaks words of
·couragement if he falters in the stern strife of life; it makes no ex-
·ting demand upon his slender store, either of muscle, of brain, or of
·nings; it tides him over the rocks and shallows of inexperience, and
·ars him on towards a manhood of assured self-respect, probity, and
·lf-dependence; it gives him, withal, the elements of a good English
·ucation and teaches him his duty to God and his fellows.

" Any destitute or homeless boy, between the ages of 10 and 20
·ars, may be admitted, if he express a willingness to become an obedi-
·t member of the household, to work for his living at any employment
·occupation to which the superintendent may assign him, and to con·
·bute out of his wages the following sum weekly, viz: $1.75, where
·ges are $3.50 or less; $2.00, where wages are over $3.50 and
·t exceeding $4.50; $2.50, where wages are over $4.50, towards the
·intenance and support of the home; and should there be parent,
·ardian, or other person or persons having the custody of the boy,
·h parent, guardian, or other person shall execute and deliver to this

447

8 E

corporation an instrument of writing, by which the person or persons so surrendering him shall obligate him, her, or themselves to receive back the boy if, after three months, the executive committee shall elect to return him, and in no way interfere with the management of the boy while at the home, nor visit him without the consent of the executive committee, nor induce, nor attempt to induce, him or any other boy to leave the home, or any family, place, or station in which he or any other boy may have been placed by the directors; and, further, that the said parent, guardian, person, or persons will not demand from the institution, or any person or persons, any compensation or reward for the services of the boy.

"Any such boy who shall not have been surrendered to this corporation in the manner herein provided may be withdrawn from the institution (or the person by whom he may be employed) by his parent or guardian, upon payment to this corporation of the expenses incurred by it in the relief, support, and instruction of such boy.

"The executive committee shall dismiss any boy whenever they shall think that the welfare of the institution will be promoted thereby."

The success of this home is attributed in a great measure to the fact that care is given to the boys outside, at their work, as well as inside. Every effort is made to render the home attractive. The library of five hundred volumes is a great source of interest to many of the boys, the importance of which cannot be overestimated.

The building is a substantial structure, thoroughly appointed throughout, with every appliance necessary for the comfort and convenience of those for whose benefit it was designed. The cost, inclusive of lot, was $46,000.

AMERICAN FEMALE GUARDIAN SOCIETY AND HOME FOR THE FRIEND-LESS, NEW YORK.

The object of this society is "to promote the cause of virtue and humanity by protecting the young, destitute, and friendless from the exposure to vice and suffering incident to their condition; also to secure for homeless children, as far as practicable, the training of the christian family." It had its origin nearly forty years ago in the efforts of a band of women, who organized an association—afterwards incorporated—with the above object in view.

To this end they employed missionary visitors, published a periodical, tracts, &c., devised effective plans for reaching the neglected poor, and visited prisons, hospitals, and localities degraded and repulsive, in season and out of season, if by any means they might save some. By memorial and petition and personal influence, they induced those in power to correct sundry abuses, establish a workhouse, place matrons in the Tombs and other prisons to have charge of their own sex, in place of men; also to enact laws for the suppression of vice and truancy. They also organized several hundred auxiliary associations, which aided

ctively in disseminating their publications and principles throughout
 land.

Presently the labors of the association began to be more and more
ned to the children. The conviction was strengthened by constant
servation that the class which furnishes much of the material for the
catombs of the outcasts and the lawless that fill our prisons with
tims and wring human hearts with sorrow, is found among the chil-
n of the street, trained in miscalled homes, and doomed early to wear
 brand of the pauper; and, furthermore, that there is a point in each
ing life where, if withdrawn from moral pitfalls into the sunlight of
ristian nurture, the child may thus be saved for this life and the
xt.

For several years the homes of sundry managers became the tempo-
y shelter for the homeless, till more permanent provision could be
ierwise made. The number of these *protégés* annually increased till
length a home for the friendless became a manifest necessity. In
46 this institution, now located at 32 East Thirtieth street, was in-
gurated, and the funds required for its erection partially contributed
small sums, from $1 upwards. In December, 1848, the edifice was com-
eted and dedicated. From that time to the present it has sheltered
er seventeen thousand beneficiaries, to most of whom it has bridged
e moral chasm between want and competence, despair and hope, peril
d safety.

The Home Chapel, 29 East Twenty-ninth street, covering three full
ts—but an appendage to the home on Thirtieth street, and connected
ith it by a bridge between the two buildings—was erected in 1856,
d furnishes school-rooms, dormitories, &c., for infants and invalids,
large chapel for Sabbath-services and anniversaries, also the pub-
shing-office, whence eight million folio pages of The Advocate and
uardian are issued annually.

The institution is *undenominational*, and wholly under the charge of
dies advised and sustained by a reliable board of counselors composed
f well-known business-men and clergymen of different denominations.
ev. Dr. Tyng, chairman of its board of counselors, in speaking of the
ome-managers at a public anniversary, gave this testimony: "Each
ne is giving more in her personal zeal and efforts than a thousand dol-
ars from the wealthy could purchase, giving what mere wealth has no
ower to measure."

Seven hundred and fifteen women and children have been, for a longer
r shorter time, inmates of the institution during a single year. Nine
hundred and twelve adults have been furnished with situations. More
than six hundred and nineteen thousand meals have been given. Upwards of eighteen thousand inmates have been received into the home
since its erection. More than three thousand five hundred children have
been provided with christian homes.

order and system are apparent in every department, and the most scrupulous neatness and cleanliness exist in every portion of the premises.

The superintendent and officers display great efficiency in caring for
the moral, physical, and intellectual welfare of the children under their
control. It is to them a labor of love, and with them kindness appears
to have produced its natural fruit, as is evident from the attachment
that exists between them and the children.

The institution is under the charge of a board of twenty-four directors,
of which A. R. Wetmore, esq., has been the president from the opening
of the asylum to the present time.

There have been three superintendents—Dr. J. D. Russ, Dr. S. D.
Brooks, and the present superintendent, Mr. E. M. Carpenter.

THE SHELTERING ARMS, NEW YORK.

The origin of The Sheltering Arms is best given in the words of its
founder and president, Rev. Thomas W. Peters, D. D. We quote from
his sermon on "The gradual growth of charities," preached before the
Protestant-Episcopal City Mission Society in 1873:

"Ten years ago, two ladies, visiting the Tombs, or city-prison, in concert with the missionary of our City Mission Society, found, from time
to time, mothers committed for drunkenness, who were sent to Blackwell's Island. Some of these women had children, who, by the removal
of the mother, were deprived of all care. Even in their degradation,
these unhappy mothers had some humanity remaining, and were concerned for their children's welfare. 'They literally lay their children at
our feet,' said one of the visiting ladies, 'imploring us to find them a
home.' At about the same time there was brought to the notice of
another lady of the same society a little blind girl, deserted by her parents, without friends, and not of an age to be received at the asylum for
the blind. Shortly after, a home was sought by a workingman for an
incurable, motherless, crippled boy. As there was no hope of his restoration, no then existing hospital or institution would receive him.
Further inquiry resulted in the unexpected discovery that there were
in the city of New York, and out of it, large numbers of children, who,
though surrounded by many asylums, were yet without a home, because
needing some necessary qualification for admission to institutions already established. It was also ascertained, in the course of these inquiries, that there were many cases of neglect of children, owing to the
usual requirement of our charitable institutions that their inmates
should be formally surrendered to the trustees. There are hundreds of
cases in which a family is abandoned by the father, thus throwing the
support of the children upon the mother, and obliging her, perhaps, to
break up the household and go out herself to service. With the hopefulness of human nature she believes the separation but temporary,
and looks for a happy home once more, at no very distant day. If she

could place her children for a few months, or a year, in good hands and under christian training, she would gladly do so, provided that, when able, she might claim them again. 'But I cannot,' said one of these deserted mothers, 'sign away my own flesh and blood.'

"There are other cases, also, among the families of the poor, which make necessary a temporary removal of the children from home. The comfort of health gives place to the famine of sickness; the father of a family is disabled, for a time, by accident or disease, and there is no money to buy food; or the mother is the sufferer, and there is no one to do the household-work, or watch over the children during the day, while the father is at his labor. For such as these, there was no place where the children could be left for a time, and claimed in returning prosperity, and without the liability of their being sent or given away beyond the parents' reach. Friends adopted, but too frequently, the unhappy alternative of placing them in wretched, squalid homes, where they were poorly kept, on a promise of future pay, and ranged the streets half clothed, and untaught, because not fitly dressed for school.

"Thus, by the directing hand of God, was indicated another work to be done, other human woes to be healed. With no promise beyond a house free of rent and a few children to inhabit it, it was resolved, in obedience to the divine Guide, to go forward. The distinguishing features of this charity were fixed upon as these: the only qualifications for the admission of a child shall be that it is not entitled to reception elsewhere and that in the institution there is a vacant bed; the children cared for there belong to their parents, not to the institution, and can be claimed by parents at will; by the introduction of the cottage-system, the children are to be distributed into separate families, with a responsible head over each.

"Gifts were soon received to furnish, and multiplying applications of little ones to inhabit, the house, so that, a few months later, on the sixth day of October, 1864, it was opened, with all its forty beds taken up. Such was the commencement of The Sheltering Arms."

Children between the ages of 2 and 10 years are received from the following classes:

1st. The blind and deaf-mutes, until the age at which they become entitled to admission at the asylums especially devoted to such unfortunates.

2d. Crippled children past hope of cure, and therefore no longer retained in ordinary hospitals.

3d. Children of poor parents, obliged on account of sickness to enter a hospital, and who commit their children for a season to our charge, with the expectation, upon recovery, of reclaiming their own.

4th. Children rendered temporarily homeless by fire or other accident.

5th. Children whose home has been broken up by the intemperance or desertion of father or mother. In such cases, the remaining parent pays, according to ability, a small sum monthly.

453

6th. Children abandoned by both parents, brought to us by friends and relatives unable to find immediately a proper home, and yet unwilling to lose control of the children or to place them beyond their reach.

Up to January, 1875, six hundred and eighty-two children have been received. The needs of some few were met by one day's hospitality. Others have remained ten years. In every case the child's necessity the limit of its stay. The cottage-system is carried out as fully as may be, and has proved a valuable aid in the training of the children, affording a good substitute for the home-life from which they are debarred. Each cottage (except the center-house) contains a dormitory, bath-room, play-room, and dining-room for thirty or thirty-five children, besides a convenient sleeping-room for the "mother" of the family. Each family is entirely separate from the others, meeting, however, at church and in school, and occasionally in the play-grounds.

The property now owned and occupied by The Sheltering Arms is situated on the corner of One hundred and twenty-ninth street and Tenth avenue. The principal building is of brick, and contains five cottages under one roof. The center-house, named the Van Horne Cottage, is used for the general purposes of the institution, and contains the office, reception-rooms, linen-rooms, kitchen, laundry, &c. The west wing is devoted to boys, and consists of two cottages, bearing respectively the names of John D. Wolfe and James E. Montgomery. The two cottages of the east wing are named after Mrs. Peter Cooper and "The Ladies' Association of the Sheltering Arms," and are occupied by girls. The school-house is a frame building, at one end of the boys' play-ground. At the end of the girls' play-ground is a brick hospital, entirely detached, and sufficiently large to meet the ordinary needs of the house.

The annual cost of each child, including *all expenses*, varies from $130 to $140. Parents or friends pay, according to their means, from two to ten dollars per month. About seventy children are received on the free list. A subscription of $138 entitles the donor to a year's support for any child of suitable age, &c. Three churches and not less than forty-three charitable persons availed themselves of this provision last year. A gift of $100 constitutes a life-member; of $500, a patron; $1,000 endows a bed, the nomination of the occupant belonging to the donor for life; $2,000 is invested as a permanent endowment of one bed, the nomination of the occupant remaining always with the donor and his heirs; a gift of $5,000 builds a cottage bearing the name of the donor.

The Sheltering Arms is under the supervision of the bishop. The affairs are managed by a board of trustees, composed of twenty-one gentlemen; this board is assisted by an association of ladies, which has assumed the entire charge of the cottage bearing its name, supplementing all deficiences in the amount received from the parents of the little occupants. This association also takes a large share in the management of the monthly paper published by the institution.

he favor and success which have attended The Sheltering Arms
i the very commencement show that the necessity for such an
itution was widely felt. Were further proof required, it could be
id in the fact that other communities have now undertaken similar
k, in many cases adopting even the very name, "Sheltering Arms,"
, matter of course, and as defining accurately the nature of the
ity.

'hen The Sheltering Arms was first projected, one long familiar with
ic charities, and who considered an institution of this character the
test want of our city, remarked of the founder, "He does not know
t a vast work he is commencing; if there were room for five hun-
i such children, in six months it would be all filled." It is true
only a beginning has been made towards affording homes to tem-
.rily-destitute children; that, where one is received, many are re-
d; that these four cottages must be multiplied tenfold; yet we are
impatient, but labor and wait, glad to do what God permits us to,
eving that, in His good time, He will send those who will lay the
.er-stone and cap the roof of other cottages to shelter the distressed.

ST. JOHN'S GUILD, NEW YORK,

n organization in New York City for the purpose of sustaining
honest poor, of either sex, in their struggle for existence, and to
·ent professional mendicancy, pauperism, and crime. It is in no way
iected with any church or religious body, its members being of the
rew, Catholic, and Protestant forms of faith, and no questions are
:d or distinctions made in respect to creed, race, or color. Its sys-
is, to have a volunteer visitor for every tenement-block in the city.
great work of this guild is to keep together the families of those
are out of employment, by affording the needed temporary relief.
y are thus soon enabled to become self-supporting, and often even
ribute towards the aid of others; whereas, once broken to pieces, such
ilies seldom recover, but become utterly demoralized, and a perma-
: charge upon the public. The widows' rent-fund, disbursed by the
ors of this society, has been the means of accomplishing a great
unt of good. The idea was originated by Mr. Francis P. Furnald,
, in a letter to the New York Herald, subscribed $500 for the purpose.
fterward reached $3,757.84; but the amount of relief afforded was
h greater than this sum would indicate, since, in some cases, bills
unting to $25 were receipted in full upon the payment of $5 by the
:ors, while many landlords freely forgave their tenants their entire
i, and some receipted bills for months in advance for their poor ten-
i, when satisfied by the visitors that they were wholly unable, through
ness and lack of work, to pay. The instances where landlords
ted worthy tenants for non-payment of rent were remarkably rare,
pared with the thousands of tenants who were temporarily unable
ieet such bills. Separate departments exist for the dispensing of

provisions, clothing, medical relief, the providing of employment, and the burial of the dead. The floating hospital for mothers with sick children has been the means of saving many thousands of little ones who were dying of malaria imbibed in their wretched homes.

FIVE POINTS HOUSE OF INDUSTRY, NO. 155 WORTH STREET, NEW YORK.

This institution was established by Rev. L. M. Pease, in 1851, and 1854 it was incorporated. It is devoted mainly to the preservation children from suffering and crime, but it receives temporarily all who have nowhere else to go. Assistance is rendered to adults as far as it can be without encouraging a dependence upon charity, and efforts are made to reform and procure labor for such women as are willing to work. Urgent cases of suffering among out-door poor are temporarily relieved until some other provision can be made for them. The institution is supported almost entirely by voluntary contribution. Since 1854 a total of 22,664 inmates have been cared for by the house.

LADIES' HOME MISSIONARY SOCIETY, (METHODIST EPISCOPAL,) OLD BREWERY, NEW YORK.

The objects of the above society are "to support one or more missionaries to labor among the poor of the city of New York, especially in the locality known as the 'Five Points;' to provide food, clothing, and other necessaries for such poor; to educate poor children and provide for their comfort and welfare, and for that purpose to maintain a school at the Five Points, in said city; and to perform kindred acts of charity and benevolence."

At the home of the mission, 61 Park Place, there was a total of 893 children taught during the year the elements of an English education and sewing. The average attendance was 429. Besides the food and clothing given away to the poor, places of employment were found for 47 adults and homes in good families furnished for 32 children.

HOME FOR LITTLE WANDERERS, OR HOWARD MISSION, NO. 40 NEW BOWERY, NEW YORK.

Children are received here, and placed in situations and in homes. During 1874, 221 children were received.

NEW YORK SOCIETY FOR THE RELIEF OF THE RUPTURED AND CRIPPLED.

This charity was incorporated in 1863, and is under the charge of a board of managers, consisting of a president, five vice-presidents, a treasurer, a corresponding secretary, a recording secretary, and twelve other persons.

The objects of the society are to supply skillfully-constructed surgico-mechanical appliances and the treatment of in- and out-door patients equiring trusses or spring supports; also bandages, lace stockings, and ther apparatus for the cure of cripples, both adults and children, on uch conditions as will make their benefits available, so far as is possible, the poorest in the city.

The character of this institution is peculiar to itself, as the managers ave yet to learn of another institution in the world that precisely cor-sponds with this in respect to the maladies treated and the age of the atients received for treatment. Children are received from the ages of to 14, and the object is to *cure* these unfortunate children of their arious afflictions, rather than to provide a home for *incurables*.

The prevailing opinion, indeed, of the uninitiated in respect to the poor, naciated, crippled children when first brought to the hospital is, that eir cure is hopeless; and such doubtless they would become were they ot timely, skillfully, and persistently treated. While in some cases a w months may suffice to restore perfect soundness, other cases, ren-ered obstinate by long neglect or unfavorable complications, may require ears to effect a like result.

It is not assumed that this institution surpasses all others in regard o the medical and surgical skill employed in the treatment of patients t is, however, believed that its advantages for the continued and suc-essful use of remedial agents in accordance with the laws of physiology nd pathology are not surpassed, if equaled, by any other hospital nown by the board to exist.

The number of patients that have been treated in the hospital are 725; hose prescribed for in the dispensary-department number 24,210. Of he results it may be concisely stated that of the whole number of patients bout 81.5 per cent. were relieved and discharged, 16.7 per cent. were con-inued under treatment, 1.6 per cent. were incurable, and 2 per cent. died.

Teachers are provided for the in-door patients, and, when their condi-ion will admit, they are taught in the common English branches and nusic; also, knitting and sewing. A professional gymnast instructs them n such athletic exercises as may best develop their physical vigor, and thus increase the efficacy of medical and surgical treatment in counter-icting the inveterate chronic diseases from which these children suffer.

The present yearly expenses of this institution exceed forty thousand dollars.

ST. BARNABAS.

The Sisterhood of the Good Shepherd, a body of Christian women, working under sisterhood-rules of the Episcopal Church, are engaged in "ministering to the poor, the sick, the homeless, the outcast, and in car-ing for little children."

Among a large amount of other work, as visiting the poor of the city and the sick in hospitals, the sisters supervise the St. Barnabas House, 306 Mulberry street, where poor and homeless persons are received, tempo-rarily, until appropriate provision can be made for them, either by pro-viding them with employment or placing them in the proper public institution. During 1874, a total of 1,888 persons were cared for in the home, to a greater or less extent, some needing only a meal, others a night's lodging, while others remained for days and weeks. No hungry or homeless person is ever sent away from the doors of this house. The day-nursery of infants is a special feature of the St. Barnabas House designed to meet the wants of mothers who are obliged to labor at day's work, and are glad to pay a small sum for the care of their infants during the day. During 1874, 105 infants were kept in the nursery. The home also furnishes an asylum for about 30 orphaned children, all there is room for. These are given the rudiments of an education, in a school kept by the Sisters in the home, and as occasion offers are placed in good families. A reading-room connected with the home offers its attractions and means of improvement to young men and boys who would otherwise be pursuing their education on the street.

A paper issued by it in April, 1874, says respecting it:

"The St. Barnabas House, 304 to 308 Mulberry street, has reached its limit of possibility in the way of accommodation. During the past season as many as 69 have lodged in one night in the 49 single beds. Throughout the year 19,221 lodgings and 94,358 meals have been furnished to people of all nationalities, colors, and religions, being 1,208 lodgings and 12,716 meals more than the previous year. Sixteen homeless children make part of our permanent family. The day-nursery receives each morning, from women going out to day's work, forty children, who are washed, fed, and taught, and returned at evening to their parents.

It is proposed, leaving 304 Mulberry street as at present, to take down the small and old building on 306, and erect in its place a five-story building 30 by 80 feet. By this means, not only will additional accommodations be furnished for the present work, but No. 308 will be set free to be used in the autumn as a lodging-house and bureau of employment for men.

The proposed building will cost $25,000. It will be commenced as soon as $10,000 shall have been received for the purpose.

HOUSE AND SCHOOL OF INDUSTRY, 120 WEST SIXTEENTH STREET, NEW YORK.

The primary design of this institution is to afford to infirm and destitute women employment in needlework, at such a rate of remuneration as may enable them to exist. This employment is given, according to circumstances, either at the residences of the applicants or at the house, where also instruction in sewing is given to such as need it. The aid of the institution is afforded, without regard to religious denomination, to such applicants as are found by the visitors of the house to be in greatest need of it. A sewing-school for the young also is maintained, open twice a week, on Wednesdays and Saturdays, and an infant industrial school, where poor neglected children are made com-

·table by baths, decent clothing, and food, and taught in the elements
common-school-instruction. For the ability to sustain this branch of
:ir work the institution expresses indebtedness to Mr. Charles L.
ace, secretary of the Children's Aid Society.

Owing to the great financial difficulties of the country, the year 1874
s not a prosperous one for the business of this house. Thus the sales
the great variety of garments and articles for household-use which
: made by the women, and with which our store is stocked, are greatly
ected. In ordinary times large numbers of shirts are purchased from
by mechanics, and their families supply themselves with coarse gar-
nts at prices very little above cost. Some articles of clothing are sold
seventy-five cents, the cost and making of which amount to sixty-
e cents. Others are sold much below cost, in order that the women
.y have good prices for their work.

A SOCIETY FOR THE PREVENTION OF CRUELTY TO CHILDREN

as organized in the city of New York in December, 1874. The officers
asist of a president, ten vice-presidents, fifteen in the board of man-
ers, a treasurer, a counsel, and a secretary. At their first meeting the
lowing circular was prepared :

"Object of the Society for the Prevention of Cruelty to Children.

" This is the society for the *prevention of cruelty to children.*
" There already exist in this city and in various parts of this State
iny excellent societies and institutions, some as charitable corpora-
ins and others as State-reformatories and asylums, for receiving and
ring for little children. Among these in our own city may be noted the
iildren's Aid Society, the Home for the Friendless, the New York
fant Asylum, the Institution for Homeless Children, the Society for
e Protection of Destitute Children, the Association for the Relief of
irls, the New York Catholic Protectory, St. Stephen's Home for
estitute Children ; and, in addition, each religious denomination has
ore or less asylums, reformatories, hospitals, and like institutions
:voted to the moral and physical culture of helpless children.
"All these and the like existing societies which are employed in this
·and and truly noble work assume the care and control of their inmates
ily after they are legally placed in their custody. It is not within their
rovince to seek out and to rescue from the dens and slums of the city
iose little unfortunates whose childish lives are rendered miserable
y the constant abuse and cruelties practiced on them by the human
rutes who happen to possess the custody or control of them. This
'ork the Society for the Prevention of Cruelty to Children undertakes
ind proposes to carry out.
"Ample laws have been passed by the legislature of this State for the
irotection of, and prevention of cruelty to, little children. The trouble
eems to be that it is nobody's business to enforce them. The societies

and institutions referred to have as much as, nay, more than, they ca___ attend to in providing for those intrusted to their care. The police an__ prosecuting officers of the people are necessarily engrossed in securing the conviction and punishment of offenders of a graver legal strip__ and, although ready to aid in enforcing the laws referred to when du__ called on so to do, can hardly be expected to seek out and prosecu__ those who claim the right to ill-treat children over whom they have an apparent legal control.

"Hence the child-beaters live in comparative security. Hence the children, hardened by brutality and cruelty, grow up to be men and women scarcely less hardened than their tyrants. The men swell the ranks of the "dangerous classes" which imperil the public peace and security, and the women are lost, body and soul, often before they are women in age and maturity.

"The Society for the Prevention of Cruelty to Children proposes to enforce, by lawful means and with energy, the laws referred to, and to secure, in like manner, the prompt conviction and punishment of every violator of any of those laws; not vindictively, not to gain public applause, but to convince those who cruelly ill-treat and shamefully neglect little children that the time has passed when this can be longer done, in this State at least, with impunity.

"And, lastly, this society, so far from interfering with the numerous societies and institutions already existing and before referred to, is intended to aid them in their noble work. It proposes to labor in the interest of no one religious denomination, and to keep entirely free from political influences of every kind. Its duties towards the children whom it may rescue will be discharged when the future custody of them is decided by the courts of justice; and the laws of this State contain ample provisions on that subject and vest that duty and responsibility in the hands of the judiciary.

"JOHN D. WRIGHT, *President.*

"NEW YORK, *December* 15, 1874."

April 21, 1875, "An act for the incorporation of societies for the prevention of cruelty to children" was passed by the legislature of New York.

This society is now at work, and will investigate and prosecute, when necessary, all cases of cruelty to children which shall come to its knowledge. It has published a pamphlet containing the "laws of the State of New York relating to children."

HOUSE OF THE GOOD SHEPHERD, NEW YORK.

This home in the country for orphan and desolate children is situated on the west bank of the Hudson River, about 40 miles from New York. It is one mile above Stony Point, and may be reached by steamboats from the foot of Harrison street, New York, or by the Hudson River lroad to Peekskill, and thence by boats. The House of the Good ¦pherd is in the township of Stony Point, Rockland County, New ·k, Tomkin's Cove Post-office. The property consists of ninety acres of l rising from the river, on which it borders for one-fifth of a mile, upon hill, giving many beautiful sites for buildings. Most of the land is l and uncultivated, used for pasture. About fifteen acres have n cleared and are in grass or cultivation. The land is well watered a brook and several springs. From the house, 160 feet above the ∍r, and surrounding grounds, an extended view, embracing features great natural beauty, presents itself.

¦he institution is under the auspices of the Protestant-Episcopal urch, and is supported by voluntary contributions. This house re-ves children from haunts of sin and poverty to a most lovely home, ·rounds them with christian and churchly influence, bringing them daily contact with and under the instruction of cultivated ladies d gentlemen, who give their best time and services, *con amore*, to ¦rist's service in the care of His lost and helpless ones. This care ¦d training are not withdrawn at the very time when their influence forming the young character is most felt, but still surrounds the ¦ild, with gentle hand molding, chastening, correcting, exciting, until, ¦th principles well established and habits of industry well formed, ¦e young man or maiden goes forth, as from a father's house, to form link in the great missionary enterprise of evangelizing the world.

In the care of the children there is an effort to realize the ideal of a ¦hristian family. They are allowed as much freedom as is consistent ¦th good order and punctual habits and are encouraged in habits of ¦ust and honor. We have no high walls, no bolts or bars. A boy ¦mes to us from the city- or village-street or country-lane. He is, per-¦ps, perfectly undisciplined, and with many bad habits. He is intro-¦ced to a boy of his own age, who is to show him the place and inform ¦m of the rules. He finds his days filled, from early morning-light ll bed-time, with duties, studies, amusements. He is assured of the ¦nd love of those who are over him. He finds himself trusted, his ·ord believed. He is taught his part in our religious services, and joins ¦ the hearty singing of God's praise. The result is that the wild, un-¦isciplined boy is transformed to a truthful, trusty, honest youth.

They work on the farm, in the house, and at trades. Children are ¦eceived from any section. The house is not merely an orphanage, but ¦ a training-school for the saving of children in need of a home. The ¦hildren are to be kept under training until fitted for the duties of life. ¦eading, writing, and arithmetic are taught. Present number of in-¦ates, 43.

POUGHKEEPSIE ORPHAN-HOUSE AND HOME FOR THE FRIENDLESS.

It is twenty years since the original charter of this institution was ¦btained from the legislature. Its object and business are there stated to be the publication and diffusion of books, papers, and tracts, and by other moral and religious means to prevent vice and moral degradation, and to maintain houses of industry and home for the relief of friend-less, destitute, or unprotected females, and for friendless or unprotected children, and for the reformation of offenders.

The following statistics will give an outline of the work of the year:

Number received during the year for the first time* 28
Number of children from Poughkeepsie 23
Number of children from county... 24
Number beyond the county-limits 2
Number of re-admissions 8
Number sent to new homes.................................... 22
Number claimed by friends 24
Number of orphans at date 14
Number of half-orphans at date 20
Average number in the family through the year 56
Number of adults in the family through the year ....:... 8

This institution derives its support from voluntary contributions; its affairs are all managed on a cash-basis, and have been so from its com-mencement. Thus far material aid has not failed them, and the past year has been one of prosperity.

OHIO.

THE CHILDREN'S HOME,

Of Cincinnati, was incorporated on the 12th of December, 1864, under the general laws of the State. Its object is to ameliorate the con-dition of poor and neglected children by procuring for such of them as may be committed to it permanent homes in the country in Christian families, where they may receive an ordinary English education and be trained in habits of industry and economy; by affording a temporary home to poor children whose parents may soon be able to support them; and by taking care of children through the day, in order that their mothers may avail themselves of outside employment. It is authorized to receive the legal care and control of all children who are properly surrendered to it by their parents or guardians or by the judge of the probate court or the mayor of the city. Over such it acquires the same authority as originally pertained to the parents.

It is supported entirely by voluntary subscriptions and has no en-dowment.

Over 1,500 children have been received since its organization and over 600 have been placed in permanent homes.

It is the duty of the superintendent or other officers of the Children's

* Number of inmates received since foundation, 754.

Home to visit these children once a year; while those who have them are expected to report to the superintendent once in three months.

The results of this work are very gratifying, especially that part which consists in placing children in country homes.

CLEVELAND INDUSTRIAL SCHOOL, CHILDREN'S AID SOCIETY AND HOME, CLEVELAND.

This institution is doing for the poor children of Cleveland a similar work to that which is accomplished for the same classes in New York and other cities by the aid- and guardian-societies there. There are day-schools for the destitute and ragged boys and girls of the city; a home for girls, also, with its school; and a farm industrial school in the country, where the boys obtain a practical knowledge of husbandry. These children belong to a class which is practically excluded from the common schools by its lack of decent clothing and cleanliness. At the industrial schools they receive clothing and food. The common-school-branches are taught, with the addition of sewing to the girls. The teachers visit the homes of their pupils in order to obtain personal information as to their necessities. In these visits, the teachers say, they find it easy to perceive the reason why their children come to school in cold weather before 8 o'clock in the morning.

The industrial schools were organized first, and afterward the Children's Aid Society started up, with the object of providing good homes for the children; but the two agencies afterward, finding themselves essentially one in their efforts, by the unanimous vote of their officers, united in their work.

It was thought advisable to have a separate home for the boys in the country, the girls remaining in the city; and soon the want was met by Mrs. Eliza Jennings, who donated a place of about twelve acres, with a large brick house and outbuildings. To this were added twenty acres adjoining, by Leonard Case, esq. Donations from friends enabled them to buy more land and build additional accommodations, so that now the society holds in trust about sixty acres of valuable land, a noble house, and beautiful school-room, well furnished, with commodious barn, stables, and all necessary farm-implements.

This charity was organized in 1857, and has now several branch schools in the city.

A condensed report of the school during the first fifteen years shows that, from the city-council, by subscriptions and donations, about $60,000 had been received and expended in carrying on its work. In that time 16,384 articles of clothing had been made and 9,991 repaired by the scholars; also a number of quilts patched in small blocks. To the scholars were given 30,555 articles of clothing, and large quantities were given to poor families, donated by individuals, ladies' benevolent societies, schools, &c. Instruction was given in the common English

9 E

branches to all, and the boys were employed, as far as possible, in the work about the buildings. The work is continuing and increasing every year.

THE HOME FOR FRIENDLESS WOMEN, TOLEDO,

is working for "the moral, spiritual, mental, social, and physical welfare" of homeless or friendless women, by giving them food, shelter, and medical attendance when necessary, and procuring employment for them when they are able to work. Many deserted wives, widows, and other even more unfortunate women have been succored in their distress and aided to help themselves.

THE CHILDREN'S HOME OF WASHINGTON COUNTY.

This institution was established by an act of the legislature of Ohio, entitled "An act for the establishment, support, and regulation of children's homes in the several counties in this State."

The county commissioners were authorized to purchase a suitable site and erect necessary buildings, to be styled the Children's Home, and to provide means by taxation for such purchase and support of the same; also to appoint three trustees, who should have the entire charge and control of the Children's Home and the inmates therein, the details of the work to be conducted and carried on the same as in similar charitable institutions.

The home is situated on the east bank of the Muskingum River, near the city of Marietta, on a farm containing one hundred and five acres.

The number provided for during the year is one hundred and four, at an expense of $7,604.63.

This was the first home established under the act providing for such institutions. Its trustees and managers were, therefore, without precedent or experience in regard to the mode in which it should be conducted, and they solicit visits of inquiry and inspection, that they may be aided by the experience and suggestions of others.

PENNSYLVANIA.

AIMWELL SCHOOL-ASSOCIATION, PHILADELPHIA.

In the year 1796 Anne Parrish, a Friend, resided in Philadelphia. Her parents were dangerously ill of yellow fever. She was strongly attached to them, and earnestly desired that they might be spared to her, resolving, if such were the case, to devote the remainder of her life to benevolent works.

They did recover, and one of the results of her dedication was the gathering of a few neglected children around her for instruction. For a time she taught them alone; but the success of her work, her delicate health, and the commiseration and sympathy aroused on account of the condition of the children of the poor for which she labored led two other 'riends to join her, and at the close of the year 1799 the association umbered eighteen. At this time the number of scholars was limited to fty, and has varied each year according to circumstances, some years ighty being the number. The number is always filled, with many wait-ig for admission.

The object is to instruct female children in the common English ranches and sewing, and to inculcate in them the principles of piety ad virtue.

Donations have been made to the association from time to time, and has received legacies, the income from which amounts to $1,500.

The association numbers 119 members.

UNION SCHOOL AND CHILDREN'S HOME, PHILADELPHIA.

This noble charity was organized to rescue neglected and destitute hildren in the district of Moyamensing. A day-school was opened for oys and girls, that an influence might be gained over them, and through iem upon the parents. As the work progressed it was found necessary) provide a home for a few little children, and from this necessity arose ie idea of establishing a "home" for destitute children. Application as made to the legislature for an act of incorporation, which was ranted in 1851, and the present name adopted.

A lot was purchased for $7,000, and on it was erected a substantial rick edifice, at a cost of $12,000. Two thousand dollars have been eceived from the State-treasury. The funds by which it has been ustained have been mostly from the benefactions of those generous itizens under whose kind auspices it has grown to its present state of sefulness and success.

Their fifteenth annual report contains the following passage: "Since he organization of this institution, on the first day of September, 1849, o the first day of January, 1865, 1,636 children have been the recipients if this charity, 945 of whom have been placed in families, and the sum if $118,321 has been collected and expended for its support."

During the month of October, 1873, the board of this institution eceived from the board of managers of the Little Wanderer's Home the following communication:

"*Resolved*, That an absolute conveyance and transfer of all the property of this corporation, real and personal, now clear of all encumbrance whatsoever, be made to the Union School and Children's Home: *Pro-vided*, That that institution will take charge of all such children here-tofore placed in homes by the Home for Little Wanderers, who may be returned to its custody, said children to be disposed of in accordance with the rules and regulations of the said Union School, &c.: *And pro-vided further*, that the said Union School will assume and pay all claims now outstanding against the Home for Little Wanderers, which are estimated not to exceed, in the whole, the sum of $1,000."

465

It was determined that, after a proper investigation, and provided the indebtedness should not exceed the sum named, the said offer should be accepted. Therefore, in accordance with a circular already issued, "this institution now will open, in the building formerly occupied by the Home for Little Wanderers, a temporary home for children and also a 'day-nursery.'"

The report of the treasurer will show that the financial crisis has, to some extent, affected our receipts, as thereby we have lost some of our largest annual contributors, and yet our work is greatly increased; and we appeal to all who may read our report to contribute of the means wherewith God has blessed them and aid us in giving timely relief to those who are ready to perish.

Our home, at the close of the year 1873, shelters 120 children; 104 have been admitted during the year, 56 placed out, and 17 returned to parents and friends.

THE WOMEN'S CHRISTIAN ASSOCIATION OF PITTSBURG AND ALLEGHENY,

In their labors for the improvement of the moral, intellectual, and social condition of women and children, have organized four distinct homes: a temporary home for destitute women, a home for aged Protestant women, a boarding-home for working-women, and a "sheltering arms." They have also, in addition, mission-work, Bible-readers' work, and an industrial school.

In the temporary home for destitute women, at 45 Chatham street, the destitute are sheltered, strangers are received and aided on their journeys, the sick cared for, and persons without employment furnished with a comfortable home until permanent situations are secured.

PITTSBURG AND ALLEGHENY HOME FOR THE FRIENDLESS.

This institution was organized in 1860, and is located in Allegheny City. The buildings cost $36,000, on a lot 125 feet front. The accommodations are ample for 150 children. As last reported, one-fourth were soldiers' orphans. The funds for its support are mainly derived from private charity. The legislature has made several appropriations, making in the aggregate the sum of $7,000.

The object of the institution is to afford a home, food, clothing, and schooling for such children as may be neglected or deserted by their parents or guardians.

SOCIETY OF THE HOME FOR THE FRIENDLESS, SCRANTON.

In response to a call from the members of the Young Men's Christian Association of Scranton, a public meeting of ladies was held in September, 1871, and a movement inaugurated in behalf of friendless women and children of the city.

A small house had been a few weeks before temporarily leased, and
rnished at the expense of the city, and had already several inmates.
though inconvenienced by repeated removals and insufficient accom-
)dations, thirty-seven persons had been received at the home at date of
it report, January, 1875—women and children whose ages ranged from
/enty years to the infant of days. This beginning developed the great
cessity of a more extended work, and a committee of ten ladies was
pointed to take preliminary steps for organization. At a subsequent
)eting a constitution was presented and approved, and fifty ladies
came members by signing the constitution and the annual payment
three dollars, and several became life-members by the payment of
ty dollars.
The society thus organized elected officers and a board of managers
r three, two, and one years and commenced their work, a report of
hich may be found in the table of statistics of orphan-asylums of
iis circular.
A lot has been secured, and arrangements are being made to erect
iereon permanent buildings.
The citizens respond heartily to the calls upon them. Many addi-
ons have been made to its list of membership, and there is great encour-
gement that the work so recently but successfully commenced will con-
nue to increase in proportion to the facilities at its command.

WISCONSIN.

THE CADLE HOME

s established on the Mission-Farm, near Green Bay, for the educa-
on and maintenance of orphan-children, for the care and relief of
ick, infirm, needy, destitute, or homeless persons, for the care and
upport of aged and infirm clergymen, and for other charitable purposes.
It owes its origin to the effort of the ladies of Christ Church, who
rganized a society to establish a home, and who, in 1867, purchased
he valuable grounds upon which the home stands. It derives its name
rom Rev. Richard F. Cadle, the first rector of Christ Church, the
iarliest Christian missionary among Protestants in all the region now
constituting the State of Wisconsin, and through him the title to the
farm was primarily acquired. It was organized in 1873, and has received
fifty-three inmates.

HOMES FOR AGED WOMEN.

These exist in almost every city of any considerable size, and are generally the outgrowth of religious organizations, each church endeavoring
to care for its own aged and helpless. Examples of these may be seen
in the Home for Aged Women of the Church of the Holy Communion,
Sixth avenue, New York, Episcopal; the Home for Aged Women, Sev-
enty-third street, New York, Presbyterian; the Ladies' Home Society of

the Baptist Churches of New York, which does a similar work; St. Luke's Home, Utica, N. Y., and the Home for the Friendless, Lombard street, Philadelphia, both Episcopal. The latter receives temporarily persons who are not members.

Similar institutions are provided in a number of cities through the beneficence of private individuals, and are open alike to persons of any and all religious beliefs, as, for example, the Louise Home in Washington, D. C., established by Hon. W. W. Corcoran, of that city. There are also homes for old men.

INDUSTRIAL SCHOOLS.

CALIFORNIA.

GOOD TEMPLARS' HOME FOR ORPHANS.

managers of the Good Templars' Home for Orphans, in Vallejo,
ate that for the past three years they have been convinced of the
ty of some employment for the children in the home other than
·suit of the educational advantages afforded them. Some light
·ial pursuit should be afforded the inmates, as a means of disci-
nd skill in workmanship. The capacity of self-helpfulness should
rly training and development in these children, and we believe
·re many light mechanical occupations which might be engaged
·r such auspices as to incur no loss. The subject has received
·arnest and careful consideration at the hands of this board, and
·eral conclusion of practicability arrived at.
·e of telegraph has been constructed to the home, whereby some
·al instruction has been given in the art of telegraphy, and with
·tisfactory results.

CONNECTICUT.

THE CONNECTICUT TRAINING-SCHOOL FOR NURSES,

ed to the State-hospital in New Haven, is modeled upon the
eneral principles as that in New York, the principal difference
that the nurses, instead of receiving $10 a month during their
·ar, receive only their board; but, if desired, they are loaned a
um of money weekly, the same to be repaid during the second
· possible. They are also required to wear a uniform-habit of
·ith white apron and cuffs. At the Bellevue school the nurses
·ply required to wear a white cap on the head to distinguish them
·hers. The same difficulty has been found here as elsewhere in
· the necessary number and quality of volunteers for this arduous
The first annual report of the school says:
a result of all the advertising for pupils, from ninety to one hun-
pplications have been received; but from some constitutional
on to thoroughness—a failing unhappily too common among

women—a large proportion of these persons applying have, on receiving the rules and finding that real work was required, withdrawn; some have done so with great regret, compelled to by their friends, but the larger part for the reason above mentioned. The places represented in the applications are New York, Massachusetts, Maine, Connecticut, Vermont, Ohio, Pennsylvania, New Jersey, Rhode Island, Michigan, Illinois, Minnesota, Virginia, and Canada, showing that the knowledge of the school is widespread."

On the whole, it is believed that the school has had during its first year a very good degree of success. The physicians and surgeons of the hospital with which it is connected report a very decided improvement in the nursing since the school commenced.

A suggestion is made to churches and other benevolent organizations as to the amount of good which might be accomplished by educating missionary nurses for the poor, and the offer is made to such organizations to train nurses for them in this school upon the payment of $5.50 weekly and the price of the uniform-dress.

DISTRICT OF COLUMBIA.

INDUSTRIAL HOME SCHOOL, GEORGETOWN.

This school takes boys and girls over 6 years of age, and instructs them in carpentry, turning, caning, sewing, and house-work. The management is unsectarian. Institution is sustained by earnings of the shop and contributions. It has done an excellent work in rescuing from helpless poverty and training to habits of useful and profitable industry large numbers of children who must otherwise have been thrown upon the town. To the younger of these it gives an education in the public schools, to the elder a knowledge of the industries above referred to.

During the past year it has been transferred to new quarters on the heights, made over to the managers by the guardians of the poor. The workshop, however, is continued in the old location in the town.

ILLINOIS.

THE ORPHAN GIRLS' HOME, CHICAGO,

Organized in 1874, takes girls from 12 to 16 years of age who have no one to care for them and no employment, (generally also lacking the skill necessary to command employment,) gives them a comfortable home and such instructions as they most need, in sewing, housework, or the elements of an English education, until there can be situations found for which they are qualified, either in families at house-work or in other occupations. About 130 girls have thus been fitted for, and aided to obtain, honorable and honest employment.

MARYLAND.

INDUSTRIAL SCHOOL, BALTIMORE.

sewing-machine school-department of the Henry Watson Child-Aid Society, Baltimore, Md., instructs about 600 pupils during the n the use of the machines and in the various descriptions of work on them, free of charge.

department for instruction in cutting and fitting dresses is a new h of work, organized June 1, 1874. Number in attendance since ization, 34; average daily attendance, 11; total number of lessons hed, 757.

s department, since its organization, has succeeded beyond expec-. It has steadily advanced in usefulness and popularity, new irs joining almost daily, gladly availing themselves of this means aining, free of charge, a lucrative and respectable livelihood.

se progress rapidly in their studies. Many who upon entering hool were ignorant of the proper use of the needle are now learn- cut and fit ladies' dresses. A very thorough system of instruction een adopted, graduating from the simpler articles of female wear- parel, such as aprons, to ladies' dresses.

ce the organization of this school (free to all applicants) its schol- ive made up, for themselves and families, 181 garments. It now ers a regular attendance of 24 scholars, ranging in age from 13 to irs.

ee of the scholars have graduated, with fair prospects of earning table livelihoods. As there is a constant and increasing demand ess-makers and seamstresses, the managers hope ere long to be ed from this and the sewing-machine-school to meet it, and thus to the girls a respectable livelihood.

T. JOSEPH'S INDUSTRIAL SCHOOL FOR GIRLS, BALTIMORE,

an Catholic,) receives girls of good character over 14 years of nd teaches them dress-making, embroidery, plain sewing, and work of all kinds. On leaving the institution the girls are pro- with good homes, some as dress-makers, some as seamstresses, thers as clerks in stores. It is supported by the labor of inmates.

ST. MARY'S INDUSTRIAL SCHOOL FOR BOYS, BALTIMORE.

man Catholic.) Besides workshops where various trades are taught, is connected with the institution a printing-office, where 13 boys mployed. A paper, entitled The Catholic Sunday Companion, is d and job-work generally is done. In the tailoring-department, ys are engaged; shoe-shop, 22; laundry, 6, and bakery, 3. There 12 boys in the institution. They are kept at school until about 12 old, and then are put at some one of the trades taught. Boys who are engaged in the workshops get about three hours' schooling a day. In this respect they are better off than many boys outside, who find it absolutely impossible to secure an apprenticeship at any trade.

MICHIGAN.

THE DETROIT INDUSTRIAL SCHOOL

Is located in the city of Detroit, and organized for the relief of the children of the poor and their instruction in the elements of knowledge and in the rudiments of mechanical arts.

It is a corporation, to continue for thirty years.

MISSOURI.

THE GIRLS' INDUSTRIAL HOME, ST. LOUIS.

The design of this institution is primarily to care for little ones who have no natural protectors or who fail to take care of them. They are taken here, not to be maintained indefinitely, but to be trained and educated for common and useful employment, to be transferred to other and more private homes as opportunity by adoption or otherwise presents.

None under 2 years nor over 12 are admitted. All are taught the common-school-branches, and those who are old enough needle-work also, including the cutting of garments and house-work. The institution is supported by contributions of the charitable.

NEW JERSEY.

THE ORPHAN ASYLUM AT NEWARK

Has recently opened an industrial department, in which the boys are instructed in the rudiments of printing, wood-carving, sign-painting, wood-engraving, carpentry, wood-turning, stone-carving, and drawing. The fixtures and apparatus obtained for the purpose, at a cost of $350, are as complete and perfect as would be required by any workmen to practice their arts. This department has as yet been but a short time in operation; still the indications are that, with very little practice, the boys will be able to save all the expense for carpenter-work of the institution, to make many holiday-articles for sale, earn some money in little jobs of printing, as cards, tags, &c., and, above all, acquire such a knowledge of the rudiments of useful trades as will be invaluable to them in after-life.

NEW YORK.

TRAINING-SCHOOL FOR NURSES, BELLEVUE HOSPITAL.

The first annual report of this school indicates that a very high degree of success has attended its efforts during its first year. This school

fers to women of fair education, good health, and ability an opportu-
ty for acquiring a useful, honorable, and lucrative profession without
ιe expenditure of any money—a profession acquired under masters of
е highest skill, physicians and surgeons of not only American but of
uropean fame. The nurses are expected to devote one year to the
quisition of their profession, during which time they are furnished
ith a home and $10 a month for their clothing. They are then required
remain a year longer to assist in training others, during which time
eir wages will be increased. The way in which this brilliant oppor-
nity has been appreciated by women in general is indicated in the
port of the secretary for 1874. She says:

" We were, at first, disappointed at the few desirable applicants who
esented themselves to be trained; but, as the knowledge of our school
adually spread over the country, we received, either through personal
terview with the superintendent or by letter, many applications from
omen offering themselves as probationers. Some were entirely unfit-
d by incapacity, physical weakness, or because, belonging to the
norant and uneducated class, they fell below our standard of admis-
on. But the majority were unwilling to devote two years to gaining
career, seeming to care little for really perfecting themselves in their
rofession. Filled as the land is with the cry for woman's work, this
ιdifference to thoroughness is the stumbling-block in the way of all edu-
ators, and has proved one of our most serious difficulties. We cannot
xact a less period from our probationers; the year of training is so
ostly that it surely is not asking too much that they should, in return,
;ive one year to training others. These applicants, numbering 73, were
rom all parts of the Union—New England, the Middle States, and the
far West, even including Colorado Territory, Minnesota, and California.

"The scarcity of such professionally-trained nurses throughout the
country was perceived in the effort to find women capable of acting as
head nurses. Advertisements, applications to doctors, and in fact
all available means, only brought us four, one of whom we were soon
forced to discharge for inefficiency.

"The probationers are rapidly being trained into good nurses. This is
shown by the fact that when, at one time, the superintendent, Miss Bow-
den, was left without head nurses, she was able unhesitatingly to place
three of the five-months' students in charge of wards. The degree of
success in the work and the appreciation of it by the hospital-authori-
ties are indicated by the fact that, whereas there was considerable hesitation in intrusting three wards to their control, they were soon requested
to undertake the nursing of the entire hospital, a thing it was not
possible for them to do, on account of a lack of a sufficient number of
workers, both of head nurses and probationers.

"Applicants are received for one month on probation, when, if found
suitable for the work, they are received as pupil nurses. They must
sign a written agreement to remain at the school for one year, and

after that time to consider themselves subject to the orders of the committee, (of whom the superintendent will make one,) for an additional
year, making two years in all, in consideration of training received.

"The instruction includes : (1) The dressing of blisters, burns, sores,
and wounds; the application of fomentations, poultices, and minor
dressings. (2) The application of leeches, externally and internally.
(3) The administration of enemas for men and women. (4) The management of trusses and appliances for uterine complaints. (5) The
best methods of friction to the body and extremities. (6) The management of helpless patients—moving, changing, giving baths in bed,
preventing and dressing bed-sores, and managing positions. (7) Ban-
daging, making bandages and rollers, lining of splints. (8) Making
patients' beds and removing sheets while the patient is in bed.

"The pupil nurses will attend the operations and assist at them. They
will be taught every kind of sick-cookery and the preparation of drinks
and stimulants for the sick ; to understand thoroughly the art of ventilation without chilling the patient, both in private houses and hospital-
wards, and all that pertains to night, in distinction from day, nursing;
to make accurate observations, and report to the physician, of the
state of secretions, expectoration, pulse, skin, appetite, temperature of
the body, intelligence, (as delirium or stupor,) breathing, sleep, condition
of wounds, eruptions, formation of matter, effect of diet, or of stimulants, or of medicines ; and to learn the management of convalescents.

"The teaching will be given by attending and resident physicians and
surgeons, at the bedside of the patients, by the superintendent, and by
the head nurses.

"The pupils will pass through the different wards, serving and being
taught, for one year. They will board and lodge at the home free of
expense, and will be paid $10 (ten dollars) a month for their clothing
and personal expenses. This sum is in no manner intended as wages,
it being considered that their education during this time will be a full
equivalent for their services.

"At the expiration of the year they will be promoted to such positions
as they may be found capable of holding, with a proportionate increase
of salary.

"When the full term of two years is ended, the nurses thus trained
will be at liberty to choose their own field of labor, whether in hospitals,
in private families, or in district-nursing among the poor. On leaving
the school they will each receive a certificate of ability and good character, signed by the physicians of the committee and the superintendent. These certificates will require to be renewed at fixed periods, in
order to prevent the public from being imposed upon and to keep up
the nurses' interest in the home."

FREE TRAINING-SCHOOL FOR WOMEN, NEW YORK.

The Women's Educational and Industrial Society of New York City
has established a Free Training-School for Women, at 47 East Tenth

reet, six doors from Broadway, where free instruction is given to women
cooking, laundry-work, house-work, all kinds of sewing, phonography,
ok-keeping, proof-reading, and writing.

Every respectable woman who applies for help is taught to work, free
expense, and, when competent, is supplied with work or placed in a
od situation.

This free instruction is afforded because in many instances the toil of
men is rendered unremunerative by their want of skill in labor. Inef-
iency and idleness too often lead to moral degradation. Because every
dividual diverted from evil courses is a direct gain to society, as well
a good to humanity, no pains are spared to guide material for labor
to those channels of useful industry from which the community derives
ch substantial benefits.

No women are received for training in household-labor without refer-
ices, which are verified before entrance to the school is permitted.
, when taught and placed in good situations, domestics fail to heed
e good advice given by the managers, to make themselves valuable to
eir employers by faithful, respectful, and willing service, they are not
gain supplied with places. If a servant has just cause for complaint
gainst her employer, as being unkind or unjust to her, the place can-
ot again be filled through the agency of the schools.

Places are provided without charge to employés.

Over 3,000 women have been trained and placed during the past year.
In cases where applicants for instruction are in straitened circum-
ances, the society provides means of support until permanent employ-
ent is obtained. Sympathy, advice, and help are cordially afforded,
nd positions are procured as each one becomes a good workwoman.
Io barriers of nationality or sectarianism are raised, the sole conditions
eing decent, womanly conduct and faithful application to work.

Realizing the fact that the needle gives occupation to thousands in the
ity, the society affords the most ample means for attaining proficiency
in all branches of sewing. Those desiring to become first-class machine-
operators are taught the use of the Wheeler & Wilson and other
machines. A thorough knowledge of hand-sewing, embroidery, and
lace-work is also imparted by competent teachers. As soon as learners
are able to manage their machines, manufacturers' work is given to them,
to be done under the supervision of teachers, and each one receives the
price of the quantity she completes, thus being enabled to earn money
after the first few days of instruction. Hundreds of women have already
been qualified for work, and are now placed where they are earning good
livelihoods.

PRINTERS' TRAINING-SCHOOL, ST. JOHNLAND.

At St. Johnland, Long Island, a charitable community, under the
auspices of the Episcopal Church, New York, the most important and
remunerative of the industries taught the crippled children sent there

.from St. Luke's Hospital is type-setting. Since its establishment, the printing-office there has been doubled in size. Its work is not, as in the beginning of the experiment, confined to composition and stereotyping, but a press is in operation, and twelve young apprentices are engaged in type-setting, book-folding, &c., under an experienced superintendent. This, besides its training of the youthful employés in a useful trade, promises to be a lucrative business. The net proceeds of the business in 1873, about two thousand dollars, ($2,000,) were not an adequate representation of its gain, the enlargement of the premises having been but recently brought into use.

INDUSTRIAL SCHOOLS OF THE CHILDREN'S AID SOCIETY, NEW YORK.

The Children's Aid Society industrial schools, so called, numbering 21 day- and 13 evening-schools, differ from the common primary schools principally in that they furnish food for the hungry, clothing for those whose need of it is very great, and instruction in sewing to girls. No industrial training is given to boys. The irregular attendance permitted in these schools, with the charitable assistance afforded, places their benefits within the reach of the large number of children in New York who are obliged to follow street-trades or other employments a portion of the day. As the circumstances of the children improve with the aid received here, they are, whenever possible, transferred to the public schools. As many as 2,296 garments were made during 1874 by the girls in these schools.

At the Girls' Lodging-House, St. Mark's Place, there are taught, in addition to plain sewing, dress-making, the use of the sewing-machine, and house-work. The sewing-machine-school turned out 933 operators in 1873 and 734 in 1874. The girls who are learning dress-making remain from four to six months and are given their board. The great difficulty with the training-class in house-work is said to be that the girls are not allowed to remain in it long enough to become thoroughly trained, so great is the demand for their services.

INDUSTRIAL SCHOOL OF THE HEBREW BENEVOLENT AND ORPHAN ASYLUM SOCIETY, NEW YORK.

This society, now over half a century old, a few years ago added to its other good work for the young an industrial school, where the older boys of the asylum are taught such vocations as enable them to provide for themselves after leaving the institution. The need for some such provision was suggested by the want of success often attending the system of binding out or securing the adoption of the children. Moreover, it was found difficult to make even this disposition of those children who were neither intellectually bright nor personally prepossessing. Accordingly a workshop was thought of, and the manufacture of boots and shoes was first introduced. The experiment was successful, netting, the first year, a profit of $229.44. Encouraged by this success and by a donation a printing-press, type, and furniture amounting to $1,079.89, another anch of industry was introduced. From the start, the printing-estab-hment differed from the shoe-factory in not receiving any appropria-ins from the board, excepting a loan of $400. Besides, the elder anch loaned a part of its earnings to the younger, and so, helping each her, both commenced their struggle for self-support and independence. ie proceeds were made use of to pay both foremen and other employés the factories, to remunerate the apprentices, and to buy presses, type, d furniture. Rapid progress was made by the younger branch, and e erection of a suitable building for the industrial school soon followed. is was provided with a large medium steam-press and a steam-paper-tter, purchased out of the funds of the society.

There are at present employed in the industrial school a foreman and sistant foreman, a proof-reader, an engineer, and a master-shoemaker. Guided by the principle that the industrial school is not a money-aking concern, but solely instituted with the view of teaching the boys useful trade, which shall enable them to earn an honorable and respect-le livelihood, they are allowed to leave the institution whenever they e so far advanced in skill and workmanship as to be able to look out r themselves. Consequently they are taught in the shortest possible ne the art of printing in all its branches, viz, news, book, and job mposition, and press-work. In fact, there is no other printing estab-hment where an apprentice is offered an opportunity for making such ogress, because there is not a printer so disinterested as to allow iskilled and inexperienced hands the free use of type and machinery, hich constitute the capital of his establishment.

Arrangements have also been made for the instruction of the boys in istrumental music, and 20 boys, for five months of the year 1874, xeived such instruction, making considerable advance in the art.

WILSON INDUSTRIAL SCHOOL AND MISSION, NEW YORK.

The primary idea of this institution is to educate the daughters of arents too poor to send them to the public schools, and to fit them for isefulness while rescuing them from the lives of ignorance and crime 'hich threaten them. Inseparable from this idea is that of interesting ind elevating the parents of the children and securing their co-opera-ion. The means used in endeavoring to accomplish these ends are, irst, the instruction of the girls in the common-school-branches and in iseful industries, the feeding of those who are hungry, the furnishing of iothing, and, when needed, of temporary lodging. Secondly, Sunday-ichools are taught, in connection with the day-schools, open every Sun-lay at half-past two o'clock. Thirdly, mothers' meetings are held every Tuesday at 1 o'clock p. m., under the direction of the missionary com-nittee, where mothers of the children in the day- and Sunday-schools 'eceive instruction in sewing and household-industries, and are allowed :o purchase materials for the clothing of themselves and families at a cheap rate, by the weekly deposit of such sums as they can spare. They also, through the kindness of friends, enjoy a monthly tea-meeting. A mission-church, organized in 1867, was an outgrowth of the Sunday- and day-schools. The institution relies wholly for support upon voluntary contributions. The managers greatly desire to establish a Kindergarten, where poor women, obliged to go out to work, may leave their young children in safety, and which may be preparatory to the day-school. The statistics of the institution for 1874 are—

Average of attendants on Sunday-school 325
Families represented in day-school 178
Children who have attended school during year 420
Average attendance 198

INDUSTRIAL TRAINING IN THE WILSON SCHOOL, NEW YORK.

In the Wilson Industrial School girls are taught, in connection with the elementary branches of a common-school-education, plain needle-work, the use of the sewing-machine, dress-making, and house-work. Each afternoon is devoted to instruction in plain needle-work, the children earning, by a system of credit-marks, the garments which they make, as well as shoes and stockings. The sewing is prepared for them by the ladies of the work-committee. During the past year there have been distributed 1,040 garments, 236 pairs of shoes, and 244 pairs of stockings.

The outfitting-department was created to give to older girls a means of support, at the same time guarding them from the temptations and influences of evil companionship, almost inseparable from factories and other large establishments. After they are proficient in plain sewing, they are taught the use of sewing- and button-hole-machines.

Every kind of ladies' and children's garments is here neatly and very cheaply made, and patronage is earnestly solicited.

In the dress-making-department girls from 15 to 20 years of age are taught, under the superintendence of a competent and experienced dress-maker. This, like the outfitting-department, is dependent on patronage. It is desired to make both these departments not only self-sustaining, but a source of revenue.

There is also a house-work-class, in which the older girls are trained in the different kinds of house-work, to fit them either for their duties in their own homes or for situations in christian families.

INDUSTRIAL SCHOOL AT THE FIVE POINTS HOUSE OF INDUSTRY.

This, to the inevitable sewing for girls, adds certain industries appropriate to boys, as tailoring, shoe-mending, and type-setting.

THE LADIES' HOME MISSIONARY SOCIETY.

At the home, 61 Park Place, New York, the ladies of this society teach sewing to the girls of their school.

THE HOUSE AND SCHOOL OF INDUSTRY, NEW YORK,

Has a sewing-school, which meets twice a week. Young girls and children are taught by two salaried teachers to sew and embroider. Work of the finest quality is executed to order by the employés of the institution, who must be expert seamstresses, many of them being ladies in reduced circumstances. An effort is made in the sewing-school to fit pupils to do this fine ordered work.

ST. JOSEPH'S INDUSTRIAL HOME, NEW YORK,

(Roman Catholic,) receives girls over years 3 of age, and teaches sewing by machine and hand, knitting, and general housework. Sustained by donation, &c.

INDUSTRIAL SCHOOLS OF THE HOME FOR THE FRIENDLESS, NEW YORK.

The Home for the Friendless, or the American Female Guardian Society, New York, has connected with it eleven "industrial schools," of similar scope and aim to the foregoing, with a yearly total attendance of over 4,000 children, averaging daily about 1,137, with 22 teachers, and as many monitors, trained from among the pupils employed. Food, clothing, and religious instruction are given these children, and industrial training to the extent of teaching the girls to sew and the older ones to cut and make garments. As in the schools of the Children's Aid Society and others, an appropriation is received from the public-school-board in proportion to the number of children in attendance.

THE NURSERY AND CHILD'S HOSPITAL, NEW YORK,

Has a training-school for the women connected with it, who are always employed in sewing, washing, or nursing. They are thus trained to earn an honest living when they leave this home. Some months ago the matron, among the other good things she has done in her care of the women, organized a sewing-room, where the women are taught the use of the sewing-machine, and among them there chanced to be a dress-maker, who instructs others in this important art. Some very neat work has been done in this department, which might compete with other and well-known establishments in the city. The steam-laundry, which has been recently arranged, has, in addition to the washing done for the inmates, been employed in doing washing for families.

THE GUILD, OR CONGREGATION OF ST. AUGUSTINE, NEW YORK,

Sustains a school, where sewing is taught the girls who attend the Sunday-school of that church.

BOYS' HOME OF INDUSTRY, ROCHESTER,

(Roman Catholic,) receives boys under 12 years of age; teaches them farming, canning fruit, &c. The institution is supported by such labor.

10 E

THE WOMAN'S CHRISTIAN ASSOCIATION, OF UTICA,

In addition to its other charitable work, as visiting the poor and sick in hospitals and in their homes, keeps a school, where instruction is given to about 150 girls and women in sewing.

THE INDUSTRIAL HOME OF THE CITY OF UTICA,

Organized in 1871, under the auspices of the Woman's Christian Association, for "the improvement of the physical, intellectual, moral, and religious condition of women, particularly of young women who are dependent upon their own exertions for support," is a boarding-house or home for worthy and respectable girls employed in the various manufacturing-establishments of the city, where such girls can live for a sum within their means, and be trained, as there may be occasion, for higher skill in the industries in which they are engaged. As in kindred homes elsewhere, provision is also made for their mental and moral improvement, through books, good papers, and the direct instructions of lady visitors.

OHIO.

The young ladies' branch of the Women's Christian Association of Cincinnati have recently established an industrial institute or school, the aims and method of which are described in the following communication, kindly furnished by Mrs. F. P. Anderson, of Cincinnati:

INDUSTRIAL SCHOOL OF THE YOUNG LADIES' BRANCH OF WOMEN'S CHRISTIAN ASSOCIATION OF CINCINNATI.

"Shortly after our organization, in November, 1870, it was suggested that, as a branch of the Women's Christian Association, we might very properly carry out a pet scheme of the association, the establishment of an industrial institute, where women of all ages might receive instruction (free of charge) in all professions or works for which woman is fitted. We were urged to open, first, departments where cooking, washing, and ironing would be taught. No means could be devised for giving instruction in these branches without a large outlay of money, and we were at the time almost penniless. We were obliged, therefore, to begin our work with a sewing-school. The use of a large room over a pork-house, in rather an undesirable part of the city, was offered by benevolent gentlemen, free of rent, and we gladly accepted it. In November, 1871, we opened with 7 scholars, and a good earnest woman to teach them, to whom we paid $33 per month. At that time we had about 16 active members, and few of any other sort. The school increased rapidly in size, and through the year the average attendance was 20. Some 700 garments were made during the year, a large proportion of them for our Bethel. As most of the girls who came to us could scarcely do more

ian thread a needle, we were obliged to confine ourselves for some time
in plain, coarse sewing. So much for the past.

We have some 204 members in all in our society at present, and of
these 36 are active members. From our active members we elect officers
id form standing and temporary committees.

We now find ourselves very comfortably and decently settled, in four
rge, well-ventilated rooms, in a fine building centrally located, the two
iper rooms devoted to teaching plain sewing, the two lower rooms to
ress-making.

Applicants to enter the school are referred to some one member of the
lmitting committee, by whom investigations are made, and, if proper
bjects, they are admitted for six months. We will not take them for
shorter time. We have printed forms, which the parents or responsi-
e parties must sign, binding the applicant to us for the time stated.
iey may remain as much longer as they will, or as may be necessary
complete their training for either plain sewing, dress-making, or both,
id we use our influence to keep them, where they show aptitude for the
ork; and, where they do not, we endeavor to induce them to go out
i house servants and make efforts to secure desirable homes for them.
ime 126 girls have been admitted since the opening of the school.
he girls in the primary department, where plain sewing is taught, are
vided into classes, the first-class girls only receiving pay. They do all
ie order-work, and have been paid at the rate of $1 per week, until
cently. Now they receive half the profits on all garments made by
iem. We entered work at the exposition of last year and this, and
iis year received the highest premium (silver medal) for ladies' and
hildren's undergarments. As some of our girls have been with us for
wo years, they are able to undertake making the most elaborate style
f undergarment. This department is open from 8 a. m. till 5 p. m.,
or five days of the week; average attendance, 18. Our superintend-
int receives $40 per month. This department will never pay of itself,
or the reason that three-fourths of the pupils are beginners.

To our dress-making-department, we take only those who understand
machine- and *hand*-sewing thoroughly; and in order to ascertain this
hey must be examined in the primary department, where they will be
letained until they are taught all that may be necessary to fit them for
he dress-making-department. For the first four months, they work with-
iut remuneration. Through the fifth month, they are paid $1.25 per
reek. The next rise is to $2, then to $2.50, and finally to $3. In
io case can the wages be raised from $1.25 until the pupil be fully fitted
o receive more. Of course we do not expect to make *dress-makers* of
ill the girls who enter this department; but, if they learn how to do all
orts of good work on dresses, they can earn from five to eight dollars
er week easily. When a pupil deserves more than $3, if we need her
ssistance, we shall propose to keep her as long as need be, and then aid
er in obtaining a good situation. As we propose to give printed cer-

tificates to girls who graduate, as it were, from either department, we presume it will be an easy matter for them to get places. We shall have an opportunity to test the efficacy of this plan shortly, as several of our girls will be ready to leave us.

Our dress-making-department is open all through the week, from 8 a. m. to 6 p. m. To the person in charge we have been paying $100 per month; from this time on we are to pay her $125 per month, and gladly do so, for this department not only pays for itself, but will soon pay the expenses of the entire school. Since June, the expenses of the school have exceeded receipts by $21 the month only. The average attendance is 15. We take 3 *novices* every spring and 3 more every fall, giving precedence to girls of the primary department always. At present there is no necessity for adding to the accommodations or number of teachers, as we are already prepared to teach all who desire to come.

CLEVELAND AID SOCIETY INDUSTRIAL SCHOOLS.

These schools teach sewing to the girls who attend, and to a small number of girls at the home housework is taught, and they are fitted for situations in families. The boys, who are on a farm in the village of West Cleveland, learn farmwork, particularly gardening, in addition to the usual common-school-branches. The Cleveland board of education furnish a teacher and an assistant to the school, which includes all the boys belonging to the farm. The larger ones spend sufficient time in field or garden to answer the purpose of a gymnasium. All have the healthy, contented look of comfortable farmer-boys. There is not a suspicion of prison-discipline about the place. The superintendent, Mr. Waterton, who has been engaged in the work since its inception—about twenty years—making it his life-work, and to whose faithful, persevering labors is due much of the success achieved, finds these neglected boys quite amenable to moral influences. The teachers, and others in charge of the children, preserve an influence over them by interesting themselves in the boys and in their pursuits, and the necessity for punishment is generally prevented by being with the boys and directing their work and play.

PENNSYLVANIA.

INDUSTRIAL TRAINING IN GIRARD COLLEGE FOR ORPHANS, PHILADELPHIA.

During the first five years of the course the pupils are instructed in reading, writing, spelling, geography, the rudiments of arithmetic, the English grammar, and the history of the United States; and during the last three the higher branches are taken up. Boys who, through idleness or incompetency, fail to make satisfactory progress in their studies, are bound out as soon after they arrive at 14 years of age as suitable places can be found for them; meantime they receive instruction in the working-classes of the institution. If a pupil indicates, by his natural capacity or his tastes and acquirements, that his mental culture is most important, he has the means for improvement. The way is open and free, and the instrumentalities and teachers are at his side ready to aid him. Pupils there receive such intellectual education as they are mentally qualified to acquire and such instruction in practical handicrafts as is best suited to their usefulness, the institution embracing the home, the college, and the workshop.

How to combine the industrial feature with the educational idea of a college was not at first understood by the managers of the institution as clearly as in the light of experience it afterward appeared. In 1864 a chair of industrial science was established, embracing the practical and theoretic teachings of various handicrafts. The labor-branches in the work-room thus arranged for were type-setting, printing, bookbinding, type-casting, stereotyping, turning, carpentering, daguerreotyping, photography, electrotyping, electroplating, and practical instruction in the electric telegraph. Shoemaking had already been taught and carried on successfully for three years.

In consequence of the increasing difficulty of finding employers willing to take boys under indentures, the working-class in 1868 had become too large for the existing facilities for manual labor, and it became necessary to enlarge them by introducing a greater variety of handicrafts; which has been done as far as the present comparatively limited capacity of the buildings would allow.

INDUSTRIAL HOME FOR GIRLS, 762 SOUTH TENTH STREET, PHILADELPHIA.

This excellent institution was opened for the reception of inmates in September, 1857, by citizens of Philadelphia, and incorporated in 1859.

The building and property now owned by the institution cost $20,900. Thirty inmates can be conveniently accommodated.

During the fourteen years it has been in operation, the lady managers have admitted 349 girls between the ages of 12 and 18 years, nearly all of whom have been put into good homes or returned to their parents, and have done well.

No appropriations have been received, either from the State or city, but the support of the institution is entirely dependent upon individual bounty.

THE INDUSTRIAL SCHOOL OF THE IMMACULATE CONCEPTION, WEST PHILADELPHIA.

(Roman Catholic.) Girls of a good moral character are received into this institution and taught dress- and shirt-making; embroidery on linen, silk, and flannel; artificial flowers; knitting, and all kinds of housework. The institution is self-supporting.

.t is found, meets a pressing want of the times, and is almost self-sustaining.

It was a significant fact, brought out at the second national convention of the thirty-six Women's Christian Associations of the United States assembled at Philadelphia, October last, that three-fourths of the number have established homes on the same plan with our own, showing plainly the need of such an institution as we represent to be not only widespread, but so apparent as to attract universal attention. The first one was founded by a Miss Bramwell, a most gifted lady, of London.

THE WOMAN'S CHRISTIAN ASSOCIATION OF PITTSBURG AND ALLE—GHENY

Have a prosperous sewing-school of about fifty pupils. The garmen made by them are given them as rewards for good conduct and e ciency.

SOUTH CAROLINA.

CHARLESTON SEWING SCHOOL.

In Charleston, S. C., about fifty children of poor parents are instructe—d by ladies of the Episcopal Church, on Saturdays, in hand-sewing an d the use of the machine, receiving the garments made by them as gift—.

TENNESSEE.

GIRLS' INDUSTRIAL HOME, KNOXVILLE.

This school had its origin in a benevolent association of Christians of several religious denominations united, which association was organized in 1873. In 1874 an Industrial Home was started, and its results for a year were so good that the work is continued, and it is hoped that soon an act of incorporation will be passed. Little street-beggars from 5 to 14 years of age are gathered up from their evil associations and trained in habits of industry and good principles. Household-labor and sewing are taught them, and it is expected that the trade of dress-making may be soon also introduced. The girls are sent to the public schools for the ordinary school-training.

WISCONSIN.

ST. ROSE'S SCHOOL, MILWAUKEE.

St. Rose's (for female orphan children, Milwaukee) receives childre over one year of age; teaches the common-school-branches, and cookin laundry-work, and sewing. Before leaving the asylum, all are provid with good situations, and generally give satisfaction.

APPENDIX A.

REPORT

OF

R. L. DUGDALE, Esq., TO ELISHA HARRIS, M. D.

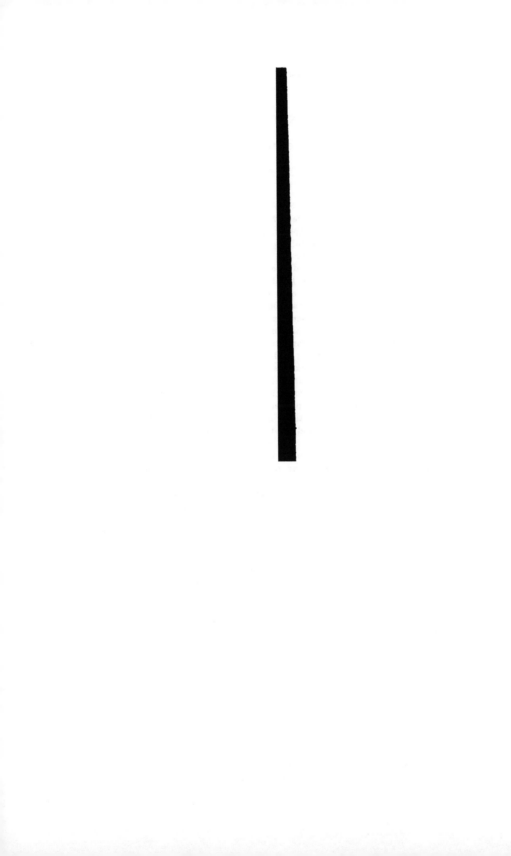

APPENDIX A.

lowing is the report referred to in the letter of transmittal:

PRISON ASSOCIATION OF NEW YORK,
58 BIBLE-HOUSE, ASTOR PLACE,
New York, June 26, 1875.

R : Your repeated request for a copy of the records and official report con-
e lineage of the stock of offenders, paupers, and unfortunates, in which
, the Mother of Criminals," appears, must be answered briefly, while I again
await the appearance of the full report, with its genealogical charts, now in
)f the State printer at Albany.

that six generations of debased womanhood and manhood, from parentage
degenerate and abandoned in habits and social state that the community
y county allowed the first and each succeeding generation of the children
·ecause so degenerate, at last have been traced and described as a conspicu-
·f criminals, vagabonds, and paupers, is certainly natural. It is simply the
iological sequences. The connection of events has been traced from the
nates of prisons, jails, and reformatories, and paupers in a particular dis-
to a characteristic parentage; and, by a retrogressive search through six
3, Mr. Dugdale, who undertook this task, completed the records which you
ioned under the synthetical title "the Mother of Criminals."

·ar 1871, the writer reported, concerning the county in which these events
red, that the relationships of pauperism and vice to crime and disorder will
inquiry by the Prison Association's committee. Fortunately Mr. Dugdale,
able and exact inquirer, found this trail of debased lineage while searching
i of a monstrous group of criminals and vicious youth last year. It is suffi-
the writer assures you that a more rigorous and trustworthy student of facts
i character than Mr. Dugdale has rarely if ever searched among the sources
,nd pauperism. His official report being a lengthy one, embodying a great
grouped statistics, it becomes necessary to respond to your requests by the
)rief abstracts, derived from that report, in the form of answers to the essen-
ions concerning which you now ask for information. As you seek to illus-
ublic duty of universal and adequate education and disciplinary training,
from actual experience will show that it is at an enormous risk to the peace,
economy, and the interests of morality in any community that vagrant and
ildren are permitted to grow up into an abandoned and degraded maturity,
e paupers or criminals, and to entail their own likeness upon successive
i8.

h great regard, faithfully yours,

ELISHA HARRIS, M. D.

IIN EATON,
nited States Commissioner of Education.

ABSTRACT OF THE COMMITTEE'S REPORT.

PRISON ASSOCIATION OF NEW YORK,
58 BIBLE HOUSE, ASTOR PLACE,
New York, June 25, 1875.

.o delay of the Prison Association's thirtieth annual report, in the State
lands, has so long postponed the publication of your special chapter concern-
nal families and their entailments in one of the counties, that I must

request of you the kindness to make a brief statement in regard to a few of the more essential points concerning that criminal and pauper stock. These points relate solely to the questions which most concern physiologists, educators, and the students of social science.

As all the points that are minutely elaborated and framed upon personal records in your full report cannot be here recited, I beg leave to ask your attention only to the following, to which you can append such replies as seem best suited to convey the truths which the facts show, without here reproducing the genealogical charts themselves. I submit these points in thirteen separate questions.

Yours,

. E. HARRIS.

RICHARD L. DUGDALE, Esq.,
 Chairman of Committee on Jails and Sources of Crime in Hudson River Counties, and Member of Executive Committee of Prison Association of New York.

———

NEW YORK, *June* 25, 1875.

SIR: As you request, I cheerfully answer the questions you have addressed to me, and I have placed your points in that order of arrangement which enables me to give the facts most accurately in the order of their occurrence. Thanking you for the opportunity of adding certain facts to those related in my report,

I remain, yours truly,   R. L. DUGDALE.

ELISHA HARRIS, M. D.,
 Corresponding Secretary, &c.

—

(1) What number of persons did you find in the jail in Ulster County who were ascertained to be kinsfolks; and by how many family names called, at what ages, and for what alleged offenses?

There were six persons passing under four different family names at the time I visited the Ulster County jail. All of them were blood-relations to each other in some degree. The oldest, a man 55 years of age, was awaiting trial for receiving stolen goods; his daughter, aged 18, but who passes for 16, held as a witness against him; her uncle, aged 42, burglary in the first degree; the illegitimate daughter of the latter's wife, aged 12 years, upon which child he had attempted rape, and who was waiting to be sent to the reformatory on Randall's Island for vagrancy; and two brothers, aged respectively 19 and 14, accused of an assault with intent to kill, they having pushed a child over a high cliff and nearly killed him by the fall. Subsequently other members of the same family, though distantly related, were arrested for minor offenses. Upon trial the oldest was acquitted; although the stolen goods were found in his house, his previous good character having been in his favor; the guilt belonged to his brother-in-law, who was living in his house, which brother-in-law is the man aged 42 above mentioned. This man is an illegitimate child, a habitual criminal, the son of an unpunished and cautious thief. He had two brothers and one sister, all of whom are thieves, the sister being the contriver of crime, while they execute it. The daughter of this woman, the girl aged 18 above mentioned, testified at the trial, which resulted in convicting her uncle and getting him sentenced for twenty years to State prison, that she was forced to accompany him upon his last expedition, that he loaded her with the stolen goods, and that he beat her on the way home, the journey being over two miles, because the load was beyond her strength to carry. When this girl was released, her father, mother, and uncle being in jail, left without a home, she was forced to make her lodging in a brothel on the outskirts of the city, and next morning she applied to the judge to be recommitted to prison, stating that she had been obliged to submit to nine men on the night previous. She has since been sent to the house of refuge. Of the two boys, one was discharged by the grand jury; the other was tried and received five years' imprisonment in Sing Sing.

(2) How many children of the same family stock did we find in the House of Refuge, and for what offenses were they or some of them committed?

Since 1870 nine of the children of the family to whom the above members belong have been sent to the House of Refuge. The offenses are: petty larceny, 1; vagrancy, 4; disorderly conduct, 4. Six are boys and three girls, six being descendants of Margaret.

(3) What is the number of generations, from the girl Margaret, counting her as the first, down to the children we found in the House of Refuge?

Counting Margaret as belonging to the first generation, some of the children above mentioned belong to the fourth generation and some to the fifth. At three points there is a sixth generation, represented by six children, and at two of the points in this genesis I find illegitimate offspring, one being the fruit of an incestuous intercourse between a man in the fourth generation with an illegitimate niece in the fifth generation, the mother being under 15 years of age at her infant's birth; the other having borne a child before 12 years old.

(4) In what line of heredity did you trace back the burglar, the boy ———, (guilty of assault or attempted homicide,) and the woman ———, who contrived plans of burglary?

The burglar, aged 42, is in the fourth generation of the illegitimate line of Margaret, as also is his sister. The boy is in the fifth generation; the girl aged 18 is in the fifth generation of Margaret on her mother's side and in the fourth generation of Margaret's sister on her father's side, both parents being descendants of the illegitimate children of the same generation as Margaret.

(5) Please describe the original habitats of this line of families, the peculiarities of their homes and social surroundings, and changes they have undergone during the past fifty years.

The ancestral breeding-spot in which this family has been nurtured nestles along the forest-covered margin of five lakes, so rocky as to be at some parts inaccessible. Most of the ancestors were squatters upon the soil, lived in log or stone houses similar to the slave-hovels, all ages, sexes, relations, and strangers "bunking" indiscriminately, and, where not producing illicit relations, evolving an atmosphere of suggestiveness that fatally broke down habits of chastity. Even to this day some of them occupy the self-same hovels built nearly a century ago. Others of these habitations have two rooms, but so firmly has habit established modes of living that they nevertheless, in many cases, only use one congregate dormitory. In many houses I found an overcrowding which was so close it suggested to my mind that these shanties were the country equivalents of the city-tenement-houses. Domesticity is impossible. The older girls, finding no privacy within a home overrun with younger brothers and sisters, purchased privacy at the risk of prudence, and the night-rambles through woods and tangles end too often in illegitimate offspring. During the last thirty years the establishment of cement-mills through this section of country has brought about the building of houses better suited to secure domesticity, and with this change alone there is no doubt that an accompanying change in personal habits is being introduced which would otherwise be impossible.

(6) What number of sisters and half-sisters, by same family name, do you find in the first generation of the unfortunate group of sisters, and were they alike socially abandoned?

Margaret is reported to have had five sisters. The parentage of these sisters has not been absolutely ascertained. The probability is that they were not all of them full sisters; that some, if not all of them, were illegitimate, and the family name, in two cases, is obscure, which accords with the supposition that at least two of the women were half-sisters to the other four, the legitimate daughters bearing a family name, the illegitimate keeping either the mother's name or adopting that of the reputed father. Five of these women in the first generation were married; the sixth one it has been impossible to trace, for she moved out of the county. Of the five that are known, three have had illegitimate children before marriage. Margaret had one bastard son, who is the grandfather and great-grandfather of the distinctively criminal line. Another sister had two illegitimate sons, who do not appear to have had any children. A third sister had four, three boys and one girl, the three oldest children being mulattoes, and the youngest, a boy, white. The fourth sister is reputed chaste, while no information could be gathered respecting the fifth in this respect, but she was the mother of one of the distinctively pauperized lines.

(7) What, briefly, is the personal record of Margaret, as given to you by old inhabitants, now living, who knew her; and when did she die ?

Margaret was a brawny and coarse white woman, temperate, but not industrious, possessing, in this last respect, the general features of most of the descendants. She did washing and chores, was not a criminal, but received help from the town. She died shortly after 1825, aged from 60 to 65 years.

(8) What number of persons and what classification does your latest analysis of the first catalogue of the descendants of these girls give ?

In my first catalogue, which forms the basis of my report to the Prison Association of New York, there are 540 persons of the blood of the five sisters who were the mothers of this stock and 169 persons who intermarried with them. Many of these latter, however, were blood-relations in the male lines of descent. Since that report was prepared for the press, 125 more names, with more or less complete histories, have been gathered, and the probabilities are that, were all the collateral branches traced, not less than 1,200 persons would form the full lineage of these six women.

The statistical analysis of the family, including the direct descendants and those who intermarried, as given in my first catalogue, is as follows :

Total number	709
Males	327
Females	319
Legitimate	337
Illegitimate	106
Of marriageable age	474
Unmarried adults	46
Married	215
Women who had bastards before marriage	24
Women who had bastards after marriage	13
Harlots	127
Total number of harlots	164
Not ascertained	95
Number who were barren or impotent	46
Kept brothels	17
Syphilitic, (notoriously)	63
Number who acquired some property	22
Number of the same who lost property	8
Number who received out-door relief	142
Number of years' individual relief	734
Number receiving alms-house-relief	64
Number of years' individual relief	96
Number of criminals	76
Number of years' imprisonment	116
Number of offenses, (indictable crimes)	115

With the exception of perhaps a dozen instances, the number of paupers and criminals is derived from the public records, and the figures are therefore very much below the truth, because the full records could not be found, a large proportion of them being destroyed. As to the diseases, the information has been furnished by several compe-

physicians; and, as to the illegitimacy, it rests on the testimony of various wit-
es, sometimes the children or grandchildren, sometimes the brothers and sisters,
etimes other relations.

) Having given the footings of your statistical analysis for the first 709 individuals
iis series of families, please state in what degrees and in what manner there seems
e a *hereditary entailment* of criminal, pauperized, and deformed moral character in
lineage; also how largely the debasing environment of these people enters into
history and causation of the hereditary entailment.

surveying the whole family, as it is mapped out in the charts accompanying the
rt, I find groups which may be considered distinctively industrious, distinctively
inal, distinctively pauper, and specifically diseased. These distinctions run along
of descent so that you can follow them with distinctness from generation to gen-
on, the breaks in the line at certain points indicating with great precision the
fying effects of disease, training, or fortuitous circumstance which have inter-
d and changed the current of the career.

to the entailment of vice, pauperism, crime, and disease, the essential object of my
iod of investigation required that the genealogical history should be divided into
lines of research : First, as to the heredity, which is defined as those traits of char-
· and physical constitution which are inherited from the parents; and, secondly, the
ronment which surrounds each individual after birth and tends to modify or deepen
riginal character. It was the object, in thus separating the two elements which
ribute to mold the growth of the individual, to determine how much of the char-
· is due to forces which are beyond immediate human control; how much to cir-
stances which, by being modified or substituted, will modify the character suffi-
ly to convert a probable criminal career into an actually honest one. The answer
iis question lies at the basis of all prison-discipline, determining in what cases
mation is possible, to what degree, and by what methods.

ie general conclusions which the examination of this group of families seems to
lish are that, where a hereditary characteristic running through several genera-
i is developed, there is also an organized social environment which runs parallel
ie heredity and tends to perpetuate the ancestral characteristics.

determining how much of the career is due to pure heredity, how much to subse-
it modifying effects, I might answer in a general way that where an inheritable
ise or a structural characteristic is organized during the ante-natal period, as, for
ince, constitutional syphilis, idiocy, or insanity, it does not seem to be greatly modi-
e by subsequent events, but dominates the fate of the individual. In this way it
ld seem that limits to mental or physical power are fixed by heredity. But when
:ome to that portion of character which is the result of post-natal development, in-
ing in this the organization and co-ordination of thought, the formation of the
, and the establishment of just moral conceptions, I find that the hereditary char-
ristics of the parents are greatly modifiable by the nature of the social environ-
.t. In other words, capacity is limited and determined mainly by heredity, but the
to which that capacity will be put is mainly governed by the impersonal training
ıgency of environment. For instance, where hereditary kleptomania exists, if
environment should be such as to become an exciting cause, the individual will be
ncorrigible thief; but if, on the contrary, he be protected from temptation, that in-
dual may lead an honest life, with some chances in favor of the entailment stop-
g there.

eredity in pauperism seems to be more fixed than heredity in crime, for very much
rime is the misdirection of faculty, and is amenable to discipline, while very much
auperism is due to the absence of vital power, the lines of pauperism being in many
's the identical lines of disease, which fact causes the successive extinction of ca-
ty from generation to generation till death supervenes.

bere are a number of other inductions which seem to be warranted by the facts
ected; inductions covering the relations of health, honesty, crime, pauperism, and
iuchery with each other, but which in greater or less degree are hypothetical

propositions which I here omit, but which you will find in my report on the "Juke" family.

(10) To what extent have special diseases invaded the families or individuals, as evinced by persons now living, whom you have seen, and as proved by medical testimony?

As might be expected among licentious people, venereal diseases are very common and in several cases hereditary, some of the lines of disease being marked by pauperism, idiocy, impotence, still-births, and deformed progeny. As to the prevalence of syphilis, 9 per cent. of those on the lists are or have been afflicted with it. This, however, only numbers those persons who have been certified to me by competent medical authority, and is much below the actual number; the judgment of those physicians who have given the information being that from 25 to 35 per cent. are afflicted with it in some form.

(11) What statistical statement will correctly express the comparative ratios of pauperism or of criminality in this unfortunate group as compared with the total population of the State as shown by the last census?

In the State at large the alms-house-pauperism amounts to .0126 per cent.; in the family it is .0902 per cent., being almost seven times more.

The number of criminals in the State at large, counting those who are in prison and those who are not, is less than 1 per cent. of the total population, the exact figures being .008 per cent. In this family it is more than 10 per cent.; but, if we take only the descendants of the illegitimate branch of Margaret, we get .2377 per cent., or nearly thirty times more than in the general community.

(12) What are the traditional characteristics of the ancestors of this lineage, and in what respects do their descendants conform to or differ from those types of character?

Originally the ancestors descended from some of the early settlers of the county, lived much as the backwoodsmen upon our frontiers now do, were a hardy, wiry, and robust people, given to hunting, fishing, and fighting by turns. As to industrial habits, they were like all hunters, averse to steady industry, working hard by spells and idling by turns. The most marked, as also the most constant, feature in all the generations is licentiousness; it is found in the generation of Margaret in the form of harlotry to the extent of 50 per cent. of the women; it is found in the total number of the women in all the generations succeeding, including only those of 12 years of age and over, to the extent of 50 per cent., so that feature seems to be a constant one from first to last. The forms of crime among the earlier members were violence to women, murder, and predatory expeditions upon the neighboring farmers. The same forms of crime are reproduced to-day. The crime of forgery appears only once in all the records, committed by a man who married into the family, while murder and attempts to murder appear in every generation, excepting the sixth, and that has no persons older than 7 years of age.

(13) The illegitimate branch of descent from Margaret (the A——,* of your group) presents the most remarkable records and lineage of crime-character, and in the sixth generation are found several children in our New York House of Refuge. What do the facts in the branch of illegitimate lineage, now referred to, show in regard to perpetual repetition of the same parental traits of criminal character, and what evidence have we that reforms can be effected in the inheritors of these traits? Under what circumstances have reforms been brought about in the instances you have reported?

In the illegitimate branch of Margaret there are three families in the sixth generation who have had six children sent to the House of Refuge. In order to clearly understand the heredity of these children, I prepared a chart† for the thirtieth annual report of the New York Prison Association, which will illustrate the following remarks completely. On examining the section relating to the illegitimate descendants of Margaret and following line 24, lines 35 and 36, and line 37, to the sixth generation, we

---

* "Ada" in the chart corresponds to Margaret in the text.
† This chart is not given in this circular. Persons desirous of pursuing this subject further are referred to the forthcoming report of the New York Prison Association.

find the children in question. So far the boys, except in line 24, are quite young and have not yet committed any open thefts, but their fate is foreshadowed if they are left to themselves. If the entire chart is examined so as to compare the brothers and sisters in the various families and in the different generations, it will be seen that in those families where the brothers have committed crime the sisters have been prostitutes; there is hardly an exception. On the other hand, very little crime occurs among the women. The explanation is perhaps to be found in the fact that the tendency of human beings is to obtain a living in the direction of least resistance; and, as this direction for women of this class is by prostitution, they enter that vocation. The brothers, being debarred from making a living in this manner, take to preying upon property. Thus the prostitute may be considered the analogue of the thief, both being the product of the same general conditions of parentage and training, the difference in the career being only an accident of sex. How essentially true is this position is shown by the fact that almost all prostitutes are thieves who are protected by their profession because their victims do not wish to make public their *liaisons* by bringing the offenders to justice.

Thus the two boys in line 36, generation 6, are seen to be brothers of harlots; one or five years more will see them enter the ranks of the criminals, adding one more example to the law above expressed. So in line 24, generation 6, we have it again demonstrated—the boy a thief, his sister a harlot.

Tracing back each of these lines, we find for line 24, mother a harlot, who kept a brothel, she dying seven years before he was committed; grandfather an unpunished thief, and a most expert sheep-stealer; grandmother a prostitute. In lines 35 and 36 we find mother a harlot, who kept a brothel, a receiver of stolen goods, and a contriver of crime; grandfather an unpunished and expert petty thief; grandmother a harlot. In line 37, mother a harlot, father a convicted felon; same grandfather and grandmother as the above. With all these children there seems to be no special wickedness of disposition. In most respects they do not compare unfavorably with the average of the children of the laboring class, except, perhaps, in respect to a tendency to licentious behavior, which is largely due to the example of their parents living in illicit and promiscuous relationships, and the tendency to tell lies, which, in the case of both the parents in the fifth generation, has become such a constitutional habit that they have become expert and reckless coiners of falsehood without purpose.

The home-influence of these children has been deplorable. They have seen debauchery in all its forms from their cradle; they have been whipped to make them steal. One of them is a harlot, with a sister keeping a brothel, as her mother also did before her; another, aged 12, has had rape attempted upon her by her step-father, if that title can be used where there has been no legal marriage. The training of these children, ranging from 8 years to 17, will have to be very different from that which they are likely to get if they are to be reclaimed; but, as they have youth upon their side, much can be expected.

This brings me to the consideration of the question of reform, of which there are three examples, two of them conspicuous ones in the fifth generation, lines 7, 25, and 26. The essential features of the lives of these three men have been the same. They were each the children of unpunished thieves, the father of the two last being an expert sheep-stealer; they committed many offenses, one of them beginning at 12 years of age and receiving an aggregate of fourteen years' imprisonment. They all committed crimes of contrivance; they all reformed before their thirty-third year, and two of the worst have since become successful in managing stone-flagging quarries of their own. It is believed that there is great significance in the fact that their reformation took place before the thirty-third year, for it is in accordance with the law of the development of mind accompanying the growth of the brain and nervous system. Explaining this fact in a brief and popular way, it may be laid down that in the growth of each individual that portion of the nervous system which brings the lungs, heart, stomach, &c., into sympathetic action with each other is first organized; then the spinal column, which chiefly brings the movements of the limbs and body under control; third, that portion of the brain which registers the impressions made upon the senses; and, fourth, the reason, the judgment, and the will, which give the adult the power to hold in check the passions which otherwise would produce crime if allowed full sway. Now, the judgment and the will are not fully organized till between the thirtieth and thirty-fifth year, and as this is the case it is easy to understand that a boy, who is a petty thief at 18 or 20, may outgrow his habits of theft as he grows older, simply because the natural tendency of the development of the brain organizes an experience which teaches that honesty is most advantageous. Before the age of full maturity is reached, say the thirty-third year, the growth of the mind is an agent spontaneously working for reformation; therefore any system of reformatory discipline and education which does not save a large proportion, at least 85 per cent., of its offenders under 20 years of age, is an administrative monstrosity, and should not be allowed to shield itself from the charge of culpable incompetence on the plea that crime is hereditary and therefore incurable. It must be distinctly accepted that the moral nature—which really means the holding of the emotions and passions under the dominion of the judgment by the exercise of will—is the last-developed of the elements of character, and, for this reason, is most modifiable by the nature of the environment. This being established, it is easy to understand the doctrine of the interchangeableness of careers in the same individual at different periods of life, as I have more fully elaborated in the report, and explains why numerous offenders become reformed, not in consequence of our prisons, but in spite of them.

The most conspicuous and uniformly noticeable trait of the true criminal is that he seems to lack the element of continuity of effort. Steady, plodding work, which is the characteristic not only of honest and successful individuals, but also of all nations that have made a mark in history, is deficient in him, and needs to be organized as a constituent of his character; thus the pre-eminent necessity of a thorough industrial training for these children who have just been sent to the reformatory. Their tendency to sexual precociousness will be checked by labor, their physiological development will become more firm and healthy, and the habit of perseverance which is such a large factor in good conduct will be organized so as to become automatic in its action, and for this reason voluntary. The direction of least resistance then will be the path of honest industry, and with this conviction as an accepted rule of conduct and the practice of it as an organized habit, reformation is secured permanently.

A fact which is noticeable, and one which seems to indicate the identity of harlotry and crime in the different sexes is that they both yield to the same general treatment, both requiring steady labor as the essential element of reform.

In taking a final and general survey of the entire progeny of the group of sisters who were the mothers of this lineage, and contrasting the illegitimate branches, which show both greater vigor, absence of disease, and large preponderance of crime, with certain legitimate branches which are distinctively pauper, debauched, and specifically diseased, it is incontestable that the criminal branches are decidedly more amenable to reform than are their pauper half-brothers or cousins, who are plunged in a condition so abject that, at points along the line of entailment, it may be said to be irreclaimable.

R. L. DUGDALE.

APPENDIX B.

STATISTICS

OF

ORPHAN AND REFORMATORY SCHOOLS

IN

THE UNITED STATES IN 1874;

BEING

STATISTICAL TABLES Nos. XXII AND XXIII OF THE REPORT OF
THE COMMISSIONER OF EDUCATION FOR THAT YEAR.

===

11 E

TABLE XXII.—*Statistics of reform-schools for 1874; from*

Number.	Name.	Location.	Date of establishment.	Control.
	1	2	3	4
1	Connecticut Industrial School for Girls......	Middletown, Conn	1870	Corporate ....
2	Connecticut Reform School	West Meriden, Conn.	1854	State.............
3	St. Mary s Reformatory......................	Chicago, Ill	1863	....
4	Sta e Reform School*	Pontiac, Ill	1871	State ....
5	Indiana Reform Institution for Girls	Indianapolis, Ind	1874	State ....
6	House of Refuge ..	Plainfield, Ind		State ....
7	Iowa State Reform School*..................	Eldora, Iowa	1868	State.............
8	House of Refuge*	Louisville, Ky	1865	Municipal ....
9	Boys' House of Refuge*	New Orleans, La	1850	Municipal ....
10	State Reform School	Cape Elizabeth, Me ..	1852	State.............
11	House of Refuge for Juvenile Delinquents *	Baltimore, Md	1855	Municipal ... ..
12	House of Reformation and Instruction for Colored Children.*	Bowie, Md	1873	Corporate ....
13	The Maryland Industrial School for Girls ..	Orange Grove Station, B. & O R R., Md.	1866	Directors ....
14	City of Boston Almshouse School............	Boston, Mass	1856	Municipal ....
15	House of Reformation for Juvenile Offenders	Boston, Mass	1827	Municipal ....
16	State Industrial School for Girls*...........	Lancaster, Mass	1856	State ....
17	Lawrence Industrial School	Lawrence, Mass.......	1874	Municipal ....
18	*House of Employment and Reformation.....	Lowell, Mass	1851	Municipal ....
19	State Primary School	Monson, Mass........	186.	State ....
20	Plummer Farm School	Salem, Mass	1870	Private ....
21	State Reform School	Westboro', Mass......	1848	State ....
22	Worcester Truant Reform School	Worcester, Mass......	1863	Municipal ....
23	Detroit House of Correction	Detroit, Mich........	1861	Municipal ....
24	Michigan State Reform School	Lansing, Mich	1856	State.............
25	Minnesota State Reform School.............	St. Paul, Minn	1868	State.............
26	New Hampshire State Reform School*......	Manchester, N. H	1855	State.............
27	New Jersey State Reform School	Jamesburg, N J	1867	State.............
28	Truant Home	Brooklyn, N Y	1857	Municipal ....
29	House of the Good Shepherd	East New York, Long Island, N Y	1868	Municipal ....
30	Industrial School...........................	New York, N Y., Hart's Island.	1868	Municipal ....
31	House of the Holy Family Association for Befriending Children and Young Girls.	New York, N. Y	1870	....
32	House of Mercy	New York, N. Y	1854	Trustees............
33	Home for Women	New York, N. Y , (273 Water street.)	1867	....
34	House of the Good Shepherd	New York, N. Y	1857	....
35	Home for Fallen and Friendless Girls	New York, N. Y , (86 West Fourth street.)	1866	Board of managers ..
36	House of Refuge	New York, N.Y., Randall's Island	1825	....
37	The Isaac T Hopper Home	New York, N. Y	1845	Private ... .
38	The Midnight Mission	New York, N. Y	1867	Trustees ....
39	Western House of Refuge*	Rochester, N. Y	1846	State.............
40	New York Catholic Protectory.............	Westchester, N. Y ...	1863	Municipal ....
41	House of Refuge*	Cincinnati, Ohio	1850	Municipal ....
42	Protectory for Boys*	Cincinnati, Ohio	1868	Brothers of St. Francis
43	Home of Refuge and Correction............	Cleveland, Ohio	1870	Municipal ....
44	The Retreat	Cleveland, Ohio	1869	....
45	State Reform School*......................	Lancaster, Ohio	1857	State.............
46	Ohio Girls' Industrial School	Lewis Centre, Ohio....	1869	State ....
47	House of Refuge	Toledo, Ohio	(c)	Municipal ....
48	House of Refuge, (white)*.................	Philadelphia, Pa	1826	Board of managers .
49	House of Refuge, (colored department)	Philadelphia, Pa	1850	State.............
50	Western House of Refuge*..................	Pittsburg, Pa	1854	Board of managers.
51	Sheltering Arms	Wilkensburg, n e a r Pittsburg, Pa.	1873	Private ....
52	Providence Reform School..................	Providence, R I	1850	Municipal ....
53	Vermont Reform School	Waterbury, Vt........	1865	State.............
54	Industrial School for Boys..................	Waukesha, Wis	1860	State.............
55	Girls' Reform School*	Washington, D. C	1873	Trustees............
56	Reform School of District of Columbia*....	Near Washington, D. C	1869	Territorial ....

* From Report of Commissioner of Education for 1873.   a Within minority.

nquiries by the United States Bureau of Education.

tendent.	Number of teachers or officers. Male.	Female.	Conditions of commitment. Age.	Other conditions.	Number.
5	6	7	8	9	
rell	2	9	8-16	Neglect, vagrancy, or vicious inclination	1
gham	9	11	10-16	Truancy of crime	2
:llian	5		7-20		3
buller	8	6	10-16	Trial by jury and conviction of crime	4
	1	5	6-16	Orphans deserted by parents, incorrigibility, &c	5
				Viciousness or crime	6
	9	7	Under 18	Vagrancy, incorrigibility, &c	7
	12	3	7-16	Petit larceny, vagrancy, and incorrigibility	8
s	6	5	6-18	Larceny, vagrancy, and truancy	9
worth	2	2	8-16	Any offense punishable by imprisonment in State prison not for life	10
	13	4	8-16	Larceny, vagrancy, and truancy	11
N. Horn	3	2	6-16	During minority	12
we	1	2	Under 18	Vagrancy, incorrigibility, poverty, &c	13
ilton	(5)		(a)	Poverty	14
iton	11	2	7-16	Truancy, larceny, and vagrancy	15
s Ames		17	7-16	Vagrancy, viciousness, and poverty	16
rown	2	3	8-16	Vagrancy, truancy, and petty crimes	17
elps	1		6-17	Truancy and misdemeanors	18
Vakefield	(8)		3-16		19
Johnson	2	3	10-16	Truancy, vagrancy, stubbornness, &c	20
epherd	22	19	7-17	During minority	21
ill		1	7-16	Truancy	22
nan	28	9			23
nson	6	6	10-16	Offenses amenable to law	24
Ribeldoffer,	2	4	(b)	Commitment by court	25
	5	9	Under 17	Offenses against the laws	26
astman	8	4	8-16	Crime against the State	27
nerest	1	1	5-14	Insubordination and truancy	28
Loretto			14-30	Destitution, desire for reformation, &c	29
unphy	6	2	10-20	Truancy, vagrancy, destitution, &c	30
C. D. Starr,	(4)		From 12	Must be depraved or fallen, or in danger from surroundings and associates	31
	1	9	Over 12	Must be fallen women	32
Boole					33
ry Magdar.		90	14-21		34
Morey					35
nes	32	23	Under 16	Must be residents of the State of New York	36
oremus				Must be women discharged from prisons	37
ek	2	2			38
on	21	11	8-16	During minority	39
eliow and Helena.	27	9	7-14	Truancy, vagrancy, and petty crimes	40
ort	10	8	7-20	During minority or will of board	41
:hael Duex	17		5-18	Poverty and orphanage	42
rson			8-20		43
ord,(mat'n)	1	2		Desire for reformation	44
			Under 16	Crime and incorrigibility	45
s, M.D	3	16	7-16	Crime, vagrancy, viciousness, or being in circumstances of want, exposure, abandonment, &c	46
owe			8-16	Petty crimes, incorrigibility, or commitment by parents or guardians	47
ver	10	12		During minority	48
erty	3	6	8-16		49
very	7	12	7-20	During minority	50
er,(matron)		1		Need of care	51
alcott	10	8	Under 18		52
Fairbank	5	9	10-16	Committed by parents or guardians	53
ickson			8-16		54
			No limit	Vagrancy, vicious life, prostitution	55
	4	4	Under 16	Until reformed or during minority	56

b Boys under 16, girls under 15.   c To be opened May 1, 1875.

TABLE XXII.—*Statistics of reform*

NOTE.— x indicates the studies

Number	Name	Number committed during the year.	Number discharged during the year.	Present inmates.					
				Sex.		Race.		Nativity.	
				Male.	Female.	White.	Colored.	Native.	Foreign.
1		10	11	12	13	14	15	16	17
1	Connecticut Industrial School for Girls	50	33		92	78	14	88	4
2	Connecticut Reform School	194	190	300		284	16	120	30
3	St. Mary's Reformatory			100		100			
4	State Reform School*	152	72	152		139	13	130	22
5	Indiana Reform Institution for Girls	100	6		104	96	8		
6	House of Refuge	265							
7	Iowa State Reform School*	70	37	146	11	157	0	152	5
8	House of Refuge*	90	63	150	24	174	0	62	25
9	Boys' House of Refuge*	160	145	118		57	61	111	7
10	State Reform School	47	27	142		138	4	42	3
11	House of Refuge for Juvenile Delinquents*	110	132	293		293		105	3
12	House of Reformation and Instruction for Colored Children.*	72		(72)			72	72	
13	The Maryland Industrial School for Girls	27	15		31	31			
14	City of Boston Almshouse School			81	27	108	0		
15	House of Reformation for Juvenile Offenders	229	208	284	20	294	10	237	67
16	State Industrial School for Girls *	20	40		110	98	12	105	5
17	Lawrence Industrial School	21	0	22	0	22	0	1	22
18	House of Employment and Reformation	49	54	28	2	30	0	24	6
19	State Primary School			362	164	497	29		
20	Plummer Farm School	10	15	30		27	3	30	0
21	State Reform School *	236	169	311		299	12	284	27
22	Worcester Truant Reform School	11	8	15		15		10	5
23	Detroit House of Correction	2,314	2,335	408	102				
24	Michigan State Reform School	109	88	243		227	16	81	28
25	Minnesota State Reform School	31	36	110	4	111	3		
26	New Hampshire State Reform School*	47	33	91	12	101	2	98	5
27	New Jersey State Reform School	138	114	184					
28	Truant Home	134	121	218	0	218	0	115	12
29	House of the Good Shepherd	357	354	0	179	179	0		
30	Industrial School, (Hart's Island)	265	51	21	3	24	3	19	3
31	House of the Holy Family Association for Befriending Children and Young Girls				100				
32	House of Mercy	73	56		79	79	0	67	12
33	Home for Women								
34	House of the Good Shepherd	216	334		456	455	1	230	226
35	Home for Fallen and Friendless Girls	67	67		26				
36	House of Refuge, (Randall's Island)	724	598	677	112	737	42	96	
37	The Isaac T. Hopper Home	352	360						
38	The Midnight Mission	160	171		21				
39	Western House of Refuge*	192	116	428		408	20		
40	New York Catholic Protectory	1,097	804	1,324	518	1,838	4	1,504	338
41	House of Refuge*	328	317	175	51	186	40	192	34
42	Protectory for Boys*	150	33	125		124	1	117	8
43	Home of Refuge and Correction	95	71	82	1				
44	The Retreat				325	319	6		
45	State Reform School*	182	118	425		415	10		
46	Ohio Girls' Industrial School	39	23	0	160	149	11	159	1
47	House of Refuge								
48	House of Refuge, (white)*	284	248	362	77	439		253	31
49	House of Refuge, (colored department)	70	60	107	45	0	152	151	1
50	Western House of Refuge*	128							
51	Sheltering Arms	10	10						
52	Providence Reform School	163	149	179	41	210	10	203	17
53	Vermont Reform School	41	32	145		141	4	143	2
54	Industrial School for Boys	113	84						
55	Girls' Reform School*								
56	Reform School of District of Columbia*	58	26	113		55	58		

* From Report of Commis

ools for 1874, &c.—Continued.

industries taught.

	Present inmates.						Studies.												
Parents illiterate.	Illiterate when committed.		Number could read only when committed.	Number could read and write when committed.	Number taught to read.	Number taught to write.	Reading, writing, spelling.	Arithmetic.	Algebra.	Book-keeping.	Geometry.	Geography.	Grammar.	History.	Philosophy.	Botany.	Physiology.	Drawing.	Music, (vocal.)	Number.
	Native parentage.	Foreign-born parentage.																		
19	**20**	**21**	**22**	**23**	**24**	**25**	**26**	**27**	**28**	**29**	**30**	**31**	**32**	**33**	**34**	**35**	**36**	**37**	**38**	
....	10	20	60	31	....	....	x	x	....	....	....	x	x	x	....	....	....	....	x	1
7	3	35	140	118	140	130	x	x	....	....	....	....	....	....	x	x	....	....	x	2
3	....	....	....	....	....	....	x	x	..	....	....	x	x	x	....	....	....	....	x	3
8	27	....	37	65	25	26	x	x	x	....	....	x	x	x	....	....	....	....	....	4
0	....	....	52	50	....	....	x	x	....	....	....	x	x	....	....	....	x	x	....	5
....	....	....	....	....	....	....														6
4	22	4	13	94	94	22	x	x	....	....	....	x	x	....	....	....	....	....	....	7
4	14	....	....	....	....	....	x	x	....	....	....	....	....	....	....	....	....	....	....	8
1	53	....	72	40	37	18	x	x	....	....	....	....	....	x	....	....	....	x	....	9
....	1	....	20	1	....	....	x	x	....	....	....	x	x	x	....	....	....	....	....	10
1	20	2	33	43	13	60	x	x	x	....	....	x	x	x	x	....	....	....	....	11
0	50	....	12	3	7	6	x	x	....	....	....	x	x	x	....	....	....	....	....	12
3	4	8	6	9	9	6	x	x	....	....	....	x	....	....	....	....	....	....	x	13
2	....	....	....	....	....	....	x	x	....	....	....	....	....	....	....	....	....	....	x	14
77	14	29	69	182	26	60	x	x	x	....	....	x	x	....	....	....	....	....	x	15
9	2	3	30	75	....	35	x	x	....	....	....	x	x	....	....	....	....	....	x	16
3	....	5	9	13	5	10	x	x	....	....	....	x	....	....	....	....	....	x	x	17
5	2	2	12	9	4	13	x	x	....	....	....	x	x	x	....	....	....	....	x	18
....	....	....	....	....	....	....	x	x	....	....	....	x	....	....	....	....	....	....	x	19
4	0	1	12	....	1	10	x	x	....	....	....	x	x	....	....	....	....	....	....	20
15	10	43	177	81	50	102	x	x	....	....	....	x	x	....	x	....	....	....	....	21
0	0	0	2	12	0	3	x	x	....	....	....	x	x	....	....	....	....	....	....	22
....	....	....	261	....	200	....	x	x	....	....	....	....	x	....	....	....	....	....	....	23
4	....	....	61	19	....	50	x	x	....	....	....	....	x	....	....	....	....	....	....	24
....	....	....	31	....	31	....	x	x	....	....	....	x	x	....	....	....	....	....	....	25
10	19	....	48	36	19	48	x	x	....	....	....	x	x	....	....	....	....	....	....	26
..	....	....	....	....	....	....	x	x	....	....	....	....	....	....	....	....	....	....	....	27
9	13	....	77	44	13	77	x	x	....	....	....	x	x	x	....	....	....	....	....	28
....	....	....	....	....	....	....	x	x	....	....	....	....	....	....	....	....	....	....	....	29
9	5	1	4	6	....	....	....	....	....	....	....	....	....	....	....	....	....	....	....	30
....	....	....	....	....	....	....	x	x	....	....	....	....	....	....	....	....	....	....	x	31
11	....	....	....	....	6	6	....	....	....	....	....	....	....	....	....	....	....	....	....	32
..	....	....	....	....	....	....	....	....	....	....	....	....	....	....	....	....	....	....	....	33
75	....	....	....	....	....	....	x	....	....	....	....	....	....	....	....	....	....	....	....	34
..	....	....	....	....	....	....														35
..	(400)	....	248	76	....	....	x	x	....	....	....	x	x	....	....	....	....	....	....	36
..	....	....	....	....	....	....														37
..	....	....	....	....	....	....														38
19	....	....	63	94	35	35	x	x	....	....	....	x	x	x	x	....	....	....	....	39
51	(415)	....	411	238	550	339	x	x	x	x	x	x	x	x	....	....	....	....	x	40
55	26	25	175	76	150	....	x	x	....	....	....	x	x	x	....	....	....	....	....	41
60	....	....	25	18	80	....	x	x	....	....	....	x	x	x	....	....	....	....	....	42
..	....	....	18	49	....	....	x	x	....	....	....	x	x	....	....	....	....	....	....	43
..	....	....	....	....	....	....	x	x	....	....	....	....	....	....	....	....	....	....	....	44
..	....	....	....	....	....	....	x	x	x	....	....	x	x	x	....	....	....	....	....	45
7	32	1	59	68	33	59	x	x	x	....	....	x	x	x	x	....	....	....	....	46
..	....	....	....	....	....	....														47
33	....	69	100	105	430	356	x	x	....	....	....	x	....	x	....	....	....	....	....	48
..	35	....	21	14	61	59	x	x	....	....	....	x	x	x	....	....	....	....	....	49
..	....	....	....	....	....	....	x	x	....	....	....	x	x	x	....	....	....	x	....	50
..	....	....	....	....	....	....														51
31	7	49	84	136	....	....	x	x	x	x	....	x	....	x	....	....	....	....	....	52
..	9	32	6	4	41	10	x	x	....	....	....	x	....	....	....	....	....	....	....	53
..	....	....	....	....	....	....	x	x	x	....	....	x	x	x	....	....	....	....	....	54
..	....	....	....	....	....	....														55
12	....	....	....	....	....	....	x	x	....	....	....	x	x	....	....	....	....	....	....	56

TABLE XXII.—*Statistics of reform-*

Number.	Baking.	Blacksmithing.	Brick-making.	Broom-making.	Brush-making.	Cane-seating.	Carpentry.	Chair-making.	Cigar-making.	Dairy-work.	Dress-making.	Farming.	Fruit-canning.	Gardening.	Glove-making.	Housework.	Knitting.	Laundry-work.	Masonry.	Paper-box-making.	Printing.	Sewing.
	39	40	41	42	43	44	45	46	47	48	49	50	51	52	53	54	55	56	57	58	59	60
1										×						×		×		×		×
2	×					×						×										
3																						
4																						
5						×					×					×	×					×
6		×	×				×				×										
7	×	×					×				×										
8											×										
9	×					×																
10			×			×					×										
11						×															
12												×										
13														×		×					×	
14																						
15											×										
16	×																					×
17																						
18											×			×							
19					×									×							
20					×						×			×							
21	×										×										
22											×										
23																						
24					×			×													
25													×								
26					×																
27																						
28												×									
29															×						×
30																						
31																	×				×
32																	×				×
33																					
34															×	×				×
35											×										
36																	×				×
37																	×				×
38																						
39																						
40	×	×				×	×				×			×							×
41	×										×									×	
42																				×	
43																				×	
44					×	×								×							×
45		×			×	×								×							
46											×										
47																					
48		×				×								×						×	
49											×									×	
50	×								×	×						×				×
51																					
52					×							×		×						
53					×		×							×						×
54			×		×						×					×		×		×
55																					
56																					

a Total expense for

Reform-schools from which no

Reform and Industrial School, Bridgeport, Ill.; Catholic Male Orphan Asylum and Reformatory, Ind Cambridge Truant Reform School, Cambridge, Mass ; House of Providence, Detroit, Mich.; ate for Boys, St. Louis, Mo , Catholic Reformatories for Boys, Buffalo, N. Y.; Institution of Mercy, York, N. Y., Nautical School Ship Mercury, New York, N. Y.; Home of Correction, Toledo, Ohio;

tools for 1874, &c.—Concluded.

			Industries.						71	72	Library.		75	76	77	78	
Shoemaking.	Shoemending.	Stereotyping.	Stone-cutting.	Straw-braiding.	Tailoring.	Tinning.	Wheelwrighting.	Wire-work.	Number committed since establishment.	Percentage of discharged known to be orderly, &c.	Number of volumes.	Increase in the past year.	Average annual cost of each inmate.	Average annual earnings of each inmate.	Annual cost of institution.	Total annual earnings of institution.	Number.
62	63	64	65	66	67	68	69	70	71	72	73	74	75	76	77	78	
									185	75	1,000	400	$192 00	$18 30	$15,752	$1,500	1
	×				×				2,279	75	1,500	0	145 98	46 80	43,795	14,040	2
×					×				1,500		50	0			10,000		3
×									260		100				25,000		4
									110		226	0	2 50		12,879	1,127	5
				66													6
	×				×				272	75	250		137 00	50 00	17,500	6,000	7
	×				×				2,055	25	400				20,000	5,000	8
	×								2,295	33	200		67 50		10,815	2,900	9
	×								1,429	60	1,400	120	172 00	28 00	24,106	4,000	10
	×			×					2,400		1,813		131 61		39,095	7,876	11
									72								12
									119		300		150 00		3,716		13
											400	185					14
									4,514		700	300					15
									830	66	1,253		178 48	4 45	22,747	542	16
									22		100				5,500		17
									1,200		500	25	100 00		3,456		18
									2,548		450	12			47,209		19
									56	80	300	50	200 00	100 00	6,000	3,000	20
	×				×				4,271	60	2,642		121 00	39 33	56,961	11,366	21
									180	50	120	10	106 21	2 47	1,503	37	22
									15,187		1,061	60					23
	×				×				1,512	70	1,800				38,727	10,838	24
	×				×	×			253	90	900	300	145 00		30,000		25
									744	7	300		182 00	62 22	24,470	16,537	26
																	27
									2,232	25	150	0	68 81	0	18,504	0	28
									1,054		198	8	35 75	15 01	37,609	8,037	29
	×				×				3,865								30
									1,000		200				10,255		31
																	32
																5,000	33
									2,024		200	20			83,731	30,088	34
																10,758	35
	×							×	15,791	73	3,995	0	141 88	56 85	121,363	42,066	36
									5,800	66							37
																9,197	38
	×				×				3,518	66	1,275		164 51	36 31	63,174	13,946	39
×	×		×		×		×		8,771		2,010	150	114 74	15 27	318,841	28,135	40
	×			×		×			3,137	75	630		148 20		a48,919	6,677	41
									550	25	627		150 00		15,000		42
	×												148 23				43
									325						2,500		44
	×				×				1,805	80	2,000		110 00		48,000	10,000	45
				×					247	60	500	0	138 48		18,000	0	46
																	47
	×								11,000	66	1,000		86 74	60 65	76,101	26,868	48
	×								2,291	65	1,500	75	161 93	41 00	21,995	5,544	49
	×				×										121,332	4,604	50
																	51
					×				2,244	60	2,362	230	104 00	50 00	41,295	10,000	52
									427	75	300		85 97	53 00	21,843	9,444	53
	×		×		×												54
																	55
					×				248	75	300		138 00		14,116		56

fifteen months.

information has been received.

Chicago, Ill ; Erring Woman's Refuge, Indianapolis, Ind ; Home of the Good Shepherd, Indianapolis, Minnesota State Reform School, St. Paul, Minn.; House of Refuge, St. Louis, Mo.; St. Louis Protector-Houston street, New York, N Y.; Home for Fallen and Friendless Girls, West Fourth street, New Home of the Good Shepherd, Baltimore, Pa.; Reform School, Vergennes, Vt.

TABLE XXIII.—PART 1.—*Statistics of orphan asylums, miscellaneous charities, and industrial schools for 1874; from replies to inquiries by the United States Bureau of Education.*

Number.	Name.	Location.	Year of incorporation.	Year of organization.	Superintendent.	Religious denomination.	Number of teachers and officers.	Total number of inmates since foundation.
	1	2	3	4	5	6	7	8
1	Church Home for Orphans	Mobile, Ala	1864	1864	Sister Harriet	Episcopal	6	340
2	Sacramento Protestant Orphan Asylum	Sacramento, Cal	1867	1867	Mrs. A. E. Peckham, matron	Undenom'l	12	
3	Ladies' Protection and Relief Society	San Francisco, Cal	1854	1853	Miss C. A. Harmon, matron	Undenom'l	4	2,000
4	Pacific Hebrew Orphan Asylum and Home Society*	San Francisco, Cal	1871	1871	Mrs. Martin	Hebrew	7	28
5	St. Boniface Orphan Asylum*	San Francisco, Cal	1866	1866	Catharine Gross	R C	2	300
6	Male Orphan Asylum*	San Rafael, Cal	1855	1855	Rev. Peter Birmingham	R C	12	
7	The Good Templars' Home for Orphans	Vallejo, Cal	1868	1868	Mrs. H. M. Chandler, matron		3	201
8	Fitch's Home*	Darien, Conn	1864	1864	Miss M. J. Davis	Undenom'l	3	89
9	Hartford Orphan Asylum	Hartford, Conn	1861		George E. Sanborne	Undenom'l	10	
10	St. Catharine Orphan Asylum	Hartford, Conn	1851	1851	Sister Rose	R C		
11	St. James's Orphan Asylum	Hartford, Conn	1862		Sister Anastasia	R C	6	1,800
12	New Haven Orphan Asylum	New Haven, Conn	1833	1833	Mrs. L. A. Kingsley, matron	Evangelical	6	1,100
13	St. Mary's Orphan Asylum	New Haven, Conn	1852			R C	23	3,000
14	Orphans' Home	Decatur, Ga	1870	1871	Rev. Joseph Carr	M. E. South		49
15	Chicago Nursery and Half-Orphan Asylum*	Chicago, Ill	1860	1860	Mrs. E. L. Hobson	Undenom'l	10	
16	Chicago Protestant Orphan Asylum	Chicago, Ill	1849	1846	Mrs. Harriet C. Bigelow	Undenom'l	2	2,500
17	Uhlich Orphan Asylum	Chicago, Ill	1869	1869	Karl Wiegmann	Evang. Luth	9	75
18	Colored Orphan Asylum	Indianapolis, Ind	1870	1870	William G. Johnson	Friends	11	133
19	German Protestant Orphan Asylum	Indianapolis, Ind	1861		George Royer	German Prot	3	
20	German and English Asylum for Orphans and Destitute	Andrew, Iowa	1864	1863	John Georg Rembold	Evang. Luth	4	190
21	Kansas Orphan Asylum and Home for Friendless Children.	Leavenworth, Kans	1866	1866	Mrs. Thomas Carney, president.	Undenom'l		185
22	St. Thomas's Orphan Asylum	Bardstown, Ky	1850	1850	Rev. Nicholas Ryan	R C	8	568
23	Convent of the Angel Guardian	Highlands, near Newport, Ky	1866	1866	Mother M. of St. Scholastica.	R C		
24	Orphanage of the Good Shepherd	Louisville, Ky	1860		Sister Sarah Clayland	Protestant	4	60
25	Protestant-Episcopal Orphan Asylum*	Louisville, Ky	1837	1838	Mrs. E. H. Bly	Prot Epis	2	468
26	St. Joseph's Orphan Asylum	Louisville, Ky	1847	1847	Sister Pacomia	R C		
27	Mount Carmel*	New Orleans, La			Mother Teresa	R C	13	
28	Female Orphan Asylum of Portland	Portland, Me			Abbe B. Bodwick, secretary	Protestant	4	
29	Annapolis Orphan Asylum*	Annapolis, Md			Mr. Richardson	Prot. Epis		

No.	Name of institution	Location			Name of officer	Denomination		
31	German Orphan Asylum						1	
32	Hebrew Orphan Asylum	Baltimore, Md	1872	1873	Rev. Abraham Hofmann	Hebrew	14	36
33	St. Anthony's Asylum	Baltimore, Md	1900	1854	Sister Mary Rosamunda	R. C	30	1,090
34	St. Francis's Orphan Asylum for Colored Children*	Baltimore, Md	1871	1829	Sister M. I. Noel	R. C		73
35	St. Mary's Female Orphan Asylum	Baltimore, Md	1818	1818	Sister Aloysia Daly	R. C		1,038
36	St. Peter's Asylum for Female Children	Baltimore, Md	1850	1850	Mrs. Ellen Binney	Prot. Epis	4	
37	St. Vincent's Male Orphan Asylum	Baltimore, Md	1840	1840	Brother James	R. C	2	
38	Shelter for Orphans of Colored Soldiers and Friendless Colored Children.	Baltimore, Md	1866		Julia Valentine	Undenom'l		950
39	The Orphan Asylum of St. Paul's Church	Baltimore, Md	1860	1860	Alice E. Bartlett	Prot. Epis	9	
40	Boston Female Orphan Asylum	Boston, Mass	1855	1855	Miss Dexter	Unitarian		
41	Church Home for Orphans and Destitute Children*	Boston, Mass	1851	1855	Rev. Justinian	Prot. Epis	1	
42	House of Angel Guardian	Boston, Mass	1843	1849	Sister Ann Alexis	R. C	12	5,383
43	St. Vincent's Orphan Asylum*	Boston, Mass	1871	1866	Sister M. A. Feruand	R. C	15	2,699
44	Protectory of Mary Immaculate*	Lawrence, Mass	1841	1849	Sister Mary	R. C	7	385
45	City Orphan Asylum*	Salem, Mass	1849	1849	Mrs. Bradbury	R. C	5	225
46	Seaman's Orphan and Children's Friend Society	Salem, Mass	1867	1867	Jamerson White, matron	Undenom'l	3	399
47	Worcester Children's Friend Society	Worcester, Mass	1848	1849	Sister Mary Gertrude	Undenom'l	43	
48	St. Anthony's Male Orphan Asylum	Detroit, Mich	1851	1856	Sister Mary Edmond	R. C	6	266
49	St. Vincent's Orphan Asylum*	Detroit, Mich	1871	1866	Brother Symphorian	R. C	4	1,660
50	D'Evereux Hall	Natchez, Miss	1856	1856	Mrs. M. S. Fife, first directress	Episcopal		193
51	Episcopal Orphan Home	St. Louis, Mo.	1845	1843	Mother Angela	Episcopal	12	500
52	German St. Vincent's Orphan Asylum	St. Louis, Mo.	1851	1850	Mrs. M. A. Winter	R. C		
53	Methodist Orphans' Home*	St. Louis, Mo.	1870	1860	Francis H. Hackemeier	Meth. Epis	13	968
54	Protestant Orphan Asylum, (German)*	St. Louis, Mo.	1850	1859	Sister Aloysa	Evangelical	3	2,105
55	St. Mary's Female Orphan Asylum*	Webster Groves, Mo.	1841	1843	Mrs. George K. Budd, president	R. C	2	2,000
56	St. Louis Protestant Orphan Asylum	St. Louis, Mo.	1871	1871	Mrs. A. R. Mock	Protestant	3	100
57	New Hampshire Orphans' Home	Franklin, N. H	1864	1864	Mrs. Mary Lockwood	Undenom'l	3	181
58	Children's Home.	Jersey City, N. J	1849	1840	Mrs. Van Vleck	Protestant	3	474
59	Orphan Asylum	Newark, N. J	1864	1863	Mrs. H. J. Hennien	Union Evan	4	144
60	Paterson Orphan Asylum Association for Orphans, Half Orphans, and Homeless Children.	Paterson, N. J				Union	2	
61	St. Vincent's Male Orphan Asylum*	Albany, N. Y	1849	1854	Brother Auphian	R. C	4	728
62	Cayuga Asylum for Destitute Children	Auburn, N. Y	1862	1862	Mrs. J. C. Rogers	Undenom'l	2	1,312
63	Davenport Institution for Orphan Girls*	Bath, N. Y	1863	1863	Elias Child	Protestant	2	65
64	Brooklyn Howard Colored Orphan Asylum Society	Brooklyn, N. Y	1866	1866	William F. Johnson	Undenom'l		
65	Orphan Asylum Society for the City of Brooklyn*	Brooklyn, N. Y	1835	1833	Mrs. J. B. Hutchinson	Undenom'l	14	2,375
66	Roman-Catholic Asylum for Boys*	Brooklyn, N. Y	1834	1834	Sister M. Baptiste	R. C		1,690
67	St. Joseph's Orphan Asylum*	Brooklyn, N. Y	1860	1861	M. May	Undenom'l		100
68	Buffalo Orphan Asylum.	Buffalo, N. Y	1835	1836	Mrs. Healy	Undenom'l	2	
69	Evangelical Lutheran St. John's Orphan Home	Buffalo and Sulphur Spring, N. Y.	1865	1864	Rev. Christian Vols.	Evang. Luth	13	113
70	Orphan Ward of Church Charity Foundation	Buffalo, N. Y	1856	1866	Mrs. Susan Graham	Prot. Epis	3	370
71	St. Mary's German Roman-Catholic Asylum	Buffalo, N. Y	1854	1853	Elias F. Schauer	R. C	2	1,190
72	St. Vincent's Asylum*	Buffalo, N. Y	1849	1848	Sister Robertine	R. C	11	235
73	Ontario Orphan Asylum*	Canandaigua, N. Y	1863	1863	Mrs. E. W. Baldwin	Protestant	6	400
74	Thomas Asylum for Orphan and Destitute Indian Children.	Collins, N. Y	1855	1855	B. F. Hall	Undenom'l	7	
75	Orphan House of the Holy Savior.	Cooperstown, N. Y	1871	1871	Susan F. Cooper	Prot. Epis	3	37

* From Report of Commissioner of Education for 1873.

TABLE XXIII.—PART 1.—*Statistics of orphan asylums, miscellaneous charities, and industrial schools for 1874, &c.*—Continued.

Number.	Name.	Location.	Year of incorporation.	Year of organization.	Superintendent.	Religious denomination.	Number of teachers and officers.	Total number of inmates since foundation
	1	2	3	4	5	6	7	8
76	St. Mary's Orphan Asylum and School	Dunkirk, N. Y.	1858	1858	Sister M. Anastasia Donovan	R. C.	4	154
77	Southern Tier Orphans' Home	Elmira, N. Y.	1866	1866	Howard Duncan	Protestant	8	535
78	Hudson Orphan and Relief Association	Hudson, N. Y.	1846	1846	Miss Elizabeth Jones, matron	Undenom'l	......	80
79	Warburg Orphan's Farm School of the Evangelical Lutheran Church.	Mt. Vernon, N. Y.	1869	1866	Rev. G. C. Holls	Evang. Luth.	4	......
80	Colored Orphan Asylum	New York, N. Y. (153d street and Boulevard.)	1838	1836	Orville K. Hutchinson	Undenom'l	24	2,014
81	Hebrew Orphan Asylum*	New York, N. Y.	1832	1822	Jacob Cohen	Hebrew	23	474
82	Leake and Watts Orphan House	New York, N. Y.	1832	1832	William H. Guest	Protestant	8	1,294
83	Orphan Asylum Society of the City of New York*	New York, N. Y.	1807	1806	Charles S. Pell	Protestant	25	2,056
84	Orphans' Home and Asylum of the Protestant-Episcopal Church.	New York, N. Y.	1859	1851	Mrs. Jane Inglee, matron	Prot. Epis	5	......
85	St. Joseph's Orphan Asylum*	New York, N. Y.	1859	1859	Sister Mary Hyacintha	R. C.	14	950
86	St. Stephen's Home	New York, N. Y.	0	1868	Sister Francis Xavier	R. C.	7	552
87	The Society for the Relief of Half-Orphan and Destitute Children.	New York, N. Y.	1837	1835	Mr. R. P. Hudson	Protestant	6	3,365
88	Poughkeepsie Orphan Asylum and Home for the Friendless.	Poughkeepsie, N. Y.	1858	1857	Mrs. C. P. Stephenson, matron	Undenom'l	2	754
89	Rochester Orphan Asylum	Rochester, N. Y.	1838	1837	Mrs. Lucia Clement, matron	Protestant	6	1,952
90	St. Mary's Orphan Boys' Asylum	Rochester, N. Y.	1864	1864	Sister M. Xavier	R. C.	14	749
91	St. Patrick's Orphan Girls' Asylum	Rochester, N. Y.	1845	1841	Sister M. de Pazzie	R. C.	7	997
92	Society for the Relief of Destitute Children of Seamen	Staten Island, N. Y.	1849	1849	Mrs. Jacob Le Roy	Undenom'l	......	......
93	Onondaga County Orphan Asylum	Syracuse, N. Y.	1845	1841	Mrs. H. M. Woods	Protestant	7	......
94	St. Joseph's Asylum	Syracuse, N. Y.	1872	1872	Sister Beata McVeal	R. C.	8	120
95	St. Vincent de Paul's Orphan Asylum	Syracuse, N. Y.	1860	1840	Sister Tatiana White	R. C.	11	600
96	St. Vincent's Female Orphan Asylum	Troy, N. Y.	1848	1848	Sarah A. Baker	R. C.	5	912
97	Troy Catholic Male Orphan Asylum	Troy, N. Y.	1864	1848	Brother Candidus	R. C.	4	......
98	Troy Orphan Asylum	Troy, N. Y.	1833	1833	Mrs. M. A. Greenman, matron	Protestant	6	1,006
99	Home of the Good Shepherd	Utica, N. Y.	1872	1872	Miss Mary Binicasse	Protestant	1	37
100	St. Vincent's Male Orphan Asylum*	Utica, N. Y.	1873	1873	Brother Clementian	Episcopal	9	683
101	Utica Orphan Asylum	Utica, N. Y.	1830	1830	Mrs. Cornelia Graham, 1st directress	Undenom'l	8	1,619

No.	Name	Location	Dates	Superintendent	Denomination	Officers	Children
110	Washington County Children's Home	Marietta, Ohio	1846 1865	S. D. Hart	Undenom'l	2	330
111	Oberlin Orphan Home	Oberlin, Ohio	1873	Linus H. Seelye	Meth. Epis	4	10
112	German Evangelical Lutheran Orphans' Asylum	Toledo, Ohio	1867	Charles Bockel	Evang. Luth		310
113	Protestant Orphans' Home	Toledo, Ohio		Miss J. A. McConnell	Undenom'l	2	312
114	McInture Children's Home	Zanesville, Ohio	1865 1865	Mrs. A. W. Ely, matron	Undenom'l		145
115	Protestant Orphan Asylum *	Allegheny, Pa	1834 1852	Mrs. E. McKelvey	Undenom'l	10	2,500
116	St. Joseph's Asylum	Allegheny, Pa	1853 1853	Sister Mary Zita	R. C.	6	430
117	Orphans' Home of the Evangelical Lutheran Church	Germantown, Pa	1860 1860	Rev. G. F. Gardner	Evang. Luth	4	355
118	Home for Friendless Children of the City and County of Lancaster	Lancaster, Pa	1860 1860	Miss Ellen Spencer, matron	Undenom'l		600
119	Association for the Care of Colored Orphans	Philadelphia, Pa	1837	Elizabeth C. Lowry	Friends	3	
120	Bethesda Children's Christian Home	Philadelphia, Pa	1860	Miss Clement	Undenom'l		198
121	Burd Orphan Asylum of St. Stephen's Church	Philadelphia, Pa	1862 1862	Rev. Gideon J. Burton, A. M., warden	Episcopal	8	104
122	Church Home for Children, (Angora)	Philadelphia, Pa	1857	Miss Purdy	Prot. Epis	4	
123	Foster Home Association	Philadelphia, Pa	1859	Mrs. S. H. Davidson	Undenom'l	4	
124	Girard College for Orphans	Philadelphia, Pa	1848	William H. Allen, president	Undenom'l	21	
125	Home for Destitute Colored Children	Philadelphia, Pa	1855	Mercy K. Williamson, president board of managers	Undenom'l	3	387
126	Jewish Foster Home and Orphan Asylum	Philadelphia, Pa	1855 1855	Mrs. Johanna Krouse	Hebrew	3	198
127	Northern Home for Friendless Children and Soldiers' Orphans Institute.*	Philadelphia, Pa	1854 1853	Miss Walk	Protestant	13	3,900
128	Philadelphia Orphan Society	Philadelphia, Pa	1815	Mrs. Stephen Colwell	Undenom'l	8	
129	St. Joseph's Roman-Catholic Orphan Asylum	Philadelphia, Pa	1807 1807	Slater Mary Gonzaga	R. C	8	1,789
130	The Southern Home for Destitute Children	Philadelphia, Pa	1857 1849	Miss Phillips, matron	Undenom'l	4	2,600
131	Union Temporary Home for Children	Philadelphia, Pa	1857	Atherton Blight	Undenom'l	3	
132	Western Provident Society and Children's Home	Philadelphia, Pa	1857 1850	Mrs. John Irwin, president board of managers	Undenom'l	6	500
133	The Orphans' Home of the Evangelical Lutheran Church	Rochester, Pa	1864	Deaconesses of the Church	Evang. Luth	3	
134	Home for Friendless Children	Wilkesbarre, Pa	1862 1860	P. H. Fithian	Undenom'l	3	194
135	Children's Home for the Borough and County of York.*	York, Pa	1865 1865	Miss S. E. Thornbury	Lutheran	2	140
136	The Orphans' Farm School*	Zelienople, Pa	1857	D. L. Debendarfer	Protestant	2	987
137	Children's Friends' Society*	Providence, R. I	1836 1858	Miss Cordelia Toner	Protestant	6	350
138	Providence Association for the Benefit of Colored Children	Providence, R. I	1839 1839	Aboy Guild	Undenom'l	4	2,500
139	St. Aloysius Orphan Asylum*	Charleston, S. C	1862 1862	S. M. Climacoas	R. C	12	
140	Charleston Orphan Asylum*	Charleston, S. C	1790 1794	Miss A. K. Irving		15	
141	Church Home*	Charleston, S. C		Mr. Chaplin	Prot. Epis	2	
142	Orphans' Home*	Decatur, S. C		Rev. W. H. Foote	Meth. Epis	3	30
143	Carolina Orphan Home	Spartanburg, S. C	1872 1872	E. C. Oliver	Methodist	3	95
144	Church Orphans' Home	Memphis, Tenn	1870 1866	Sisters of the Order of St. Mary	Episcopal	9	
145	Leath Orphan Asylum*	Memphis, Tenn	1852 1859	J. M. Peabody	Protestant		700
146	Protestant Home of Industry*	Nashville, Tenn	1846 1841	Mrs. Glasco	Protestant	3	
147	Protestant Orphan Asylum*	Nashville, Tenn	1846 1845	Mrs. A. G. Montague	Protestant	2	600

* From Report of Commissioner of Education for 1873.

TABLE XXIII.—PART 1.—*Statistics of orphan asylums, miscellaneous charities, and industrial schools for 1874, &c.*—Concluded.

Number.	Name.	Location.	Year of incorporation.	Year of organization.	Superintendent.	Religious denomination.	Number of teachers and officers.	Total number of inmates since foundation.
	1	2	3	4	5	6	7	8
148	Providence Orphan Asylum	Burlington, Vt.	1866	1854	Sister Mary Magdalen	R. C	12	765
149	St. Mary's Orphan Asylum	Elm Grove, Wis	1869	1859	Sister M. Salesia	R. C	7	...
150	Milwaukee Orphan Asylum	Milwaukee, Wis	1852	1850	Maria P. Mason, matron	Undenom'l	3	732
151	St. Rose's—for female orphan children	Milwaukee, Wis	1848		Sister Camilla	R. U	6	7,090
152	Taylor Orphan Asylum*	Racine, Wis	1867	1872	Miss M. J. Weston	Protestant		33
153	St. Clemilanus Orphan Asylum	St. Francis Station, Wis	1850	1846	C. Wapelhorst	R. C	12	443
154	National Home for Destitute Colored Women and Children.	Washington, D. C.	1863	1863	Miss Eliza Heacock	Union	4	679
155	St. Joseph's Male Orphan Asylum*	Washington, D. C.	1855	1856	Sister M. Irene	R. C	7	402
156	Washington City Orphan Asylum*	Washington, D. C.		1815				

* From Report of Commissioner of Education for 1873.

TABLE XXIII.—PART 1.—*Statistics of orphan asylums, miscellaneous charities, and industrial schools for 1874, &c.*—Continued.

Number	Name.	Conditions of admission. Age.	Conditions of admission. Other conditions.	How supported.	Industries taught.	Provision for children who have left the institution.
	1	9	10	11	12	18
1	Church Home for Orphans	Under 10		Charity	Housework and sewing	
2	Sacramento Protestant Orphan Asylum	Boys under 10, girls under 12		State appropriation, subscriptions, donations, &c.		Returned to friends or adopted.
3	Ladies' Protection and Relief Society	Boys 1 month to 11 years, girls all ages		Legislative appropriation and contributions.	Housework	Placed in homes.
4	Pacific Hebrew Orphan Asylum and Home Society.*	3 years		Appropriations and contributions.		
5	St. Boniface Orphan Asylum*	Under 16	All orphans, foundlings, &c.	Appropriations and contributions		
6	Male Orphan Asylum*	6-12		Charitable contributions.		
7	The Good Templars' Home for Orphans	2-12		Lodge contributions, State aid, and donations.		
8	Fitch's Home*	4-14	Soldiers' orphans	Donations and State appropriations.	Sewing and housework	None.
9	Hartford Orphan Asylum	3-12		Endowment and contributions		Sent to trades or farms or housework.
10	St. Catherine Orphan Asylum	3 years		Charity and donations	Housework	
11	St. James's Orphan Asylum	3 years		Charity and donations	Farming, trades, and housework.	
12	New Haven Orphan Asylum	2-10	Freedom from contagious disease, and poverty.	Contributions and town appropriation.	Sewing and housework.	
13	St. Mary's Asylum	3 years		Charity and donations.	Housework	
14	Orphans' Home	5-10		Contributions and annual subscriptions.	Housework and farming	
15	Chicago Nursery and Half-Orphan Asylum*	Under 14	Orphanage and destitution.	Endowment and contributions.		Placed in good homes.
16	Chicago Protestant Orphan Asylum			Contributions.		
17	Uhlich Orphan Asylum	Under 14		Voluntary contributions	General work	Good homes.
18	Colored Orphan Asylum	Under 14		Contributions and subscriptions.		Provided with homes.
19	German Protestant Orphan Asylum			Donations.		
20	German and English Asylum for Orphans and Destitute Children.	2-18			Needle-work of all kinds.	
21	Kansas Orphan Asylum and Home for Friendless Children.	Under 16		Contributions and charitable entertainments.		Good Christian homes.

* From Report of Commissioner of Education for 1873.

TABLE XXIII.—PART 1.—*Statistics of orphan asylums, miscellaneous charities, and industrial schools for 1874, &c.*—Continued.

Number.	Name.	Conditions of admission.		How supported.	Industries taught.	Provision for children who have left the institution.
		Age.	Other conditions.			
1	1	9	10	11	12	13
22	St. Thomas's Orphan Asylum	Over 2		Collections in the diocese	Farming	Apprenticed to mechanics and farmers, and some sent to colleges.
23	Convent of the Angel Guardian	3-15		Industry and charitable contributions.	Sewing and housework	
24	Orphanage of the Good Shepherd	2-6		Voluntary subscriptions.	Printing	
25	Protestant-Episcopal Orphan Asylum*	Under 18	Orphanage or destitution.	Endowment and contributions		
26	St. Joseph's Orphan Asylum	Under 19		Donations and subscriptions of members of St. Joseph's Orphan Society.		
27	Mount Carmel*	6-14		Contributions.		
28	Female Orphan Asylum of Portland	1-10	Generally received by bond of surrender.	Subscriptions, donations, &c.	House and needle work	Adopted or bound out to service.
29	Annapolis Orphan Asylum*	3-18		Subscriptions and contributions.		
30	Baltimore Orphan Asylum	2-12		Subscriptions, donations, and endowment.		
31	German Orphan Asylum*	From 2 years		By German General Society	Sewing	None.
32	Hebrew Orphan Asylum	3-11	Full health	Contributions of members, &c.	Sewing, knitting, and fancy needle-work.	
33	St. Anthony's Asylum	1-12		Contributions and collections		
34	St. Francis's Orphan Asylum for Colored Children.	From 3 years		Collections		
35	St. Mary's Female Orphan Asylum	3-12		Contributions and ground-rent.	Plain sewing	Transferred to industrial school at 15 years of age, and taught trades.
36	St. Peter's Asylum for Female Children	4-9		Endowment and charity	Sewing and housework	Outfit of clothing and homes or trades provided.
37	St. Vincent's Male Orphan Asylum	7-12		Endowment and contributions		Homes provided.
38	Shelter for Orphans of Colored Soldiers and Friendless Colored Children.	9-12		Appropriations and contributions.		
39	The Orphan Asylum of St. Paul's Church.	Under 17		Contributions and endowment	Sewing and housework	
40	Boston Female Orphan Asylum.	3 years		Contributions and endowment	Sewing, knitting, and house-	

	4-5	Conditions	Contributions	Industries	Disposition
41	Church Home for Orphans and Destitute Children				
42	House of Angel Guardian	7-15	If destitute, must be resident of the diocese	Payments on account of some pupils, contributions and concerts, &c., given by pupils.	Tailoring and baking	Adopted or returned to parents or guardians.
43	St. Vincent's Orphan Asylum*	1-16		Collections and donations		
44	Protectory of Mary Immaculate*	From 18 mons		Contributions		
45	City Orphan Asylum*	From 18 mons		Donations and industry		
46	Seaman's Orphan and Children's Friend Society.	3 years		Endowment and subscriptions	Housework	Adopted or provided with homes in families.
47	Worcester Children's Friend Society	9-12	Healthy, and parents residents of Salem.	Contributions and endowment	Housework	Adopted or provided with homes in families.
48	St. Anthony's Male Orphan Asylum	4-12		Charitable contributions	Sewing	
49	St. Vincent's Orphan Asylum	3-12		An annual fair	None	Provided with homes.
50	D'Evereux Hall	4-15		Contributions		Boys bound out at 12 years of age to farmers or mechanics.
51	Episcopal Orphan Home	Under 12	Destitution	Endowment, subscriptions, and donations.	Sewing and housework	Placed in families.
52	German St. Vincent's Orphan Asylum	Under 11	Orphanage	Voluntary contributions	Needle work, housework, and gardening.	
53	Methodist Orphan Home*	Under 16	Orphanage and destitution.	Contributions		
54	Protestant Orphan Asylum, (German)*	9 months-10 years.		Pay and contributions		
55	St. Mary's Female Orphan Asylum*	5-12		Contributions		Placed in homes.
56	St. Louis Protestant Orphan Asylum			Endowment and donations		Adopted into families.
57	New Hampshire Orphans' Home.	3-14		Contributions and endowment	Farming and housework	
58	Children's Home	4-10		Contributions		
59	Orphan Asylum	9-10		Endowment, appropriations, and contributions.	Sewing, knitting, painting, engraving, stone and wood carving, carpentry, &c.	
60	Paterson Orphan Asylum Association for Orphans, Half-Orphans, and Homeless Children.	3-10		Contributions solicited by trustees	Housework and gardening.	Placed in homes.
61	St. Vincent's Male Orphan Asylum*	7-14		Appropriations and contributions		Placed in good homes.
62	Cayuga Asylum for Destitute Children	2-12		County appropriation, and contributions.		
63	Davenport Institution for Orphan Girls*	5-9		Donations and endowment		
64	Brooklyn Howard Colored Orphan Asylum	2-10		Contributions and subscriptions.		Provided with homes.
65	Orphan Asylum Society for the City of Brooklyn.*	3-12		State appropriations and contributions.		
66	Roman Catholic Asylum for Boys*	4-12		Voluntary contributions.		
67	St. Joseph's Orphan Asylum*			Voluntary contributions.		
68	Buffalo Orphan Asylum	2-12	Orphanage	Voluntary contributions.		
69	Evangelical Lutheran St. John's Orphan Home.	2-12		Appropriations, contributions, and produce of the Orphans' Farm.	Housework, sewing, knitting, farming, and mat-making.	

* From report of Commissioner of Education for 1873.

TABLE XXIII.—PART 1.—*Statistics of orphan asylums, miscellaneous charities, and industrial schools for 1874, &c.*—Continued.

Number.	Name.	Conditions of admission.		How supported.	Industries taught.	Provision for children who have left the institution.
		Age.	Other conditions.			
1	1	9	10	11	12	13
70	Orphan Ward of Church Charity Foundation.	3–10	Orphans or half-orphans of Protestant parentage.	Contributions of Protestant-Episcopal churches of Buffalo.	Gardening, sewing, and housework.	Situations provided.
71	St. Mary's German Roman-Catholic Asylum		Destitute orphans of St. Mary's parish.	Contributions of St. Mary's parish and appropriations.	Housework, sewing, and knitting.	Placed in families, boys for trades, girls for housework.
72	St. Vincent's Asylum	From 5 years		Appropriations.	Dressmaking, fancy needle-work, and plain sewing.	
73	Ontario Orphan Asylum*	Under 12	Free from imbecility.	Contributions and donations		
74	Thomas Asylum for Orphan and Destitute Indian Children.	Under 12	Orphanage and destitution.	Indian Bureau and State of New York.		
75	Orphan House of the Holy Savior.	Boys, 3–7; girls, 3–12	Orphanage and destitution.	Contributions	Gardening, sewing, and housework.	Provided with homes or fitted for self-support.
76	St. Mary's Orphan Asylum and School	From 2 years		Contributions and board of education.	Sewing and housework	
77	Southern Tier Orphans' Home	Under 12		Contributions	Housework	
78	Hudson Orphan and Relief Association	Under 12		Endowment, appropriations, and contributions.		
79	Wartburg Orphans' Farm School of the Evangelical Lutheran Church.	6–10		Contributions	Gardening, farming, sewing, and housework.	The children have a permanent home in the institution, to which they may return in case of sickness or when out of employment.
80	Colored Orphan Asylum	2–10	Must be orphans, half-orphans, or destitute children of the State of New York.	Endowment, city appropriations, donations, and payment of board.	Gardening, sewing, and housework.	Returned to friends, or indentured at the age of 12.
81	Hebrew Orphan Asylum*	Over 5	Must be orphans or half-orphans.	Contributions		
82	Leake and Watts Orphan House	3–12	Must be entire orphans.			Indentured to trades or to farming.
83	Orphan Asylum Society of the City of New York.*	Under 10		Legacies, appropriations, and subscriptions.		
84	Orphans' Home and Asylum of the Protestant Episcopal Church.	3–8	Orphanage	Voluntary contributions	Sewing and housework	Returned to friends or placed in good homes.

No.	Name	Ages	Conditions of admission	Means of support	Industrial training	What becomes of the children
						trades, or in higher schools.
87	The Society for the Relief of Half-Orphans and Destitute Children.	4-10	Must be half-orphans or destitute.	Voluntary contributions	Sewing and housework	None.
88	Poughkeepsie Orphan Asylum and Home for the Friendless.	2-12	Must be healthy	Voluntary contributions	Sewing, knitting, and basket-making.	Indentured or adopted.
89	Rochester Orphan Asylum	Under 12	Orphanage and destitution.	Contributions and board from city and county for pauper children.	Sewing and housework	Indentured or adopted.
90	St. Mary's Orphan Boys' Asylum	3-14		Donations and contributions		Adopted or returned to friends.
91	St. Patrick's Orphan Girls' Asylum	3-16		Donations and contributions		Adopted or returned to friends.
92	Society for the Relief of Destitute Children of Seamen.			Subscriptions and donations		Homes provided.
93	Onondaga County Orphan Asylum	2-12		Endowment and appropriations		
94	St. Joseph's Asylum	Under 11		Contributions	Manual labor for the elder boys.	Adopted or returned to friends.
95	St. Vincent de Paul's Orphan Asylum			Contributions and endowment	Needle-work and domestic economy.	Homes or situations provided.
96	St. Vincent's Female Orphan Asylum	3-12		Appropriations, fairs, and collections.	Sewing and housework	Good homes provided.
97	Troy Catholic Male Orphan Asylum	5-12	Must be surrendered to the entire control of the institution, or a nominal price paid for their support.	Appropriations and contributions	Farming and gardening	Homes in families.
98	Troy Orphan Asylum	3-10	Destitution and friendlessness.	Appropriations and contributions	None	Returned to friends, adopted, or indentured with families in the country.
99	House of the Good Shepherd *	No limits		Voluntary offerings		
100	St. Vincent's Male Orphan Asylum *	4-14	Must be indigent orphans.	Contributions, subscriptions, legacies, &c.		Returned to friends or adopted.
101	Utica Orphan Asylum	2-14	Destitution	Contributions and subscriptions		Employment provided.
102	Orphan Asylums	6-12	Must be healthy and intelligent, and be bound legally to institution until majority.	Contributions, produce of field and garden, and board, wages, &c.	Gardening and housework.	
103	German Methodist Orphan Asylum				Farming, gardening, sewing, housework, fancy-work, &c.	
104	Cincinnati Orphan Asylum *		Orphanage and destitution.	Endowment and contributions		
105	General German Protestant Orphan Asylum.			By members and donations	Sewing, knitting, &c.	
106	Cleveland Orphan Asylum *	2-10		Endowment		Bound out till 18 years of age to good families, for which the child receives schooling, board, and $100 cash.

* From Report of Commissioner of Education for 1873.

12 E

TABLE XXIII.—PART 1.—*Statistics of orphan asylums, miscellaneous charities, and industrial schools for 1874, &c.*—Continued.

Number	Name.	Conditions of admission.		How supported.	Industries taught.	Provision for children who have left the institution.
		Age.	Other conditions.			
	1	9	10	11	12	13
107	Orphan Asylum I. O. B. B	4-12		Contributions	None	Taught trades in the places from which they came.
108	Montgomery County Children's Home	Under 16		County taxation	Housework and gardening	Indentured or adopted. At 16 years of age adopted or put to trades.
109	Ebenezer Orphan Asylum	2-12	Orphanage and destitution.	Contributions and endowment	Farming and housework	
110	Washington County Children's Home	Under 16		Appropriation and county taxation	Farming, gardening, and housework.	Indentured or adopted.
111	Oberlin Orphan Home	1-3	Must be entirely destitute	Unsolicited donations		
112	German Evangelical Lutheran Orphans' Asylum.	From 2 years	Admitted free of charge, if destitute orphans, others charged from $2 to $6 per month.	Contributions of members of the society, charity, and income of farm.		Trades or situations provided.
113	Protestant Orphans' Home	No limit	Destitution	Contributions	Housework	Adopted in families.
114	McIntire Children's Home	3-12		Allowance from John McIntire's estate and contributions.	Sewing, knitting, and housework.	Good homes provided.
115	Protestant Orphan Asylum	Under 14	Orphanage and youth.	Contributions and endowment.	Knitting, sewing, dress making, and tucking.	
116	St. Joseph's Asylum			Contributions		
117	Orphans' Home of the Evangelical Lutheran Church.	Over 2	Orphanage and destitution.	Contributions, appropriations, and endowment.	Shoe-mending and caning, sewing and housework.	Boys indentured to trades, girls indentured in Christian families.
118	Home for Friendless Children of the City and County of Lancaster.	Under 12	Must be white children surrendered by parents or committed by the court or mayor of Lancaster.	County and State appropriations and contributions.	Gardening, sewing, and housework.	Indentured, girls until 18, boys until 21 years of age.
119	Association for the Care of Colored Orphans.	Under 12		Contributions and subscriptions.		Homes in families provided.
120	Bethania Children's Christian Home	Under 12		Donations and payment of board.	Sewing and housework	
121	Burd Orphan Asylum of St. Stephen's Church.	4-9	Baptized in the P. E. Church and father.	Endowment	Sewing and housework	Outfit of clothing and $30.

No.	Institution	Age	Character	Appropriations, subscriptions, and donations.	Industries taught	Disposition of children
122	Church Home for Children, (Angora)	2-12		Subscriptions and donations	Sewing, knitting, and housework.	Provided with homes in families.
123	Foster Home Association			Endowment	Carpentry, gardening, and shoemaking.	Sent to trades or schools.
124	Girard College for Orphans	3-12			Gardening and housework.	None.
125	Home for Destitute Colored Children	Over 4		Contributions and legacies	Sewing, knitting, and housework.	
126	Jewish Foster Home and Orphan Asylum	3-12		Members' dues, contributions, and endowment.		
127	Northern Home for Friendless Children and Soldiers' Orphan Institute.*	3-12		Donations and contributions.		
128	Philadelphia Orphan Society	2-12		Subscriptions, donations, and legacies.		
129	St. Joseph's Roman-Catholic Orphan Asylum.	3-7	Orphanage and destitution.	Voluntary contributions	Sewing and housework	Bound out until of age and then receive two new suits of clothes.
130	The Southern Home for Destitute Children.	2 mos-6 yrs		Appropriations and contributions		Homes as servants.
131	Union Temporary Home for Children.			Subscriptions, donations, and board of children.		Homes in families.
132	Western Provident Society and Children's Home.	4-12		Contributions	None	Homes provided.
133	The Orphans' Home of the Evangelical Lutheran Church.			Contributions and donations.	Farming, gardening, sewing, and housework.	
134	Home for Friendless Children			Voluntary contributions.	Gardening and housework.	
135	Children's Home for the Borough and County of York.*	Under 12		Subscriptions and donations.		
136	The Orphans' Farm School*	Under 10		Charity		
137	Children's Friends Society*	2-12		Endowment and contributions.		
138	Providence Association for the Benefit of Colored Children.	From 3 yrs		Charity	Sewing and housework.	Placed in families.
139	St. Aloysius Orphan Asylum	3-14		Fairs and contributions.	Sewing and housework.	Situations in families.
140	Charleston Orphan Asylum*	Over 12		Appropriations and contributions		
141	Church Home*	10 or under.		Contributions		
142	Orphans' Home*			Contributions		
143	Carolina Orphan Home		Orphanage and destitution.	Voluntary contributions	Gardening and printing.	
144	Church Orphans' Home	2 or over	Needing the charity of the Church.	Contributions		
145	Leath Orphan Asylum	Under 20		Contributions	Farming and housework.	
146	Protestant House of Industry*	8-14		Industry		
147	Protestant Orphan Asylum*	Boys, under 10; girls, all ages.		Contribution and appropriations		
148	Providence Orphan Asylum	2-12	Orphanage.	Contributions	Chair-seating, sewing, and dressmaking.	Returned to guardians or placed in good homes during minority.
149	St. Mary's Orphan Asylum	Under 18	Orphanage	Labor of sisterhood and proceeds of schools.	Sewing, dressmaking, and housework.	Good homes provided.

* From Report of Commissioner of Education for 1873.

TABLE XXIII.—PART 1.—*Statistics of orphan asylums, miscellaneous charities, and industrial schools for 1874, &c.*—Continued.

Number	Name.	Conditions of admission.		How supported.	Industries taught.	Provision for children who have left the institution.
		Age.	Other conditions.			
	1	9	10	11	12	13
150	Milwaukee Orphan Asylum	Girls, 2-12; boys, 2-10.	Orphanage and destitution.	Contributions and appropriations.	Cane-seating, sewing, knitting and housework.	Returned to friends, adopted, or placed at service.
151	St Rose's—for female orphan children	Over 1 year.		Fairs and donations.	Sewing and housework.	Placed in families or at trades.
152	Taylor Orphan Asylum*	Under 14.		Endowment		
153	St. Chrisostom Orphan Asylum	Under 12.		Contributions		
154	National Home for Destitute Colored Women and Children.	1-12		Donations	Gardening, sewing, and housework.	Good homes provided.
155	St Joseph's Male Orphan Asylum*	5-12		Voluntary contributions		
156	Washington City Orphan Asylum*	2-12		Voluntary contributions		

*From Report of Commissioner of Education for 1873.

TABLE XXIII.—Part I.—*Statistics of orphan asylums, institutions, etc., for 1873* —

Number	Name	Amount of permanent fund.	Income.	Expenditure.	Sex.		Race.		Parent-age.		Orphanage.			Instruction: No. taught—					Library.	
		14	15	16	Male. 17	Female. 18	White. 19	Colored. 20	Natives. 21	Foreign. 22	Orphans. 23	Half-orphans. 24	Foundlings. 25	Reading. 26	Writing. 27	Arithmetic. 28	Drawing. 29	Music. 30	Number of volumes. 31	Increase in the past year. 32
1	Church Home for Orphans	80	$4,537	$6,621	1	38	39	0	36	3	32		1	9	25	25		3		
2	Sacramento Protestant Orphan Asylum	8,000		15,000	32	43	75		50	25	17	57	1						300	50
3	Ladies' Protection and Relief Society		10,000	9,000	(120)		169					56							500	100
4	Pacific Hebrew Orphan Asylum and Home Society*		10,000	1,560	19	6	25	1	13	12	12	13							100	100
5	St. Boniface Orphan Asylum*		1,200		10	9	14		15	4	4	11		15	14	14				
6	Male Orphan Asylum*		35,000	35,000	270		270				130	140		270	270	270	2		1,312	100
7	The Good Templars' Home for Orphans	0	10,000	10,000	38	16	55	2	18		16	46	0	46	30					
8	Fitch's Home*	0	5,544	5,544	20	16	42	0			14	46		44	30	40		60	1,675	15
9	Hartford Orphan Asylum	0			40	18	58		11		14	35			30				100	0
10	St. Catharine Orphan Asylum	0	500	500	23	33	53	0	20		33									
11	St. James's Orphan Asylum	0			54		54													
12	New Haven Orphan Asylum	40,000	13,000	12,000	70	45	115	1	19		30	86		100	100		90	100	500	40
13	St. Mary's Orphan Asylum					12				37										
14	Orphans' Home	1,497	3,065	2,947	14	12	26	0		131	16	13	1	26	26	26		1	800	100
15	Chicago Nursery and Half Orphan Asylum*		10,000	10,000	67	60	127	0		40	35	73	4	60	60					
16	Chicago Protestant Orphan Asylum				70	60	130			15	7	11								
17	Uhlich Orphan Asylum		8,969	7,092	13	13	26	0	11	13	10	34								
18	Colored Orphan Asylum				30	14	0	44	44	0	10			16	14	14			75	0
19	German Protestant Orphan Asylum	0	2,500	2,314	7	3	10	1	22			23		10	10					
20	German and English Asylum for Orphans and Destitute Children	0			70	55	125	0	40	85	50	39		14	10	14				
21	Kansas Orphan Asylum and Home for Friendless Children	0	4,000	4,000	39	33	90	0	70	20	50	75	5						40	0
22	St. Thomas's Orphan Asylum	0			90		90			6	18	40		90	90	90				
23	Convent of the Angel Guardian		4,000	4,000	40	64	40	0	30		9	15		53	53	53		0	800	
24	Orphanage of the Good Shepherd		4,763	4,763		31	31				12	18	1	31	31	31		0		
25	Protestant Episcopal Orphan Asylum*	12,000	6,000	5,500	53	37	56			59	61	24	0						200	
26	St. Joseph's Orphan Asylum					97														
27	Mount Carmel*		2,375	2,375		36	36							60	60		10	0		
28	Female Orphan Asylum of Portland	8,000	7,000			30			18	18	12	21		60	12			0		
29	Annapolis Orphan Asylum*					3	3		3		7		0	3	3	3				

* From Report of the Commissioner of Education for 1873.

TABLE XXIII.—PART 1.—*Statistics of orphan asylums, miscellaneous charities, and industrial schools for 1874, &c.*—Continued.

Number	Name	14 Amount of permanent fund.	15 Income.	16 Expenditure.	Sex. 17 Male.	Sex. 18 Female.	Race. 19 White.	Race. 20 Colored.	Parentage. 21 Natives.	Parentage. 22 Foreign.	Orphanage. 23 Orphans.	Orphanage. 24 Half-orphans.	Orphanage. 25 Foundlings.	Instruction: No. taught— 26 Reading.	27 Writing.	28 Arithmetic.	29 Drawing.	30 Music.	Library. 31 Number of volumes.	Library. 32 Increase in the past year.
30	Baltimore Orphan Asylum	$13,500	$3,500	$3,500	44	62	106	0			35	71	0							
31	German Orphan Asylum*		5,500	7,000	79	14	93	0	93		18	75	0	21	21	90	3			
32	Hebrew Orphan Asylum		9,237	9,390	65	71	136		9	101	60	76		110	90	90	90	90	520	40
33	St. Anthony's Asylum		1,172	1,172				29			10	16	3							
34	St. Francis's Orphan Asylum for Colored Children*	3,000	1,559	9,169		111	117		75	42	51	66		90	90	90		50	350	56
35	St. Mary's Female Orphan Asylum	3,300	1,333	1,333	0	59	59		39	20	19	11	6	70	64	58	10		130	10
36	St. Peter's Asylum for Female Children	6,500	6,000	6,500	0	84	84		73	12	40	35		84	51	51		51	430	64
37	St. Vincent's Male Orphan Asylum				85															
38	Shelter for Orphans of Colored Soldiers and Friendless Colored Children				57	53														
39	The Orphan Asylum of St. Paul's Church		10,000	10,000	43	49	107		85	11	11	10	0	40	40	40	0	84	250	10
40	Boston Female Orphan Asylum		22,953	24,425		107	92				11	69		90	39	40	10	42		0
41	Church Home for Orphans and Destitute Children*	0	15,485	16,850		215	185		112	73	39	57		185	185	185	10			
42	Home of Angel Guardian				185				70	147	98	93	4	93	93	93	10	10		
43	St. Vincent's Orphan Asylum*					217	215		31	57	28	47	2	58	58	34	4	10		
44	Protectory of Mary Immaculate*				39	39	97				12	30		46	46	46	10	10		
45	City Orphan Asylum*	30,000	8,000	8,000	39	38	34		24	10	12	10		40	40	40	10	10	150	10
46	Seaman's Orphan and Children's Friend Society	14,000	5,740	2,685	96	15	34		12	63	76	98		90	10	10	4	30	90	18
47	Worcester Children's Friend Society		4,631	4,046	28	73	72		36	57	40	15		10	10	47			250	
48	St. Anthony's Male Orphan Asylum		5,000	4,000	45	0	45		38		60	4		73	75	73		30	350	60
49	St. Vincent's Orphan Asylum	0			37	65	73	0		7	40	40	2	73	73	36	30	43	300	
50	D'Everenx Hall		5,500	5,500	84	13	53			114	102	41	0	38	38	30				
51	Episcopal Orphan Home	0	6,000	6,000	10	33	43				14	43	1				30			
52	German St. Vincent's Orphan Asylum		9,445	9,815		144	144					71		15	15	15				
53	Methodist Orphans' Home*	0				12	53		90	113		80		90	90	75	1		250	
54	Protestant Orphan Asylum, (German)*					139	139			133	102	60		162	162	162			350	
55	St. Mary's Female Orphan Asylum				1	175	176		25										200	125
56	New Hampshire Orphans' Home	$28,000																	285	
57	Children's Home	30,000	4,000	4,000										10	10	16	0			

		First Cost																					
	and Homeless Children.																						
61	St. Vincent's Male Orphan Asylum*	6,500	12,719	12,073	111	65	0	111	103		0	86	31	103		99	63	63		64		150	33
62	Cayuga Asylum for Destitute Children		4,664	4,112	65		29	84	12		67	31	12		65	63	44				106	
63	Davenport Institution for Orphan Girls*	18,100	18,100	18,100		31	31	30	31		9		31		63	35	35			53		
64	Brooklyn Howard Colored Orphan Asylum Society		50,989	63,304	156	89	68	245	169	10	207	34	26	30	230	220		30			302	55
65	Orphan Asylum Society for the City of Brooklyn*		51,974	51,940	335	59	29	334	229	5	190	145	46	75	330	289	143		50		100	
66	Roman-Catholic Asylum for Boys*		14,140	13,990	34	20	20	70	45	0	4	5	24		97	21	21		30		500	
67	St. Joseph's Orphan Asylum*			7,000	42	36	30	40	73	0	35	7	12	46	30	30	21		30		400	
68	Buffalo Orphan Asylum	45,000	12,517	12,505	40	28	37	73	42	0	7	5	17		30	30	18				394	60
69	Evangelical Lutheran St. John's Orphan Home		5,311	5,446	21	20	19	36	12	0	24	6	37		30	30	14		30		410	25
70	Orphan Ward of Church Charity Foundation		2,296	1,262	19	19	8	30	19	0	9	6	9		30						90	0
71	St. Mary's German Roman-Catholic Asylum					113		113	65	3	32	24	105		109	109	109					
72	St. Vincent's Asylum		9,097	9,000	23	58	15	36	30	1	89	6		15	35	35	30			15		
73	Ontario Orphan Asylum	1,000	9,744	9,744	61	57	43	75		2	90		30	116			39				302	55
74	Thomas Asylum for Orphan and Destitute Indian Children		4,339	9,639	9	15	15	15		0	11	4		30	10	14	14		7	30	100	
75	Orphan House of the Holy Savior*		2,165	2,165	31	15	10	21	13	0	37	5	15		15	14	0		28	3	200	100
76	St. Mary's Orphan Asylum and School	2,000	9,942	9,942	34	10	40	43		4	10	10	40	32	42	42	0		3		100	
77	Southern Tier Orphans' Home		7,300	6,700	66	53	40	58	13	0	43	47	13	13	45	40	30				237	
78	Hudson Orphan and Relief Association		6,151	6,163	35	28	26	63	61	6	16	10	40	61	29	29	115			20		
79	Wartburg Orphans' Farm School of the Evangelical Lutheran Church	30,000	36,044	38,900	196	88	88	113	270	294	174	44	110	270	212	224	163				518	25
80	Colored Orphan Asylum																					
81	Hebrew Orphan Asylum		70,656	69,285	139	51	55	190	98	3	145	44	102	24	178	178	164			284	570	25
82	Leake and Watts Orphan House				86	50	50	136	108	0	70	28	108		122	122	124				350	
83	Orphan Asylum Society of the City of New York*		53,041	52,725	96	63	30	161	94	1	121	16	30	106	153	153	133				400	100
84	Orphans' Home and Asylum of the Protestant Episcopal Church		14,301	15,136	66	71	20	157	98	0	15	102	11		86	86	86	0	137		200	100
85	St. Joseph's Orphan Asylum*		39,564	17,234	98	81	81	180	190	1	137	78	113	113	171	171	171	12			200	30
86	St. Stephen's Home	30,000	18,000	18,000	50	62	62	110	4	0	34	24	4		90	90	40	6			100	30
87	The Society for the Relief of Half-Orphan and Destitute Children	35,000	18,000	18,000	121	87	71	206	176	46	200	84	176		291	291	115	0	12		237	
88	Poughkeepsie Orphan Asylum and Home for the Friendless.	6,000	9,667	6,986	38	10	28	63		0	10	18	5		40	40	40	0			650	0
89	Rochester Orphan Asylum		7,089	5,214	67	23	23	83	24	0	53	15	24		43	43	43				300	
90	St. Mary's Orphan Boys' Asylum			4,487	113	23	23	111	17	1	85	20	17		95	95	53	8			200	
91	St. Patrick's Orphan Girls' Asylum					104		103	30		85	21	30		92	92	56	0				
92	Society for the Relief of Destitute Children of Seamen	31,585	16,936	17,019	72	42	42	113	94	1	57	12	94		74	74	30				650	
93	Onondaga County Orphan Asylum		16,884	16,464	60	63	42	63		0	53	12			149	149	109	95	95		270	12
94	St. Joseph's Asylum		20,881	20,881	191	127	0	127	115	0	54	30	115	113	117	117	41	117	117		200	
95	St. Vincent de Paul's Orphan Asylum		12,563	12,563	115		0			0	55	16	113	113	100	100	64	2	2			15
96	St. Vincent's Female Orphan Asylum		18,597	18,330	130	41	0	95		0	112	25	11	119	115	115	85	46	82		290	
97	Troy Catholic Male Orphan Asylum	36,168	12,437	13,299	54	21	41	95	54	0	18	4	54	44	95	95	90	0	0		450	
98	Troy Orphan Asylum				14	14	21	37	12	0	23	14	12	51	16	16	14	0	95			
99	House of the Good Shepherd*		9,363	9,586	59	32	21	52	20	0	47	59	20	20	76	76	40	14			250	50
100	St. Vincent Male Orphan Asylum*	149,115	12,708	12,743	65	34	34	53	12	0	12	10	12	12	99	99	30	1			567	
101	Utica Orphan Asylum		10,800	10,500	74	76	56	150	148	0	70		148		100	100	25		150		200	
102	Orphan Asylums		6,412	6,412	28	14	14	44	0	0	17	19	0		40	40	40	0	40		300	60
103	German Methodist Orphan Asylum	33,000	10,874	10,272	67	26	26	61	44	0	67	17	41	41						57	536	
104	Cincinnati Orphan Asylums*		12,000	12,000	45	51	51	96	55	1	36	85	91	91	61	61	61		41	60		96
105	General German Protestant Orphan Asylum	13,364	12,843		39	51		61	52		11	39	53	33	30			16				280	
106	Cleveland Orphan Asylum*	60,000	56,000	26,000	114	95	95	95		29	176	36	212	212	197	197	197	89	89		450	0
107	Orphan Asylum I. O. O. B.																				1,000	

* From Report of Commissioner of Education for 1873.

TABLE XXIII.—PART 1.—*Statistics of orphan asylums, miscellaneous charities, and industrial schools for 1874, &c.—Concluded.*

Number.	Name.	Amount of permanent fund.	Income.	Expenditure.	Sex. Male.	Sex. Female.	Race. White.	Race. Colored.	Parentage. Natives.	Parentage. Foreign.	Orphanage. Orphans.	Orphanage. Half-orphans.	Orphanage. Foundlings.	Instruction: No. taught— Reading.	Writing.	Arithmetic.	Drawing.	Music.	Library. Number of volumes.	Library. Increase in the past year.
105	Montgomery County Children's Home	$40,000	$8,000	$8,000	63	31	94	0	90	4	50	33	5	30	90	90	24	0	35	35
106	Ebenezer Orphan Asylum		14,625	14,490	60	40	100		94	6	36	64		91	62	72	17	100	400	
107	Washington County Children's Home			18,000	54	40		16		40		4		64			15		50	50
108	Oberlin Orphan Home			2,000	4	2	6	0	6	0	4	2		1		1			75	9
109	German Evangelical Lutheran Orphans' Asylum	0	2,989	2,925	27	21	48		6	42	7	29	1	27	35	27	8	27	0	0
110	Protestant Orphans' Home	0	3,446	10,852	31	12	41		23	22		36		97	97	78	65	12	75	28
111	McIntire Children's Home	0	3,000	16,917	87	59	146	0		5				123	73	73	60	69		
112	Protestant Orphan Asylum		30,753	16,000	52	44	96				54	0	0	63	63	63	69	69	300	33
113	St. Joseph's Asylum	12,300	9,000	9,340	42	20	62		11	51	14	54		62	48	42	0	54	300	
114	Orphan's Home of the Evangelical Lutheran Church	5,000	9,000	9,000	81	32	113		93	20	20	93	0	56	71	56	36	113	0	0
115	Home for Friendless Children of the City and County of Lancaster																			
116	Association for the Care of Colored Orphans		1,879	1,879	4	3		41	25					30	30	71		39	300	71
117	Bethesda Children's Christian Home				0	60	60	0	0	0				60	30	50		20		13
118	Burd Orphan Asylum of St. Stephen's Church				0	83					14	46		83	83	83		15	300	
119	Church Home for Children, (Angora)																			
120	Foster Home Association																			
121	Girard College for Orphans		600,000		530		530							530	530	530	530	550	5,000	
122	Home for Destitute Colored Children	26,300	7,717	6,666	27	14		41	41	0	34			34	34	34	4		3,375	100
123	Jewish Foster Home and Orphan Asylum	8,500	6,693	6,693	21	17	38		0	38	22			34	38	38	100	15	300	100
124	Northern Home for Friendless Children, and Soldiers' Orphan Insti- tute.		63,001	63,001	223	109	332	0		0	13	340		320	320	300				
125	Philadelphia Orphan Society						133							90	90	90				
126	St. Joseph's Roman-Catholic Orphan Asylum				46	44	133							135	135	100				
127	The Southern Home for Destitute Children						All	41	41					19						
128	Union Temporary Home for Children		7,503	7,503	40	45	85			0					55		0		270	83
129	Western Provident Society and Children's Home	2,477				40										42				
130	The Orphans' Home of the Evangelical Lutheran Church		7,706																	
131	Home for Friendless Children																			
132	Orphan's Home for the Borough and County of York															45				
133	The Orphans' Farm School																			

136	Providence Asylum Society*	13,434	4,081	3,407																100
137	Providence Association for the Benefit of Colored Children		14,000	14,000															400	
139	St. Aloysium Orphan Asylum		26,000	26,000															1,770	
140	Charleston Orphan Asylum*																			
141	Church Home*																			
142	Orphans' Home*	30,000	2,300	2,300												19		75		
143	Carolina Orphan Home																	200	60	
144	Church Orphans' Home.	13,000	14,000	2,500												4		600	181	
145	Louth Orphan Asylum		2,100	2,500																
146	Protestant House of Industry*		6,000	5,738																
147	Protestant Orphan Asylum*	1,000																150		
148	Providence Orphan Asylum*																			
149	St. Mary's Orphan Asylum	0	9,636	8,548												0		200	10	
150	Milwaukee Orphan Asylum	0	1,200													0				
151	St. Rose's—for female orphan children																			
152	Taylor Orphan Asylum*		10,000	7,000																
153	St. Clemillanus Orphan Asylum		6,603	6,562														290	38	
154	National Home for Destitute Colored Women and Children	3,350	8,969	5,138																
155	St. Joseph's Male Orphan Asylum*																			
156	Washington City Orphan Asylum*																			

* From Report of the Commissioner of Education for 1873.

TABLE XXIII.—PART 2.—*Statistics of soldiers' orphans' homes.*

Number.	Name.	Location.	Year of incorporation.	Year of organization.	Superintendent.	Religious denomination.	Number of teachers and officers.	Total number of inmates since foundation.
	1	2	3	4	5	6	7	8
1	Soldiers' Orphans' Home	Mansfield, Conn	1864	1866	A. H. Coe	Undenom'l	24	147
2	Union Home and School*	New York, N. Y	1861	1861	Mrs. E. B. Hull	Protestant	24	3,373
3	Soldiers and Sailors' Orphans' Home*	Xenia, Ohio	1870	1870	Dr. L. D. Griswold	Undenom'l	34	742
4	Soldiers' Orphan Home	Andersonburg, Pa	1866	1866	M. Molyer	Undenom'l	2x	464
5	Bridgewater Soldiers' Orphan School	Bristol, Pa	1869	1868	James Stitzer	Undenom'l	12	25
6	St. Paul'n Orphan Home*	Butler, Pa	1868	1867	Rev. J. B. Thompson	Ref'd German	5	63
7	White Hall Soldiers' Orphan School	Camp Hill, Pa	1866	1866	J. A. Moore, (principal)	Undenom'l	7	556
8	Soldiers' Orphan School	Chester Springs, Pa	1866	1866	Mrs. E. H. Moore	Undenom'l	16	472
9	Dayton Soldiers' Orphan School	Dayton, Pa	1866	1866	Hugh McCandless	Undenom'l	16	400
10	Harford Soldiers' Orphan School	Harford, Pa	1866	1866	H. S. Sweet	Undenom'l	20	435
11	Prosaler Orphan Home*	Loisville, Pa	1868	1865	Rev. P. Willard, A. M	Evang. Luth	9	175
12	Soldiers' Orphan School*	McAllisterville, Pa	1868	1864	J. H. Smith	Methodist	17	564
13	Soldiers' Orphan School	Mansfield, Pa	1867	1867	Prof. F. A. Allen	Undenom'l	14	418
14	Soldiers' Orphan School*	Mercer, Pa	1868	1868	John G. White	Undenom'l	6	306
15	Lincoln Institution	Philadelphia, Pa	1866	1866	Edward L. Pearson	Episcopal	6	250
16	Soldiers' Orphans' Institute*	Philadelphia, Pa	1866	1866	Dr. A. Harshberger	Undenom'l	12	406
17	Phillipsburg Soldiers' Orphan School*	Phillipsburg, Pa	1865	1865	Rev. W. G. Taylor	Undenom'l	2x	480
18	Soldiers' Orphan School*	Titusville, Pa	1867	1867	Gurdon N. Berry	Undenom'l	2x	414
19	Dunlar Camp Soldiers' Orphan School*	Near Uniontown, Pa	1866	1866	Rev. A. H. Waters	Undenom'l	4	401
20	Soldiers' Orphans' Home a	Madison, Wis	1866	1866	R. W. Burton	Undenom'l	2x	683
21	National Soldiers' and Sailors' Orphans' Home*	Washington, D. C	1866	1866	Mrs. Frost, (matron)	Undenom'l	7	

* From Report of Commissioner of Education for 1873. a Closed December 15, 1874. All inmates under 14 years of age were sent to their friends. Entitled to State aid until 14 years of age at the rate of $5 per month.

Number	Name.	Conditions of admission. Age.	Conditions of admission. Other conditions.	How supported.	Industries taught.	Provision for children who have left the institution.
	1	9	10	11	12	13
1	Soldiers' Orphans' Home*		Must be soldiers' orphans	Appropriations and contributions.		
2	Union Home and School*		Must be soldiers' or sailors' children.	Appropriations and contributions.		
3	Soldiers' and Sailors' Orphans' Home*	2–16		State appropriations	Sewing and housework.	Places provided if mothers wish it.
4	Soldiers' Orphan Home		Must be soldiers' orphans	Appropriations and donations	Agriculture and housework.	
5	Bridgewater Soldiers' Orphan School	8 years old.	Must be soldiers' orphans	State appropriations		
6	St. Paul's Orphan Home*	3–16	Must be white	Appropriations and contributions.	Farming and housework	Returned to guardians, or trades and professions found for them.
7	White Hall Soldiers' Orphan School	3–16		Appropriations		Returned to guardians..
8	Soldiers' Orphan School	8 years old.	Must be soldiers' orphans	By the State	Domestic duties	Returned to mothers, or provided with home.
9	Dayton Soldiers' Orphan School		Must be soldiers' orphans born before 1866.	State appropriations	Farming and shoemaking, sewing and housework.	
10	Harford Soldiers' Orphan School	Under 16 years		State appropriations	Agriculture and domestic duties.	
11	Pressler Orphan Home*	Under 11 years.		Appropriations and contributions.		
12	Soldiers' Orphan School*	From 7 years.	Must be soldiers' orphans	Appropriations	Gardening, farming, sewing, and housework.	
13	Soldiers' Orphan School	8–16	Must be soldiers' orphans	Appropriations		
14	Soldiers' Orphan School*	Under 16 years	Must be soldiers' orphans.	Appropriations	All pupils employed in stores or at trades.	Boys may remain at the institution after 16 years of age by paying $3 per week.
15	Lincoln Institution	Over 13 years		Appropriation, contribution, and endowment.		
16	Soldiers' Orphans' Institute*	8–16	Must be orphans of Pennsylvania soldiers.	Appropriations		
17	Phillipsburg Soldiers' Orphan School*	8–16	Must be soldiers' orphans	State appropriations	Farming, gardening, and domestic duties.	Provided for by mother, guardian, or Grand Army of the Republic.
18	Soldiers' Orphan School*	5–16	Must be soldiers' orphans and destitute.	Appropriations		
19	Dunbar Camp Soldiers' Orphan School.			State appropriation		
20	Soldiers' Orphans' Home a	4–14		State appropriation	Farming and shoemaking	
21	National Soldiers' and Sailors' Orphans' Home.*	6–16		Congressional appropriation		

* From Report of Commissioner of Education for 1873.   a Closed December 15, 1874.   All inmates under 14 years of age were sent to their friends.   Entitled to State aid until 14 years of age at the rate of $5 per month.

TABLE XXIII.—PART 2.—*Statistics of soldiers' orphans' homes*—Concluded.

Number.	Name.	Amount of permanent fund.	Income.	Expenditure.	Sex. Male.	Sex. Female.	Race. White.	Race. Colored.	Parentage. Native.	Parentage. Foreign.	Orphanage. Orphans.	Orphanage. Half orphans.	Orphanage. Foundlings.	Instruction: No. taught— Reading.	Writing.	Arithmetic.	Drawing.	Music.	Library. Number of volumes.	Library. Increase in the past year.
	1	14	15	16	17	18	19	20	21	22	23	24	25	26	27	28	29	30	31	32
1	Soldiers' Orphans' Home		$47,976	$40,233	134	67	201	0	54	71	58	132		195	195	169	110			32
2	Union Home and School		(a)		400	200	582	5			75	525	0	550	550	550	550		1,000	400
3	Soldiers' and Sailors' Orphans' Home																			0
4	Soldiers' Orphan Home																			
5	Bridgewater Soldiers' Orphan School		5,000	5,000	50	39	41	68			19	70		89	89	89	110	89	300	0
6	St. Paul's Orphan Home		(b)		29	12		0			4	31		35	35	30		80		
7	White Hall Soldiers' Orphan School		(c)		137	76	213				213									
8	Dayton Soldiers' Orphan School		30,000	30,600	106	57	163		912			150		163	208	208	208	213	350	0
9	Harford Soldiers' Orphan School		21,382	21,382	120	93	215			3		215		215	215	140	190	163	900	163
10	Pressler Orphan Home		11,200	10,000	88	56	144	0	144		10	134	4	144	144	141	100	215	165	0
11	Soldiers' Orphan School		25,044		125	58	135	6			33	75		170	160	160	144	144	600	100
12	Soldiers' Orphan Home		(d)		83	68	151	0	151		151			151	151	144		100	800	0
13	Soldiers' Orphan School				129	103	225	6				226		226	226	144	226	300	300	
14	Lincoln Institution		32,000	30,000	173	50	225	0				245	4	225	225	225	226	226		
15	Soldiers' Orphans' Institute				74				239					74	74	74	50			
16	Phillipsburg Soldiers' Orphan School		25,000	47,300	149	92	237	2	185	52	147			220	220	220	220		1,000	150
17	Soldiers' Orphan School		25,000	25,049	65	62	147		170	10	137	167		147	147	147	50		1,500	
18	Dunbar Camp Soldiers' Orphan School		37,246		99	81	178				133			168	168	168				
19	Soldiers' Orphans' Home		20,000	20,000	80	57	137					133		135	135	135		135	300	
20	National Soldiers' and Sailors' Orphans' Home		15,140	15,106	30	28	58				12	46	0	58	58	58			700	0
21																				347	

* From Report of Commissioner of Education for 1873.

a $175 per child over 10 years of age: $140 under 10 years of age.
b State appropriation of $150 per annum for each child over 10 years of age.
c State appropriation of $150 per annum for each child over 10 years of age.
d State appropriation of $150 per annum for each child over 10 years of age; $115 per annum for each child under 10 years.
e Closed December 15, 1874. All inmates under 14 years of age were sent to their friends. Entitled to State aid until 14 years of age, at the rate of $5 per month.

Number	Name.	Location.	Year of incorporation.	Year of organization.	Superintendent.	Religious denomination	Number of teachers and officers.	Total number of inmates since foundation.
	1	2	3	4	5	6	7	8
1	Chicago Foundlings' Home	Chicago, Ill	1872	1872	George E. Shipman, M. D	Undenom'l	6	1,500
2	House of Providence	Detroit, Mich	1869	1869	Sister Mary Stella	R. C	4	505
3	New York Infant Asylum	New York, N. Y	1865	1865	Miss Amanda M. Judson	Undenom'l		
4	Nursery and Child's Hospital	New York, N. Y	1854	1854	Mary A. Du Bois	Undenom'l		
5	The New York Foundling Asylum Society	New York, N. Y	1869	1869	Mother M. Regina	R. C		5,000
6	St. Vincent's Home	Philadelphia, Pa	1855	1855	Sister Mary Joseph	R. C		
7	Providence Nursery	Providence, R. I	1872	1872	Mrs. Carruthers	Undenom'l	5	150
8	St. Joseph's Orphan Asylum for Small Female Children	Milwaukee, Wis	1860	1860	Sister Camilla	R. C	4	
9	St. Ann's Infant Asylum	Washington, D. C	1863	1860	Sister Agnes	R. C		

TABLE XXIII.—PART 3.—*Statistics of infant asylums*—Continued.

Number.	Name.	Conditions of admission.		How supported.	Industries taught.	Provision for children who have left the institution.
		Age.	Other conditions.			
	1	9	10	11	12	13
1	Chicago Foundlings' Home	Under 3 months		Contributions	None	Adopted.
2	Home of Providence	Under 5 years		Contributions		
3	New York Infant Asylum	Under 2 years		Subscriptions, donations, and State.		
4	Nursery and Child's Hospital			Appropriations, contributions, and donations.		Provided with homes or adopted.
5	The New York Foundling Asylum Society			Contributions and donations.		
6	St. Vincent's Home	Under 7 years		Contributions and appropriations.		Returned to parents or adopted.
7	Providence Nursery	Under 5 years		Private subscription		
8	St Joseph's Orphan Asylum for Small Female Children.			St. Rose's Asylum		
9	St. Ann's Infant Asylum	Under 5 years		Charity		

524

Number.	Name.	Amount of permanent fund	Income.	Expenditure.	Sex.		Race.		Parentage.		Orphanage.			Instruction: Number taught—					Library.	
					Male.	Female.	White.	Colored.	Native.	Foreign.	Orphans.	Half-orphans.	Foundlings.	Reading.	Writing.	Arithmetic.	Drawing.	Music.	Number of volumes.	Increase in the past year.
	1	14	15	16	17	18	19	20	21	22	23	24	25	26	27	28	29	30	31	32
1	Chicago Foundling's Home	0	$53,771	$53,771	97	98	49	4	90	15			34						0	0
2	House of Providence				90	95	45		80											
3	New York Infant Asylum																		
4	Nursery and Child's Hospital																		
5	The New York Foundling Asylum Society	0			(307)	5	14		7			14								
6	St. Vincent's Home				9														
7	Providence Nursery				(57)														
8	St. Joseph's Orphan Asylum for Small Female Children				50	50	67	3												
9	St. Ann's Infant Asylum																		

TABLE XXIII.—PART 4.—Statistics of miscellaneous charities.

Number	Name.	Year of incorporation.	Year of organization.	Superintendent.	Religious denomination.	Number of teachers and officers.	Total number of inmates since foundation.	Conditions of admission.	
								Age.	Other conditions.
1	2	3	4	5	6	7	8	9	10
1	Hebrew Widows and Orphans' Society*	1864	1864	Jacob Mandlebaum	Jewish				
2	Union for Home Work	1871	1871	Mrs. C. L. Sluyter	Undenom'l				
3	Home of the Friendless	1866	1866	Mrs. William Hillhouse	Undenom'l				
4	Appleton Church Home*	1870	1870	Sister Margaret	Episcopal	1	25	2–12	No conditions.
5	Home for the Friendless	1859	1859	Mrs. Joel Grant	Undenom'l	10		10–18	
6	Newsboys and Bootblacks' Association	1867	1865	W. B. Billings, gen'l supt.	Undenom'l	9	a 447	9–20	
7	Boys' Home Association	1867	1866	John H. Lynch	Protestant	3	664		
8	Home of the Friendless		1854	Mrs. James F. Atkinson	Undenom'l				
9	The Henry Watson Children's Aid Society	1861	1861	William C. Palmer	Undenom'l				
10	Home for the Friendless Children of the Eastern Shore of Maryland	1870	1871	Miss Lillie W. Tiffy	Prot. Epis.	2	21	3–8	Certificate of health.
11	Boston Asylum and Farm-School for Indigent Boys	1832	1832	William A. Morse	Undenom'l	5	1,550	8–12	Good health and not immoral.
12	Home for Friendless Women and Children	1863	1863	Caroline L. Rice, president	Undenom'l	3	409	Under 14	Healthy, intelligent, and dependent.
13	State Public School for Dependent Children	1871	1874	Zelotes Truesdel	Undenom'l	11	193	4–16	
14	Home for the Friendless*	1862	1862	Mrs. M. Stewart	Undenom'l	2	3,000	Males, under 10; females, from 5 men.	
15	Home of Providence			Sisters of Charity	R. C				
16	Home of the Friendless, or Old Ladies' Home	1870	1873		Undenom'l		500		Aged dependent women.
17	Mission Free School	1861	1854	Mary E. Tucker	Unitarian	1	300		Poverty.
18	Orphanage of the Church Charity Foundation of Long Island	1851	1850	Sisters Julia and Elizabeth	Prot. Epis.	4	300	4–10	Any destitute children may be received, but the children of the church have the preference.
19	RC Johnland	1870	1865	Rev. W. A. Muhlenberg, D.D.	Prot. Epis.				
20	Home for Aged Women of the Church of the Holy Communion			Sister Catherine	Prot. Epis.		256		
21	Home for the Friendless	1849	1834	Miss S. C. Wilcox	Undenom'l		30,000		Destitute and homeless.

No.	Name	Location	Year	Year	No.	No.	Denomination	Officer	Age admitted	Age range	Conditions
26	Methodist-Episcopal Church. Ladies' Home Society.	New York, N. Y.						Mrs. D. C. Hays			
27	New York Juvenile Asylum.	New York, N. Y.	1851	1853	44	17,772	Baptist. / Undenom'l	Elisha M. Carpenter		7-14	Truant and disobedient children of the city of New York.
28	New York Society for Relief of the Ruptured and Crippled.	New York, N. Y.	1863	1863	13	722	Undenom'l	James Knight, M. D		4-14	
29	Presbyterian Home for Aged Women.	New York, N. Y.	1866	1866			Presbyt'n	Mrs. Sheafe.	65 or over		Destitution.
30	St. Barnabas House.	New York, N. Y.			4		Prot. Epis	Rev. Stephen F. Holmes.	No limits		
31	St. John's Guild.	New York, N. Y.	1870	1870	7	7,500	Undenom'l	Rev. Alvah Wiswall			No conditions.
32	St. Vincent's Home for Boys.	New York, N. Y.	1870	1872			R. C.	Rev. J. C. Drumgoole	Under 21		Needing protection and a home.
33	Shelter for Respectable Girls.	New York, N.Y., (322 Sixth avenue.)					Prot. Epis.	Sister Catherine.			
34	The Sheltering Arms.	New York, N. Y.	1864	1864	5	689	Prot. Epis.	Rev. T. M. Peters, D.D.		2-10	
35	Children's Home*.	Rochester, N. Y.	1853	1854	6	791	Prot. Epis.	S. R. Woodruff.		5-17	
36	Church Home.	Rochester, N. Y.	1869	1868	4		Prot. Epis.	Miss H. A. Neeley, matron	No limits		
37	The House of the Good Shepherd.	Stony Point, N.Y.	1870	1866	3	167	Prot. Epis.	Rev. M. Gay.		2-10	
38	Industrial Home of the City of Utica.	Utica, N. Y.	1871	1871			Undenom'l	Mrs. M W. Bussey			
39	St. Luke's Home, with hospital department.	Utica, N. Y.	1869	1869	6	60	Prot. Epis.	Rev. Edwin M. Van Deusen, D.D.	No limits		
40	City Infirmary for Children*.	Cincinnati, Ohio.	1852	1852	11	503	Protestant.	Arthur Hill	Under 16.		Poor and infirm, of any age. Homeless and destitute.
41	The Children's Home*.	Cincinnati, Ohio.	1864	1864	4	1,700	Undenom'l	William T. Haydock.			
42	Cleveland Children's Aid Society and Home.	Cleveland, Ohio.	1857	1857			Undenom'l				
43	Cleveland Industrial School*.	Cleveland, Ohio.	1865	1867	9	5,154	Protestant.	Robert Waterton			
44	The Home for Friendless Women.	Toledo, Ohio.	1873			52	Undenom'l	Mrs. Dr. S. H. Bergen.			
45	Pittsburg and Allegheny Home for the Friendless.*	Allegheny, Pa.	1860	1860	7		Protestant.	Mrs. F. J. Neel.	Boys under 8; girls all ages.		
46	Almwell School Association*	Philadelphia, Pa.	1850	1850			Friends	Miss E. S. Lorry, secretary			
47	Bishop Potter Memorial House.	Philadelphia, Pa.		1867	3	37	Prot. Epis	The Bishop of the Diocese			
48	The Home for the Homeless.	Philadelphia, Pa.	1870				Prot. Epis	Mrs. Anna F. Lex	No limits		
49	Temporary Home for Destitute Women.	Scranton, Pa.	1870				Undenom'l	Mrs. F. R. Brunot.	No limits		
50	Society of the Home for the Friendless.	Charleston, S. C.	1871		3		Prot. Epis.	Mrs. C. H. Dond			
51	Church Home for Destitute Ladies of the Episcopal Church.		1871					John F. Chaplin			
52	Holy Communion Church Institute.	Charleston, S. C.	1866	1866	9		Prot. Epis	Rev. A. T. Porter.			Orphanage or desertion of parents.
53	Wheeling Hospital and Orphan Asylum.	Wheeling, W. Va.	1856	1853	10		R. C.	Sister M. Stanialaus.	2-10		
54	The Cadle Home.	Green Bay, Wis.	1872	1873			Episcopal	Bishop of the diocese, pres't.			
55	Children's Hospital of District of Columbia.	Washington, D. C.	1870	1870	3	53	Undenom'l	Miss A. C. Macgrudor.	No limits		Requiring medical and surgical attention.
56	Church Home of the Epiphany*.	Washington, D. C.	1871	1871			Prot. Epis	Miss Janette Shriver			
57	St. John's Hospital for Children*.	Washington, D. C.	1870	1870	4	92	Prot. Epis	Sister Lilly			Sickness and need.

* From Report of Commissioner of Education for 1873.　　a Since reorganisation in 1873.　　b Since incorporation $98,000 has been received and $107,000 expended.

TABLE XXIII.—PART 4.—*Statistics of miscellaneous charities*—Continued.

Number.	Name.	How supported.	Industries taught.	Provision for children who have left the institution.	Amount of permanent fund.	Income.	Expenditure.
	1	11	12	13	14	15	16
1	Hebrew Widows and Orphans' Society *	Contributions from members				$4,926	$4,926
2	Union for Home Work	Contributions, subscriptions, and donations					
3	Home of the Friendless	Voluntary contributions				4,086	2,575
4	Appleton Church Home *	Endowment and subscriptions				2,000	2,000
5	Home for the Friendless	Voluntary charity	Caning chairs, tailoring, shoe-making, and printing	Placed in families or schools		16,007	15,066
6	Newsboys and Bootblacks' Association	Voluntary contributions		Placed in homes	$0	$0	4,000
7	Boys' Home Association	Contributions, and in part self-supporting				10,983	10,950
8	Home of the Friendless	Contributions and donations	Dress-making, hand and machine sewing.		0		7,000
9	The Henry Watson Children's Aid Society	Contributions and donations					
10	Home for the Friendless Children of the Eastern Shore of Maryland	Voluntary contributions	Housework	None as yet	5,000	1,348	1,983
11	Boston Asylum and Farm-School for Indigent Boys	Contributions and fund	Farming	Good homes provided	100,000	11,000	12,000
12	Home for Friendless Women and Children	Contributions	Sewing and housework	Placed in homes or at service	0	6,515 (a)	5,478
13	State Public School for Dependent Children	State appropriations	Farming, sewing, and housework	Indentured	0		
14	Home for the Friendless *	Contributions					
15	Home of Providence	Contributions and donations	Sewing and laundry-work	Homes in Roman-Catholic families.		5,978	2,830
16	Home of the Friendless, or Old Ladies' Home.	Endowment and contributions				8,000	
17	Mission Free School	Contributions by Unitarian Church		Placed in homes			3,000
18	Orphanage of the Church Charity Foundation of Long Island	Contributions of P. E. Church in the diocese of Long Island	Type-setting, molding, and presswork, sewing and housework				
19	St. Johnland	Contributions and donations	Type-setting and stereotyping				
20	Home for Aged Women of the Church of the Holy Communion	Contributions and donations					
21	Home for the Friendless, 32 East Thirtieth street	Donations, subscriptions, bequests, and appropriations				64,470	65,546
22	Home and School of Industry, 120 West Sixteenth street	Subscriptions and donations	Hand and machine sewing				
23	Howard Mission	Contributions and donations					

No.	Institution	Support	Industries taught	Disposition of inmates			
25	Ladies' Home Missionary Society of the Methodist-Episcopal Church.						
26	Ladies' Home Society	Donations and subscriptions.					
27	New York Juvenile Asylum	Appropriations and contributions.	Tailoring, shoe-making, farming, and sewing.	Three-fourths returned to friends; one-fourth sent to homes in Illinois.	0	103,536	29,402
28	New York Society for Relief of the Ruptured and Crippled.	Appropriations by county, and contributions.	Needle-work.		0	41,100	42,568
29	Presbyterian Home for Aged Women	Donations and subscriptions.					
30	St. Barnabas House	Voluntary contributions.					
31	St. John's Guild	Self-supporting in part, and contributions.				32,702	32,016
32	St. Vincent's Home for Boys	Contributions and donations.	None		0	6,034	15,209
33	Shelter for Respectable Girls, 332 Sixth avenue.						4,970
34	The Sheltering Arms.	Voluntary contributions.	Housework, sewing, fancy-work.	Returned to parents or friends	3,500	20,942	19,458
35	Children's Home*	City tax and contributions.	Housework.			8,445	6,811
36	Church Home*	Subscriptions and donations.	House and farm work, and shoe-making.	Returned to parents or guardians	300	4,174	3,973
37	The House of the Good Shepherd	Voluntary contributions.		Sent to situations or trades.	0	8,606	8,520
38	Industrial Home of the City of Utica.	Annual subscriptions and donations				2,390	3,296
39	St. Luke's Home, with hospital department.	Voluntary contributions and board of inmates.	Sewing	None.	7,000	5,000	40,000
40	City Infirmary for Children*	Appropriations.					
41	The Children's Home	Voluntary contributions.		Placed in country homes.	0	10,000	10,000
42	Cleveland Children's Aid Society and Home.	City appropriations, subscriptions, and donations.	Sewing, knitting, housework, farming, and gardening.	Provided with homes in families			
43	Cleveland Industrial School*	Appropriations and contributions.				4,800	4,700
44	The Home for Friendless Women	Contributions, subscriptions, and donations.	Sewing and housework.			10,096	10,096
45	Pittsburg and Allegheny Home for the Friendless.*	Contributions.				9,005	10,939
46	Almwell School Association*	Appropriations and contributions.					
47	Bishop Potter Memorial House	Voluntary contributions.				1,500	1,500
48	The Home for the Homeless	Voluntary contributions.					
49	Temporary Home for Destitute Women	Contributions and donations.					897
50	Society of the Home for the Friendless.	Contributions, donations, and life-memberships.				5,963	5,963
51	Church Home for Destitute Ladies of the Episcopal Church.	Subscriptions.			3,000	7,000	
52	Holy Communion Church Institute.	Contributions and board of inmates	Dressmaking and housework.	Provided with situations as servants, trades-women, or teachers.	0		
53	Wheeling Hospital and Orphan Asylum	Charity.					
54	The Cadle Home	Voluntary contributions				874	510
55	Children's Hospital of District Columbia*						
56	Church Home of the Epiphany*	Contributions.					
57	St. John's Hospital for Children*	Charitable contributions.				5,959	5,761

* From Report of Commissioner of Education for 1873.

a Since incorporation $98,000 has been received and $107,000 expended.

TABLE XXIII.—PART 4.—*Statistics of miscellaneous charities—Concluded.*

		Sex.		Race.		Parentage.		Orphanage.			Instruction: Number taught—					Library.	
	Name.	Male.	Female.	White.	Colored.	Natives.	Foreign.	Orphans.	Half-orphans.	Foundlings.	Reading.	Writing.	Arithmetic.	Drawing.	Music.	Number of volumes.	Increase in the past year.
Number.	1	17	18	19	20	21	22	23	24	25	26	27	28	29	30	31	32
1	Hebrew Widows and Orphans' Society *																
2	Union for Home Work		20	20	0	20	0										
3	Home of the Friendless		170	167	3	87	147	10	10		16	11	14	10	8	100	0
4	Appleton Church Home *										70	70	40		0	350	200
5	Home for the Friendless *	64		20						1							50
6	Newsboys and Bootblacks' Association	All.				4	4	4	4	4	All.	All.	All.			1,000	
7	Boys' Home Association	53	0	53	0	28	25	35	12	0	53	53	53				
8	Home of the Friendless																
9	The Henry Watson Children's Aid Society																
10	Home for the Friendless Children of the Eastern Shore of Maryland	0	18	18	0	18	0	4	14	0	13	13				0	0
11	Boston Asylum and Farm-School for Indigent Boys	92	0	92	0	84	6	90	52	0	92	92	92	0	93	900	0
12	Home for Friendless Women and Children	15	19	33	1	18	16		30							0	0
13	State Public School for Dependent Children	133	60	180	13	152	41	31	89	0	184	66	132	45	184	60	60
14	Home for the Friendless *	9	10	19	0		10	1	18		4	2	4				
15	Home of Providence		45														
16	Home of the Friendless or Old Ladies' Home																
17	Mission Free School	9	8	17	0	2	15	2	15		69	69	69				
18	Orphanage of the Church Charity Foundation of Long Island	47	22	60					40								
19	St. Johnland																
20	Home for Aged Women of the Church of the Holy Communion													50			
21	Home for the Friendless, 32 East Thirty-third street		81	136	0	3	1				221	75	115			200	
22	Howard and Sea-School of Industry, 120 West Sixteenth street	All.									All.	All.	All.	All.	All.		
23	Howard Mission																

27	New York Juvenile Asylum	83	93	176	0	72	104	15	82	1	133	107	97	0	0	400	50
28	New York Society for Relief of the Ruptured and Crippled																
29	Presbyterian Home for Aged Women																
30	St. Barnabas House																
31	St. John's Guild	180	439	175	5	36	144	67	33	0	70	70	70	10	120	325	100
32	St. Vincent's Home for Boys																
33	Shelter for Respectable Girls, 329 Sixth avenue.																
34	The Sheltering Arms	65	65	130	0	80	50	0	60	0	110	100	100	10		400	50
35	Children's Home*	47	9	52	4	18	37	4	45		31	12	28		34	300	
36	Church Home	25	9	34	0			9	97		43	43	43		43	500	50
37	The House of the Good Shepherd	31	22	43	0	18	25	9	28	2	43	43	43			500	300
38	Industrial Home of the City of Utica.																
39	St. Luke's Home, with hospital department.	9	24	33	0	31	9		0							500	300
40	City Infirmary for Children*	329	283	463	40	20	33	5	30	2	26	21	10	30			
41	The Children's Home*	30	23	53	0	20				1	40	40	30				
42	Cleveland Children's Aid Society and Home.																
43	Cleveland Industrial School*	41						70	140	70	280	240	220	20		500	200
44	The Home for Friendless Women*		26	67				5	15		26	16	15				
45	Pittsburg and Allegheny Home for the Friendless.*		70	70	0						70	70	70	70			
46	Almwell School Association*																
47	Bishop Potter Memorial House.																
48	The Home for the Homeless																
49	Temporary Home for Destitute Women.																
50	Society of the Home for the Friendless.	1	22	23	0	17	6		4		12	12	12	12	12		
51	Church Home for Destitute Ladies of the Episcopal Church.																
52	Holy Communion Church Institute	13	63	74	2	10	37	30	16	1	41	41	41	3	3		
53	Wheeling Hospital and Orphan Asylum.	6	7	13	0	3	10	9	4	0							
54	The Cradle Home.	16	9	91	4	25											
55	Children's Hospital of District of Columbia.*																
56	Church Home of the Epiphany*																
57	St. John's Hospital for Children*	11	13	94	0												

* From Report of Commissioner of Education for 1873.

TABLE XXIII.—PART 5.—Statistics of industrial schools.

Number	Name.	Location.	Year of incorporation.	Year of organization.	Superintendent.	Religious denomination.	Number of teachers and officers.	Total number of inmates since foundation.
1	2	3	4	5	6	7	8	
1	Industrial School*.	San Francisco, Cal	1856	1859	George F. Harris.	Undenom'l.	92	1,507
2	Connecticut Training-School for Nurses.	New Haven, Conn		1873	Miss Townsend.	Undenom'l.	7	17
3	Orphan Girls' Home.	Chicago, Ill	1874	1874	Mrs. C. W. Haskins.	Undenom'l.	7	130
4	St. Joseph's Industrial School for Girls.	Baltimore, Md. (corner Carey and Lexington streets)	1865	1865	Sister Josepha.	R. C.	8	540
5	Detroit Industrial School.	Detroit, Mich	1862	1857	Mrs. C. Van Husan, cor. secretary	Union Evang.	2	9,000
6	Girls' Industrial Home.	St. Louis, Mo	1854	1854	Mrs. John S. Thomson	Undenom'l.	10	
7	Brooklyn Industrial School	Brooklyn, N. Y. (No. 1 Concord street.)		1854	Mrs. Hines.	Undenom'l.	10	
8	Industrial School, or St. Paul's Female Orphan Asylum*.	Brooklyn, N. Y.	1834	1834	Sister M. Constantia.	R. C	20	1,470
9	Children's Aid Society Industrial Schools	New York, N. Y., (19 East Fourth street.)	1853	1853	J. W. Skinner	Undenom'l.	77	30,000
10	Five-Points House of Industry	New York, N. Y.	1854	1850	William F. Barnard	Undenom'l.		98,664
11	Industrial School of St. Augustine's Chapel, Trinity Parish	New York, N. Y. (262 Bowery)	1870	1870	Arthur C. Kimber	Episcopal.	17	
12	Industrial School of the Hebrew Orphan Asylum	New York, N. Y.	1860	1860	S. Arnheim, principal	Jewish		58
13	Rivington Street Newsboys' Home and Industrial School	New York, N. Y.	1853	1853	George Calder	Undenom'l.	8	18,469
14	St. Joseph's Industrial Home	New York, N. Y.	1869	1869	Sister Mary Agnes.	R. C	19	598
15	Training-School for Nurses, Bellevue Hospital	New York, N. Y.	1872	1872	Miss Bowden	Undenom'l.	5	99
16	Wilson's Industrial School and Mission*	New York, N. Y.	1853	1853	Mrs. E. G. Janeway, secretary	Protestant.		
17	Women's Educational and Industrial Society Training School.	New York, N. Y., (47 East Tenth street.)	1873	1873	Mrs. C. L. Hodges	Undenom'l.		3,000
18	Boys' Home of Industry	Rochester, N. Y	1873	1873	Sister M. Gertrude.	R. C	6	94
19	Industrial School of Young Ladies, Branch of Woman's Christian Association.	Cincinnati, Ohio		1870	Mrs. Newcomb and Miss Huff.	Protestant		180
20	Industrial School*.	Cincinnati, Ohio	1866	1866	Mother M. Scholastica.	R. C.	11	500
21	Industrial Home for Girls*	Philadelphia, Pa	1857	1857	Mrs. Reeves	Protestant.		349

TABLE XXIII.—PART 5.—*Statistics of industrial schools.*—Continued.

Number	Name (1)	Age (9)	Other conditions (10)	How supported (11)	Industries taught (12)	Provision for children who have left the institution (13)
1	Industrial School*	Under 18	.....	Appropriations by city and county.	.....	.....
2	Connecticut Training-School for Nurses	14-90	Good health and good moral character.	Contributions and hospital fund.	Nursing the sick	Good homes in families.
3	Orphan Girls' Home	12-16	.....	Contributions.	Housework and sewing.	Good homes, and employment as dressmakers, seamstresses, or clerks.
4	St. Joseph's Industrial School for Girls	Over 14	Good moral character.	By the industry of the inmates.	Dress-making, sewing, embroidery, and fancy-work.	
5	Detroit Industrial School		No conditions	Subscriptions and interest of fund.	Housework	Placed in homes for adoption.
6	Girls' Industrial Home	2-12		Collections and occasional festivals or concerts.	Sewing, cutting garments, and housework.	
7	Brooklyn Industrial School	Boys, 10 years; girls, 14 years.		Contributions.	Sewing	
8	Industrial School, or St. Paul's Female Orphan Asylum.*	3-15		Voluntary contributions	.....	None.
9	Children's Aid Society Industrial Schools.		Poverty and destitution.	Charity and school fund.	Sewing, dress-making, and crocheting.	Returned to parents or provided with homes.
10	Five-Points House of Industry	2½-13		Voluntary contributions	Tailoring, repairing shoes, type-setting, and sewing.	
11	Industrial School of St. Augustine's Chapel, Trinity Parish.		Must attend Sunday-school	Appropriations from vestry of Trinity Church.	Sewing	
12	Industrial School of the Hebrew Orphan Asylum.	14 years old	Proficient in elementary education.	Self-supporting.	Printing, shoemaking, instrumental music.	They receive $200 besides their savings, and are fitted to earn their living.
13	Rivington Street Newsboys' Home and Industrial School.	7-18		Appropriations and contributions.	Sewing and knitting	Permanent homes as servants.
14	St. Joseph's Industrial Home	Over 3 years		Donations.	Washing, sewing, knitting, and housework.	
15	Training-School for Nurses, Bellevue Hospital.	21 years old	Good health and good moral character.	Contributions and hospital funds.	Nursing the sick.	
16	Wilson's Industrial School and Mission*			Contributions and donations.	.....	

* From Report of Commissioner of Education for 1873.

TABLE XXIII.—PART 5.—Statistics of industrial schools—Continued.

Number	Name	Conditions of admission		How supported	Industries taught	Provision for children who have left the institution.
		Age.	Other conditions.			
1	1	9	10	11	12	18
17	Women's Educational and Industrial Society Training-School.					
18	Boys' Home of Industry	Under 12.		Contributions......	Cooking, laundry-work, house-work, phonography, book-keeping, proof-reading, and writing.	Returned to friends or provided with situations in stores, &c.
19	Industrial School of Young Ladies, Branch of Woman's Christian Association.			Industry of inmates ..	Sewing......	
20	Industrial School*	Under 18		Self-supporting in part, and subscriptions.		
21	Industrial Home for Girls*	Under 18	Poverty	Industry and charity. Voluntary contributions	Dress- and shirt-making, embroidery, knitting, fancy-work, and house-work.	
22	Industrial School of Immaculate Conception.	5-21	Good moral character.	Pension paid for pupils, and work of inmates.	Sewing	
23	Industrial School			Contributions......	Housework and sewing...	Placed in homes.
24	Girls' Industrial Home	5-14		Industry......		
25	Protestant House of Industry*	8-14		Earnings of shop and contributions.	Carpentry, cane-seating, sewing, and housework.	
26	Industrial Home School	6 years old				

534

* From Report of Commissioner of Education for 1873.

No.	Name	Amount of permanent fund.	Income.	Expenditure.	Male.	Female.	White.	Colored.	Native.	Foreign.	Orphans.	Half-orphans.	Foundlings.	Reading.	Writing.	Arithmetic.	Drawing.	Music.	Number of volumes.	Increase in the past year.
		14	15	16	17	18	19	20	21	22	23	24	25	26	27	28	29	30	31	32
1	Industrial School*	90	$1,500	$1,500	901	57 9	941	17	96	160	96	69		938	938	938				32
2	Connecticut Training-School for Nurses.																	6		
3	Orphan Girls' Home.				0	130	130	0	30	100	100	30	0	36	36	130			75	75
4	St.-Joseph's Industrial School for Girls.	4,075	5,050	3,910	(130)	30	36	4	90	100	30	21		130	68	36	0	6	140	25
5	Detroit Industrial School.	0	4,130	4,130	60	75	135	4	18	16	22	21		60	50	50	35			
6	Girls' Industrial Home.			1,800		56	75	6	22	50	22	44		41	25	43			100	
7	Brooklyn Industrial School.																			
8	Industrial School, or St. Paul's Female Orphan Asylum.*				0	541	541	0		541	350	191		450	350	450	198			
9	Children's Aid Society Industrial Schools.	0	33,527	34,396	167	163	381	12	80	241	10	50	0	330	330	232		174	1,000	
10	Five-Points House of Industry.	17,100	175	175	1	320													1,000	
11	Industrial School of St. Augustine's Chapel, Trinity Parish.																			
12	Industrial School of the Hebrew Orphan Asylum.				90	0	96	0	24	4	14	14	0	98	28	98	35	6	100	100
13	Rivington Street Newsboys' Home and Industrial School.		11,850	11,850	385	150	372	3	94	283	130	90	4	375	320	209		240	370	90
14	St.-Joseph's Industrial Home.		96,200	96,067	0	198	198	0			90	100		190	170	170		25	600	
15	Training-School for Nurses, Bellevue Hospital.				19												198			
16	Wilson's Industrial School and Mission.		11,639	11,440	(190)	198	198	0		541			1	198	198	198	198			
17	Women's Educational and Industrial Society Training-School.					1,000														
18	Boys' Home of Industry.	0		6,046	21	0	21	0	12	9	21			21	21	21				
19	Industrial School of Young Ladies, Branch of Woman's Christian Association.				40	40	40	0												
20	Industrial School*		3,056	6,094	0	60	60	0	60	60	10	40		60	45	46			100	
21	Industrial Home for Girls*				0	97	97	0	20	70	90	41		97	57	57				
22	Industrial School of Immaculate Conception.				0	90	90	0		1				60	60	60				
23	Industrial School.		1,772	1,615	0	13	13	0	12		9	10								
24	Girls' Industrial Home.	400	2,500	2,500	0	20	20	0			7	12							30	
25	Protestant House of Industry*			4,176																
26	Industrial Home School.	0	3,586	4,176	14	7	21	0	21		3	18		20	20	20				

* From Report of Commissioner of Education for 1873.

List of orphan asylums, miscellaneous charities, and industrial schools from which no information has been received.

Name.	Location.
PART I.—*Orphan asylums.*	
Male Orphan Asylum and Industrial School	Mobile, Ala.
Sheltering Arms	Mobile, Ala.
Orphans' Home	Montgomery, Ala.
Protestant Orphan Asylum	Montgomery, Ala.
St. Francis Orphan Asylum for Girls	New Haven, Conn.
Female Orphan Asylum	Wilmington, Del.
Scandinavian Orphan Asylum	Berlin, Ill.
Boys' Asylum, Roman Catholic	Chicago, Ill.
St. Paul's Orphan Asylum	Chicago, Ill.
St. Aloysius Orphan Asylum of St. Boniface Church	Quincy, Ill.
Roman Catholic Asylum	Ft. Wayne, Ind.
Community of the Poor Handmaids of Jesus Christ	Hesse Cassel, Allen County Ind.
Orphan Asylum	Rensselaer, Ind.
St. Ann's Orphan Asylum	Vincennes, Ind.
St. Vincent's Male Orphan Asylum	Vincennes, Ind.
St. Vincent's Orphan Asylum	Leavenworth, Kans.
German Orphan Asylum	Covington, Ky.
St. John's Orphan Asylum	Covington, Ky.
St. Vincent's Female Orphan Asylum	Louisville, Ky.
Protestant-Episcopal Children's Home	New Orleans, La.
St. Joseph's Orphan Asylum	New Orleans, La.
St. Mary's Orphan Asylum	New Orleans, La.
St. Theresa Female Orphan Asylum	New Orleans, La.
St. Vincent's Home for Boys	New Orleans, La.
The Kelso Home for Orphans of the Methodist-Episcopal Church of Baltimore.	Baltimore, Md.
State Alms-House, (orphans' department)	Hampden County, Mass.
St. Patrick's Orphan Asylum	Lawrence, Mass.
State Alms-House, (orphans' department)	Plymouth County, Mass.
Protestant Orphan Asylum	Detroit, Mich.
St. Joseph's Orphan Asylum	St. Paul, Minn.
Orphan Asylum	Shakopee, Minn.
St. Mary's Orphan Asylum	Natchez, Miss.
Home of Guardian Angel	St. Louis, Mo.
Home of the Good Shepherd	St. Louis, Mo.
Mulanphy Orphan Asylum for Females	St. Louis, Mo.
St. Bridget's Half-Orphan Asylum	St. Louis, Mo.
St. Joseph's Half-Orphan Asylum	St. Louis, Mo.
St. Philomena Orphan Asylum and School	St. Louis, Mo.
Orphan Asylum	Virginia City, Nev.
St. Mary's Orphan Asylum	South Orange, N. J.
Orphan Asylum of the Church of the Holy Trinity	Brooklyn, N. Y.
St. Joseph's Boys' Orphan Asylum	Buffalo, (Lime Stone Hill) N. Y.
St. Mary's Orphan Asylum	Canandaigua, N. Y.
St. Mary's Orphan Asylum	Clifton, Long Island, N. Y.
St. Joseph's Orphan Asylum	Erie, N. Y.
St. Patrick's Orphan Asylum	Newburg, N. Y.
Children's Fold	New York, N. Y.
St. Vincent de Paul's Asylum	New York, N. Y.
Sisters of St. Dominick's Orphan Asylum	New York, N. Y.
County Alms-House, (orphans' department)	Onondaga Hill, N. Y.
St. Joseph's Orphan Asylum, (German)	Rochester, N. Y.
St. Mary's Orphan Asylum	Rondout, N. Y.
St. Mary's Orphan Asylum	Syracuse, N. Y.
German Orphan Asylum	Utica, N. Y.
Orphan Asylum	Oxford, N. C.
Cincinnati Colored Orphan Asylum	Cincinnati, Ohio.
House of Preservation of Children	Cincinnati, Ohio.
St. Aloysius Orphan Asylum	Cincinnati, Ohio.
German Orphan Asylum	Cleveland, Ohio.
St. Joseph's Orphan Asylum	Cleveland, Ohio.
St. Mary's Female Orphan Asylum	Cleveland, Ohio.
St. Joseph and St. Peter's Asylum	Cumminsville, Ohio.
Asylum of Franciscan Sisters	Delphos, Ohio.
Citizen's Hospital and Orphan Asylum	Tiffin, Ohio.
St. Vincent's Orphan Asylum	Toledo, Ohio.
German Catholic Orphan Asylum	Allegheny, Pa.
St James' Orphan Asylum	Lancaster, Pa.
Emmons Institute	Middletown, Pa.
St. John's Male Orphan Asylum	Philadelphia, Pa.
St. Vincent's Orphan Asylum	Philadelphia, Pa.
Allegheny County Home	Pittsburg, Pa.
St. Paul's Roman-Catholic Asylum	Pittsburg, Pa.
Orphan's Home of the Shepherd of Lambs	Womelsdorf, Pa.
Boys' Orphan Asylum, (Roman Catholic)	Charleston, S. C.
State Orphan Asylum for Colored Children	Charleston, S. C.

List of orphan asylums, miscellaneous charities, industrial schools, &c.—Concluded.

Name.	Location.
ornwell Orphanage	Clinton, S. C.
almetto Orphan Asylum	Columbia, S. C.
anfield Colored Orphan Asylum.a	Memphis, Tenn.
. Peter's Orphan Asylum	Memphis, Tenn.
ounty Asylum, (orphans' department)	Nashville, Tenn.
rphan Asylum	Burlington, Vt.
. Mary's Orphan Asylum	Norfolk, Va.
. Joseph's Orphan Asylum	Richmond, Va.
. Joseph's Orphan Asylum	Milwaukee, Wis.
. Vincent's Female Orphan Asylum	Washington, D. C.
herokee Orphan Asylum	Indian Territory.
. Genovefa Female Orphan Asylum	Vancouver, Wash.
. Vincent's Male Orphan Asylum	Vancouver, Wash.

PART II.—*Soldiers' orphans' home.*

oldiers' Orphan Home	Normal, Ill.
oldiers' Orphans' Home	Cedar Falls, Iowa.
oldiers' Orphans' Home	Davenport, Iowa.
oldiers' Orphans' Home	Glenwood, Iowa.
nion Orphan Asylum	Baltimore, Md.
oldiers' Orphan School	Mount Joy, Pa.

PART III.—*Infant asylums.*

ursery	Hartford, Conn.
. Vincent's Infant Asylum	Baltimore, Md.
assachusetts Infant Asylum	Brookline, Mass.
oundlings' Home	Detroit, Mich.
. Mary's Asylum for Foundlings and Infants	Buffalo, N. Y.
ursery of the Church of the Holy Communion	New York, N. Y.
fants' Nursery and Hospital	Randall's Island, N. Y.
hildren's Day Home Society, (Tibbit's Mansion)	Troy, N. Y.

PART IV.—*Miscellaneous charities.*

rinity Church Home	New Haven, Conn.
. Vincent's House of Providence	Chicago, Ill.
ome for the Friendless	Indianapolis, Ind.
he Home	Baltimore, Md.
ouse of Providence	Detroit, Mich.
ouse of Shelter	Detroit, Mich.
utheran Orphan Asylum and Hospital	Kirkwood, Mo.
ouse of Shelter	Albany, N. Y.
ouse of the Good Shepherd	Brooklyn, N. Y.
gleside Home	Buffalo, N. Y.
. Stephen's Home	Buffalo, N. Y.
ome for the Friendless	Rochester, N. Y.
ouse of the Good Shepherd	Syracuse, N. Y.
. Joseph's House of Providence	Syracuse, N. Y.
ome of the Friendless	Cincinnati, Ohio.
thel Home	Cleveland, Ohio.
ome for Friendless Women	Toledo, Ohio.
urch Home	Allegheny, Pa.
ome for the Friendless	Harrisburg, Pa.
urch Home	Pittsburg, Pa.
ome for the Friendless	Pittsburg, Pa.
elter Home	Providence, R. I.

PART V.—*Industrial schools.*

Elizabeth House of Industry	New Orleans, La.
Mary's Industrial School for Boys	Baltimore, Md.
Mary's Industrial School for Boys	Boston, Mass.
Mary's Industrial School	Dedham, Mass.
ate Industrial School for Girls	Lancaster, Mass.
Vincent's Industrial School	Newark, N. J.
Vincent's Industrial School	Albany, N. Y.
artha Industrial School	Buffalo, N. Y.
Mary's Industrial School	Buffalo, N. Y.
dustrial School of the Sisters of Mercy	New York, N. Y.
rinity Church Industrial School	Rondout, N. Y.
John's Industrial School	Syracuse, N. Y.
ury Warren Free Institute	Troy, N. Y.
dustrial School of Guardian Angels	Cincinnati, Ohio.
ome of Industry	Allegheny, Pa.
dustrial Home School	Washington, D. C.
. Rose's Industrial School	Washington, D. C.

a Now a free school for colored children.

TABLE XXIII.—*Memoranda.*

Name.	Location.	Remarks.
Boys' Home	Baltimore, Md ...	See Boys' Home Association, identical.
Orphans' Home, (German) .	Baltimore, Md ...	See German Orphan Asylum, identical.
Orphan Asylum............	Bath, N. Y	See Davenport Institution for Orphan Girls, identical.
Orphans' Home	Brooklyn, N. Y...	See St Joseph's Orphan Asylum, identical
Orphan Society for the City of Brooklyn.	Brooklyn, N. Y ..	See Orphan Asylum Society for the City of Brooklyn, identical.
Industrial School, Hart's Island.	New York, N. Y..	See Table XXII.
Protestant Half-Orphan Asylum.	New York, N. Y..	See the Society for the Relief of Half-Orphan and Destitute Children, identical.
Soldiers' Orphan School....	Cassville, Pa	Closed.
Catholic Home for Destitute Orphan Girls	Philadelphia, Pa .	See St. Joseph's Roman-Catholic Orphan Asylum, identical.
Union School and Children's Home.	Philadelphia, Pa .	See the Southern Home for Destitute Children, identical.

INDEX.

EFORMATORY SCHOOLS.

CONNECTICUT.

nnecticut Industrial School for
p. 7.
icut State Reform School, p. 10.

DISTRICT OF COLUMBIA.

form School of the District of
bia, p. 10.

INDIANA.

Reformatory for Women and
p. 12.

IOWA.

form School, p. 13.

KENTUCKY.

le House of Refuge, p. 13.

MARYLAND.

d Industrial School for Girls, p. 14.
use of Refuge for Juvenile Delin-
of the City of Baltimore, p. 14.

MASSACHUSETTS.

mary School at Monson, p. 15.
form School at Westboro', p. 16.

MAINE.

form School, p. 17.

MICHIGAN.

louse of Correction, p. 18.
ngan State Reform School, p. 18.

NEW HAMPSHIRE.

ichool of the State of New Hamp-
, 20.

NEW JERSEY.

ney State Reform School, p. 21.

NEW YORK.

The Truant Home, p. 22.
Western House of Refuge, p. 23.
New York House of Refuge, p. 24.
The New York Catholic Protectory, p. 27.
Monastery of the Good Shepherd, p. 29.
The Isaac T. Hopper Home, p. 30.

OHIO.

Cincinnati House of Refuge, p. 32.
House of Refuge and Correction, p. 34.
The Ohio Reform School, p. 35.

PENNSYLVANIA.

House of Refuge, p. 38.
Pennsylvania Reform School, p. 39.
The Sheltering Arms, p. 40.

RHODE ISLAND.

Providence Reform School, p. 41.

WISCONSIN.

The Wisconsin Industrial School for Boys,
p. 41.

Review of Reformatories:
Labor as a means of reformation, p. 42.
Mental and moral discipline also neces-
sary, p. 43.
Physical treatment called for, p. 43.
Further means, p. 44.
The family-system of reform, p. 45.
Necessity for some earnest action, p. 47.
The earlier the action the more of
hope, p. 50.
Education indispensable, p. 51.
Adult-reformation, p. 53.

HOMES AND SCHOOLS FOR CHIL-
DREN.

CALIFORNIA.

Good Templars' Home for Orphans, p. 57.

CONNECTICUT.

Hartford Orphan Asylum, p. 57.
New Haven Orphan Asylum, p. 57.

DISTRICT OF COLUMBIA.

National Soldiers' and Sailors' Orphans'
Home, p. 59.

ILLINOIS.

Protestant Orphan Asylum, p. 60.
Chicago Nursery and Half-Orphan Asylum, p. 61.

MARYLAND.

The Hebrew Orphan Asylum of Baltimore,
p. 62.

NEW HAMPSHIRE.

The New Hampshire Orphans' Home and
School of Industry, p. 62.

NEW JERSEY.

Newark Orphan Asylum, p. 62.

NEW YORK.

Davenport Orphanage, p. 64.
Buffalo Orphan Asylum, p. 64.
Thomas Asylum for Orphan and Destitute
Indian Children, p. 65.
The Hebrew Benevolent and Orphan Asy-
lum Society, p. 65.
Orphan Asylum Society in the city of New
York, p. 66.
St. Joseph's Asylum, p. 66.
The Society for the Relief of Half-Orphan
and Destitute Children of the City of
New York, p. 66.
Orphans' Home and Asylum, p. 68.
Colored Orphan Asylum, p. 68.
Rochester Orphan Asylum, p. 69.
Troy Orphan Asylum, p. 69.
St. Vincent's Female Orphan Asylum, p. 70.

OHIO.

German Protestant Orphan Asylum, p. 70.
Cincinnati Orphan Asylum, p. 71.
Cleveland Orphan Asylum, p. 71.
The Jewish Orphan Asylum of Cleveland,
p. 72.
Ebenezer Orphan Institute of the Evangel-
ical Association of North America, p. 72.
Protestant Orphan Home of the City of
Toledo, p. 73.

PENNSYLVANIA.

The Orphans' Home and Asylum for the
Aged and Infirm of the Evangelical
Lutheran Church, p. 73.

PENNSYLVANIA—Concluded.

Girard College for Orphans, p. 74.
The Burd Orphan Asylum, p. 75.
The Jewish Foster Home Society, p. 76.
Western Provident Society and Childi
Home of Philadelphia, p. 76.
St. Joseph's Female Orphan Asylum, p
The Orphans' Home of the Evange
Lutheran Church, p. 77.
Protestant Orphan Asylum of Pitts
and Allegheny, p. 77.
Home for Destitute Colored Children, j
The Home for Friendless Children for
Borough of Wilkesbarre and Coun
Luzerne, p. 78.
Children's Home for Borough and Co
of York, p. 78.
The Orphans' Farm School of the Eva
ical Lutheran Church, p. 78.

RHODE ISLAND.

Providence Children's Friend Society,

SOUTH CAROLINA.

Charleston Orphans' Home, p. 79.

TENNESSEE.

The Nashville Protestant Orphan Asy
p. 79.

WISCONSIN.

Milwaukee Orphans' Asylum, p. 79.

HOMES AND SCHOOLS FOR S
DIERS' ORPHANS.

NEW YORK.

The Union Home and School, p. 81.

OHIO.

Ohio Soldiers' and Sailors' Orphans' H
p. 81.

PENNSYLVANIA.

Lincoln Institution, p. 83.
Mansfield Soldiers' Orphans' Home, p.
McAlesterville Soldiers' Orphans' Sch
p. 84.
Cassville Soldiers' Orphans' School, p.
Mercer Soldiers' Orphans' Home, p. 86.
Bridgewater Soldiers' Orphans' Sch
p. 86.
St. Paul's Orphan Home, p. 57.

PENNSYLVANIA—Concluded.

burg Soldiers' Orphan School, p. 87.
lle Soldiers' Orphan School, p. 88.
n Home for Friendless Children
oldiers' Orphans' Institute, p. 88.
wn Soldiers' Orphan Home, p. 90.
  Springs Soldiers' Orphan School
iterary Institute, p. 90.
  Soldiers' Orphans' School, p. 90.
l Soldiers' Orphans' School, p. 91.
' Orphans' School at Andersonburg,

Hall Soldiers' Orphans' Home, p. 92.

INFANT-ASYLUMS.

DISTRICT OF COLUMBIA.

's Infant Asylum, p. 93.

ILLINOIS.

) Foundlings' Home, p. 93.

MICHIGAN.

of Providence, p. 94.

NEW YORK.

undling Asylum of the City of New
. p. 94.
rk Infant Asylum, p. 95.
 and Child's Hospital, p. 95.
irsery for the Children of Poor
en, p. 96.
y's Hospital for Children, p. 96.

PENNSYLVANIA.

cent's Home, p. 96.
ildren's Hospital of Philadelphia,

RHODE ISLAND.

ovidence Nursery, p. 97.

SCELLANEOUS CHARITIES.

CONNECTICUT.

for Home Work, p. 99.
for the Friendless, p. 99.

ILLINOIS.

for the Friendless, p. 100.

MARYLAND.

Ienry Watson Children's Aid So-
, p. 102.
of the Friendless, p. 102.

MASSACHUSETTS.

The Home for Friendless Women and Children, p. 102.

MICHIGAN.

Detroit Industrial School, p. 103.
The Michigan State Public School, p. 103.

MISSOURI.

Home of the Friendless or Old Ladies'
Home, p. 105.

NEW YORK.

Brooklyn Industrial School No. 1, p. 105.
Church Charity Foundation, p. 105.
The Orphans' Home of the Church Charity
Foundation, p. 107.
St. Johnland, p. 108.
Children's Aid Society, p. 108.
Aid society schools and the new educa-
tion law, p. 109.
Country Home, p. 109.
Flower Mission, p. 110.
Children's Lodging-Houses, p. 110.
American Female Guardian Society and
Home for the Friendless, p. 114.
The Industrial Home for Women, p. 116.
The Sheltering Arms, p. 118.
St. John's Guild, p. 121.
Five Points House of Industry, p. 122.
Ladies' Home Missionary Society, p. 122.
Home for Little Wanderers, or Howard
Mission, p. 122.
New York Society for the Relief of the
Ruptured and Crippled, p. 122.
St. Barnabas, p. 123.
House and School of Industry, p. 124.
Society for the Prevention of Cruelty to
Children, p. 125.
House of the Good Shepherd, p. 126.
Poughkeepsie Orphans' House and Home
for the Friendless, p. 127.

OHIO.

The Children's Home, p. 128.
Cleveland Industrial School, Children's
Aid Society and Home, p. 129.
The Home for Friendless Women, p. 130.
The Children's Home of Washington
County, p. 130.

PENNSYLVANIA.

Aimwell School Association, p. 130.
Union School and Children's Home, p. 131.

208

PENNSYLVANIA—Concluded.

The Women's Christian Association of Pittsburg and Allegheny, p. 132.
Pittsburg and Allegheny Home for the Friendless, p. 132.
Society of the Home for the Friendless, p. 132.

WISCONSIN.

The Cadle Home, p. 133.
Homes for Aged Women, p. 133.

INDUSTRIAL SCHOOLS.

CALIFORNIA.

Good Templars' Home for Orphans, p. 135.

CONNECTICUT.

The Connecticut Training-School for Nurses, p. 135.

DISTRICT OF COLUMBIA.

Industrial Home School, p. 156.

ILLINOIS.

The Orphan Girls' Home, p. 136.

MARYLAND.

Industrial School, p. 137.
St. Joseph's Industrial School for Girls, p. 137.
St. Mary's Industrial School for Boys, p. 137.

MICHIGAN.

The Detroit Industrial School, p. 138.

MISSOURI.

The Girls' Industrial Home, p. 128.

NEW JERSEY.

The Orphan Asylum at Newark, p. 138.

NEW YORK.

Training School for Nurses, p. 138.
Free Training-School for Women, p. 140.
Printers' Training-School, p. 141.
Industrial Schools of the Children's Aid Society, p. 142.

NEW YORK—Concluded.

Industrial School of the Hebrew lent and Orphans' Asylum Society
Wilson Industrial School and p. 143.
Industrial training in the Wilson p. 144.
Industrial School at the Five Point of Industry, p. 144.
The Ladies' Home Missionary p. 144.
The House and School of Industr
St. Joseph's Industrial Home, p. 14
Industrial Schools of the Home Friendless, p. 145.
The Nursery and Child's Hospital
The Guild or Congregation of St tine, p. 145.
Boys' Home of Industry, p. 145.
The Woman's Christian Associatio
The Industrial Home of the City p. 146.

OHIO.

Industrial School of the Young Branch of Women's Christian tion of Cincinnati, p. 146.
Cleveland Aid Society Industrial p. 148.

PENNSYLVANIA.

Industrial training in Girard Co Orphans, p. 148.
Industrial Home for Girls, p. 149.
The Industrial School of the Imr Conception, p. 149.
The Boarding-Home for Working. p. 150.
The Woman's Christian Associa Pittsburg and Allegheny, p. 150

SOUTH CAROLINA.

Charleston Sewing School, p. 150.

TENNESSEE.

Girls' Industrial Home, p. 150.

WISCONSIN.

St. Rose's School, p. 150.

CIRCULARS OF INFORMATION

OF THE

BUREAU OF EDUCATION.

No. 7–1875.

CONSTITUTIONAL PROVISIONS IN REGARD TO EDUCATION IN
THE SEVERAL STATES OF THE AMERICAN UNION.

WASHINGTON:
GOVERNMENT PRINTING OFFICE.
1875.

LETTER.

DEPARTMENT OF THE INTERIOR,
BUREAU OF EDUCATION,
Washington, D. C., September 1, 1875.

ι: Educational interests, although commonly subjects of legislation,
argely dependent upon the statute-law, have, from the very begin-
of our State governments, been more or less within the limitations
;uarantees of our State constitutions, and many of their most valued
res have by this means been placed beyond chance of change,
than by a modification of the organic law.

¯eral of the larger States embraced no provisions having direct
:nce to educational subjects in their first constitutions, nor for
· years afterward; but in the successive revisions that have since
made, one after another has extended these pledges, guarantees,
;rants to the various interests relating to education, literature, and
ce, until there is not now a single State in the American Union in
ı these interests are not recognized and guarded. A careful study
e subject will lead to the remark, that the ideas of one have been
ted by another, according as these several instruments have been
ılted and followed in the preparation of new plans of government
the revision of old ones. This process of construction and amend-
is going on every year, and the study of fundamental principles in
·nment becomes, in one part of the country or another, a frequent
ct of immediate practical importance with those who may be
;ed with these responsible duties or who may feel an interest in
uccess of the labors of those who are so charged. The merits of
several principles come under the direct personal inspection of
· citizen who thoughtfully studies the plan submitted for his ap-
ıl or rejection; and with the increasing intelligence which it is the
nce of education to impart, we may reasonably hope that every
;e in the organic law will be an improvement, and that these frames
vernment will in each change present a principle justified by expe-
e and well founded in justice and wisdom.

e frequent occasions that arise for information as to constitutional
sions in regard to educational subjects have led me to request Dr.
klin B. Hough, of Lowville, N. Y., to prepare this Circular as the
answer that can be given to these inquiries. It is believed to be
ılete in all that expressly relates to educational, literary, or scientific
ars in the constitution of each of the States, from the beginning

545

down to the present time. It contains no remark showing preference
of one over another, and no note other than such as tends to illustrate
or explain the subject-matter of the text, or to show how the several
requirements of the constitutions have been carried into effect. It is
accompanied by a classified summary, in which are briefly stated the
principal features of the several State constitutions in such an order that
their origin, successive changes, and present condition may be known.
This synopsis does not refer to the rejected constitutions, most of which
are given in smaller type in the text, or in the form of notes, nor is it
claimed as complete in the minor details, although, it is hoped, sufficiently full to show historically and comparatively every important fact
or principle that has been, or that is, a part of the organic law in each of
the States of the American Union. A concise index has been added, to
further facilitate the use of this circular.

I recommend the publication of this material as a Circular of Information.

Very respectfully, your obedient servant,

JOHN EATON,
Commissioner.

Hon. C. DELANO,
Secretary of the Interior. •

Approved, and publication ordered.

B. R. COWEN,
Acting Secretary.

CONTENTS.

		Page.
ibama, constitutional provisions, 1819 and 1868		9
zansas, constitutional provisions, 1836		12
constitutional provisions, 1868		13
lifornia, constitutional provisions, 1849		16
constitutional provisions, 1862		17
nnecticut, constitutional provisions, 1818		17
laware, constitutional provisions, 1792		18
rida, constitutional provisions, 1845, 1861, 1865, and 1868		19
rgia, constitutional provisions, 1777 and 1798		22
constitutional provisions, 1868		23
nois, constitutional provisions, 1818		23
constitutional provisions, 1862, (not adopted,) and 1870		25
liana, constitutional provisions, 1816		28
constitutional provisions, 1851		29
va, constitutional provisions, 1844. (Not adopted)		31
constitutional provisions, 1846		32
constitutional provisions, 1857		33
nsas, constitutional provisions, 1859		36
constitutional provisions, Topeka convention, 1855. (Not adopted)		36
constitutional provisions, Lecompton convention, 1857. (Not adopted)		36
constitutional provisions, Leavenworth convention, 1858. (Not adopted)		37
constitutional provisions, 1859		38
ntucky, constitutional provisions, 1850		40
uisiana, constitutional provisions, 1845		41
constitutional provisions, 1852		42
constitutional provisions, 1864		43
constitutional provisions, 1868		44
ine, constitutional provisions, 1820		45
ryland, constitutional provisions, 1864		46
constitutional provisions, 1867		48
ssachusetts, constitutional provisions, 1780		48
constitutional provisions, 1853. (Not adopted)		51
constitutional provisions, 1857		51
higan, constitutional provisions, 1835		52
constitutional provisions, 1850		53
constitutional provisions, 1861		55
constitutional provisions, 1867. (Not adopted)		55
nnesota, constitutional provisions, 1858		57
ssissippi. constitutional provisions, 1817		57
constitutional provisions, 1868		58
ssouri, constitutional provisions, 1820		59
constitutional provisions, 1865		60
braska, constitutional provisions, 1867		62
constitutional provisions, 1871. (Not adopted)		62
vada, constitutional provisions, 1864		65
v Hampshire, constitutional provisions, 1784		67

	Page.
New Jersey, constitutional provisions, 1844	68
New York, constitutional provisions, 1821	68
constitutional provisions, 1846	69
constitutional provisions, 1867. (Not adopted.)	70
North Carolina, constitutional provisions, 1776	70
constitutional provisions, 1868	71
Ohio, constitutional provisions, 1802	74
constitutional provisions, 1851	75
constitutional provisions, 1874. (Not adopted)	75
Oregon, constitutional provisions, 1857	76
Pennsylvania, proprietary concessions	77
constitutional provisions, 1776	78
constitutional provisions, 1790, 1838, and 1873	79
Rhode Island, constitutional provisions, 1842	80
South Carolina, constitutional provisions, 1868	81
Tennessee, constitutional provisions, 1796 and 1834	83
constitutional provisions, 1870	84
Texas, constitutional provisions, 1845	84
constitutional provisions, 1866	85
constitutional provisions, 1869	87
Vermont, constitutional provisions, 1786 and 1793	89
Virginia, constitutional provisions, 1851 and 1870	90
West Virginia, constitutional provisions, 1861	92
constitutional provisions, 1872	93
Wisconsin, constitutional provisions, 1846. (Not adopted.)	97
constitutional provisions, 1848	97
Territory of Colorado, proposed provisions, 1865	99
Territory of New Mexico, proposed provisions, 1850	100
proposed provisions, 1870	101
Classified summary	103
Index	116

CONSTITUTIONAL PROVISIONS

RELATING TO

)UCATION, LITERATURE, AND SCIENCE

IN THE

SEVERAL STATES OF THE AMERICAN UNION,

INCLUDING

FORMER PROVISIONS, AS WELL AS THOSE NOW IN FORCE, AND THOSE PROPOSED BY
CONSTITUTIONAL CONVENTIONS BUT NOT ADOPTED;

WITH

A CLASSIFIED ABSTRACT OF THE MORE IMPORTANT FEATURES,
AND EXPLANATORY NOTES.

PREPARED BY

FRANKLIN B. HOUGH.

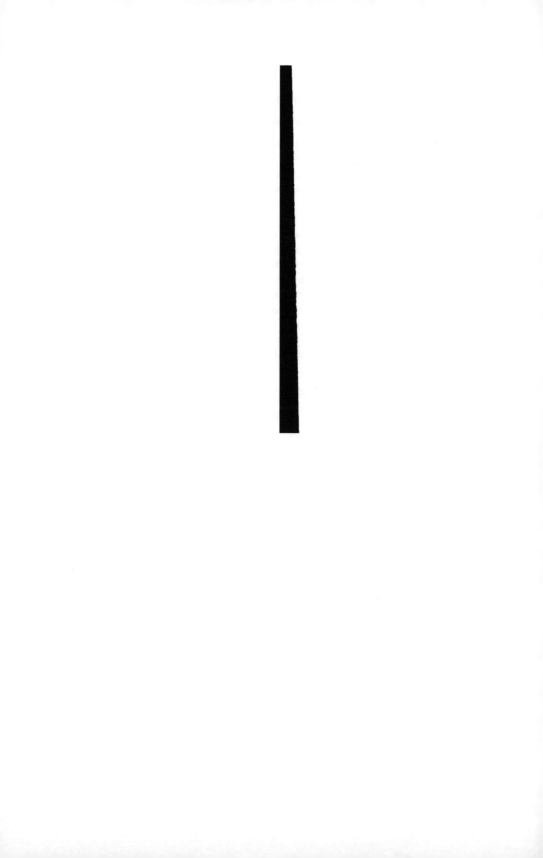

ALABAMA.

CONSTITUTION OF ALABAMA, AS ADOPTED IN 1819.

Education.

Schools and the means of education shall forever be encouraged in this State; and the general assembly shall take measures to preserve from unnecessary waste or damage such lands as are, or hereafter may be, granted by the United States, for the use of schools, within each township in this State, and apply the funds which may be raised from such lands in strict conformity to the object of such grant. The general assembly shall take like measures for the improvement of such lands as have been or may be hereafter granted by the United States to this State for the support of a seminary of learning; and the moneys which may be raised from such lands by rent, lease, or sale, or from any other quarter, for the purpose aforesaid, shall be and remain a fund for the exclusive support of a State-university,* for the promotion of the arts, literature, and the sciences; and it shall be the duty of the general assembly, as early as may be, to provide effectual means for the improvement and permanent security of the funds and endowments of such institution.

CONSTITUTION OF ALABAMA, AS AMENDED IN 1868.

Article IX.—Taxation.

SECTION 1. All taxes levied on property in this State shall be assessed in exact proportion to the value of such property: *Provided, however,* That the general assembly may levy a poll-tax not exceeding one dollar and fifty cents on each poll, which shall be applied exclusively in aid of the public-school-fund.

Article XI.—Education.

SECTION 1. The common schools and other educational institutions of the State shall be under the management of a board of education,

---

* The code of 1852 defines the university-fund as the sum of $250,000, for the permanent security of which and the punctual payment of the interest thereon at the rate of 6 per cent. a year forever the faith and credit of the State were pledged.

By an act of Congress approved March 2, 1827, the legislature of Alabama was authorized to sell its school-land, with the consent of the inhabitants of the towns in which it was located, and to invest the proceeds in some productive funds. The share due to each township and district was to be in proportion to the value of lands in each. If insufficient for the support of schools, the income might be invested until the principal was sufficient for the maintenance of schools.

The Revised Code of 1867, Title VIII, Chapter 1, Article I–III, more fully defines the present law with reference to school-lands, trustees, and surveys, and, chapter 2, the university-lands and site.

consisting of a superintendent of public instruction and two members from each congressional district. The governor of the State shall be *ex officio* a member of the board, but shall have no vote in its proceedings.

§ 2. The superintendent of public instruction shall be president of the board of education, and have the casting vote in case of a tie; he shall have the supervision of the public schools of the State and perform such other duties as may be imposed upon him by the board and the laws of the State; he shall be elected in the same manner and for the same term as the governor of the State, and receive such salary as may be fixed by law. An office shall be assigned him in the capitol of the State.

§ 3. The members of the board shall hold office for a term of four years, and until their successors shall be elected and qualified. After the first election under the constitution, the board shall be divided into two equal classes, so that each class shall consist of one member from each district. The seats of the first class shall be vacated at the expiration of two years from the day of election, so that one-half may be chosen biennially.

§ 4. The members of the board of education, except the superintendent, shall be elected by the qualified electors of the congressional districts in which they are chosen, at the same time and in the same manner as the members of Congress.

§ 5. The board of education shall exercise full legislative powers in reference to the public educational institutions of the State; and its acts, when approved by the governor or when re-enacted by two-thirds of the board in case of his disapproval, shall have the force and effect of law unless repealed by the general assembly.

§ 6. It shall be the duty of the board to establish throughout the State, in each township, or other school-district which it may have created, one or more schools, at which all the children of the State between the ages of five and twenty-one years may attend, free of charge.

§ 7. No rule or law affecting the general interest of education shall be made by the board without a concurrence of a majority of its members. The style of all acts of the board shall be, "Be it enacted by the Board of Education of the State of Alabama."

§ 8. The board of education shall be a body politic and corporate, by the name and style of the Board of Education of the State of Alabama. Said board shall also be a board of regents of the State University, and when sitting as a board of regents of the university shall have the power to appoint the president and faculties thereof.

The president of the university shall be *ex officio* a member of the board of regents, but shall have no vote in its proceedings.

§ 9. The board of education shall meet annually at the seat of government, at the same time as the general assembly, but no session shall continue longer than twenty days, nor shall more than one session be

d in the same year, unless authorized by the governor. The mem-
s shall receive the same mileage and daily pay as the members of
general assembly.

10. The proceeds of all lands that have been or may be granted by
United States to the State, for educational purposes, of the swamp-
ds,* and of all lands or other property given by individuals or appro-
ated by the State for like purposes, and of all estates of deceased
sons who have died without leaving a will or heir, and all moneys
ch may be paid as an equivalent for exemption from military duty,
ll be and remain a perpetual fund, which may be increased but not
inished, and the interest and income of which, together with the
ts of all such lands as may remain unsold, and such other means as
general assembly may provide, shall be inviolably appropriated to
cational purposes, and to no other purpose whatever.

11. In addition to the amount accruing from the above sources, one-
of the aggregate annual revenue of the State shall be devoted
lusively to the maintenance of public schools.

12. The general assembly may give power to the authorities of the
ool-districts to levy a poll-tax on the inhabitants of the district in
of the general school-fund, and for no other purpose.

13. The general assembly shall levy a specific annual tax upon all rail-
d, navigation, banking, and insurance corporations, and upon all in-
ance and foreign-bank and exchange agencies, and upon the profits of
ign bank-bills issued in this State by any corporation, partnership,
persons, which shall be exclusively devoted to the maintenance of
lic schools.

14. The general assembly shall, as soon as practicable, provide for
establishment of an agricultural college,† and shall appropriate the
hundred and forty thousand acres of land donated to this State for
support of such a college, by the act of Congress passed July 2, 1862,‡
he money or scrip, as the case may be, arising from the sale of said
d, or any lands which may hereafter be granted or appropriated for
purpose, for the support and maintenance of such college or schools,
may make the same a branch of the University of Alabama for in-
ction in agriculture, in the mechanic arts, and the natural sciences
nected therewith, and place the same under the supervision of the
nts of the university.

---

riginally granted to the States by act of September 28, 1850, for construction of
s for reclaiming these lands ; confirmed to the States March 3, 1857.

n act approved February 26, 1872, created a board of directors of the Agricultural
Mechanical College of Alabama, and defined their powers. It was located at Au-
, Lee County, upon lands deeded by the East Alabama Male College on the 17th of
uary, 1872, the State reserving the right of removal of the institution if the gen-
welfare should demand it.

ict donating public lands to the several States and Territories for the benefit of
ulture and the mechanic arts, approved July 2, 1862, chapter 130, second ses-
Thirty-seventh Congress.—*Statutes at Large*, XII, 503.

ARKANSAS.

CONSTITUTION OF ARKANSAS AS ADOPTED IN 1836.

Article IX. General provisions—Education.

. . . . . Knowledge and learning, generally diffused through a
. . . . as to the preservation of a free government, and
. . . . . the opportunities and advantages of education through the
. . . . part of the State being highly conducive to this end, it shall
be the duty of the general assembly to provide by law for the improvement of such lands as are, or hereafter may be, granted by the United
. . . . to this State for the use of schools, and to apply any funds which
. . . derived from such land, or from any other source, to the accom

---

. . . . . for the government of this bureau was approved August 12, 1868.—*Laws of
. . . . . . 1868, p. . .*

.

lishment of the object for which they are or may be intended. The
general assembly shall, from time to time, pass such laws as shall be
calculated to encourage intellectual, scientific, and agricultural improvements, by allowing rewards and immunities for the promotion and
improvement of arts, science, commerce, manufactures, and natural history, and countenance and encourage the principles of humanity, industry, and morality.

[The above section was included in the constitution of 1864–'65, as Art.
VIII, § 1.]

Constitution of Arkansas, as amended in 1868.

Article I.—Bill of rights.

Section 23. Religion, morality, and knowledge being essential to
good government, the general assembly shall pass suitable laws to protect every religious denomination in the peaceable enjoyment of its own
mode of public worship, and to encourage schools and the means of
instruction.

Article VI.—Executive department.

Section 1. The executive department of this State shall consist of
a governor, lieutenant-governor, secretary of state, auditor, treasurer,
attorney-general, and superintendent of public instruction, all of whom
shall hold their several offices for the term of four years and until their
successors are elected and qualified. They shall be chosen by the qualified electors of this State at the time and places of choosing the members of the general assembly.

§ 18. The governor, chief justice, secretary of state, treasurer, auditor, attorney-general, and superintendent of public instruction shall
severally reside, and keep all public records, books, papers, and documents which may pertain to their respective offices, at the seat of government.

§ 19. The returns of every election for governor, lieutenant-governor,
secretary of state, treasurer, auditor, attorney-general, and superintendent of public instruction shall be sealed up and transmitted to the
seat of government by the returning-officers, and directed to the presiding officer of the senate, who, during the first week of the session, shall
open and publish the same in presence of the members then assembled.
The person having the highest number of votes shall be declared elected,
but if two or more shall have the highest and equal number of votes
for the same office, one of them shall be chosen by a joint vote of both
houses. Contested elections shall likewise be determined by both houses
of the general assembly in such manner as is or may hereafter be prescribed by law.

§ 21. The auditor, treasurer, attorney-general, and superintendent of
public instruction shall perform such duties as are now or may hereafter be prescribed by law.

§ 22. In case of the death, impeachment, removal from the State, or other disability of the secretary of state, treasurer, auditor, attorney-general, and superintendent of public instruction, the vacancies in their several offices thus occasioned shall be filled by appointment of the governor, which appointment shall be made for the unexpired terms of said offices, or until said disabilities are removed, or until elections are held to fill said vacancies.

§ 24. The officers of the executive department mentioned in this article shall, at stated times, receive for their services a compensation, to be established by law, which shall not be diminished during the period for which they shall have been elected or appointed.

§ 25. The officers of the executive department and judges of the supreme court shall not be eligible, during the period for which they may have been elected or appointed to their respective offices, to any position in the gift of the qualified electors or of the general assembly of this State.

Article IX.—Education.

SECTION 1. A general diffusion of knowledge and intelligence among all classes being essential to the preservation of the rights and liberties of the people, the general assembly shall establish and maintain a system of free schools* for the gratuitous instruction of all persons in this State between the ages of five and twenty-one years; and the funds appropriated for the support of common schools shall be distributed to the several counties in proportion to the number of children and youths therein between the ages of five and twenty-one years, in such manner as shall be prescribed by law; but no religious or other sect or sects shall ever have any exclusive right to, or control of, any part of the school-funds of this State.

§ 2. The supervision of public schools shall be vested in a superintendent of public instruction, and such other officers as the general assembly shall provide. The superintendent of public instruction shall receive such salary and perform such duties as shall be prescribed by law.

§ 3. The general assembly shall establish and maintain a State-university,† with departments for instruction in teaching, in agriculture, and the natural sciences as soon as the public-school-fund will permit.

---

* An act for organizing and maintaining a system of free schools in Arkansas was approved July 23, 1868.—*Acts of the General Assembly of the State of Arkansas*, 1868, pp. 163-197.

† An act establishing an industrial university ,was approved July 23, 1868. It required, in addition to the usual course of study prescribed in universities, that the science and practice of agriculture, the mechanic arts, engineering, and military science should be taught. The location was left to be decided by bids from individuals, counties, cities, townships, incorporated towns, corporations, or otherwise, their offers being open till the first day of the next session of the general assembly.—*Acts of Arkansas*, 1868, p. 323.

By acts approved March 13, 1873, further provision was made with reference to the university, which had been located at Fayetteville, Washington County.—*Acts of Arkansas*, 1871, p. 201; 187. p. 26.

§ 4. The proceeds of all lands that have been, or hereafter may be, ·anted by the United States to this State, and not otherwise appro-·iated by the United States or this State ; also, all mines, stocks, bonds, nds, and other property now belonging to any fund for purposes of ¦ucation ; also, the net proceeds of all sales of land and other prop-·ty and effects that may accrue to this State by escheat, or from sales estrays, or from unclaimed dividends or distributive shares of the tates of deceased persons, or from fines, penalties, or forfeitures; so, any proceeds of the sales of public lands which may have been or ny be hereafter paid over to this State, (Congress consenting;) also, l the grants, gifts, or devises that have been or hereafter may be made this State, and not otherwise appropriated by the terms of the grant, ft, or devise, shall be securely invested and sacredly preserved as a ıblic school-fund, which shall be the common property of the State, e annual income of which fund, together with one dollar *per capita*, be annually assessed on every male inhabitant of this State over the ʒe of twenty-one years, and so much of the ordinary annual revenue ' the State as may be necessary, shall be faithfully appropriated for .tablishing and maintaining the free schools and the university in this ·ticle provided for, and for no other use or purposes whatever.

§ 5. No part of the public-school-fund shall be invested in the stocks · bonds or other obligations of any State, or any county, city, town, · corporation. The stocks belonging to any school-fund or university-.nd shall be sold in such manner and at such times as the general ¡sembly shall prescribe, and the proceeds thereof, and the proceeds of ıe sales of any lands or other property which now belong or may ɜreafter belong to said school-fund, may be invested in the bonds of ıe United States.

§ 6. No township or school-district shall receive any portion of the ¦hool-fund unless a free school shall have been kept therein for not ss than three months during the year for which distribution thereof ¦ made. The general assembly shall require by law that every child, [sufficient mental and physical ability, shall attend the public schools, uring the period between the ages of five and eighteen years, for a ·rm equivalent to three years, unless educated by other means.

§ 7. In case the public-school-fund shall be insufficient to sustain a ·ee school at least three months in every year in each school-district in ıis State, the general assembly shall provide by law for raising such eficiency by levying such tax upon all taxable property in each county,· ɔwnship, or school-district as may be deemed proper.

§ 8. The general assembly shall, as far as it can be done without in-·inging upon vested rights, reduce all lands, moneys, or other property ¡ed or held for school-purposes in the various counties of this State ¡to the public-school-fund herein provided for.

§ 9. Provision shall also be made, by general laws, for raising such ım or sums of money, by taxation or otherwise, in each school-district as may be necessary for the building and furnishing of a sufficient number of suitable school-houses for the accommodation of all the pupils within the limits of the several school-districts.

Article X.—Finances, taxation, public debt, and expenditures.

SECTION 1. The levying of taxes by the poll is grievous and oppressive; therefore the general assembly shall never levy a poll-tax excepting for school-purposes.

§ 2. Laws shall be passed taxing, by a uniform rule, all money-credits, investment in bonds, joint-stock-companies, or otherwise; and also all real and personal property according to its true value in money; but all burying-grounds, public-school-houses, houses used exclusively for public worship, institutions of purely public charity, and public property used exclusively for any public purpose shall never be taxed.

§ 15. The principal arising from the sale of all lands donated to the State for school purposes shall be paid into the treasury, and the State shall pay interest thereon for the support of schools at the rate of six per cent. per annum.

CALIFORNIA.

CONSTITUTION OF CALIFORNIA, AS ADOPTED IN 1849.

Article IX.—Education.

SECTION 1. The legislature shall provide for the election by the people of a superintendent of public instruction, who shall hold his office for three years,* and whose duties shall be prescribed by law, and who shall receive such compensation as the legislature may direct.†

§ 2. The legislature shall encourage, by all suitable means, the promotion of intellectual, scientific, moral, and agricultural improvement. The proceeds of all lands that may be granted by the United States to this State for the support of schools, which may be sold or disposed of, and the five hundred thousand acres of land granted to the new States, under an act of Congress distributing the proceeds of the public lands among the several States of the Union, approved A. D. 1841, and all estates of deceased persons who may have died without leaving a will or heir, and also such per cent. as may be granted by Congress on the sale of lands in this State, shall be and remain a perpetual fund, the interest of which, together with all the rents of the unsold lands, and such other means as the legislature may provide, shall be inviolably appropriated to the support of common schools throughout the State.

§ 3. The legislature shall provide for a system of common schools‡ by which a school shall be kept up and supported in each district at

---

* Changed in 1862 to four years.

† This section was superseded by an amendment adopted in 1862, as subsequently noticed.

‡ A State-board of education was organized by an act approved April 6, 1863.

least three months in every year; and any school-district neglecting to keep up and support such a school may be deprived of its proportion of the interest of the public fund during such neglect.

§ 4. The legislature shall take measures for the protection, improvement, or other disposition of such lands as have been or may hereafter be reserved or granted by the United States, or any person or persons, to the State for the use of a university; and the funds accruing from the rents or sale of such lands, or from any other source, for the purpose aforesaid, shall be and remain a permanent fund, the interest of which shall be applied to the support of said university, with such branches as the public convenience may demand, for the promotion of literature and the arts and sciences, as may be authorized by the terms of such grant. And it shall be the duty of the legislature, as soon as may be, to provide effectual means for the improvement and permanent security of the funds of said university.*

AMENDMENT TO CONSTITUTION OF CALIFORNIA, ADOPTED IN 1862.

Article IX.

SECTION 1. A superintendent of public instruction shall, at the special election for judicial officers to be held in the year 1863, and every four years thereafter, at such special elections, be elected by the qualified voters of the State, and shall enter upon the duties of his office on the first day of December next after his election.

CONNECTICUT.

[This State remained under the colonial charter of 1662 until 1818, when the present constitution was adopted. That instrument gave no express directions or privileges with respect to education, but guaranteed all the rights of English subjects, and very ample powers of self-government, in all things not contrary to the laws and statutes of the realm.]

CONSTITUTION OF CONNECTICUT, AS ADOPTED IN 1818.

Article VIII.—Of Education.

SECTION 1. The charter of Yale College, as modified by agreement with the corporation thereof, in pursuance of an act of the general assembly, passed in May, 1792, is hereby confirmed. †

---

* A State-university was organized by act approved March 23, 1868, pursuant to this section of the constitution, and to consist of, first, colleges of arts; secondly, a college of letters; and, thirdly, such professional and other colleges as might be added thereto or connected therewith. The colleges of arts were to consist of the following: A State-college of agriculture; a State-college of mechanic arts; a State-college of mines; a State-college of civil engineering, and such other colleges of arts as the board of regents might be able, and find it expedient, to establish. The third class was to embrace colleges of medicine, law, and other like professional colleges. The university has been located at Oakland.

† "An act for enlarging the powers and increasing the funds of Yale College" appointed William Hart, John Trumbull, and Andrew Kingsbury as commissioners, to

§ 2. The fund called the *school-fund** shall remain a perpetual fund the interest of which shall be inviolably appropriated to the support and encouragement of the public or common schools throughout the State, and for the equal benefit of all the people thereof. The value and amount of said fund shall, as soon as practicable, be ascertain in such manner as the general assembly may prescribe, published, a recorded in the comptroller's office; and no law shall ever be ma authorizing said fund to be diverted to any other use than the encour agement and support of public or common schools, among the severa school-societies, as justice and equity shall require.

AMENDMENT ADOPTED IN OCTOBER, 1855.

Article XI.

Every person shall be able to read any article of the constitution, any section of the statutes of this State, before being admitted as elector.

DELAWARE.

CONSTITUTION OF DELAWARE, AS AMENDED IN 1792.

Article VIII.

SECTION 12. The legislature shall, as soon as conveniently may be, provide by law, for * * * * establishing schools and promoting arts and sciences. †

[The same continued in the amended constitution of 1831, as a part of Article VII, § 11.]

---

perform certain duties specified with regard to balances due to the State, which were appropriated to Yale College upon condition of the acceptance, on the part of the president and corporation, of certain modifications in their corporate powers, of which legal evidence was to be filed in the office of the secretary of state.

An additional act was passed May, 1796, by which a claim of 50 per cent. of sums collected on certain balances was relinquished to the college on condition that the latter should transfer $13,726.39 in deferred stock of the United States to the State treasurer. The president and corporation were by this act required to report annually to the general assembly an account of receipts and expenditures of the moneys belonging to the college.

* The school-fund of Connecticut was established May, 1795, from moneys arising from the sale of the lands known as the Western Reserve in Northern Ohio. The capital of this fund amounted on the 2d day of September, 1872, to $2,044,190.81, of which the sum of $204,812.61 was invested in bank-stocks, $130,000 in State-bonds $1,683,211.69 in contracts, bonds, and mortgages against individuals residing in Connecticut, Massachusetts, New York, and Ohio, and the remainder was in cash. The disbursements for the year ended March 31, 1874, amounted to $144,043.21, including a dividend of $1 *per capita* to 133,530 children entitled to its benefits. The fund is managed by commissioners, who report its condition annually to the general assembly, with details of investment and expenditure.

† An act was passed February 9, 1796, to create a fund, sufficient to establish schools in this State, from marriage- and tavern-licenses until 1806, and such other money and estate as might thereafter be granted for this purpose. The State-treasurer was constituted the trustee of this fund and his powers and duties defined.

FLORIDA.

CONSTITUTION OF FLORIDA, PREPARED IN 1839; IN FORCE FROM 1845.

Article X.—Education.

The proceeds of all lands granted by the United States for the use of schools shall remain a perpetual fund, the interest of which shall be used for the benefit of said schools, and for no other purpose.*

CONSTITUTION OF FLORIDA, AS AMENDED IN 1861.

Article X.—Education.

SECTION 1. The proceeds of all lands that have been granted by the united States for the use of schools and a seminary or seminaries of learning shall be and remain a perpetual fund, the interest of which, gether with all moneys, derived from any other source, applicable to e same object, shall be inviolably appropriated to the use of schools id seminaries of learning, respectively, and to no other purpose.

§ 2. The general assembly shall take such measures as may be necessary to preserve from waste or damage all land so granted and appropriated to the purposes of education.

CONSTITUTION OF FLORIDA, AS AMENDED IN 1865.

Article X.—Education.

SECTION 1. The proceeds of all lands for the use of schools and a seminary or seminaries of learning shall be and remain a perpetual und, the interest of which, together with all moneys accrued from any ther source, applicable to the same object, shall be irrevocably appropriated to the use of schools and seminaries of learning, respectively, nd to no other purpose.

§ 2. The general assembly shall take such measures as may be necessary to preserve from waste or damage all lands so granted or appropriated for the purpose of education.

CONSTITUTION OF FLORIDA, AS AMENDED IN 1868.

Article IV.

SECTION 22. The legislature shall provide by general law for incorporating such municipal, educational, mechanical, mining, and other useful companies or associations as may be deemed necessary.

---

* The register of the land-office had previously been charged with the duty of selecting the various lands that had been or might be granted to Florida for the seminaries f learning.—*Act of December* 26, 1835.

By an act passed March 15, 1843, the sheriffs of the several counties were declared o be commissioners of the school-fund in their several counties, and the governor was directed to appoint five " trustees of the seminary-lands," and their duties were defined.

consisting of a superintendent of public instruction and two members from each congressional district. The governor of the State shall be *ex officio* a member of the board, but shall have no vote in its proceedings.

§ 2. The superintendent of public instruction shall be president of the board of education, and have the casting vote in case of a tie; he shall have the supervision of the public schools of the State and perform such other duties as may be imposed upon him by the board and the laws of the State; he shall be elected in the same manner and for the same term as the governor of the State, and receive such salary as may be fixed by law. An office shall be assigned him in the capitol of the State.

§ 3. The members of the board shall hold office for a term of four years, and until their successors shall be elected and qualified. After the first election under the constitution, the board shall be divided into two equal classes, so that each class shall consist of one member from each district. The seats of the first class shall be vacated at the expiration of two years from the day of election, so that one-half may be chosen biennially.

§ 4. The members of the board of education, except the superintendent, shall be elected by the qualified electors of the congressional districts in which they are chosen, at the same time and in the same manner as the members of Congress.

§ 5. The board of education shall exercise full legislative powers in reference to the public educational institutions of the State; and its acts, when approved by the governor or when re-enacted by two-thirds of the board in case of his disapproval, shall have the force and effect of law unless repealed by the general assembly.

§ 6. It shall be the duty of the board to establish throughout the State, in each township, or other school-district which it may have created, one or more schools, at which all the children of the State between the ages of five and twenty-one years may attend, free of charge.

§ 7. No rule or law affecting the general interest of education shall be made by the board without a concurrence of a majority of its members. The style of all acts of the board shall be, "Be it enacted by the Board of Education of the State of Alabama."

§ 8. The board of education shall be a body politic and corporate, by the name and style of the Board of Education of the State of Alabama. Said board shall also be a board of regents of the State University, and when sitting as a board of regents of the university shall have the power to appoint the president and faculties thereof.

The president of the university shall be *ex officio* a member of the board of regents, but shall have no vote in its proceedings.

§ 9. The board of education shall meet annually at the seat of government, at the same time as the general assembly, but no session shall continue longer than twenty days, nor shall more than one session be

in the same year, unless authorized by the governor. The mem-
shall receive the same mileage and daily pay as the members of
general assembly.

l0. The proceeds of all lands that have been or may be granted by
United States to the State, for educational purposes, of the swamp-
s,* and of all lands or other property given by individuals or appro-
:ed by the State for like purposes, and of all estates of deceased
ons who have died without leaving a will or heir, and all moneys
h may be paid as an equivalent for exemption from military duty,
be and remain a perpetual fund, which may be increased but not
nished, and the interest and income of which, together with the
3 of all such lands as may remain unsold, and such other means as
general assembly may provide, shall be inviolably appropriated to
ational purposes, and to no other purpose whatever.

l. In addition to the amount accruing from the above sources, one-
of the aggregate annual revenue of the State shall be devoted
sively to the maintenance of public schools.

2. The general assembly may give power to the authorities of the
ol-districts to levy a poll-tax on the inhabitants of the district in
f the general school-fund, and for no other purpose.

3. The general assembly shall levy a specific annual tax upon all rail-
, navigation, banking, and insurance corporations, and upon all in-
nce and foreign-bank and exchange agencies, and upon the profits of
gn bank-bills issued in this State by any corporation, partnership,
ersons, which shall be exclusively devoted to the maintenance of
ic schools.

4. The general assembly shall, as soon as practicable, provide for
stablishment of an agricultural college,† and shall appropriate the
hundred and forty thousand acres of land donated to this State for
upport of such a college, by the act of Congress passed July 2, 1862,‡
e money or scrip, as the case may be, arising from the sale of said
, or any lands which may hereafter be granted or appropriated for
purpose, for the support and maintenance of such college or schools,
may make the same a branch of the University of Alabama for in-
tion in agriculture, in the mechanic arts, and the natural sciences
ected therewith, and place the same under the supervision of the
its of the university.

iginally granted to the States by act of September 28, 1850, for construction of
for reclaiming these lands ; confirmed to the States March 3, 1857.

act approved February 26, 1872, created a board of directors of the Agricultural
lechanical College of Alabama, and defined their powers. It was located at Au-
Lee County, upon lands deeded by the East Alabama Male College on the 17th of
ary, 1872, the State reserving the right of removal of the institution if the gen-
elfare should demand it.

t donating public lands to the several States and Territories for the benefit of
lture and the mechanic arts, approved July 2, 1862, chapter 130, second ses-
hirty-seventh Congress.—*Statutes at Large*, XII, 503.

Article XII.—Industrial resources.

SECTION 1. A bureau of industrial resources shall be established, to be under the management of a commissioner, who shall be elected at the first general election, and shall hold his office for the term of four years.

§ 2. The commissioner of industrial resources* shall collect and condense statistical informati n concerning the productive industries of the State, and shall make, or cause to be made, a careful, accurate, and thorough report upon the agriculture and geology of the State, and annually report such additions as the progress of scientific development and extended explorations may require. He shall, from time to time, disseminate among the people of the State such knowledge as he may deem important concerning improved machinery and production, and for the promotion of their agricultural, manufacturing, and mining interests; and shall send out to the people of the United States and foreign countries such reports concerning the industrial resources of Alabama as may best make known the advantages offered by the State to emigrants, and shall perform such other duties as the general assembly may require.

§ 3. It shall be the duty of the general assembly, at the first session after the adoption of this constitution, to pass such laws and regulations as may be necessary for the government and protection of this bureau, and also to fix and provide for the compensation of the commissioner.

§ 4. This bureau shall be located and the commissioner shall reside at the capital of the State, and he shall annually make a written or printed report to the governor of the State, to be laid before the general assembly at each session.

§ 5. In case of the death, removal, or resignation of the commissioner, the governor, with approval of the senate, shall have power to appoint a commissioner for the unexpired term.

ARKANSAS.

CONSTITUTION OF ARKANSAS, AS ADOPTED IN 1836.

Article IX.—General provisions—Education.

SECTION 1. Knowledge and learning, generally diffused through a community, being essential to the preservation of a free government, and diffusing the opportunities and advantages of education through the various parts of the State being highly conducive to this end, it shall be the duty of the general assembly to provide by law for the improvement of such lands as are, or hereafter may be, granted by the United States to this State for the use of schools, and to apply any funds which may be raised from such land, or from any other source, to the accom

---

* An act for the government of this bureau was approved August 12, 1868.—*Laws of Alabama*, 1868, p. 55.

ishment of the object for which they are or may be intended. The
:neral assembly shall, from time to time, pass such laws as shall be
Jculated to encourage intellectual, scientific, and agricultural improve-
ents, by allowing rewards and immunities for the promotion and
1provement of arts, science, commerce, manufactures, and natural his-
ry, and countenance and encourage the principles of humanity, indus-
y, and morality.

[The above section was included in the constitution of 1864–'65, as Art.
III, § 1.]

Constitution of Arkansas, as amended in 1868.

Article I.—Bill of rights.

SECTION 23. Religion, morality, and knowledge being essential to
)od government, the general assembly shall pass suitable laws to pro-
·ct every religious denomination in the peaceable enjoyment of its own
.ode of public worship, and to encourage schools and the means of
istruction.

Article VI.—Executive department.

SECTION 1. The executive department of this State shall consist of
governor, lieutenant-governor, secretary of state, auditor, treasurer,
:torney-general, and superintendent of public instruction, all of whom
iall hold their several offices for the term of four years and until their
iccessors are elected and qualified. They shall be chosen by the qual-
.ed electors of this State at the time and places of choosing the mem-
:rs of the general assembly.

§ 18. The governor, chief justice, secretary of state, treasurer, audi-
·r, attorney-general, and superintendent of public instruction shall
·verally reside, and keep all public records, books, papers, and doc-
nents which may pertain to their respective offices, at the seat of gov-
nment.

§ 19. The returns of every election for governor, lieutenant-governor,
cretary of state, treasurer, auditor, attorney-general, and superin-
udent of public instruction shall be sealed up and transmitted to the
at of government by the returning-officers, and directed to the presid-
g officer of the senate, who, during the first week of the session, shall
·en and publish the same in presence of the members then assembled.
ie person having the highest number of votes shall be declared elected,
it if two or more shall have the highest and equal number of votes
r the same office, one of them shall be chosen by a joint vote of both
iuses. Contested elections shall likewise be determined by both houses
' the general assembly in such manner as is or may hereafter be pre-
ribed by law.

§ 21. The auditor, treasurer, attorney-general, and superintendent of
iblic instruction shall perform such duties as are now or may here-
ter be prescribed by law.

§ 22. In case of the death, impeachment, removal from the State, or other disability of the secretary of state, treasurer, auditor, attorney-general, and superintendent of public instruction, the vacancies in their several offices thus occasioned shall be filled by appointment of the governor, which appointment shall be made for the unexpired terms of said offices, or until said disabilities are removed, or until elections are held to fill said vacancies.

§ 24. The officers of the executive department mentioned in this article shall, at stated times, receive for their services a compensation, to be established by law, which shall not be diminished during the period for which they shall have been elected or appointed.

§ 25. The officers of the executive department and judges of the supreme court shall not be eligible, during the period for which they may have been elected or appointed to their respective offices, to any position in the gift of the qualified electors or of the general assembly of this State.

Article IX.—Education.

SECTION 1. A general diffusion of knowledge and intelligence among all classes being essential to the preservation of the rights and liberties of the people, the general assembly shall establish and maintain a system ✓ of free schools * for the gratuitous instruction of all persons in this State between the ages of five and twenty-one years ; and the funds appropriated for the support of common schools shall be distributed to the several counties in proportion to the number of children and youths therein between the ages of five and twenty-one years, in such manner as shall be prescribed by law ; but no religious or other sect or sects shall ever have any exclusive right to, or control of, any part of the school-funds of this State.

§ 2. The supervision of public schools shall be vested in a superintendent of public instruction, and such other officers as the general assembly shall provide. The superintendent of public instruction shall receive such salary and perform such duties as shall be prescribed by law.

§ 3. The general assembly shall establish and maintain a State-university, † with departments for instruction in teaching, in agriculture, and the natural sciences as soon as the public-school-fund will permit.

* An act for organizing and maintaining a system of free schools in Arkansas was approved July 23, 1868.—*Acts of the General Assembly of the State of Arkansas,* 1868, pp. 163–197.

† An act establishing an industrial university ,was approved July 23, 1868. It required, in addition to the usual course of study prescribed in universities, that the science and practice of agriculture, the mechanic arts, engineering, and military science should be taught. The location was left to be decided by bids from individuals, counties, cities, townships, incorporated towns, corporations, or otherwise, their offers being open till the first day of the next session of the general assembly.—*Acts of Arkansas,* 1868, p. 323.

By acts approved March 13, 1873, further provision was made with reference to the university, which had been located at Fayetteville, Washington County.—*Acts of Arkansas,* 1871, p. 201; 187. p. 26.

§ 4. The proceeds of all lands that have been, or hereafter may be, granted by the United States to this State, and not otherwise appropriated by the United States or this State; also, all mines, stocks, bonds, lands, and other property now belonging to any fund for purposes of education; also, the net proceeds of all sales of land and other property and effects that may accrue to this State by escheat, or from sales of estrays, or from unclaimed dividends or distributive shares of the estates of deceased persons, or from fines, penalties, or forfeitures; also, any proceeds of the sales of public lands which may have been or may be hereafter paid over to this State, (Congress consenting;) also, all the grants, gifts, or devises that have been or hereafter may be made to this State, and not otherwise appropriated by the terms ot the grant, gift, or devise, shall be securely invested and sacredly preserved as a public-school-fund, which shall be the common property of the State, the annual income of which fund, together with one dollar *per capita*, to be annually assessed on every male inhabitant of this State over the age of twenty-one years, and so much of the ordinary annual revenue of the State as may be necessary, shall be faithfully appropriated for establishing and maintaining the free schools and the university in this article provided for, and for no other use or purposes whatever.

§ 5. No part of the public-school-fund shall be invested in the stocks or bonds or other obligations of any State, or any county, city, town, or corporation. The stocks belonging to any school-fund or university-fund shall be sold in such manner and at such times as the general assembly shall prescribe, and the proceeds thereof, and the proceeds of the sales of any lands or other property which now belong or may hereafter belong to said school-fund, may be invested in the bonds of the United States.

§ 6. No township or school-district shall receive any portion of the school-fund unless a free school shall have been kept therein for not less than three months during the year for which distribution thereof is made. The general assembly shall require by law that every child, of sufficient mental and physical ability, shall attend the public schools, during the period between the ages of five and eighteen years, for a term equivalent to three years, unless educated by other means.

§ 7. In case the public-school-fund shall be insufficient to sustain a free school at least three months in every year in each school-district in this State, the general assembly shall provide by law for raising such deficiency by levying such tax upon all taxable property in each county, township, or school-district as may be deemed proper.

§ 8. The general assembly shall, as far as it can be done without infringing upon vested rights, reduce all lands, moneys, or other property used or held for school-purposes in the various counties of this State into the public-school-fund herein provided for.

§ 9. Provision shall also be made, by general laws, for raising such sum or sums of money, by taxation or otherwise, in each school-district as may be necessary for the building and furnishing of a sufficient number of suitable school-houses for the accommodation of all the pupils within the limits of the several school-districts.

Article X.—*Finances, taxation, public debt, and expenditures.*

SECTION 1. The levying of taxes by the poll is grievous and oppressive; therefore the general assembly shall never levy a poll-tax excepting for school-purposes.

§ 2. Laws shall be passed taxing, by a uniform rule, all money-credit investment in bonds, joint-stock-companies, or otherwise; and also all real and personal property according to its true value in money; but burying-grounds, public-school-houses, houses used exclusively for public worship, institutions of purely public charity, and public property used exclusively for any public purpose shall never be taxed.

§ 15. The principal arising from the sale of all lands donated to the State for school purposes shall be paid into the treasury, and the State shall pay interest thereon for the support of schools at the rate of six per cent. per annum.

CALIFORNIA.

CONSTITUTION OF CALIFORNIA, AS ADOPTED IN 1849.

Article IX.—*Education.*

SECTION 1. The legislature shall provide for the election by the people of a superintendent of public instruction, who shall hold his office for three years,* and whose duties shall be prescribed by law, and who shall receive such compensation as the legislature may direct.†

§ 2. The legislature shall encourage, by all suitable means, the promotion of intellectual, scientific, moral, and agricultural improvement. The proceeds of all lands that may be granted by the United States to this State for the support of schools, which may be sold or disposed of, and the five hundred thousand acres of land granted to the new States, under an act of Congress distributing the proceeds of the public lands among the several States of the Union, approved A. D. 1841, and all estates of deceased persons who may have died without leaving a will or heir, and also such per cent. as may be granted by Congress on the sale of lands in this State, shall be and remain a perpetual fund, the interest of which, together with all the rents of the unsold lands, and such other means as the legislature may provide, shall be inviolably appropriated to the support of common schools throughout the State.

§ 3. The legislature shall provide for a system of common schools‡ by which a school shall be kept up and supported in each district at

---

* Changed in 1862 to four years.
† This section was superseded by an amendment adopted in 1862, as subsequently noticed.
‡ A State-board of education was organized by an act approved April 6, 1863.

least three months in every year; and any school-district neglecting to keep up and support such a school may be deprived of its proportion of the interest of the public fund during such neglect.

§ 4. The legislature shall take measures for the protection, improvement, or other disposition of such lands as have been or may hereafter be reserved or granted by the United States, or any person or persons, to the State for the use of a university; and the funds accruing from the rents or sale of such lands, or from any other source, for the purpose aforesaid, shall be and remain a permanent fund, the interest of which shall be applied to the support of said university, with such branches as the public convenience may demand, for the promotion of literature and the arts and sciences, as may be authorized by the terms of such grant. And it shall be the duty of the legislature, as soon as may be, to provide effectual means for the improvement and permanent security of the funds of said university.*

AMENDMENT TO CONSTITUTION OF CALIFORNIA, ADOPTED IN 1862.

Article IX.

SECTION 1. A superintendent of public instruction shall, at the special election for judicial officers to be held in the year 1863, and every four years thereafter, at such special elections, be elected by the qualified voters of the State, and shall enter upon the duties of his office on the first day of December next after his election.

CONNECTICUT.

[This State remained under the colonial charter of 1662 until 1818, when the present constitution was adopted. That instrument gave no express directions or privileges with respect to education, but guaranteed all the rights of English subjects, and very ample powers of self-government, in all things not contrary to the laws and statutes of the realm.]

CONSTITUTION OF CONNECTICUT, AS ADOPTED IN 1818.

Article VIII.—Of Education.

SECTION 1. The charter of Yale College, as modified by agreement with the corporation thereof, in pursuance of an act of the general assembly, passed in May, 1792, is hereby confirmed. †

---

* A State-university was organized by act approved March 23, 1868, pursuant to this section of the constitution, and to consist of, first, colleges of arts; secondly, a college of letters; and, thirdly, such professional and other colleges as might be added thereto or connected therewith. The colleges of arts were to consist of the following: A State-college of agriculture; a State-college of mechanic arts; a State-college of mines; a State-college of civil engineering, and such other colleges of arts as the board of regents might be able, and find it expedient, to establish. The third class was to embrace colleges of medicine, law, and other like professional colleges. The university has been located at Oakland.

† "An act for enlarging the powers and increasing the funds of Yale College" appointed William Hart, John Trumbull, and Andrew Kingsbury as commissioners, to

§ 2. The fund called the *school-fund** shall remain a perpetual fund, the interest of which shall be inviolably appropriated to the support and encouragement of the public or common schools throughout the State, and for the equal benefit of all the people thereof. The value and amount of said fund shall, as soon as practicable, be ascertained in such manner as the general assembly may prescribe, published, and recorded in the comptroller's office; and no law shall ever be made authorizing said fund to be diverted to any other use than the encoagement and support of public or common schools, among the several school-societies, as justice and equity shall require.

AMENDMENT ADOPTED IN OCTOBER, 1855.

Article XI.

Every person shall be able to read any article of the constitution, or any section of the statutes of this State, before being admitted as an elector.

DELAWARE.

CONSTITUTION OF DELAWARE, AS AMENDED IN 1792.

Article VIII.

SECTION 12. The legislature shall, as soon as conveniently may be, provide by law, for * * * * establishing schools and promoting arts and sciences. †

[The same continued in the amended constitution of 1831, as a part of Article VII, § 11.]

---

perform certain duties specified with regard to balances due to the State, which were appropriated to Yale College upon condition of the acceptance, on the part of the president and corporation, of certain modifications in their corporate powers, of which legal evidence was to be filed in the office of the secretary of state.

An additional act was passed May, 1796, by which a claim of 50 per cent. of sums collected on certain balances was relinquished to the college on condition that the latter should transfer $13,726.39 in deferred stock of the United States to the State-treasurer. The president and corporation were by this act required to report annually to the general assembly an account of receipts and expenditures of the moneys belonging to the college.

* The school-fund of Connecticut was established May, 1795, from moneys arising from the sale of the lands known as the Western Reserve in Northern Ohio. The capital of this fund amounted on the 2d day of September, 1872, to $2,044,190.81, of which the sum of $204,812.61 was invested in bank-stocks, $130,000 in State-bonds $1,683,211.69 in contracts, bonds, and mortgages against individuals residing in Connecticut, Massachusetts, New York, and Ohio, and the remainder was in cash. The disbursements for the year ended March 31, 1874, amounted to $144,043.21, including a dividend of $1 *per capita* to 133,530 children entitled to its benefits. The fund is managed by commissioners, who report its condition annually to the general assembly, with details of investment and expenditure.

† An act was passed February 9, 1796, to create a fund, sufficient to establish schools in this State, from marriage- and tavern-licenses until 1806, and such other money and estate as might thereafter be granted for this purpose. The State-treasurer was constituted the trustee of this fund and his powers and duties defined.

FLORIDA.

CONSTITUTION OF FLORIDA, PREPARED IN 1839; IN FORCE FROM 1845.

Article X.—Education.

The proceeds of all lands granted by the United States for the use of schools shall remain a perpetual fund, the interest of which shall be used for the benefit of said schools, and for no other purpose.*

CONSTITUTION OF FLORIDA, AS AMENDED IN 1861.

Article X.—Education.

SECTION 1. The proceeds of all lands that have been granted by the United States for the use of schools and a seminary or seminaries of learning shall be and remain a perpetual fund, the interest of which, together with all moneys, derived from any other source, applicable to the same object, shall be inviolably appropriated to the use of schools and seminaries of learning, respectively, and to no other purpose.

§ 2. The general assembly shall take such measures as may be necessary to preserve from waste or damage all land so granted and appropriated to the purposes of education.

CONSTITUTION OF FLORIDA, AS AMENDED IN 1865.

Article X.—Education.

SECTION 1. The proceeds of all lands for the use of schools and a seminary or seminaries of learning shall be and remain a perpetual fund, the interest of which, together with all moneys accrued from any other source, applicable to the same object, shall be irrevocably appropriated to the use of schools and seminaries of learning, respectively, and to no other purpose.

§ 2. The general assembly shall take such measures as may be necessary to preserve from waste or damage all lands so granted or appropriated for the purpose of education.

CONSTITUTION OF FLORIDA, AS AMENDED IN 1868.

Article IV.

SECTION 22. The legislature shall provide by general law for incorporating such municipal, educational, mechanical, mining, and other useful companies or associations as may be deemed necessary.

---

* The register of the land-office had previously been charged with the duty of selecting the various lands that had been or might be granted to Florida for the seminaries of learning.—*Act of December* 26, 1835.

By an act passed March 15, 1843, the sheriffs of the several counties were declared to be commissioners of the school-fund in their several counties, and the governor was directed to appoint five "trustees of the seminary-lands," and their duties were defined.

Article V.—Executive department.

SECTION 17. The governor shall be assisted by a cabinet of administrative officers, consisting of a secretary of state, attorney-general, comptroller, treasurer, surveyor-general, superintendent of public instruction, adjutant-general, and commissioner of immigration. Such officers shall be appointed by the governor and confirmed by the senate, and shall hold their offices the same time as the governor,* or until their successors shall be qualified.

§ 19. *   *   *   * The governor shall appoint in each county a county-treasurer, county-surveyor, and county-superintendent of common schools, and five county-commissioners, each of whom shall hold his office for two years, and the duties of each shall be prescribed by law. Such officers shall be subject to removal by the governor, when in his judgment the public welfare will be advanced thereby : *Provided,* No officer shall be removed except for willful neglect of duty, or a violation of the criminal-laws of the State, or for incompetency.

§ 20. The governor and cabinet shall constitute a board of commissioners of State-institutions, which board shall have supervision of all matters connected therewith, in such manner as shall be prescribed by law.

Article VII.—Administrative department.

SECTION 1. There shall be a cabinet of administrative officers, consisting of a secretary of state, attorney-general, comptroller, treasurer, surveyor-general, superintendent of public instruction, adjutant-general, and commissioner of immigration, who shall assist the governor in the performance of his duties.

§ 7. The superintendent of public instruction shall have the administrative supervision of all matters pertaining to public instruction, the supervision of buildings devoted to educational purposes, and the libraries belonging to the university and common schools. He shall organize a historical bureau for the purpose of accumulating such matter and information as may be necessary for compiling and perfecting the history of the State. He shall also establish a cabinet of minerals and other natural productions.

§ 10. Each officer of the cabinet shall make a full report of his official acts, of the receipts and expenditures of his office, and of the requirements of the same, to the governor at the beginning of each regular session of the legislature, or whenever the governor shall require it. Such reports shall be laid before the legislature by the governor at the beginning of each regular session thereof. Either house of the legislature may, at any time, call upon any cabinet-officer for any information required by it.

---

* Four years.

Article VIII.—Education.

SECTION 1. It is the paramount duty of the State to make ample provision for the education of all the children residing within its borders, without distinction or preference.

§ 2. The legislature shall provide a uniform system of common schools and a university, and shall provide for the liberal maintenance of the same. Instruction in them shall be free.

§ 3. There shall be a superintendent of public instruction, whose term of office shall be four years, and until the appointment and qualification of his successor. He shall have general supervision of the educational interests of the State. His duties shall be prescribed by law.

§ 4. The common-school-fund, the interest of which shall be exclusively applied to the support and maintenance of common schools and purchase of suitable libraries and apparatus therefor, shall be derived from the following sources: The proceeds of all lands that have been or may hereafter be granted to the State by the United States for educational purposes; donations by individuals for educational purposes; appropriations by the State; the proceeds of lands or other property which may accrue to the State by escheat or forfeiture; the proceeds of all property granted to the State, when the purpose of such grant shall not be specified; all moneys which may be paid as an exemption from military duty; all fines collected under the penal laws of this State; such portion of the *per apita* tax as may be prescribed by law for educational purposes; twenty-five per centum of the sales of public lands which are now or which hereafter may be owned by the State.

§ 5. A special tax of not less than one mill on the dollar of all taxable property in the State, in addition to the other means provided, shall be levied and appropriated annually for the support and maintenance of common schools.

§ 6. The principal of the common-school-fund shall remain sacred and inviolate.

§ 7. Provision shall be made by law for the distribution of the common-school-fund among the several counties in the State, in proportion to the number of children residing therein between the ages of four and twenty-one years.

§ 8. Each county shall be required to raise annually, by tax, for the support of common schools therein, a sum not less than one-half of the amount apportioned to each county for that year from the income of the common-school-fund. Any school-district neglecting to establish and maintain for at least three months in each year, such school or schools as may be provided by law for such district, shall forfeit its portion of the common-school-fund during such neglect.

§ 9. The superintendent of public instruction, secretary of state, and attorney-general shall constitute a body-corporate, to be known as the

Board of Education of Florida. The superintendent of public instruction shall be the president thereof. The duties of the board of education shall be prescribed by the legislature.

Article XII.—Taxation and finance.

SECTION 1. The legislature shall provide for a uniform and equal rate of taxation, and shall prescribe such regulations as shall secure a just valuation of all property, both real and personal, excepting such property as may be exempted by law, for municipal, educational, literary, scientific, religious, or charitable purposes.

Article XVI.—Miscellaneous.

SECTION 4. The salary of * * * each cabinet-officer shall be $3,000.*

§ 5. The salary of each officer shall be payable quarterly, upon his own requisition.

§ 15. The governor, cabinet, and supreme court shall keep their offices at the seat of government. But in case of invasion or violent epidemics the governor may direct that the offices of the government shall be removed temporarily to some other place. The session of the legislature may be adjourned for the same reason to some other place; but in such case of removal all the departments of the government shall be removed to one place. But such removal shall not continue longer than the necessity for the same shall continue.

§ 27. The property of all corporations, whether heretofore or hereafter incorporated, shall be subject to taxation, unless such corporation be for religious, educational, or charitable purposes.

GEORGIA.

CONSTITUTION OF GEORGIA, AS ADOPTED IN 1777.

LIV. Schools shall be erected in each county, and supported at the general expense of the State, as the legislature shall hereafter point out.

[The above was not continued in the revision of 1789, educational affairs being left without mention, subject to such regulation as the general assembly might deem necessary and proper, it being authorized to pass all laws for the good of the State, and not repugnant to the constitution.]

CONSTITUTION OF GEORGIA, AS AMENDED IN 1798.

Article IV.

SECTION 13. The arts and sciences shall be promoted in one or more seminaries of learning, and the legislature shall, as soon as con-

---

* Reduced to $2,000 by an amendment ratified in 1871.

niently may be, give such further donations and privileges to those
ready established,* as may be necessary to secure the objects of
eir institution; and it shall be the duty of the general assembly, at
eir next session, to provide effectual measures for the improvement
d permanent security of the funds and endowments of such institu-
ons.

CONSTITUTION OF GEORGIA, AS AMENDED IN 1868.

Article VI.—Education.

SECTION 1. The general assembly, at its first session after the adop-
n of this constitution, shall provide a thorough system of general
ucation,† to be forever free to all children of the State, the expense
which shall be provided for by taxation or otherwise.

§ 2. The office of State-school-commissioner is hereby created. He
all be appointed by the governor, with the consent of the senate,
d shall hold his office for the same term as the governor. The gen-
l assembly shall provide for the said commissioner a competent salary
d necessary clerks. He shall keep his office at the seat of govern-
nt.

ILLINOIS.

ORDINANCE ADOPTED BY THE CONVENTION WHICH FORMED THE
CONSTITUTION OF ILLINOIS, AUGUST 26, 1818.

Whereas the Congress of the United States, in the act entitled "An
to enable the people of the Illinois Territory to form a constitution
l State-government, and for the admission of such State into the
ion on an equal footing with the original States," passed the 18th of
ril, 1818,‡ have offered to this convention, for their free acceptance or
ection, the following propositions, which, if accepted by the conven-
n, are to be obligatory upon the United States, viz:

'1st. That section numbered sixteen, in every township, and when
h section has been sold or otherwise disposed of, other lands equiva-
t thereto, and as contiguous as may be, shall be granted to the State,
the use of the inhabitants of such township, for the use of schools.

'2d. That all salt-springs within such State, and the lands reserved
the use of the same, shall be granted to the said State for the use of

---

Acts were passed in July, 1783, and February, 1784, for the establishment of a seat
earning in Georgia. This object was more fully provided for by an act passed
uary 27, 1785, which created a board of visitors for the general superintendence
regulation of the literature of this State, and in particular of the university.
ther board of trustees was also created, and these two boards united, or a majority
hem, were to compose the "Senatus Academicus of the University of Georgia."

An act to establish a system of public instruction, under this requirement, was
roved July 28, 1870. The former laws regulating common schools and school-funds
given in *Irwin's Revised Code*, sections 1269 to 1302 inclusive.

Statutes at Large, III, 428.

the said State, and the same to be used under such terms and conditions and regulations as the legislature of said State shall direct, provided the legislature shall never sell nor lease the same for a longer term than ten years at any one time.

"3d. That 5 per cent. of the net proceeds of the land lying within such State, and which shall be sold by Congress from and after the 1st day of January, 1819, after deducting all expense incident to the same, shall be reserved for the purposes following, viz: Two-fifths to be disbursed under the direction of Congress, in making roads leading to the State, the residue to be appropriated by the legislature of the State for the encouragement of learning, of which one-sixth part shall be exclusively bestowed on a college or university.

"4th. That thirty-six sections, or one entire township, which shall be designated by the President of the United States, together with the one heretofore reserved for that purpose, shall be reserved for the use of a seminary of learning, and vested in the legislature of the said State, to be appropriated solely to the use of such seminary by the said legislature."

And whereas the foregoing propositions are offered on the condition that this convention shall provide by ordinance, irrevocable without the consent of the United States, that every and each tract of land sold by the United States from and after the 1st day of January, 1819, shall remain exempt from any tax laid by order or under the authority of the State, whether for State, county, or township, or any other purpose whatever: *   *   *   *   *   *   *

Therefore this convention, on behalf of and by the authority of the people of the State, do accept of the foregoing propositions;   *
*   *   *   *   * And this convention do further ordain and declare that the foregoing ordinance shall not be revoked without the consent of the United States.   *   *   *

[The constitution of Illinois was revised by a convention and a new form adopted in 1847–'48. The only references made to education in that instrument are the following:]

Article IX.

SECTION 3. The property of the State and counties, both real and personal, and such other property as the general assembly may deem necessary for school, religious, and charitable purposes, may be exempted from taxation.

§ 5. The corporate authorities of counties, townships, school-districts, cities, towns, and villages may be vested with power to assess and collect taxes for corporate purposes, such taxes to be uniform with respect to persons and property within the jurisdiction of the body imposing the same. And the general assembly shall require that all the property within the limits of municipal corporations belonging to individuals shall be taxed for the payment of debts contracted under authority of law.

AMENDMENTS PROPOSED IN 1862, BUT NOT ADOPTED.

[A convention held in this State in 1862 prepared a constitution
hich was rejected by the people. Its article upon *revenue* allowed the
gislature to exempt from taxation such property as it might deem nec-
sary for school, religious, and charitable purposes, by general laws.
s other educational provisions were as follows:]

Article VII.

SECTION 6. The general assembly may provide that all taxes and assessments for
ste, county, city, school, or any other purpose, may be collected by the same person.

Article X.—Education.

SECTION 1. The general assembly shall encourage, by all suitable means, the pro-
tion of intellectual, scientific, moral, and agricultural improvement.

2. The principal of all funds and moneys arising from the sale of lands and other
perty which have been or may hereafter be granted, entrusted, or donated to this
ate for educational purposes shall forever be held inviolate; and the income arising
refrom shall be applied to the support of common schools.

3. The general assembly shall provide for a uniform, thorough, and efficient sys-
a of free schools throughout the State.

4. There shall be a State-superintendent of public instruction, who shall be
cted at the same time and in the same manner as members of the general assembly,
o shall hold his office for two years, and until his successor shall be elected and
alified; whose powers, duties, and compensation shall be prescribed by law; which
npensation shall not be altered during his term of office; and he shall receive no
ser allowance whatever.

CONSTITUTION OF ILLINOIS, AS AMENDED IN 1870.

Article IV.—Legislative department.

SPECIAL LEGISLATION PROHIBITED.

SECTION 22. The general assembly shall not pass local or special
ws in any of the following-enumerated cases, that is to say :

  *   *   *   *   *

oviding for the management of common schools.

  *   *   *   *

Article V.—Executive department.

SECTION 1. The executive department shall consist of a governor,
utenant-governor, secretary of state, auditor of public accounts,
easurer, superintendent of public instruction, and attorney-general,
no shall each, with the exception of the treasurer, hold his office for
e term of four years from the second Monday next after his election,
id until his successor is elected and qualified. They shall, except
e lieutenant-governor, reside at the seat of government during their
rm of office, and keep the public records, books, and papers there,
id shall perform such duties as may be prescribed by law.

ELECTIONS.

§ 3. An election for governor, lieutenant-governor, secretary of state,
auditor of public accounts, and attorney-general shall be held on the

Tuesday next after the first Monday of November, in the year of our Lord 1872, and every four years thereafter; for superintendent of public instruction, on the Tuesday next after the first Monday of November, in the year 1870, and every four years thereafter; and for treasurer, on the day last above mentioned, and every two years thereafter, at such places and in such manner as may be prescribed by law.

§ 5. * * * Neither the governor, lieutenant-governor, auditor of public accounts, secretary of state, superintendent of public instruction, nor attorney-general, shall be eligible to any other office during the period for which they shall have been elected.

STATE-OFFICERS OTHER THAN GOVERNOR AND LIEUTENANT-GOVERNOR.

§ 20. If the office of auditor of public accounts, treasurer, secretary of state, attorney-general, or superintendent of public instruction shall be vacated by death, resignation, or otherwise, it shall be the duty of the governor to fill the same by appointment, and the appointee shall hold his office until his successor shall be elected and qualified, in such manner as may be provided by law. An account shall be kept by the officers of the executive department, and of all the public institutions of the State, of all moneys received or disbursed by them severally, from all sources and for every service performed, and a semi-annual report thereof be made to the governor, under oath; and any officer who makes a false report shall be guilty of perjury and punished accordingly.

§ 21. The officers of the executive department, and of all the public institutions of the State, shall, at least ten days preceding each regular session of the general assembly, severally report to the governor, who shall transmit such report to the general assembly, together with the reports of the judges of the supreme court, of defects in the constitution and laws; and the governor may at any time require information in writing, under oath, from the officers of the executive department, and all officers and managers of State-institutions, upon any subject relating to the condition, management, and expenses of their respective offices.

[Section 23 provides that the officers named in this article shall receive for their services a salary to be established by law,* which shall not be increased or diminished during their official terms, and forbids the taking of other fees, costs, perquisites of office, or other compensation.]

Article VIII.—Education.

SECTION 1. The general assembly shall provide a thorough and efficient system of free schools, whereby all the children of this State may receive a good common-school-education.†

* Salary paid superintendent of public instruction, $3,500.

†An act to establish and maintain a system of free schools was passed, in pursuance of this article, April 1, 1872.—*Laws of Illinois*, 1871–'72, p. 700.

§ 2. All lands, moneys, or other property, donated, granted, or received for school, college, seminary, or university purposes, and the proceeds thereof, shall be faithfully applied to the objects for which such gifts or grants were made.

§ 3. Neither the general assembly nor any county, city, town, township, school-district, or other public corporation, shall ever make any appropriation, or pay from any public fund whatever, anything in aid of any church or sectarian purpose, or to help support or sustain any school, academy, seminary, college, university, or other literary or scientific institution controlled by any church or sectarian denomination whatever; nor shall any grant or donation of land, money, or other personal property ever be made by the State or any such public corporation to any church or for any sectarian purpose.

§ 4. No teacher, State, county, township, or other district school-officer shall be interested in the sale, proceeds, or profits of any book, apparatus, or furniture used or to be used in any school in this State, with which such officer or teacher may be connected, under such penalties as may be provided by the general assembly.

§ 5. There may be a county-superintendent of schools in each county, whose qualifications, powers, duties, compensation, and time and manner of election and term of office shall be prescribed by law.*

Article IX.—Revenue.

SECTION 3. The property of the State, counties, and other municipal corporations, both real and personal, and such other property as may be used exclusively for agricultural and horticultural societies, for schools, religious, cemetery, and charitable purposes, may be exempted from taxation, but such exemption shall be only by general laws.

[Section 12 forbids county, city, township, school-district, or other municipal corporations from becoming indebted more than 5 per cent. on the value of taxable property therein, and further provides as follows:] "Any county, city, township, school-district, or other municipal corporation incurring any indebtedness as aforesaid, shall, before or at the time of doing so, provide for the collection of a direct annual tax sufficient to pay the interest on such debt as it falls due, and also to pay and discharge the principal thereof within twenty years from the time of contracting the same."

[This section was not to be construed to prevent any county, city, township, school-district, or other municipal corporation from issuing its bonds in compliance with a vote of the people taken prior to the adoption of this constitution and in pursuance of law.]

---

* The school-law of 1871 provides for the election in 1873, and every four years thereafter, of a county-superintendent of schools, as authorized by the above constitutional provision.

INDIANA.

CONSTITUTION OF INDIANA, ADOPTED IN 1816.

Article IX.

SECTION 1. Knowledge and learning generally diffused through a community being essential to the preservation of a free government, and spreading the opportunities and advantages of education through the various parts of the country being highly conducive to this end, it shall be the duty of the general assembly to provide by law for the improvement of such lands as are or hereafter may be granted by the United States to this State for the use of schools, and to apply any funds which may be raised from such lands, or from any other quarter, to the accomplishment of the grand object for which they are or may be intended. But no lands granted for the use of schools or seminaries of learning shall be sold by authority of this State prior to the year 1820; and the moneys which may be raised out of the sale of any such lands, or otherwise obtained for the purposes aforesaid, shall be and remain a fund for the exclusive purpose of promoting the interests of literature and the sciences, and for the support of seminaries and the public schools. The general assembly shall, from time to time, pass such laws as shall be calculated to encourage intellectual, scientifical, and agricultural improvement, by allowing rewards and immunities for the promotion of the arts, sciences, commerce, manufactures, and natural history, and to countenance and encourage the principles of humanity, industry, and morality.

§ 2. It shall be the duty of the general assembly, as soon as circumstances will permit, to provide by law for a general system of education, ascending in regular gradation from township-schools to State university, wherein tuition shall be gratis and equally open to all.*

§ 3. And for the promotion of such salutary end, the money which shall be paid as an equivalent by persons exempt from militia duty, except in times of war, shall be exclusively, and in equal proportions, applied to the support of county-seminaries; also all fines assessed for any breach of the penal laws shall be applied to said seminaries in the counties wherein they shall be assessed.

* * * * * * *

§ 5. The general assembly, at the time they lay off a new county, shall cause at least 10 per cent. to be reserved out of the proceeds of the sale of town-lots in the seat of justice of such county, for the use of a public library for such county; and at the same session they shall incorporate a library-company, under such rules and regulations as will best secure its permanence and extend its benefits.

---

* Acts were passed January 31, 1824, providing for public schools in congressional townships and seminaries in counties. The law relating to township-schools was revised in 1831.

Extract from an ordinance passed by the convention for preparing the constitution of Indiana in 1816.

"*Be it ordained,* • • • That we do, for ourselves and our posterity, gree, determine, declare, and ordain that we will, and do hereby, accept the propositions of the Congress of the United States as made and contained in their act of the 19th day of April, 1816, entitled " An act to enable the people of the Indiana Territory to form a State-government and constitution, and for the admission of such State into the Union on an equal footing with the original States."•

CONSTITUTION OF INDIANA, AS AMENDED IN 1851.

[Among the restrictions upon legislation imposed by § 22, Art. IV, of the constitution of Indiana (1851) is the following:]

"The general assembly shall not pass local or special laws in any of the following-enumerated cases, that is to say:
•   •   •   •   •   •   •

"Providing for supporting common schools and for the preservation of school-funds."
•   ‹

Article VIII.—Education.

SECTION 1. Knowledge and learning generally diffused throughout a community being essential to the preservation of a free government, it shall be the duty of the general assembly to encourage, by all suitable means, moral, intellectual, scientific, and agricultural improvement, and to provide by law for a general and universal system of common schools, wherein tuition shall be without charge and equally open to all.

§ 2. The common-school-fund shall consist of the congressional-township-fund and the lands belonging thereto; the surplus-revenue-fund;† the saline-fund, ‡ and the lands belonging thereto; the bank-tax-fund,

---

• These conditions, so far as concerned educational affairs, were as follows:

First. That the section numbered sixteen in every township, and, when such section as been sold, granted, or disposed of, other lands equivalent thereto, and most contiguous to the same, shall be granted to the inhabitants of such township for the use of schools.

Fourth. That one entire township, which shall be designated by the President of the United States, in addition to the one heretofore reserved for that purpose, shall be reserved for the use of a seminary of learning, and vested in the legislature of the said State, to be appropriated solely to the use of such seminary by the said legislature.— *United States Statutes at Large*, III, 289.

† Known in some States as the " United States deposit-fund."

‡ Derived from a grant of Congress to the State, upon the passage of an enabling-act, in 1816, which gave all salt-springs within the Territory of Indiana, and the land reserved for the use of the same, together with such other lands as might by the President of the United States be deemed necessary and proper for working them, not exceeding in all thirty-six entire sections of land. It was to be used under such terms,

and the fund arising from the one hundred and fourteenth section of the charter of the State Bank of Indiana;[*] the fund to be derived from the sale of county-seminaries,[†] and the money and property heretofore held for such seminaries; from the fines assessed for breaches of the penal laws of the State, and from all forfeitures which may accrue; all lands and other estate which shall escheat to the State for the want of heirs or kindred entitled to the inheritance; all lands that have been, or may hereafter be, granted to the State, where no special purpose is expressed in the grant, and the proceeds of the sales thereof, including the proceeds of the sales of the swamp-lands granted to the State of Indiana by the act of Congress of 28th of September, 1850,[‡] after deducting the expense of selecting and draining the same; taxes on the property of corporations that may be assessed for common-school-purposes.

§ 3. The principal of the common-school-fund shall remain a perpetual fund, which may be increased, but shall never be diminished; and the income thereof shall be inviolably appropriated to the support of common schools, and to no other purpose whatever.

§ 4. The general assembly shall invest, in some safe and profitable manner, all such portions of the common-school-fund as have not here-

conditions, and regulations as the legislature might direct, but was not to be sold nor leased longer than ten years at a time.—*Statutes at Large*, III, 290.

Permission was granted by Congress for the sale of the school-lands of Indiana, by an act approved May 24, 182?.—*Statutes at Large*, IV, 298.

Permission was further given, by an act approved July 21, 1852, for the sale of unsold saline lands.—*Ibid.*, X, 15.

* The bank-charter, approved January 28, 1834, provided for the creation of a sinking-fund, consisting of unapplied balances of loans procured on the part of the State for its stock in the State Bank, or for the purpose of being loaned to stockholders to enable them to meet their stock-installments in the bank; the semi-annual payments of interest on the State-loans to stockholders, and the sums that might be received in payment of said loans; the dividends that might be declared and paid by the State Bank on the State-stock, and the dividends accruing on such portions of the stock belonging to the other stockholders as shall have been paid for by the loan on the part of the State, and which shall not have been repaid by such stockholders. The principal and interest on this sinking-fund was to be reserved and set apart for the purpose of liquidating and paying off the loan or loans, and the interest thereon, that might be negotiated on the part of the State for the payment of its stock in the State Bank, and the second and third installments on the shares of the other stockholders in said bank, and for no other purpose, until said loans, and the interest thereon, and incidental expenses, were paid; after which the residue of said fund was to be appropriated to the cause of common-school-education, in such manner as the general assembly might thereafter direct.

† An act approved June 12, 1852, provided for the sale of county-seminaries and the property belonging thereto, and for the transfer of the proceeds thereof to the common-school-fund, after deducting advances made to individuals and for the repayment of such advances. The sale was to be made by the county-treasurer and county-auditor, or the clerk of the circuit-court doing the business of the county-auditor, upon notice and in manner specified.—*Revised Statutes of Indiana*, 1851, I, 437.

‡ *Statutes at Large*, IX, 519. The total amount of swamp-lands granted to the State of Indiana, up to September 30, 1871, was 1,354,732 acres.—*Report of the Secretary of the Interior*, 1871-'72.

fore been intrusted to the several counties, and shall make such pro-
sion by law for the distribution among the several counties of the
terest thereof.*

§ 5. If any county shall fail to demand its proportion of such interest
· common-school-purposes, the same shall be re-invested for the benefit
such county.

§ 6. The several counties shall be held liable for the preservation of
much of the said fund as may be intrusted to them and for the pay-
·nt of the annual interest thereon.

§ 7. All funds held by the State shall remain inviolate, and be faith-
ly and exclusively applied to the purposes for which the trust was
·ated.

§ 8. The general assembly shall provide for the election, by the voters
the State, of a State-superintendent of public instruction, who shall
ld his office for two years and whose duties and compensation shall
prescribed by law.

Article X.—Finance.

Section 1. The general assembly shall provide by law for a uniform
·d equal rate of assessment and taxation, and shall prescribe such regula-
·ns as shall secure a just valuation for taxation of all property, both
al and personal, excepting such only, for municipal, educational, liter-
y, scientific, religious, or charitable purposes, as may be specially
empted by law.

IOWA.

[The first constitution prepared for this State, in the autumn of 1844,
fore an enabling-act had been passed by Congress, did not prove
ceptable to the people, and was defeated by a vote of 7,235 to 7,656.
· article upon education was as follows :]

Article X.—Education and school-lands.

Section 1. The legislature, by joint vote, shall appoint a superintendent of public
truction, who shall hold his office for three years, and whose duty shall be prescribed
law, and who shall receive such compensation as the legislature may direct.

· 2. The legislature shall encourage, by all suitable means, the promotion of intel-
tual, scientific, moral, and agricultural improvement. The proceeds of all lands
·t have been, or hereafter may be, granted by the United States to this State for the
·port of schools which shall hereafter be sold or disposed of, and the 500,000 acres
land granted to the new States under an act of Congress distributing the proceeds
the public lands among the several States of the Union, approved A. D. 1841, and
estates of deceased persons who may have died without leaving a will or heirs, and
o such per cent. as may be granted by Congress on the sale of lands in this State,
·ll be and remain a perpetual fund, the interest of which, together with all the rents
the unsold lands, shall be inviolably appropriated to the support of schools through-
·t the State.

· 3. The legislature shall provide for a system of common schools, by which a school
·ll be kept up and supported in each school-district at least three months in every

---

* Provision was made for this investment in an act approved June 14, 1852.—*Revised*
statutes of Indiana, 1852, I, 439.

year; and any school-district neglecting to keep up and support such a school may be deprived of its equal proportion of the interest of the public fund during such neglect.

§ 4. As soon as the circumstances of the State will permit, the legislature shall provide for the establishment of libraries, one at least in each township; and the money which shall be paid by persons as an equivalent for exemption from military duty, and the clear proceeds of all fines assessed in the several counties for any breach of the penal laws shall be exclusively applied to the support of said libraries.

§ 5. The legislature shall take measures for the protection, improvement, or other disposition of such lands as have been or may hereafter be reserved or granted by the United States, or any person or persons, to this State for the use of a State-university; and the funds accruing from the rents or sale of such lands, or from any other source, for the purpose aforesaid, shall be and remain a permanent fund for the support of said university, with such branches as the public convenience may hereafter demand for the promotion of literature, the arts and sciences, as may be authorized by the terms of such grant; and it shall be the duty of the legislature, as soon as may be, to provide effectual means for the improvement and permanent security of the funds of said university.

CONSTITUTION OF IOWA, AS ADOPTED IN 1846.

Article X.—Education and school-lands.

SECTION 1. The general assembly shall provide for the election, by the people, of a superintendent of public instruction, who shall hold his office for three years, and whose duties shall be prescribed by law and who shall receive such compensation as the general assembly may direct.

§ 2. The general assembly shall encourage, by all suitable means, the promotion of intellectual, scientific, moral, and agricultural improvement. The proceeds of all lands that have been or hereafter may be granted by the United States to this State for the support of schools, which shall hereafter be sold or disposed of, and the five hundred thousand acres of land granted to the new States under an act of Congress distributing the proceeds of the public lands among the several States of the Union, approved A. D. 1841, and all estates of deceased persons who may have died without leaving a will or heir, and also such per cent. as may be granted by Congress on the sale of lands in this State shall be and remain a perpetual fund, the interest of which, together with all the rents of the unsold lands, and such other means as the general assembly may provide, shall be inviolably appropriated to the support of common schools throughout the State.

§ 3. The general assembly shall provide for a system of common schools, by which a school shall be kept up and supported in each school-district at least three months in every year; and any school-district neglecting to keep up and support such school may be deprived of its proportion of the interest of the public fund during such neglect.

§ 4. The money which shall be paid by persons as an equivalent for exemption from military duty, and the clear proceeds of all fines collected in the several counties for any breach of the penal laws, shall be exclusively applied, in the several counties in which such money is paid lne collected, among the several school-districts of said counties, in proportion to the number of inhabitants in such districts, to the port of common schools or the establishment of libraries, as the gen-assembly shall, from time to time, provide by law.

5. The general assembly shall take measures for the protection, im-vement, or other disposition of such lands as have been or may here-r be reserved or granted by the United States, or any person or per-s, to this State, for the use of a university ; and the funds accruing n the rents or sale of such lands, or from any other source, for the pose aforesaid, shall be and remain a permanent fund, the interest hich shall be applied to the support of said university, with such nches as the public convenience may hereafter demand, for the pro-ion of literature, the arts and sciences, as may be authorized by the us of such grant. And it shall be the duty of the general assembly, oon as may be, to provide effectual means for the improvement and nanent security of the funds of said university.*

CONSTITUTION OF IOWA, AS AMENDED IN 1857.
Article IX.—Education and schools.
First.—Education.

ECTION 1. The educational interests of the State, including common ools and other educational institutions, shall be under the manage-it of a board of education, which shall consist of the lieutenant-gov-or, who shall be the presiding officer of the board and have the cast-vote in case of a tie, and one member to be elected from each judi-district in the State.

2. No person shall be eligible as a member of said board who shall have attained the age of twenty-five years, and shall have been one r a citizen of the State.

3. One member of said board shall be chosen by the qualified elect-f each district, and shall hold the office for the term of four years, until his successor is elected and qualified. After the first election er this constitution, the board shall be divided, as nearly as prac-ble, into two equal classes, and the seats of the first class shall be ited after the expiration of two years, and one-half of the board l be chosen every two years thereafter.

4. The first session of the board of education shall be held at the of government, on the first Monday of December after their elec-; after which the general assembly may fix the time and place of ting.

5. The session of the board shall be limited to twenty days, and but session shall be held in any one year, except upon extraordinary sions, when, upon the recommendation of two-thirds of the board, governor may order a special session.

The objects of the constitution with respect to education are more fully defined by
XII, Chapters 1, 2, and 3, of the Code of Iowa.

§ 6. The board of education shall appoint a secretary, who shall be the executive officer of the board, and perform such duties as may be imposed upon him by the board and the laws of the State. They shall keep a journal of their proceedings, which shall be published and distributed in the same manner as the journals of the general assembly.

§ 7. All rules and regulations made by the board shall be published and distributed to the several counties, townships, and school-districts, as may be provided for by the board, and when so made, published, and distributed, they shall have the force and effect of law.

§ 8. The board of education shall have full power and authority to legislate and make all needful rules and regulations in relation to common schools and other educational institutions that are instituted; to receive aid from the school- or university-fund of this State; but all acts, rules, and regulations of said board may be altered, amended, or repealed by the general assembly; and, when so altered, amended, or repealed, they shall not be re-enacted by the board of education.

§ 9. The governor of the State shall be, *ex officio*, a member of said board.

§ 10. The board shall have no power to levy taxes or make appropriations of money. Their contingent expenses shall be provided for by the general assembly.

§ 11. The State-university shall be established at one place,* without branches at any other place, and the university-fund shall be applied to that institution, and no other.

§ 12. The board of education shall provide for the education of all the youths of the State, through a system of common schools, and such schools shall be organized and kept in each school-district at least three months in each year. Any district, failing for two consecutive years to organize and keep up a school as aforesaid, may be deprived of its portion of the school-fund.

§ 13. The members of the board of education shall each receive the same per diem during the time of their session, and mileage going to and returning therefrom, as members of the general assembly.

§ 14. A majority of the board shall constitute a quorum for the transaction of business; no rule, regulation, or law, for the government of common schools or other educational institutions, shall pass without the concurrence of a majority of all the members of the board, which shall be expressed by the yeas and nays on the final passage. The style of all acts of the board shall be, " Be it enacted by the Board of Education of the State of Iowa."

§ 15. At any time after the year 1863 the general assembly shall have power to abolish or reorganize the board of education, and provide for the educational interests of the State in any other manner that to them shall seem best and proper.

---

* The Iowa State University was chartered in 1857, and organized at Iowa City in 1860.

Second.—*School-funds and school-lands.*

SECTION 1. The educational and school-funds and lands shall be nder the control and management of the general assembly of this tate.

§ 2. The university-lands and the proceeds thereof, and all moneys elonging to said fund, shall be a permanent fund for the sole use of the tate university. The interest arising from the same shall be annually ppropriated for the support and benefit of said university.

§ 3. The general assembly shall encourage, by all suitable means, the romotion of intellectual, scientific, moral, and agricultural improvement. The proceeds of all lands that have been, or hereafter may be, ranted by the United States to this State for the support of schools hich may have been or shall hereafter be sold or disposed of, and the ive hundred thousand acres of land granted to the new States, under n act of Congress distributing the proceeds of the public lands among he several States of the Union, approved in the year of our Lord one housand eight hundred and forty-one, and all estates of deceased persons who may have died without leaving a will or heir, and also such er cent. as has been or may hereafter be granted by Congress on the ale of lands in this State, shall be and remain a perpetual fund, the nterest of which, together with all rents of the unsold lands, and such ther means as the general assembly may provide, shall be inviolably ppropriated to the support of common schools throughout the State.

§ 4. The money which may have been, or shall be, paid by persons as n equivalent for exemption from military duty, and the clear proceeds f all fines collected in the several counties for any breach of the penal aws, shall be exclusively applied, in the several counties in which such noney is paid, or fine collected, among the several school-districts of aid counties, in proportion to the number of youths subject to enumeration in such districts, to the support of common schools or the establishment of libraries, as the board of education shall from time to time rovide.

§ 5. The general assembly shall take measures for the protection, improvement, or other disposition of such lands as have been, or may hereafter be, reserved or granted by the United States, or any person or ersons, to this State, for the use of the university, and the funds accruing from the rents or sales of such lands, or from any other source for he purpose aforesaid, shall be and remain a permanent fund, the interest of which shall be applied to the support of said university for the romotion of literature and the arts and sciences, as may be authorized y the terms of such grant. And it shall be the duty of the general assembly, as soon as may be, to provide effectual means for the improvement and permanent security of the funds of said university.

§ 6. The financial agents of the school-funds shall be the same that by law receive and control the State- and county-revenues for other civil purposes, under such regulations as may be provided by law.

§ 7. The money subject to the support and maintenance of common schools shall be distributed to the districts, in proportion to the number of youths between the ages of five and twenty-one years, in such manner as may be provided by the general assembly.

KANSAS.*

ORDINANCE PRECEDING THE WYANDOTTE CONSTITUTION, ADOPTED IN 1859.

Whereas the Government of the United States is the proprietor of a large portion of the lands included in the limits of the State of Kansas, as defined by this constitution; and whereas the State of Kansas will possess the right to tax said lands for purposes of government and other

---

* Before the adoption of the Wyandotte constitution, three forms of constitution had been prepared, viz:

TOPEKA CONSTITUTION.

[A convention, in the free-State interest, met at Topeka, in October, 1855, and prepared a constitution which was not adopted. It contained the following article:]

Education.—Article VII.

SECTION 1 The principal of all funds arising from the sale or other disposition of lands or other property granted or intrusted to this State for educational and religious purposes, shall forever be preserved inviolate and undiminished, and the income arising therefrom shall be faithfully applied to the specific objects of the original grants or appropriations.

§ 2. The general assembly shall make such provision, by taxation or otherwise, as, with the income arising from the school-trust-fund, will secure a thorough and efficient system of common schools throughout the State; but no religious or other sect or sects shall ever have any exclusive right to, or control of, any part of the school-funds of this State.

§ 3. The general assembly may take measures for the establishment of a university, with such branches as the public convenience may hereafter demand, for the promotion of literature, the arts, science, medical, and agricultural instruction.

§ 4. Provision may be made by law for the support of normal schools, with suitable libraries and scientific apparatus.

LECOMPTON CONSTITUTION.

[A pro-slavery convention reported at Lecompton on the 5th of September, 1857, a form of constitution, which did not receive final sanction. Its educational article was as follows:]

Article XIV.—Education.

SECTION 1. A general diffusion of knowledge being essential to the preservation of the rights and liberties of the people, schools and the means of education shall be forever encouraged in this State.

§ 2. The legislature shall take measures to preserve from waste and damage such lands as have been or hereafter may be granted by the United States, or lands or funds which may be received from other sources, for the use of schools within this State, and shall apply the funds which may arise from such lands, or from any other sources, in in strict conformity with the object of the grant.

§ 3. The legislature shall, as soon as practicable, establish one common school, or

purposes : Now, therefore, be it enacted by the people of Kansas that the right of the State of Kansas to tax such lands is relinquished forever, and the State of Kansas will not interfere with the title of the United States to such lands, nor with any regulation of Congress in relation thereto, nor tax non-residents higher than residents, provided, always, that the following condition be agreed to by Congress :

SECTION 1. Sections unnumbered 16 and 36 in each township in the State, including Indian reservations and trust-lands, shall be granted to the State for the exclusive use of common schools, and when either of said sections, or any part thereof, has been disposed of, other lands of equal value, as nearly contiguous thereto as possible, shall be substituted therefor.

§ 2. That 72 sections of land shall be granted to the State for the erection and maintenance of a State-university.

§ 6. That five per centum of the proceeds of the public land in Kansas,

more, in each township in the State, where the children of the township shall be taught gratis.

§ 4. The legislature shall have power to make appropriations from the State-treasury for the support and maintenance of common schools wherever the funds accruing from the lands donated by the United States, or the funds received from other sources, are insufficient for that purpose.

§ 5. The legislature shall have power to pass laws for the government of all common schools within this State.

LEAVENWORTH CONSTITUTION.

[A third convention, composed of free-soil men, was held at Leavenworth and reported a constitution on the 3d of April, 1858, which also failed to receive recognition. Its educational article was as follows :]

Article VII.—Education.

SECTION 1. The stability and perpetuity of free republican institutions depend upon the intelligence and virtue of the people: Therefore, it is declared to be the duty of the State to establish by law, at the earliest possible period, a uniform system of free schools, in which every child in the State shall be entitled to receive a good common-school-education at the public expense.

§ 2. The principal of all school-funds, from whatever source, shall be the common property of the State, and may be increased, but shall forever be preserved inviolate and undiminished.

§ 3. The income of the school-fund shall be devoted exclusively to the support of schools; and, together with any funds raised in any other manner for school-purposes, shall be distributed through the county or township-treasurer to the several school-districts, in some equitable proportion to the number of children and youth resident therein between the ages of five and twenty-one years

§ 4. The school-lands shall never be sold until such sale is authorized by a free and fair vote of the people of Kansas, but, subject to valuation every three years, may be leased at a per centum established by law.

§ 5. No religious sect or sects shall ever have any right to, or control of, any part of the school funds of this State.

§ 6. The general assembly shall make such provision, by location or otherwise, as, with the income arising from the school-fund, will secure throughout the State the maintenance of a thorough and uniform system of common schools, which shall be kept up and supported in each district at least four months in each year, and shall be

disposed of after the admission of the State into the Union, shall be paid to the State for a fund, the income of which shall be used for the support of common schools.

§ 7. That the 500,000 acres of land to which the State is entitled under the act of Congress entitled "An act to appropriate the proceeds of the sales of public lands and grant pre-emption rights," approved September 4, 1841, shall be granted to the State for the support of common schools.

§ 8. That the lands hereinbefore mentioned shall be selected in such manner as may be prescribed by law; such selections to be subject to the approval of the Commissioner of the General Land-Office of the United States.

CONSTITUTION OF KANSAS, ADOPTED IN 1859.

Article I.—Executive.

SECTION 1. The executive department shall consist of a governor, lieutenant-governor, secretary of state, auditor, treasurer, attorney-general, and superintendent of public instruction, who shall be chosen by the electors of the State, at the time and place of voting for members of the legislature, and shall hold their offices for the term of two years from the second Monday of January next after their election, and until their successors are elected and qualified.

* * * * * *

§ 14. Should either the secretary of state, auditor, treasurer, attorney-general, or superintendent of public instruction become incapable of performing the duties of his office for any of the causes specified in the thirteenth section of this article,* the governor shall fill the vacancy until the disability is removed or a successor is elected and qualified. Every such vacancy shall be filled by election at the first general election that occurs more than thirty days after it shall have happened; and the person chosen shall hold the office for the unexpired term.

§ 15. The officers mentioned in this article shall, at stated times, receive for their services a compensation, to be established by law, which shall neither be increased nor diminished during the period for which they shall have been elected.

---

open and free to every child in the State between the ages of five and twenty-one years.

§ 7. As the means of the State will admit, educational institutions of a higher grade shall be established by law, so as to form a complete system of public instruction, embracing the primary, normal, preparatory, collegiate, and university departments.

§ 8. At the first election of State-officers, and biennially thereafter, the people shall elect a superintendent of public instruction, whose duties and compensation shall be prescribed by law.

§ 9. At the first election of State officers, and biennially thereafter, there shall be elected by the people a commissioner of school-lands, who shall have the charge of the school-lands and the principal of the school-fund, whose duties and compensation shall be prescribed by law.

* Impeachment, displacement, resignation, death, or otherwise.

§ 16. The officers of the executive department, and of all public State-institutions, shall, at least ten days preceding each regular session of the legislature, severally report to the governor, who shall transmit such reports to the legislature.

Article VI.—Education.

SECTION 1. The State-superintendent of public instruction shall have the general supervision of the common-school-funds and educational interests of the State, and perform such other duties as may be prescribed by law. A superintendent of public instruction shall be elected in each county, whose term of office shall be two years and whose duty and compensation shall be prescribed by law.

§ 2. The legislature shall encourage the promotion of intellectual, moral, scientific, and agricultural improvement, by establishing a uniform system of common schools and schools of higher grade, embracing normal, preparatory, collegiate, and university departments.

§ 3. The proceeds of all lands that have been or may be granted by the United States and the State, for the support of schools, and the five hundred thousand acres of land granted to the new States under an act of Congress distributing the proceeds of public lands among the several States of the Union, approved September 4, A. D. 1841, and all estates of persons dying without heir or will, and such per cent. as may be granted by Congress on the sale of lands in this State shall be the common property of the State, and shall be a perpetual school-fund, which shall not be diminished, but the interest of which, together with all the rents of the lands, and such other means as the legislature may provide by law or otherwise, shall be inviolably appropriated to the support of common schools.

§ 4. The income of the State-school-funds shall be distributed annually, by order of the State-superintendent, to the several county-treasurers, and thereon to the treasurers of the several school-districts, in equitable proportion to the number of children and youth resident therein between the ages of five and twenty-one years: *Provided*, That no school-district in which a common school has not been maintained at least three months in each year shall be entitled to receive any portion of such funds.

§ 5. The school-lands shall not be sold unless such sale be authorized by a vote of the people at a general election; but, subject to a revaluation every five years, they may be leased for any number of years not exceeding twenty-five, at a rate established by law.

§ 6. All money which shall be paid by persons as an equivalent for exemption from military duty, the clear proceeds of estrays, ownership of which shall vest in the taker-up, and the proceeds of fines for any breach of the penal laws shall be exclusively applied, in the several counties in which the money is fined or fines collected, to the support of common schools.

§ 7. Provision shall be made by law for the establishment at some eligible and central point of a State-university * for the promotion of literature and the arts and sciences, including a normal and agricultural department. All funds arising from the sale or rents of lands granted by the United States to the State for the support of a State-university, and all other grants, donations, or bequests, either by the State or by individuals, for such purposes, shall remain a perpetual fund, to be called the " university-fund," the interest of which shall be appropriated to the support of the State-university.

§ 8. No religious sect or sects shall ever control any part of the common-school- or university-funds of the State.

§ 9. The State-superintendent of public instruction, secretary of state, and attorney-general shall constitute a board of commissioners for the management and investment of the school-funds. Any two of said commissioners shall be a quorum.

KENTUCKY.

[The constitutions of 1792 and 1799 contained no educational provisions.]

CONSTITUTION OF KENTUCKY, AS AMENDED IN 1850.

Article XI.—Concerning education.

SECTION 1. The capital of the fund called and known as the "common-school-fund," consisting of $1,225,768.42, for which bonds have been executed by the State to the board of education, and $73,500 of stock in the Bank of Kentucky; also, the sum of $51,223.29, balance of interest on the school-fund for the year 1848, unexpended, together with any sum which may be hereafter raised in the State by taxation, or otherwise, for purposes of education, shall be held inviolate, for the purpose of sustaining a system of common schools. The interest and dividends of said funds, together with any sum which may be produced for that purpose by taxation or otherwise, may be appropriated in aid of common schools, but for no other purpose. The general assembly shall invest said $51,223.29 in some safe and profitable manner; and any portion of the interest and dividends of said school-fund, or other money or property raised for school-purposes, which may not be needed in sustaining common schools, shall be invested in like manner.† The general assembly shall make provision by law for the payment of the interest of said school-fund: *Provided*, That each county shall be entitled to its proportion of the income of said fund; and, if not called for for common-school-purposes, it shall be re-invested from time to time for the benefit of such county.

* A State-university was incorporated at Lawrence, Kans., in 1864. It reported in 1873 a corps of 11 instructors and an attendance of 81 male and 77 female students.

† The receipts of the school-fund of Kentucky for the year ended October 10, 1871, were $859,700.62; balance in treasury at beginning of year, $70,586.80; total, $930,287.72. The details of investment, receipts, and expenditures are reported annually by the auditor of public accounts.

2. A superintendent of public instruction shall be elected by the
lified voters of this Commonwealth, at the same time the governor
elected, who shall hold his office for four years, and his duties and
ry shall be prescribed and fixed by law.

LOUISIANA.

The first constitution of this State, adopted in 1812, contained no
icational provisions.]

CONSTITUTION OF LOUISIANA, AS AMENDED IN 1845.

Title VII.—Public education.

ARTICLE 133. There shall be appointed a superintendent of public
ication, who shall hold his office for two years. His duties shall be
scribed by law. He shall receive such compensation as the legisla-
e may direct.

ART. 134. The legislature shall establish free public schools through-
t the State, and shall provide means for their support, by taxation on
)perty or otherwise.

ART. 135. The proceeds of all lands heretofore granted by the United
ates to this State for the use or support of schools, and of all lands which
y hereafter be granted or bequeathed to the State, and not expressly
inted or bequeathed for any other purpose, which hereafter may be
iposed of by the State, and the proceeds of the estates of deceased
rsons to which the State may become entitled by law, shall be held
the State as a loan, and shall be and remain a perpetual fund, on
lich the State shall pay an annual interest of six per centum; which
erest, together with all the rents of the unsold lands, shall be appro-
ated to the support of such. schools; and this appropriation shall
nain inviolable.

ART. 136. All moneys arising from the sales which have been made,
may hereafter be made, of any lands heretofore granted by the United
ites to this State, for the use of a seminary of learning, and from any
id of donation that may hereafter be made for that purpose, shall be
l remain a perpetual fund, the interest of which, at six per cent. per
num, shall be appropriated to the support of a seminary of learning for
promotion of literature and the arts and sciences; and no law shall
er be made diverting said fund to any other use than to the establish-
nt and improvement of said seminary of learning.

ART. 137. A university shall be established in the city of New
leans. It shall be composed of four faculties, to wit: one of law, one
medicine, one of the natural sciences, and one of letters.

ART. 138. It shall be called the "University of Louisiana;" and the
edical College of Louisiana, as at present organized, shall constitute
e faculty of medicine.

ART. 139. The legislature shall provide by law for its further organization and government, but shall be under no obligation to contribute to the establishment or support of said university by appropriations.

CONSTITUTION OF LOUISIANA, AS AMENDED IN 1852.

Title VIII.—Public education.

ARTICLE 135. There shall be elected a superintendent of public education, who shall hold his office for the term of two years. His duties shall be prescribed by law, and he shall receive such compensation as the legislature may direct: *Provided*, That the general assembly shall have power, by a vote of the majority of the members elected to both houses, to abolish the said office of superintendent of public education whenever in their opinion said office shall be no longer necessary.[*]

ART. 136. The general assembly shall establish free public schools throughout the State, and shall provide for their support by general taxation on property or otherwise; and all moneys so raised or provided shall be distributed to each parish, in proportion to the number of free white children between such ages as shall be fixed by the general assembly.[†]

ART. 137. The proceeds of all lands heretofore granted by the United States to this State for the use or support of schools, and of all lands which may hereafter be granted or bequeathed to the State, and not expressly granted or bequeathed for any other purpose, which hereafter may be disposed of by the State, and the proceeds of the estates of deceased persons, to which the State may become entitled by law, shall be held by the State as a loan, and shall be and remain a perpetual fund, on which the State shall pay an annual interest of six per cent., which interest, together with the interest on the trust-funds deposited with this State by the United States, under the act of Congress approved June 23, 1836, and all the rents of the unsold lands, shall be appropriated to the support of such schools; and this appropriation shall remain inviolable.

ART. 138. All moneys arising from the sales which have been, or may hereafter be, made of any lands heretofore granted by the United States to this State for the use of a seminary of learning, and from any kind of donation that may hereafter be made for that purpose, shall be and remain a perpetual fund, the interest of which, at six per cent. per annum, shall be appropriated to the support of a seminary of learning, for the promotion of literature and the arts and sciences; and no law shall ever be made diverting said fund to any other use than to the establishment and improvement of said seminary of learning.

---

[*] The office of parish-superintendent of schools was abolished March 18, 1852.

[†] Fixed, by an act approved April 28, 1853, at from six to sixteen years; provided that any white person under twenty-one years of age might have the right of at least two years' tuition under this act.

ART. 139. The University of Louisiana in New Orleans, as now established, shall be maintained.

ART. 140. The legislature shall have power to pass such laws as may be necessary for the further regulation of the university, and for the promotion of literature and science, but shall be under no obligation to contribute to the support of said university by appropriations.

CONSTITUTION OF LOUISIANA, AS AMENDED IN 1864.

Title XI.—Public education.

ART. 140. There shall be elected a superintendent of public education, who shall hold his office for the term of four years. His duties shall be prescribed by law, and he shall receive a salary of $4,000 per annum until otherwise provided by law: *Provided*, That the general assembly shall have power, by a vote of a majority of the members elected to both houses, to abolish the said office of superintendent of public education whenever in their opinion said office shall be no longer necessary.

ART. 141. The legislature shall provide for the education of all children of the State, between the ages of six and eighteen years, by maintenance of free public schools, by taxation or otherwise.

ART. 142. The general exercises in the common schools shall be conducted in the English language.

ART. 143. A university shall be established in the city of New Orleans. It shall be composed of four faculties, to wit: one of law, one of medicine, one of the natural sciences, and one of letters. The legislature shall provide by law for its organization and maintenance.

ART. 144. The proceeds of all lands heretofore granted by the United States to this State, for the use or purpose of the public schools, and of all lands which may hereafter be granted or bequeathed for that purpose, and the proceeds of the estates of deceased persons to which the State may become entitled by law, shall be and remain a perpetual fund, on which the State shall pay an interest of six per cent., which interest, together with the interest of the trust-fund deposited with the State by the United States under the act of Congress approved June 23, 1836, and all the rents of unsold lands, shall be appropriated to the purpose of such schools, and this appropriation shall remain inviolable.

ART. 145. All moneys arising from the sales which have been, or may hereafter be, made of any lands heretofore granted by the United States to this State, for the use of a specific seminary of learning, or from any kind of donation that may hereafter be made for that purpose, shall be and remain a perpetual fund, the interest of which, at six per cent. per annum, shall be appropriated to the promotion of literature and the arts and sciences; and no law shall ever be made diverting said fund to any other use than to the establishment and improvement of said seminary of learning, in such manner as it may deem proper.

ART. 146. No appropriation shall be made by the legislature for the support of any private school or institution of learning; but the highest encouragement shall be granted to public schools throughout the State.

CONSTITUTION OF LOUISIANA, AS AMENDED IN 1868.

Title VII.—Public education.

ART. 135. The general assembly shall establish at least one free public school in every parish throughout the State, and shall provide for its support by taxation or otherwise. All children of this State, between the years of six and twenty-one, shall be admitted to the public schools or other institutions of learning sustained or established by the State in common, without distinction of race, color, or previous condition. There shall be no separate schools or institutions of learning established exclusively for any race by the State of Louisiana.[*]

ART. 136. No municipal corporation shall make any rules or regulations contrary to the spirit and intention of article 135.

ART. 137. There shall be elected by the qualified voters of this State a superintendent of public education, who shall hold his office for four years. His duties shall be prescribed by law, and he shall have the supervision and the general control of all public schools throughout the State. He shall receive a salary of $5,000 per annum, payable quarterly, on his own warrant.

ART. 138. The general exercises in the public schools shall be conducted in the English language.

ART. 139. The proceeds of all lands heretofore granted by the United States for the use and support of public schools, and of all lands or other property which may be granted or bequeathed to the State, and not granted or bequeathed expressly for any other purpose, which may hereafter be disposed of by the State, and the proceeds of all estates of deceased persons to which the State may be entitled by law shall be held by the State as a loan, and shall be and remain a perpetual fund, on which the State shall pay an annual interest of six per cent., which interest, with the interest of the trust-fund deposited with this State by the United States, under the act of Congress approved June the twenty-third, 1836, and the rent of the unsold land, shall be appropriated to the support of such schools; and this appropriation shall remain inviolable.

ART. 140. No appropriations shall be made by the general assembly for the support of any private school or any private institution of learning whatever.

ART. 141. One-half of the funds derived from the poll-tax herein

---

[*] The educational system of Louisiana was remodeled by an act approved March 10, 1869, by which the common schools and such high and normal schools as might be established and maintained by the State were placed under the management of a State board of education, consisting of a superintendent of public education, and one member to be appointed from each congressional district of the State and two from the State at large.—*Acts of Louisiana*, 1869, p. 175.

)vided for shall be appropriated exclusively to the support of the free
blic schools throughout the State and the University of New Orleans.
ART. 142. A university shall be established and maintained in the
y of New Orleans. It shall be composed of a law, a medical, and a
legiate department, each with appropriate faculties. The general
embly shall provide by law for its organization and maintenance :
)vided, That all departments of this institution of learning shall be
:n in common to all students capable of matriculating. No rules or
·ulations shall be made by the trustees, faculties, or other officers of
d institution of learning nor shall any laws be made by the general
embly violating the letter or spirit of the articles under this title.
ART. 143. Institutions for the support of the insane, the education
l support of the blind, and the deaf and dumb, shall always be fos-
ed by the State, and be subject to such regulations as may be
:scribed by the general assembly.

MAINE.

Constitution of Maine, as adopted in 1820.

Article VIII.—Literature.

A general diffusion of education being essential to the promotion of
) rights and liberties of the people; to promote this important object,
' legislature are authorized, and it shall be their duty, to require the
eral towns to make suitable provision, at their own expense, for the
)port and maintenance of public schools; and it shall further be their
ty to encourage and suitably endow, from time to time, as the circum-
nces of the people may authorize, all academies, colleges, and semi-
·ies of learning within the State: *Provided*, That no donation, grant,
endowment shall at any time be made by the legislature to any
·rary institution now established, or which may be hereafter estab-
ied, unless, at the time of making such endowment, the legislature
the State shall have the right to grant any further powers to alter,
it, or restrain any of the powers vested in any such literary institu-
ı as shall be judged necessary to promote the best interests thereof.
The State of Maine, formerly belonging to Massachusetts, was organ-
l by permission of that State, as provided by an act of its legisla-
e passed June 19, 1819, and formally declared by the convention of
ine, October 19, 1819, which act was declared a part of the constitu-
ı of the latter State. Among the provisions of this act of Massachu-
ts was the following:]
Seventh. All grants of lands, franchises, immunities, corporate or other
bts, and all contracts for or grants of land not yet located, which have
n or may be made by the said Commonwealth before the separation
said district shall take place, and having or to have any effect within
, said district, shall continue in full force after the said district shall
:ome a separate State. But the grant which has been made to the
:sident and trustees of Bowdoin College out of the tax laid upon the

banks within this Commonwealth shall be charged upon the banks within the said district of Maine, and paid according to the terms of said grant; and the president and trustees and the overseers of said college shall have, hold, and enjoy their powers and privileges in all respects, so that the same shall not be subject to be altered, limited, annulled, or restrained, except by judicial process, according to the principles of law; and in all grants hereafter to be made, by either State, of unlocated land within the said district, the same reservations shall be made for the benefit of schools and of the ministry as have heretofore been usual in grants made by this Commonwealth. And all lands heretofore granted by this Commonwealth to any religious, literary, or eleemosynary corporation or society shall be free from taxation while the same continues to be owned by such corporation or society."

MARYLAND.

[The charter to Lord Baltimore, granted in 1632, contained no specific mention of schools, but gave very ample powers of government, and under this a system of free schools was enacted in 1696, and more fully provided for in each county in 1732. The constitution of Maryland, adopted in 1776, and its amendments in 1812 and 1835, did not refer to educational subjects.]

CONSTITUTION OF MARYLAND, AS AMENDED IN 1864.

Article VIII.—Education.

SECTION 1. The governor shall, within thirty days after the ratification by the people of this constitution, appoint, subject to the confirmation of the senate at its first session thereafter, a State-superintendent of public instruction, who shall hold his office for five years, and until his successor shall have been appointed and shall have been qualified. He shall receive an annual salary of $2,500, and such additional sum for traveling and incidental expenses as the general assembly may by law provide; shall report to the general assembly, within thirty days after the commencement of its first session under this constitution, a uniform system of free public schools, and shall perform such other duties pertaining to his office as may from time to time be prescribed by law.*

§ 2. There shall be a State-board of education, consisting of the governor, the lieutenant-governor, the speaker of the house of delegates, and the State-superintendent of public instruction, which board shall perform such duties as the general assembly may direct.

---

* A new article was added to the code of public general laws, March 24, 1865, providing a uniform system of free public schools for the State of Maryland and repealing all existing laws inconsistent therewith. A school-system was reported to the house of delegates by the superintendent of public instruction on the 2d day of February, 1868.

§ 3. There shall be in each county such number of school-commis-
oners as the State-superintendent of public instruction shall deem
necessary, who shall perform such duties and receive such compensa-
on as the general assembly or State-superintendent may direct; the
hool-commissioners of Baltimore City shall remain as at present con-
ituted, and shall be apportioned as at present, by the mayor and city-
uncil, subject to such alterations and amendments as may be made
om time to time by the general assembly or the said mayor and city-
uncil.

§ 4. The general assembly, at its first session after the adoption of
is constitution, shall provide a uniform system of free public schools,
y which a school shall be kept open and supported free of expense for
ution in each school-district for at least six months in each year; and,
 case of failure on the part of the general assembly so to provide, the
stem reported to it by the State-superintendent of public instruction
all become the system of free public schools of the State: *Provided*,
hat the report of the State-superintendent shall be in conformity with
e provisions of this constitution, and such system shall be subject to
ch alterations, conformable to this article, as the general assembly
ay from time to time enact.

§ 5. The general assembly shall levy, at each regular session after the
loption of this constitution, an annual tax of not less than ten cents on
ch hundred dollars of taxable property throughout the State, for the
pport of free public schools, which tax shall be collected at the same
me and by the same agents as the general State-levy, and shall be
aid into the treasury of the State, and shall be distributed under such
gulations as may be prescribed by law among the counties and the city
f Baltimore in proportion to their respective populations between the
ges of five and twenty years: *Provided*, That the general assembly
all not levy any additional school-tax upon particular counties, unless
ch county expresses by popular vote its desire for such tax. The city
f Baltimore shall provide for its additional school-tax as at present, or
s may hereafter be provided by the general assembly or by the mayor
nd city-council of Baltimore.

§ 6. The general assembly shall further provide by law, at its present
ssion, after the adoption of this constitution, a fund for the support of
ee public schools of the State, by the imposition of an annual tax of
t less than five cents on each one hundred dollars of taxable property
roughout the State, the proceeds of which tax shall be known as the
blic-school-fund, and shall be invested by the treasurer, together with
s annual interest, until such time as said fund shall by its own increase
d any addition which may be made to it from time to time, together
ith the present school-fund, amount to $6,000,000, when the tax of ten
nts on the one hundred dollars, authorized by the preceding section,
ay be discontinued in whole or in part, as the general assembly may
irect. The principal fund of six millions, herein provided, shall remain

forever inviolate as the free public-school-fund of the State, and the annual interest of said school-fund shall be disbursed for educational purposes only, as may be prescribed by law.

CONSTITUTION OF MARYLAND, AS AMENDED IN 1867.

Article VIII.—Education.

SECTION 1. The general assembly, at its first session after the adoption of this constitution, shall, by law, establish throughout the State a thorough and efficient system of free public schools, and shall provide by taxation or otherwise for their maintenance.*

§ 2. The system of public schools, as now constituted, shall remain in force until the end of the said first session of the general assembly, and shall then expire, except so far as adopted or continued by the general assembly.

§ 3. The school-fund of the State shall be kept inviolate, and appropriated only to the purposes of education.†

MASSACHUSETTS.

[Neither the great charter of New England, granted in 1620, nor the colonial charters of the Plymouth and Massachusetts Bay Colonies, nor the provincial charter of 1691, contained any specific requirements, powers, or privileges in reference to education, the general powers of government being amply sufficient for all occasions that might arise with respect to this object.

The first imperfect draft of a constitution, reported in 1778, but not accepted by the people, was equally silent upon this subject.]

CONSTITUTION OF MASSACHUSETTS, AS ADOPTED IN 1780.

[Extract from Part II of Frame of Government. Chapter V, "The University at Cambridge, and encouragement of literature," &c.]

Article I.—The University.‡

SECTION 1. Whereas our wise and pious ancestors, so early as the year 1636, laid the foundation of Harvard College, in which university

*A new system of free public schools was enacted March 30, 1868, superseding all former laws inconsistent therewith.

† The aggregate of school-money received by the State of Maryland for the year ended September 30, 1873, was $460,539.81, of which $388,566.97 was from the State-school-tax, $58,972.84 from the free-school-fund, and $13,000 from the academic fund.

‡ Mr. John Adams, afterward President of the United States, was the author of this article, which, in its essential features, was afterward incorporated into the constitutions of New Hampshire and Maine. This account of the origin of the thought is given by himself in a statement written in 1809, and quoted in Quincy's History of Harvard University, and more fully in the Life and Works of John Adams, edited by his grandson, Charles Francis Adams, (vol. iv, p. 257.) There were only one or two slight verbal alterations from the draft of its author:

"In traveling from Boston to Philadelphia, in 1774-'5-'6-'7, I had several times amused

many persons of great eminence have, by the blessing of God, been initiated in those arts and sciences which qualified them for public employments, both in church and state; and whereas the encouragement of arts and sciences and all good literature tends to the honor of God, the advantage of the christian religion, and the great benefit of this and the other United States of America, it is declared that the presi-

nyself at Norwalk, Conn., with the very curious collection of birds and insects, of American production, made by Mr. Arnold, a collection which he afterward sold to Jovernor Tryon, who sold it to Sir Ashton Lever, in whose apartments in London I afterward viewed it again. This collection was so singular a thing that it made a deep impression on me, and I could not but consider it a reproach to my country that so little was known even to herself of her natural history.

"When I was in Europe, in the years 1778 and 1779, in the commission to the King of France, with Dr. Franklin and Arthur Lee, I had opportunity to see the King's collection and many others, which increased my wishes that nature might be examined and studied in my own country as it was in others.

"In France, among the academicians and other men of science and letters, I was frequently entertained with inquiries concerning the Philosophical Society at Philadelphia, and with eulogiums on the wisdom of that institution and encomiums on some publications of their transactions.

"These conversations suggested to me the idea of such an establishment in Boston, where I knew there was as much love of science, and as many gentlemen capable of pursuing it, as in any other city of its size.

"In 1779 I returned to Boston in the French frigate La Sensible, with the Chevalier de la Luzerne and Mr. Marbois. The corporation of Harvard College gave a public dinner in honor of the French embassador and his suite, and did me the honor of an invitation to dine with them. At the table, in the philosophy-chamber, I chanced to sit next to Dr. Cooper. I entertained him during the whole of the time we were together with an account of Arnold's collections I had seen in Europe, the compliments I had heard in France upon the Philosophical Society at Philadelphia, and concluded with proposing that the future legislature of Massachusetts should institute an academy of arts and sciences.

"The doctor at first hesitated; thought it would be difficult to find members who would attend it; but his principal objection was that it would injure Harvard College, by setting up a rival to it that might draw the attention and affections of the people in some degree from it. To this I answered, first, that there were certainly men of learning enough that might compose a society sufficiently numerous; and, secondly, that instead of being a rival to the university it would be an honor and advantage to it; that the president and principal professors would undoubtedly be always members of it, and the meetings might be ordered wholly or in part at the college, and in that room. The doctor at length appeared better satisfied, and I entreated him to propagate the idea and the plan as far and as soon as his discretion would justify. The doctor accordingly did diffuse the project so judiciously and effectually, that the first legislature under the constitution adopted and established it by law.*

"Afterward, when attending the convention for framing the constitution, I mentioned the subject to several of the members, and when I was appointed by the sub-committee to make a draft of a project of a constitution, to be laid before the convention, my mind and heart were so full of the subject I inserted Chapter V, section 2.

"I was somewhat apprehensive that criticism and objection would be made to the section, and particularly that the 'natural history' and the 'good humor' would be stricken out, but the whole was received very kindly, and passed the convention unanimously without amendment."

* The American Academy of Arts and Sciences was incorporated May 4, 1780.

4 E

dent and fellows of Harvard College, in their corporate capacity, and
their successors in that capacity, their officers and servants, shall have,
hold, use, exercise, and enjoy all the powers, authorities, rights, liberties, privileges, immunities, and franchises which they now have, or are
entitled to have, hold, use, exercise, and enjoy ; and the same are hereby
ratified and confirmed unto them, the said president and fellows of Harvard College, and to their successors, and to their officers and servants
respectively, forever ;

§ 2. And whereas there have been, at sundry times, by divers persons,
gifts, grants, devises of houses, lands, tenements, goods, chattels, legacies, and conveyances, heretofore made, either to Harvard College, in
Cambridge, in New England, or to the president and fellows of Harvard College, or to the said college by some other description, under
several characters successively, it is declared that all the said gifts,
grants, devises, legacies, and conveyances are hereby forever confirmed
unto the president and fellows of Harvard College, and to their successors,
in the capacity aforesaid, according to the true intent and meaning of the
donor or donors, grantor or grantors, devisor or devisors.

§ 3. And whereas, by an act of the general court of the colony of Massachusetts Bay, passed in the year 1642, the governor and deputy governor,
for the time being, and all the magistrates of that jurisdiction, were, with
the president and a number of the clergy in the said act described, consti
tuted the overseers of Harvard College, and it being necessary in this new
constitution of government to ascertain who shall be deemed successors
to the said governor, deputy governor, and magistrates, it is declared
that the governor, lieutenant-governor, council, and senate of this Commonwealth are, and shall be, deemed their successors, who, with the president of Harvard College for the time being, together with the ministers
of the Congregational churches in the towns of Cambridge, Watertown,
Charlestown, Boston, Roxbury, and Dorchester, mentioned in the said act,
shall be, and hereby are, vested with all the powers and authority belonging or in any way appertaining to the overseers of Harvard College: *Provided*, That nothing herein shall be construed to prevent the legislature
of this Commonwealth from making such alterations in the government
of the said university as shall be conducive to its advantage and the
interest of the republic of letters, in as full a manner as might have been
done by the legislature of the late province of the Massachusetts Bay.

The encouragement of literature.

CHAPTER V, SECTION 2. Wisdom and knowledge, as well as virtue,
diffused generally among the body of the people, being necessary for the
preservation of their rights and liberties, and as these depend on spreading the opportunities and advantages of education in the various parts
of the country, and among the different orders of the people, it shall be
the duty of the legislatures and magistrates, in all future periods of this
Commonwealth, to cherish the interests of literature and the sciences, and

seminaries of them, especially the university at Cambridge, public
ools and grammar schools in the towns; to encourage private socie-
and public institutions by rewards and immunities for the promotion
agriculture, arts, sciences, commerce, trades, manufactures, and a nat-
l history of the country ; to countenance and inculcate the principles
umanity and general benevolence, public and private charity, industry
l frugality, honesty and punctuality in their dealings, sincerity,
d humor, and all social affections and generous sentiments among the
ple.

ENDMENT ADOPTED BY THE LEGISLATURE OF MASSACHUSETTS IN
1856 AND 1857, AND RATIFIED MAY 1, 1857.

ARTICLE XX. No person shall have the right to vote, or to be eligible
office under the constitution of this Commonwealth, who shall not be
e to read the constitution in the English language and write his
ne: *Provided, however*, That the provisions of this amendment shall not
ly to any person prevented by a physical disability from complying
h its requisitions, nor to any person who now has the right to vote,
to any person who shall be sixty years of age or upwards at the time
s amendment shall take effect.

AMENDMENTS PROPOSED IN 1853.

A constitutional convention met in this State in 1853, and submitted
new constitution and a series of amendments of the constitution to
people, all of which were disapproved at an election. The changes
ommended were as follows:]

HAPTER XII, § 1. [Corresponding with Chapter V, of former and present constitution,
cle I as it now stands, with the following addition:] But the legislature shall
ays have full power and authority, as may be judged needful for the advance-
t of learning, to grant any further powers to the president and fellows of Harvard
ege, or to alter, limit, annul, or restrain any of the powers now vested in them:
vided, The obligation of contracts shall not be impaired; and shall have the like
er and authority over all corporate franchises hereafter granted for the purposes
ducation in this Commonwealth.

ARTICLES II and III continued without change. A new article was
posed, as follows:]

RT. IV. It shall be the duty of the legislature, as soon as may be, to provide for
enlargement of the school-fund of the Commonwealth until it shall amount to a
not less than $2,000,000; and the said fund shall be preserved inviolate, and the
me thereof shall be annually appropriated for the aid and improvement of the
mon schools of the State, and for no other purpose.

Chapter V, § 2, continued without change, as § V of Chapter XII
the proposed constitution.

he following proposition was submitted to a separate vote, and de-
ted by a vote of 65,111 to 65,512:]

ROPOSITION NUMBER SIX.—All moneys raised by taxation in the towns and cities
the support of public schools, and all moneys which may be appropriated by the

State for the support of common schools, shall be applied to and expended in no other schools than those which are conducted according to law, under the order and superintendence of the authorities of the town or city in which the money is to be expended, and such money shall never be appropriated to any religious sect, for the maintenance, exclusively, of its own schools.

MICHIGAN.

CONSTITUTION OF MICHIGAN, AS PREPARED IN 1835, AND IN FORCE FROM 1837 TO 1850.

Article X.—Education.

SECTION 1. The governor shall nominate, and by and with the advice and consent of the legislature in joint vote shall appoint, a superintendent of public instruction, who shall hold his office for two years, and whose duties shall be prescribed by law.*

§ 2. The legislature shall encourage, by all suitable means, the promotion of intellectual, scientifical, and agricultural improvement. The proceeds of all lands that have been or hereafter may be granted by the United States to this State, for the support of schools, which shall hereafter be sold or disposed of, shall be and remain a perpetual fund; the interest of which, together with the rents of all such unsold lands, shall be inviolably appropriated to the support of schools throughout the State.

§ 3. The legislature shall provide for a system of common schools, by which a school shall be kept up and supported in each school-district, at least three months in every year; and any school-district neglecting to keep up and support such school may be deprived of its equal proportion of the interest of the public fund.

§ 4. As soon as the circumstances of the State will permit, the legislature shall provide for the establishment of libraries, one at least in each township; and the money which shall be paid by persons as an equivalent for exemption from military duty, and the clear proceeds of all fines assessed in the several counties for any breach of the penal laws, shall be exclusively applied to the support of such libraries.†

§ 6. The legislature shall take measures for the protection, improvement, or other disposition of such lands as have been or may hereafter be reserved or granted by the United States to this State for the support of a university; and the funds accruing from the rents or sale of such lands, or from any other source for the purpose aforesaid, shall be and remain a permanent fund for the support of said university, with such branches as the public convenience may hereafter demand for the promotion of literature, the arts and sciences, and as may be authorized

---

* An act to define the duties of superintendent of public instruction was passed March 28, 1836, in pursuance of this section of the constitution.

† The Revised Statutes of Michigan, adopted in 1846, Title XI, chapter 58, section 114, provide for the organization and management of township-libraries, that might be formed by the board of school-inspectors, under this provision of the constitution.

y the terms of such grant. And it shall be the duty of the legislature, s soon as may be, to provide more effectual means for the improveient and permanent security of the funds of said university.

ORDINANCE ADOPTED BY THE CONVENTION WHICH FORMED THE CONSTITUTION OF MICHIGAN IN 1835.

Be it ordained by the convention assembled to form a constitution for the State of Michigan, in behalf and by authority of the people of said State, that the following propositions be submitted to the Congress of the United States, which, if assented to by that body, shall be obligatory n this State:

1st. Section numbered sixteen in every surveyed township of the public lands, and where such section has been sold or otherwise disposed f, other lands equivalent thereto, and as contiguous as may be, shall e granted to the State for the use of schools.

2d. The seventy-two sections of land set apart and reserved for the se and support of a university, by an act of Congress approved on the 0th day of May, 1826, entitled "An act concerning a seminary of learnng in the Territory of Michigan," shall, together with such further uantities as may be agreed upon by Congress, be conveyed to the State, and shall be appropriated solely to the use and support of such niversity in such manner as the legislature may prescribe.

*　　*　　*　　*　　*　　*　　*

7th. The first Senators and Representatives elected to Congress from his State are hereby authorized and empowered to make or assent to uch other propositions, or to such variations of the propositions herein made, as the interests of the State may require; and any such changes or new propositions, when approved by the legislature, shall be as obigatory as if the assent of this convention were given thereto; and all tipulations entered into by the legislature in pursuance of the authorty herein conferred shall be considered articles of compact between he United States and this State; and the legislature is hereby further uthorized to declare, in behalf of the people of Michigan, if such decaration be proposed by Congress, that they will never interfere with he primary disposal under the authority of the United States of the acant lands within the limits of this State.

CONSTITUTION OF MICHIGAN, AS AMENDED IN 1850.

Article XIII.—Education.

SECTION 1. The superintendent of public instruction shall have the general supervision of public instruction, and his duties shall be prescribed by law.*

§ 2. The proceeds from the sales of all lands that have been, or here-

---

* The duties of this office are prescribed by an act passed April 4, 1851, which took effect July 4 of that year.—*Laws of Michigan,* 1851, p. 116.

after may be, granted by the United States to the State for educational purposes, and the proceeds of all lands or other property given by individuals or appropriated by the State for like purposes, shall be and remain a perpetual fund, the interest and income of which, together with the rents of all such lands as may remain unsold, shall be inviolably appropriated and annually applied to the specific objects of the original gift, grant, or appropriation.

§ 3. All lands the title of which shall fail from a defect of heirs shall escheat to the State ; and the interest on the clear proceeds from the sales thereof shall be appropriated exclusively to the support of primary schools.

§ 4. The legislature shall, within five years from the adoption of this constitution, provide for and establish a system of primary schools, whereby a school shall be kept, without charge for tuition, at least three months in each year, in every school-district in the State, and all instruction in said schools shall be conducted in the English language.

§ 5. A school shall be maintained in each school-district at least three months in each year. Any school-district neglecting to maintain such school shall be deprived for the ensuing year of its proportion of the income of the primary-school-fund, and of all funds arising from taxes for the support of schools.

[§ 6. *There shall be elected in each judicial circuit, at the time of the election of the judge of such circuit, a regent of the university, whose term of office shall be the same as that of such judge. The regents thus elected shall constitute the board of regents of the University of Michigan.]

§ 7. The regents of the university, and their successors in office, shall continue to constitute the body-corporate known by the name and title of "The Regents of the University of Michigan."

§ 8. The regents of the university shall, at their first annual meeting, or as soon thereafter as may be, elect a president of the university, who shall be *ex officio* a member of their board, with the privilege of speaking but not of voting. He shall preside at the meetings of the regents, and be the principal executive officer of the university. The board of regents shall have the general supervision of the university, and the direction and control of all expenditures from the university interest-fund.

§ 9. There shall be elected at the general election in the year 1852 three members of a State board of education, one for two years, one for four years, and one for six years ; and at each succeeding biennial election there shall be elected one member of such board, who shall hold his office for six years. The superintendent of public instruction shall be *ex officio* a member and secretary of such board. The board shall have the general supervision of the State normal school, and their duties shall be prescribed by law.

* This section was superseded in 1861 by an amendment given below.

. Institutions for the benefit of those inhabitants who are deaf,
, blind, or insane, shall always be fostered and supported.

.. The legislature shall encourage the promotion of intellectual,
ific, and agricultural improvement, and shall, as soon as practi-
provide for the establishment of an agricultural school.* The leg-
re may appropriate the twenty-two sections of salt-spring-lands
inappropriated, or the money arising from the sale of the same,
 such lands have been already sold, and any land which may here-
be granted or appropriated for such purpose, for the support and
enance of such school, and may make the same a branch of the
rsity for instruction in agriculture and the natural sciences con-
l therewith, and place the same under the supervision of the regents
 university.

. The legislature shall also provide for the establishment of at
one library in each township; and all fines assessed and collected
 several counties and townships for any breach of the penal laws,
be exclusively applied to the support of such libraries.

IDMENT ADOPTED IN 1861, IN PLACE OF SECTION 6, AS ABOVE
GIVEN.†

There shall be elected in the year 1863, and at the election of a
e of the supreme court, eight regents of the university, two of
 shall hold their office for two years, two for four years, two for
·ars, and two for eight years. They shall enter upon the duties of
office on the first day of January next succeeding their election.
·ery regular election of a justice of the supreme court thereafter,
shall be elected two regents, whose term of office shall be eight
. When a vacancy shall occur in the office of regent, it shall be
by appointment of the governor. The regents thus elected shall
tute the board of regents of the University of Michigan

AMENDMENTS PROPOSED IN 1867.

e constitution of Michigan as amended by convention in 1867 (but
itified) provided for the election of a superintendent of public inion for a term of two years, and for the filling of vacancies in this
by the governor, or by the governor and senate. His salary was
$2,500, unless changed by law, and he was not allowed to receive
ither fees or perquisites. All specific State taxes were to be
·d in paying the interest on primary-school, university, and other
tional funds, and the interest on and principal of the State debt, in
·der here mentioned, until the extinguishment of the State debt,
than the amounts due to educational funds, when such specific

---

 Michigan State Agricultural College was incorporated in 1855, and organized
' at Lansing.
 a amendment was ratified by a vote of 4,363 to 1,901.

taxes were to be added to and constitute a part of the primary-school interest-fund. The educational article was as follows:]

Article XII.—Education.

SECTION 1. Religion, morality, and knowledge being necessary to good government and the happiness of mankind, schools and the means of education shall forever be encouraged.

§ 2. Institutions for the benefit of those inhabitants who are deaf, dumb, blind, or insane, shall always be fostered and supported.

§ 3. The legislature shall provide for a system of primary schools, by which a school shall be maintained in each school-district in the State, free of charge for tuition, at least four months in the year. The instruction shall in all cases be conducted in the English language.

§ 4. The legislature shall provide for the establishment and maintenance of a library in each township, and of at least one in each city. And all moneys belonging to the public derived from fines, penalties, forfeitures, or recognizances imposed or taken in the several counties, cities, or townships, for any breach of the penal laws of the State, after deducting the actual costs of collection, shall be apportioned in the same manner as is the income of the primary-school-fund, and paid over to the several cities and townships of the county in which such money accrued, for the support of such libraries: *Provided,* That the legislature may authorize any township, by a vote of its electors, to apply its portion of said money to the direct support of its primary schools.

§ 5. There shall be elected eight regents of the university, whose term of office shall be eight years, two of whom shall be elected in every second year, on the day of the annual township-election, so as to succeed the regents now in office as their several terms shall expire. When a vacancy shall occur in the office of regent, it shall be filled by appointment by the governor. The chief-justice of the supreme court shall be *ex officio* a member of the board of regents.

§ 6. The regents of the university and their successors in office shall continue to constitute the body-corporate known by the name and title of "The Regents of the University of Michigan."

§ 7. The regents of the university shall, as often as necessary, elect a president of the university, who shall be *ex officio* a member of their board, with the privilege of speaking but not of voting. He shall preside at the meetings of the regents, and be the principal executive officer of the university. The board of regents shall have the general supervision of the university, and the direction and control of all expenditures from the university interest-fund.

§ 8. There shall be elected three members of a State board of education, whose term of office shall be six years, one of whom shall be elected in every second year, at the time of the election of regents of the university. They shall enter upon the duties of their office on the first day of January next succeeding their election. The superintendent of public instruction shall be *ex officio* a member and secretary of such board. The board shall have the general supervision of the State normal school, and their duties shall be prescribed law.

§ 9. The legislature shall provide for the support and maintenance of an agricultural college for instruction in agriculture and the natural sciences connected therewith.

§ 10. The proceeds from the sale of all lands that have been, or hereafter may be, granted by the United States to the State for educational purposes, and the proceeds of all lands or other property given by individuals or appropriated by the State for like purposes, shall be and remain a perpetual fund, the interest and income of which, together with the rents of all such lands as may remain unsold, shall be inviolably appropriated and annually applied to the specific objects of the original grant, gift, or appropriation.

§ 11. All lands the title of which shall fail from a defect of heirs shall escheat to the State; and the interest on the clear proceeds from the sale thereof shall be appropriated exclusively to the support of primary schools.

MINNESOTA.

CONSTITUTION OF MINNESOTA, AS ADOPTED IN 1858.

Article VIII.—School-funds, education, and science.

SECTION 1. The stability of a republican form of government depend-
g mainly upon the intelligence of the people, it shall be the duty of
e legislature to establish a general and uniform system of public
hools.

§ 2. The proceeds of such lands as are or hereafter may be granted by
e United States for the use of schools, within each township in this
ate, shall remain a perpetual school-fund to the State, and not more
an one-third of said lands may be sold in two years, one-third in five
ars, and one-third in ten years ; but the lands of the greatest valua-
m shall be sold first : *Provided*, That no portion of the said lands
all be sold otherwise than at public sale. The principal of all funds
ising from sales or other disposition of lands, or other property
anted or intrusted to this State in each township for educational pur-
ises, shall forever be preserved inviolate and undiminished ; and the
come arising from the lease or sale of said school-lands shall be dis-
ibuted to the different townships throughout the State, in proportion
the number of scholars in each township between the ages of five
d twenty-one years, and shall be faithfully applied to the specific
jects of the original grants or appropriations.

§ 3. The legislature shall make such provisions, by taxation or other-
se, as, with the income arising from the school-fund, will secure a
orough and efficient system of public schools in each township in the
ate.

§ 4. The location of the University of Minnesota, as established by
isting laws, is hereby confirmed, and said institution is declared to
the University of the State of Minnesota. All the rights, immunities,
inchises, and endowments heretofore granted or conferred, are hereby
rpetuated unto the said university, and all lands which may hereafter
granted by Congress, or other donations for said university-purposes,
all vest in the institution referred to in this section.

MISSISSIPPI.

CONSTITUTION OF MISSISSIPPI, AS ADOPTED IN 1817.

Article VI.

SECTION 16. Religion, morality, and knowledge being necessary to
od government, the preservation of liberty, and the happiness of man-
nd, schools and the means of education shall forever be encouraged
this State. [Continued in the amended constitutions of 1832 and 1865
Art. VII, § 14.]

Constitution of Mississippi, as amended in 1868.

Article VIII.—School-funds, education, and science.

Section 1. As the stability of a republican form of government depends mainly upon the intelligence and virtue of the people, it shall be the duty of the legislature to encourage by all suitable means the pro—motion of intellectual, scientific, moral, and agricultural improvement, by establishing a uniform system of free public schools, by taxation or otherwise, for all children between the ages of five and twenty-one years, and shall, as soon as practicable, establish schools of higher grade.

§ 2. There shall be a superintendent of public education elected at the same time and in the same manner as the governor, who shall have the qualification of the secretary of state, and hold his office for four years, and until his successor shall be elected and qualified, whose duties shall be the general supervision of the common schools and the educational interests of the State, and who shall perform such other duties pertaining to his office, and receive such compensation as shall be prescribed by law. He shall report to the legislature for its adoption, within twenty days after the opening of its first session under this constitution, a uniform system of free public schools.

§ 3. There shall be a board of education, consisting of the secretary of state, the attorney-general, and the superintendent of public education, for the management and investment of the school-funds, under the general direction of the legislature, and to perform such other duties as may be prescribed by law. The superintendent and one other of said board shall constitute a quorum.

§ 4. There shall be a superintendent of public education in each county, who shall be appointed by the board of education, by and with the advice and consent of the senate, whose term of office shall be two years, and whose compensation and duties shall be prescribed by law: *Provided*, That the legislature shall have the power to make said office of county-school-superintendent of the several counties elective, as other county-officers are.

§ 5. A public school or schools shall be maintained in each school-district at least four months in each year. Any school-district neglecting to maintain such school or schools shall be deprived for that year of its proportion of the income of the free-school-fund, and of all funds arising from taxes for the support of schools.

§ 6. There shall be established a common-school-fund, which shall consist of the proceeds of the lands now belonging to the State, heretofore granted by the United States; and of the lands known as "swamp-lands," except the "swamp-lands" lying and situated on Pearl River, in the counties of Hancock, Marion, Lawrence, Simpson, and Copiah; and of all lands now or hereafter vested in the State by escheat or purchase or forfeiture for taxes; and the clear proceeds of all fines collected in the several counties for any breach of the penal laws; and all moneys received for licenses granted under the general laws of the State for the sale of intoxicating liquor, or keeping of dram-shops; all moneys paid as an equivalent for persons exempt from military duty; and the funds arising from the consolidation of the congressional-township-funds, and the lands belonging thereto, together with all moneys donated to the State for school-purposes; which funds shall be securely invested in United States bonds, and remain a perpetual fund, which may be increased but not diminished, the interest of which shall be inviolably appropriated for the support of free schools.

§ 7. The legislature may levy a poll-tax not to exceed two dollars a head in aid of the school-fund, and for no other purpose.

§ 8. The legislature shall, as soon as practicable, provide for the establishment of an agricultural college or colleges; and shall appropriate the two hundred and ten thousand acres of land donated to the State for the support of such a college, by the act of Congress passed July 2, A. D. 1862, or the money or scrip, as the case may be, arising from the sale of said lands or any lands which may hereafter be granted or appropriated for such purpose

§ 9. No religious sect or sects shall ever control any part of the school or university funds of this State.

§ 10. The legislature shall, from time to time, as may be necessary, provide for the levy and collection of such other taxes as may be required to properly support the system of free schools herein adopted; and all school-funds shall be divided *pro rata* among the children of school ages.

MISSOURI.

CONSTITUTION OF MISSOURI, AS ADOPTED IN 1820.

Article VI.

SECTION 1. Schools and the means of education shall forever be encouraged in this State; and the general assembly shall take measures to preserve from waste or damage such lands as have been, or hereafter may be, granted by the United States for the use of schools within each township in this State, and shall apply the funds which may arise from such lands in strict conformity to the object of the grant; and one school or more shall be established in each township as soon as practicable and necessary, where the poor shall be taught gratis.

§ 2. The general assembly shall take measures for the improvement of such lands as have been, or hereafter may be, granted by the United States to this State for the support of a seminary of learning; and the funds accruing from such lands, by rent or lease, or in any other manner, or which may be obtained from any other source for the purposes aforesaid, shall be and remain a permanent fund to support a university, for the promotion of literature and of the arts and sciences; and it shall be the duty of the general assembly, as soon as may be, to provide effectual means for the improvement and permanent security of the funds and endowments of such institution.

ORDINANCE ADOPTED BY THE CONVENTION WHICH FORMED THE CONSTITUTION OF MISSOURI, JULY 19, 1820.

Whereas the act of Congress of the United States of America, approved March 6, 1820, entitled "An act to authorize the people of Missouri Territory to form a constitution and State government, and for the admission of such State into the Union on an equal footing with the original States, and to prohibit slavery in certain Territories," contains certain requisitions and provisions, and, among other things, has offered to this convention when formed, for and in behalf of the people inhabiting this State, for their free acceptance or rejection, the five following propositions, which, if accepted by this convention in behalf of the people as aforesaid, are to be obligatory on the United States, viz:

" 1st. That section numbered sixteen in every township (when such section has been sold or otherwise disposed of, other lands equivalent thereto and as contiguous as may be) shall be granted to the State, for the use of the inhabitants of such township, for the use of schools.

   *   *   *   *   *   *   *

" 5th. That thirty-six sections, or one entire township, which shall be designated by the President of the United States, together with the other lands heretofore reserved for that purpose, shall be reserved for the use of a seminary of learning, and vested in the legislature of said State, to be appropriated solely for the use of such seminary, by the legislature:"

Now this convention, for and in behalf of the people inhabiting this State, and by the authority of the said people, do accept the five before-recited propositions offered by Congress, under which they are assembled. * * * And this convention, for and in behalf of the people inhabiting this State, and by the authority of the said people, do further ordain, agree, and declare that this ordinance shall be irrevocable, without the consent of the United States.   *   *   *

CONSTITUTION OF MISSOURI, AS AMENDED IN 1865.

Article II.

SECTION 19. After the first day of January, 1876, every person who was not a qualified voter prior to that time, shall, in addition to the other qualifications required, be able to read and write, in order to become a qualified voter, unless his inability to read or write shall be the result of a physical disability.

Article IX.—Education.

SECTION 1. A general diffusion of knowledge and intelligence being essential to the preservation of the rights and liberties of the people, the general assembly shall establish and maintain free schools for the

gratuitous instruction of all persons in this State between the ages of
five and twenty-one years.

§ 2. Separate schools may be established for children of African
descent. All funds provided for the support of public schools shall be
appropriated in proportion to the number of children, without regard to
color.

§ 3. The supervision of public instruction shall be vested in a board
of education, whose powers and duties shall be prescribed by law. A
superintendent of public schools, who shall be the president of the board,
shall be elected by the qualified voters of the State. He shall possess
the qualifications of a State senator, and hold his office for the term of
four years, and shall perform such duties and receive such compensation as may be prescribed by law. The secretary of state and attorney-
general shall be *ex officio* members, and, with the superintendent, compose said board of education.

§ 4. The general assembly shall also establish and maintain a State
university, with departments for instruction in teaching, in agriculture,
and in natural science, as soon as the public fund will permit.

§ 5. The proceeds of all lands that have been or hereafter may be
granted by the United States to this State, and not otherwise appropriated by this State or the United States; also all moneys, stocks, bonds,
funds, and other property now belonging to any fund for purposes of
education; also the net proceeds of all sales of lands and other property
and effects that may accrue to the State by escheat, or from sales of
strays, or from unclaimed dividends, or distributive shares of the
estates of deceased persons, or from fines, penalties, and forfeitures; also,
any proceeds of the sales of public lands which may have been or hereafter may be paid over to this State, (if Congress will consent to said
appropriation;) also, all other grants, gifts, or devises that have been
or hereafter may be made to this State, and not otherwise appropriated
by the terms of the grant, gift, or devise, shall be securely invested and
sacredly preserved as a public-school-fund, the annual income of which
and, together with so much of the ordinary revenue of the State as
may be necessary, shall be faithfully appropriated for establishing and
maintaining the free schools and the university in this article provided
for, and for no other uses or purposes whatsoever.

*§ 6. No part of the public-school-fund shall ever be invested in the

---

*This section was ratified at an election held in November, 1872, by a vote of 231,228
to 8,197. It takes the place of the following:

"§ 6. No part of the public-school-fund shall ever be invested in the stock, or bonds,
other obligations of any S'ate, or of any county, city, town, or corporation. The
stock of the Bank of the State of Missouri, now held for school-purposes, and all other
stocks belonging to any school or university fund, shall be sold in such manner and at
such time as the general assembly shall prescribe, and the proceeds thereof, and the
proceeds of the sales of any lands or other property which now belong or may
hereafter belong to said school-fund, may be invested in the bonds of the United
States. All county-school-funds shall be loaned upon good and unincumbered real-
estate security, with personal security in addition thereto."

stock, or bonds, or other obligations of any other State, or of any county, city, town, or corporation. The stock of the Bank of the State of Missouri, now held for school-purposes, and all other stocks belonging to any school- or university-fund, shall be sold in such manner and at such time as the general assembly shall prescribe, and the proceeds thereof, and the proceeds of the sales of any lands or other property which now belong or may hereafter belong to said school-fund, may be invested in the bonds of the State of Missouri or of the United States. All county-school-funds shall be loaned upon good and sufficient unincumbered real-estate-security, with personal security in addition thereto.

§ 7. No township or school-district shall receive any portion of the public-school-fund unless a free school shall have been kept therein for not less than three months during the year for which distribution thereof is made. The general assembly shall have power to require by law that every child of sufficient mental and physical ability shall attend the public schools, during the period between the ages of five and eighteen years, for a term equivalent to sixteen months, unless educated by other means.

§ 8. In case the public-school-fund shall be insufficient to sustain a free school at least four months in every year, in each school-district in this State, the general assembly may provide by law for the raising of such deficiency by levying a tax on all the taxable property in each county, township, or school-district, as they may deem proper.

§ 9. The general assembly shall, so far as can be done without infringing upon vested rights, reduce all lands, moneys, and other property used or held for school-purposes, in the various counties of this State, into the public-school-fund herein provided for; and in making distribution of the annual income of such fund, shall take into consideration the amount of any county or city funds appropriated for common-school-purposes, and make such distribution as will equalize the amount appropriated for common schools throughout the State.

NEBRASKA.[*]

Constitution of Nebraska, as adopted in 1867.

Article I.

Section 16. * * * Religion, morality, and knowledge, however, being essential to good government, it shall be the duty of the legislature to pass suitable laws to protect every religious denomination in the peaceable enjoyment of its own mode of public worship, and to encourage schools and means of instruction.

---

[*] A convention was called in Nebraska for revising their organic law in the summer of 1871, and it reported a form of constitution, which was rejected by a vote of 7,986 to 8,627. This abortive constitution proposed the election, as one of the executive department, of a superintendent of public instruction, with a term of two years, an office at the seat of government, and a requirement to report to the legislature within ten days

Education.

SECTION 1. The principal of all funds arising from the sale or other disposition of lands, or other property, granted or intrusted to this State for educational and religious purposes, shall forever be preserved inviolate and undiminished; and the income arising therefrom shall be faithfully applied to the specific objects of the original grants or appro-

after the beginning of each regular session. His salary was to be $2,000, and he could hold no other office, nor receive other fees or perquisites. The salary might be re-adjusted by the legislature once in five years, but could not be increased or diminished during any term. The article relating to education was as follows:

"Article VII.—Education.

" SECTION 1. All funds and lands set apart for educational purposes shall be under the control and management of the legislature.

"§ 2. All lands, money, or other property, granted, or bequeathed, or in any manner conveyed to this State for educational purposes, shall be used and expended in accordance with the terms of such grant, bequest, or conveyance.

"§ 3. The following are hereby declared to be perpetual funds for common-school-purposes, of which the annual interest or income only can be appropriated, to wit:

" First. Such per centum as has been or may hereafter be granted by Congress on the sale of lands in this State.

"Second. All moneys arising from the sale or leasing of sections number 16 and 36 in each township in this State, and the lands selected or that may be selected in lieu thereof.

"Third. The proceeds of all lands that have been or may hereafter be granted to this State, where, by the terms and conditions of such grant, the same are not to be otherwise appropriated.

"Fourth. The net proceeds of lands and other property and effects that may accrue to the State by escheat or forfeiture, or from unclaimed dividends, or distributive shares of the estates of deceased persons.

" Fifth. All moneys, stocks, bonds, lands, and other property now belonging to the common-school-fund.

"Sixth. All other grants, gifts, and devises that have been or may hereafter be made to this State, and not otherwise appropriated by the terms of the grant, gift, or devise, the interest arising from all of the funds mentioned in this section, together with all rents of the unsold school-lands, and such other means as the legislature may provide, shall be exclusively applied to the following objects, to wit:

" 1st. To the support and maintenance of common schools in each school-district in the State, and the purchase of suitable libraries and apparatus therefor.

"2d. Any residue of such funds as shall be appropriated to the support and maintenance of academies, normal schools, and schools of an intermediate grade between the common schools and the university, and the purchase of suitable libraries and apparatus therefor.

"§ 4. All fines, penalties, and license-moneys arising under the general laws of the State shall belong and be paid over to the counties, respectively, where the same may be levied or imposed; and all fines, penalties, and license-moneys arising under the rules, by-laws, or ordinances of cities, villages, towns, precincts, or other municipal subdivision less than a county, shall belong and be paid over to the same respectively. All such fines, penalties, and license-moneys shall be appropriated exclusively to the use and support of common schools in the respective subdivisions where the same may accrue, and to the purchase of suitable libraries and apparatus therefor.

"§ 5. The legislature shall provide by law for the establishment of district-schools,

priations. The legislature shall make such provisions, by taxation or otherwise, as, with the income arising from the school-trust-fund, will secure a thorough and efficient system of common schools throughout the State ; but no religious sect or sects shall ever have any exclusive right or control of any part of the school-funds of this State.

§ 2. The university-lands, school-lands, and all other lands which

which shall be as nearly uniform as practicable, and such schools shall be free and without charge for tuition to all children between the ages of five and twenty-one years.

"§ 6. Provision shall be made by law for the equal distribution of the income of the fund set apart for the support of common schools among the several school-districts of the State, in proportion to the number of children and youth resident therein between the ages of five and twenty-one years, and no appropriation shall be made from said fund to any district for the year in which a school shall not be maintained at least three months.

"§ 7. No university, agricultural-college, common-school, or other lands, which are now held or may hereafter be acquired by the State for educational purposes, shall be sold for less than seven dollars per acre.

"§ 8. All funds belonging to the State for educational purposes, the interest and income whereof only are to be used, shall be deemed trust-funds held by the State, and the State shall supply all losses thereof that may in any manner accrue, so that the same shall remain forever inviolate and undiminished ; and such funds, with the interest and income thereof, are hereby solemnly pledged for the purposes for which they are granted and set apart, and shall not be transferred to any other fund for other uses.

"§ 9. The general government of the University of Nebraska shall, under the direction of the legislature, be vested in a board of regents, to be styled the Board of Regents of the University of Nebraska, one member of which shall be elected in each judicial district by the electors thereof. Their duties, powers, and term of office shall be prescribed by law ; and they shall receive no compensation, but may be re-imbursed their actual expenses incurred in the discharge of their duties.

"§ 10. Schools for the benefit of the deaf and dumb and the blind shall be fostered and supported.

"§ 11. The supervision of public instruction shall be vested in the State-superintendent of public instruction and such other officers as the legislature shall provide.

"§ 12. The secretary of state, treasurer, attorney-general, and commissioner of public lands and buildings shall constitute a board of commissioners for the sale, leasing, and general management of all lands and funds set apart for educational purposes, and for the investment of school-funds, in such manner as may be prescribed by law.

"§ 13. No sectarian instruction shall be allowed in any school or institution supported in whole or in part by the public funds set apart for educational purposes; nor shall the State accept any grant, conveyance, or bequest of money, lands, or other property to be used for sectarian purposes."

This constitution also proposed to exempt school-property from taxation. A separate clause was submitted, as follows :

"*Compulsory education and reformatory schools* —The legislature <u>may</u> require, by law, that every child of sufficient mental and physical ability, between the ages of eight and sixteen years, unless educated by other means, shall in all cases, when practicable, attend a public school supported by the common-school-fund for some definite length of time each year, to be fixed by law; and may establish a school or schools for the safe-keeping, education, employment, and reformation of all children under the age of sixteen years, who, for want of proper parental care, or other cause, are growing up in mendicity, ignorance, idleness, or vice, which school shall constitute a part of the system of common schools."

have been acquired by the Territory of Nebraska, or which may hereafter be acquired by the State of Nebraska for educational or school-purposes, shall not be aliened or sold for a less sum than five dollars per acre.

NEVADA.

Constitution of Nevada, as adopted in 1864.

Article V.

Section 22. The secretary of state, State-treasurer, State-comptroller, surveyor-general, attorney-general, and superintendent of public instruction shall perform such other duties as may be prescribed by law.

Article XI.—Education.

Section 1. The legislature shall encourage by all suitable means the promotion of intellectual, literary, scientific, mining, mechanical, agricultural, and moral improvement, and also provide for the election by the people, at the general election, of a superintendent of public instruction, whose term of office shall be two years from the first Monday of January, A. D. 1865, and until the election and qualification of his successor, and whose duties shall be prescribed by law.

§ 2. The legislature shall provide for a uniform system of common schools,* by which a school shall be established and maintained in each school-district at least six months in every year; and any school-district neglecting to establish and maintain such a school, or which shall allow instruction of a sectarian character therein, may be deprived of its portion of the interest of the public-school-fund during such neglect or infraction; and the legislature may pass such laws as will tend to secure a general attendance of the children in each school-district upon said public schools.

§ 3. All lands included in the sixteenth and thirty-sixth sections, in every township, donated for the benefit of public schools, in the act of the Thirty-eighth Congress, to enable the people of Nevada Territory to form a State-government;† the thirty thousand acres of public lands granted by an act of Congress, approved July 2, 1862, for each Senator and Representative in Congress; and all proceeds of lands that have been or may be hereafter granted or appropriated by the United States to this State, and also the five hundred thousand acres of land granted to the new States under the act of Congress distributing the proceeds of the public lands among the several States of the Union, approved A. D. 1841,‡ provided that Congress makes provision for or authorizes

* The school-system of Nevada was organized as required in the constitution, by an act approved March 20, 1865.—*Compiled Laws of Nevada*, II, 253.

† Sections 16 and 36 in every township were granted for schools, by § 7 of the enabling-act, approved March 21, 1864, chapter 37, first session Thirty-eighth Congress.

‡ Act of September 4, 1841, chapter 16, first session Twenty-seventh Congress.—*Statutes at Large*, V, 455.

such division to be made for the purpose therein contained ; all estates that may escheat to the State ; all of such per cent. as may be granted by Congress on the sale of land ; all fines collected under the penal laws of the State ; all property given or bequeathed to the State for educational purposes ; and all proceeds derived from any or all of such sources, shall be, and the same hereby are, solemnly pledged for educational purposes, and shall not be transferred to any other fund for any other uses ; and the interest thereon shall, from time to time, be appor - tioned among the several counties in proportion to the ascertained num bers of the persons between the ages of six and eighteen years in the different counties ; and the legislature shall provide for the sale of float ing land-warrants to cover the aforesaid lands, and for the investmen of all proceeds derived from any of the above-mentioned sources ir United States bonds or the bonds of this State: *Provided*, That th interest only of the aforesaid proceeds shall be used for educational purposes, and any surplus interest shall be added to the principal sum *And provided further*, That such portions of said interest as may b necessary may be apportioned for the support of the State-university

§ 4. The legislature shall provide for the establishment of a State university, which shall embrace departments for agriculture, mechani arts, and mining, to be controlled by a board of regents, whose dutie shall be prescribed by law.*

§ 5. The legislature shall have power to establish normal schools, and such different grades of schools, from the primary department to the university, as, in their discretion, they may deem necessary ; and all professors in said university, or teachers in said schools, of whatever grade, shall be required to take and subscribe to the oath as prescribed in Article XV of this constitution. No professor or teacher who fails to comply with the provisions of any law framed in accordance with the provisions of this section shall be entitled to receive any portion of the public moneys set apart for school-purposes.

§ 6. The legislature shall provide a special tax of one-half of one mill on the dollar, on all taxable property in the State, in addition to the other means provided for the support and maintenance of said uni- versity and common schools: *Provided*, That at the end of ten years they may reduce said tax to one-quarter of one mill on each dollar of taxable property.

§ 7. The governor, secretary of state, and superintendent of public instruction shall, for the first four years and until their successors are elected and qualified, constitute a board of regents, to control and man-

---

* By an act approved March 7, 1873, the State University, as described in section 4, Article XI, of the constitution, was located at the town of Elko, provided the people of that town, within one year, conveyed to the board of regents of the State of Nevada the title of not less than twenty thousand acres, with buildings for a preparatory de- partment costing at least $10,000, and furnished ready for the use of at least one hun- dred pupils.

age the affairs of the university and the funds of the same, under such regulations as may be provided by law. But the legislature shall, at its regular session next preceding the expiration of the term of office of the said board of regents, provide for the election of a new board of regents and define their duties.*

§ 8. The board of regents shall, from the interest accruing from the first funds which come under their control, immediately organize and maintain the said mining department in such manner as to make it most effective and useful: *Provided*, That all the proceeds of the public lands donated by act of Congress approved July 2, 1862, for a college for the benefit of agriculture, the mechanic arts, and including military tactics, shall be invested by the said board of regents in a separate fund, to be appropriated exclusively to the benefit of the first-named departments to the university, as set forth in section four above; and the legislature shall provide that, if, through neglect or any other contingency, any portion of the fund so set apart shall be lost or misappropriated, the State of Nevada shall replace said amount so lost or misappropriated in said fund, so that the principal of said fund shall remain forever undiminished.

§ 9. No sectarian instruction shall be imparted or tolerated in any school or university that may be established under this constitution.

NEW HAMPSHIRE.

[The first constitution, adopted in 1776, made no allusion to educational affairs.]

CONSTITUTION OF NEW HAMPSHIRE, AS AMENDED IN 1784, AND SINCE CONTINUED.

Extract from Part II of Form of Government, entitled "Encouragement of literature, &c."

"Knowledge and learning, generally diffused through a community, being essential to the preservation of a free government, and spreading the opportunities and advantages of education through the various parts of the country, being highly conducive to promote this end, it is the duty of the legislators and magistrates, in all future periods of this government, to cherish the interest of literature and the sciences, and all seminaries and public schools; to encourage private and public institutions, rewards and immunities for the promotion of agriculture, arts, sciences, commerce, trades, manufactures, and natural history of the country; to countenance and inculcate the principles of humanity and general benevolence, public and private charity, industry and economy, honesty and punctuality, sincerity, sobriety, and all social affections and generous sentiments among the people."

---

* The election, term, and duties of a board of regents are provided for by an act approved March 5, 1869.

NEW JERSEY.

CONSTITUTION OF NEW JERSEY, AS AMENDED IN 1844.

Article VII.

SECTION 6. The fund for the support of free schools, and all money, stock, and other property which may hereafter be appropriated for that purpose, or received into the treasury under the provisions of any law heretofore passed to augment the said fund, should be securely invested, and remain a perpetual fund; and the increase thereof, except so much as it may be judged expedient to apply to an increase of the capital, shall be annually appropriated to the support of public schools, for the equal benefit of all the people of the State; and it shall not be competent for the legislature to borrow, appropriate, or use the said fund, or any part thereof, for any other purpose, under any pretext whatever.

[In 1873 a commission was appointed to prepare and recommend to the legislature such amendments to the constitution as they might deem proper. They proposed, among other changes, an addition to Article VII, section 6, above given, as follows :]

"A general diffusion of knowledge and intelligence being essential to the preservation of the rights and liberties of the people, the legis- lature shall establish and maintain public schools for the gratuitous instruction of all persons in this State between the ages of five and eighteen. The term 'free schools,' used in this constitution, shall be construed to mean schools that aim to give to all a rudimentary educa- tion, and not to include schools designed to fit or prepare pupils to enter college, or schools controlled by, or under the influence of, any creed. religious society, or denomination whatever."

NEW YORK.

[The first constitution of this State was adopted in 1777, and con- tained no provisions relating directly to education. It was amended in 1801, by a convention, but without insertion of any features bearing upon this subject.]

CONSTITUTION OF NEW YORK, AS AMENDED IN 1821.

Article VII.

SECTION 10. The proceeds of all lands belonging to this State, ex- cept such parts thereof as may be reserved or appropriated to public use or ceded to the United States, which shall hereafter be sold or dis- posed of, together with the fund denominated the common-school-fund, shall be and remain a perpetual fund, the interest of which shall be in- violably appropriated and applied to the support of common schools throughout this State.   *   *   *   *   *

CONSTITUTION OF NEW YORK, AS AMENDED IN 1846.

Article IX.

SECTION 1. The capital of the common-school-fund,* the capital of he literature-fund,† and the capital of the United States deposit-fund‡ hall be respectively preserved inviolate. The revenues of the said ommon-school-fund shall be applied to the support of common schools; he revenues of the said literature-fund shall be applied to the support f academies, and the sum of twenty-five thousand dollars of the reve- ues of the United States deposit-fund shall each year be appropriated o and made a part of the capital of the said common-school-fund.

---

* The school-fund of the State of New York was created by an act passed April 5, 805, which gave the net proceeds of 500,000 acres of vacant lands, to be sold by the urveyor-general, (Simeon De Witt,) and invested as a permanent fund. It was to be oaned to persons or bodies-corporate, for literary purposes, safely secured, until the acome reached $50,000 annually, when the income was to be annually applied to chool-purposes. It reached this point in 1813, and from this date the school-system f New York has a continuous history. No distribution was actually made until 1815. y subsequent donations from various sources the school-fund had been increased to 1,155,827.40 on the day when the constitution of 1821 went into full effect, and there ere, besides this, 991,660 acres of unsold lands then belonging to it. In many of the arly sales of lands under State-authority, and in the lands in Central New York given as ounties to officers and soldiers of the Revolution, there was a reservation of a mile quare in each township for gospel and schools, and a like amount for literature. here were also large donations of land, or of the proceeds of land-sales, to colleges, libra- ies, and other literary objects. The annual report of the superintendent of public nstruction gives the amount of capital and mode of investment of the common-school- und for each year from the beginning. Its amount at intervals of ten years was as ollows:

805	$26,774 10	1845	$2,090,632 41
815	934,015 13	1855	2,457,520 86
825	1,319,886 46	1865	2,765,703 77
835	1,875,191 71	1874	3,029,165 55

Its investment in 1874 was $50,000 in bank-stock, $1,165,057.24 in State-stocks, 36,000 in comptroller's bonds, and $1,310,866.28 money in the treasury.

† The literature-fund originated with the granting of certain lands for literary pur- oses, and was largely increased by four lotteries granted in 1801, by which the sum of 100,000 was raised for the joint benefit of academies and common schools, but chiefly he proceeds of sales of lands, arrears of quit-rents, profits on the sale of State-stocks, nd other appropriations which have been added from time to time. The capital of the terature-fund on the 30th of September, 1874, was $271,980.76, and the revenue $50,157.13. he investment was chiefly in State-stocks, ($242,347,) and it is managed by the comp- roller. The expenditure is under the direction of the regents of the university.

‡ The United States deposit-fund is a part of the sum of $37,468,859.97 distributed mong the States June 23, 1836, of which $5,352,694.38 came to the State of New York. t was distributed among the counties on the basis of population and loaned on securi- ies of real estate. Of its income the sum of $25,000 is added annually to the capital f the school-fund, and the remainder applied to the schools and academies of the State, nder the direction of the superintendent of public instruction and the regents of the niversity. At the close of the fiscal year, September 30, 1874, the capital of this fund mounted to $4,014,520.71, and the revenue for the preceding year was $254,148.05.

AMENDMENTS PROPOSED BY THE CONVENTION OF 1867–'68.

[A constitutional convention was held in 1867–'68, and a new form of constitution was recommended, but not adopted. It contained the following provisions in reference to educational affairs:]

Article IX.

SECTION 1. The capital of the common-school-fund, the capital of the literature-fund, the capital of the United States deposit-fund, the capital of the college-land-scrip-fund, and the capital of the Cornell endowment-fund, as it shall be paid into the treasury, shall each be preserved inviolate. The revenues of the common-school-fund shall be applied to the support of common schools; the revenues of the literature-fund shall be applied to the support of academies, and the sum of $25,000 of the revenue of the United States deposit-fund shall each year be appropriated to, and make a part of, the capital of the common-school-fund; the revenues of the college-land-scrip-fund shall each year be appropriated and applied to the support of the Cornell University, in the mode and for the purposes defined by the act of Congress donating public lands to the several States and Territories, approved July 2, 1862, so long as the university shall fully comply with and perform the conditions of the act of the legislature establishing it; and the revenues of the Cornell endowment-fund shall each year be paid to the trustees of the Cornell University for its use and benefit.

§ 2. The legislature shall provide for the free instruction in the common schools of this State of all persons between seven and twenty years of age.

[In 1872–'73 a commission, appointed for the purpose, made sundry recommendations of change in the constitution of the State of New York, some of which have been adopted, but none of these affected the provisions relating to education as they previously existed.]

NORTH CAROLINA.

CONSTITUTION OF NORTH CAROLINA, AS FIRST ADOPTED IN 1776.

Form of government, &c.

Whereas, [recital of preamble omitted.] Wherefore, in our present state, in order to prevent anarchy and confusion, it becomes necessary that government should be established in this State: Therefore, we, the representatives of the freemen of North Carolina, chosen and assembled in congress for the express purpose of framing a constitution, under the authority of the people, most conducive to their happiness and prosperity, do declare that a government for this State shall be established in manner following, to wit:

[Here follows a series of sections relating to the organization, powers, and duties of the legislature, among which is the following:]

41. That a school or schools shall be established by the legislature, for the convenient instruction of youth, with such salaries to the masters, paid by the public, as may enable them to instruct at low prices; and all useful learning shall be duly encouraged and promoted, in one or more universities.*

---

* In 1866 an amended constitution was submitted to the people and rejected. It contained, in Art. VII, § 2, a provision identical with § 41, as above given, excepting that the words "general assembly" were substituted for the word "legislature."

CONSTITUTION OF NORTH CAROLINA, AS AMENDED IN 1868.

Article I.—Declaration of rights.

SECTION 7. The people have a right to the privilege of education, and it is the duty of the State to guard and maintain that right.

Article III.—Executive department.

SECTION 1. The executive department shall consist of a governor, (in whom shall be vested the supreme executive power of the State,) a lieutenant-governor, a secretary of state, an auditor, a treasurer, a superintendent of public works, a superintendent of public instruction, and an attorney-general, who shall be elected for a term of four years, by the qualified electors of the State, at the same time and places, and in the same manner, as members of the general assembly are elected. Their term of office shall commence on the first day of January next after their election, and continue until their successors are elected and qualified: *Provided,* That the officers first elected shall assume the duties of their office ten days after the approval of this constitution by the Congress of the United States, and shall hold their offices four years from and after the first day of January, 1869.

§ 7. The officers of the executive department, and of the public institutions of the State, shall, at least five days previous to each regular session of the general assembly, severally report to the governor, who shall transmit such reports, with his message, to the general assembly; and the governor may, at any time, require information in writing from the officers in the executive department upon any subject relating to the duties of their respective offices, and shall take care that the laws be faithfully executed.

§ 13. The respective duties of the secretary of state, auditor, treasurer, superintendent of public works, superintendent of public instruction, and attorney-general shall be prescribed by law. If the office of any of said officers shall be vacated by death, resignation, or otherwise, it shall be the duty of the governor to appoint another until the disability be removed or his successor be elected and qualified. Every such vacancy shall be filled by election, at the first general election that occurs more than thirty days after the vacancy has taken place, and the person chosen shall hold the office for the remainder of the unexpired term fixed in the first section of this article.

§ 14. The secretary of state, auditor, treasurer, superintendent of public works, and superintendent of public instruction shall constitute, *ex officio,* the council of the State, who shall advise the governor in the execution of his office, and three of whom shall constitute a quorum; their advice and proceedings in this capacity shall be entered in a journal, to be kept for this purpose exclusively and signed by the members present, from any part of which any member may enter his dissent; and such journal shall be placed before the general assembly when called for by either house. The attorney-general shall be, *ex officio*, the legal adviser of the executive department.

§ 15. The officers mentioned in this article shall, at stated periods, receive for their services a compensation, to be established by law, which shall neither be increased nor diminished during the time for which they shall have been elected, and the said officers shall receive no other emolument or allowance whatever.

§ 17. There shall be established in the office of secretary of state a bureau of statistics, agriculture, and immigration, under such regulations as the general assembly may provide.

Article IX.—Education.

SECTION 1. Religion, morality, and knowledge being necessary to good government and happiness of mankind, schools and the means of education shall forever be encouraged.

§ 2. The general assembly, at its first session under this constitution, shall provide, by taxation and otherwise, for a general and uniform system of public schools, wherein tuition shall be free of charge to all the children of the State between the ages of six and twenty-one years.

§ 3. Each county of the State shall be divided into a convenient number of districts, in which one or more public schools shall be maintained at least four months in every year; and if the commissioners of any county shall fail to comply with the aforesaid requirements of this section they shall be liable to indictment.

§ 4. The proceeds of all lands that have been, or hereafter may be, granted by the United States, and not otherwise specially appropriated by the United States or heretofore by this State; also, all moneys, stocks, bonds, and other property now belonging to any fund for purposes of education ; also, the net proceeds that may accrue to the State from sales of estrays or from fines, penalties, and forfeitures; also, the proceeds of all sales of the swamp-lands belonging to the State; also, all money that shall be paid as an equivalent for exemption from military duty ; also, all grants, gifts, or devises that may hereafter be made to this State, and not otherwise appropriated by the grant, gift, or devise, shall be securely invested and sacredly preserved as an irreducible educational fund, the annual income of which, together with so much of the ordinary revenue of the State as may be necessary, shall be faithfully appropriated for establishing and perfecting in this State a system of free public schools, and for no other purposes or uses whatsoever.

§ 5. The University of North Carolina, with its lands, emoluments, and franchises, is under the control of the State, and shall be held to an inseparable connection with the free public-school-system of the State.*

§ 6. The general assembly shall provide that the benefits of the university, as far as practicable, be extended to the youth of the State free of expense for tuition; also, that all the property which has heretofore

---

* This university was wholly suspended during the war, and not again revived until *September*, 1875.

accrued to the State, or shall hereafter accrue, from escheats, unclaimed dividends, or distributive shares of the estates of deceased persons, shall be appropriated to the use of the university.

§ 7. The governor, lieutenant-governor, secretary of state, treasurer, auditor, superintendent of public works, superintendent of public instruction, and attorney-general shall constitute a State-board of education.

§ 8. The governor shall be president and the superintendent of public instruction shall be secretary of the board of education.

§ 9. The board of education shall succeed to all the powers and trusts of the president and directors of the literature-fund of North Carolina, and shall have full power to legislate and make all needful rules and regulations in relation to free public schools and the educational fund of the State; but all acts, rules, and regulations of said board may be altered, amended, or repealed by the general assembly; and, when so altered, amended, or repealed, they shall not be re-enacted by the board.

§ 10. The first session of the board of education shall be held at the capital of the State, within fifteen days after the organization of the State-government under this constitution; the time of future meeting may be determined by the board.

§ 11. A majority of the board shall constitute a quorum for the transaction of business.

§ 12. The contingent expenses of the board shall be provided for by the general assembly.

§ 13. The board of education shall elect trustees for the university as follows: one trustee for each county in the State, whose term of office shall be eight years. The first meeting of the board shall be held within ten days after their election; and at this and every subsequent meeting ten trustees shall constitute a quorum. The trustees at their first meeting shall be divided as equally as may be into four classes. The seats of the first class shall be vacated at the expiration of two years; of the second class, at the expiration of four years; of the third class, at the expiration of six years; of the fourth class, at the expiration of eight years; so that one-fourth may be chosen every second year.

§ 14. The board of education and the president of the university shall be, *ex officio*, members of the board of trustees of the university, and shall, with three other trustees, to be appointed by the board of trustees, constitute the executive committee of the trustees of the University of North Carolina, and shall be clothed with the powers delegated to the executive committee under the existing organization of the institution. The governor shall be, *ex officio*, president of the board of trustees and chairman of the executive committee of the university. The board of education shall provide for the more perfect organization of the board of trustees.

§ 15. All the privileges, rights, franchises, and endowments heretofore granted to or conferred upon the board of trustees of the University of

North Carolina by the charter of 1789, or by any subsequent legislation, are hereby vested in the board of trustees authorized by this constitution, for the perpetual benefit of the university.

§ 16. As soon as practicable after the adoption of this constitution the general assembly shall establish and maintain, in connection with the university, a department of agriculture, of mechanics, of mining, and of normal instruction.

§ 17. The general assembly is hereby empowered to enact that every child of sufficient mental and physical ability shall attend the public schools, during the period between the ages of six and eighteen years, for a term of not less than sixteen months, unless educated by other means.

OHIO.*

Constitution of Ohio, as adopted in 1802.

Article VIII.

That the general, great, and essential principles of liberty and free government may be recognized and forever unalterably established, we declare:

* * * * * * *

3. That all men have a natural and indefeasible right to worship Almighty God, [here the rights of conscience and of religious worship are declared, and disqualifications from office on account of religion forbidden.] But religion, morality, and knowledge being essentially necessary to the good government and the happiness of mankind, schools and the means of instruction shall forever be encouraged by legislative provision not inconsistent with the rights of conscience.

* * * * * * *

---

* This being the first State organized out of "the Territory Northwest of the river Ohio," it may be proper to notice in this connection the provisions of certain ordinances of the Continental Congress having reference to education. The first of these in which there is a distinct recognition of the claims of schools, was passed May 20, 1785, and was entitled "An ordinance for ascertaining the mode of disposing of lands in the western territory." The provision was as follows:

"There shall be reserved the lot No. 16 of every township for the maintenance of public schools within the said township; also, one-third part of all gold, silver, lead, and copper mines, to be sold or otherwise disposed of, as Congress shall hereafter direct."

Salt-springs and lead-mines were reserved by subsequent laws, but the reservations with respect to mines of gold, silver, and copper were not continued. The townships here alluded to were six miles square, the same as those since surveyed, and the reservation of section 16 has been uniformly continued for the benefit of schools in all subsequent land-sales.

An ordinance for the government of the territory northwest of the river Ohio, passed July 13, 1787, contained, as a part of the compact between Congress, representing the original States, and the inhabitants of the said territory, the following:

"Article III. Religion, morality, and knowledge being necessary to good government and the happiness of mankind, schools and the means of education shall forever be encouraged."

25. That no law shall be passed to prevent the poor in the several counties and townships within this State from an equal participation in the schools, academies, colleges, and universities within this State which are endowed, in whole or in part, from the revenue arising from the donations made by the United States for the support of schools and colleges ; and the doors of the said schools, academies, and universities shall be open for the reception of scholars, students, and teachers of every grade, without any distinction or preference whatever contrary to the intent for which said donations were made.

* * * * * * *

27. That every association of persons, when regularly formed within this State, and having given themselves a name, may, on application to the legislature, be entitled to receive letters of incorporation to enable them to hold estates, real and personal, for the support of their schools, academies, colleges, universities, and other purposes.

CONSTITUTION OF OHIO, AS AMENDED IN 1851.

Extract from Article I, Section 7.—Bill of rights.

* * * Religion, morality, and knowledge, however, being essential to good government, it shall be the duty of the general assembly to pass suitable laws to protect every religious denomination in the peaceable enjoyment of its own mode of public worship, and to encourage schools and means of instruction.

Article VI.—Education.

SECTION 1. The principal of all funds arising from the sale or other disposition of lands or other property granted or intrusted to this State for educational and religious purposes shall forever be preserved inviolate and undiminished; and the income arising therefrom shall be faithfully applied to the specific objects of the original grants or appropriations.

§ 2. The general assembly shall make such provisions, by taxation or otherwise, as, with the income arising from the school-trust-fund, will secure a thorough and efficient system of common schools throughout the State; but no religious or other sect or sects shall ever have any exclusive right to, or control of, any part of the school-funds of the State.

CONSTITUTION FOR THE STATE OF OHIO, PREPARED BY A CONVENTION IN 1874, BUT REJECTED BY THE PEOPLE AT AN ELECTION.

Article I.—Bill of rights.

SECTION 7. [Freedom of religious faith and worship affirmed.] * * * Religion, morality, and knowledge, however, being essential to good government, it shall be the duty of the general assembly to pass laws to protect every religious denomination in the peaceable enjoyment of its own mode of public worship, and to encourage schools and the means of instruction.

Article II.—Legislative.

SECTION 29. All laws of a general nature shall have a uniform operation throughout the State. No act, or part of an act, except such as relates to public schools, public buildings, or public bridges, shall be passed to take effect upon a vote of the people to be affected thereby, except as otherwise provided in this constitution ; nor shall any act be passed conferring special powers or privileges upon any county, township, city, village, or other municipality, not conferred upon all counties, townships, cities, villages, and municipalities of the same general class.

Article VI.—Education.

SECTION 1. The principal of all funds arising from the sale or other disposition of lands and other property, granted or intrusted to the State for educational or religious purposes, shall forever be preserved inviolate and undiminished ; and the income therefrom shall be faithfully applied to the specific objects of the original grants and trusts.

§ 2. The general assembly shall make such provision, by taxation or otherwise, as, with the income arising from the school-trust-fund, will secure a thorough and efficient system of common schools throughout the State. No religious or other sect shall ever have exclusive right to, or control of, any part of the school-funds of the State.

§ 3. Women, having such qualifications as to age, citizenship, and residence as may be prescribed for electors, shall be eligible to any office under the school-laws, except that of State-commissioner of common schools.

Article XIII.—Revenue and taxation.

SECTION 4. The general assembly may provide by general laws for exemption from taxation of all burial-grounds, public-school-houses, houses used exclusively for public worship, institutions of purely public charity, public libraries, public property used exclusively for any public purpose, and personal property to an amount not exceeding $200 to each individual ; but such laws shall be subject to alteration or repeal, and the value of property so exempted shall, from time to time, be ascertained and published, as may be directed by law.

OREGON.

[In 1843, the inhabitants of Oregon, as well those professing allegiance to the United States as those claiming to be British subjects, united in adopting a primitive form of government, which contained no provisions with reference to education. The legislature elected under this organic law attempted in 1845 to enact a law in relation to public schools, but failed. In August, 1848, a territorial form of government was provided by Congress, and in 1859 Oregon was admitted into the Union as a State.]

CONSTITUTION OF OREGON, AS ADOPTED IN 1857.

Article VIII.—Education and school-lands.

SECTION 1. The governor shall be superintendent of public instruction, and his powers and duties in that capacity shall be such as may be prescribed by law; but after the term of five years from the adoption of this constitution, it shall be competent for the legislative assembly to provide by law for the election of a superintendent, to provide for his compensation, and prescribe his powers and duties.*

---

* The governor continues to act as State-superintendent of schools in this State.

§ 2. The proceeds of all the lands which have been, or hereafter may be, granted to this State for educational purposes, (excepting the lands heretofore granted to aid in the establishment of a university;) all the moneys and clear proceeds of all property which may accrue to the State by escheat or forfeiture; all moneys which may be paid as exemption from military duty; the proceeds of all gifts, devises, and bequests made by any person to the State for common-school-purposes; the proceeds of all property granted to the State, when the purposes of such grant shall not be stated; all the proceeds of the five hundred thousand acres of land to which this State is entitled by the provisions of an act of Congress entitled "An act to appropriate the proceeds of the sales of the public lands, and to grant pre-emption rights," approved the 4th of September, 1841, and also the 5 per centum of the net proceeds of the sales of public lands to which this State shall become entitled, on her admission into the Union, (if Congress shall assent to such appropriation of the two grants last mentioned,) shall be set apart as a separate and irreducible fund, to be called the common-school-fund, the interest of which, together with all other revenues derived from the school-lands mentioned in this section, shall be exclusively applied to the support and maintenance of common schools in each school-district and purchase of suitable libraries and apparatus therefor.

§ 3. The legislative assembly shall provide by law for the establishment of a uniform and regular system of common schools.

§ 4. Provision shall be made by law for the distribution of the income of the common-school-fund among the several counties of this State, in proportion to the number of children resident therein between the ages of four and twenty years.

§ 5. The governor, secretary of state, and State-treasurer shall constitute a board of commissioners for the sale of school- and university-lands and for the investment of the funds arising therefrom, and their powers and duties shall be such as may be prescribed by law : *Provided*, That no part of the university-funds, or of the interest arising therefrom, shall be expended until the period of ten years from the adoption of this constitution, unless the same shall be otherwise disposed of, by the consent of Congress, for common-school-purposes.

PENNSYLVANIA.

PROPRIETARY CONCESSIONS IN FAVOR OF EDUCATION DURING THE COLONIAL PERIOD.

[A frame of government granted by William Penn, the proprietor of Pennsylvania, April 20, 1682, contained the following requirements with respect to education within the province :]

"XII. That the governor and provincial council shall erect and order all publick schools, and encourage and reward the authors of useful sciences and laudable inventions in the said province.

"XIII. That for the better management of the powers and trusts aforesaid, the provincial council shall, from time to time, divide itself into four distinct and proper *committees*, for the more easy administration of the affairs of the province, which divides the seventy into four eighteens, every one of which eighteen shall consist of six out of each of the three orders or yearly elections, each of which shall have a distinct portion of business, as followeth : * * * * Fourth, a committee of manners, education, and arts, that all wicked and scandalous living may be prevented, and that youth may be successively trained up in virtue and useful knowledge and arts; the quorum of each of which committees being six, that is, two out of each of the three orders or yearly elections as aforesaid, making a constant and standing council of twenty-four, which shall have the power of the provincial council, being the quorum of it, in all cases not excepted in the fifth article. * * * * "

[A frame of government granted in 1683, contained in Article X the same provisions as those in Article XII above cited. An act was passed November 7, 1696, confirming this frame of government, reciting its provisions, and changing its form in some places. The educational provisions thus modified were as follows :]

"*Be it further enacted by the authority aforesaid*, That the governor and council shall erect and order all public houses, and encourage and reward the authors of useful sciences and laudable inventions in the said province and territories thereof.

"*And be it further enacted, &c.*, That the governor and council shall, from time to time, have the care and management of all public affairs relating to the peace, safety, justice, treasury, trade, and improvement of the province and territories, and to the good education of youth and sobriety of the manners of the inhabitants therein as aforesaid."

CONSTITUTION OF PENNSYLVANIA, AS ADOPTED IN 1776.

ARTICLE XLIV. A school or schools shall be established in each county by the legislature for the convenient instruction of youth, with such salaries to the masters, paid by the public, as may enable them to instruct youth at low prices ; and all useful learning shall be duly encouraged and promoted in one or more universities.

XLV. Laws for the encouragement of virtue and prevention of vice and immorality shall be made and constantly kept in force, and provision shall be made for their due execution; and all religious societies or bodies of men heretofore united or incorporated for the advancement of religion or learning, or for other pious and charitable purposes, shall be encouraged and protected in the enjoyment of the privileges, immunities, and estates which they were accustomed to enjoy, or could of right have enjoyed, under the laws and former constitution of this State.

Constitution of Pennsylvania, as amended in 1790.

Article VII.

SECTION 1. The legislature shall, as soon as conveniently may be, provide by law for the establishment of schools throughout the State, in such manner that the poor may be taught *gratis.*

§ 2. The arts and sciences shall be promoted in one or more seminaries of learning.

Constitution of Pennsylvania, as amended in 1838.

Article VII.—*Education.*

SECTION 1. The legislature shall, as soon as conveniently may be, provide by law for the establishment of schools throughout the State, in such manner that the poor may be taught *gratis.*

§ 2. The arts and sciences shall be promoted in one or more seminaries of learning.

Constitution of Pennsylvania, as amended in 1873.*

Article III.—*Legislation.*

SECTION 7. The general assembly shall not pass any local or special law * * * regulating the affairs of counties, cities, townships, wards, boroughs, or school-districts, * * * erecting new townships or boroughs, changing township-lines, borough-limits, or school-districts, * * * creating offices, or prescribing the powers and duties of officers in counties, cities, boroughs, townships, election- or school-districts; * * * regulating the management of public schools, the building or repair of school-houses, and the raising of money for such purposes. * * *

Article IV.—*The executive.*

SECTION 1. The executive department of this Commonwealth shall consist of a governor, lieutenant-governor, secretary of the Commonwealth, attorney-general, auditors-general, State-treasurer, secretary of internal affairs, and a superintendent of public instruction.†

§ 20. The superintendent of public instruction shall exercise all the powers and perform all the duties of the superintendent of common schools, subject to such changes as may be made by law.

---

* Took effect January 1, 1874.

† By section 8 of this article the office of superintendent of public instruction is required to be filled, for terms of four years, upon nomination of the governor and with the advice and consent of two-thirds of all the members of the senate. Vacancies in this office are to be filled by the governor during the recess of the senate, but during their next session he must nominate a candidate for their confirmation or rejection. Executive sessions are held with open doors.

Article X.—Education.

SECTION 1. The general assembly shall provide for the maintenance and support of a thorough and efficient system of public schools, wherein all the children of this Commonwealth above the age of six years may be educated, and shall appropriate at least one million of dollars each year for that purpose.

§ 2. No money raised for the support of the public schools of the Commonwealth shall be appropriated to or used for the support of any sectarian school.

§ 3. Women twenty-one years of age and upwards shall be eligible to any office of control or management under the school-laws of this State.

RHODE ISLAND.

[The colonial charter granted to Rhode Island by Charles II, in July, 1663, proved so well suited to the wants of the people of this State, that it remained their organic law until the adoption of the present constitution in 1842. It contained no provision with direct reference to education.]

CONSTITUTION OF RHODE ISLAND, ADOPTED IN 1842.

Article XII.—Of education.

SECTION 1. The diffusion of knowledge, as well as of virtue, among the people being essential to the preservation of their rights and liberties, it shall be the duty of the general assembly to promote public schools, and to adopt all means which they may deem necessary and proper to secure to the people the advantages and opportunities of education.

§ 2. The money which now is, or which may hereafter be, appropriated by law for the establishment of a permanent fund for the support of public schools, shall be securely invested and remain a perpetual fund for that purpose.

§ 3. All donations for the support of public schools, or for other purposes of education, which may be received by the general assembly, shall be applied according to the terms prescribed by the donors.

§ 4. The general assembly shall make all necessary provision by law for carrying this article into effect. They shall not divert said money or fund from the aforesaid uses, nor borrow, appropriate, nor use the same, or any part thereof, for any other purpose, under any pretext whatever.

SOUTH CAROLINA.

[A constitution was first adopted in this State in 1776. It was revised in 1778 and 1790, and amended in 1808, 1810, 1816, 1820, 1828, 1854, and 1856, but without including any provisions relating to education. The same remark applies to the constitution of 1865.]

CONSTITUTION OF SOUTH CAROLINA, AS AMENDED IN 1868.

Article X.—Education.

SECTION 1. The supervision of public instruction shall be vested in a State-superintendent of education, who shall be elected by the qualified electors of the State, in such manner and at such time as the other State-officers are elected; his powers, duties, term of office, and compensation shall be defined by the general assembly.

§ 2. There shall be elected, biennially, in each county, by the qualified electors thereof, one school-commissioner, said commissioners to constitute a State-board of education, of which the State-superintendent shall, by virtue of his office, be chairman; the powers, duties, and compensation of the members of said board shall be determined by law.

§ 3. The general assembly shall, as soon as practicable after the adoption of this constitution, provide for a liberal and uniform system of free public schools throughout the State, and shall also make provision for the division of the State into suitable school districts. There shall be kept open, at least six months in each year, one or more schools in each school-district.

§ 4. It shall be the duty of the general assembly to provide for the compulsory attendance, at either public or private schools, of all children between the ages of six and sixteen years, not physically or mentally disabled, for a term equivalent to twenty-four months at least: *Provided*, That no law to that effect shall be passed until a system of public schools has been thoroughly and completely organized, and facilities afforded to all the inhabitants of the State for the free education of their children.

§ 5. The general assembly shall levy, at each regular session after the adoption of this constitution, an annual tax on all taxable property throughout the State for the support of public schools, which tax shall be collected at the same time and by the same agents as the general State-levy, and shall be paid into the treasury of the State. There shall be assessed on all taxable polls in the State an annual tax of one dollar on each poll, the proceeds of which tax shall be applied solely to educational purposes: *Provided*, That no person shall ever be deprived of the right of suffrage for the non-payment of said tax. No other poll- or capitation-tax shall be levied in the State, nor shall the amount assessed on each poll exceed the limit given in this section. The school-tax shall be distributed among the several school-districts of the State in proportion to the respective number of pupils attending the public schools. No religious sect or sects shall have exclusive right to or control of any part of the school-funds of the State, nor shall sectarian principles be taught in the public schools.

§ 6. Within five years after the first regular session of the general assembly following the adoption of this constitution, it shall be the duty of the general assembly to provide for the establishment and support of a State normal school, which shall be open to all persons who may wish to become teachers.

§ 7. Educational institutions for the benefit of all the blind, deaf and dumb, and such other benevolent institutions as the public good may require, shall be established and supported by the State, subject to such regulations as may be prescribed by law.

§ 8. Provisions shall be made by law, as soon as practicable, for the establishment and maintenance of a State-reform-school for juvenile offenders.

§ 9. The general assembly shall provide for the maintenance of the State University, and, as soon as practicable, provide for the establishment of an agricultural college, and shall appropriate the land given to this State for the support of such a college by the act of Congress passed July second, one thousand eight hundred and sixty-two, or the money or scrip, as the case may be, arising from the sale of said lands, or any lands which may hereafter be given or appropriated for such purpose, for the support and maintenance of such college, and may make the same a branch of the State University, for instructions in agriculture, the mechanic arts, and the natural sciences connected therewith.

§ 10. All the public schools, colleges, and universities of this State, supported in whole or in part by the public funds, shall be free and open to all the children and youths of the State, without regard to race or color.

§ 11. The proceeds of all lands that have been, or hereafter may be, given by the United States to this State for educational purposes, and not otherwise appropriated by this State or the United States, and of all lands or other property given by individuals, or appropriated by the State for like purposes, and of all estates of deceased persons who have died without leaving a will or heir, shall be securely invested and sacredly preserved as a State school-fund; and the annual interest and income of said fund, together with such other means as the general assembly may provide, shall be faithfully appropriated for the purpose of establishing and maintaining free public schools, and for no other purposes or uses whatever.

ORDINANCE X.—An ordinance instructing the general assembly to provide for appropriating the citadel for educational purposes, passed March 16, 1868.

We, the people of South Carolina, in convention met, do ordain : That the general assembly is hereby instructed to provide, by suitable laws, for the appropriation of the citadel and grounds, in the city of Charleston, for educational purposes, said building and grounds to be devoted to the establishment of an institution of learning, which shall be a body politic and corporate, and shall be managed by a board of trustees, and their successors, who shall be chosen by the general assembly, and shall be subject to visitation by and under its authority.

ιid institution of learning shall have power to establish schools of law
ιd medicine, and to issue diplomas that shall entitle the holders to
:actice said professions, as shall be prescribed by law.

TENNESSEE.

CONSTITUTION OF TENNESSEE, AS ADOPTED IN 1796.

Article I.

SECTION 24. No member of the general assembly shall be eligible to
ιɔ office or place of trust, except to the office of a justice of the peace
· a trustee of any literary institution, where the power of appointment
ι such office or place of trust is vested in their own body.

CONSTITUTION OF TENNFSSEE, AS AMENDED IN 1834.

Article XI.

SECTION 10. Knowledge, learning, and virtue being essential to the
·eservation of republican institutions, and the diffusion of the opportu-
ties and advantages of education throughout the different portions
˙ the State being highly conducive to the promotion of this end, it
ιall be the duty of the general assembly, in all future periods of this
overnment, to cherish literature and science. And the fund called the
ɔmmon-school-fund, and all the lands and proceeds thereof, dividends,
tocks, and other property of every description whatever, heretofore by
aw appropriated by the general assembly of this State for the use of
ɔmmon schools, and all such as shall hereafter be appropriated, shall
emain a *perpetual fund*, the principal of which shall never be diminished
ιʏ legislative appropriation; and the interest thereof shall be inviolably
ppropriated to the support and encouragement of common schools
ιroughout the State, and for the equal benefit of all the people thereof;
ιd no law shall be made authorizing said fund, or any part thereof, to
ι diverted to any other use than the support and encouragement of
mmon schools; and it shall be the duty of the general assembly to
point a board of commissioners for such term of time as they may
inιk proper, who shall have the general superintendence of said fund,
ɑ who shall make a report of the condition of the same, from time to
ne, under such rules, regulations, and restrictions as may be required
˙ law: *Provided*, That if at any time hereafter a division of the public
ιnds of the United States, or of the money arising from the sale of
ɑch lands, shall be made among the individual States, the part of such
ɑnds or money coming to this State shall be devoted to the purposes
ɔf education and internal improvement, and shall never be applied to
ɑnʏ other purpose.

§ 11. The above provisions shall not be construed to prevent the
legislature from carrying into effect any laws that have been passed in

favor of the colleges, universities, or academies, or from authorizing heirs or distributees to receive and enjoy escheated property, under such rules and regulations as from time to time may be prescribed by law.

Amendment of 1870.

[The amended constitution of 1870 contains in Article XI, § 12, the same general declaration and provisions as formerly existed, down to and including the pledge that "no law shall be made authorizing said fund, or any part thereof, to be diverted to any other use than the support and encouragement of common schools." In place of the succeeding portions the following is substituted:]

"The State-taxes derived hereafter from polls shall be appropriated to educational purposes, in such manner as the general assembly shall, from time to time, direct by law. No school established or aided under this section shall allow white and negro children to be received as scholars together in the same school. The above provision shall not prevent the legislature from carrying into effect any laws that have been passed in favor of the colleges, universities, or academies, or from authorizing heirs or distributees to receive and enjoy escheated property under such laws as may be passed from time to time."

TEXAS.

[No provision with reference to education was included in the constitution of the Republic of Texas, adopted in 1836.]

CONSTITUTION OF TEXAS, AS ADOPTED IN 1845.

Article X.—Education.

SECTION 1. A general diffusion of knowledge being essential to the preservation of the rights and liberties of the people, it shall be the duty of the legislature of this State to make suitable provision for the support and maintenance of public schools.

§ 2. The legislature shall, as early as practicable, establish free schools throughout the State and shall furnish means for their support by taxation on property; and it shall be the duty of the legislature to set apart not less than one-tenth of the annual revenue of the State derived from taxation, as a perpetual fund, which fund shall be appropriated to the support of free public schools; and no law shall ever be made diverting said fund to any other use; and until such time as the legislature shall provide for the establishment of such schools in the several districts of the State, the fund thus created shall remain as a charge against the State, passed to the credit of the free-common-school-fund.

§ 3. All public lands which have been heretofore, or which may hereafter be, granted for public schools to the various counties, or other political divisions in this State, shall not be alienated in fee, nor disposed of otherwise than by lease, for a term not exceeding twenty years, in such manner as the legislature may direct.

§ 4. The several counties in this State which have not received their quantum of lands for the purposes of education shall be entitled to the same quantity heretofore appropriated by the congress of the Republic of Texas to other counties.*

Constitution of Texas, as Amended in 1866.

Article X.—Education.

Section 1. A general diffusion of knowledge being essential to the preservation of the rights and liberties of the people, it shall be the duty of the legislature of this State to make suitable provisions for the support and maintenance of public schools.

§ 2. The legislature shall, as early as practicable, establish a system of free schools throughout the State; and, as a basis for the endowment and support of said system, all the funds, lands, and other property heretofore set apart and appropriated, or that may hereafter be set apart and appropriated, for the support and maintenance of public schools, shall constitute the public-school-fund; and said fund, and the income derived therefrom, shall be a perpetual fund exclusively for the education of all the white scholastic inhabitants of this State, and no law shall ever be made appropriating said fund to any other use or purpose whatever. And until such time as the legislature shall provide for the establishment of such system of public schools in the State, the fund thus created, and the income derived therefrom, shall remain as a charge against the State, and be passed to the credit of the free-common-school-fund.

§ 3. And all the alternate sections of land reserved by the State out of grants heretofore made, or that may hereafter be made, to railroad-companies or other corporations of any nature whatever, for internal improvements or for the development of the wealth and resources of the State, shall be set apart as a part of the perpetual school-fund of the State; and the legislature shall hereafter appropriate one-half of the proceeds resulting from all sales of the public lands to the perpetual public-school-fund.

§ 4. The legislature shall provide, from time to time, for the sale of lands belonging to the perpetual public-school-fund, upon such time and terms as it may deem expedient: *Provided*, That in cases of sale the preference shall be given to actual settlers: *And provided further*, That

---

* An act of the Republic of Texas, approved January 26, 1839, granted to each county three leagues of land, for the purpose of establishing a primary school or academy. The lands were to be located in the county, if good lands could be found vacant, and they might be surveyed in any-sized tracts of not less than 160 acres. If lands proper for this use did not exist in the county, they might be surveyed upon any of the vacant lands of the republic at the expense of the county.

The same act directed a tract of fifty leagues of land to be set apart for the establishment and endowment of two colleges or universities, thereafter to be created, the cost of survey being paid by the general treasury.

the legislature shall have no power to grant relief to purchasers by granting further time of payment, but shall, in all cases, provide for the forfeiture of the land to the State for the benefit of a perpetual public-school-fund; and that all interest accruing upon such sales shall be a part of the income belonging to the school-fund, and subject to appropriations annually for educational purposes.

§ 5. The legislature shall have no power to appropriate, or loan, or invest, except as follows, any part of the principal sum of the perpetual school-fund for any purpose whatever; and it shall be the duty of the legislature to appropriate annually the income which may be derived from said fund, for educational purposes, under such system as it may adopt; and it shall, from time to time, cause the principal sum now on hand and arising from sales of land, or from any other source, to be invested in the bonds of the United States of America, or the bonds of the State of Texas, or such bonds as the State may guarantee.

§ 6. All public lands which have been heretofore, or may be hereafter, granted for public schools to the various counties or other political divisions in this State, shall be under the control of the legislature, and may be sold on such terms and under such regulations as the legislature shall by law prescribe; and the proceeds of the sale of said lands shall be added to the perpetual school-fund of the State. But each county shall receive the full benefit of the interest arising from the proceeds of the sale of the lands granted to them respectively: *Provided*, That the lands already patented to the counties shall not be sold without the consent of such county or counties to which the lands may belong.

§ 7. The legislature may provide for the levying of a tax for educational purposes, provided the taxes levied shall be distributed from year to year, as the same may be collected, and provided that all the sums arising from said tax which may be collected from Africans, or persons of African descent, shall be exclusively appropriated for the maintenance of a system of public schools for Africans and their children; and it shall be the duty of the legislature to encourage schools among these people.

§ 8. The moneys and lands heretofore granted to, or which may hereafter be granted for the endowment of, one or more universities, shall constitute a special fund for the maintenance of said universities; and until the university or universities are located and commenced, the principal and the interest arising *from* the investment of the principal shall be invested in the like manner and under the same restrictions as provided for the investment and control of the perpetual public-school-fund in sections four and five of this article of the constitution; and the legislature shall have no power to appropriate the university-fund for any other purpose than that of the maintenance of said universities; and the legislature shall, at an early day, make such provisions by law as will organize and put into operation the university.

§ 9. The four hundred thousand acres of land that have been surveyed and set apart, under the provisions of a law approved 30th August, A.

D. 1856, for the benefit of a lunatic-asylum, a deaf-and-dumb-asylum, a blind-asylum, and an orphan-asylum, shall constitute a fund for the support of such institutions, one-fourth part to each; and the said fund shall never be diverted to any other purpose. The said lands may be sold and the fund invested under the same rules and regulations as provided for the lands belonging to the school-fund. The income of said fund only shall be applied to the support of such institutions, and, until so applied, shall be invested in the same manner as the principal.

§ 10. The governor, by and with the advice and consent of two-thirds of the senate, shall appoint an officer to be styled the superintendent of public instruction. His term of office shall be four years, and his annual salary shall not be less than $2,000, payable at stated times; and the governor, comptroller, and superintendent of public education shall constitute a board, to be styled a board of education, and shall have the general management and control of the perpetual school-fund and common schools, under such regulations as the legislature may hereafter prescribe.

§ 11. The several counties in this State which have not received their quantum of the lands for the purposes of education shall be entitled to the same quantity heretofore appropriated by the congress of the Republic of Texas, and the State, to other counties. And the counties which have not had the lands to which they are entitled for educational purposes located shall have the right to contract for the location, surveying, and procuring the patents for said lands, and of paying for the same with any portion of said lands so patented, not to exceed one-fourth of the whole amount to be so located, surveyed, and patented, to be divided according to quality, allowing to each part a fair proportion of land, water, and timber.

CONSTITUTION OF TEXAS, AS AMENDED IN 1869.[*]

Article IX.—Public schools.

SECTION 1. It shall be the duty of the legislature of this State to make suitable provisions for the support and maintenance of a system of public free schools for the gratuitous instruction of all the inhabitants of this State between the ages of six and eighteen years.

§ 2. There shall be a superintendent of public instruction, who, after the first term of office, shall be elected by the people; the first term of office shall be filled by appointment of the governor, by and with the advice and consent of the senate. The superintendent shall hold his office for the term of four years. He shall receive an annual salary of $2,500, until otherwise provided by law. In case of vacancy in the of-

---

[*] The stability of educational institutions in this State is further secured by an act of Congress approved March 30, 1870, which made the following stipulation as one of the conditions of admission to representation in Congress, after the interruption occasioned by the late war: " That the constitution of Texas shall never be so amended as to deprive any citizen or class of citizens of the United States of the school-rights and privileges secured by the constitution of said State."

fice of superintendent, it shall be filled by appointment of the governor, until the next general election.

§ 3. The superintendent shall have the supervision of the public free schools of the State and shall perform such other duties concerning public instruction as the legislature may direct. The legislature may lay off the State into convenient school-districts, and provide for the formation of a board of school-directors in each district. It may give the district-boards such legislative powers in regard to the schools, school-houses, and school-fund of the district as may be deemed necessary and proper. It shall be the duty of the superintendent of public instruction to recommend to the legislature such provisions of law as may be found necessary, in the progress of time, to the establishment and perfection of a complete system of education, adapted to the circumstances and wants of the people of this State. He shall, at each session of the legislature, furnish that body with a complete report of all the free schools in the State, giving an account of the condition of the same, and the progress of education within the State. Whenever required by either house of the legislature, it shall be his duty to furnish all information called for in relation to public schools.

§ 4. The legislature shall establish a uniform system of public free schools throughout the State.

§ 5. The legislature at its first session, or as soon thereafter as may be possible, shall pass such laws as shall require the attendance on the public free schools of the State of all the scholastic population thereof for the period of at least four months of each and every year: *Provided*, That when any of the scholastic inhabitants may be shown to have received regular instruction for said period of time in each and every year from any private teacher having a proper certificate of competency, this shall exempt them from the operation of the laws contemplated by this section.

§ 6. As a basis for the establishment and endowment of said public free schools, all the funds, lands, and other property heretofore set apart and appropriated, or that may hereafter be set apart and appropriated, for the support and maintenance of public schools, shall constitute the public-school-fund. And all sums of money that may come to this State hereafter from the sale of any portion of the public domain of the State of Texas shall also constitute a part of the public-school-fund. And the legislature shall appropriate all the proceeds resulting from sales of public lands of this State to such public-school-fund. And the legislature shall set apart, for the benefit of public schools, one-fourth of the annual revenue derivable from general taxation; and shall also cause to be levied and collected an annual poll-tax of one dollar on all male persons in this State, between the ages of twenty-one and sixty years, for the benefit of public schools. And said fund and the income derived therefrom, and the taxes herein provided for school-purposes, shall be a perpetual fund, to be applied, as needed, exclusively for the education of all the scholastic inhabitants of this State; and no law shall ever be made appropriating such fund for any other use or purpose whatever.

§ 7. The legislature shall, if necessary, in addition to the income derived from the public-school-fund and from the taxes for school-purposes provided for in the foregoing section, provide for the raising of such amount by taxation, in the several school-districts in the State, as will be necessary to provide the necessary school-houses in each district, and insure the education of all the scholastic inhabitants of the several districts.

§ 8. The public lands heretofore given to counties shall be under the control of the legislature, and may be sold under such regulations as the legislature may prescribe; and in such case the proceeds of the same shall be added to the public-school-fund.

§ 9. The legislature shall, at its first session, and from time to time thereafter, as may be found necessary, provide all needful rules and regulations for the purpose of carrying into effect the provisions of this article. It is made the imperative duty of the legislature to see to it that all the children in the State, within the scholastic age, are without delay provided with ample means of education. The legislature shall annually appropriate for school-purposes, and to be equally distributed among all the scholastic population of the State, the interest accruing on the school-fund and the income derived from taxation for school-purposes; and shall from time to time, as may be necessary, invest the principal of the school-fund in the bonds of the United States Government, and in no other security.

VERMONT.

[A very imperfect form of constitution was adopted by the inhabitants upon the "New Hampshire grants," in 1777. It was without provision for educational institutions, and was superseded in 1786 by a more formal frame of government, which, with the revisions of 1793 and of later years, has since continued. It recognized the claims of education and imposed upon the legislature the duty of providing and maintaining schools of learning by the State.]

CONSTITUTION OF VERMONT, AS AMENDED IN 1786 AND CONTINUED IN 1793.

[Extract from Chapter II.—Plan or Frame of Government.]

41. Laws for the encouragement of virtue and prevention of vice and immorality ought to be constantly kept in force and duly executed. And a competent number of schools ought to be maintained in each town for the convenient instruction of youth, and one or more grammar-schools be incorporated and properly supported in each county in this State. * * * *

VIRGINIA.

[No educational provisions were introduced into the constitution of 1776 nor in the revision of 1830.]

CONSTITUTION OF VIRGINIA, AS AMENDED IN 1851.

Article IV.—Subdivision of taxation and finance.

SECTION 24. A capitation-tax, equal to the tax assessed on land of the value of two hundred dollars, shall be levied on every white male inhabitant who has attained the age of twenty-one years; and one equal moiety of the capitation-tax upon white persons shall be applied to the purposes of education in primary and free schools; but nothing herein contained shall prevent exemptions of taxable polls in cases of bodily infirmity.

[The above section was continued in the revision of 1864, in which it is numbered as § 22 of Article IV.]

CONSTITUTION OF VIRGINIA, AS AMENDED IN 1870.*

Article VII.—County-organizations.

SECTION 1. * * * * And there shall be appointed, in the manner provided for in Article VIII,† one superintendent of schools: Provided, That counties containing less than eight thousand inhabitants may be attached to adjoining counties for the formation of districts for superintendents of schools: Provided, also, That in counties containing thirty thousand inhabitants there may be appointed an additional superintendent of schools therein. All regular elections for county-officers shall be held on the first Tuesday after the first Monday in November, and all officers elected or appointed under this provision shall enter upon the duties of their offices on the first day of January next succeeding their election, and shall hold their offices for the term of three years, except that the county- and circuit-court-clerks shall hold their offices for four years.

SCHOOL-DISTRICTS.

§ 3. Each township shall be divided into so many compactly-located school districts as may be deemed necessary: Provided, That no school-district shall be formed containing less than one hundred inhabitants. In each school district there shall be elected or appointed annually one school-trustee, who shall hold his office three years: Provided, That at the first election held under this provision there shall be three trustees elected, whose terms shall be one, two, and three years, respectively.

---

*An act of Congress approved January 26, 1870, for the admission of this State to representation in Congress, after the interruption of the war, contains the following stipulation: "That the constitution of Virginia shall never be so amended or changed as to deprive any citizen or class of citizens of the United States of the school-rights and privileges secured by the constitution of said State."

†Election by joint ballot of the legislature, within thirty days after organization, and every four years after.

Article VIII.—Education.

SECTION 1. The general assembly shall elect, in joint ballot, within thirty days after its organization under this constitution, and every fourth year thereafter, a superintendent of public instruction. He shall have the general supervision of the public free-school-interests of the State, and shall report to the general assembly for its consideration, within thirty days after his election, a plan for a uniform system of pub-' lic free schools.

§ 2. There shall be a board of education, composed of the governor, superintendent of public instruction, and attorney-general, which shall appoint, and have power to remove, for cause and upon notice to the incumbents, subject to confirmation by the senate, all county-superintendents of public free schools. This board shall have, regulated by law, the management and investment of all school-funds, and such supervision of schools of higher grades as the law shall provide.

§ 3. The general assembly shall provide by law, at its first session under this constitution, a uniform system of public free schools, and for its gradual, equal, and full introduction into all the counties of the State, by the year 1876, or as much earlier as practicable.

§ 4. The general assembly shall have power, after a full introduction of the public free-school-system, to make such laws as shall not permit parents and guardians to allow their children to grow up in ignorance and vagrancy.

§ 5. The general assembly shall establish, as soon as practicable, normal schools, and may establish agricultural schools and such grades of schools as shall be for the public good.

§ 6. The board of education shall provide for uniformity of text-books and the furnishing of school-houses with such apparatus and library as may be necessary, under such regulations as may be provided by law.

§ 7. The general assembly shall set apart, as a permanent and perpetual " literary fund," the present literary funds of the State, the proceeds of all public lands donated by Congress for public-school-purposes, of all escheated property, of all waste and unappropriated lands, of all property accruing to the State by forfeiture, and all fines collected for offenses committed against the State, and such other sums as the general assembly may appropriate.

§ 8. The general assembly shall apply the annual interest on the literary fund, the capitation-tax provided for by this constitution for public free-school-purposes, and an annual tax upon the property of the State of not less than one mill, nor more than five mills, on the dollar, for the equal benefit of all the people of the State, the number of children between the ages of five and twenty-one years in each public free-school-district being the basis of such division. Provision shall be made to supply children attending the public free schools with necessary text-books, in cases where the parent or guardian is unable, by reason of poverty, to furnish them. Each county and public free-school-district may raise additional sums by a tax on property for the support of public free schools. All unexpended sums of any one year in any public free-school district shall go into the general school-fund for redivision the next year: *Provided*, That any tax authorized by this section to be raised by counties or school-districts shall not exceed five mills on a dollar in any one year and shall not be subject to redivision, as hereinbefore provided in this section.

§ 9. The general assembly shall have the power to foster all higher grades of schools under its supervision, and to provide for such purpose a permanent educational fund.

§ 10. All grants and donations received by the general assembly for educational purposes shall be applied according to the terms prescribed by the donors.

§ 11. Each city and county shall be held accountable for the destruction of school-property that may take place within its limits by incendiaries or open violence.

§ 12. The general assembly shall fix the salaries and prescribe the duties of all school-officers and shall make all needful laws and regulations to carry into effect the public free-school-system provided for by this article.

WEST VIRGINIA.

CONSTITUTION OF WEST VIRGINIA, AS ADOPTED IN 1861.

Article VIII.—Taxation and finance.

SECTION 1. Taxation shall be equal and uniform throughout the State, and all property, both real and personal, shall be taxed in proportion to its value, to be ascertained as directed by law. No one species of property from which a tax may be collected shall be taxed higher than any other species of property of equal value; but property used for educational, literary, scientific, religious, or charitable purposes, and public property, may by law be exempted from taxation.

Article X.—Education.

SECTION 1. All money accruing in this State, being the proceeds of forfeited, delinquent, waste, and unappropriated lands, and of lands heretofore sold for taxes and purchased by the State of Virginia, if hereafter redeemed or sold to others than this State; all grants, devises, or bequests that may be made to this State for the purpose of education, or where the purposes of such grants, devises, or bequests are not specified; this State's personal share of the literature-fund of Virginia, whether paid over or otherwise liquidated, and any sums of money, stocks, or other property which this State shall have the right to claim from all persons who may die without leaving a will or heir, and of all escheated lands; the proceeds of any taxes that may be levied on the revenues of any corporation hereafter created; all moneys that may be paid as an equivalent for exemption from military duty; and such sums as may from time to time be appropriated by the legislature for the purpose, shall be set apart as a separate fund, to be called the school-fund, and invested, under such regulations as may be prescribed by law, in the interest-bearing securities of the United States or of this State; and the interest thereof shall be annually applied to the support of free schools throughout the State, and to no other purpose whatever. But any portion of such interest remaining unexpended at the close of a fiscal year shall be added to and remain a part of the capital of the school-fund.

§ 2. The legislature shall provide as soon as practicable for the establishment of a thorough and efficient system of free schools. They shall provide for the support of such schools by appropriating thereto the interest of the invested school-fund, the net proceeds of all forfeitures, confiscations, and fines accruing to this State under the laws thereof, and by general taxation on persons or property, or otherwise. They shall also provide for raising in each township, by the authority of the people thereof, such a proportion of the amount required for the support of free schools therein as shall be prescribed by general laws.

§ 3. Provision may be made by law for the election and prescribing the duties of a general superintendent of free schools for the State, whose term of office shall be the same as that of the governor, and for a county-superintendent of each county; and for the election in the several townships, by the voters thereof, of such officers not specified in this constitution as may be necessary to carry out the objects of this article; and for the organization, whenever it may be deemed expedient, of a State-board of instruction.

§ 4. The legislature shall foster and encourage moral, intellectual, scientific, and agricultural improvement; they shall, whenever it may be practicable, make suitable provision for the blind, mute, and insane, and for the organization of such institutions of learning as the best interests of general education in the State may demand.

CONSTITUTION OF WEST VIRGINIA, AS AMENDED IN 1872.

Article VII.—Executive department.

SECTION 1. The executive department shall consist of a governor, secretary of state, State-superintendent of free schools, auditor, treasurer, and attorney-general, who shall be, *ex officio*, reporter of the court of appeals. Their terms of office, respectively, shall be four years, and shall commence on the fourth day of March next after their election. They shall, except the attorney-general, reside at the seat of government during their terms of office, and keep there the public records, books, and papers pertaining to their respective offices, and shall perform such duties as may be prescribed by law.

§ 2. An election for governor, State-superintendent of free schools, auditor, treasurer, and attorney-general shall be held at such times and places as may be prescribed in this constitution or by general law.

* * * * * * *

§ 4. Neither the governor, State-superintendent of free schools, auditor, treasurer, nor attorney-general, shall hold any other office during the term of his service. The governor shall be ineligible to said office for the four years next succeeding the term for which he was elected.

*   *   *   *   *   *   *

§ 17. If the office of auditor, treasurer, State-superintendent of free schools, or attorney-general shall become vacant by death, resignation, or otherwise, it shall be the duty of the governor to fill the same by appointment, and the appointee shall hold his office until his successor shall be elected and qualified in such manner as may be provided by law. The subordinate officers of the executive department and the officers of all public institutions of the State shall keep an account of all moneys received or disbursed by them, respectively, from all sources, and for every service performed, and make a semi-annual report thereof to the governor, under oath or affirmation; and any officer who shall willfully make a false report shall be deemed guilty of perjury.

§ 18. The subordinate officers of the executive department and the officers of all the public institutions of the State shall, at least ten days preceding each regular session of the legislature, severally report to the governor, who shall transmit such report to the legislature; and the governor may at any time require information in writing, under oath, from the officers of his department, and all officers and managers of State-institutions, upon any subject relating to the condition, management, and expenses of their respective offices.

§ 19.   *   *   *   The State-superintendent of free schools [shall receive] fifteen hundred [dollars;]   *   *   *   and no additional emolument or allowance, except as herein otherwise provided, shall be paid or made out of the treasury of the State to any of the foregoing executive officers on any account.

Article X.—Taxation and finance.

SECTION 1.   *   *   *   *   No one species of property, from which a tax may be collected, shall be taxed higher than any other species of property of equal value; but property used for educational, literary, religious, or charitable purposes, all cemeteries, and public property, may by law be exempted from taxation.

§ 2. The legislature shall levy an annual capitation-tax of one dollar upon each male inhabitant of the State who has attained the age of twenty-one years, which shall be annually appropriated to the support of free schools. Persons afflicted with bodily infirmity may be exempted from this tax.

§ 7. County-authorities shall never assess taxes in any one year the aggregate of which shall exceed 95 cents per one hundred dollars valuation, except for the support of free schools, payment of indebtedness existing at the time of the adoption of this constitution; and for the payment of any indebtedness, with the interest thereon, created under the succeeding section, unless such assessment, with all questions involving the increase of such aggregate, shall have been submitted to the vote of the people of the county and have received three-fifths of all the votes cast for and against it.

Article XII.—Education.

SECTION 1. The legislature shall provide, by general law, for a thorough and efficient system of free schools.

§ 2. The State-superintendent of free schools shall have a general supervision of free schools and perform such other duties in relation thereto as may be prescribed by law. If, in the performance of any such duty imposed upon him by the legislature, he shall incur any expenses, he shall be re-imbursed therefor: *Provided*, The amount does not exceed five hundred dollars in any one year.

§ 3. The legislature may provide for county-superintendents and such other officers as may be necessary to carry out the objects of this article, and define their duties, powers, and compensation.

§ 4. The existing permanent and invested school-fund, and all money accruing to this State from forfeited, delinquent, waste, and unappropriated lands, and from lands heretofore sold for taxes and purchased by the State of Virginia, if hereafter redeemed or sold to others than this State; all grants, devises, or bequests that may be made to this State for the purposes of education, or where the purposes of such grants, devises, or bequests are not specified; this State's just share of the literary fund of Virginia, whether paid over or otherwise liquidated; and any sums of money, stocks, or property which this State shall have the right to claim from the State of Virginia for educational purposes; the proceeds of the estates of persons who may die without leaving a will or heir, and of all escheated lands; the proceeds of any taxes that may be levied on the revenues of any corporation; all moneys that may be paid as an equivalent for exemption from military duty; and such sums as may, from time to time, be appropriated by the legislature for the purpose, shall be set apart as a separate fund, to be called the "school-fund," and invested, under such regulations as may be prescribed by law, in the interest-bearing securities of the United States or of this State; or, if such interest-bearing securities cannot be obtained, then said "school-fund" shall be invested in such other solvent interest-bearing securities as shall be approved by the governor, superintendent of free schools, auditor, and treasurer, who are hereby constituted the "board of the school-fund," to manage the same under such regulations as may be prescribed by law; and the interest thereof shall be annually applied to the support of free schools throughout the State, and to no other purpose whatever. But any portion of said interest remaining unexpended at the close of a fiscal year shall be added to and remain a part of the capital of the "school-fund:" *Provided*, That all taxes which shall be received by the State upon delinquent lands, except the taxes due to the State thereon, shall be refunded to the county or district by or for which the same were levied.

§ 5. The legislature shall provide for the support of free schools by appropriating thereto the interest of the invested " school-fund," the net proceeds of all forfeitures and fines accruing to this State under the laws thereof, the State-capitation-tax, and by general taxation on persons and property or otherwise. It shall also provide for raising in each county or district, by the authority of the people thereof, such a proportion of the amount required for the support of free schools therein as shall be prescribed by general laws.

§ 6. The school-districts into which any county is now divided shall continue until changed in pursuance of law.

§ 7. All levies that may be made by any county or district for the purpose of free schools shall be reported to the clerk of the county-court, and shall, under such regulations as may be prescribed by law, be collected by the sheriff, or other collector, who shall make annual settlement with the county-court, which settlements shall be made a matter of record by the clerk thereof, in a book to be kept for that purpose.

§ 8. White and colored persons shall not be taught in the same schools.

§ 9. No person connected with the free-school-system of the State, or with any educational institution of any name or grade under State-control, shall be interested in the sale, proceeds, or profits of any book or other thing used or to be used therein, under such penalties as may be prescribed by law : *Provided*, That nothing herein shall be construed to apply to any work written or thing invented by such person.

§ 10. No independent free-school-district or organization shall hereafter be created, except with the consent of the school-district or districts out of which the same is to be created, expressed by a majority of the voters voting on the question.

§ 11. No appropriation shall hereafter be made to any State normal school or branch thereof, except to those already established and in operation or now chartered.

§ 12. The legislature shall foster and encourage moral, intellectual, scientific, and agricultural improvement; it shall, whenever it may be practicable, make suitable provision for the blind, mute, and insane, and for the organization of such institutions of learning as the best interests of the general education in the State may demand.

WISCONSIN.

[A convention was first held in Wisconsin while still a Territory, for the preparation of a constitution, in the autumn of 1846, under an enabling-act of Congress approved August 6 of that year. Their work was not approved by the people, and Wisconsin remained two years longer under a territorial government. The educational article prepared in 1846 bears a notable resemblance to that subsequently adopted, and was as follows:]

Article —.—Education—Schools and school-fund.

SECTION 1. The supervision of public instruction shall be vested in a State-superintendent and such other officers as the legislature may direct. The State-superintendent shall be chosen by the electors of the State once in every two years. The legislature shall provide for filling vacancies in the office of State-superintendent and prescribe his powers and duties.

§ 2. There shall be a State-fund for the support of public schools throughout the State, the capital of which shall be preserved inviolate. All moneys that may be granted by the United States to this State, and the clear proceeds of all property, real or personal, that has been or may be granted as aforesaid for educational purposes, or for the use of the State, where the purposes of the grant are not specified, and all moneys, and the clear proceeds of all property which may accrue to the State by forfeiture or escheat, shall be appropriated to and made a part of the capital of said fund. The interest on said fund, together with the rents on all property until sold, shall be inviolably appropriated to the support of said schools annually. Provision shall be made by law for an equal and equitable distribution of the income of the State-school-fund amongst the several towns, cities, and districts, for the support of schools therein, respectively, in some just ratio to the number of children attending such schools, respectively.

§ 3. Provision shall be made by law requiring the several towns and cities to raise a tax on the taxable property therein, annually, for the support of public schools in said towns and cities, respectively. The amount of such tax for each year shall not be less, in any town or city, than, with the amount receivable by such town or city from the State-school-fund, will produce an amount equal to $1 50 for every scholar therein.

§ 4. The legislature shall provide for a system of public schools, which shall be as nearly uniform as may be throughout the State; and, inasmuch as the public schools should be equally free to children of all religious persuasions, no book of religious doctrine or belief, and no sectarian instruction, shall be used or permitted in any public school.

§ 5. The legislature shall provide for the establishment of libraries, one, at least, in each town and city; and the money which shall be paid as an equivalent for exemption from military duty and the clear proceeds of all fines assessed in the several counties for any breach of the penal laws shall be exclusively applied to the support of said libraries.

CONSTITUTION OF WISCONSIN, AS ADOPTED IN 1848.

Article X.—Education.

SECTION 1. The supervision of public instruction shall be vested in a State-superintendent and such other officers as the legislature shall direct. The State-superintendent shall be chosen by the qualified electors of the State, in such manner as the legislature shall provide; his powers, duties, and compensation shall be prescribed by law: *Provided,* That his compensation shall not exceed the sum of $1,200 annually.

§ 2. The proceeds of all lands that have been or hereafter may be granted by the United States to this State for educational purposes, (except the lands heretofore granted for the purposes of a university,) and all moneys and clear proceeds of all property that may accrue to the

7 E

State by forfeiture or escheat, and all moneys which may be paid as an equivalent for exemption from military duty, and the clear proceeds of all fines collected in the several counties for any breach of the penal laws, and all moneys arising from any grant to the State, where the purposes of such grant are not specified, and the five hundred thousand acres of land to which the State is entitled by the provisions of an act of Congress entitled "An act to appropriate the proceeds of the sales of the public lands, and to grant pre-emption rights," approved the 4th day of September, 1841; and also 5 per centum of the net proceeds of the public lands to which the State shall become entitled on her admission into the Union, (if Congress shall consent to such appropriation of the two grants last mentioned,) shall be set apart as a separate fund, to be called the school-fund, the interest of which, with all other revenues derived from the school-lands, shall be exclusively applied to the following objects, to wit: (1) To the support and maintenance of common schools in each school-district, and the purchase of suitable libraries and apparatus therefor. (2) The residue shall be appropriated to the support and maintenance of academies and normal schools, and suitable libraries and apparatus therefor.

§ 3. The legislature shall provide by law for the establishment of district-schools, which shall be as nearly uniform as practicable; and such schools shall be free and without charge for tuition to all children between the ages of four and twenty years; and no sectarian instruction shall be allowed therein.

§ 4. Each town and city shall be required to raise by tax, annually, for the support of common schools therein, a sum not less than one-half the amount received by such town or city respectively for school-purposes from the income of the school-fund.

§ 5. Provision shall be made by law for the distribution of the income of the school-fund among the several towns and cities of the State, for the support of common schools therein, in some just proportion to the number of children and youth residing therein between the ages of four and twenty years; and no appropriation shall be made from the school-fund to any city or town for the year in which said city or town shall fail to raise such tax, nor to any school-district for the year in which a school shall not be maintained at least three months.

§ 6. Provision shall be made by law for the establishment of a State-university at or near the seat of the State-government, and for connecting with the same, from time to time, such colleges in different parts of the State as the interests of education may require. The proceeds of all lands that have been or may hereafter be granted by the United States to the State for the support of a university shall be and remain a perpetual fund, to be called the "university-fund," the interest of which shall be appropriated to the support of the State-university; and no sectarian instruction shall be allowed in such university.

§ 7. The secretary of state, treasurer, and attorney-general shall constitute a board of commissioners for the sale of the school· and university-lands, and for the investment of the funds arising therefrom. Any two of the commissioners shall be a quorum for the transaction of all business pertaining to the duties of their office.

§ 8. Provision shall be made by law for the sale of all school- and university-lands, after they have been appraised; and when any portion of such lands ·shall be sold, and the purchase-money shall not be paid at the time of the sale, the commissioners shall take security by mortgage upon the land sold for the·sum remaining unpaid, with 7 per cent. interest thereon, payable annually at the office of the treasurer. The commissioners shall be authorized to execute good and sufficient conveyance to all purchasers of such lands, and to discharge any mortgages taken as security when the sum due thereon shall have been paid. The commissioners shall have power to withhold from sale any portion of such lands when they shall deem it expedient; and shall invest all moneys arising from the sale of such lands, as well as all other university- and school-funds, in such manner as the legislature shall provide, and shall give such security for the faithful performance of their duties as may be required by law.

TERRITORY OF COLORADO.

[In 1865 the inhabitants of this Territory, acting, as they supposed, under an enabling-act which had been passed by Congress in 1864, elected delegates to a convention which prepared a State-constitution. Their proceedings were deemed irregular by the President, who declined to issue the proclamation required to give them validity. This form of constitution provided for the election of a superintendent of public instruction, as one of the executive departments, to hold office two years and to report annually to the legislature. He was to have a salary of $1,000. The title of all property of religious, educational, or charitable incorporations was to be vested in trustees elected by the members of those corporations. The educational article of this constitution was as follows :]

Article XIII.—Education. ·

SECTION 1. The State-superintendent of public instruction shall have the general supervision of the educational interests of the State and perform such other duties as may be provided by law.

§ 2. A county-superintendent of public instruction shall be elected in each county, whose term of office shall be two years, and whose duties and compensation shall be prescribed by law.

§ 3. The legislative assembly shall encourage the promotion of intellectual, moral, scientific, and agricultural improvement, by establishing a uniform system of public schools of higher grade, embracing normal, preparatory, and university-departments; but no religious institution of a strictly sectarian character shall receive the aid of the State.

TERRITORY OF NEW MEXICO.

[The inhabitants of New Mexico, in the summer of 1850, voted to accept a constitution prepared as a basis of State-government, but not approved by Congress. The educational article was as follows :]

Article VII.—Education.

SECTION 1. A general diffusion of knowledge being essential to the preservation of the rights and liberties of the people, it shall be the duty of the legislature of this State to make suitable provisions for the support and maintenance of public schools.

§ 2. The legislature shall, at as early a day as practicable, establish free schools throughout the State, and shall furnish means for their support by taxation ; and it shall be the duty of the legislature to set apart not less than one-twelfth of the annual revenue of the State derived from taxation as a perpetual fund, which fund shall be appropriated to the support of free public schools ; and no law shall be made diverting said fund to any other use.

§ 3. The supervision of public instruction shall be vested in a State-superintendent, and such other officers as the legislature may direct, the powers and duties of which officers shall be prescribed by law. The secretary of state shall, by virtue of his office, be the State-superintendent, for which he shall receive no extra compensation under any pretense whatever.

§ 4. The proceeds of all lands that have been or may be granted to the State for the support of schools, and all estates of persons dying without heir or will, and such percentage as may be granted by Congress on the sale of lands in this State shall be the common property of the State, and shall be a perpetual school-fund, which shall not be diminished ; but the interest and such other means as the legislative assembly may provide, by tax or otherwise, shall be inviolably appropriated to the support of common schools.

§ 5. The income of the State-school-fund shall be disbursed annually, by order of the State-superintendent, in the manner provided by law.

§ 6. All money which shall be paid by persons as an equivalent for exemption from military duty, the clear proceeds of estrays, and the proceeds of all fines for any breach of the penal laws, shall be exclusively applied to the support of common schools.

§ 7. The legislative assembly shall provide for the protection, improvement, or other disposition of such lands as have been or may hereafter be reserved or granted by the United States, or by any person or persons, to this State for the use of a university; and the funds accruing from the same, or from any other source for the purposes aforesaid, shall be and remain a permanent fund, the interest of which shall be applied to the support of the said university for the promotion of literature and the arts and sciences, as may be authorized by the terms of such grants ; and it shall be the duty of the legislative assembly, as soon as may be, to provide effectual means for the improvement and permanent security of the funds of said university.

§ 8. The legislative assembly shall provide by law who shall be commissioners of the school-fund.

[In 1870 a constitution was prepared for the "State of New Mexico," in anticipation of its admission into the Union, but, failing in this, it has never had effect. Its educational features were embraced in the following article :]

Article VIII.—Education.

SECTION 1. The education of the masses, and the diffusion of knowledge among them, being essential in order to preserve the rights and liberties of the people and maintain a free government, it shall be the duty of this State to provide by law for the maintenance of public schools.

§ 2. The legislature shall, as soon as practicable, establish schools in all the counties in the State, and maintain them by an equal tax; and it shall be the duty of the legislature to set apart one-twelfth of the gross income of the State derived from taxation as a perpetual fund, which fund shall be apportioned for the maintenance of public schools, in proportion to the population; and no law shall be passed diverting said fund to any other use.

§ 3. The superintendence of public instruction will be conferred upon a superintendent of public schools, and such other officers as may be prescribed by law; and, until otherwise provided, the secretary of state shall be, *ex officio*, superintendent of public schools.

CLASSIFIED SUMMARY.

NOTE.—The dates given in the following summary are those of first introduction mentioned into the constitutions of the provisions, and it will be understood that they have been since continued, unless it is otherwise mentioned:

RIGHT OF EDUCATION:

The people have a right to the privileges of an education, and it is the duty of the State to guard this right. N. C., 1868.

EDUCATIONAL QUALIFICATION OF VOTERS:

Must be able to read. Conn., 1855.
Must read English, and write their names. Mass., 1859.
May be required to read, after January, 1876. Mo., 1865.

OBJECTS TO BE PROMOTED BY THE STATE:

Agriculture, arts, science, commerce, trades, manufactures, and natural history. Mass., 1780.
Arts and sciences. Del., 1792; Ga., 1798.
Arts, sciences, commerce, manufactures, and natural history. Ind., 1816; Ark., 1836.
Arts, sciences, commerce, trades, manufactures, and natural history. N. H., 1784.
General diffusion of education. Me., 1820.
General diffusion of knowledge. Tex., 1845.
Humanity, general benevolence, public and private charity, industry, economy, honesty, punctuality, sincerity, sobriety, social affections, and generous sentiments. N. H., 1784. [The same, excepting "frugality" in place of "economy," and "good humor" in place of "social affections."] Mass., 1780.
Humanity, industry, and morality. Ind., 1816; Ark., 1836.
Intellectual, literary, scientific, mechanical, agricultural, and moral improvements. Nev., 1864.
Intellectual, scientific, and agricultural improvements. Ind., 1816; Mich., 1853; Ark., 1836.
Intellectual, scientific, moral, and agricultural improvement. Iowa, 1846; Cal., 1849; Ind., 1851; Kans., 1859; Miss., 1868.
Intelligence and stability. Minn., 1858.
Intelligence, virtue, and stability. Miss., 1868.
Knowledge and intelligence. Mo., 1865; Ark., 1868; N. J., 1873.

OBJECTS TO BE PROMOTED BY THE STATE—Continued.

Knowledge and learning. N. H., 1784; Ind., 1816; Ark., 1836.

Knowledge and virtue. R. I., 1842.

Knowledge, learning, and virtue. Tenn., 1834.

Literature and science. Mass., 1780; N. H., 1784; Tenn., 1834.

Literature, arts, and science. Mo , 1820; Mich., 1835; Iowa, 1846; Kans., 1859.

Moral, intellectual, scientific, and agricultural improvements. W. Va., 1861.

Religion, morality, and knowledge. Miss., 1817; Ohio, 1851; Nebr., 1867; Ark., 1868; N. C., 1868.

Virtue, and prevention of vice. Vt., 1786.

Virtue, and prevention of vice and immorality. Pa., 1776.

Wisdom and knowledge, as well as virtue. Mass., 1780.

ESTABLISHMENT AND MAINTENANCE OF SCHOOLS :

Schools to be encouraged. N. H.. 1784; Vt., 1786; Del., 1792; Ohio, 1802; Ala., 1819; Me., 1820; Mo., 1820; Ark., 1836; Tex., 1845; La., 1845; Oreg., 1857; Minn., 1858; Nebr., 1867; Fla., 1868; Miss., 1868; Pa., 1873.

Public and private schools to be encouraged by rewards and immunities. Nev., 1864.

Schools and means of education to be encouraged. Miss., 1817.

Schools to be free. Wis., 1848.

Free schools to be established. Ind., 1816; Mich., 1850; La., 1852; W. Va., 1861; Md., 1867; Ala., 1868; Ark., 1868; Ga., 1868; Miss., 1868; N. C., 1868; S. C., 1868; Tex., 1869; Ill., 1870; Va., 1870.

Free schools as early as practicable by tax. Tex., 1845.

Schools to be kept in each county at State expense. Ga., 1777 to 1789.

A school or schools in each county. Pa., 1776.

At least one free school in every parish. La., 1864.

One or more schools to be kept in each township. Mo., 1820.

Schools to be kept in every township. Minn., 1858; W. Va., 1861.

Free common schools to be kept in each district. Ala., 1868; Ark., 1868.

Free schools defined as "elementary." N. J., 1873.

Public to pay salaries so as to enable youth to be taught. Pa., 1776.

Schools for the poor to be gratis. Pa., 1790; Mo., 1820.

Poor entitled to privileges of education. Ohio, 1802.

Schools must be taught three months in a year. Mich., 1835; Iowa, 1846; Wis., 1848; Cal., 1849; Kans., 1859; Mo., 1865; Ark., 1868; Fla., 1868.

Schools must be taught four months in a year. Miss., 1868; N. C., 1868.

Schools must be taught six months in a year. Md., 1864 to 1867; S. C., 1868; Nev., 1869.

Schools for whites of scholastic age. Tex., 1866.

GENERAL SUPERINTENDENCE OF SCHOOLS:

Title of chief officer :

"General superintendent of free schools." W. Va., 1861.

[Governor to act as superintendent until the office is created by law.] Oreg., 1857.

"State school-commissioner." Ga., 1868.

"Superintendent of public education." Miss., 1868.

"Superintendent of public education." La., 1845, 1852, 1864; [may be abolished, La., 1868;] Wis., 1848; Cal., 1849; Mich., 1850; Ind., 1851; Md., 1864 to 1867; Nev., 1864; Tex., 1866; Ala., 1868; Ark., 1868; Fla., 1868; N. C., 1868; S. C., 1868; Ill., 1870; Va., 1870; Pa., 1873.

"Superintendent of public schools." Mo., 1865.

Election or appointment of chief officer :

[Elected by the people, except as follows :]

By joint ballot of general assembly. Va., 1870.

By the governor and senate. Mich., 1835; Md., 1864 to 1867; Tex., 1866 to 1869; Ga., 1868.

By the board of education, with the consent of the senate, but may be made elective by law, with a term of two years. Miss., 1868.

Term of chief officer :

Two years. Mich., 1835; La., 1845 to 1864; Ind., 1851; Kans., 1859; Nev., 1864.

Three years. Iowa, 1846; Cal., 1849 to 1862.

Four years. Ky., 1850; W. Va., 1861; Cal., 1862; La., 1864; Mo., 1865; Tex., 1866; Ark., 1868; Fla., 1868; N. C., 1868; Ill., 1870; Va., 1870.

Five years. Md., 1864.

Same as that of the governor. W. Va., 1861; Ala., 1868; Fla., 1868; Ga., 1868.

To be fixed by law. Wis., 1848; S. C., 1868.

Salary of chief officer :

[To be fixed by law, except in the following cases:]

Not over $1,200. Wis., 1848.

Fifteen hundred dollars and expenses, not over $500. W. Va., 1872.

Two thousand dollars. Fla., since 1871.

Twenty-five hundred dollars. Md., 1864, (till changed by law;) Tex., 1869.

Three thousand dollars. Fla., 1868 to 1871.

Four thousand dollars. La., 1864 to 1868.

Five thousand dollars. La., 1868.

Location of chief office :

At the seat of government. Ky., 1850; Kans., 1859; Ark., 1868; Fla., 1868; Ga., 1868; Ill., 1870; W. Va., 1872.

May be removed in certain cases mentioned. Fla., 1868.

GENERAL SUPERINTENDENCE OF SCHOOLS—Continued.

Relations of the chief officer to the government:

One of the executive department; Kans., 1859; Ark., 1868; Fla., 1868; N. C., 1868; Ill., 1870; W. Va., 1872; Pa., 1873.

One of a cabinet of administrative officers. Fla., 1868.

One of a council of State. N. C., 1868.

Special duties of chief officer:

To report a plan for a system of education. Md., 1864 to 1867; Miss., 1868; Tex., 1869; Va., 1870.

To report condition of schools. Fla., 1868; N. C., 1868; Ill., 1870; W. Va., 1872.

To organize a historical bureau and a cabinet. Fla., 1868. (A bureau of industrial resources to be formed under a commission. Ala., 1868.)

OTHER SUPERINTENDENCE OF SCHOOLS:

The legislature may provide other methods. Wis., 1848; Ark., 1868.

Women may be elected to school offices. Pa., 1873.

County school commissioners to be elected biennially; to form a State board of education. S. C., 1868.

The legislature may direct the appointment of school commissioners in each county. Md., 1864 to 1867.

County school superintendents must be elected in each county. Kans., 1859; W.Va., 1861; Fla., 1868; Va., 1870. [May be elected in each county.] Ill., 1870; W. Va., 1872.

BOARDS AND COMMISSIONS IN CHARGE OF EDUCATIONAL AFFAIRS:

Board of commissioners of State institutions, (cabinet.) Fla., 1868.

Board of commissioners in charge of school-fund, appointed by the general assembly, and reporting annually. Tenn., 1834.

Board of commissioners for the sale of school and university lands. Wis., 1848; Oreg., 1857.

Board of education, (with powers and duties more or less defined.) Mich., 1850; Iowa, 1857; Md., 1864 to 1867; Tex., 1866; Ala., 1868; Fla., 1868; Miss., 1868; N. C., 1868; Va., 1870.

Board of instruction. W. Va., 1861.

Board of regents of the university, (with limited legislative powers and specific duties.) Mich., 1850; (for term of four years, till changed.) Nev., 1864; (same as board of education, with powers with respect to the university and agricultural college.) Ala., 1868.

Board of school-fund. W. Va., 1872.

LOCAL SCHOOL LEGISLATION:

Baltimore school-taxes and school-commissioners to continue as before. Md., 1864 to 1867.

LOCAL SCHOOL LEGISLATION—Continued.

Local legislation forbidden with respect to common schools. Ill., 1870; (with respect to common schools and school-fund,) Ind., 1851; (with respect to schools and school-houses,) Pa., 1873.

MINIMUM TERM OF SCHOOLS TO ENTITLE TO A SHARE IN THE SCHOOL-MONEYS:

Three months. Ark., 1868; Cal., 1849; Fla., 1868; Iowa, 1846; Kans., 1859; Mich., 1835; Wis., 1848.
Four months. Miss., 1868.
Six months. Nev., 1864.

SECTARIAN SCHOOLS FORBIDDEN FROM RECEIVING SCHOOL-MONEYS:

Ark., 1836; Wis., 1848; Ohio, 1851; Kans., 1859; Nev., 1864; Nebr., 1867; S. C., 1868; Ill., 1870; Pa., 1873. [Schools becoming sectarian to forfeit right to State aid.] Nev., 1864. [Religious sects not to control.] Miss., 1868.

LANGUAGE TAUGHT IN SCHOOLS:

To be taught in English. Mich., 1850.
General exercises to be in English. La., 1864.

ALLEGIANCE OF TEACHERS:

Teachers required to take the oath required of public officers by the constitution. Nev., 1864.

DISTINCTIONS OF RACE AND COLOR; PREFERENCES:

No preference to be shown in schools by the State. Ohio, 1802.
No distinctions of race or color allowed. S. C., 1868.
No distinctions of race, color, or previous condition allowed. La., 1868.
No municipal law to be passed contrary to the article relating to color. La., 1868.
Funds to be applied without regard to color. Mo., 1865.
Schools to be provided for white scholastic inhabitants. Tex., 1866 to 1869.
Whites and negroes not allowed in same schools. Tenn., 1870.
Separate schools for whites and colored. W. Va., 1872.
Separate schools *may* be provided for Africans. Mo., 1865.
School-taxes on Africans to be applied for their benefit. Tex., 1866.
Schools to be encouraged among Africans. Tex., 1866 to 1869.
Schools for benefit of all the children. Va., 1870.

SCHOOL AGES FOR WHICH PROVISION IS MADE:

Over six years. Pa., 1873.
Four to twenty years. Wis., 1848; Oreg., 1857.
Four to twenty-one years. Fla., 1868.

SCHOOL AGES FOR WHICH PROVISION IS MADE—Continued.

Five to eighteen years. N. J., 1873.

Five to twenty years. Md., 1864.

Five to twenty-one years. Iowa, 1857; Minn., 1858; Kans., 1859; Mo., 1865; Ala., 1868; Ark., 1868; Va., 1870.

Six to eighteen years. Nev., 1864; Tex., 1869.

Six to twenty-one years. La., 1868; N. C., 1868.

To be fixed by law. La., 1852 to 1868.

COMPULSORY ATTENDANCE:

May be required by law. Nev., 1864.

May be required, after schools are established. Va., 1870.

To be required at least 16 months between 6 and 18 years. N. C., 1868.

May be required between 5 and 18 years. Ark., 1868.

May be required 16 months between 5 and 18 years. Mo., 1865.

Scholastic population may be required to attend 4 months in each year. Tex., 1869.

May be required to attend 24 months between 6 and 16 years, after schools are fully established. S. C., 1868.

CONSOLIDATION OR DIVISION OF COUNTIES FOR SCHOOL-SUPER-VISION :

Counties of less than 8,000 inhabitants may be annexed to others, and those of over 30,000 may be divided. Va., 1870.

SCHOOL-DISTRICTS:

A board of school-directors in each, with legislative powers. Tex., 1869.

Each town to be divided into districts with at least 100 inhabitants, and 3 trustees. Va., 1870.

Local laws affecting school-districts forbidden. Pa., 1873.

New districts to be formed only on the vote of a majority of those interested. W. Va., 1872.

State to be divided into school-districts. N. C., 1868; S. C., 1868.

SCHOOL-HOUSES:

To be built by tax. Tex., 1869; by tax or otherwise. Ark., 1868.

To be free of tax. Ill., 1847; Ind., 1851; Ark., 1868; Fla., 1868.

SCHOOL-APPARATUS :

Apparatus to be furnished to schools. Wis., 1848; Oreg., 1857.

SCHOOL-LIBRARIES:

To be established. Wis., 1848; Oreg., 1857; Va., 1870.

May be established. Iowa, 1846, 1857.

No teacher or school-officer to be interested in sale of books or apparatus. Ill., 1870.

THER LIBRARIES:

County libraries: 10 per cent. on town lots at county-seat for this object. Ind., 1816.

At least one library in each township; military exemption-money and fines for violation of penal laws applied. Mich., 1835.

EXT-BOOKS:

Text-books to be uniform. Va., 1870.

Text-books to be furnished to the poor. Va., 1870.

No school-officer to be concerned in school-books or other thing used in schools, except those of his own authorship. W. Va., 1872.

ESPONSIBILITY FOR THE SAFE-KEEPING OF SCHOOL-PROPERTY:

Each city or town to be accountable for the destruction of school-property from incendiarism or violence. Va., 1870.

CHOOL-LANDS, AND REVENUES ARISING THEREFROM:

Lands granted by State. N. Y., 1821.

Lands received from, or to be given by the United States, and the proceeds of sales to be applied to schools. Ind., 1816; Ill., 1818; Ala., 1819; Mo., 1820; Tenn., 1834; Mich., 1835; Ark., 1836; Fla., 1845; La., 1845; Iowa, 1846; Wis., 1848; Cal., 1849; Kans., 1859; Nev., 1864; Nebr., 1867; Miss., 1868; N. C., 1868.

Swamp-lands. Ind., 1851; Ala., 1868; N. C., 1868.

Swamp-lands, except in certain counties. Miss., 1868.

Forfeited, waste, and unappropriated lands. W. Va., 1861.

Lands not otherwise appropriated. Wis., 1848; La., 1845; Ind., 1851; Mo., 1865; Ark., 1868; N. C., 1868; Oreg., 1868; W. Va., 1872.

The 500,000 acres granted in 1841 to new States. Iowa, 1846; Cal., 1849; Oreg., 1857; Kans., 1849; Nev., 1864.

Such percentage on the sale of lands as may be allowed by Congress Iowa, 1846; Cal., 1849; Kans., 1859; Nev., 1864; N. C., 1868.

Five per cent. on net proceeds of public lands. Wis., 1848; Oreg., 1857.

Twenty-five per cent. of sales of public lands. Fla., 1868.

Half the proceeds of public lands. Tex., 1866.

Alternate sections of lands reserved in railroad grants. Tex., 1866.

School-lands not to be sold, but leased for not less than 20 years. Tex., 1845.

Floating land-warrants to be sold for benefit of schools. Nev., 1864.

Lands not to be sold without a vote, but may be leased 25 years. Kans., 1859.

In selling lands for school-fund, preference to be given to settlers. Tex., 1866.

Lands not to be sold before 1820. Ind., 1816.

Not over a third sold in 2 years, another third in 5 years, and remaining third in 10 years. Minn., 1858.

SCHOOL-LANDS, AND REVENUES ARISING THEREFROM—Continued.

Lands of greatest valuation to be first sold; sales public. Minn., 1858.

Rents of lands applied to school purposes. Mo., 1820; La., 1845; Cal., 1849; Iowa, 1851; Minn., 1858; Kans., 1859; Ala., 1868.

SCHOOL-FUNDS; REVENUES; TAXATION FOR SCHOOL-PURPOSES:

Capital inviolable. Ind., 1816; Conn., 1818; Mo., 1820; N. Y., 1821; Tenn., 1834; R. I., 1842; N. J., 1844; Iowa, 1846; Wis., 1848; Ky., 1850; Ohio, 1851; Kans., 1859; Tex., 1866; Md., 1867; Miss., 1868; S. C., 1868.

United States deposit fund of 1836. Ind., 1851; La., 1864.

Sum of $25,000 a year added to school-fund from N. Y., 1846.

Taxes to be raised, if funds do not allow a school to be kept 4 months in a year. Mo., 1865.

Taxes by towns or cities for schools must equal half the sum received from school-fund. Wis., 1848; Fla., 1868.

A tax of 5 cents per $100 to be raised till it amounts to $6,000,000. Md., 1864 to 1867.

Bonds and stocks granted. Ark., 1868.

At least $1,000,000 a year to be granted for schools. Pa., 1873.

Tax of one to five mills per $1, on valuation. Va., 1870.

Taxes to such extent as may be necessary. Tex., 1866; Va., 1866; Ark., 1868; N. C., 1868; W. Va., 1872.

Tax on corporations. Ind., 1851; W. Va., 1861.

Ten per cent. of annual revenue for schools. Tex., 1845.

One-fifth of aggregate annual revenue of State for schools. Ala., 1868.

Twenty-five per cent. of taxation for schools. Tex., 1869.

Tax of 10 cents per $100 or more. Md., 1864 to 1867.

Tax of half a mill for university and schools; may be reduced to ¼ mill in 10 years. Nev., 1864.

Tax for schools to be collected with other taxes. Md., 1864 to 1867; S. C., 1868.

Tax-sales applied to schools. Miss., 1868; W. Va., 1872.

Tax of at least 1 mill on a dollar. Fla., 1868.

Particular extra school-tax on counties if requested by vote. Md., 1864 to 1867.

Right of taxation of United States lands abandoned. Kans., 1859.

Certain specific taxes specified in detail. Ala., 1868.

Bank-tax fund. Ind., 1851.

County seminary-fund. Ind., 1851; La., 1845; Iowa, 1846; Cal., 1849; Mich., 1850; Kans., 1859; W. Va., 1861.

Distributive shares in estates of deceased persons. Mo., 1865; Ala., 1868; Ark., 1868; S. C., 1868.

CHOOL-FUNDS, &c.—Continued.

Escheats. Wis., 1848; Mich., 1850; Ind., 1851; Oreg., 1857; W. Va., 1861; Nev., 1864; Mo., 1865; Ark., 1868; Fla., 1868; Miss., 1868; Va., 1870.

Estrays. Kans., 1859; Mo., 1865; Ark., 1868; N. C., 1868.

Excise licenses. Miss., 1868.

Fines for violation of penal laws. Ind., 1816; Iowa, 1846; Wis., 1848; Kans., 1859; Nev., 1864; Mo., 1865; Ark., 1868; Fla., 1868; Miss., 1868; N. C., 1868; Va., 1870; W. Va., 1872.

Forfeitures. Wis., 1848; Ind., 1851; Oreg., 1857; Ark., 1868; Fla., 1868; Va., 1870; W. Va., 1872.

Individual grants. Iowa, 1846; Kan., 1859; Oreg., 1857; W. Va., 1861; Ala., 1868; Fla., 1868.

Saline fund. Ind., 1851.

State grants. Ala., 1868; Fla., 1868.

Military exemption moneys. Ind., 1816; Iowa, 1846; Wis., 1848; Oreg., 1857; Kans., 1859; W. Va., 1861; Ala., 1868; Fla., 1868; Miss., 1868; N. C., 1868.

Mines. Ark., 1868.

Penalties. Mo., 1865; Ark., 1868; N. C., 1868.

Unclaimed dividends. Mo., 1865; Ark., 1868.

OLL-TAXES FOR SCHOOL-PURPOSES:

Poll taxes may be raised. Va., 1850; Ala., 1868; Ark., 1868; Fla., 1868; Miss., 1868; S. C., 1868; Tenn., 1870; Tex., 1869; W. Va., 1872.

Right of suffrage not lost for non-payment of, S. C., 1868.

Half for free schools and half for University of New Orleans. La., 1868.

EBTS OF SCHOOL-DISTRICTS:

Not to exceed 5 per cent. of valuation of taxable property. Ill., 1870.

ANAGEMENT OF SCHOOL-FUNDS:

To be managed by same financial agents as State and county funds. Iowa, 1857.

Unexpended balances to be added yearly. W. Va., 1861.

Mode of investment prescribed. La., 1852; Nev., 1864; Mo., 1865; Tex., 1866; Ark., 1868; Miss., 1868; W. Va., 1872.

All money and property to be reduced to the public-school fund, so far as may be, under vested rights. Mo., 1865.

Fund may be increased but not diminished. Iowa, 1846; Ind., 1851; Ala., 1868.

To remain in charge of State till schools are established. Tex., 1845.

Bank-stock to be sold. Mo., 1865.

MANAGEMENT OF SCHOOL-FUNDS—Continued.

Managed by superintendent of public instruction. Kans., 1859.
Commissioners for management provided. Kans., 1859.

SCHOOL-FUNDS OF THE PARENT STATE:

To be shared by the new State. W. Va., 1861.
Grants for educational purposes confirmed. Me., 1820.

EDUCATIONAL INSTITUTIONS EXEMPT FROM TAXATION:

Ill., 1847; Ind., 1851; W. Va., 1861; Fla., 1868; W. Va., 1861.

INCORPORATION OF INSTITUTIONS FOR EDUCATION:

To be provided for. Ohio, 1802.

COUNTY SCHOOL LANDS AND FUNDS:

Funds to be loaned on real estate, with personal securities. Mo., 1865.
Counties to receive their share of lands for schools. Tex., 1845.
County school-lands may be sold. Tex., 1866.
Funds to be safely guarded. Ind., 1851.
Funds not used to be re-invested. Ind., 1851.
Lands sold for taxes, to benefit the counties where the land is located. W. Va., 1872.
Counties liable for safe-keeping of county school-funds. Ind., 1851.

GRADED SYSTEMS OF EDUCATION:

To be a gradation from township-schools to university. Ind., 1816.
Schools to be established, grading from primary to university. Nev., 1864.

ACADEMIES AND SEMINARIES:

To be encouraged. Mass., 1780.
One or more seminaries of learning to be established. Ga., 1798.
Uniform schools of higher grade to be established. Kans., 1857.
Seminaries of learning and instruction in arts and sciences to be established. Mo., 1820; La., 1845.
Grants to specific seminaries inviolable. La., 1864.
Literature-fund inviolable. N. Y., 1821.
Literary fund to be provided. Va., 1870.
No grants to be made to private schools. La., 1864.
County seminaries to be established. Ind., 1816 to 1851.
One or more grammar-schools to be established in each county. Tex., 1866.
Higher seminaries may be established. Va., 1870.
Academies, colleges, and seminaries of learning may be endowed, with right of repeal. Me., 1820.
Residue of certain funds to be applied to academies. Wis., 1848.
654

ORMAL SCHOOLS:

May be established. Nev., 1864.
Shall be established. Kans., 1859; [within five years,] S. C., 1868.
To be in university. N. C., 1868.
Certain residue funds applied to. Wis., 1848.
No new normal schools to be established. W. Va., 1872.

OLLEGES EXISTING ON THE ADOPTION OF THE CONSTITUTION:

Rights of Bowdoin College confirmed. Me., 1820.
Rights of Harvard University confirmed. Mass., 1780.
Rights of Yale College confirmed. Conn., 1818.

NIVERSITIES:

One or more universities to be established. Pa., 1776.
One or more seminaries, to be established. Pa., 1790.
A university may be established with branches. Mich., 1835; Iowa,
1846, [without branches.] Iowa, 1857.
A State university of arts, literature, and science to be formed.
Ala., 1819; Cal., 1849; Kans., 1859.
One or more universities to be founded. N. C., 1776.
A State university to be established with instruction in agriculture
and natural sciences. Ark., 1836; Kans., 1859; Mo., 1865; Fla.,
1868; Ill., 1870.
The University of New Orleans established, and its organization
prescribed. La., 1845.
Location of university as established by law, and its rights con-
firmed. Minn., 1858.
Part of educational funds to be applied to a university. Nev., 1864.
A university to be organized at an early day. Tex., 1866.
University to form part of school-system, free of tuition, and aided
by escheats, unclaimed dividends, and distributive, shares of
estates. N. C., 1868.
A free State university to be founded. S. C., 1868.
Citadel and grounds in Charleston granted for educational purposes.
S. C., 1868.
Mining to be taught in university. Nev., 1864; N. C., 1868.
Agricultural instruction may form a branch of university. Kans.,
1859; Ala., 1868; N. C., 1868.
Mechanics to be taught in university. N. C., 1868.
University lands to be protected. Ala., 1819; Mo., 1820; Mich.,
1835; Iowa, 1846; Wis., 1848; Cal., 1849; Kans., 1859; Tex.,
1866; Neb., 1867; S. C., 1868.
One township for a seminary. Ind., 1816.
Lands for a university asked for. Kans., 1859.
Lands granted for. Nev., 1864.

δ E   655

AGRICULTURAL SCHOOLS:

Funds provided for. Mich., 1850; Miss., 1868; S. C., 1868; Va. 1868.

Land granted for a separate agricultural college. Nev., 1864.

STATE REFORM SCHOOL:

To be provided for juvenile offenders. S. C., 1868.

EDUCATION AND SUPPORT OF UNFORTUNATE CLASSES:

Provision to be made for the blind and deaf and dumb. La.; S. C., 1868.

Provision for the deaf and dumb, blind, and insane. Mich., 1850; Va., 1850.

Provision for the blind and insane. W. Va., 1861. ·

A tract of 400,000 acres to be surveyed for the benefit of the deaf and dumb and blind. Tex., 1866.

INDEX.

A.

	Page.
Academies, funds of, New York	69
—— to be established, Maine	45
—— and seminaries, (summary)	112
Adams, Charles Francis, citation from work edited by	48
Adams, John, author of educational article in constitution of Massachusetts	48
African children, education of, Texas	86
—— separate schools for:	
Missouri	61
Tennessee	84
Ages of children entitled to school privileges:	
Alabama	10
Arkansas	14, 15
Iowa	36
Kansas	37, 38, 39
Louisiana	42, 43
Maryland	47
Minnesota	57, 58
Mississippi	58
Missouri	62
Nebraska	67
New Jersey	68
New York	70
North Carolina	72
Oregon	77
Pennsylvania	80
South Carolina	81
Texas	87, 88
Summary	107
Agricultural colleges and instruction in—	
Alabama	11
Arkansas	14
Michigan	55, 56
Mississippi	59
Missouri	61
Nevada	66
North Carolina	74
South Carolina	88
—— improvement—	
Indiana	28, 29
Iowa	35
Kansas	36, 39, 40
Mississippi	58
Nevada	65, 66, 67
New Hampshire	67
—— survey, Alabama	12
Alabama, constitution of, 1819	9

Page.

Alabama, constitution of, 1868 9
Allegiance of teachers, (summary) 107
American Academy of Arts and Sciences 49
Apparatus for normal school, Kansas 36
—— teachers and school officers not to be interested in sale of, Illinois 27
Arts, encouragement of:
     Arkansas 13
     Delaware 17
     Georgia 22
     Iowa 33
     Kansas 36
     Louisiana 42
     Massachusetts 49
     Michigan 52
     New Hampshire 67
Arkansas, constitution of, 1836 12
—— constitution of, 1864–'65 13
—— constitution of, 1868 13
Arnold, Mr., collections of 49
Attendance, compulsory, (summary) 108
Auburn, Ala., agricultural and mechanical college at 11

B.

Baltimore, school commissioners of 47
Bank of Kentucky, stock in 40
Bank-tax fund, Indiana 29
Banks, taxes upon, Maine 46
Benevolence, inculcation of:
     Massachusetts 51
     New Hampshire 67
Blind, institutions for:
     Louisiana 45
     Michigan 55, 56
     South Carolina 82
     Texas 87
Board of commissioners for sale of school lands:
     Kansas 40
     Nebraska 64
—— of Education:
     Alabama 9, 10, 11
     Florida 22
     Iowa 33, 34
     Maryland 46
     Michigan 54, 56
     Mississippi 58
     Missouri 61
     North Carolina 73
     South Carolina 81
Boards and commissions, (summary) 104
—— of regents, (see regents of university.)
Bonds for school purposes forbidden, Illinois 27
Boston, minister of Congregational Church in 50
—— philosophical society formed at 49
Bowdoin College, rights of, Maine 45
Bureau of industrial resources, Alabama 12
Bureau of statistics, agriculture, and immigration, North Carolina 72

C.

	Page.
Cabinet of administrative officers, Florida	22
California, constitution of, 1849	18
—— amendment of, 1862	19
Cambridge, ministers of Congregational Church in	50
Charity, inculcation of:	
Massachusetts	51
New Hampshire	67
Charleston, S. C., citadel at, given for educational purposes	82
Charlestown, Mass., minister of Congregational Church in	50
Citadel at Charleston, S. C., given for educational purposes	82
Classified summary	103
Colleges existing on the adoption of constitution, (summary)	113
—— to be established, Maine	45
Color and race, (summary)	107
Colored children, education of, Texas	86
—— to be educated separately:	
Missouri	61
Tennessee	84
—— no distinction in schools for, South Carolina	82
Commerce, encouragement of:	
Arkansas	13
Massachusetts	51
New Hampshire	67
Commissioner of industrial resources, Alabama	12
Committee of manners, education, and arts, Pennsylvania	78
Common-school fund. (See School-fund.)	
Compulsory attendance at schools: *NED 64*	
North Carolina	74
South Carolina	81
Texas	88
Summary	108
Congress, limitations imposed by, Texas	87
Connecticut, constitution of, 1818	17
Consolidation of counties	108
Continental Congress, ordinances of	74
Cooper, Dr	49
Copiah County, Mississippi, swamp-lands in	58
Copper-mines, income from	74
Cornell University, endowment-fund	70
Corporations, educational:	
Florida	21
Ohio	75
Council of the State, North Carolina	71
Counties to have the benefit of school-lands, Texas	86, 86
County school-funds, Indiana	31
County school-lands and funds, (summary)	112
County seminaries, Indiana	28, 30
County superintendent of education, Mississippi	58

D.

Deaf and dumb, institutions for:	
Louisiana	45
Michigan	55, 56
South Carolina	82

	Page.
Deaf and dumb, institutions for:	
Texas	87
Debts of school-districts limited	111
Delaware, constitutions of, 1792 and 1831	18
De Witt, Simeon	69
Distinctions of race and color, (summary)	107
Dividends, unclaimed, Arkansas	15
Dorchester, Mass., minister of Congregational Church in	50

E.

Economy, inculcation of, New Hampshire	67
Educational qualification of voters, (summary)	103
Education and support of unfortunate classes, (summary)	114
—— the people have the right to, North Carolina	71
Election of officers:	
Alabama	10
Arkansas	13
California	16
English, reading of, a qualification of voters, Massachusetts	51
—— to be taught in schools:	
Louisiana	43, 44
Michigan	54, 56
Escheated property, given to school-fund:	
Alabama	11
Arkansas	15
Michigan	54, 56
Mississippi	58
Missouri	61
Nebraska	63
Nevada	65
North Carolina	73
Oregon	77
—— heirs not to be prevented from enjoyment of, Tennessee	84
Establishment of schools, (summary)	104
Estrays, proceeds of sales of:	
Arkansas	15
Kansas	39
Executive department:	
Arkansas	13
Florida	22
Illinois	25
Kansas	38
North Carolina	71
Pennsylvania	79
Exemption of educational property from taxation:	
Florida	22
Oregon	76
summary	112
(See Military exemptions.)	

F.

Fayetteville, Ark., university at	14
Fines applicable to school purposes:	
Alabama	11
Arkansas	15

	Page.
Fines applicable to school purposes:	
Iowa	32, 35
Kansas	39
Massachusetts..	58
Missouri	63
Nebraska	63
North Carolina	72
Oregon	77
—— applied to libraries, Michigan	55, 56
Florida, constitutions of, 1839, 1861, and 1868	21
Frame of government of Pennsylvania, 1682..................................	77
——, 1683, 1696	78
Franklin, Dr	49
Free schools defined, New Jersey...	68
—— system of to be reported, Mississippi...................................	58
Frugality, promotion of, Massachusetts	51
Furniture for schools, teachers, &c., not to be interested in sale of, Illinois......	27

G.

General superintendence of schools, (summary)	104
—— legislation to be provided for schools :	
Illinois	25
Indiana...	29
—— laws to be passed for erecting and changing school-districts, Pennsylvania.	79
Generous sentiments, inculcation of, New Hampshire.......................	67
Geological survey, Alabama..	12
Georgia, constitution of, 1777	22
—— constitution of, 1798..	22
—— constitution of, 1868..	23
Gold-mines, income from	74
Governor to be superintendent of schools, Oregon	76
Graded systems of education, (summary)......................................	112
Grammar-schools, encouragement of, Massachusetts	51
Grants for school purposes:	
Alabama...	9, 11
Arkansas	15
California	16
Florida	21
Illinois	27
Louisiana..	41, 42, 43, 44
Michigan	53, 54, 56
Minnesota	57
Missouri	61
Nebraska	63
Nevada	65
North Carolina...	72
Oregon	77
Texas	84, 85

H.

Hancock County, Mississippi, swamp-lands in.................................	58
Hart, William, commissioner Yale College....................................	17
Harvard College, foundation and rights of, Massachusetts	48, 49, 50, 51
Honesty, promotion of :	
Massachusetts...	51
New Hampshire..	67

Page

Humanity, promotion of:
Arkansas 13
Massachusetts... 51
New Hampshire.. 67

I.

Illinois, ordinance of convention of 1818............................. 23
—— constitution of, 1847-'48... 24
—— constitution proposed in 1862.................................... 25
—— constitution of, 1870.. 25
Improvements in arts, &c., to be encouraged:
Arkansas 13
California 16
Delaware 18
Georgia... 22
Iowa 33
Kansas 36
Louisiana... 42
Massachusetts... 49
Michigan 52
North Carolina.. 67
Indiana, constitution of, 1816....................................... 28
—— constitution of, 1856.. 29
Indian reservations, Kansas.. 37
Industrial resources, Alabama.. 12
Industry, promotion of:
Arkansas 13
Massachusetts... 51
New Hampshire... 67
Insane, institutions for:
Louisiana... 45
Michigan 55,56
Intelligence, promotion of:
Arkansas 14
California.. 16
Indiana... 28,29
Iowa 32,35
Kansas 39
Michigan 52,55,56
Minnesota 57
Mississippi 58
Intestate estates, certain interests arising from, given to schools:
Alabama... 11
Arkansas 15
Iowa 31,32,35
Kansas 39
Louisiana... 41,42,43,44
Nebraska 63
North Carolina.. 73
South Carolina.. 84
Investment of school-funds:
Arkansas 15,16
California 16
Indiana... 30

	Page.
Investment of school-funds:	
Missouri	61
New Jersey	68
New York	69
Texas	86
Iowa, constitution proposed in 1844	31
—— constitution of, 1846	32
—— constitution of, 1857	33
Iowa City, University at	34

J.

| Juvenile offenders, school for, South Carolina | 82 |

K.

Kansas, constitution of, 1859	36
Kentucky, constitution of, 1850	40
Kingsbury, Andrew, commissioner Yale College	17
Knowledge, promotion of:	
Arkansas	12, 14
Indiana	28, 29
Kansas	36
Massachusetts	50
Michigan	56
Mississippi	57, 58
Nebraska	62
North Carolina	67
Ohio	72
Oregon	74, 75
Rhode Island	80
Tennessee	83
Texas	84, 85

L.

Lands for school purposes:	
Alabama	9, 11
Arkansas	12, 15
California	16, 17
Florida	19
Georgia	24
Illinois	27
Indiana	28
Iowa	32, 33, 35
Kansas	36, 38
Louisiana	41, 42, 43, 44
Michigan	52, 53, 44
Minnesota	57
Mississippi	58
Missouri	59
Nebraska	63, 64
Nevada	65
New York	68, 70
North Carolina	72
Ohio	75
Oregon	77
South Carolina	82
Tennessee	83
Texas	85, 86, 87, 89

Page.
Lands for school purposes:
      Virginia 91
      West Virginia 93
      Wisconsin 97, 98
Language taught in schools, (summary) 107
Lansing, agricultural college at 55
Law department in University, Louisiana 41, 45
Law-school may be established, South Carolina 83
Lawrence County, Mississippi, swamp-lands in 58
Lawrence, University of Kansas at 40
Lead-mines, income from 74
Learning, diffusion of:
      Indiana 28, 29
      New Hampshire 67
      Tennessee 83
Leavenworth constitution, Kansas 37
Lecompton constitution, Kansas 36
Lee, Arthur 49
Legislative powers of board of education:
      Alabama 10
      Iowa 34
Leven, Sir Ashton, collections owned by 49
Libraries:
      Iowa 32, 33
      Michigan 52, 55, 56
—— normal school, Kansas 36
—— summary 108, 109
License-moneys given to school-fund:
      Mississippi 59
      Nebraska 63
Literary institutions, members of general assembly not eligible to, South Carolina 83
Literary qualifications of voters:
      Connecticut 18
      Massachusetts 51
      Missouri 60
Literature, promotion of:
      Iowa 33
      Louisiana 42
      Massachusetts 49
      Michigan 52
      Nevada 65
      New York 69
      New Hampshire 67
      Tennessee 83
Literature-fund:
      New York 69, 70
      North Carolina 73
Local school legislation, (summary) 104
Louisiana, constitution of, 1845 41
—— constitution of, 1852 42
Lunatic asylum, Texas 87
Luzerne, Chevalier de la 49

M.

	Page.
Maine, constitution of, 1820	45
Management of school-funds, (summary)	111, 112
Manufactures, encouragement of:	
Arkansas	13
Massachusetts	51
Marbois, M	49
Marion County, Mississippi, swamp-lands in	58
Marriage-licenses, proceeds of, before 1806, Connecticut	18
Maryland, constitution of, 1864	46
—— constitution of, 1867	48
Massachusetts, constitution of, 1870	48
—— constitution proposed in 1853	51
—— act of State of, enabling Maine to organize a State	45
Mechanical improvement:	
Nevada	65, 66
Mechanic arts:	
Nevada	67
North Carolina	74
South Carolina	82
Medical instruction:	
Kansas	36
Louisiana	41, 45
South Carolina	83
Michigan, constitution of, 1835	52
—— constitution of, 1850	53
—— amendment of, 1861	55
—— abortive constitution of, 1867	55
Military exemptions, moneys derived from:	
Iowa	32, 35
Kansas	39
Michigan	52
Mississippi	59
North Carolina	72
Oregon	77
Military tactics, Nevada	67
Mines, income from, appropriated for schools	74
Minimum term of schools, to entitle to public moneys, (summary)	107
Mining department of university:	
Nevada	67
North Carolina	74
Mining improvement, Nevada	65, 66
Minnesota, constitution of, 1858	57
Mississippi, constitution of, 1817, 1832, and 1865	57
—— constitution of, 1868	58
Missouri, constitution of, 1820	58
—— constitution of, 1865	60
Morality, promotion of:	
Arkansas	13
Iowa	35
Kansas	39
Michigan	56
Mississippi	57, 58
Nebraska	62
North Carolina	72

Page.

Morality, promotion of:
Nevada 65
Ohio... 74,75

N.

Natural history, promotion of:
Arkansas 13,14
Massachusetts... 51
New Hampshire.. 67
Natural sciences to be taught:
Louisiana.. 41
Michigan 55,56
Missouri 61
South Carolina.. 82
Nebraska, constitution of, 1867.. 62
———— abortive constitution of, 1870.............................. 63
Nevada, constitution of, 1864... 65
New Hampshire, constitution of, 1784............................... 67
New Jersey, constitution of, 1844 68
New Orleans University, Louisiana..................................... 41,43
New York, constitution of, 1821... 68
———— constitution of, 1846.. 69
———— constitution proposed in 1867–'68......................... 70
Normal schools:
Kansas 36,38,39,40
Michigan 54,56
Missouri 61,74
Nevada... 66
South Carolina... 82
summary 113
North Carolina, constitution of, 1776 70
———— constitution of, 1868.. 71
Norwalk, Conn., museum at.. 49

O.

Oakland, Cal., University at.. 17
Oath required of teachers, Nevada..................................... 66
Objects to be promoted by the state, (summary) 103
Ohio, constitution of, 1802... 74
———— constitution of, 1851.. 75
———— constitution proposed in 1874 75
Ordinance of convention, 1816, Indiana............................. 29
———— preceding the Wyandotte constitution of Kansas 36
———— of Michigan convention 53
———— of Missouri convention, 1820............................... 60
———— relating to citadel for educational purposes, South Carolina........... 82
Ordinances of Continental Congress................................... 74
Oregon, constitution of, 1857.. 76
Orphan asylum, Texas... 87

P.

Parent State, school-funds of, (summary)............................ 112
Pearl River, swamp-lands on... 58
Penn, William, concessions by 77
Pennsylvania, proprietary concessions................................ 77

666

	Page.
Pennsylvania, constitution of, 1776	78
—— constitution of, 1790, 1838, 1873	79
Philosophical Society of Philadelphia	49
Poll-taxes for school purposes:	
Alabama	9, 11
Arkansas	15, 16
Mississippi	59
South Carolina	81
Tennessee	84
Texas	88
summary	111
Poor not to be prevented from school privileges, Ohio	75
Preferences of race and color, (summary)	107
Preparatory department of University Kansas	38, 39
Primary department of University Kansas	38
—— free schools, Michigan	54, 56
Propositions of Congress accepted:	
Illinois	23
Missouri	60
Provincial council of Pennsylvania, duties of	78
Punctuality, promotion of:	
Massachusetts	51
New Hampshire	67

Q.

Quincy's History of Harvard cited	48
Quit-rents, funds from, New York	69

R.

Race, distinctions of, (see Color,) summary	107
Reading a qualification for voting:	
Connecticut	18
Massachusetts	51
—— may be made a qualification, Missouri	60
Reform-school to be established, South Carolina	82
Regents of university:	
Alabama	10, 11
Michigan	54, 55, 56
Nevada	66, 67
Religion, protection of:	
Arkansas	13
Michigan	96
Mississippi	57
Nebraska	62
North Carolina	72
Ohio	74, 75
Religious sects not to control the schools or the school-fund:	
Arkansas	14
Illinois	25
Mississippi	59
Nebraska	64
South Carolina	81
Responsibility with respect to school-property	109
Rewards to be offered for the promotion of the arts, Indiana	28

	Page.
Rhode Island, constitution of, 1842	80
Right of education, North Carolina	71
Roxbury, minister of Congregational Church in	50

S.

Salary of cabinet officers, Florida	22
Salaries of masters to be paid by State, North Carolina	70
Sale of school-lands, Minnesota	57
Saline land, Indiana	29, 30
Salt-springs, Illinois	23
——— income from, in territory northwest of river Ohio	74
School-ages, (summary) 107, 108	
School-apparatus	108
School-books, teachers and school-officers not to be interested in sale of, Illinois.	27
School-commissioner, Georgia	23
——— county :	
Maryland	47
South Carolina...	81
School-districts, (summary)	108
School-fund :	
Alabama..	9, 11
Arkansas...	14, 15
California	16
Connecticut	18
Florida	21
Iowa 32, 34, 35	
Kansas	36, 39
Kentucky...	40
Maryland	47, 48
Massachusetts..	51
Mississippi...	58
Missouri	59, 62
Nebraska	63
Nevada	66
New Jersey..	68
New York..68, 69, 70	
Ohio...	75, 76
Oregon	77
Rhode Island	80
Tennessee	83
Texas..84, 85, 86, 87, 88, 89	
summary..110, 111	
School-houses, taxation for, Arkansas..	16
School-lands, (see Lands for school purposes,) summary 109, 110	
School-libraries, (summary)..	108
Schools to be encouraged or maintained :	
Alabama..	9, 10
Arkansas	14, 15
California	16
Connecticut...	18
Delaware	18
Florida	21
Georgia	22, 23
Illinois	25
Indiana...	30, 31

Page.

ıools to be encouraged or maintained:

Iowa	31
Kansas	37, 39
Kentucky	40
Louisiana	41, 42, 43, 44
Maine	46
Maryland	46, 47, 48
Massachusetts	50
Michigan	52
Mississippi	57
Missouri	61
Nebraska	62
Nevada..	65
New Hampshire	67
New Jersey	68
New York	69
North Carolina	70
Ohio	74, 75
Oregon	77
Pennsylvania	78, 79, 80
Rhode Island	80
South Carolina	81
Tennessee	83
Texas	84, 85, 87
Vermont	89
Virginia	90, 91
West Virginia	93, 95
Wisconsin	97

ence, encouragement of:

Arkansas	13
Delaware	18
Georgia	22
Indiana	28, 29
Iowa	33, 35
Kansas	36, 39
Louisiana	42
Massachusetts	49 57
Michigan	52, 55, 56
Mississippi	58
New Hampshire	67
Pennsylvania	78, 79
Tennessee	83

t of government, tempory change of, Florida	22

tarian schools not to receive public moneys:

Illinois	27
Kansas	36, 37, 40
Nevada	67
Pennsylvania	80
South Carolina	81
summary	107

ınaries, lands granted for, Florida	21
— to be encouraged, Maine	45
— summary	112
ninary fund, Missouri	59, 60

Page.

Separate schools for African children:
        Missouri 61
        Tennessee 84
Silver-mines, income from 74
Simpson County, Mississippi, swamp-lands in 58
Sincerity, inculcation of, New Hampshire 67
Sobriety, inculcation of, New Hampshire 67
Social affections, inculcation of, New Hampshire 67
South Carolina, constitutions before 1868 80
——— constitution of, 1868 81
——— ordinance of convention of, 1868 82
State bank, Indiana 30
State reform-school, South Carolina 82
Summary, classified 103
Superintendent of public education:
        Louisiana 42, 43, 44
        Mississippi 58
Superintendent of public instruction:
        Alabama 10
        Arkansas 14
        California 16
        Illinois 25, 26
        Indiana 31
        Iowa 31, 32
        Kansas 38, 39
        Kentucky 41
        Louisiana 41
        Maryland 46
        Michigan 52, 55
        Nebraska 64
        Nevada 65
        North Carolina 71
        Pennsylvania 72
        South Carolina 81
        Texas 87, 88
Superintendent of public schools, Missouri 61
Surplus revenue fund, Indiana 29
Swamp-lands:
        Alabama 11
        Indiana 30
        Mississippi 58
        North Carolina 72

T.

Tavern licenses given to schools before 1805, Connecticut 18
Taxation for school purposes:
        Alabama 9, 11
        Arkansas 15
        Florida 22
        Illinois 24, 25
        Louisiana 41, 42, 44
        Maryland 47
        Minnesota 57
        Mississippi 58, 59
        Nebraska 64

Page.

tion for school purposes:

Nevada 66
North Carolina.. 72
Ohio 75
South Carolina 81
Texas 84, 85, 88
Summary 110

- exemption of educational institutions from:

Arkansas 16
Florida 22
Georgia 24
Illinois 27
Indiana 31
West Virginia...... ....92, 94

- of United States lands, right relinquished, Kansas...................... 37
s not to be levied by board of education, Iowa......................... 34
essee, constitutions of, 1796 and 1834.................... 83
- amendment of constitution of, 1870 84
itory northwest of the river Ohio 74
s, constitution of, 1845.. 84
- constitution of, 1866.. 85
- constitution of, 1869 87
-books, (summary) 109
ka constitution, Kansas 36
-lots, reservation of 10 per centum in sale of, Indiana.................. 28
s to support schools, Maine 45
ship libraries:

Iowa 32
Michigan 55, 56
ships, survey of, and school-lots in.................................... 72
es, promotion of:

Massachusetts... 51
New Hampshire... 67
bull, John, commissioner Yale College 17
-fund of 1836:

Louisiana 42, 43, 44
New York 69, 70
-lands. (See Lands for school purposes.)

U.

tunate classes, education and support of, (summary).. 114
d States deposit-fund:

Louisiana 42, 43, 44
New York..69, 70
rsities:

Alabama 9, 11
Arkansas 14, 15
California 17
Georgia 23
Indiana 29
Iowa 33, 34, 35
Kansas 36, 37, 38, 39, 40
Louisiana...41, 42, 43, 45
Michigan 52
Minnesota 57

	Page.
Universities:	
Missouri	59, 61
Nebraska	63, 64
Nevada	66
North Carolina	70, 72, 73
Pennsylvania	78, 79
South Carolina	82
Texas	85, 86
summary	113
University-fund. (See Universities.)	
University-lands. (See Universities.)	

V.

Vermont, constitutions of, 1786 and since	89
Virginia, constitutions of, 1851 and 1870	90
Virtue, promotion of:	
Massachusetts	50
Rhode Island	80
Tennessee	83
Voters, literary qualifications of:	
Connecticut	18
Massachusetts	51
Missouri	60

W.

Watertown, minister of Congregational church in	50
Western reserve, Ohio, proceeds of sale of	20
West Virginia, constitution of, 1861	92
—— constitution of, 1872	93
Wisconsin, constitution proposed in 1846	96
—— constitution of, 1848	97
Women eligible to school offices :	
Ohio	76
Pennsylvania	80
Wyandotte constitution, Kansas	36

Y.

Yale College, Connecticut	17, 18

○

OF THE

BUREAU OF EDUCATION.

No. 8–1875.

SCHEDULE FOR THE PREPARATION OF STUDENTS' WORK FOR THE
CENTENNIAL EXHIBITION, AS REPORTED BY THE COMMITTEE
OF THE DEPARTMENT OF SUPERINTENDENCE OF
THE NATIONAL EDUCATIONAL ASSOCIATION,
APPOINTED AT MINNEAPOLIS IN 1875.

WASHINGTON:
GOVERNMENT PRINTING OFFICE.
1875.

CONTENTS.

Page.

Letter of the Commissioner of Education to the Secretary of the Interior.......   5

STUDENT'S WORK AT THE CENTENNIAL:

Classification of material... 7, 8

General rules.. 8

Class I.—Examination-manuscripts prepared according to prescribed rules.. 8–10

Class II.—Special work for the preparation of which no rules are prescribed 10, 11

Class III.—Material arranged and presented to illustrate systems of instruction 11

Drawing and penmanship 11, 13

APPENDIX:

Resolutions of National Educational Association regarding exhibition of educational development... 14–15

Model title pages recommended by committee of superintendents........... 15

LETTER.

DEPARTMENT OF THE INTERIOR,
BUREAU OF EDUCATION,
Washington, D. C., November 27, 1875.

SIR : The desire that specimens of the actual school-work of students should be shown at Philadelphia has been expressed by many educators, and this work is included in the classification furnished by the Centennial Commission.

The difficulty has been to devise a uniform plan for the preparation of students' work.

The department of superintendence of the National Educational Association, in session at Minneapolis in August, 1875, considered the subject, and, after full discussion, referred to a committee the preparation of a suitable schedule, in accordance with the provisions of which all such specimens of scholars' work should be prepared. It was understood that the recommendations of this committee would be accepted as the standard. Many inquiries in reference to the methods of preparing school-work have been addressed to this Office. As furnishing a satisfactory answer to these inquiries, and in accordance with the requests of members of the National Educational Association, I recommend the publication, by this Bureau, of the report of this committee, with the schedule as adopted by them.

Very respectfully, your obedient servant,

JOHN EATON,
Commissioner.

Hon. Z. CHANDLER,
Secretary of the Interior.

Approved and publication ordered.

Z. CHANDLER,
Secretary.

STUDENTS' WORK*

AT THE

NATIONAL CENTENNIAL EXHIBITION,
1876.

At the request of Hon. John Eaton, United States Commissioner of Education, a committee of the superintendents' section of the National Educational Association was appointed at its last meeting, held at Minneapolis during August, 1875, to draught rules to govern the preparation and exhibition of pupils' and students' work at the National Centennial Exhibition to be held at Philadelphia in 1876. This committee has given the subject due consideration, and would respectfully submit the rules appended.

A. J. RICKOFF,
Supt. of City-Schools, Cleveland, Ohio;
J. L. PICKARD,
Supt. of City-Schools, Chicago, Ill.;
J. H. SMART,
State Supt. of Pub. Inst., Indiana;
Committee.

CLASSIFICATION.

All material which may be offered for exhibition will be classified as follows:

I. Examination-manuscripts prepared according to prescribed rules.

II. Special work for the preparation of which no rules are prescribed.

III. Material arranged and presented to illustrate systems of instruction.

On account of peculiarities of organization or administration, it may be difficult for an institution or the public schools of a town or city to exhibit in some one of the classes above named, while in another it might

---

* Officers of systems and institutions of education participating in preparing students' work are desired to forward the material to the superintendents of public instruction for their respective States or Territories. Special attention is also invited to the other suggestions contained in the resolutions passed by the Department of Superintendence of the National Educational Association, which are presented in the Appendix.

be able to make a display which would be creditable to itself and to the whole country. It is, therefore, left to managers of schools and school-systems of every grade to exhibit in any class or classes they may elect.

Class I affords an opportunity for the public schools of towns and cities and separate institutions of learning of every grade to compare their own work with the work of others, performed under like conditions.

Class II provides for the exhibition of anything that may be looked upon as of value in the line of educational products. Here no limit is prescribed in time or other conditions of preparation. As a condition of exhibition, however, it is required that the circumstances of the preparation be fully stated.

Class III opens the door for the exhibition of such products of the school-room as will serve to illustrate the working of a course of study or a system of instruction. In this class the smallest district school or private institution may have an opportunity to exhibit its plans and ways of working. Here a principal of a single school or one subordinate teacher in a large unorganized mass of schools may submit illustrations of a plan or process of instruction, methods of recitation, &c., in one or more branches of study, though the number of pupils he represents may be comparatively insignificant.

No contribution will be received in any one of the three classes for purposes of competition.

GENERAL RULES.

(*a*) No article shall be exhibited unless the class to which it belongs be stamped or otherwise plainly marked on the article itself or on the cover containing it.

(*b*) It is recommended that all manuscript-work, especially in Class I, be written on letter-paper, 8¼ by 10½ inches in size.

(*c*) The questions to be answered should be written or printed directly above each answer in all manuscripts in arithmetic; and in all other subjects the same course should be pursued, or the answers should be so framed that the question may be plainly indicated thereby. The latter is the better plan.

(*d*) Every set or collection of manuscripts on any subject must be accompanied by the full list of questions presented the class in that subject, which list should be inserted immediately after the appropriate title page.

CLASS I.

EXAMINATION-MANUSCRIPTS.

RULE 1. *Who may be examined.*—None but *bonâ fide* pupils of the schools and of the particular grade of schools purporting to be represented shall be permitted to contribute anything for exhibition in Class I.

RULE 2. *Time of examination.*—All manuscripts to be exhibited in this class shall be prepared from the 1st to the 15th of February. Not more than four hours shall be allowed for the writing of a paper on any one branch of study, which time shall include the entire work from the time the questions are placed before the pupil to the completion of the copy submitted.

RULE 3. *The ground of examination.*—The ground or limit of the examination shall be the work done within the current school-year up to the time of the examination and work preliminary thereto, according to the course of study of the institution or schools preparing the work, which course of study shall accompany all manuscripts sent for exhibition.

RULE 4. *Questions, by whom prepared and precautions to be observed.*—The questions for examination shall be prepared by the superintendent of schools or some other person not engaged in the instruction of the class or classes under examination, and the utmost care shall be taken that no information in regard to the nature or topics of the questions be circulated among the pupils and that no previous intimation of the ground of examination, except as in Rule 3, be given to the teachers of the classes to be examined.

RULE 5. *Manuscripts to be exhibited.*—All schools, colleges, technical schools, special schools, and school systems of towns and cities exhibiting in Class I may be represented, first, by papers prepared as above from one entire class of each grade, in which pen and ink are used in writing, and, second, by not less than one paper in ten selected from all the other manuscripts prepared in the examination.

[NOTE.—It is to be understood that when any grade of pupils, fifth-year grade, for example, is examined, all the pupils in that grade throughout the entire town or city system shall be examined in all branches upon which written examinations are required for transfer; and that thereafter, for each of the subjects, the manuscripts of some one entire class of that grade be taken for exhibition, and also one-tenth of all the other manuscripts of that grade; and, further, that the exhibition of manuscripts of entire classes and selected manuscripts shall be especially subject to the following rule:]

RULE 6. *Title page and declaration of chief officers.*—A title page, after model A, for the papers of entire classes, or after model B for selected papers, shall be inserted in every volume, collection, or set of manuscripts designed for exhibition in Class I; and no papers shall be admitted for exhibition in this class unless accompanied by a declaration from the principal executive officer of the school or other institution of learning thereby represented, that said papers were executed in accordance with the above rules and Rule 7, as below.

NOTE.—The course of study in some towns and cities is divided into eight grades, to correspond approximately with the average time taken for completing the course assigned to primary and grammar schools.

In such cases it will be easy to fill this blank; but, when the number of grades does not correspond with the average number of years thus required, it is desirable that the blank be so filled as to show approximately what year of the course is represented by the manuscripts.

In the title page marked A it might be well to insert the name of the teacher of the class under the words " one entire class represented."

RULE 7. *Headings of manuscripts and declarations of students or pupils.*—Every manuscript of every pupil or student should be headed, in the pupil's own handwriting, with his name, age, grade, or class, the name of the school or institution of which his class is a part, and the date of the examination. At the foot of the last page it should contain, also in the pupil's own handwriting, a minute of the time taken for the writing of the paper, which must include the whole time elapsing from the putting of the questions before the pupil to the handing in of the copy exhibited. On the completion and handing in of any manuscript or specimen for exhibition under Class I the student or pupil should make the following declaration on a separate slip of paper, over his own signature, viz: "This accompanying manuscript was written by myself, without aid from any source."

The manuscripts of every class shall be accompanied by a written declaration, by the teacher or by the one who had charge of the pupils of the class at the time of the examination, that the entire work of the class was done under his own eye and that all the regulations were observed as herein prescribed. These certificates, written on separate sheets of paper, shall be sent to the superintendent or other officer having the direction of the examination. They need not, however, be sent to the Exhibition. (See Rule 6.)

CLASS II.

SPECIAL PRODUCTS.

Bound volumes or portfolios of examination-papers prepared at any previous time in regular examinations, and without reference to the Centennial or any other "exhibition."—An exact statement of what it purports to be should accompany each collection of this class. Such statement should set forth whether the collection is from an entire class or whether the papers are selected; and, if selected, what part of an entire grade is represented; also, the time occupied in the examination, the rules under which it was conducted, and all such other information as may be necessary to enable any one to judge of the merit of the exhibition. In Class II may be included also any work of students or pupils connected with, or incident to, school-work, such as collections of insects, plants, shells, &c., collected and arranged by pupils or graduates of schools, colleges, or other institutions of learning: specimens of manual skill in the construction of models of any sort prepared for the illustration of school studies; drawings and specimens of penmanship of special merit; in short, anything which may be fairly exhibited as results of school instruction or training. Every production in this class should be accompanied by a statement of the age, sex, and class of the pupil, the time occupied in producing the article, whether it was made with or without the assistance of professors or teachers, and of all the circumstances which should enter into an estimate of its educational value or bearing.

It is not necessary that students or pupils contributing to this class be members of the schools represented during the current year. All that is required is that they should have been *boná-fide* members of the school represented and that the work be directly traceable as the result of school instruction.

CLASS III.

MATERIAL TO ILLUSTRATE SYSTEMS OF INSTRUCTION.

Specimens of examination-papers, exercises in review, regular lessons or class-exercises of any nature which may be adapted to exhibit and illustrate the course and method pursued in any line of study or instruction, from the commencement to the end thereof, in any public, private, or corporate institution or system of institutions of learning.—The value of any exhibition in this class will not depend so much upon the excellence of the specimens submitted as upon the clearness with which they may show, in outline and in detail, the plans and processes of instruction pursued. The specimens should be few, and it is quite indispensable that they be accompanied by written or printed explanations, as the case may seem to demand. More will depend in this department than in any other upon the judgment, invention, and taste of teachers and school officers; more, indeed, than upon the skill with which the schemes may be carried out in practice. Exhibitions in this class may also consist of proposed schemes or syllabuses of instruction in any department of literature, science, or art, without accompanying specimens from pupils, if, from the nature of the case, illustration be impracticable. If, however, any scheme is submitted as one which has been adopted in any institution or system of schools, it is not to be accepted as such, unless it be explicitly stated by the highest executive officer of such institution or system that it has been as regularly and systematically carried out in practice as any other work required in the school or schools under his or her care.

DRAWING AND PENMANSHIP.

All exhibitions in drawing and penmanship shall be stamped or otherwise plainly marked as entered for exhibition in Class I, II, or III, as the case may be; and the preparation and display of the same shall be governed by all the rules for the respective classes, and in addition thereto by the following

SPECIAL RULES FOR PENMANSHIP.

Specimens in penmanship shall be written on paper of the ordinary size of the writing books commonly used in the schools, and shall consist of not less than eight or ten lines of poetry or prose, the selection to be announced only at the time of writing. (See Rule 3.)

No written copy shall be permitted, either on blackboard or elsewhere, in sight of the pupil at the time of writing. Not more than two hours shall be given to the writing of such a specimen after the matter to be written is placed before the pupil.

SPECIAL RULES FOR LABELING DRAWINGS.

The labels are the underscored words, and they are to be used to designate drawings according to the explanations annexed.

In the drawing of problems, the thing required shall be written out in the pupil's own handwriting on the same sheet and side of the sheet with the drawing.

FROM FLAT COPY.

Free-hand.—Drawings from flat copy, without the use of a rule, straight-edge, or measure of any kind at any step of the work.

Semi free-hand.—Case 1. Drawings from flat copies, in which the construction-lines were made with a rule or in which points were located by the aid of rule or measure.

Case 2. Drawings made on paper having construction-lines or points either made in or printed on the paper.

Instrumental.—Drawings of machines, geometrical or architectural problems, or any kind of drawings made from flat copy, and in which mechanical appliances have been used.

FROM DICTATION.

Free-hand.—Drawing made entirely free-hand, line by line or part by part, at dictation of teachers, no rule or measure of any kind being allowed.

Semi-free-hand.—Drawings in which distances were measured or construction-points were located, but otherwise free-hand.

Instrumental.—Drawings in which the rule or measure was freely used.

FROM MEMORY.

Free-hand.—Drawings made entirely free-hand.

Semi-free-hand.—Drawings in which construction-lines only were made or construction-points were located with the rule or by measure.

Instrumental.—Drawings from memory with the free use of mechanical aids.

MECHANICAL.

The solution of problems.—Whether geometrical, in mechanical contrivance or architectural arrangement, either from the object or to satisfy given conditions or dimensions, or both, wrought out by the pupils, in the execution of which the usual mathematical principles and mechanical aids are made use of.

OBJECT-DRAWING.

From the object, without the use of vanishing-points, horizon-lines, or projections.
From objects in alto-rilievo, as above.
From objects in demi-rilievo.
From objects in basso-rilievo.

OBJECT-DRAWING FROM DICTATION.

The teacher stating the position in which the object is supposed to be, the pupil makes the drawing without seeing the object in that position.

PERSPECTIVE.

Drawings of problems made by mathematical perspective.
Drawings from the object with the use of mathematical perspective.
Drawings made with the use of elementary perspective, either as the solution of a problem or from the object.

DESIGNS: FREE-HAND, SEMI-FREE-HAND, OR INSTRUMENTAL, AS THE CASE MAY BE.

Entirely original.—Designs made from natural objects in which the particular natural objects from which they are taken are manifest.
Original combinations.—Designs made up of elements taken from other designs and recombined, making new arrangements.
Original with given elements.—Designs in which given elements are combined, the plan and arrangements being the pupil's.
Elements and arrangements given.—Designs in which the elements and arrangement of the elements are given by the teacher.
NOTE.—If tracing-paper be used in any part of the work presented under the head of design, the fact must be stated.

APPENDIX.

The following papers embody : (1) The resolutions respecting education at the Centennial, passed by the superintendents' section of the National Educational Association at its meeting in Minneapolis, August 5, 1875, out of the third of which resolutions grew the rules herewith presented; and (2) the models A and B recommended for the title pages of student's work to be exhibited.

1.—RESOLUTIONS.

Hon. J. H. Smart, of Indiana, chairman of a special committee to draught resolutions in regard to the exhibition of educational development at the approaching Centennial at Philadelphia, reported the following, which were received, discussed, and adopted *seriatim :*

Whereas a communication has been received from the Hon. John Eaton, United States Commissioner of Education, in which the National Educational Association, now assembled, is requested to take into consideration the interests of the educational department of the coming Centennial Exposition and to make suggestions in relation thereto: Therefore,

Resolved, That we heartily second the efforts of the Commissioner to secure an adequate representation of our educational products at the Centennial, and that we will co-operate with him in every practicable way to make the enterprise a success.

Resolved, That, in accordance with the Commissioner's request, we make the following suggestions, viz :

(1) In our opinion, wall-space of not less than 2,000 feet in length, with accompanying counter and floor space, will be needed for the proper display of our educational products.

(2) The amount of wall-space occupied by each State should be limited to 100 feet in length.

(3) All products of the schools, executed by pupils, except such as may be classed as "special products," should be made during the month of January, 1876.[*]

(4) We respectfully recommend that there be formed an Exposition Committee, consisting of one agent appointed from each of the States and Territories represented at the Centennial, by the chief educational officer in conference with the national Commissioner of Education, whose duty it should be to co-operate with the Commissioner in the superintendence of the educational department at Philadelphia.[†]

---

[*] The committee into whose charge this matter was given adopted, after consultation, the month of February, (1-15,) instead of January, as may be seen under Rule 2, Class I, in the preceding pages.

[†] Hon. Mr. Smart, by whom these resolutions were presented, proposes that suggestion 4, under resolution second, be made, for greater clearness, to read thus :

"We respectfully recommend that the chief educational officer of each State and Territory which displays educational products at the Centennial be invited to appoint an agent, whose duty it shall be to represent his State or Territory at Philadelphia, to see that the educational products thereof are properly arranged and cared for, and to act in conjunction with other agents in forming a committee of inspection to co-operate with the United States Commissioner of Education in the superintendence of the educational department."

Resolved, That a committee of three be appointed to prepare and submit to General Eaton rules and regulations by which pupils and students shall be governed in the preparation of such products as may be executed by them.

Resolved, That we recommend that an international educational congress be held at some time during the Centennial Exposition, and that we also recommend that arrangements therefor be made by the United States Commissioner of Education.

Resolved, That we respectfully recommend to the Commissioner of Education that the appointment of delegates to the international congress be made through the chief educational officers of the several States and Territories.

The superintendents' section then adjourned *sine die*.

2—MODEL TITLE PAGES A AND B, RECOMMENDED BY THE COMMITTEE OF SUPERINTENDENTS.

TITLE PAGE, MODEL A.

(Name of institution or school system.   Location.)

MANUSCRIPTS OF EXAMINATION

OF

(Insert here the grade or grades of the class or classes examined.)

BEING THE —— YEAR OF THE COURSE

IN

(Insert here the subjects of the examination.)

HELD

(Insert here the date of examination.)

ONE ENTIRE CLASS REPRESENTED.

(The name of the teacher may here be inserted.)

The class has pursued this study —— ——.
Whole number of pupils in the grade, ——. Average age, ——.
Whole number of pupils in the class represented, ——. Average age, ——.
The number represented is —— per cent. of the whole number in the grade.
Total enrollment in all the schools at the time of examination, ——.

TITLE PAGE, MODEL B.

(Name of institution or school system.   Location.)

MANUSCRIPTS OF EXAMINATION

OF

(Insert here the grade or grades of the class or classes examined.)

BEING THE —— YEAR OF THE COURSE

IN

(Insert here the subjects of the examination.)

HELD

(Insert here the date of examination.)

SELECTED PAPERS.

The class has pursued this study —— ——.
Whole number of pupils in the grade, ——. Average age, ——.
Number of pupils represented by the selections, ——. Average age, ——.
The number represented is —— per cent. of the whole number in the grade.
Total enrollment in all the schools at the time of examination, ——.

Lightning Source UK Ltd.
Milton Keynes UK
UKHW020623120219

337137UK00005B/544/P

9 780266 983187